Parenting Representations

The study of parents from their own perspective, not just as socializing agents of their children, has been long neglected. This book summarizes and presents the new and surging literature on parenting representations, namely parents' views, emotions, and internal world regarding their parenting. Within this area, several prominent researchers typically coming from the attachment tradition suggested various ways of assessing parenting representations, mostly by way of semi-structured interviews. This book presents their conceptualizations and includes detailed descriptions of their interviews and their coding schemes. In addition, a review and summary of the growing number of findings in this domain and an integrated conceptualization that serves as a theoretical base for future research are presented. Finally, the clinical implications of the study of parenting representations are discussed at large. Clinical notions and conceptualizations regarding parenting representations are presented and thoroughly discussed, including detailed case studies that demonstrate, among other things, intergenerational transmission of representations.

Ofra Mayseless received her Ph.D. from the Psychology Department of Tel-Aviv University in Israel in 1984. She is a certified clinical psychologist and a professor of Developmental Psychology at the Faculty of Education at the University of Haifa in Israel. She has taught in University of California, Berkeley, and Mills College, California, as well as in the University of British Columbia and Simon Fraser University in Vancouver, BC, Canada. She is a member of the American Psychological Association, the Society for Research in Child Development (SRCD), International Association for Relationship Research (IARR), International Society for the Study of Behavior Development, and the International Society for Research on Adolescence. She has written more than 50 articles and chapters in the area of close relationships, in particular adolescents' and adults' attachment and caregiving manifestations.

Cambridge Studies in Social and Emotional Development

General Editor: Carolyn Shantz, *Wayne State University*

Advisory Board: Nancy Eisenberg, Robert N. Emde,
Willard W. Hartup, Lois W. Hoffman, Franz J. Mönks,
Ross D. Parke, Michael Rutter, and Carolyn Zahn-Waxler

Recent books in the series:

Conflict in Child and Adolescent Development
Edited by Carolyn Uhlinger Shantz and Willard W. Hartup

Children in Time and Place
Edited by Glen H. Elder, Jr., John Modell, and Ross D. Parke

Disclosure Processes in Children and Adolescents
Edited by Ken J. Rotenberg

Morality in Everyday Life
Edited by Melanie Killen and Daniel Hart

The Company They Keep
Edited by William M. Bukowski, Andrew F. Newcomb,
and Willard W. Hartup

Developmental Science
Edited by Robert B. Cairns, Glen H. Elder, and Jane E. Costello

Social Motivation
Edited by Jaana Juvonen and Kathryn R. Wentzel

Emotional Development
By L. Alan Sroufe

Comparisons in Human Development
Edited by Jonathan Tudge, Michael J. Shanahan, and
Jaan Valsiner

continued after the Index

Parenting Representations

Theory, Research, and Clinical Implications

Edited by

OFRA MAYSELESS
University of Haifa

CAMBRIDGE
UNIVERSITY PRESS

CAMBRIDGE UNIVERSITY PRESS
Cambridge, New York, Melbourne, Madrid, Cape Town, Singapore, São Paulo

Cambridge University Press
40 West 20th Street, New York, NY 10011-4211, USA

www.cambridge.org
Information on this title: www.cambridge.org/9780521828871

First published 2006

Printed in the United States of America

A catalog record for this publication is available from the British Library.

Library of Congress Cataloging in Publication Data

Parenting representations : theory, research and clinical implications /
edited by Ofra Mayseless.
    p.   cm. – (Cambridge studies in social and emotional development)
Includes bibliographical references and index.
ISBN-13: 978-0-521-82887-1 (hardback)
ISBN-10: 0-521-82887-2 (hardback)
1. Parenting.   2. Parents–Psychology.   3. Parents–Attitudes.
I. Mayseless, Ofra, 1953–   II. Title.   III. Series.
HQ755.8.P3916   2006
306.874 – dc22   2005031230

ISBN-13   978-0-521-82887-1 hardback
ISBN-10   0-521-82887-2 hardback

אורי מייסלס

This book is dedicated to my precious, wonderful son – Ouri Mayseless.

On August 20, 2003, not yet 22 years old, he was killed with his friend, Oren Simon, by a careless driver in the painfully beautiful, lush green landscapes of Alaska, far from his home – Israel.

Ouri was a bright-eyed child with a breathtaking life force, a creativity that always took us by surprise, an endless curiosity, and an open heart to love and embrace everybody – a heart of gold. From early on, I was highly curious to see what would become of him. How would he integrate these extraordinary capacities? I was sure it would be something unexpected and astonishing. Ouri grew up to be an amazing young person, naive, yet mature, fun-loving and yet highly dedicated and serious in his studies and sport pursuits, extremely bright, and above all exceptionally imaginative and creative. He studied electrical engineering and was a top A student. He had a wonderful, amazingly loving relationship with his one (and only) girlfriend, in which intimacy, trust, respect, and love were so vibrant and glowing – they both served as a model couple for their friends and for us. Before his last semester of studies, he went on a trip to Alaska. He wanted a relatively safe place of nature, to relax, have fun, and to contemplate.

As we flew to Alaska to bring him back home with us and I was all torn from within, I was struck by the sharp, excruciating realization that as a researcher whose passionate professional life was devoted to the study of the marvelous encompassing love of parents for their children, I now was witnessing firsthand how unbearable, unthinkable, and crushing such a blow to this bond can be.

Psychologists often wonder what makes people choose a certain subject for research; why researchers find certain topics challenging and captivating. For me the answer seemed quite obvious. I was fascinated with the strong force of loving and caring, which is manifested all around us in myriad ways and relations but which seemed to me to be most powerful, all-encompassing, and so wonderfully giving in the case of parents. I have been, of course, aware of the obvious evolutionary "explanation," but this did not "explain" or clarify what I found so fascinating – the love (physical, emotional, cognitive, and behavioral) that parents have and express toward their children. Out of this focus grew the work on this volume, as I found like-minded scholars who were attracted to understand, reveal, and uncover more about the working of the parents' mind and soul.

Little did I know that an almost impossible lesson about parenting awaited me just as I was about to finalize the work on this volume.

My friends and colleagues were not sure that I would be able to touch these topics again as they so directly bear upon my pain. But for me, the work on this volume and in particular my other parallel path to find meaning "through time and space" have been like a lighthouse in the middle of the storm. I did not search to elude pain, nor did I sink into it and embrace it, but in my personal life as in my professional life I wanted to see what does it mean. And mostly, I wanted to understand why.

I miss my son incessantly – in a physical sense as a part torn from my own body leaving me cut open, in an emotional sense as a flowing love and energy that now does not have an earthly address, and in a psychological sense as a friend and companion, as a growing evolving wonderful person, and as a fun and bright ally.

Ouri had two names and they both become him so well – *Ouri* which means in Hebrew *my Light* and *Shmuel* (in English – Samuel – who was a prophet and by God's order nominated the first and second kings of Israel – *Shaul* and *David*). The meaning of the word *Shmuel* in Hebrew is "given/received from God." I believe in a way Ouri had some of the qualities reflected in his two names – having both *Truth* and *Love* as his inner guiding lights, with a highly inquisitive mind and a passion to give and help others – he was God's present to me.

I know that in a different sphere Ouri knows about this book and about this dedication, and that he – there – and I – here – know that it does not even come close to expressing how and what I feel for him and what he might have been able to accomplish – had he lived.

I know that like me when writing this dedication, his heart is aching and his tears are running, but he is content that the mission has been accomplished.

Contents

List of Illustrations   *page* xi

List of Tables   xiii

List of Appendixes   xv

List of Contributors   xvii

Preface   xix

Acknowledgments   xxiii

Part One Theoretical Perspectives

1 Studying Parenting Representations as a Window to Parents'
   Internal Working Model of Caregiving   3
   Ofra Mayseless

2 Maternal Representations of Relationships: Assessing
   Multiple Parenting Dimensions   41
   Donna R. Steinberg and Robert C. Pianta

3 Social Cognitive Approaches to Parenting
   Representations   79
   Duane Rudy and Joan E. Grusec

Part Two Research Applications

4 Communicating Feelings: Links Between Mothers'
   Representations of Their Infants, Parenting, and Infant
   Emotional Development   109
   *Katherine L. Rosenblum, Carolyn J. Dayton, and
   Susan McDonough*

5   The Dual Viewpoints of Mother and Child on Their
    Relationship: A Longitudinal Study of Interaction and
    Representation   149
    Anat Scher, Judith Harel, Miri Scharf, and Liora Klein

6   Modeling and Reworking Childhood Experiences: Involved
    Fathers' Representations of Being Parented and of Parenting
    a Preschool Child   177
    Inge Bretherton, James David Lambert, and Barbara Golby

7   Maternal Representations of Parenting in Adolescence and
    Psychosocial Functioning of Mothers and Adolescents   208
    Ofra Mayseless and Miri Scharf

8   Like Fathers, Like Sons? Fathers' Attitudes to Childrearing
    in Light of Their Perceived Relationships with Own Parents,
    and Their Attachment Concerns   239
    Ruth Sharabany, Anat Scher, and Judit Gal-Krauz

Part Three Clinical Implications

9   Intergenerational Transmission of Dysregulated Maternal
    Caregiving: Mothers Describe Their Upbringing and
    Childrearing   265
    Judith Solomon and Carol George

10 Good Investments: Foster Parent Representations of Their
    Foster Children   296
    John P. Ackerman and Mary Dozier

11 Intergenerational Transmission of Experiences in
    Adolescence: The Challenges in Parenting Adolescents   319
    Miri Scharf and Shmuel Shulman

12 Interplay of Relational Parent–Child Representations from a
    Psychoanalytic Perspective: An Analysis of Two
    Mother–Father–Child Triads   352
    Hadas Wiseman, Ruth Hashmonay, and Judith Harel

13 Why Do Inadequate Parents Do What They Do?   388
    Patricia M. Crittenden

Index   435

Illustrations

4.1 The affective tone of mothers' representations of their infants
by WMCI typology classifications   *page* 129

4.2 Mothers' emotion displays across the Still Face procedure,
from the initial Free Play episode to Reengagement following
the Still Face: Maternal positive affect   134

4.3 Mothers' emotion displays across the Still Face procedure,
from the initial Free Play episode to Reengagement following
the Still Face: Maternal hostile/angry behavior   135

13.1 Six memory systems as a function of cognitive and affective
information   394

13.2 The Dynamic-Maturational Model of attachment   400

13.3 A clustering of parental representation organized around a
patterned gradient of covarying psychological processes   404

Tables

2.1 Descriptive Statistics for CPAP-PDI Construct Means after
    Adjustment for Skewness ($N = 80$)   *page* 57
2.2 Significant Correlations Representational Dimensions
    ($N = 80$)   58
2.3 Correlations between Demographic Variables, Maternal
    Psychological Characteristics, Maternal Behavior, and
    CPAP-PDI   60
4.1 Representational Typology Categories for the WMCI   124
4.2 Conceptual Grid Linking Elements of the Affective
    Organization of Parenting with Assessment Measures
    Employed in the Michigan Family Study   127
4.3 Correlations between Affective Tone Scales and Maternal
    Affective Behavior during the Still Face Procedure   133
5.1 Reliability Coefficients, Inter-correlations among the
    Parenting Representation Scales, and Correlations with Child
    Variables   159
5.2 Spearman Correlation Coefficients of Mother's Parenting
    Representations with Early Mother–Infant Interaction and
    with Child's Representations of the Mother Figure   160
6.1 Percentages and Frequencies of Men Who Mentioned
    Specific Topics When Comparing Themselves to Their
    Mothers and Fathers in Terms of Similarities and Differences   192
7.1 Caregiving Characteristics of Mothers in Adequate/Balanced,
    Flooded, and Restricted Categories of Parenting
    Representations   217
7.2 Cross-Tabulation of Mothers' Attachment and Parenting
    Representations   225

7.3 Parenting Representations as a Function of Mothers' Three
     Categories AAI   225
7.4 Parenting Representations as a Function of Mothers' Four
     Categories AAI   227
7.5 The Association between Mothers' Parenting Representations
     and Their Sons' Coping with Military Service – Time 2   228
7.6 Individuation of Sons as a Function of Their Mothers'
     Parenting Representations Categories   229
7.7 The Association between Mothers' Parenting Representations
     and Their Sons' Individuation – Time 3   230
8.1 Fathers' Attitudes to Childrearing and Their Perceived
     Relationships with Own Mother and Father   249
8.2 Fathers' Attachment-Related Concerns, Perceived
     Relationships with Own Mother and Father, and Their
     Childrearing Attitudes: Pearson Correlations   250
9.1 Life Events Summary   274
12.1 Interplay among Mother–Father–Child Relational
     Representations   370

Appendixes

2.1 Parent Development Interview, adapted from Aber, Slade,
   Berger, Bresgi, & Kaplan, 1985   *page* 69
2.2 Description of Parent Development Interview Constructs   70
4.1 The Working Model of the Child Interview   139
5.1 The Parenting Interview: Coding Scales   170
8.1 The Items Used from the CRPR (Block, 1981) and the
   Relationship Scales   257
10.1 "This is My Baby" Interview   312

Contributors

John P. Ackerman, M. A.
Department of Psychology,
  University of Delaware

Inge Bretherton, Ph.D.
Department of Human Development
  and Family Studies, University of
  Wisconsin-Madison

Patricia M. Crittenden, Ph.D.
Family Relations Institute

Carolyn J. Dayton, M.A., MSW
Department of Psychology, Michigan
  State University

Mary Dozier, Ph.D.
Department of Psychology, University
  of Delaware

Judit Gal-Krauz
University of Haifa, Israel

Carol George, Ph.D.
Mills College, Oakland, CA

Barbara Golby
Elmhurst Hospital

Joan E. Grusec, Ph.D.
Department of Psychology, University
  of Toronto

Judith Harel, Ph.D.
Department of Psychology, University
  of Haifa, Israel

Ruth Hashmonay, Ph.D.
Faculty of Education, University of
  Haifa, Israel

Liora Klein
University of Haifa, Israel

James David Lambert
Edgewood College

Ofra Mayseless, Ph.D.
Faculty of Education, University of
  Haifa, Israel

Susan McDonough, Ph.D., MSW
Center for Human Growth and
  Development, University of
  Michigan

Robert C. Pianta, Ph.D.
University of Virginia

Katherine L. Rosenblum, Ph.D.
Center for Human Growth and
  Development, University of
  Michigan

Duane Rudy
University of Toronto

Miri Scharf, Ph.D.
Faculty of Education, University of Haifa, Israel

Anat Scher, Ph.D.
Faculty of Education, University of Haifa, Israel

Ruth Sharabany, Ph.D.
Department of Psychology, University of Haifa, Israel

Shmuel Shulman, Ph.D.
Department of Psychology, Bar-llan University, Ramat Gan, Israel

Judith Solomon, Ph.D.
Early Childhood Mental Health Program, Children's Hospital of Oakland, Oakland, CA

Donna R. Steinberg, Ph.D.
Dartmouth College

Hadas Wiseman, Ph.D.
Faculty of Education, University of Haifa, Israel

Preface

This book grew out of my deep interest in caregiving, a central encompassing motivation that, as I see it, "makes the world go round." Parenting seemed to me to be the prototypical example of this motivation, yet the most taken for granted. From my own experience as a mother, I knew how powerful this bond and commitment to the well-being, happiness, and survival of your children is, and how central in my being, though not always in my doing. As I was focusing more on this emotion/feeling/bond/motivation, it became clearer to me that our motivation to give care, our love for our children, and the great many concessions and sometimes sacrifices that we are willing to make for them without expectation to be reciprocated and for the "sole" purpose that they will be healthy, happy, and fulfilled are not at all the same as our needs to be nurtured and protected. In other words, I became quite convinced that the caregiving motive is very distinct from attachment. Yet, unlike attachment which has been examined and studied from various angles, caregiving and in particular parenting have been much less explored.

This last statement is not fully true because developmental researchers as well as clinicians have devoted considerable contemplation and study efforts to uncover what a good parent is. In an effort to understand this issue, they explored for the most part parental behaviors and practices (and less so parental emotions and cognitions) and in particular looked at the effects of these on child outcomes. Thus, in most of the extant literature on parenting, the effects of parents' actions and practices on their children were the focus of the investigation in an attempt to provide the world with a valid answer to the question how best to parent. Parents were viewed as a vehicle to promote the child's success, welfare, and well-being. The focus on the parental subjective world, parents' feelings and thoughts, emotions and attributions, love and hate, dedication and guilt were considered less central in and of themselves. For example, whereas it seemed quite natural to fund investigations aimed at uncovering normative changes within the child, few such studies were conducted with regards to the normative development of parenting, before and after people become parents.

Recently (for the past two decades), a surge of interest in the subjective world of the parents has emerged. This involved a focus on the parents' subjective experience and grew out of the social cognition literature (as reviewed in Rudy and Grusec – Chapter 3), the psychoanalytic literature (see chapters by Scharf and Shulman – Chapter 11 – and by Wiseman, Hashmonay, and Harel – Chapter 12), and the attachment paradigm (see a review in Mayseless – Chapter 1 – and Steinberg and Pianta – Chapter 2). Most of the chapters in this volume reflect the growing interest within this latter paradigm – the attachment point of view – in parental representations as reflecting their internal subjective world.

As reviewed in Mayseless (Chapter 1), most researchers used interviews to explore parents' mind, which they analyzed in various ways. The chapters in this volume present a diverse set of studies with such interviews and describe the interviews they used and their coding scheme. Steinberg and Pianta (Chapter 2) present their work with the adapted version of the *Parent Development Interview* (PDI), which includes also issues of achievement and compliance. They demonstrate that these concerns have unique associations with child and mother characteristics as well as with her behavior and that they are distinct from attachment-related issues. Applying another adaptation of the PDI with mothers of six-year-old children, Scher, Harel, Scharf, and Klein (Chapter 5) show that mothers' sensitivity in infancy is associated with their parenting representations, which in turn are correlated with the children's representations of the maternal figure. Using the *Working Model of the Child Interview* (WMCI), Rosenblum, Dayton, and McDonough (Chapter 4) show that mothers' representations have a marked effect on emotion activation and regulation of mothers and infants. Finally, applying the *Parenting Representations Interview-Adolescence* (PRI-A) with mothers of adolescents, Scharf and Mayseless (Chapter 7) show that mothers' representations are associated with their own AAI and with the sons' psychosocial functioning one year and three years later.

In two chapters, the fathers', not mothers', parenting representations are assessed using interviews – the *Parent Attachment Interview* by Bretherton, Lambert, and Golby (Chapter 6) and questionnaires by Sharabany, Scher, and Gal-Krauz (Chapter 8). In both chapters the associations of these representations with the fathers' perceived relationships with their own parents are described. Both studies suggest that fathers learn from their own fathers what not to do; that is, instead of emulation, fathers use compensation and reworking to define their own paternal role vis-à-vis that of their fathers.

Solomon and George (Chapter 9) too examine how parents' experiences with their own parents affect their parenting and the child's functioning. They suggest that childhood experiences of helplessness exhibited in a parental rage pattern are associated with similar helpless parenting representations and child's disorganized attachment. Four other chapters directly address clinical issues related to parenting representations. Ackerman and Dozier (Chapter 10) examine representations of foster parents and demonstrate the significant and central role of parental investment assessed using a special parenting interview (*This is My Baby Interview*). Like Solomon and George, Scharf and Shulman (Chapter 11) examine intergenerational transmission of parenting. They look at parents of adolescents and use interviews to examine the parents' own experiences as adolescents as well as their current parenting. Using case studies they demonstrate the powerful, and in many cases unsuccessful, attempts of parents to correct and undo past experiences with their own parents when they themselves were adolescents in their current relationships with their adolescents. Similarly, Wiseman, Hashmonay, and Harel (Chapter 12) examine processes of intergenerational transmission as they observe the connection between parents' representations of the child and the child's representations using the WMCI and the Core Conflictual Relational Theme method. Similar to Scher et al., they describe powerful associations between these two sets of representations. Interestingly, the three chapters that present clinical cases (Chapters 9, 11, and 12) underscore in particular cases of role reversal and enmeshment. Each suggests different ways by which parents can succeed to break the chain of intergenerational transfer of negative experiences.

Different conceptual issues are addressed in all the chapters. Here I would like to pinpoint in particular three of the chapters. Rudy and Grusec (Chapter 3) address the extant literature in social cognition that has been applied to parenting representations. This literature provides a rich conceptual base for researchers focusing on parents' minds. Similarly, Mayseless (Chapter 1) provides an overview of studies of parenting representations and offers a general conceptual model as well as highlights future directions. Finally, Crittenden (Chapter 13) presents a challenging and valuable model of parenting representations of parents whose parenting goes awry. This model can serve as a very significant point of departure for clinicians who wish to understand "what's on this parent's mind" when treating parents who mistreat, neglect, or abuse their children.

Together this whole collection of chapters presents new ideas, avenues for research, and clinical implications in the realm of parenting representations, as well as new insights into parents' mind and soul – their feelings, emotions, and cognitions, their origin and their effect on children.

Acknowledgments

This work would not have been done had I not received extensive help from many people. First and foremost of them is Miri Scharf, my dear friend and colleague – whose encouragement, great ideas, and above all good and sound advice helped steer this work in the right direction at so many junctions. Other friends as well and in particular Anat Scher, Hadas Wiseman, and Ruth Sharabany have been highly helpful at different phases, when the idea first came up and when I was wholly invested in it, and at different levels, professional and personal.

Naama and Oded, my children, are the ones from whom I learned firsthand about parenting and about this great gift. They are the well and source of my love and insights – flowing and originating in them.

On a different sphere, the work on this topic and on this book would not have been realized at all – had I not my husband, Meir, at my side serving as my "holding environment" and anchor, a web of confidence and security.

Finally, I would like to thank my colleagues and friends who have contributed to this volume. Their enthusiastic participation, openness to my requests and suggestions, and professional investment in writing the chapters have made it a successful realization.

PART I

Theoretical Perspectives

PART I

Theoretical Perspectives

1 Studying Parenting Representations as a Window to Parents' Internal Working Model of Caregiving

Ofra Mayseless

Abstract

This chapter examines the concept of parenting representations as embedded in the conceptualization of attachment theory regarding the caregiving behavioral system. The growing body of research on parenting representations is extensively reviewed, and the notion of "internal working model of caregiving" is presented in relation to the extant literature. In general, strong reliability and validity of various schemes for coding interviews assessing parenting representations are demonstrated, and their distinctiveness with regards to state of mind with respect to attachment is noted. The implications of this research and the concept of Internal Working Models (IWM) of caregiving are discussed, and future directions for theory and research are suggested.

Historical Overview

What's on a Parent's Mind

The study of parenting has a long history in clinical and developmental psychology. For the most part, researchers treated parents as the independent variable and were interested in them insomuch as they affected the normal or pathological development of children. The interest in the parent, in most cases the mother, as a subject in and of itself, and the focus on the parent's own desires, wishes, thoughts, and affective world, has developed mostly in the last two decades. Four major fields of research displayed such a focus: (1) researchers in the psychoanalytic tradition (e.g., Kraemer, 1996; Stern, 1989; Stern-Bruschweiler & Stern, 1989; see a review in Wiseman, Hashmonay, & Harel, this volume), (2) scholars of a feminist outlook (e.g., Ruddick, 1989), (3) researchers taking the social cognition perspective in developmental psychology (see a review in Rudy & Grusec, this volume), and (4) scholars in the tradition of attachment theory. This chapter focuses on the last-named, and examines the concept of parenting representations as embedded in the conceptualization of attachment theory regarding the caregiving behavioral system.

Attachment has been the major guiding theory in the area of emotional and social development for the past two decades and is one of the most influential theories in developmental psychology. From the start, Bowlby (1969/1982; 1973), the founder of the theory, discussed two relevant and reciprocal behavioral systems: attachment and caregiving. Attachment referred to the motivational system of the infant to receive care whereas caregiving referred to the motivational system of the parents to give care and protection. Since the inception of the theory, the study of attachment processes has flourished and evinced an increasing number of advances in theory and conceptualizations, as well as in measures (see, for example, the recent *Handbook of Attachment* edited by Cassidy & Shaver, 1999).

The study of the parenting motivational system lagged behind. But in the past few years interest in the caregiving system has surged and is exemplified by several publications. George and Solomon suggested that researchers should devote similar research efforts to the caregiving system as they have to the attachment behavioral system (George & Solomon, 1989). Following Bowlby, they further advocated that the two systems, though related, are separate, and each should be studied in its own right. In 1996 they edited a special issue of the *Infant Mental Health Journal* devoted to caregiving, which published several empirical studies of caregiving processes (e.g., George & Solomon, 1996). In the recent *Handbook of Attachment,* they wrote a central chapter on the caregiving system (George & Solomon, 1999a). A book highlighting caregiving from an attachment perspective has been written by Heard and Lake (1997) presenting the authors' perspective on the issue, including also a clinical focus. More recently, a major theoretical target article in *Psychological Inquiry* (Bell & Richard, 2000) was devoted to caregiving, with more than a dozen commentaries by prominent researchers in developmental psychology and other related areas.

Theoretical interest in the parenting motivational system (the caregiving behavioral system) has been paralleled by an empirical attempt to assess parents' views, emotions, and internal world regarding their parenting. This has culminated in a new and expanding area of research involving *parenting representations*. Several researchers in different laboratories have suggested various ways of assessing these. They have mostly employed semi-structured interviews, and have developed various different ways of analyzing those interviews (e.g., Bretherton, Biringen, Ridgeway, Maslin, & Sherman, 1989; Benoit, Zeanah, Parker, Nicholson, & Coolbear, 1997; Aber, Belsky, Slade, & Crnic, 1999; see the review below). Though not openly stated, their focus on parenting representations seems to reflect an attempt to examine and investigate parents' Internal Working Models (IWMs) regarding caregiving (see the next section). In many respects that research followed the breakthrough in the development of the Adult Attachment Interview (AAI) with its new conception and method, which provided a way to assess adults' IWMs regarding attachment (Hesse, 1999).

In this chapter, I first present the concept of Internal Working Models and briefly describe the innovation in conceptualization and research following the development of the AAI (a thorough discussion of the research with the AAI can be found in Hesse, 1999). I then extensively review the growing body of research on parenting representations and summarize its main findings. Finally, I discuss the implications of this research and the concept of the Internal Working Model of caregiving, suggesting future directions for theory and research.

The Place of Internal Working Models in Bowlby's Theory

One of the major postulates of Bowlby's (1969/1982) theorizing was that the two motivational systems, attachment and caregiving, are not drives but function as behavioral systems that are characterized by several distinct features. First, behavioral systems are organized as goal-corrected, with specific set goals rather than a pre-wired sequence of behaviors. Behaviors change and adjust to serve the different goals, and this adjustment involves a feedback loop. Similar behaviors may reflect the operation of different goals and the same goal may be served by different behaviors in the same individual and across different individuals. The meanings of specific sequences of behaviors derive from the goals that govern them. In addition, Bowlby suggested that the different behavioral systems (e.g., attachment and caregiving) need to be coordinated in various ways to allow the achievement of the distinct goals. Finally, behavioral systems are seen as governed by higher processes of integration and control, and hence include IWMs, namely representations of the world and how the relevant set goals can be achieved. According to Bowlby (1969/1982; p. 82), working models include a model of the environment (social and non-social) as well as a representation of the person's own skills and potentialities. Because behavioral systems are seen as governed by these IWMs and because the significance of behaviors depends on the meaning imparted to them by these IWMs, researchers started focusing on the study of IWMs as a major avenue to understand the workings of behavioral systems, in particular the behavioral system of attachment (Main, Kaplan, & Cassidy, 1985).

Several researchers tried to elucidate and clarify the concept of Internal Working Model, in particular regarding the attachment behavioral system (e.g., Bretherton & Munholland, 1999; Collins & Read, 1994; Crittenden, 2000). First, it was claimed that these representations are built on actual experiences, and in the case of attachment on actual experiences with caregivers in attachment-related circumstances. Second, IWMs were seen as serving to regulate, interpret, and predict the person's as well as the caregiver's attachment-related behaviors, thoughts, and feelings. IWMs were not seen just as reflecting a reality but also as regulating and in some cases creating a reality. Third, IWMs were seen as somewhat flexible to some extent in that they can be updated in light of a person's new experiences and information, and modified by a person's changing capacities to interpret and reflect on different experiences. Fourth, the representations of the environment and the self were seen as involving several distinct memory systems: procedural, semantic, and episodic, at various levels of consciousness and involving varying degrees of affective load. Finally, IWMs were also seen as reflecting the operation of diverse defensive processes that serve to protect the person from unbearable anxiety and psychological suffering. These defensive processes are involved in all facets of the IWMs such as the representations of the environment and the self, the goals set, and the plans adopted.

The Adult Attachment Interview: A Conceptual and Assessment Breakthrough

With regard to the attachment behavioral system, the Adult Attachment Interview (AAI) and its coding (Main & Goldwyn, 1998) proved a very powerful means for gaining some understanding of working models of attachment. The AAI is an hour-long structured interview designed to arouse memories and emotions related to attachment experiences. Interviewees are requested to give a general description of their relationships with their parents (and of other caregivers who acted in an attachment-related capacity) and to support these descriptions by specific biographical incidents. Additionally, they are asked about specific experiences of separation, rejection, or abuse. Furthermore, they are asked to explain their parents' behavior, to describe the nature of their current relationship with their parents, and to assess the influence of childhood experiences on their development and personality. The interviews are audiotaped and transcribed verbatim; the coding is based on the transcript. Scores are assigned to inferred childhood experiences of love, rejection, involvement, inattentiveness (neglect), and pressure to achieve exerted by each parent, and to the respondent's state of mind with regard to idealization, anger, derogation, insistence upon inability to recall childhood, passivity, and coherence. Some of the AAI scales refer to the content of the representations (e.g., parental love), but major coding is based on how the coder views the interviewee's reflections, evaluations, and defensive processes, what has been termed the *state of mind with respect to attachment*.

Specifically, from the transcript the interviewee's emotional access and openness to past attachment-related experiences are assessed, as well as the coherence in describing them. Adults with a *secure* (*autonomous*) state of mind with respect to attachment have somewhat easier access to past experiences, positive or negative, which they tend to describe openly and coherently. Insecure adults do not access past experiences easily, or they describe them incoherently. Specifically, *dismissing* adults tend to restrict the importance of attachment in their own lives, or to idealize their parents without being able to illustrate their positive evaluations with concrete evidence. They seem to use the defensive strategy of minimizing attachment behavior and feelings. They often appear to lack memory of childhood experiences related to attachment. *Preoccupied* adults are still greatly involved and preoccupied with their past attachment experiences and are, therefore, not able to describe them coherently and reflectively. They may express passivity or anger when describing current attachment relationships with their parents. In addition, a fourth category was proposed, for people who are *unresolved* with respect to loss or trauma. Such individuals are also placed in one of the other three major categories as a forced categorization.

The AAI was first developed and validated (Main et al., 1985) against the behavior in the Strange Situation of infants of the interviewed adults. Correspondence between the classification of the adult's IWM according to the interview and the infants' attachment classification served to validate the AAI (van IJzendoorn, 1995). In addition, the AAI was related, as anticipated, to observed parenting behaviors (Hesse, 1999). In all, the AAI has proved a valuable and valid measure of the internal working model of attachment as regards parent–child relationships (Hesse, 1999).

The development of the AAI was a major leap forward for understanding IWMs. Specifically, it demonstrated that with regard to predicting children's attachment relationships, the overt content of the caregiver's IWM as well as the presumed quality of the relationships with his or her own parents as deduced from the interview by the coders are not as important as the current affective and defensive stance with regard to attachment experiences. Secure adults seem to be free to evaluate these experiences, good or bad; dismissing adults seem to reject parts of these experiences, whereas preoccupied adults seem to be over involved in them without the capacity to emotionally disengage and reflect on them.

The success in using the AAI to uncover an important part of a person's IWM in respect of attachment led to attempts by several groups of investigators (see the following sections) to examine parenting representations using similarly constructed interviews. These contained questions about the child and the parent's relationship with him or her instead of questions pertaining to the parent's own parents or caregivers. Though not explicitly stated, these efforts can be seen as aimed to uncover the parents' IWMs regarding their caregiving. The following sections review these efforts extensively.

Assessments of Parenting Representations: Coding Schemes and Findings

In presenting the different ways of assessing and examining parenting representations, I have chosen to organize the review according to the different researchers or assessment methods. I then review studies with a more particular focus on a specific clinical population or a special aspect of the representation. As happens so often in science, many of these investigations started around the same point in time in different laboratories, by different researchers often with only partial knowledge of the others' work at first. The order in which these studies are reviewed does not reflect their importance or their temporal sequence.

The Parent Attachment Interview (PAI): Bretherton and Her Colleagues

Within the attachment tradition, Bretherton and her colleagues (Bretherton et al., 1989) were among the first to suggest examining parents' representations regarding their parenting, and voiced surprise at researchers' neglect of the parental side of attachment till then. On the basis of Main's Adult Attachment Interview, Bretherton and her colleagues devised an in-depth structured yet open-ended interview, the *Parent Attachment Interview* (PAI), which focused on parents' attachment experiences with a specific child. Bretherton and her colleagues used the term attachment but referred to the parental side, namely the parent's provision of caregiving and the caregiving bond that characterizes most of these relationships. They chose the term "parental attachment" advisedly. In their own words,

> It is not only the infant who keeps tabs on the parent, and who becomes distressed upon separation; parents also tend to keep a watchful eye on their infant, to intervene when the infant is getting into a potentially painful or harmful situation, to experience feelings of alarm when the infant's whereabouts are not known or the infant's well-being is in danger, and to feel relief when the child is found or the danger past. In our view the term "caregiving", though often used to describe the parental side of the attachment relationship, does not sufficiently reflect the depth of the parent-to-child bond. (Bretherton et al., 1989; p. 205)

The interview adapted for mothers of toddlers included structured questions followed by probes asking for examples and elaborations (see Bretherton, Lambert, & Golby, this volume). The questions revolved around the following issues: mother's thoughts and feelings at the baby's birth, the baby's personality, experiences at nighttime and during other separations, autonomy-related negotiations, compliance issues, mother's feelings such as joy, anger, worry, or guilt, comparisons with her own parents' caregiving, and projection into the future. The interview was first administered to 37 mothers of two-year-olds as part of a longitudinal study which included assessments of a number of other constructs (e.g., temperament, maternal personality, attachment Q-sort). Data analysis included content analysis, which focused on the mother's thoughts and feelings regarding particular attachment issues, and a global analysis using a nine-point scale assessing sensitivity/insight concerning the mother's relationship with the infant (see Bretherton et al., this volume). Content analyses exposed meaningful variations among the mothers as well as several joint themes such as quite high tolerance of inconvenient attachment behavior at night. The sensitivity/insight scale was significantly associated with security of attachment as indexed in the Strange Situation, attachment Q-sort, and attachment story completions. The scale was also significantly and positively associated with the child's perceived attention span and sociability and negatively with the child's emotionality. Similarly, it was positively associated with mother's extroversion and cohesive and adaptable family relations.

In another study with 40 mothers and their toddlers (Biringen, Matheny, Bretherton, Renouf, & Sherman, 2000), the interview was further scored using Westen's (1991) six dimensions of the SCORS-Q: Affect tone of relationship schemas, Understanding of social causality, Experience and management of aggressive impulses, Cognitive structure/complexity of representations, Capacity for emotional investment in moral standards, and Self-esteem. Associations between these scores as well as the sensitivity/insight score and mother's sensitivity and structuring during observations with her child at 18, 24, and 39 months were examined. Several aspects of the maternal representation (but not the global scale of sensitivity/insight) were associated with the mother's behavior. For example, experience and management of aggressive impulses, capacity for emotional investment in moral standards, and particularly self-esteem were associated with observed maternal sensitivity at 18 months. By 24 and 39 months, observed maternal structuring during the interactions was significantly associated with the mother's self-esteem, which refers to her having realistically positive views of herself in the relationship.

Lately the PAI was used to examine maternal representations in divorced mothers (Golby & Bretherton, 1999), and as reported in this volume (Bretherton et al.) it was also administered to intact couples including the fathers. In both cases parents' interviews were subjected to a content analysis aiming to identify themes and categories of responses rather than quantitatively assess specific dimensions in parents' representations. For example, in the divorced-mothers study themes of resiliency were identified and highlighted.

In general the PAI has been employed mostly with parents of toddlers and pre-school children, and has been analyzed qualitatively and also by use of quantitative scales reflecting global aspects of the interview narrative such as insight/sensitivity or self-esteem and sense of competence in the maternal role. It has shown moderate association with a diverse set of measures of attachment security of the child and was associated with mother's behavior during an observed interaction with the child.

Parent Development Interview (PDI): Aber, Slade, and Colleagues

At the same time as Bretherton and her colleagues devised the PAI, Aber and his colleagues (Aber et al., 1985) developed a somewhat similar interview, the Parent Development Interview (PDI), to assess parenting representations. In general the interview addressed similar issues and had a similar format: open-ended questions, followed by probes with a request for specific examples and elaboration. This interview asked the parents to describe the relationships with the child, not his or her personality as in the PAI. In addition parents were asked what they liked or disliked about their child, how different or similar they were to the child and to their own parents, pleasures and difficulties in their relationship with the child, and their own strengths and weaknesses as parents. They were asked about separations and various feelings and challenging situations (e.g., mother could not give the child her full attention). The PDI is distinguished by the specific coding scheme developed by Slade and her colleagues (Slade, Belsky, Aber, & Phelps, 1999). In this coding scheme, three general dimensions are assessed by means of several rating scales which are scored based on the interview as a whole: (1) parents' representation of their own affective experience, (2) parents' representation of their child's affective experience, and (3) parenting state of mind or thought processes. Parents' own affective experience is measured on scales assessing anger, neediness, separation distress, guilt, joy and pleasure, and sense of competence and efficacy. Child's affective experience is measured on scales assessing child's anger, separation distress, and dependence–independence. Finally, scales for state of mind assess general coherence and richness of perception, the latter adapted from Zeanah, Benoit, Hirshberg, Barton, and Regan (1994).

In a large sample of 125 mothers of first-born *male* toddlers, the PDI was administered twice: when the children were 15 and 28 months old (Aber et al., 1999; Slade et al., 1999). In addition mothers were administered the AAI and observed twice at home with their toddlers. Though they assessed quite a large number of separate constructs in the PDI, following factor analyses the researchers used three major scales: (1) coherence/joy, comprising coherence, richness of perception, and joy–pleasure; (2) anger, comprising degree, acknowledgment, and modulation of parental anger; and (3) guilt/separation distress, comprising parent's degree and acknowledgment of guilt and separation distress. The other scales were not included in the analyses in that study. Coherence/joy was negatively associated with anger to a small to moderate degree.

In terms of validation, these researchers (Aber et al., 1999, Slade et al., 1999) reported that mothers with an autonomous state of mind assessed by the AAI scored highest on the joy–pleasure/coherence dimension of the PDI, and mothers classified as dismissing on the AAI scored highest on the anger dimension of the PDI. In addition, the joy–pleasure/coherence dimension was positively associated with a general scale of positive mothering as observed on the two home visits. Thus, parenting representations of toddlers as measured on global scales reflecting content (i.e., anger) as well as thought processes (i.e., coherence) were associated, as expected, with mothers' state of mind with respect to attachment and their behavior with their toddlers.

Parenting representations were stable across this year at a range of 20–25% of explained variance. Additionally, there was a general increase in anger as the children moved into the terrible-twos; anger at 15 months contributed negatively to joy/coherence, whereas coherence/joy contributed negatively to anger a year later, after accounting for simple stability between identical scales. Daily parenting-related hassles contributed to anger identified in the interview at 28 months, and positive mothering as observed on the home visits contributed to joy/pleasure over and above the stability of parenting representations. Together, these findings demonstrated that parenting representations sensitively reflect changes in the relationships and in the general parenting context.

In another sub-sample ($N = 40$) of a larger sample of middle class mothers of infants (girls and boys), the PDI was again administered along with the AAI (Slade, Grienenberger, Bernbach, Levy, & Locker, 2001). Mothers and infants were also observed in the Strange Situation. This time the PDI was analyzed by the application of a modified assessment of what Fonagy terms reflective function (Fonagy, 1996; Fonagy & Target, 1998). Mother's reflective function in the PDI was manifested in her capacity to attribute mental states to her child and to herself in relation to the child, namely to keep the baby in mind and reflect on the baby's experience. Mothers' reflective function was associated, as expected, with autonomous state of mind in the AAI, with infants' attachment security in the Strange Situation, and with mothers' low levels of atypical maternal behaviors assessed by the AMBIANCE coding scheme (Lyons-Ruth, Bronfman, & Parsons, 1999) during the Strange Situation. The authors advise caution in interpreting this result because of the small sample and the small to moderate association between mother's AAI and child's attachment security. Still, they report that this moderate association was fully mediated by maternal reflective functioning as attested in her parenting interview. Again, parenting representations as assessed with the PDI proved associated with maternal state of mind with regard to attachment, the child's attachment security, and maternal behavior.

Parent Development Interview (PDI): Modification by George and Solomon

Modifying the PDI, George and Solomon (1989) extended the use of the interview to mothers of older children (aged six years) and incorporated changes relevant to parenting in this age group (for example, they included questions regarding separation to go to school). In the first study, with 32 mother–child dyads, they suggested two complementary rating scales, which were applied to the whole transcript: a *secure base* scale, which assesses how effective the mother is as a secure base for her child, and how much she displays a goal-corrected partnership with her child; and a *competence* rating scale, which assesses how far she fosters autonomy and growth in her child, who reacts positively to these endeavors. Both scales reflect *maternal strategies and behaviors*, unlike the coding of the PDI which focuses on the *relationships between the mother and the child*. The two scales correlated highly, and were also strongly correlated with attachment security of the child as exhibited in a reunion procedure in the laboratory; but they were weakly associated with Q-sort items derived from observations of child's behavior at home.

Subsequently, George and Solomon (1989) suggested a somewhat different way of analyzing the interview, again focusing on the maternal side. They relied on their elaborate theoretical model (Solomon & George, 1996) of different parenting strategies for giving protection: *flexible protection, distant care, close care,* and the partial or full *abdication of the protective role* (Solomon, George, & De Jong, 1995). They developed four rating scales reflecting these general parenting strategies, which in turn are expected to yield different attachment patterns in the child. The four scales, *secure base, rejection, uncertainty,* and *helplessness,* are expected to be associated with secure attachment (flexible care), avoidant attachment (distant care), ambivalent attachment (close care), and disorganized or controlling attachment (abdication of protection), respectively. They are based on the whole interview and on the content of the interview, as well as its narrative style reflecting the mother's thought processes. Depending on her highest score, a mother could be categorized into one of the four caregiving strategies. In the sample described previously, George and Solomon reported strong association between these scales, and the caregiving categories based on them, and the mothers' corresponding AAI categories, as well as the child's corresponding attachment categorization determined following a reunion procedure (Solomon & George, 1996).

A similar interview was applied with a larger sample of 144 mothers (married and divorced) and their toddlers (Solomon & George, 1999). The interview was again coded with the secure base scale as a global assessment of parenting representations. In addition, for divorced or separated mothers another scale, psychological protection, was used to analyze the questions pertaining to father's visits. This scale assesses the extent to which the mother is judged as taking active measures to avoid or mitigate the child's distress during paternal visitation. The two measures correlated moderately, and both were independently associated with infant's attachment security in the Strange Situation. Replicating the findings in the small sample of six-year-olds, this study showed a clear association of parenting representations with infants' attachment security, too.

In sum, like Bretherton and her colleagues (e.g., Bretherton et al., 1989) and Aber, Slade, and their colleagues (e.g., Aber et al., 1999; Slade et al., 1999), George and Solomon also demonstrated a significant association between mothers' parenting representations (specifically, the secure base scale) with mothers' autonomous state of mind with respect to attachment as assessed by the AAI as well as with attachment security of their children (one-year-olds and six-year-olds). George and Solomon further suggested an interesting and promising conceptualization of four caregiving strategies assessed by four general scales applied to the whole interview and categories based on these scales.

Parent Development Interview (PDI): Modifications by Pianta and Colleagues

The PDI was modified by Button Pianta, and Marvin (2001) as well. As described more fully in Chapter 2 (Steinberg & Pianta), these researchers suggested extending the examination of parenting representations beyond attachment-related aspects, affect, and thought processes (i.e., narrative style) to issues of compliance and achievement in the mother–child relationship and to issues of boundaries between the two. They suggested using a coding scheme that marks the existence of a certain theme or issue on a question-by-question basis rather than relying on a global coding of the whole interview. They examined a large sample of 112 mothers with children aged one to four years, including children diagnosed with cerebral palsy or epilepsy and a control group. Mothers' representations proved to reflect their children's clinical status: children with more severe disability were associated with less mention of compliance issues and more pain; and pain was positively associated with longer time since the diagnosis. Enmeshment in thought processes was associated with experiencing more worry and pain in the relationship and more pressuring behavior in a problem-solving task. Representations of worry about the child's future were associated with less support and less positive affect in an interaction with the child.

The same interview was applied in Australia by Shamir-Essakow, Ungerer, Rapee, and Safier (2004) to examine mothers' representations of 103 children aged three to four years (of whom 71 were identified as inhibited). Maternal anxiety was associated with higher levels of anger, worry, and guilt in the caregiving representations. Mothers of inhibited children described more incidences of comforting and safe haven and lower levels of neutralizing/defensiveness in their thought processes regarding caregiving than other mothers. In the inhibited group, mothers who had secure children as assessed by the preschool version of the Strange Situation scored higher on perspective taking and lower on neutralizing/defensiveness and emotion invalidation in their caregiving representations than mothers of insecure children. In sum, the research using this extended coding scheme found significant associations between parenting representations and mothers' behavior with the child; also, parenting representations reflected the different nature of the child's clinical condition or temperament and were associated with the child's attachment security. This approach, which considers other issues besides attachment, may be an important extension of other ways of analyzing the interviews.

Working Model of the Child Interview (WMCI): Zeanah and Benoit

About the same time as Bretherton and her colleagues developed the PAI, and Aber and his colleagues devised the PDI, Zeanah and his colleagues (Zeanah, Keener, Stewart, & Anders, 1985; Zeanah, Keener, & Anders, 1986) started examining mothers' and fathers' prenatal perceptions and feelings with regard to their expected infant (see later). Consequently, Zeanah and Benoit (1995) developed the Working Model of the Child Interview (WMCI: see Wiseman et al., this volume) to assess parents' perceptions and subjective experience of their infants, and their relationships with their infants.

Similar to the other interviews (the PAI or the PDI), the WMCI is an hour-long structured interview, which includes general questions followed by probes eliciting examples and elaborations. It was administered to parents from as early as pregnancy to when the child was five. It begins with a developmental history of the infant, from conception and birth. Parents are asked to describe impressions of the child's personality and behavior, in what way the infant is like or unlike the parents, and times when the infant is upset or difficult. They are asked about their relationships, what in the child pleases and displeases them, and how they envision the child in the future. Besides being audiotaped and transcribed, as in the other interviews, this one can be analyzed from videotapes by means of continuous Likert scales.

Eight primary Likert scales refer to richness of perception, openness to change, intensity of involvement, coherence, caregiving sensitivity, acceptance, infant difficulty, and fear for safety. Eight secondary rating scales assess the affective tone of the representations: joy, anxiety, pride, anger, guilt, indifference, disappointment, and other emotions expressed by the caregiver. The transcripts are categorized into one of three categories of representations: balanced, disengaged, or distorted. Balanced representations are characterized by moderate to high coherency, high levels of involvement, acceptance, and sensitive caregiving; also moderate to high scores on openness to change and richness of perception, joy, and pride, and low scores on anxiety, anger, disappointment and indifference. Balanced representations are expected to be associated with secure attachment.

Disengaged representations are characterized by coolness, emotional distance, and indifference, and are expected to be associated with avoidant attachment. Distorted representations reflect internal inconsistency within the representation and are expected to predict ambivalent attachment. The parent may be confused or anxious, self-involved, and insensitive, and may have unrealistic expectations of the infant. Intense feelings, both positive and negative, are expressed. In distorted representations the parent's interview evinces high scores on intensity of involvement, anxiety, and/or anger.

The WMCI was first administered to 45 mothers of infants (Zeanah et al., 1994) and showed a significant concurrent association with the infants' Strange Situation classification (69% concordance). A second study (Benoit, Parker, & Zeanah, 1997) replicated and extended these findings with a sample of 85 mothers. Again, mothers' categories of parenting representations were significantly concurrently associated with infants' Strange Situation classifications; in particular the balanced-secure concordance was apparent. In this sample the WMCI was administered during the third trimester of pregnancy also. High stability of categorizations (80%) was demonstrated, in particular regarding the balanced and distorted categories. Prenatally assessed WMCI categories also significantly predicted Strange Situation classifications. Again, the balanced-secure concordance was the most prominent.

Benoit, Zeanah, Parker, Nicholson, and Coolbear (1997) also examined the parenting representations of several at-risk groups: mothers of infants with failure to thrive, mothers of toddlers with sleep disorders, and mothers of infants seen in a general infant psychiatry clinic ($N = 54$), and compared them with a group of mothers of matched controls ($N = 45$). As expected, the prevalence of insecure representations (disengaged and distorted) was greater in each clinical group than in the control groups, with 81% insecure as opposed to 62%, respectively. Mothers in the clinical groups differed significantly from controls on several of the specific scales. They scored lower on richness of perception, openness to change, intensity of involvement, sensitivity, acceptance, and joy.

Another at-risk sample consisting of 50 preterm babies was examined by Cox, Hopkins, and Hans (2000). They administered a modified version of the PAI to mothers of 19-month-old infants but used the WMCI coding scheme. They found a significant association between mothers' parenting representations (balanced, disengaged, and distorted classifications) and the infants' secure/insecure Strange Situation classification. When specific insecure parenting representations and Strange Situation categories were examined, there was a significant association between the balanced and the secure classifications and between the disengaged and the avoidant ones, but not between the distorted representation and infants' ambivalent and disorganized classifications.

These studies were extended by Rosenblum, McDonough, Muzik, Miller, and Sameroff (2002). With a sample of 100 mothers, these researchers (see also Rosenblum, Dayton, & McDonough, this volume) showed that mother's representations were associated with her behavior during a still-face procedure with her seven-month-old infant. Specifically, only babies of mothers with balanced representations returned to a high level of positive affect during the reengagement phase following the still-face episode, and the levels of maternal positive affect of mothers with balanced representations mediated this effect. In addition, disengaged representations were associated with maternal rejection as observed during the still-face procedure, and infants of mothers with disengaged representations demonstrated more negative affect during the initial baseline episode.

In a large sample of 206 mothers, Huth-Bocks, Levendosky, Bogat, and von Eye (2004) administered the WMCI to pregnant women along with a questionnaire measure of their attachment experiences. Risk factors such as domestic violence, low SES, and single parenthood were also assessed. A year later, infants were observed in the Strange Situation. The authors used six major scales from the WMCI, related to thought processes and to content of the representations (richness of perception, openness to change, coherence, caregiving sensitivity, self as mother, and acceptance), to model mothers' prenatal representations of caregiving in Structural Equations Modeling. Maternal attachment experiences were significantly related to their prenatal representations of caregiving, which were significantly related to the infant's attachment. Maternal risk factors were strongly associated with mothers' prenatal representations of caregiving. In an extension of this last point, Huth-Bocks, Levendosky, Theran, and Bogat (2004) looked more closely at the association between domestic violence and prenatal representations. They showed that domestic violence was associated with more negative and insecure parenting representations (e.g., more anger, depression, and anxiety, a well as a perception of the not yet born infant as more difficult, lower openness to change, and lower acceptance).

In sum, the WMCI has been used fairly extensively by various researchers, including the original group who developed the coding scheme and others. Maternal representations as assessed using the WMCI with pregnant women as well as with mothers of preschool children, demonstrated high stability and the expected association with (1) the Strange Situation classifications of the infants, (2) maternal positive and negative affect during interaction with the baby, (3) the baby's emotion regulation, (4) maternal perceived attachment experiences, and (5) clinical status or risk factors. The balanced and the disengaged categories proved more informative than the distorted one. Similarities to and differences from the mother's state of mind with regard to attachment have not yet been explored.

Parenting Representations Interview – Adolescence (PRI-A): Mayseless and Scharf

Extending the examination of parenting representations to parents of adolescents, Mayseless and Scharf (this volume; 2001) devised an extensive interview, the PRI-A (Parenting Representations Interview – Adolescence), which builds on the PAI, the PDI, and the WMCI but adds aspects relevant to parenting of adolescents, such as monitoring, enabling autonomy, and partnership/mutuality (Scharf & Mayseless, 1997/2000). Mayseless and Scharf (2001) used scales referring to narrative style (i.e., balanced, restricted, and flooded) and scales referring to the content of the representations. These included scales for the mother (competence and self-understanding), the child (confidence in the child, child's understanding), the relationship (warmth/affection, monitoring, enhancing autonomy, mutuality/partnership, role-reversal, push to achieve, and capacity to envision future relationships with the child), and strength of various negative feelings (anger, guilt, worry, pain) (Scharf, Mayseless, & Kivenson-Baron, 1997/2000). With a sample of 82 mother–adolescent son dyads (Scharf, Mayseless, & Kivenson-Baron, 2004), these authors found mothers' representations to be associated with their state of mind as assessed by the AAI (Mayseless & Scharf, this volume) and their physical and psychological symptoms (Mayseless & Scharf, 2001). In general, autonomous mothers differed from preoccupied mothers in their evincing higher competence, self- and child understanding, confidence in the child, warmth/affection, partnership/mutuality, autonomy promotion, monitoring, and balanced representations. Preoccupied mothers were most conspicuous in their role reversal and flooded parenting representations and their high levels of symptoms. Dismissing mothers showed the lowest levels of negative emotions regarding their parenting and the highest level of restriction in their narrative.

Mothers' parenting representations were also associated, as expected, with the son's AAI (Mayseless, Scharf, Kivenson-Baron, & Scharf, 2005). Specifically, in contrast to dismissing adolescents, autonomous adolescents had mothers whose representations reflected higher levels of competence, warmth/affection, monitoring, and partnership/mutuality. Finally, mothers' parenting representations were associated with psychosocial functioning of their sons concurrently and at two other points in time: a year later during their home-leaving transition to mandatory military service and four years later at the end of the three-year military service (Mayseless et al., 2005). For example, mother's competence, her confidence in her child, and partnership/mutuality were concurrently associated with the son's secure attachment style, the son's capacity to provide emotional support, and the quality of his relationship with his best friend – notably emotional closeness and balanced relatedness.

These same qualities in mothers' parenting representations as well as warmth/affection and a flooded narrative (reversed) were associated with better coping with the home-leaving transition to mandatory military service as indexed by the son's and peers' reports. Finally, some of these qualities in maternal representations as well as mother's understanding of herself and her son, and degree of balance in the narrative, were predictive of the son's level of individuation four years later. By extending research of parenting representations to parents of adolescents, and including outcomes not assessed previously, this study attests to the importance of mothers' parenting representations in predicting a host of psychosocial outcomes in their sons. These associations still need to be examined with adolescent girls and with fathers' parenting representations as well.

Assessment of Particular Aspects in the Representations

Applying a specific interview to examine resolution of their child's diagnosis, Pianta, Marvin, and their colleagues (Pianta, Marvin, Britner, & Borowitz, 1996; Marvin & Pianta, 1996; Sheeran, Marvin, & Pianta, 1997; Welch, Pianta, Marvin, & Saft, 2000) suggested that facing a diagnosis of a child with a disability is a crisis and is experienced by parents as loss or trauma which they need to resolve to be able to care effectively for their child. Resolution was assessed by the capacity to integrate the experience of the diagnosis and its consequences into parenting representations and to reorient and refocus on problem solving in the present and the future. In a large sample ($N = 97$), Sheeran et al. (1997) found that mothers who were resolved felt less stressed with their parenting and perceived more support from their family, and their husbands felt more satisfied in the marriage. In addition, mothers' resolution of the diagnosis was significantly associated with infants' attachment security as assessed by the Strange Situation (Marvin & Pianta, 1996), but was not related to qualities of feeding interactions (Welch et al., 2000) or to diagnosis type, severity of condition, developmental age, and time since receiving the diagnosis (Pianta et al., 1996). Thus, the general concept of parenting representations can be extended to include coping, at the representational level, with child's disability or diagnosis of a chronic illness.

In another application of an interview to assess a particular aspect of parenting representations, Dozier and her colleagues (e.g., Bates & Dozier, 2002; Tyrrell & Dozier, 1999) examined foster parents' representations; they focused on several specific aspects by designing specialized questions. In a study comparing biological mothers with foster mothers ($N = 50$), Tyrrell and Dozier (1999) investigated mothers' perceived attachment-related difficulties of the infant, and mothers understanding of attachment strategies (e.g., their capacity to explain why a child would avoid a mother after a separation and their understanding that the child nevertheless needed the caregiver but had difficulty expressing it). Mothers' understanding of attachment strategies was significantly related to their observed sensitivity during a home visit. Foster and biological mothers showed no difference in such knowledge and sensitivity, but as expected, the former perceived more attachment-related difficulties than the latter. Mothers' capacity to reflect on attachment-related issues and understand them was associated with their greater observed sensitivity.

In another study, Bates and Dozier (2002) again focused on specific dimensions in the foster mothers' parenting representations and designed an interview that specifically focuses on these issues: the "This is My Baby Interview" (TIMB: see Ackerman & Dozier, this volume). This quite short interview (compared with the PDI or the WMCI) takes about 10 minutes and inquires about mother's view of the baby's personality, whether she ever wished she could raise the child to adulthood, missing the child, how she views the effect of the current relationships on the child, and what she wants for the baby for now and in the future. Three dimensions are scored: *Acceptance* (i.e., pleasure, delight, and respect), *commitment*, and *belief in her influence* on the child. In the study, these dimensions were quite highly intercorrelated. The results ($N = 48$) indicated that autonomous mothers (as assessed by the AAI) were more accepting and had stronger belief in their capacity to influence the infants in their care when these children were placed earlier than when they were placed later. Child's age at placement was not associated with these parenting representations for non-autonomous mothers. The parenting representations of autonomous mothers sensitively reflected the contextual important variable of child's age at placement.

Focusing on foster mothers' investment, Ackerman and Dozier (2003; described in Ackerman & Dozier, this volume) found that high levels of caregiver investment were associated with more positive self-evaluations among school-age foster children and lower levels of aggressive response biases towards peers. Furthermore, as indicated in the chapter in this volume

(Ackerman & Dozier), foster mothers' representations indicative of investment proved an important predictor of other indicators of psychosocial development of children. Caregiver representations reflecting investment may serve
as a protective factor in foster children's psychosocial development.

Parenting Representations Before the Baby Is Born

Several researchers were interested in the images and expectations that parents
have of their child during pregnancy, namely even before the child is born,
and how these change after the birth as the parents begin to form a relationship
with a "real" baby.

Zeanah et al. (1985; 1986) examined mothers' and fathers' prenatal perceptions of their infant using a quantitative self-report questionnaire. They
asked parents to report on the infant's temperament as presumed during the
third trimester of pregnancy, and then one month and six months postnatally. Parents were also interviewed regarding the infant's personality and
their relationship with the infant at the same points in time, and these interviews were analyzed qualitatively (Zeanah, Zeanah, & Stewart, 1990). Parents
were able to give prenatal descriptions of their child, and these were associated with those obtained postnatally. These perceptions (e.g., activity level,
affect, sociability) varied considerably, and, as expected, parents' descriptions became richer and fuller with infant's age. Parents harbor images of
their children before they are born and these representations are associated
with those they hold later on, after they form an actual relationship with their
child.

Ammaniti, Baumgartner, and Candelori et al. (1992) similarly explored
the content and structure of maternal representations using an interview
and a questionnaire asking mothers for descriptions of themselves and the
baby with a sample of 23 primiparous women in their third trimester of
pregnancy. Already then the research exposed a complex set of representations of the mothers and their baby (Ammaniti, 1991). In the interview
mothers were asked to describe themselves as mothers and their as yet
unborn baby. These descriptions were similar in general style (e.g., richness
of description, coherence). However, their separate descriptions of themselves, their own mothers, and their expected baby, using a list of adjectives, were quite different. In most cases mothers had more positive views
of their coming baby than of themselves or their mothers. Fave-Viziello,
Antonioli, Cocci, and Invernizzi (1993) found similar results and emphasized that these representations evolve and change after the baby is born.
In particular, representations of the mother of herself as a mother and of

her baby seem to change, reflecting the actual relationships formed between the two.

A similar finding was reported by Ilicali and Fisek (2004), who asked each of 23 pregnant women and 22 mothers of infants to describe five different significant figures, namely her child, herself as mother, herself as a person, her own mother, and her partner, using a list of 18 adjectives. In addition these authors used a brief interview with the same women, which was analyzed in reference to several scales: coherence, congruence of affect, richness, and flexibility, as well as positiveness of perceptions of each of the persons described. There were no significant differences between the mothers-to-be and the actual mothers. Mothers' representations showed a strong association between self as mother and self as person, and a moderate association between self as mother and the perception of the child. For the pregnant women, perception of the child and the self as person were moderately associated with perceptions of partner. Interestingly, perception of own mother was not significantly associated with perceptions of other figures. These findings underscore that while the pregnant women entertained various images and perceptions of their as yet unborn child, these representations, though mostly projective, reflected only moderately their perceptions of other important figures in their lives.

Using a similar method with two large groups of high- and low-risk pregnant women in Finland ($N = 84$ and 296, respectively), Pajulo, Savonlahti, Sourander, Piha, and Helenius (2001) found that representations of child, self, own mother, and partner were more negative in the high-risk group. Still, child ratings were the most positive of all, and were the closest to those of the low-risk group. These results attest to the association of clinical risk and representations of the child and the mother even before the child is born; yet they show a tendency in future mothers to a positivity bias in their perceptions of the as yet unborn child, one noted by Stern (1991) and discussed by him as indicating an adaptive process.

Changes in Parents' Representations Following Therapy

Changes in maternal representations following therapy were also examined (Cramer & Stern, 1988). Cramer et al. (1990) examined maternal representations of 38 mothers of children less than 30 months old who were referred to therapy because of various symptoms such as sleep and behavior disorders. Dyads underwent two kinds of a brief (less than 10 sessions) mother–infant psychotherapy. Mothers were asked to fill out questionnaires, were observed interacting with their child, and engaged in an interview termed *R* developed by an international research group (Stern et al., 1989) and also employed by Ilicali and Fisek (2004). The interview examines representations of the child, the mother in her mothering role, the mother and father as persons, and the mother's own mother. It probes for affects, wishes, anxieties, and self-esteem and asks the mother to evaluate past and present influences on her mothering. Therapy success was evaluated one week and six months following termination of the therapy by means of questionnaires, observed interaction between mother and child, and the *R* interview.

Maternal representations became more positive following the therapy, showing a medium effect size, and this improvement was retained at the six-month follow-up. Specifically, infants were seen as calmer, more affectionate, more independent, and less aggressive. Mothers perceived themselves as happier, more active, calmer, and with higher self-esteem when relating to themselves as persons, but surprisingly showed no change in their perceptions of themselves as mothers. Their own mothers were perceived as more anxious but also as more available and more satisfied in their role as mothers. Finally, mothers felt less sadness in their relationship with the child, and more positive affect overall. Some of these effects, in particular positive changes in self-esteem and in positive affective tone, persisted even 12 months following the intervention (Robert-Tissot et al., 1996). Though not targeted directly in the psychotherapeutic interventions, parenting representations reflected the change in the relationships brought about by the psychotherapy.

General Discussion

General Summary of Research

The rich body of studies reviewed above demonstrates the burgeoning interest of developmental researchers and clinicians in assessing parenting representations. Most of the studies used measures modeled after the AAI, namely a structured or a semi-structured interview of an hour to an hour and a half. The questions pertained to the child, the mother, and in particular their relationship, and respondents were asked to supply concrete examples besides general descriptions. Researchers tended to include a core of questions pertaining to several major issues such as parents' general descriptions of the child and the relationship, positive and negative emotions, and comparison with their own childhood experiences. Depending on their focus, researchers were quite ready to include additional questions. The WMCI, concentrating on pregnancy, includes a large section pertaining to this experience. George and Solomon (1989), when referring to mothers of six-year-olds, added questions relevant to this age group. Mayseless and Scharf (this volume) included questions about letting go and individuation when they adjusted the interview to mothers of adolescents. Other researchers centering on specific aspects devised shorter interviews for these dimensions only (e.g., investment by foster mothers). In all, a great deal of flexibility in questions and issues is evident.

The interviews also heavily borrowed from the AAI as regards their analysis. In most cases interviews are audiotaped and the transcripts are coded (but note the analysis of videotaped or audiotaped WMCI). The suggested codes are quite diverse, reflecting researchers' flexibility and experimentation in the domain. Most researchers followed the AAI coding scheme by including codes for content of the interview and codes for thought processes, most notably coherence of the transcript. They also tried to capture the richness of parental experiences by developing and using scales for aspects not assessed in the AAI. For example, parental competence or self-esteem proved a prominent issue assessed by most researchers. Most researchers found that various feelings such as joy, anxiety, anger, or guilt need to be coded as well, as central dimensions in parenting representations. Some of the coding scales were derived from theoretical considerations (e.g., monitoring and autonomy promotion in interviews of mothers of adolescents; the scales proposed by George and Solomon (1996) to capture the four caregiving strategies). Codes were also devised bottom-up, whereby certain themes emerged from the interview and led researchers to develop a scale for them.

The interviews differed somewhat in their kinds of analysis. The PAI concentrated on parenting representations of the *child*, and the PDI, as employed by Aber, Slade, and their colleagues, centered on the *relationship* with the child. George and Solomon's (1996) conceptualization was on the *mother's* caregiving *strategies*, classifying the parent's representation of self as a caregiver. The WMCI in its categories concentrated on the *narrative style* of the representations.

Because most researchers extended insights from attachment research and the study of attachment representations to the study of parenting representations, most systems of analysis heavily relied on attachment notions also with regard to validation and prediction. Researchers looked for associations between parenting representations and attachment security of the infants/children or associations with parent's state of mind with regard to attachment. Accordingly, interviews were mostly coded to afford such a correspondence. Scales relevant to the three or four categories of attachment were suggested (e.g., Solomon & George, 1996), and/or mothers' representations were categorized into three or four categories corresponding to the attachment categorizations (e.g., WMCI). Even without such prior planning, factor analyses or other data reduction procedures eventually yielded three or four composite scales roughly corresponding to the attachment categories (e.g., Aber et al., 1999). This may have to do with the nature of the representations, the kinds of questions asked, and the kinds of scales proposed, but most of all it seems related to the kinds of outcome assessed. When correspondence with attachment categories was sought, scales that do not assess these aspects were dropped from the analysis (e.g., Aber et al., 1999). The approach of Pianta and his colleagues (see an extended delineation of this approach in Steinberg & Pianta, this volume) may be quite promising in proposing to assess other aspects besides attachment-related dimensions, and to broaden the array of outcomes examined. Mayseless and Scharf (this volume) went in this direction when assessing monitoring, autonomy promotion, and maternal competence, and observing outcomes in a variety of domains (e.g., self-concept, close relationship, coping).

Altogether, the current set of studies demonstrates several remarkable qualities. First, the schemes reported in these studies exhibit high *reliability* as examined in various ways. Specifically, (1) interjudge reliability was high, (2) composite scales showed good internal reliability, (3) when composite scales were used their intercorrelations warranted using them as separate dimensions, and (4) the aspects of the representations assessed proved quite stable over several months and even over a year – before and after the child's birth.

Second, these diverse coding schemes displayed concurrent and predictive *validity*. Specifically, parenting representations as assessed by these schemes showed impressive association with infants' and children's attachment classifications, and with mothers' state of mind with respect to attachment. In addition, parenting representations, as assessed by these coding schemes, showed significant associations in the predicted direction with maternal behaviors, as observed at home and in the laboratory, as well as with indicators of the child's psychosocial functioning. These different associations were obtained retrospectively, concurrently, and even prospectively, attesting to impressive predictive validity of the coding of parenting representations. Parenting representations as assessed by these coding schemes reflected the nature of the parenting context (e.g., divorce, domestic violence) and the clinical status of the child, and reflected transformations in the relationship due to developmental changes or therapy.

Third, though parenting representations were associated, as anticipated, with AAI categories, these associations were not so strong as to suggest that the two measures assess the same construct. This moderate to small association was apparent when mothers' AAI and parenting representations were assessed in adolescence. At that stage we would expect parenting representations to become shaped and influenced not only by the mother's history of attachment relationships (her IWM with regard to attachment) but also by the long and rich relationship together and the personality of the adolescent. Yet this moderate level of association between attachment and parenting representations was also apparent when mothers were assessed in the early months of caring for their new-born baby, when the history of their relationship had just begun. The association as well as the distinctiveness between attachment and caregiving in mothers' representations were demonstrated.

More than 1,300 parents participated in the studies reviewed above, done by over 10 different research teams in seven countries (Australia, Canada, Finland, Italy, Israel, Turkey, and the United States) with normal and clinical samples. This impressive body of research attests to the significance of assessing parenting representations, which have a distinct role in parents' experience and inner world.

On this solid basis, several issues and challenges that await further elaboration and examination can be identified. They concern conceptual and theoretical considerations, as well as assessment aspects.

Assessment Aspects: Diversity of Coding Schemes

One of the central issues related to the assessment of parenting representations is how best to code the interviews. In the studies just reviewed, researchers used categories mostly modeled after the AAI as well as specific scales. The specific scales referred to (1) the content of the representations, (2) non-content aspects of the representations (e.g., richness of perception), and (3) narrative style or thought processes (e.g., coherence, reflective function). Content-focused scales covered various domains: (a) parental perception of the self as a parent (e.g., competence, self-esteem), (b) parental perception of the child (e.g., confidence in the child, shy), (c) the relationship (e.g., mutuality), and (d) parents' feelings and emotions (e.g., joy, delight, guilt). In most cases attachment aspects in the representations were more prominent. Some researchers extended this focus and included other aspects more distant from attachment processes such as limit setting and playing. The diversity of coding approaches makes it difficult to compare results across different studies and leaves the reader wondering what might be the distinctiveness of different yet related aspects, such as mother's competence and her self-esteem. Because the different schemes of coding were not included together in one dataset, how far the differences in focus capture distinct aspects in parenting representations is unclear. The question arises whether one scheme of coding the interviews is "better" in any way than another in showing the essence of parenting representations. Should we focus on non-content aspects or narrative style, as in the coding of the AAI, or should we pay attention to the specific content of the representations? Should we limit ourselves to attachment-related issues, or include the host of other issues parents grapple with? Another dilemma relates to the place of emotions in the representations and how best to code them. Should we code their mere existence, their degree, or their containment?

This diversity partly reflects the richness of the inner parental world, which includes various dimensions and facets. In this respect, it is interesting to note that the different aspects identified in the schemes for assessing parenting representations are in most cases only moderately correlated; similarly when mothers' cognitions were examined, domains of parenting cognitions were relatively independent (Bornstein & Cote, 2003). Recognizing the existence of this wealth and variety, as yet only partly charted, researchers apparently sought to do it justice and refrained from limiting it by imposing a pre-selected set of dimensions. Future research may need to address this diversity and explore the distinctiveness of various coding schemes and foci (e.g., emotions, cognitions, thought processes); eventually a more coherent way of charting and assessing parenting representations may emerge.

Caregiving Representations: Demarcation from the AAI

The study of parenting representations reviewed here emanated from the attachment tradition and was based on insights gained by the AAI. It further used a similar format of interview and coding schemes. Thus, a major conceptual and empirical question that needs to be addressed by researchers interested in parenting representations is to what degree parenting representations are similar to the construct that is assessed by the AAI, and whether they have a unique and distinct place. This question should be tackled at the conceptual and empirical levels: at the theoretical level it may be possible to distinguish between state of mind with regard to attachment – the construct assessed by the AAI – and parenting representations (see the next section); but at the assessment level these two constructs might be so bound together that the one just reproduces or reflects the other. As reviewed in previous sections, empirical research has demonstrated a significant but small to moderate association between the two representations, mostly at the secure/insecure divide, thus validating the uniqueness of parenting representations at the empirical level.

Note that on the theoretical level parenting representations reflect the operation of the caregiving behavioral system, whereas the AAI reflects the operation of the attachment behavioral system. George and Solomon (1996; 1989; 1999a; 1999b) lucidly articulated the differences between the attachment and the caregiving behavioral systems. Both revolve around goals of protection, but whereas attachment is related to the goal of receiving care and protection, the goal of the caregiving behavioral system is providing such care and protection – most notably to your child. The AAI revolves around relationships with attachment figures mostly in childhood, whereas parenting representations relate to a parent's relationship with a particular child or with several children. Furthermore, as highlighted in the next section, caregiving may be construed as much broader in scope than attachment as it includes a wide range of set goals, a diverse array of relationships, and a broad span of contributing sources. Although attachment and caregiving representations, in particular parenting representations, are expected to be related because they have a similar origin (Dozier, 2000; see the following discussion), they are nevertheless expected to be distinct and to be only moderately associated. As the relationship with a particular child develops and evolves, the IWM with regard to caregiving of that child should become more distinct from the parent's general IWM with regard to attachment as assessed by the AAI (Slade & Cohen, 1996).

Internal Working Models of Caregiving

Just as the attachment behavioral system is seen as governed and regulated by a mental model, so is the caregiving behavioral system. As summarized by Bretherton and Munholland (1999; p. 91), "What is often overlooked is that Bowlby's conception of the working model is a very general one. It applies to *all* representations and is not restricted to working models of self and other in attachment relationships" (emphasis in original). Each caregiver (e.g., a parent) is expected to have a mental model of the environment (social and non-social), including the care-receiver (i.e., the child) and himself or herself in the capacity of caregiver, as well as how the relevant set goals of the caregiving behavioral system can be achieved. Like the mental models of attachment, the IWMs of caregiving (a) are based on actual experiences in caregiving-related circumstances; (b) serve to regulate, interpret, and predict the care-receiver and the caregiver's caregiving-related behaviors, thoughts, and feelings; (c) reflect reality but also regulate and create it; (d) are flexible to some extent and can be updated by new experiences and self-reflections; (f) involve several distinct memory systems: procedural, semantic, and episodic, at various levels of consciousness and with varying degrees of affective load; and (g) reflect the operation of various defensive processes that serve to protect the caregiver from unbearable anxiety and psychological suffering.

To understand the scope of the IWM of caregiving, the distinction between the function of a behavioral system and its set goals (Bowlby, 1969) is important. The function is viewed as the evolutionary purpose of the behavioral system, of which a person may or may not be aware, while the set goals are the proximal aims in terms of actual end states of the organism. The attachment behavioral system is conceptualized as a "safety regulating system," that is, its main function is seen as promoting a person's own safety, both physically and psychologically, in the context of close relationships (Crittenden, 2000; p. 370). Feeling comforted (not stressed) and secure through the actions or the presence of an attachment figure is considered the set goal of the system (Goldberg, Grusec, & Jenkins, 1999; Kobak, 1999; Waters & Cummings, 2000).

How were the functions and the set goals of the caregiving system construed? Some scholars (e.g., George & Solomon, 1999a) contend that the function of the caregiving behavioral system is the survival of the young, so the set goal is to keep the child safe; the caregiving behavioral system was seen as mirroring the set goal of attachment. Others (e.g., Mayseless, 1996) suggest that the function of the caregiving behavioral system is the survival of one's offspring to maturity and reproduction. This more general function is promoted through three separate and specific set goals: (a) to keep the child safe; (b) to keep the child happy and content; and (c) to promote the child's efficacy and capacity to manage in the world. Other researchers have suggested somewhat different set goals. For example, discussing the nurturance motive, Fogel, Melson, and Mistry (1986) suggested that "nurturance is the provision of guidance, protection and care for the purpose of fostering developmental change congruent with the expected potential for change of the object of nurturance" (p. 55). Objects of nurturance can be human (infants, age-mates, elderly) as well as pets, plants, and even art, and the set goal is very broad and involves fostering the realization of the object's potential for growth. Similarly, Ruddick (1989) discusses three main goals: sustaining life, fostering growth, and training to be an acceptable member of society.

One of the things researchers examining parenting representations from an attachment perspective would need to do is define the scope of the IWM of caregiving: what does it include? Is it related only to security regulation goals? Or are other aspects, such as teaching, limit setting, or autonomy promotion, included too? As indicated by the research reviewed above, researchers interested in parenting representations for the most part did not limit themselves to issues of protection but were keen to explore a much wider array of parenting functions. The IWM of caregiving seems to encompass a much broader domain of representations of thoughts, behavioral sequences, feelings, plans, and defensive processes than the IWM of attachment.

Sources of Caregiving Representations

Another issue highly relevant to the IWM of caregiving is related to the sources of these representations. Biology, hormonal levels, and individual differences in temperament probably play an important role (Bell, 2001). Like attachment representations, parenting representations are based on actual experiences. But because they develop later in life than attachment representations, and are activated in full at an older age, the period of relevant experiences seems to be much longer, starting even before the person becomes a parent, let alone afterwards. First, these sources include experiences of the person as a child in a relationship with a caregiver. Children are able to represent both sides of the interaction – themselves as care-receivers in an attachment capacity and the caregiver in a caregiving capacity. Though they may not be aware of all the internal workings, conflicts, affects, thoughts, and plans of the caregiver they do construct a theory – a representation of the caregiver's behavior, and they internalize specific memories – procedural and episodic – from what they imagine is the caregiver's side (see a discussion in Crittenden, this volume). Similarly, one's own feelings, interpretations, defensive processes, and sequences of actions internalized during such interactions that are experienced as a care-receiver may serve as ways to understand and comprehend the child's point of view when this becomes needed.

Caregiving representations can also be based on other experiences of being cared for by other people. They can also reflect a host of situations in which the child acts as a caregiver before becoming a parent (e.g., to an ailing grandfather, a sibling, or a pet). Vicarious learning and internalization of other models, actual (e.g., mother of a best friend; other parents) or fictional (e.g., a character in a TV show or a book), probably take place as well. Even before individuals assume an actual caregiving relationship with a child, most of them have probably already developed a broad and multifaceted IWM with regard to caregiving. This developmental realization is reflected in the capacity to investigate parenting representations even before a baby is born and to predict actual behaviors of the parent towards the baby (see review of studies in previous sections). Of course, as the relationship between a parent and a child progresses and unfolds, the IWM increasingly reflects the actual relationships with that child and the contribution of the child's own personality and behavior (i.e., child effects).

One or Many IWMs of Caregiving?

In that sense, a parent may possess different IWMs for different children or different care-receivers, partly reflecting the specific history of the relationships and the contributions of the care-receiver. Consequently, future research should examine parenting representations with different children and investigate their similarities and distinctiveness. A related theoretical and empirical question is the structural associations between these different IWMs. Do they form a coherent set? How similar are they? Do they reflect a hierarchical structure? For example, a parent may have a general IWM with regard to caregiving encompassing individual instances (cases) of IWM with specific children, all subsumed under the generalized representation. Alternatively the internal organization of these different representations may be more modular and interconnected and they may all operate at the same level of generalization and abstraction.

Related to this issue is the specific place of parenting within the caregiving behavioral system. Parental caring for children is often treated as the prototypical example of the caregiving behavioral system but not the exclusive one. When Bowlby described the caregiving system, he referred mostly but not exclusively to the parent–child relationships. For example, he mentioned caring for siblings or caring for a parent as manifestations of this motivational system. Clearly, adults (and older children) develop caregiving relationships with other figures as well. These include siblings, students, clients, day-care children, and also spouses. Research within the attachment tradition has already applied attachment notions to each of these relationships. For example, the attachment relationships of children to professional caregivers have been examined quite extensively (Howes, 1999). Similarly, attachment notions have been widely applied to highlight the bond a client forms with a therapist and to explain many central processes in psychotherapy (Slade, 1999). A large body of research also examined the relationships children form with their teachers as partly reflecting attachment processes (Pianta, Nimetz, & Bennett, 1997). In each of these relationships the caregiver's side was also examined, albeit to a lesser extent.

Are these relationships governed by the same caregiving motivational system? Pertinent to this question is a study that compared the caregiving representations of mothers and day-care caregivers (*metapelet*) in the kibbutz setting (Ben-Aaron, Eshel, & Yaari, 1999). The researchers administered to the mothers and the *metapelet* a similar interview, with 10 open-ended questions pertaining to the perception of the child and the caregiver's role in the relationship. As expected, significant differences emerged between mothers and *metapelet*. For example, mothers presented more elaborate and positive descriptions of their child. In addition, mothers' emotional tone was more anxious but at the same time more enthusiastic. Still, the application of the same interview to mothers and professional caregivers, and the fact that these caregivers were able to provide elaborate and meaningful responses that could be significantly coded and compared to those of mothers, provides some support for the possibility that a general motivational system governs a diverse array of caregiving relationships.

Several very challenging empirical questions are related to this issue. For example, can we assess and identify a person's general caregiving representations, or IWMs, encompassing all the caregiving relationships, and also examine the distinct representations or IWMs with regards to specific classes of relationships (e.g., own children, clients)? Are these organized in a hierarchy or in other interconnected ways? IWMs might be organized along various different dimensions. These might include groupings according to non-egalitarian relationships (e.g., children, clients) vs. egalitarian relationships (e.g., friends, spouses), filial relationships (e.g., children, spouse, grandparents) vs. non-filial (e.g., friends), or the level of emotional investment in the relationships (high vs. low). Furthermore, might people differ in the way these representations, or IWMs, are organized? Cultural salience of various dimensions might be implicated in such distinct organization. This point of view opens up a considerable number of exciting research questions and a very broad, new, and challenging avenue for future research.

Future Directions

Although quite diverse, the study of parenting representations can be greatly enhanced by cross-fertilization with other areas of research pertaining to the mental world of parents. As indicated above, researchers have been quite open in their exploration of various dimensions and aspects. However, the assessment of representation was mostly done by means of interviews. An interview which probes at different dimensions and aspects provides a rich and fruitful avenue to explore parenting representations especially at the formative stage, when the boundaries of the phenomenon are not clear and the concept is fluid and still demands structure and conceptualization. Yet as indicated by some research that included both interviews and questionnaires (Ilicali & Fisek, 2004), and as evident in the review chapter by Rudy and Grusec (this volume), many specific aspects related to parenting representations have been explored using other measures, such as questionnaires, and some very interesting and significant findings have emerged with these instruments (see Sharabany,

Scher, & Gal-Krauz, this volume). In some cases, a striking resemblance to specific scales devised for coding the interviews appears (e.g., maternal perceived competence, or maternal delight). In other cases, very fruitful and promising conceptualizations assessed by questionnaires and the "parenting cognitions" literature such as power attributions (Bugental, Johnston, New, & Silvester, 1998), parental goals, and parental attitudes (Bornstein & Cote, 2004; Bornstein, Cote, & Venuti, 2001) have not been directly assessed in the interviews. Their inclusion in them or their concurrent assessment by other measures may greatly enrich our understanding of the motivational, cognitive, emotional, and behavioral strata of parenting representations. The two as yet almost unrelated bodies of investigation, parenting cognitions and parenting representations assessed by the AAI tradition, will benefit tremendously from cross-fertilization.

Similarly, notions addressed by the feminist and psychoanalytic points of view are also highly important. For example, the discussion within these paradigms of maternal subjectivity stresses the ambivalence and the strong negative emotions including hatred that mothers harbor as they care for their children (e.g., Kraemer, 1996; Parker, 1996). They further underscore the importance of understanding how mothers cope with these emotions and how most of them find the way to overcome them and provide good enough, sensitive mothering. These issues are less addressed in the current conceptualizations based on the attachment paradigm.

The coding scheme developed so far focused on three important aspects of the representations: their content, the affective domain, and thought processes, including defensive ones. However, as cogently discussed by Crittenden (this volume), parents' caregiving representations also include non-verbal aspects: procedural as well as imaged (experienced) facets that are not easily captured by verbal means such as questionnaires or even in-depth interviews. Other means, such as drawing or clay sculpturing, may reveal an as yet uncharted realm of the parental mental world. In this respect insight from art therapy research may prove helpful, just as it has when applied to assess attachment relationships (e.g., Pianta, Longmaid, & Ferguson, 1999).

Most of the studies to date focused on mothers, but some (e.g., Bretherton, Lambert, & Golby; this volume) included fathers and started looking at their representations as well. As indicated in two chapters in this volume (Bretherton et al.; Sharabany et al.), fathers' representations and internal reworking of their experiences as children may be different and in some cases more complex than mothers' owing to cohort changes in fathers' role as caregivers. Future research may well remedy the relative neglect of investigating fathers' representations and explore this issue as well.

34   *O. Mayseless*

Finally when devising the questions in the interviews, more especially when devising the coding schemes, researchers, while in most cases departing from the AAI tradition, still adjusted to the richness of the parents' internal world and did not limit themselves to attachment-related notions or dimensions. In contrast, when they examined various outcomes, researchers often focused on attachment-related aspects such as maternal AAI, child's attachment pattern, and maternal sensitivity. When other outcomes were examined (e.g., Bretherton et al., this volume; Rosenblum et al., this volume; Mayseless & Scharf, this volume) it became clear that they may be distinctively related to different facets of the representations. As research now moves from the first level, which involved proving the feasibility of the assessment of parenting representations, and demonstrating its reliability and its validity vis-à-vis core empirical measures of attachment, a broadening of assessed outcomes is called for.

References

Aber, J. L., Belsky, J., Slade, A., & Crnic, K. (1999). Stability and change in mothers' representations of their relationship with their toddlers. *Developmental Psychology, 35*, 1038–47.

Aber, J. L., Slade, A., Berger, G., Bresgi, I., & Kaplan, M. (1985). *The Parent Development Interview*. Unpublished manuscript.

Ackerman J. & Dozier, M. (this volume). Good investments: Foster parent representations of their foster children.

Ackerman, J. & Dozier, M. (2003). The influence of caregiver investment on foster children's representations of self and others. Unpublished manuscript.

Ammaniti, M. (1991). Maternal representations during pregnancy and early infant-mother interactions. *Infant Mental Health Journal, 12*, 246–55.

Ammaniti, M., Baumgartner, E., Candelori, C., Perucchini, P., Pola, M., Tambelli, R., & Zampino, F. (1992). Representations and narratives during pregnancy. *Infant Mental Health Journal, 13*, 167–82.

Bates, B. & Dozier, M. (2002). The importance of maternal state of mind regarding attachment and infant age at placement to foster mothers' representations of their foster infants. *Infant Mental Health Journal, 23*, 417–31.

Bell, D. C. (2001). Evolution of parental caregiving. *Personality and Social Psychology Review, 5*, 216–29.

Bell, D. C. & Richard, A. J. (2000). Caregiving the forgotten element in attachment. *Psychological Inquiry, 11*, 69–83.

Ben-Aaron, M., Eshel, Y., & Yaari, G. (1999). Mother and caregiver representations of toddlers in a kibbutz setting. *British Journal of Medical Psychology, 72*, 189–201.

Benoit, D., Parker, K. C. H., & Zeanah, C. H. (1997). Mothers' representations of their infants assessed prenatally: Stability and association with infants' attachment classifications. *Journal of Child Psychology and Psychiatry and Allied Disciplines, 38*, 307–13.

Benoit, D., Zeanah, C. H., Parker, K. C. H., Nicholson, E., & Coolbear, J. (1997). "Working Model of the Child Interview": Infant clinical status related to maternal perceptions. *Infant Mental Health Journal, 18*, 107–21.

Biringen, Z., Matheny, A., Bretherton, I., Renouf, A., & Sherman, M. (2000). Maternal representation of the self as parent: Connections with maternal sensitivity and maternal structuring. *Attachment and Human Development, 2*, 218–32.

Bornstein, M. H. & Cote, L. R. (2003). Cultural and parenting cognitions in acculturating cultures: 2. Patterns of prediction and structural coherence. *Journal of Cross Cultural Psychology, 34*, 350–73.

Bornstein, M. H. & Cote, L. R. (2004). Mothers' parenting cognitions in cultures of origin, acculturating cultures, and cultures of destination. *Child Development, 75*, 221–35.

Bornstein, M. H., Cote, L. R., & Venuti, P. (2001). Parenting beliefs and behaviors in northern and southern groups of Italian mothers of young infants. *Journal of Family Psychology, 15*, 663–75.

Bowlby, J. (1969/1982). *Attachment and Loss: Volume 1. Attachment.* 2nd Edition. New York: Basic Books.

Bowlby, J. (1973). *Attachment and Loss: Volume 2. Separation.* New York: Basic Books.

Bretherton, I., Biringen, Z., Ridgeway, D., Maslin, C., & Sherman, M. (1989). Attachment: The parental perspective. *Infant Mental Health Journal, 10*, 203–21.

Bretherton, I., Lambert, J. D., & Golby, B. (this volume). Modeling and reworking childhood experiences: Involved fathers' representations of being parented and of parenting a preschool child.

Bretherton, I. & Munholland, K. A. (1999). Internal working models in attachment relationships: A construct revisited. In J. Cassidy & P. R. Shaver (Eds.), *Handbook of Attachment: Theory, Research, and Clinical Applications.* New York: Guilford Press, pp. 89–111.

Bugental, D. B., Johnston, C., New, M., & Silvester, J. (1998). Measuring parental attributions: Conceptual and methodological issues. *Journal of Family Psychology, 12*, 459–80.

Button, S., Pianta, R. C., & Marvin, R. S. (2001). Mothers' representations of relationships with their children: Relations with parenting behavior, mother characteristics, and child disability status. *Social Development, 10*, 455–72.

Cassidy, J. & Shaver, P. R. (Eds.) (1999). *Handbook of Attachment: Theory, Research, and Clinical Applications.* New York: Guilford Press.

Collins, N. L. & Read, S. J. (1994). Cognitive representations of attachment: The content and function of working models. In K. Bartholomew & D. Perlman (Eds.), *Advances in Personal Relationships.* London: Jessica Kingsley, pp. 53–90.

Cox, S. M., Hopkins, J., & Hans, S. L. (2000). Attachment in preterm infants and their mothers: Neonatal risk status and maternal representations. *Infant Mental Heath Journal, 21*, 464–80.

Cramer, B., Robert-Tissot, C., Stern, D. N., Serpa-Rusconi, S., De Muralt, M., Besson, G., Falacio-Espasa, F., Bachmann, J. P., Knauer, D., Berney, C., & D'arcis, U. (1990). Outcome evaluation in brief mother-infant psychotherapy: A preliminary report. *Infant Mental Health Journal, 11*, 278–300.

Cramer, B. & Stern, D. N. (1988). Evaluation of changes in mother-infant brief psychotherapy: A single case study. *Infant Mental Health Journal, 9*, 20–45.

Crittenden, P. M. (2000). A dynamic-maturational exploration of the meaning of security and adaptation: Empirical, cultural, and theoretical considerations. In P. M. Crittenden & A. H. Claussen (Eds.). *The Organization of Attachment Relationships: Maturation, Culture, and Context*. New York: Cambridge University Press, pp. 358–84.

Crittenden, P. M. (this volume). Why do inadequate parents do what they do?

Dozier, M. (2000). Motivation for caregiving from an ethological perspective. *Psychological Inquiry, 11*, 97–100.

Fave-Viziello, G. F., Antonioli, M. E., Cocci, V., & Invernizzi, R. (1993). From pregnancy to motherhood: The structure of representative and narrative change. *Infant Mental Health Journal, 14*, 4–16.

Fogel, A., Melson, G. F., & Mistry, J. (1986). Conceptualizing the determinants of nurturance: A reassessment of sex differences. In A. Fogel & G. F. Melson (Eds.), *Origins of Nurturance: Developmental, Biological and Cultural Perspectives on Caregiving*. Hillsdale, NJ: Erlbaum, pp. 53–67.

Fonagy, P. (1996). The significance of the development of metacognitive control over mental representations in parenting and infant development. *Journal of Clinical Psychoanalysis, 5*, 67–86.

Fonagy, P. & Target, M. (1998). Mentalization and the changing aims of child psychoanalysis. *Psychoanalytic Dialogues, 8*, 87–114.

George, C. & Solomon, J. (1989). Internal working models of caregiving and security of attachment at age six. *Infant Mental Health Journal, 10*, 222–37.

George, C. & Solomon, J. (1996). Representational models of relationships: Links between caregiving and attachment. *Infant Mental Health Journal, 17*, 198–216.

George, C. & Solomon, J. (1999a). Attachment and caregiving: The caregiving behavioral system. In J. Cassidy & P. R. Shaver (Eds.), *Handbook of Attachment: Theory, Research, and Clinical Applications*. New York: Guilford Press, pp. 649–70.

George, C. & Solomon, J. (1999b). The development of caregiving: A comparison of attachment theory and psychoanalytic approaches to mothering. *Psychoanalytic Inquiry, 19*, 618–46.

Golby, B. J. & Bretherton, I. (1999). Resilience in postdivorce mother-child relationships. In H. I. McCubbin & E. A. Thompson (Eds.), *The Dynamics of Resilient Families. Resiliency in Families*. Thousand Oaks, CA: Sage, pp. 237–69.

Goldberg, S., Grusec, J. E., & Jenkins, J. M. (1999). Confidence in protection: Arguments for a narrow definition of attachment. *Journal of Family Psychology, 13*, 475–83.

Heard, D. & Lake, B. (1997). *The Challenge of Attachment for Caregiving*. London: Routledge.

Hesse, E. (1999). The Adult Attachment Interview: Historical and current perspectives. In J. Cassidy & P. R. Shaver (Eds.), *Handbook of Attachment: Theory, Research, and Clinical Applications*. New York: Guilford Press, pp. 395–433.

Howes, C. (1999). Attachment relationships in the context of multiple caregivers. In J. Cassidy & P. R. Shaver (Eds.), *Handbook of Attachment: Theory, Research, and Clinical Applications*. New York: Guilford Press, pp. 671–87.

Huth-Bocks, A. C., Levendosky, A. A., Bogat, G. A., & von Eye A. (2004a). The impact of maternal characteristics and contextual variables on infant–mother attachment. *Child Development, 75*, 480–96.

Huth-Bocks, A. C., Levendosky, A. A., Theran, S. A., & Bogat, G. A. (2004b). The impact of domestic violence on mothers' prenatal representations of their infants. *Infant Mental Health Journal, 25*, 79–98.

Ilicali, E. T. & Fisek, G. O. (2004). Maternal representations during pregnancy and early motherhood. *Infant Mental Health Journal, 25*, 16–27.

Kobak, R. (1999). The emotional dynamics of disruptions in attachment relationships: Implications for theory, research, and clinical intervention. In J. Cassidy & P. R. Shaver (Eds.), *Handbook of Attachment: Theory, Research, and Clinical Applications*. New York: Guilford Press, pp. 21–43.

Kraemer, S. B. (1996). "Betwixt the dark and the daylight" of maternal subjectivity: Meditations on the threshold. *Psychoanalytic Dialogues, 6*, 765–91.

Lyons-Ruth, K., Bronfman, E., & Parsons, E. (1999). Maternal frightened, frightening, or atypical behavior and disorganized infant attachment patterns. In J. Vondra & D. Barnett (Eds.), *Atypical Patterns of Infant Attachment: Theory, Research and Current Directions. Monographs of the Society for Research in Child Development, 64*, 67–96.

Main, M. & Goldwyn, R. (1998). *Adult Attachment Scoring and Classification Systems, Version 6.3*. Unpublished manual, University of California, Berkeley.

Main, M., Kaplan, N., & Cassidy, J. (1985). Security in infancy, childhood, and adulthood: A move to the level of representation. *Monographs of the Society for Research in Child Development, 50 (1–2)*, 66–104.

Marvin, R. S. & Pianta, R. C. (1996). Mothers' reactions to their child's diagnosis: Relations with security of attachment. *Journal of Clinical Child Psychology, 25*, 436–45.

Mayseless, O. (1996). *Tending and caregiving*. Unpublished manuscript, University of Haifa, Israel.

Mayseless, O. & Scharf, M. (2001). *Maternal representations of parenting, socioemotional functioning, and coping of mothers and adolescent sons with a stressful separation*. Paper presented at the biennial meeting of Society for Research in Child Development, April, Minneapolis, Minnesota.

Mayseless, O., & Scharf, M. (this volume). Maternal representations of parenting in adolescence and psychosocial functioning of mothers and adolescents.

Mayseless, O., Scharf, M., Kivenson-Baron, I., & Schnarch, R. (2005). Mothers' attachment and caregiving representations and their adolescent sons' functioning and state of mind with regard to attachment. Unpublished manuscript, University of Haifa.

Pajulo, M., Savonlahti, E., Sourander, A., Piha, J., & Helenius, H. (2001). Prenatal maternal representations: Mothers at psychosocial risk. *Infant Mental Health Journal, 22*, 529–44.

Parker, R. (1996). *Torn in Two*. London: Virago.

Pianta, R. C., Longmaid, K., & Ferguson, J. E. (1999). Attachment-based classifications of children's family drawings: Psychometric properties and relations with children's adjustment in kindergarten. *Journal of Clinical Child Psychology, 28*, 244–55.

Pianta, R. C., Marvin, R. S., Britner, P. A., & Borowitz, K. C. (1996). Mothers' resolution of their children's diagnosis: Organized patterns of caregiving representations. Special issue: The caregiving system. *Infant Mental Health Journal, 17*, 239–56.

Pianta, R. C., Nimetz, S. L., & Bennett, E. (1997). Mother-child relationships, teacher-child relationships, and school outcomes in preschool and kindergarten. *Early Childhood Research Quarterly, 12,* 263–80.

Robert-Tissot, C., Cramer, B., Stern, D. N., Rusconi-Serpa, S., Bachmann, J. P., Falacio-Espasa, F., Knauer, D., De Muralt, M., Berney, C., & Mendiguren, G. (1996). Outcome evaluation in brief mother-infant psychotherapies: Report on 75 cases. *Infant Mental Health Journal, 17,* 97–114.

Rosenblum, K. L., McDonough, S., Muzik, M., Miller, A., & Sameroff, A. (2002). Maternal representations of the infant: Associations with infant response to the still face. *Child Development, 73,* 999–1015.

Rosenblum, K. L., Dayton, C. L., & McDonough, S. (this volume). Communicating feelings: Links between mothers' representations of their infants, parenting and infant emotional development.

Rudy, D. & Grusec, J. (this volume). Social cognitive approaches to parenting.

Ruddick, S. (1989). *Maternal Thinking: Towards a Politics of Peace.* New York: Ballantine Books.

Scharf, M. & Mayseless, O. (1997/2000). *Parenting Representations Interview – Adolescence (PRI-A).* Unpublished manuscript, University of Haifa.

Scharf, M., Mayseless, O., & Kivenson-Baron, I. (1997/2000). *Coding Manual of the Parenting Representations Interview – Adolescence (PRI-A).* Unpublished manuscript, University of Haifa.

Scharf, M., Mayseless, O., & Kivenson-Baron, I. (2004). Adolescents' attachment representations and developmental tasks in emerging adulthood. *Developmental Psychology, 40,* 430–44.

Scharf, M. & Shulman, S. (this volume). Intergenerational transmission of experiences in adolescence: The challenges in parenting adolescents.

Shamir-Essakow, G., Ungerer, J. A., Rapee, R. M., & Safier, R. (2004). Caregiving representations of mothers of behaviorally inhibited and uninhibited preschool children. *Developmental Psychology, 40,* 899–910.

Sharabany, R., Scher, A., & Gal-Krauz, J. (this volume). Like fathers like sons? Fathers' attitudes to childrearing in light of their perceived relationships with own parents, and their attachment concerns.

Sheeran, T., Marvin, R. S., & Pianta, R. C. (1997). Mothers' resolution of their child's diagnosis and self-reported measures of parenting stress, marital relations, and social support. *Journal of Pediatric Psychology, 22,* 197–212.

Slade, A. (1999). Attachment theory and research: Implications for the theory and practice of individual psychotherapy with adults. In J. Cassidy & P. R. Shaver (Eds.), *Handbook of Attachment: Theory, Research, and Clinical Applications.* New York: Guilford Press, pp. 575–94.

Slade, A., Belsky, J., Aber, J. L., & Phelps, J. (1999). Mothers' representations of their relationships with their toddlers: Links to adult attachment and observed mothering. *Developmental Psychology, 35,* 611–19.

Slade, A. & Cohen, L. J. (1996). The process of parenting and the remembrance of things past. *Infant Mental Health Journal, 17,* 217–38.

Slade, A., Grienenberger, J. Bernbach, E., Levy, D., & Locker, A. (2001). *Maternal reflective functioning and attachment: Considering the transmission gap.* Paper presented at the Biennial Meeting of the Society for Research in Child Development, Minneapolis, MN.

Solomon, J., George, C., & De Jong, A. (1995). Children classified as controlling at age six: Evidence of disorganized representational strategies and aggression at home and school. *Development and Psychopathology, 7*, 447–64.

Solomon, J. & George, C. (1996). Defining the caregiving system. Toward a theory of caregiving. *Infant Mental Health Journal, 17*, 183–97.

Solomon, J. & George, C. (1999). The caregiving system in mothers of infants: A comparison of divorcing and married mothers. *Attachment and Human Development, 1*, 171–90.

Steinberg, D. & Pianta R. C. (this volume). Maternal representations of relationships: Assessing multiple parenting dimensions.

Stern, D. N. (1989). The representation of relational patterns: Developmental considerations. In A. J. Sameroff & R. Emde (Eds.), *Relationship Disturbances in Early Childhood: A Developmental Approach.* New York: Basic Books, pp. 52–69.

Stern, D. N. (1991). Maternal representations: A clinical and subjective phenomenological view. *Infant Mental Health Journal, 12*, 174–86.

Stern, D. N., Robert-Tissot, C., Besson, G., Serpa-Rusconi, S., de Muralt, M., Cramer, B., & Palacio-Espasa, F. (1989). L'Entretien"R": une methode d'evaluation de representations maternelles. In S. Lbovici, P., Mazet, & J. P. Visier (Eds.), *L'evaluation des interactions precoces entre le bebe et ses partnaires.* Paris, Eshel; Geneve: Medicine et Hygiene, pp. 131–49.

Stern-Bruschweiler, N. & Stern, D. N. (1989). A model for conceptualizing the role of the mother's representational world in various mother-infant therapies. *Infant Mental Health Journal, 10*, 142–56.

Tyrrell, C. & Dozier, M. (1999). Foster parents' understanding of children's problematic attachment strategies: The need for therapeutic responsiveness. *Adoption Quarterly, 2*, 49–64.

van IJzendoorn, M. (1995). Adult attachment representations, parental responsiveness, and infant attachment: A meta-analysis on the predictive validity of the Adult Attachment Interview. *Psychological Bulletin, 117*, 387–403.

Waters, E. & Cummings, E. M. (2000). A secure base from which to explore close relationships. *Child Development, 71*, 164–72.

Welch, K., Pianta, R. C., Marvin, R. S., & Saft, E. W. (2000). Feeding interactions for children with cerebral palsy: Contributions of mother's psychological state and children's skills and abilities. *Journal of Developmental and Behavioral Pediatrics, 21*, 123–9.

Westen, D. (1991). Social cognition and object relations. *Psychological Bulletin, 109*, 429–55.

Wiseman, H., Hashmonay, R., & Harel, J. (this volume), Interplay of relational parent-child representations from a psychoanalytic perspective: An analysis of two mother-father-child triads.

Zeanah, C. H. & Benoit, D. (1995). Clinical applications of a parent perception interview in infant mental health. *Child and Adolescent Psychiatric Clinics of North America, 4*, 539–54.

Zeanah, C. H., Benoit, D., Hirshberg, L., Barton, M. L., & Regan, C. (1994). Mothers' representations of their infants are concordant with infant attachment classifications. *Developmental Issues in Psychiatry and Psychology, 1*, 1–14.

Zeanah, C. H., Keener, M. A., & Anders, T. F. (1986). Adolescent mothers' prenatal fantasies and working models of their infants. *Psychiatry, 49*, 193–203.

Zeanah, C. H., Keener, M. A., Stewart, L., & Anders, T. A. (1985). Prenatal perception of infant personality: A preliminary investigation. *Journal of the American Academy of Child Psychiatry, 24*, 204–10.

Zeanah, C. H., Zeanah, P. D., & Stewart, L. K. (1990). Parents' constructions of their infants' personalities before and after birth: A descriptive study. *Child Psychiatry and Human Development, 20*, 191–206.

2 Maternal Representations of Relationships
Assessing Multiple Parenting Dimensions

Donna R. Steinberg and Robert C. Pianta

Abstract

This chapter describes a series of studies using an adapted version of the Parent Development Interview (PDI) to assess dimensions of parenting in addition to attachment, such as parents' orientation towards achievement and compliance, and the business of caretaking. The results demonstrate the following points regarding maternal representations: 1) maternal representations of not only attachment, but also discipline and teaching, seem to be organized and measurable; 2) these three parenting dimensions are not redundant; 3) they relate to characteristics of the child (such as birth order, verbal IQ, disability status, and gender) and characteristics of the mother (such as age, education, income, sensitivity with her child, and psychological adjustment); and 4) they differentially predict aspects of maternal behavior, even when maternal education and psychological characteristics are taken into account. Anger, perspective-taking, and achievement were found to be particularly important dimensions of maternal representations.

Originally, Bowlby developed attachment theory to explain the nature of children's bonds to their parents in terms of their biological function, and to account for disturbing behaviors observed in infants subjected to prolonged separations from significant attachment figures (1969). With further developments in attachment theory, Main, Kaplan, and Cassidy (1985) suggested that parents' mental representations of their own childhood attachment experiences strongly influence the quality of their child's attachment to them. Mental representations, also called internal working models or representational models, are cognitive structures that develop when individuals are exposed to many similar, yet different, experiences. For instance, if a child usually receives a warm hug from a parent when the child has been injured, then that child will come to view the parent as a source of comfort. The child will learn to seek out the parent when hurt. As such, representational models promote understanding and guide behavior (Johnson-Laird, 1983; Schank & Abelson, 1977). Bowlby (1973) suggested that internal working models of the self and one's parents play a major role in the intergenerational transmission of attachment patterns. The relation between internal working models and behavior in relationships, as well as the consistency of such behavior, has been supported empirically with the successful development of measures that assess internal working models of relationships (e.g., Main, Kaplan, & Cassidy, 1985; Fonagy, Steele, & Steele, 1991; van IJzendoorn, 1995). Given the treatment and policy applications that have grown from this line of research, a focus on representations is now a major feature of research on attachment and interpersonal relationships.

Most measures of representations, such as the Adult Attachment Interview (AAI) (George, Kaplan, & Main, 1985) and the Parent Attachment Interview (PAI) (Bretherton et al., 1989), assess only the attachment aspect of relationships. More recently, there has been attention to establishing links between non-attachment representational aspects of the parent–child relationship (such as concern with achievement, compliance, and meeting a child's physical needs) and qualitites of parent–child interaction (Aber et al., 1999; Slade et al., 1999).

The studies described in this chapter used the PDI to assess dimensions of parenting in addition to attachment, such as parents' orientation towards achievement and compliance, and the business of caretaking. The PDI was developed by Aber and colleagues in 1985, and as described in this chapter, adapted by Pianta and Marvin at the Child Parent Attachment Project. In a series of studies, Pianta and colleagues (Button, Pianta, & Marvin, 2001; Messina-Sayre, Pianta, Marvin, & Saft, 2001) demonstrated that what mothers say about the multiple aspects of their relationships with their children relates to an assortment of interactive behaviors and to key characteristics of the child. The results of these studies suggest that maternal representations are differentiated and organized, relate to characteristics of the mother and child, and predict mother–child interaction, even when demographic information, and maternal characteristics are taken into account. As such, these results confirm a number of basic assumptions about parent–child relationships as dyadic systems (Emde, 1989; Pianta, 1999).

Literature Review

Researchers generally agree that there is a strong interdependence among how people were parented, their intimate relationships, and the parenting of their own offspring. One explanation for findings of intergenerational similarity is that individuals develop internal working models of self and other. Craik (1943), one of the first modern theorists to describe mental models, posited that human beings create unconscious representations of their surroundings (Johnson-Laird, 1983). When exposed to many similar experiences, people create unconscious "memory averages" of them. The more a specific aspect of an event occurs, the more likely it is to be incorporated into the mental model (Schank & Abelson, 1977). These actual experiences become translated into simpler, more easily accessible versions than the entities they represent.

By facilitating understanding, mental models guide behavior efficiently. Because mental models are activated automatically, and serve as templates, each new situation does not have to be processed in its entirety (Schank & Abelson, 1977). A person may recall a typically occurring event, even if it was not the accurate one, in place of the less likely one. In such a way, even when not explicitly mentioned, information may be falsely recalled by "default." Conversely, what a person perceives and remembers guides the maintenance of the mental model. Thus, an individual's perception and memory provide the "evidence" that an event is probable, which in turn fuels the continuation of the mental model (Beck, 1995). Mental models of relationships begin to form early in life. They are, in part, a measure of a person's current state of mind and therefore, incorporate an individual's interpretations of events. Although resistant to change, internal working models can be altered when individuals are exposed to new circumstances and experiences. Through new relationships and events, either positive or negative in nature, many individuals consciously and unconsciously alter their mental representations of important relationships (Beck, 1995).

Mental models have been examined from the perspectives of both cognitive and attachment researchers. Although there are many different, yet overlapping, internal working models that an individual may make use of, perhaps the most studied one in relation to parenting is that in which the attachment function of the child–mother relationship is the focus. The relative wealth of research on the attachment relationship was inspired largely by Bowlby's landmark publication, "On Attachment," which merged theories of evolution, cognitive psychology, systems theory, and object relations theory to describe the attachment relationship between children and their primary caretakers, usually their mothers (Bowlby, 1969, 1973, 1980).

Internal Working Models of Attachment

Bowlby originally described attachment as an inborn system designed, like other behavioral systems, to contribute to the survival of the species. Attachments are expressed behaviorally at first but persist throughout life in both representational and behavioral form. Like other mental models, a model of attachment provides a map of previous experiences so that an individual can react automatically in new, but relationally and situationally familiar situations. This model allows for the prediction of others' attachment-related or caregiving-related behaviors and their interpretation. Furthermore, the attachment model guides what an individual remembers or recalls about these behaviors and experiences.

Early studies of attachment representations used the Adult Attachment Interview (AAI), developed by George, Kaplan, and Main in 1985. The AAI is a semi-structured interview composed of 15 questions with standardized probes. The content and process of answers are coded. Contradictions and seemingly unnoticed incoherencies are as important as the views the speaker deliberately expresses. Classification as Autonomous, Dismissing, Preoccupied, or Unresolved/disorganized is derived from the form and content of the language used by the respondent during interview. Adults who are coherent and consistent when speaking about their childhood experiences, and who also have relevant, clear, and succinct responses, are classified as Autonomous. Similarly, individuals who come from more challenging backgrounds, but who speak coherently when discussing and evaluating positive and negative childhood experiences, are also classified as Autonomous. Adults are classified as Dismissing when they describe their attachment figures in very positive terms, but then contradict or are unable to support their claims later in the interview when asked for specific examples. Adults classified as Preoccupied display a confused, angry, or passive preoccupation with their parents. Finally, when Unresolved adults speak of attachment relationships, they demonstrate lapses of logic and executive function around trauma or loss (Main et al, 1985; van IJzendoorn, 1995).

In a landmark study, Main and her colleagues (1985) linked mothers' current state of mind with respect to their own parent relationships to their (12–18-month-old) child's behavior towards the mother in the Strange Situation (Ainsworth et al., 1978). Specifically, parents classified with the AAI as autonomous had children classified in the Strange Situation as secure.

Dismissing parents tended to have avoidant infants; preoccupied parents tended to have ambivalent infants, and unresolved parents tended to have disorganized infants. Main et al.'s findings were that for mothers, the relation is $r = 0.62$, $p < 0.001$, and for fathers, the relation is $r = 0.37$, $p < 0.05$. Several studies replicated these seminal findings to varying degrees; then, Van IJzendoorn (1995) integrated these results in a meta-analytic study that provided evidence for the links between mothers' representations of attachment and children's attachment status. Utilizing 18 samples, with $N = 854$, van IJzendoorn's meta-analysis revealed a combined effect size of 1.06 in the expected direction for the secure versus insecure split.

Following on the work of Main and colleagues on adult attachment, Bretherton and colleagues (1989) reasoned that an interview based on a parent's relationship with a particular child would produce similar relations to observable child–parent attachment-related behaviors. This idea led to the development of the Parent Attachment Interview (PAI) (Bretherton et al., 1989), which is much like the AAI in that it asks structured questions calling for open-ended answers.

Like the AAI, the PAI probes for specific events to support initial descriptions of the relationship, but is intended to be a more direct way to relate mental representations of attachment with parenting behaviors and child Strange Situation classifications. Where the AAI assesses a person's representation with respect to his or her own parents, the PAI assesses the person's representation of his or her own child. Bretherton et al. used a sample of 37 mothers of 25-month-old children to design their global coding system. The interviews are coded on a nine-point scale to assess the parent's sensitivity and insight concerning her or his relationship with the child. High scores (6 or more) on the sensitivity/insight scale are given if the interview conveys that the parent responds sensitively and appropriately to the child and has insight into the parent's own and the child's behavior and personality. On the other hand, low-scoring parents (those who receive less than 5) talk about "correct" behaviors, but then describe their own behavior as contrary to these general statements. Low scores are also assigned when parents fail to make obvious connections between their own and their child's behavior, or when they repeatedly express confusion about why the child behaves a certain way. In addition, low scores are given if the parent describes over or under-controlling behaviors by either the parent or the child, but also express helplessness about it. Finally, low scores also are given if the parent consistently talks about the child as if he or she was a possession.

In Bretherton's sample, the sensitivity/insight scale at 25 months correlated significantly (ranging from 0.38 to 0.60) with a number of attachment-related assessments: 1) the Strange Situation at 18 months, 2) Bretherton, Ridgeway, and Cassidy's (1990) Attachment Story Completion Task (a representational assessment administered to the child) at 37 months, and 3) the Waters and Dean (1985) Attachment Q-sort Security (a mother report measure of descriptions of attachment-related child behavior) at 25 months and at 37 months. Thus, researchers repeatedly find significant relations between what mothers say about the attachment-related aspects of their relationships with their children and actual observed mother, child, and dyad behaviors.

Broadening the Focus on Representations: Parenting Relationships

Attachment is only one component of the child–parent relationship, so capturing the complexity involved in caregiving likely requires conceptualization and measurement of representational dimensions not solely focused on attachment. For example, parents' state of mind with respect to attachment explains only about 12% of the variation in their responsiveness to their children (van Ijzendoorn, 1995). Therefore, examination of broader parent representations seems warranted.

The Working Model of the Child Interview (WMCI), developed by Zeanah et al. in 1993, assesses parents' internal working model of a particular child. It, too, is a semi-structured interview designed to assess parents' perceptions and subjective experiences with their young children. The WMCI begins with an optional section on developmental history, including a description of the pregnancy, labor, delivery, and the child's early development. The interview continues with a non-optional section where parents are asked to describe their child's personality, pick five adjectives which describe their child, and say which of their parents the child resembles most in personality. Parents are asked how they chose their child's name, what makes their child unique compared to other children, and how they handle their child's misbehaviors. Parents also are asked about their relationship with their child, the changes in the relationship over time, and how these changes have affected both parent and child. Subjects are asked to describe typical situations with their child, such as the child getting upset or sick. Lastly, parents are asked about their expectations for their child's future.

Zeanah and colleagues (1993) designed a coding system for the interview transcripts of 45 mother–infant dyads using 15 Likert-type scales. The scales assess what parents say about their relationship with their child, and how they say it, including the affect they demonstrate. In addition to the Likert-type scales, mothers are assigned to one of three global categories: Balanced, Disengaged, Distorted. These classifications are similar to the Ainsworth attachment classifications and are based on how the parents modulated their affect. Classification as Balanced is given to mothers who are straightforward, convey a rich description of their relationship with their child, and seem open to new information about their child. Classification as Disengaged is given to mothers who seem detached from their infant and who give impoverished descriptions of their child and their relationship with their child. Finally, the Distorted classification is assigned when mothers contradict themselves, share confusing narratives, and seem to distort the reality of their relationship with their child.

The Parent Development Interview (PDI), by Aber et al. (1985), is another semi-structured interview that probes for an assortment of parenting themes, and thus can assess qualities of the parent–child relationship in addition to attachment. Unlike the Zeanah et al. (1993) IWMC system just described, which assesses the parent's representation of a particular child, the PDI assesses the parents' representation of their *relationship* with that child. For instance, where the IWMC interview asks parents to provide adjectives describing the child, the PDI asks for adjectives describing the parent's relationship with the child. Although this may appear to be a non-important distinction, the focus on conceptualizing, recalling, and describing a relationship is more closely aligned with the probing used in the AAI than is a more general approach to asking about the child. The original PDI consists of 45 questions regarding a parent's behaviors, emotions, beliefs, and attributions about self and a specific child. Like the AAI, the PDI probes for specific relational experiences and emotions across a number of themes. Parents are asked what they like most and least about their child, and how their child is similar or different from themselves and their partner and to describe specific incidents when interactions between parent and child did and did not go well. Parents also are asked to pick five adjectives to describe their relationship with their child, and to describe themselves as parents. They are asked what parenting-related situations elicit various feelings for them. Parents are questioned about their reactions to situations that are typical with toddlers, and how they think their child feels in these situations. Lastly, parents are asked to recount how their child has changed them and describe how their experiences with their own parents have affected them and/or their child. Appendix 2.1 contains a list of adapted interview questions.

The coding system developed by Slade et al. (1993) assesses three general dimensions of parenting: 1) parents' awareness of their affective experience in the parent–child relationship, 2) parents' awareness of their child's affective experience in the relationship, and 3) parents' overall understanding of the relationship. Because the PDI assesses a number of interrelated themes, it can

48   *D. Steinberg and R. Pianta*

be used to better understand parents' multifaceted internal working models of parenting without being limited solely to attachment.

Researchers have used the PDI to relate internal working models of parenting to their own attachment status and to their parenting behaviors. In a sample of 125 mothers of 12 to 21 month old first-born sons, Slade et al. (1999) found that three factors (joy–pleasure/coherence, anger, and guilt/separation) described the scales used to code responses. The first factor pertains to how mothers represent joy and pleasure in their relationships with their children; mothers who spoke about the joy and pleasure in their relationships with their toddlers were also rated to have highly coherent and rich representations. The second factor relates to how mothers talk about anger. Some mothers' representations contained a high degree of anger that was poorly modulated, whereas others expressed a low degree of anger that was well-modulated. The final factor relates to the extent to which mothers talk about guilt and separation distress in the relationship with their toddler. Correlations among these factors were: 0.27 for Joy–Pleasure/Coherence and Anger, 0.04 for Joy–Pleasure/Coherence and Guilt–Separation Distress, and 0.14 for Anger and Guilt–Separation Distress.

Mothers classified as autonomous on the AAI scored highest on the joy–pleasure/coherence factor of the PDI and mothers classified as dismissing on the AAI scored highest on the anger factor of the PDI. They also found that mothers scoring higher on the joy–pleasure/coherence factor on the PDI were less negative and more positive with their children. Similarly, mothers scoring higher on the anger dimension were less sensitive and more negative with their children. They did not find that the guilt/separation factor correlated with AAI classification or mothering.

Contrary to predictions, Slade et al. (1999) found that mothers' state of mind with respect to attachment with their own parents did not predict to positive parenting once the joy–pleasure/coherence factor on the PDI was controlled. Positive parenting was a measurement comprised of positive loadings on the variables positive affect, sensitivity, and cognitive stimulation, and a negative loading on detachment. One explanation for this result had to do with their sample's restriction to boys. Van IJzendoorn and colleagues (1991) also did not find adult-attachment differences in sensitive responsiveness with a sample of boys in mother–son dyads, but did find differences with a sample of girls in mother–daughter dyads. Another important difference that may account for this finding is that unlike prior investigations, Slade et al. (1999) used assessments of mothering based on naturalistic observations in the home at a time when fathers were present, not exclusively dyadic structured situations in a laboratory.

Aber and colleagues (1999) further investigated the stability and change in maternal representations of their relationships with their male toddlers in a study of the dynamic association of representations and daily parenting experiences with the child. They administered the PDI twice when the children were 15 and 28 months of age. Using the same sample as above, Aber and colleagues (1999) found that there were no changes in average levels of mothers' joy–pleasure/coherence and guilt/separation distress from 15 to 28 months, but that there was a significant increase in mothers' level of anger. This increase in anger occurred during the "terrible twos," a period notable for intense parent–child conflict and negotiation. They also found bi-directional effects in that mothers whose representations have more pleasure and coherence at 15 months were less likely to represent their relationships as angry at 28 months, over and above that predicted by their original level of anger at 15 months. Similarly, anger at 15 months predicted joy–pleasure/coherence at 28 months, over and above joy–pleasure/coherence at 15 months. Although anger and joy–pleasure/coherence seem to be mutually influential during this period, neither affected nor were affected by levels of guilt/separation.

Finally, Aber et al. (1999) found that both quality of mothering and features of mothers' everyday life (as measured by daily parenting hassles) contribute to changes in mothers' representations during toddlerhood. More specifically, positive mothering at the height of negativity during toddlerhood predicted an increase in the joy–pleasure/coherence dimension of parenting. Parenting hassles (but not negative mothering or non-parenting hassles) during the same time period predicted an increase in the anger dimension of parenting. Neither daily hassles nor quality of mothering predicted changes in mothers' guilt/separation distress. These findings confirmed yet again the view that parents' representations of relationships with their child are embedded within a system comprised of interactive behaviors, life experiences, and individual characteristics of the parent and child.

Furthermore, George and Solomon (1996) used an edited version of the PDI, and coded mothers' responses along four 7-point rating scales: secure base, rejection, uncertainty, and helplessness. These scales were specifically designed to predict the child's attachment security under the hypotheses that these constructs reflect the caregiving equivalent of the four attachment strategies used by children. These four qualities relate to theorized aspects of the parent's representational model of self as caregiver, in relation to the attachment function of the parent–child relationship. In a sample of 32 mother–child pairs, mothers were assigned a caregiving classification that was the highest of the four scales. For instance, a mother who scored higher on the rejection scale than on the secure base, uncertainty, or helplessness scales would be assigned a "rejecting" caregiver classification. Mother's caregiving classifications corresponded significantly (81% match) with her child's classification in a modified version of the Strange Situation. As expected, secure caregivers had secure children, rejecting caregivers had avoidant children, uncertain caregivers had ambivalent children, and helpless mothers had insecure-controlling (disorganized) children. Furthermore, caregiving classifications matched mother's adult attachment classifications on the AAI, again providing evidence of the dynamic, systemic associations among representations of attachment and caregiving, and parenting outcomes such as the child's attachment status.

In summary, research supports that representations of the parenting relationship influence, and are influenced by, the parents' own attachment status, child characteristics, and parenting behavior. The PDI at one age has been used to predict representations later in time, and yet child factors, such as age and gender, have also influenced internal working models, as have quality of mother–child interactions and stressors outside the mothers' role as a parent. Given the success of the line of research on representations related to attachment only, and that there are other important components in parent–child relationships, there was reason to assess parenting representations more broadly.

Research on the CPAP Adaptation of the Parent Development Interview

Several limitations to the current systems of measuring and validating parents' mental representations of caregiving have been discussed (Pianta, O'Connor, & Marvin, 1993; George & Solomon, 1996). As stated earlier, most studies have examined only internal working models with respect to attachment, which leaves untapped the multiple other parenting domains, such as disciplinarian, teacher, and physical caretaker. Another limitation has to do with the use of global rating scales and categorical systems. Most studies utilize global rating scales and categorical systems to capture information related to complex representational systems. These systems have clear advantages for capturing global, qualitative aspects of very complicated constructs expressed in the course of lengthy interviews conducted by Main and colleagues (1985). But by design, global coding methods of parenting classifications may not be well-suited for examining the multiple dimensions of behaviors, emotions, and thoughts that comprise the representational system.

To address these limitations, Pianta, O'Connor, and Marvin (1993) developed a new coding system for an abbreviated version of the PDI at the Child-Parent Attachment Project (see Appendix 2.2). The adapted PDI reflects the original work of Aber and colleagues (1985). Because remaining emotionally and physically available (i.e., being a secure base) is only one function among many played by parents (Pianta et al., 1993; Emde, 1989), the adapted PDI and its corresponding coding system also assess parents' view of themselves as disciplinarian, teacher, and caretaker with a specific child. It was theorized that parents of multiple children would have different representations for each child because representations depend, in part, on characteristics of the child such as gender, special needs based on disability, and birth order. The adapted PDI is a semi-structured interview consisting of 15 questions designed to include themes such as separation, caregiving, and teaching. Similar to the AAI and other assessments of internal models of relationships, the adapted PDI probes for specific incidents in response to most questions, and asks participants to report their feelings and their child's feelings in these situations.

Pianta, O'Connor, Morog, Button, Dimmock, and Marvin developed the coding system for the adapted PDI, herein referred to simply as the CPAP-PDI, at the Child-Parent Attachment Project (CPAP) in 1995. Each question is coded on a four-point scale for 11 different constructs. The constructs fall into one of three categories: content, process, and affect. The four content scores are: compliance, business of caretaking, the child's achievement, or providing a secure base. The business of caretaking was scored, for example, if a parent mentions giving the target child a bath, or making dinner for the family. Two process codes are scored if either the parent's response reflects the child's point of view (perspective-taking), or the parent strategically avoids negative affect (neutralizing). An example of neutralizing is if a parent mentions feeling angry at the child, and then veers away from it by stating, "but it really wasn't that bad." Finally, five affect codes (anger, pleasure, guilt, worry/anxiety, and pain) are scored if the parent articulates feeling one of these emotions. Appendix 2.2 contains a more detailed description of each construct.

Furthermore, each construct was rated along a four-point scoring system. A response was scored "0" if the parent showed no evidence of the construct. A response was scored "1" if the parent gave vague or minimal evidence of a construct. A "2" was scored if evidence of the construct was articulated clearly, and "3" was given for strong, multiple or detailed evidence of a construct. Each construct was summed across each question of the interview, so in this sense, the adapted PDI is unlike other coding systems that assess the interview as a whole. Unless otherwise stated, analyses were conducted with this construct sum.

Button, Pianta, and Marvin (2001) conducted the first reliability and validity studies on the CPAP-PDI coding system. Button and her colleagues coded

112 interviews of mothers of a heterogeneous group of children, including a large percentage of children with disabilities. The CPAP sample included four groups of mothers: 1) those with children with severe cerebral palsy ($n = 34$), 2) those with children with moderate cerebral palsy ($n = 24$), 3) those with children with epilepsy ($n = 19$), and 4) a control group of typically developing children ($n = 35$). Intraclass correlations for the sum of each construct ranged from 0.73 to 0.83, with SEM's ranging from 0.10 to 0.17. Button et al. (2001) found that, compared with mothers of children with epilepsy or children with no diagnosis, representations of mothers of children with cerebral palsy contained less compliance-related content. These differences suggest that parents' representational model of parenting reflected characteristics of the child related to disability. Button et al. (2001) also found that individual CPAP-PDI constructs of worry and enmeshment were associated with mothers' behavior in a problem-solving task. Mothers whose narratives indicated greater worry tended to be less sensitive and less supportive in this setting. Mothers whose narratives expressed greater enmeshment were more likely to pressure their child and be over-involved.

Messina-Sayre et al. (2001) used a sub-sample of the one described above to examine the extent to which parenting representations predicted the feeding interactions of mothers and their children with cerebral palsy. Like studies of typically developing children (e.g., Slade et al., 1999; Aber et al., 1999), Messina-Sayre et al.'s study revealed many relations between the CPAP-PDI and maternal behaviors. Mothers' representations accounted for significant variance, beyond that accounted for by the child's developmental status, for maternal sensitivity and maternal delight. The more mothers' expressed compliance-related concern, the less sensitivity, acceptance and delight they exhibited during feeding. Greater emotional pain was associated with more hostility. Mothers experiencing greater worry displayed more sensitivity and delight with their children. Messina-Sayre et al.'s (2001) findings regarding worry are interesting in light of Button et al.'s. It is not that all "good" constructs related to all "good" behaviors, and all "bad" constructs related to all "bad" behaviors in research on the CPAP-PDI. Rather, these results seem to reflect the importance of specificity when considering different measurements of maternal behavior. The problem-solving task was increasingly mentally and physically taxing for both child and mother. Higher levels of worry, or anxiety, may interfere with sensitivity when the caregiver is stressed. On the other hand, the feeding situation involved everyday, predictable behaviors for the mother–child dyad. It may be that with routine tasks, worry does not interfere, or is even beneficial, with the perspective-taking abilities related to sensitivity.

Overall, Messina-Sayre's study is an important contribution to the study of mental models of parenting. Maternal affective experience was an important element of the representational model of parenting and appeared to be the aspect of representation most closely linked to maternal behavior. However, future work was needed on a more normative sample to identify whether these relations between CPAP-PDI scales and maternal behavior held in more typical parenting situations, or reflected the more atypical variations in parenting a child with a disability. It also was important for future work on the PDI to control for possible confounds such as child's gender and developmental level.

As such, this line of work with the CPAP-PDI was extended by using a sample of typically developing children, which was a sub-sample of the mother/child pairs who participated in the prospective National Institute of Child Health and Human Development (NICHD) Study of Early Child Care. The longitudinal design of the study provided advantages in that earlier measures could be used to predict behavior at a later date, moving beyond correlational analyses. The primary hypotheses of this study were that the multidimensional nature of mothers' representational models of their relationship with their child, as assessed by the CPAP-PDI, would be 1) measurable, and 2) related to characteristics of both the child and the mother. Furthermore, it was hypothesized that the CPAP-PDI would predict maternal behavior, independent of maternal education and personality factors.

Method

Participants

The sample consisted of 74 mother/child pairs who participated in the National Institute of Child Health and Human Development (NICHD) Study of Early Child Care at the University of Virginia Site, one of ten national sites. These 74 mothers and children (40 girls and 34 boys) are a subset of the larger NICHD Virginia sample. The dyads participated in all of the lab procedures at both 36 and 54 months, and the mothers completed the Parent Development Interview at 42 months. The mothers were contacted soon after their infants were born and were invited to participate in a longitudinal study. When the infants were one month old, the mother's mean age was 28 ($SD = 5.5$, range 18–40) years. There were 32 first-born children in the sample. There were 25 second-born, 14 third-born, two fourth-born, and two fifth-born children. The mothers, fathers, and babies were predominantly Caucasian (greater than

85%). Ten percent of the children were African American, and less than 5% were Asian or Pacific Islander. The representation of other ethnic minorities was minimal. Sixty percent of the mothers reported attaining at least a high school degree. The average years of mothers' education was 14 (*SD* = 2.8, ranging from 7 to 21). At 36 months, approximately 14% of the mothers reported receiving Public Assistance.

Procedures

Participants in this study were recruited originally for the NICHD Study of Early Child Care, a national study with an initial sample of 1,364 families located in 10 different cities across the United States. All sites collected data to examine the effects of childcare on children and their families. Data were collected in the home when the children were 1, 6, 15, 24, 36, and 54 months. Data also were collected in the lab at 15, 24, 36, and 54, months. An additional home visit was made at 42 months to collect PDI data, which was specific to the Virginia site.

The present study utilizes measures from several domains. First, demographic measures were collected when the children were first born. Second, mothers' personality characteristics and behaviors were assessed at every visit. Third, measures of child characteristics and behaviors were collected at 36 and 54 months. Finally, mother–child interactions were assessed at the 36- and 54-month lab visits.

Measures

Measures of Maternal Characteristics
Maternal Psychological Adjustment. A composite measure of maternal psychological adjustment was created using the (reversed) average of the Center for Epidemiological Studies Depression Scale (CES-D) (Radloff, 1977), obtained at 1, 6, 15, 24, and 36 months, and the NEO Personality Inventory (Costa & McCrae, 1985), which was administered at 1 month. Three scales of the NEO were utilized: 1) Neuroticism, the extent to which the mother indicated she is anxious, hostile, and depressed (reversed); 2) Agreeableness, the extent to which she is trusting, helpful, and forgiving; and 3) Extraversion, the extent to which she is sociable, fun-loving, and optimistic. Higher scores indicated better adjustment.

Parent Development Interview. The PDI used in this study was adapted from Aber et al.'s work (1985) by Pianta et al. (1993) and was administered at

42 months. The interviews were administered in standardized fashion by research assistants for the NICHD Study of Early Child Care. Interviews were audiotaped, and then transcribed. All interviews were coded independently by at least two of the four coders. Eleven interviews were coded separately by all four coders. Teams of coders changed throughout the coding process so that each coder worked about equally as often with the other three coders. Coders established consensus on disagreements through review of the transcript and reference to the coding manual.

The constructs were summed across the interview, and then adjustments were made to construct means by changing the outliers' values to $+/-2\,SD$ from the mean. Each of the 80 mothers interviewed had summation scores on 11 constructs. There were 35 outliers out of a possible 880 data points, with Anger and Compliance having more outliers each (6 and 5, respectively) than any other construct. As such, means and standard deviations changed little as a result of the adjustments. However, the skewness values decreased so that all but two constructs, Anger and Worry, fell within normal limits. Although a limitation, the skewness values of Anger (0.72) and Worry (0.77) still were considered adequate for analyses. All of the analyses utilized the mean construct scores after adjusting for skewness.

Intraclass correlations on inter-rater agreement for the sum of constructs are presented in Table 2.1. Overall reliabilities for this study were comparable to those in the CPAP sample. There is one notable exception. In this sample of typically developing children, the Enmeshment construct was rare, and therefore, a particularly challenging code on which to become reliable. Therefore, the Enmeshment construct was dropped from all analyses. Multiple regression analyses required that the data be reduced due to the small sample size. A composite was created by summing Achievement, Comfort, and Perspective with the five Affect codes. Theory and results of initial principle component analyses guided the creation of this composite. Alpha for the composite was 0.81. Unless otherwise stated, all future references to the CPAP-PDI are to this variable, called the CPAP-PDI composite.

Measures of Child Characteristics. Three qualities of the child were utilized. The first was language competence, assessed with the Verbal Comprehension scale of the Reynell Developmental Language Scale (Reynell, 1991). This measure of verbal comprehension was used as a proxy for IQ. The Reynell was administered by trained assistants at the 36-month laboratory visit. The internal consistency was 0.93 for the Verbal Comprehension scale. The mean Reynell Verbal Comprehension Standard Score was 96, $SD = 17$, with a range of 62–136. Children's gender and birth order were the two other child characteristics considered in this study.

Assessment of Mother–Child Interaction

Three Boxes Procedures. At 36 months, mother–child interaction was observed in the laboratory using a modified version of the Three Boxes Procedure (Vandell, 1979), in which the mother and child were presented with three containers of age-appropriate toys. A set of washable markers, stencils, and paper was in the first container; a set of dress-up clothes and a cash register was in the second container, and a set of Duplo blocks with a picture of a model that could be copied was in the third. The mother was instructed to have her child play with the toys in each of the three containers in a specified order for 15 minutes. Mothers and children were videotaped in the semi-structured play interactions. These videotapes were shipped to a central location for coding. Two teams of six coders received intensive supervision and met on a regular basis through the period of formal scoring to maintain reliability. Two coders served as members of both teams. A composite score of maternal sensitivity was created from three different seven-point scales: 1) mothers' supportive presence, 2) respect for the child's autonomy, and 3) hostility (reversed). Intercoder reliability on the composite was 0.84 (Winer, 1971). Cronbach alpha was 0.78. The average Maternal sensitivity score was 17.2 ($SD = 3.0$). Similarly, at 54 months, mothers and children were videotaped during a structured interaction, and tapes were coded by trained observers. Maternal sensitivity again represents a composite of supportive presence, respect for autonomy, and (reversed) hostility. Intercoder reliability was 0.82. Cronbach's alpha for the composite was 0.84.

At 54 months, mother–child dyads returned to the laboratory and, again, their interaction during a structured play was videotaped and sent to a central location for coding. The procedure at this age was similar to that at 36 months, but assessment used age-appropriate activities, including a puzzle task and an etch-a-sketch maze copying task. Maternal stimulation at 54 months represents a teaching composite created by summing mother's stimulation of cognitive development and mother's quality of assistance. Interrater reliability for maternal stimulation was 0.89. Cronbach's alpha for the composite was 0.84. Maternal Positive Caregiving at 54 months was created by calculating a proportional weighted sum of all the mother ratings (supportive presence, respect for autonomy, (reversed) hostility, cognitive stimulation, quality of assistance, and confidence). Interrater reliablity was 0.87. Cronbach's alpha for the Positive Caregiving composite was 0.91.

Table 2.1. *Descriptive Statistics for CPAP-PDI Construct Means after Adjustment for Skewness (N = 80)*

Construct	Mean	SD	Range	Skewness	ICC
(N = 11)					
Compliance	0.88	0.32	0.35–1.56	0.45	0.90
Business	0.48	0.29	0–1.09	0.42	0.67
Achievement	0.56	0.35	0–1.29	0.39	0.90
Comfort/Safe Haven	0.31	0.13	0.12–0.59	0.51	0.51
Perspective Taking	1.16	0.34	0.35–1.87	0.35	0.89
Neutralize	0.50	0.24	0.06–0.98	0.17	0.82
Anger	0.39	0.23	0–0.93	0.72	0.86
Pleasure	1.04	0.31	0.35–1.73	0.22	0.70
Guilt	0.17	0.12	0–0.43	0.34	0.77
Worry/Anxiety	0.35	0.14	0–0.68	0.77	0.77
Pain/Burden	0.81	0.37	0.18–1.57	0.49	0.92

Results

The following section first provides descriptive information about the CPAP-PDI scales, including correlations among the CPAP-PDI constructs, and associations between the CPAP-PDI and child and mother variables. Second, multiple regression analyses are presented. The CPAP-PDI was used to predict mother–child behavior, above and beyond what could be predicted by maternal educational level and psychological health.

Descriptive Analyses

On average, mothers of these four-year-olds tended to speak more about their child's compliance than any other topic, and the least about their child's comfort seeking behaviors. They tended to mention their child's achievement and the business of caring for their child about equally. Regarding mothers' emotional experience, they spoke more about the pleasure in their relationships with their children than any of the individual negative emotions. When speaking of their negative affect, they mention the pain and burden associated with parenting more than they did either their anger, worry, or guilt. No inferential conclusions were drawn about these trends. Table 2.1 presents descriptive statistics and intraclass correlations (ICCs) for each construct.

Intercorrelations were calculated among the CPAP-PDI constructs in order to examine associations among different dimensions of the mothers' representational systems. There were 35 significant correlations, which are presented

Table 2.2. *Significant Correlations Representational Dimensions (N = 80)*

Construct	1	2	3	4	5	6	7	8	9	10	11
1. Compliance	–		0.38**	0.38**	0.57**		0.56**			0.22*	0.22*
2. Business		–					0.23*	0.24*			0.33**
3. Achievement			–	0.27*	0.64**	0.25*	0.36**	0.48*	0.39**	0.41**	
4. Comfort				–	0.53**			0.33**	0.30**		0.35**
5. Perspective					–		0.46**	0.47**	0.31**	0.41*	0.41*
6. Neutralize						–			-0.30**		
7. Anger							–	0.25*	0.32**		0.41**
8. Pleasure								–	0.31**	0.27*	0.42**
9. Guilt									–	0.41**	0.39**
10. Worry										–	0.32**
11. Pain											–

$^*p < 0.05$; $^{**}p < 0.01$.

in Table 2.2. The general pattern of moderate ($r = 0.30 - 0.40$) correlations suggests that verbalizations about one aspect of representations were associated with other aspects in ways that are not surprising, but also that these dimensions are not redundant, reflecting a differentiated representational system. For instance, mothers who spoke about their child's compliance also tended to speak about their own feelings of anger, worry, and pain. Similarly, mothers who neutralized, or avoided, negative affect tended also not to speak about their own emotions, and in fact, were less likely to talk about their feelings of guilt compared to other mothers. Mothers who spoke about their child's comfort-seeking behaviors also mentioned their own feelings of pleasure, and took their child's perspective, yet they did not speak about their feelings of anger. Thus, it is not the case that constructs are redundant.

Maternal Representations and Child Characteristics

Correlations between CPAP-PDI constructs and child characteristic variables were calculated in order to test the hypothesis that characteristics of the child would be related to maternal representations. When children had higher IQs, mothers spoke more often about compliance ($r = 0.24$, $p < 0.05$), achievement ($r = 0.31, p < 0.01$), and anger ($r = 0.34, p < 0.01$). Later born children tended to have mothers who took their child's perspective more often ($r = 0.29, p < 0.05$), and spoke more often about the pleasure in their relationship with their child ($r = 0.23, p < 0.05$), than did mothers of first-born children. To test for differences between the representations of mothers of girls and mothers of boys, t-tests were performed. Two constructs (Comfort and Perspective) evidenced significant differences between boys and girls. Mothers of boys spoke about their child's use of them as a secure base, and took their child's perspective, more often than mothers of girls. There were no differences in mothers' representations as a function of child gender in the CPAP sample.

Maternal Representations and Maternal Characteristics

Variables pertaining to maternal behavioral and demographic characteristics were correlated with the constructs of the CPAP-PDI. In general, mothers who were older, had more education, and displayed greater sensitivity also spoke more about their child's achievement, and their own feelings of pleasure, anger, and guilt. Furthermore, three measures of maternal behavior at 54 months (Maternal Positive Caregiving, Maternal Stimulation, and Maternal Sensitivity) were correlated with the constructs of the CPAP-PDI, and the composite measure. There were multiple associations, with the highest being between Achievement and Maternal Stimulation. These correlations are presented in Table 2.3.

Prediction of Mother–Child Interaction

To examine the extent to which maternal representations accounted for parent behavior, above and beyond what could be predicted by her educational level and psychological adjustment, multiple regression analyses were used. Three measures of maternal behavior, Maternal Stimulation, Maternal Positive Caregiving, and Maternal Sensitivity, were the dependent variables. Hierarchical multiple regression was utilized with block entry. In three separate regressions, three blocks of variables were entered. Due to concern about limited degrees of freedom, only selected variables were entered in each of the blocks. Maternal Education was entered in the first block. Maternal Psychological Adjustment was entered in the second block, and the CPAP-PDI composite was entered in the third block. When the CPAP-PDI was significant, follow-up analyses examined which of the constructs were the most powerful predictors. Each of the individual CPAP-PDI constructs comprising the composite were entered in the last block (in place of the CPAP-PDI composite). Because Pain, Worry, and Guilt were considered theoretically similar, and more similar than the other Affect codes, they were summed and entered as one variable, named Negative Affect. Follow-up analyses were conducted on each of the maternal behavior measures. Interactions examining the extent

Table 2.3. *Correlations between Demographic Variables, Maternal Psychological Characteristics, Maternal Behavior, and CPAP-PDI*

	Mothers' Age	Mothers' Education	Income to Needs Ratio	Mothers' Psych Health	Maternal Sensitivity (36 months)	Maternal Sensitivity (54 months)	Maternal Stimulation
	$(N = 75)$	$(N = 75)$	$(N = 72)$	$(N = 71)$	$(N = 74)$	$(N = 71)$	$(N = 71)$
Compliance					0.24*	0.29*	0.35**
Business							
Achievement	0.31**	0.32**	0.26*	0.243*	0.38**		0.46**
Comfort		0.28*					
Perspective					0.33*	0.24*	0.42**
Neutralize				0.25*			
Anger	0.24*	0.31**			0.35**		0.35**
Pleasure	0.34**	0.36**	0.33**		0.40**		0.35**
Guilt	0.26*	0.35**	0.30*		0.27*		
Worry							
Pain		0.29*					
PDI Composite	0.28*		0.41**		0.43**	0.26*	0.45**

* $p < 0.05$ (two-tailed); ** $p < 0.01$ (two-tailed).

to which associations between representations and behavior were moderated by mother's education or psychological adjustment (CPAP-PDI by Maternal Education, and CPAP-PDI by Maternal Psychological Adjustment) were tested as an additional block and were found to be nonsignificant.

As expected, in each model, the covariates of education and psychological adjustment significantly predicted aspects of the mothers' behavior when interacting with her child. The CPAP-PDI composite significantly predicted (R-square Change $= 0.054$, Beta $= 0.254$, Total R-Square $= 0.347, p < 0.05$, two-tailed) one of the three variables, Maternal Stimulation at 54 months, even when Maternal Education and Psychological Adjustment were taken into account. The composite approached significance for Positive Caregiving (R-square Change $= 0.031$, Beta $= 0.194$, Total R-Square $= 0.31, p < 0.10$, two-tailed). Follow-up analyses revealed that Anger (R-square Change $=$ 0.059, Beta $= 0.262, p < 0.05$, two-tailed), Perspective (R-square Change $=$ 0.075, Beta $= 0.287$, $p < 0.01$, two-tailed), and Achievement (R-square Change $= 0.058$, Beta $= 0.261, p < 0.05$, two-tailed), individually associated with Maternal Stimulation. Anger (R-square Change $= 0.059$, Beta $= 0.264$, $p < 0.05$, two-tailed), and Perspective (R-square Change $= 0.052$, Beta $=$ $0.239, p < 0.05$, two-tailed), but not Achievement, also individually associated with Positive Caregiving in follow-up analyses. As such, Achievement serves as a link between a specific aspect of representations, and the parenting behavior one would expect. Contrary to expectations, the CPAP-PDI did not account for significant increments in explained variance for Maternal Sensitivity at 54 months.

Discussion

The results described in this study, and others using the PDI to assess mothers' representations of their relationships with their child, demonstrate the following points regarding maternal representations (Button et al., 2001; Messina–Sayre et al., 2001; Slade et al., 1999; Aber et al., 1999). First, maternal representations of not only attachment, but also discipline and teaching, seem to be organized and measurable. Second, these three parenting dimensions are only moderately correlated, meaning they are not redundant. Third, they relate to characteristics of the child (such as birth order, verbal IQ, disability status, and gender) and characteristics of the mother (such as age, education, income, sensitivity with her child, and psychological adjustment). Fourth, they differentially predict aspects of maternal behavior, even when maternal education and psychological characteristics are taken into account. The different aspects of maternal representations (that of compliance, achievement, and comfort) uniquely predict mother–child behavior. That is, the different aspects of the caregiving role differently contribute to different maternal behaviors. These findings in the studies on the CPAP-PDI are similar to other studies of mental models (e.g., Bretherton et al., 1989). The findings of specific, differentiated associations between dimensions of mothers' representations and their behavior with their child suggests a level of specificity not often reported in this interaction.

Results of this study suggest that qualities of the child, such as birth order, verbal IQ, and gender show scattered associations with maternal representations of their relationship with that child. With regard to birth order, mothers of later born children spoke more about the pleasure in their relationship and their child's comfort seeking behaviors than did mothers of first-born children. As Dunn, Kendrick, and McNamee's (1981) study revealed, after the birth of a second child, there are marked changes in the interaction between first-borns and their mothers. There is a sharp decrease in maternal attention, including play, and an increase in punitive and restrictive maternal behaviors. Furman (1995) offered two reasons to account for these changes. First, the mother has the demands of a newborn, which can lead to significant changes in the mother's behavior toward the first-born. Second, many first-born children display an increase in distress or problem behavior when their siblings are born (Dunn, Kendrick, & MacNamee, 1981; Thomas et al., 1961; Shrader & Leventhal, 1968). Based on these studies, the results showing mothers of later-borns expressing more pleasure in their relationships with their child are not surprising.

This study also suggests that child's gender also plays an important, but limited, role in a mother's mental model of the parent–child relationship. Mothers of boys spoke about their child's comfort seeking behaviors, and took their son's perspective, to a greater extent than mothers of girls. These results are interesting in light of previous studies on gender in parent–child relationships, which suggest that there are circumstances associated with differential treatment of a child based on gender. For example, Lamb and colleagues (1982) found that nontraditional parents (where father planned to be the child's primary caretaker) interacted preferentially with their three-month-old daughters, whereas the reverse was true for traditional parents. Similarly, Cowan, Cowan, and Kerig (1993) found that maritally dissatisfied fathers, but not mothers, tended to treat their daughters more negatively than they did their sons. Across studies of parental attitudes, there are consistent findings when individuals are shown the same baby dressed as a boy or a girl and asked to describe the child. Babies thought to be girls are described as frail and sweet, whereas babies thought to be boys are described as tough and sturdy (Condry & Condry, 1976 as cited in Fagot, 1995). In these studies, parental attitudes and behaviors towards their child were different depending on the child's gender. Because mental models are thought to guide behavior, and behaviors and attitudes towards children are different based on child gender, it follows that the mental models of these relationships are different based on gender as well, although in this study, associations were not strong.

However, to some extent, these differences in mental models based on the child's gender may be masking developmental differences between boys and girls. Another possible explanation for the difference in maternal mental models involving the comforting of sons more than daughters concerns the differences between boys and girls at age four. In general, at age four, boys can be considered less mature or independent than girls. As opposed to the interpretation that mothers favor their sons over their daughters, it is possible that boys at this age seek more comfort from their mothers than do girls. This interpretation makes sense given that differences in maternal representations based on gender were not found in the CPAP sample, which contained children ranging in age from 14 to 52 months.

Although associations between representations and child characteristics were moderate, characteristics of the mothers, such as their education level, psychological adjustment, and family income, were more strongly related to their representations as measured by the PDI. Mothers' mention of their child's achievement and their feelings of anger, pleasure, and guilt were particularly associated with demographic and maternal psychological characteristic variables. Because of these relations, it was necessary to account for the demographic and maternal psychological characteristics when using maternal representations to predict mother–child interaction. These relations were similar to those of Messina-Sayre et al. (2001), who also needed to account for maternal education when predicting mother–child interaction.

Mothers' self-reported psychological health was found to be positively correlated with neutralizing, but this finding is not surprising. Neutralizing, or not acknowledging one's own negative affect, is thought to interfere with a parent's ability to recognize and respond to a child's emotional needs (Haft & Slade, 1989). Mothers who neutralize, by definition, are more likely than others to state that they do not experience, or only mildly experience, negative affect. Thus, it is not surprising that mothers with high neutralizing scores on the PDI did not endorse negative affect on the paper-and-pencil measures of psychological adjustment. It may be that minimizing, but only to a certain extent, one's own experience of negative affect can be a positive way to cope with painful feelings. This interpretation of the Neutralizing construct is supported by cognitive research on depressed and non-depressed individuals, which underscores that depressed people attend equally to negative, neutral, and positive stimuli, whereas non-depressed people "avoid" negative stimuli, attending with a positive, and protective, bias (McCabe & Gotlib, 1995; Gotlib, McLachlan, & Katz, 1988). It may be that mothers who attend to positive interactions or emotions preferentially over negative ones (a form of neutralizing) have a protective bias, which in turn paves the way for more positive interactions with their children. In a separate set of exploratory analyses, there was modest evidence suggesting a nonlinear relationship between Neutralizing and maternal sensitivity. The idea that negative feelings, experienced in moderate amounts, is optimal may pose a challenge to assessment in general. However, with the PDI coding system, how a parent uses language (the degree to which they neutralize) is taken into account not only in any given answer, but also across the interview.

Although it was initially assumed that mothers' representations of anger would reflect negative qualities of the parent–child relationship, the inverse was found. While counter to findings of some researchers (i.e., Aber et al., 1999; Slade et al., 1999), the level of anger expressed in this sample was low. As such, this association may hold only for low levels of anger. Unlike other coding systems (e.g., Slade et al., 1993), anger was coded for its expression, but no clinical judgment was made as to how insightful the mother seemed regarding her angry feelings. Mothers' expression of anger in the PDI seems to be functioning as a measure of openness to explore and ability to express negative feelings. Thus, mothers' expression of moderate anger has functioned as a measure of positive parenting. It is not surprising, then, that mothers who were willing and able to express their anger tended to have high levels of education, in addition to having children with high intelligence. This finding is also more easily understood when keeping in mind that the mothers in this study were not a part of a clinical sample. While the moderate expression of anger can be viewed as positive, it is important to remember that mothers in this study tended to express low levels of anger in comparison to their feelings of pleasure. It may be useful to think of mother's expression of anger as reflective of her defensiveness. Mothers who are less defensive are more able to describe their feelings of anger with integrity.

This finding in relation to anger is also interesting given work in clinical samples and in attachment research. For example, in a prospective study, Gjerde (1995) found that depressive disorders in women were related to problems expressing anger. In that study, depressed women seemed to lack the capacity to experience anger. Instead of using their feelings of anger to overcome obstacles, depressed women seem to turn their anger inward and become passive. Bretherton (1985) described early studies of attachment (Main, Tomasini, & Tolan, 1979; Main & Stadtman, 1981) which found that mothers of infants classified as avoidant in the Strange Situation were generally low in emotional expressiveness, even in response to the sometimes highly aggressive behaviors of their children. Along these lines, many maltreated toddlers seem to inhibit the expression of negative affect when interacting with their mothers (Crittenden & DiLalla, 1988; Lynch & Cicchetti, 1991). Although it is highly unlikely that all mothers who do not express their anger are depressed, were abused as children, or maltreat their own children, there seems to be important links between the open expression of moderate levels of anger, feelings of empowerment and/or safety, and positive parenting.

The emotion of anger, the ability to take the child's perspective, and the description of the child's achievement emerged as important aspects of the mental model of parenting as they relate to the utilized measures of mother–child behaviors. These would seem to be important dimensions of parents' processing of their relationship with their child. It was surprising that mothers' expression of pleasure was not found to be significant predictors of parent–child interaction, as was found in the Button and Messina-Sayre sample (Button et al., 2001; Messina-Sayre et al., 2001). It may be there are differences in important characteristics of the mental model depending on the particular choice of mother–child interaction (e.g., a play situation or a problem-solving task). In addition, as discussed above, it may be that there are differences across either samples or coders, or both.

In summary, diverse aspects of parenting representations, in addition to that related to attachment, are not only measurable, but it can also predict parenting behavior. Furthermore, there were more relations overall between maternal representations and qualities of the mother, such as her education level and psychological health, than there were relations between maternal representations and child characteristics. These findings are in accordance with Bowlby's theory (Bowlby, 1969), which states that the mother brings much more complexity to the parent–child relationship than does the child. Again, it is not the case that all maternal characteristics are related to all aspects of representations. The ones for which there is no relation, such as mother's psychological adjustment and her mention of any negative affect, also make theoretical sense.

In particular, there were several associations, as expected, between mothers' representations and their behavior with their child. Given Bretherton et al.'s (1989) findings that mothers who took their child's perspective were more likely to have securely attached children, it is not surprising that with the PDI, mothers who took their child's perspective had more positive interactions with their child. Similarly, Aber et al. (1999) found that a pleasure-coherence dimension of mental models related to positive parenting behaviors. As such, the result that mothers who often mention their pleasure in the relationship, and their child's comfort seeking behaviors, also have positive interactions with their children, was expected. It was also not surprising that the more a mother spoke about her child's achievement, the more intellectual stimulation and the higher quality of teaching she provided for her child.

There are some important limitations of these studies. First, the data were skewed, necessitating the adjustment of outliers. Even so, some of the constructs remained slightly skewed according to some statisticians (Snedecor & Cochran, 1980). It is unclear how much the slight skewness of the Anger construct confounds these results. Even so, the Perspective and Achievement constructs were not skewed, and they also accounted for significant increases in explained variance in maternal behavior. A second limitation involves the small sample size, and subsequent concern about degrees of freedom, which restricted the number of variables entered in the regression model. A third limitation has to do with the interview itself. These results must be considered in light of the interview questions, many of which elicited descriptions of the negative aspects of parenting. An interview which probed more often for positive memories or experiences may have produced different findings. For example, there may have been more robust findings regarding the pleasure involved in the mother–child relationship had there been more instances for parents to talk about their positive feelings in their relationship with their child. Thus, it is important to note this contextual issue. Finally, these early studies are exploratory in nature. Repeated correlational tests were utilized and many of the correlations revealed were not specifically predicted. Replication of these findings in future studies on maternal representations would increase the confidence in these results, and therefore enhance the understanding of maternal representations and mother–child interaction.

Direction for Future Research

The results of the CPAP-PDI studies are promising in terms of contributing to the understanding of maternal representations and mother–child interaction, but need to be repeated due to the exploratory nature of this work. A larger sample would be beneficial in future studies and another fruitful line of study would be on clinically referred mother–child dyads. A comparison between a clinical sample and a non-clinical sample could further illuminate various aspects of parenting representations and how they relate to behavior. Further research is needed to more clearly understand the complex interplay between specific dimensions of mental models and behavior, and to make stronger predictions across numerous types and forms of mother–child interaction.

Three minor modifications of how the CPAP-PDI is utilized may be helpful in better understanding mental models of parenting. First, for each of the constructs, parents' answers have been averaged across the interview. Another avenue to explore is to use ratios (for instance, "pain to pleasure") for the PDI constructs, which may eliminate the need to account for differences in length of response, and may also uncover further findings. Second, the Compliance construct may have stronger findings if the coding is changed to allow for the tracking of both child compliance and noncompliance. These two compliance-related constructs could be summed if necessary, which would be identical to the current coding system. Although such a change would complicate an already complex coding system, it may be worthwhile when trying to predict child compliance. Third, a measure of "positive neutralizing" may be used to further understand the links between acknowledgment and understanding of one's own affect and an individual's behaviors. A code can be added for parents who minimize the positive aspects of their relationships with their children. This code may be linked to children classified with an insecure-avoidant attachment to their mothers.

Aside from these minor changes, there are a number of potentially beneficial investigations of parenting representations to continue. It may be important and clinically useful to study mental representations in parents of older children and the changes in representations over time. Similarly, how representations differ among siblings could also be enlightening, as the parent remains a "common denominator." It is unclear how significant individual child differences might be, even though children contribute less to complexity to mother–child relationships than do parents (Bowlby, 1969). It also may be advantageous to investigate many possible mediating factors to changes in representations. For example, as Aber et al. (1999) have explained, mothers who described more pleasure in their relationships with their children were less likely to represent their relationships as angry about one year later, even when accounting for earlier levels of anger. Other possible mediating factors include economic stability and a supportive relationship with a partner. The extent to which psychotherapy supports changes in representational models of parenting could also be a worthwhile line of study, as could examining the changes in relative contribution of child characteristics in the parents' representational models as the children mature. Another important consideration is to study paternal representations. Adding a code for "play" would be useful when comparing fathers' and mothers' representations as fathers spend proportionately more time playing with their children than mothers do (Fagot, 1995). Other important considerations are to examine how the qualities of adult love relationships, and the stressors associated with single parenthood, relate to mental models.

Finally, one controversy in the literature centers around how mental models are transmitted across generations (Fox, 1995). In order to gain a clearer understanding of the interplay between biology and the environment, studying mental models in relation to behaviors and demographics in parents of adopted children would be an important step in understanding intergenerational transmission of relational processes. Along the lines of how representational models are transmitted, an important step would be to analyze subtle uses of language. There is a difference between a parent saying, "It is time for you to go to bed," and "I would like for you to go to bed now." Over time, such subtleties may contribute to different representations of the next generation of caregivers.

Summary

The PDI is a measure of mental models that assesses more of the complexity involved in parent–child relationships than only attachment-related aspects. In addition, studies on the CPAP-PDI contribute to research on maternal representations because the CPAP-PDI involves a measure of mental models that is less interpretive, and therefore requires less clinical training than most other interview coding systems. The studies on the CPAP-PDI were conducted on two different samples: a homogeneous one, and a group of children with varying degrees of cerebral palsy. Multiple relations were found between maternal representations and child characteristics, maternal characteristics, and demographic variables. Maternal representations, as measured by the CPAP-PDI, predicted mother–child interaction, even when maternal education and psychological adjustment were taken into account. When constructs were used individually, three components of maternal representations (Anger, Perspective, and Achievement) predicted maternal stimulation. Only two aspects of maternal representations (Anger and Perspective, but not Achievement) predicted maternal caregiving. This finding makes theoretical sense, and suggests that representations differentially predict aspects of maternal behavior. Findings were more limited when maternal sensitivity was controlled in addition to the other variables.

Appendix 2.1
Parent Development Interview, adapted from Aber, Slade, Berger, Bresgi, & Kaplan, 1985

1. a. Choose three words that tell about your relationship with (child's name). Now, please give me a specific experience or particular incident for the first adjective.
   b. Please give me a specific experience or particular incident for the second adjective.
   c. Please give me a specific experience or particular incident for the third adjective.
2. Describe a time in the last week when you and (child's name) really clicked.
3. Now describe a time in the last week when you and (child's name) really weren't clicking.
4. Are there any experiences in (child's name's) life that you feel were particularly challenging or difficult for him/her?
5. All parents struggle with knowing how much to push their child to do what is difficult versus how much not to push. What kinds of situations bring this dilemma up for you?
6. Tell me a time recently when (child's name) misbehaved.
7. What gives you the most joy in being a parent?
8. What gives you the most pain or difficulty in being a parent?
9. When you worry about (child's name), what do you find yourself worrying about most?
10. How confident are you that you will be able to soothe (child's name) when s/he is upset? How do you do it?
11. Do you ever feel angry as a parent? What kinds of situations make you feel this way? How do you handle your angry feelings?
12. Do you ever feel guilty as a parent? What kinds of situations make you feel this way? How do you handle your guilty feelings?
13. Every parent has at least occasional doubts about whether they are doing a good job or not. What kinds of situations bring doubts up for you and how do you handles these feelings?
14. Do you ever feel needy as a parent? What kinds of situations make you feel this way? How do you handle your needy feelings?
15. Now we're going to talk about when you and (child's name) are separated from one another. Tell me about a separation when you have to leave or when s/he has to leave you. What is hard for you about these separations? What is easy for you? How does (child's name) typically respond to these separations?

Appendix 2.2
Description of Parent Development Interview Constructs

In the present scoring system, parents' mental representations of their relationship with their child are assessed with respect to three areas: a) content or themes represented, b) process or *how* the parent represents him/herself and the content, and c) affective tone of representations. Together, these three areas provide a fairly comprehensive view of the representational system with respect to a given parent–child relationship, from the parents' perspective. These three areas are conceptually distinct (to some degree) and can provide qualitatively different information. The 14 scales are classified into these three areas. The Content area includes "Mentions compliance," "Ineffectiveness of compliance/control management," "Mentions business of caregiving," "Mentions child's achievement," and "Comfort/Safe haven." The Process area includes "Perspective-taking," "Enmeshment," "Neutralize," and "Confusion of response." The Affect area includes "Anger," "Positive Affect," "Guilt," "Worry/Anxiety about the future," and "Pain/Burden." The system, as developed, is open-ended.

A four-point scale (0–3) was adopted to score each response to a single question in the interview on each scale. A completed scoring will have all questions in the PDI scored on all scales in the scoring system. Scoring criteria for each scale point are given subsequently.

General Code Points for Each Scale:

0 = no evidence of construct; parent's response does not include any reference to construct or related issues.

1 = vague, minimal evidence of construct; parent's response includes reference to topics "close" to the construct being assessed; parent may also mention the construct but does not give a clear (full, complete) example.

2 = clear evidence; there is clear evidence the parent mentions the dimension directly or the dimension is clearly a part of the parent's response, although no episodic example is given, or little detail or elaboration is present.

3 = detailed, elaborated, or episodic description; parent offers a qualitative or quantitative extension of a "3" response. These are often prototypic examples or definitions of a given construct. Sometimes the word "very" will serve to increase a "2" response to a "3" response. For example, "it was a very tiring time" would be scored a "3," whereas "it was a tiring time" would be scored a "2."

For these scales ONLY content involving the parent and the TARGET CHILD is coded. For example, if the parent discusses non-compliant interactions with a child other than the target, these are not coded on these scales.

Mentions Compliance/Control. This scale measures whether the parent's response refers to the child's compliance with parental (or other) rules or struggles over parent's (vs. the child's) control in the situation or class of situations being discussed. (This scale does not measure problems with compliance, but simply whether compliance is mentioned in the response.) There must be an explicit reference to the target child. There is no assumption that this scale is positive or negative (i.e., distinguishes good and bad parenting); it simply reflects how dominant the theme of behavior management/compliance is in the parent's working model of him/herself as a parent. At the high end compliance is clear in the response; at the low end it is not present.

This scale can be tricky when coding parents' experiences with infants, but the coder should code what the parent says, even if the **coder** knows that a three-month-old child is not capable of compliance per se ("he was fussing at me all day, he just would not do what I wanted"). If the parent frames the content as compliance, then it is coded on this scale. When discussing an infant and there is clearly no reference to compliance ("he was sick that day and fussed all morning"), score a "0."

Mentions Business of Caregiving. Parent mentions caregiving behaviors involving direct personal contact with the child such as diapering, feeding, dressing, bathing, rocking, putting to bed, hygiene, giving medicine, etc. Often, caregiving examples may overlap with other codes (e.g., if parent reports having difficulty putting the child to bed), and that is okay. This scale reflects the extent to which the parent reports self as directly involved in the care of the child at the behavioral level.

NOTE: Taking the child to a sitter, the doctor's, providing treatment or rehabilitation, or arranging daycare for the child are all NOT considered direct physical caregiving as defined for the purposes of this scale. These parenting behaviors are NOT scored here.

Mentions Child's Achievement/Performance. This scale measures the parent's references to the child's performance of skills and behaviors or more general reference to developmental progress. The scale assesses the parent's mental occupation with the child's developmental progress. The key to scoring interview content is the parent's indication of the **progression** aspect of the child's behavior, and not just reference to child behavior in general or absence of a skill (e.g., "he's starting to learn to walk" vs. "he can't walk"). A mention of time is a very good clue that the parent is thinking about progress. The high end is an explicit, detailed example of the child's progress in a certain area of development (social, motor, cognitive, language, self-help).

Comfort/Save Haven/Secure Base. Parent mentions him/herself comforting, soothing, or having contact with the (distressed or not) child in response to separation/threat/fear/disequilibrium on the part of the child or parent gives example of child's secure base behavior. Particularly salient are instances in which the parent reports the child was distressed by something, sought the parent, and the parent comforted the child. These are instances of prototypic comfort/safe-haven behavior, and when they are reported in a detailed manner they should be given a 3. At the lower end of the scale are examples in which there appears to be evidence for general comfort or physical contact situations.

Process Codes: Perspective Taking, Neutralizing/Defensive

This set of scales reflects process dimensions of the parent's representational system. Included are scales for constructs reflecting aspects of the parent's differentiation from the child (Perspective-Taking, Enmeshment), the processing of affect in the representations (Neutralizing), and indicators of disorganization in mental processes when discussing the relationship with the child (Confusion of Response).

As before, the coder should focus ONLY on content relevant to the TARGET CHILD and not code (on these scales) content referring to a sibling or another child, or children in general. Also, on these scales it is important the coder have a sense of the overall scale descriptor before assigning a particular code, because it is impossible to script each example in an anchor-point description.

Perspective-Taking. Parent's response indicates that s/he views the child with independent states, thoughts, and feelings (these must be tenable, believable, not misattributions). Simply labeling feelings (i.e., something internal to the child) (e.g., "she felt sad," "things have been hard for her," "he does better with a sitter than he used to") are scored a "1" because they do not qualify as real perspective-taking. If s/he describes the idea of taking the child's perspective, score a "1." In order to receive a score of "3," the parent must provide an example indicating awareness of the child's perspective – including a description of the child's state and a NARRATED link between the child's state and the reason for that state. If the state is described and plausible reasons are included in the answer but NOT narrated, the response is coded a "2" and if the state is described without the answer including plausible reasons for the state, it is coded a "1." Examples of hypothetical perspective taking, for example, "if she wanted to go to the park and I said no she'd be pretty mad," are coded IF the example is related to plausible real-life situations but NOT coded if it is far in the future or not related to current parent–child interactions, for example, "I worry about how he feels when he gets to school" said of a 12-month-old.

Neutralize. The overriding theme of this code is the parent's attempt to distance him/herself from the NEGATIVE affective component of the question. The code is akin to the avoidant or dismissing strategy in discussions of attachment, in which emotion in the context of a discussion/interaction is dismissed, neutralized, or avoided. If the end result of the response does not seem to neutralize negative affect or somehow avoid the question, neutralize should not be scored at the high end. A parent who delays in responding to the question, but then goes on to talk at length about something else or discusses other feelings, is not neutralizing. The scale is designed to reflect the degree to which a parent "backs away from" discussion of emotion in the interview, and may take many forms – including not responding or denying in response to a question about feelings ("I don't know"), or more sophisticated forms in which the parent responds with great detail for events, etc. but does not provide any information about his/her feelings.

Affect Codes: Anger, Pleasure, Guilt, Worry/Anxiety about the Future, Sadness/Pain

The 0–3 scale is also used for the affective tone expressed in the response. Use primarily verbal expressions when coding. It is not necessary that the parent display the affect both verbally and nonverbally in order to receive a score of "3."

Note: Unlike the other sets of scales, the parent's response is coded if any relevant content is included, even if it refers to another child or experience other than the target child. If the parent clearly expresses one of the affects listed below in any modality, a score of "3" should be given, even if the affect is directed toward/in response to something other than the child (e.g., doctors, scornful neighbors). The hypothesis is that if an affect is stimulated during this parent interview, it is part of his/her "representational space."

Affect Codes: Code the highest level present in the response.

0 = no evidence
1 = vague or oblique reference (e.g., "frustration" for anger)
2 = solid or clear example of affect (e.g., "yes I feel angry").
3 = multiple, strong, or detailed expressions of a particular affect being coded (e.g., "it felt so wonderful to watch him take his first step," "I was so angry I could have. . . .").

Anger. Parent mentions feeling angry (or related synonym, e.g., frustrated) or gives an example that includes his/her anger. "Frustration" is likely to be coded as a "1."

Pleasure. Parent expresses or mentions feeling a positive affect that can take any of several forms, or describes affection between themselves and the child. Examples of positive affects include happiness, joy, close, pride, loving, etc. Or, parent mentions physical affection or gives an example that includes his/her physical affection (e.g., a hug, warm touching, cuddling, child in lap in affectionate manner, etc.). Or, parent mentions being proud of child/child's accomplishments, etc., or parent gives an example that includes his/her pride in the child. Score a "1" if the feeling is vaguely positive (e.g., "understanding").

Guilt. Parent mentions feeling guilty or gives an example that includes his/her guilt, such as "I'm sorry I punished him." A vague reference to guilt, such as, "I wish I had done something else," would be scored a "1."
    NOTE: Many responses that seem like guilt may also be coded under "Pain/Burden."

Worry/Anxiety About the Future. Parent mentions feeling worried/anxious or gives an example that includes his/her worry/anxiety that is **in response to thinking about the future** or what the child might experience that might be negative. These could include expectations. The primary issue in parent's response is uncertainty of child outcome – not parent feeling bad because of something that happened. Reports about how the parent thought in the past – "we wondered if he would live" – are scored as well.

Pain/Burden. Parent reports (or shows) feelings of pain, sadness or reports being overwhelmed, burdened, or encumbered with respect to being a parent, the parental role, or about the child's own tough experiences. This code is a fairly frequent element of many responses so coders should be alert to this.

References

Aber, J. L., Belsky, J., Slade, A., & Crnic, K. (1999). Stability and change in mothers' representations of their relationship with their toddlers. *Developmental Psychology, 35*, 1038–47.

Aber, J. L., Slade, A., Berger, B., Bresgi, I., & Kaplan, M. (1985). *The Parent Development Interview*. Unpublished manuscript, New York: Barnard College, Department of Psychology.

Ainsworth, M. S., Blehar, M. C., Waters, E., & Wall, S. (1978). *Patterns of Attachment: A Psychological Study of the Strange Situation*. Hillsdale, NJ: Lawrence Erlbaum Associates.

Beck, J. S. (1995). *Cognitive Therapy: Basics and Beyond*. New York: Guilford Press.

Bowlby, J. (1969). *Attachment and Loss: Volume I. Attachment*. New York: Basic Books.

Bowlby, J. (1973). *Attachment and Loss: Volume 2. Separation*. New York: Basic Books.

Bowlby, J. (1980). *Attachment and Loss: Volume 3. Loss, Sadness, and Depression*. New York: Basic Books.

Bretherton, I. (1985). Attachment theory: Retrospect and prospect. In I. Bretherton & E. Waters (Eds.), *Growing points of attachment theory and research. Monographs of the Society for Research in Child Development, 50*, (1–2, serial No. 209), 3–37.

Bretherton, I., Biringen, Z., Ridgeway, D., Maslin, C., & Sherman, M. (1989). Attachment: The parental perspective. *Infant Mental Health Journal, 10 (3)*, 203–21.

Bretherton, I., Ridgeway, D., & Cassidy, J. (1990). Assessing internal working models of the attachment relationship: An attachment story completion task for 3-year-olds. In Greenberg, Ciccetti, & Cummings (Eds.), *Attachment in the Preschool Years*. Chicago: University of Chicago Press, pp. 273–308.

Button, S., Pianta, R. C., & Marvin, R. S. (2001). Mothers' representations and child disability. *Social Development, 10 (4)*, 455–72.

Condry, J. & Condry, S. (1976). Sex differences: A study of the eye of the beholder. *Child Development, 47 (3)*, 812–19.

Costa, P. & McCrae, R. (1985). *The NEO Personality Inventory Manual*. Odessa, FL: Psychological Assessment Resource.

Cowan, P. A., Cowan, C. P., & Kerig, P. K. (1993). Mothers, fathers, sons, and daughters: Gender differences in family formation and parenting style. In D. Field, & P. A. Cowan, (Eds), *Family, Self, and Society: Toward a New Agenda for Family Research.* (pp. 165 95). Hillsdale, NJ; Hove, UK: Lawrence Erlbaum Associates.

Craik, K. J. W. (1943). *The Nature of Explanation*. Oxford, England: University Press, Macmillan.

Crittenden, P. M. & DiLalla, D. L. (1988). Compulsive compliance: The development of an inhibitory coping strategy in infancy. *Journal of Abnormal Child Psychology, 16 (5)*, 585–99.

Dunn, J., Kendrick, C., & MacNamee, R. (1981). The reaction of first-born children to the birth of a sibling: Mothers' reports. *Journal of Child Psychology and Psychiatry, 22 (1),* 1–18.

Emde, R. N. (1989). The infant's relationship experience: Developmental and affective aspects. In R. N. Emde & A. J. Sameroff (Eds.), *Relationship Disutrbances in Early Childhood: A Development Approach.* New York: Basic Books, pp. 35–51.

Fagot, B. (1995). Parenting of boys and girls. In M. H. Bornstein (Ed.) *Handbook of Parenting, Vol. 1: Children and Parenting.* Hillsdale, NJ; Hove, UK: Lawrence Erlbaum Associates, Inc., pp. 163–83.

Fonagy, P., Steele, H., & Steele, M. (1991). Maternal representations of attachment during pregnancy predict the organization of infant-mother attachment at one year of age. *Child Development, 62,* 891–905.

Fox, N. (1995). Of the way we were: Adult memories about attachment experiences and their role in determining infant-parent relationships: A commentary on van IJzendoorn (1995). *Psychological Bulletine, 117,* 404–10.

Furman, W. (1995). Parenting siblings. In M. H. Bornstein (Ed.), *Handbook of Parenting, Vol. 1: Children and Parenting.* Hillsdale, NJ; Hove, UK: Lawrence Erlbaum Associates, Inc., pp. 143–62.

George, C., Kaplan, N., & Main, M. (1985). *An Adult Attachment Interview.* Unpublished manuscript, University of California at Berkeley.

George, C. & Solomon, J. (1996). Representational models of relationships: Links between caregiving and representation. *Infant Mental Health Journal, 17,* 198–216.

Gjerde, P. F. (1995). Alternative pathways to chronic depressive symptoms in young adults: Gender differences in developmental trajectories. *Child Development, 66 (5),* 1277–300.

Gotlib, I. H, McLachlan, A. L., & Katz, A. N. (1988). Biases in visual attention in depressed and nondepressed individuals. *Cognition and Emotion, 2 (3),* 185–200.

Haft, W. & Slade, A. (1989). Affect attunement and maternal attachment: A pilot study. *Infant Mental Health Journal, 10 (3),* 157–72.

Johnson-Laird, P. K. (1983). *Mental Models: Towards a Cognitive Science of Language, Inference, and Consciousness.* Cambridge, MA: Harvard University Press.

Kendrick, C. & Dunn, J. (1982). Protest or pleasure? The response of first-born children to interactions between their mothers and infant siblings. *Journal of Child Psychology and Psychiatry, 23 (2),* 117–29.

Lamb, M. F., Frodi, A. M., Hwang, C. P., Frodi, M., & Steinberg J. (1982). Effect of gender and caretaking role on parent-infant interaction. In R. N. Emde & R. J. Harmon (Eds.), *The Development of Attachment and Affiliative Style.* New York: Plenum Press, 109–18.

Lynch, M. & Cicchetti, D. (1991). Patterns of relatedness in maltreated and nonmaltreated children: Connections among multiple representational models. *Development and Psychopathology, 3 (2),* 207–26.

Main, M., Kaplan, N., & Cassidy, J. (1985). Security in infancy, childhood and adulthood: A move to the level of representation. *Monographs of the Society for Research in Child Development, 50* (1–2, Serial No. 209).

Main, M. & Stadtman, J. (1981). Infant response to rejection of physical contact by the mother. Aggression, avoidance, and conflict. *Journal of the American Academy of Child Psychiatry, 20*, 292–307.

Main, M., Tomasini, L., & Tolan, W. (1979). Differences among mothers of infants judged to differ in security. *Developmental Psychology, 15 (4)*, 472–3.

McCabe, S. B. & Gotlib, I. H. (1995). Selective attention and clinical depression: Performance on a deployment-of-attention task. *Journal of Abnormal Psychology, 104 (1)*, 241–5.

Messina–Sayre, J., Pianta, R. C., Marvin, R. S., & Saft, E. W. (2001). Mothers' representations of relationships with their children: Relations with mother characteristics and feeding sensitivity. *Journal of Pediatric Psychology, 26 (6)*, 375–84.

Pianta, R. C. (1999). *Enhancing Relationships between Children and Teachers*. Washington, D.C.: American Psychological Association.

Pianta, R. C., O'Connor, T. G., & Marvin, R. S. (1993). *Measuring Representations of Parenting: An Interview-based System*. Unpublished manuscript, University of Virginia, Charlottesville.

Radloff, L. (1977). The CES-D Scale: a self-reported depression scale for research in the general populatoin. *Applied Biological Measurement, 1*, 385–401.

Reynell, J. (1991). Reynell Developmental Language Scales (U.S. Edition). Los Angeles: Western Psychological Service.

Schank, R. C. & Abelson, R. P. (1977). *Scripts, Plans, Goals and Understanding: An Inquiry into Human Knowledge Structures*. Oxford, England: Lawrence Erlbaum.

Shrader, W. K. & Leventhal, T. (1968). Birth order of children and parental report of problems. *Child Development, 39 (4)*, 1164–75.

Slade, A., Aber, J. L., Cohen, L., Fiorello, C. A., Meyer, J., DeSear, & Waller (1993). *Parent Development Interview Coding System*. Manuscript.

Slade, A., Belsky, J., Aber, J. L., & Phelps, J. (1999). Mothers' representations of their relationships with their toddlers: Links to adult attachment and observed mothering. *Developmental Psychology, 35*, 611–19.

Snedecor, G. W. & Cochran, W. G. (1980). *Statistical Methods*. Ames Iowa State University Press.

Thomas, A., Birch, H. G., Chess, S., & Robbins, L. C. (1961). Individuality in responses of children to similar environmental situations. *American Journal of Psychiatry, 117*, 798–803.

van IJzendoorn, M. (1995). Adult attachment representations, parental responsiveness, and infant attachment: A meta-analysis on the predictive validity of the adult attachment interview. *Psychological Bulletin, 117 (3)*, 387–403.

van IJzendoorn, M. H., Kranenburg, M., Zwart-Woudstra, A., van Busschbach, A., & Lambermom, M. (1991). Parental attachment and children's socioemotional development: Some findings on the validity of the Adult Attachment Interview in the Netherlands. *International Journal of Behavioral Development, 14*, 375–94.

Vandell, D. L. (1979). The effects of a playgroup experience on mother-son and father-don interaction. *Developmental Psychology, 15*, 379–85.

Waters, E. & Deane, K. (1985). Defining and assessing individual difference in attachment relationships: Q-methodology and the organization of behavior in infancy and early childhood. In I. Bretherton and E. Waters (Eds.), *Growing points of attachment theory and research. Monographs of the Society for Research in Child Development, 50* (1–2, serial No. 209), 41–65.

Winer, B. J. (1971). *Statistical Principles in Experimental Design.* New York: McGraw-Hill.

Zeanah, C. H., Benoit, D., Hirshberg, L., & Barton, M. L. (1993). *Working Model of the Child Interview: Rating Scales and Classifications.* Unpublished manuscript, New Orleans: Louisiana State University School of Medicine.

3 Social Cognitive Approaches to Parenting Representations

Duane Rudy and Joan E. Grusec

Abstract

Social cognitive theorists have studied parenting cognitions that include perspective-taking ability, socialization goals, and attributions made for actions of the self and of the child. These are described, with a focus on their links to parenting actions and child outcomes. The distinction between controlled and automatic cognition and its role in parenting cognitions is discussed, with the former involving movement between the mobilization and minimization of cognitive activity regarding parent–child interactions. It is argued that inappropriate reliance on mobilization or minimization leads to difficulties in information-processing and emotion regulation which result in maladaptive parenting behavior. Finally, similarities and differences between social cognitive and attachment approaches to mental representations of parenting are discussed.

Cognitive constructs have played a prominent role in attempts to understand the impact of parenting on children's social, emotional, and cognitive outcomes. For many years, childrearing attitudes – cognitive events that predispose the individual to act either positively or negatively toward their object – were the dominant focus of researchers and theorists. Indeed, attitudes were assumed to be the preeminent parenting construct (Holden & Buck, 2002) because they were considered to be good predictors of parenting behavior, markers of the emotional climate parents provided to their children, and, therefore, seen to have a major impact on children's development Psychoanalysts (e.g., Horney, 1933) argued that parenting behavior was determined by unconscious emotional reactions parents had to the way they themselves had been parented, with these unconscious reactions having an effect on their own, conscious, attitudes. Thus, Levy (1943) developed the concept of "overprotection," or excessive parental control and intrusion into the life of the child.

He argued that this behavior was rooted in the fact that the parents' emotional needs had been unmet in childhood and that the attitudinal residue of this early experience manifested itself either in overprotection or its behavioral opposite, rejection.

These early approaches were based on the belief that attitudes have their origins in the unconscious. As the unconscious became an increasingly unpopular concept among academics, however, attitudes came to be treated as straightforward events that were accessible to conscious awareness. As well, the notion of overprotection was supplanted by ideas about acceptance and rejection, and these became the object of intensive investigation that continues to this day, with these attitudes generally found to relate at least weakly to social, emotional, and cognitive outcomes in children (Maccoby & Martin, 1983).

The study of attitudes is not without its problems. Links between attitudes and behavior are not all that impressive (Holden & Buck, 2002). In a critique of the predominant approach to their investigation, the use of questionnaires, Holden and Edwards (1989) pointed out many flaws in the design of these questionnaires as well as less than impressive attention to issues of standardization. Although Holden and Edwards urged investigators to improve their ways of assessing attitudes, changes in approach have not been striking. One of the reasons for this slowness to change is what Holden and Buck (2002) refer to as "turf erosion": Socialization theorists have turned to other sorts of mental constructs that they believe may hold greater promise for elucidating the linkages between parents' thoughts and their actions. These mental constructs comprise an extensive array of events that include beliefs about children's development, about childrearing, and about parenting self-efficacy. They also include perspective-taking ability, the goals parents have for children during socialization, and the attributions they make for their own actions and those of their children. We turn now to a description of some of these new mental constructs, how they operate, and what the relation is between them, parenting actions, and child outcomes. We then make a distinction between controlled and automatic processes of cognition, and speculate as to how automatic processes of emotion regulation may influence parental cognition, emotion, and behavior. In this way, we revisit the focus of early researchers who were concerned with the unconscious aspects of parents' attitudes.

The review must be selective, given space limitations. We have chosen those most relevant to representations of caregiving relationships that have been studied by attachment theorists and that are the primary focus of this edited volume. Although the study of parenting cognitions, much of it influenced by social cognitive theories, has progressed largely independent of the work on representations of caregiving relationships, we will also point out similarities and points of overlap as well as distinctive contributions of this particular approach to parenting cognitions. After all, those who study parenting, regardless of their theoretical perspective and starting points, are looking at the same phenomena. The absence of overlap in findings would be, then, a most surprising and disconcerting observation.

Parenting Cognitions

We begin this survey with a discussion of general goals that parents have when socializing their children, then move to a discussion of parenting self-efficacy, as well as to attributional approaches that focus on parents' ability to control and guide the behavior of their children. There is some degree of overlap in these mental constructs, with each of them having some similar implications for parent emotionality and problem-solving ability, as well as for parenting behavior and child outcomes. We then briefly consider the role of parental perspective-taking and parents' knowledge of their children. In all cases, researchers have been interested in linking these cognitions to parent affect, parenting behavior, and, ultimately to child outcomes.

Parenting Goals

Among the various cognitions considered by developmental researchers are feelings about values that are to be instilled into children, values such as obedience, respect for others, and independence. At another level, however, parents also have more general or overarching outcomes they hope to achieve in their dealings with their children. One dichotomy that has characterized approaches to socialization is that between short- and long-term goals. Basic to the thinking of developmental theorists has been the idea that the desirable outcome of socialization is that children internalize, or take over, the values of others and make them their own (Bugental & Goodnow, 1998). Less desirable are short-term goals geared toward obtaining immediate compliance, less desirable because they do not ensure that positive social behaviors will continue in the absence of surveillance and the presence of external contingencies. Short-term goals are also considered to be parent-centered because their focus is on compliance with parental wishes, whereas long-term goals are considered to be child-centered because their focus is on teaching values that are ultimately seen by the child to be acceptable independent of external pressures. Dix (1992) has expanded the basic dichotomy between parent- and child-centered goals by adding a third set of goals, those having to do with ensuring that the child's desires are met.

In an attempt to identify the range of goals parents actually report in their daily interactions with their children, Hastings and Grusec (1998) surveyed parents, asking them what they had hoped to achieve in situations in which they and their children were having a disagreement about appropriate behavior. The goals they reported reduced to four categories: parent-centered, child-centered, relationship-centered, and safety-centered. Safety needs little comment. Parents have a basic role as protectors of their children, a role that plays a central part in the understanding of attachment relationships. The Hastings and Grusec (1998) findings make clear, however, that in addition to the usual dichotomy of child vs. parent-focused activity, parents also concern themselves with the nature of the relationship they have with their children, attempting to achieve dyadic harmony and mutual satisfaction in contentious interactions. Moreoever, what they hope to achieve determines the actions they direct toward the child. Thus, these parents reported that their parent-centered goals were more likely to be associated with punishment or threats of punishment, child-centered with reasoning, and relationship with negotiation, compromise, and acceptance.

Self-Efficacy

According to Bandura (1977; 1986), self-efficacy refers to beliefs individuals have about their abilities in specific domains. These beliefs guide their behavior by determining what they attempt to achieve and how much effort they put into those attempts. Thus, two individuals may have the same objective ability level but, to the extent that their perceptions of that ability level differ, they will perform at different levels of adequacy. Self-efficacy beliefs, of course, are reinforced by the outcomes of these different levels of performance: People with high self-efficacy persist at tasks until they are successful and so their beliefs are strengthened. Those with low self-efficacy do not persist and so they fail, with a consequent strengthening of their low self-efficacy belief. In addition, low self-efficacy leads to preoccupation with the self and negative emotional arousal that further interferes with performance. According to Bandura (1977), self-efficacy beliefs are affected by four variables. These are actual performance, as noted above; vicarious experience, that is, watching others engage in a particular task and being successful or unsuccessful; emotional arousal, for example, depression; and social persuasion.

Teti, Gelfand, and Pompa (1990) and Teti and Gelfand (1991) applied self-efficacy notions in the domain of parenting. They asked mothers of infants to rate their ability to care for their infants, including such activities as soothing, amusing, and understanding the needs of their babies. These investigators report that mothers who rated themselves as low in caregiving self-efficacy were cold, unemotional, and disengaged when interacting with their babies. As well, they were not appropriately responsive to their infants' signals and they exhibited hostility and anger toward them. Teti and his collaborators (1990) also found that low self-efficacy was related to mothers' lack of social support, having children with difficult temperaments, and maternal depression levels. These links accord with the variables proposed to affect self-efficacy: mothers with a strong social support network would be more likely to have relatives and friends who would reassure them about their parenting ability as well as model effective behavior; mothers of children with easy tempera- ments would be more likely to experience success in their interactions with their babies; and those who were depressed would be more prone to perform poorly in the parenting role because their negative emotional arousal would selectively activate memories of failure and thereby interfere with perfor- mance. Finally, these investigators found that self-efficacy mediated between social support, temperament, and depression and parenting behavior. Thus, when the effect of self-efficacy was controlled for, the correlation between maternal behavior and social support, temperament, and depression was sub- stantially reduced.

In extensions of this early work to parenting practices with older children, others (e.g., Bondy & Mash, 1999) have found that low self-efficacy is linked to a coercive parenting style, although the link between self-efficacy and parenting practice may not always be direct. Thus, in a study of rural single- parent African American families, Brody, Flor, and Gibson (1999) found no direct link from self-efficacy beliefs to competence-promoting parenting practices (operationalized as the existence of family routines, positive mother– child interactions, and maternal involvement in the child's school). Instead, efficacy beliefs were related to the goals mothers set for their children (e.g., being well-educated and well-behaved), with goals being linked to parenting practices that, in turn, were linked to academic and psychosocial competence through their influence on the child's ability to self-regulate or plan ahead.

Attributional Approaches

Attribution theory has played a major role in the thinking of social psychol- ogists, and its proposals about the ways in which people find reasons for their own actions and those of others have been incorporated into analyses of parenting and parent–child relationships. Indeed, Miller (1995) proposed that parents are especially likely to make attributions about their children because the parenting situation has many aspects that promote the search for causes of behavior, including the expectation of continued interaction, the desire for control, and the occurrence of ambiguous or novel behavior. Parents also make attributions about their own behavior. In many cases their ideas are embedded in complex schemas that involve both conscious and unconscious ideation and are associated with strong affect. As we will discuss subsequently, these schemas narrow attention, selectively guide memory retrieval, and can interfere with reflective appraisal of and coping with the parenting challenge. In this way they impair the ability to parent effectively. It should be noted that these features of attributional schemas overlap to a considerable extent with those of self-efficacy constructs. Although the focus is somewhat different, there is also overlap in the impact of these various aspects of thinking on parenting affect and behavior.

Weiner (e.g., 1985) has proposed that individuals use three dimensions in making inferences about causality: locus, stability, and controllability. Thus, they attribute events either to causes in the self (e.g., personality) or in the environment (e.g., external pressure), to causes that are either fixed (e.g., intelligence) or variable (e.g., fatigue), and to causes over which they either have or do not have control (e.g., lack of effort vs. lack of ability). Of particular interest are the patterns of causal inference that have implications for the way in which individual responsibility for an action is assigned. If a child, for example, engages in a misdemeanor that is seen to be internally driven, a stable feature of behavior, and something over which that child has control, then the child will be seen as responsible and the parent is likely to react with anger and strong disciplinary action. Parents who attribute children's antisocial actions to stable dispositional factors, for example, seeing them as intentional and under the child's control, report feeling more negative affect as well as being more punitive in their response (Dix & Grusec, 1985; Dix, Ruble, & Zambarano, 1989). The suggestion is that negative affect increases the probability of forceful action and, also, that people believe that those who behave badly intentionally deserve more punishment than those whose bad behavior was unintentional. When attributions are accurate, then parenting practices should be optimal, that is, children who know that an action is wrong need strong interventions to motivate compliance and those who do not know that it is wrong need explanations and guidance. When the attributions are incorrect, however, they lead to maladaptive parenting because parents are using motivation when they should be using explanation and guidance or they are using explanation and guidance when they should be using motivation.

Attributions, as noted, lead to emotional arousal. They share, then, with attitudes and with self-efficacy, a mechanism for motivating or driving parenting behavior. However, emotional arousal can also trigger attributions. Dix, Reinhold, and Zambarano (1990), for example, found that mothers who were experiencing a negative mood were more likely to blame their children for a misdeed as well as feel more upset over noncompliance and report higher levels of disapproval. Similarly, Sameroff, Seifer, and Elias (1982) note that depressed mothers are more likely to see their noncompliant children as being deviant. Finally, although there is not great deal of research addressed to the issue, it seems that this negative attributional style, that is, assuming children's undesirable behavior is intentional, is to some extent stable. Thus, parents who score high on measures of authoritarianism (a relatively stable feature of parenting) are also more likely to make dispositional attributions for their children's misdeeds (Dix et al., 1989).

A parent's atttributional style has implications for children's behavior. For example, mothers' negative or hostile attributional biases predict, over time, children's externalizing behaviors (Nix et al., 1999). Similarly, MacKinnon et al. (1992), in a study of mother–child dyadic aggression, report that the most aggressive dyads are those where both mother and son have similar hostile attributional patterns.

Parenting researchers, as well as looking at attributions made for children's actions, have also considered attributions parents make concerning their own behavior, specifically control, as well as the relation they see between their own control and that of their children. We now describe two of these programs of research.

Illusory Control. Donovan, Leavitt, and Walsh (1990, 1997, 2000) identified three groups of mothers on the basis of their estimation of the degree of control they reported themselves to have over a baby's crying when, in fact, they had none. High "illusory control" mothers, relative to the others, differed on a number of dimensions relevant to effective parenting. They were depressed and they displayed a negative attributional style, being more inclined to attribute their own failures to internal, stable, and uncontrollable causes. They showed a reduced ability to solve problems following experience with an insoluble problem. High illusory control mothers also experienced heart acceleration when confronted with infant cries, a marker of defensive arousal and in contrast to heart deceleration that correlates with orienting responses and a problem-solving orientation. Finally, Donovan and colleagues (1997) found that high illusory control mothers were not able to perceive differences between cries that varied in their fundamental frequency, another indication of impaired information-processing.

High illusory control has an impact on parenting and child outcomes. Donovan et al. (2000) assessed illusory control when mothers had infants who were five months of age. When the baby was 24 months old, the dyad returned to the lab where they were observed in a playroom setting. High illusory control mothers used more negative control (e.g., displays of anger and annoyance, criticism, and threats) when they were trying to persuade their children to clean up the playroom. In turn, their children defied them, with the negativity of the dyadic interaction escalating. In contrast, mothers who had been identified as moderate in illusory control were more inclined to use directives and prohibitions, with little defiance or noncompliance by their children. Children of mothers who were low in illusory control were also inclined to be noncompliant, but this noncompliance did not escalate, presumably because they did not experience the same sorts of threats to their autonomy as children with high illusory control mothers.

Power Schemas. Dix and his colleagues in the work described in the previous sections, have focused on the attributions parents make for their children's behavior and Donovan and colleagues in the work described in the previous sections, on the attributions parents make for their own behavior. Bugental and colleagues (for a review of the work, see Bugental & Happaney, 2002) have focused on both, looking at perceptions of control that mothers have for their own behavior and the behavior of their children. The important outcome in this analysis is the relative level of control each member of the dyad is perceived to have, with these perceptions consolidated in "power schemas." These power schemas are stable across time, they come to mind automatically when mothers find themselves in challenging situations with their children, and they involve implicit rather than "on-line" processes, that is, they operate outside conscious awareness.

Bugental has explored at length features of parenting of mothers who feel they have less power or control than their children (in comparison to those where the mother sees herself as high in power, or sees both herself and her child as having equivalent amounts of power, either high or low). Low power mothers engage in abusive and coercive behavior when there is a possibility of exercising control over children, or they become unassertive and submissive when this possibility does not exist. They deliver inconsistent and confusing messages to their children, either speaking in a sarcastic or condescending fashion, or adopting a tone of voice that does not match the valence of the message (Bugental, Mantyla, & Lewis, 1989; Bugental & Lewis, 1999). They derogate their children, and are more strict and coercive with them (Bugental & Happaney, 2001). When providing feedback on a dynamometer to indicate how well a child is performing on a task, they press harder than necessary after failure trials, an indication of arousal that manifests itself in greater-than-necessary force (Bugental et al., 2000).

Accompanying this behavioral pattern is one of physiological arousal comparable to that of high illusory control mothers – increased heart rate indicative of defensive arousal that reflects mobilization for defense rather than orienting and increased problem-solving (Bugental et al., 1993). Indeed, mothers with low power schemas, when faced with a difficult child, show impaired information-processing abilities, unable to perform as well on a cognitively demanding task as those who do not see themselves as so helpless. Presumably these mothers are impaired in their parenting abilities because they have less cognitive capacity available to address the problem of childrearing. As well, low power mothers display pessimistic thinking (Bugental et al., 2000), another psychological feature that makes it less likely they can perform effectively. The automaticity or unconscious nature of their power schema is demonstrated by the fact that low power mothers, when engaged in a competing task, can make judgments about power differentials (e.g., in response to the question "Who is bossier, you or your child"?) with a shorter latency than mothers who do not have these power schemas (Bugental et al., 1997).

Not surprisingly, this pattern of parental functioning takes its toll on the responsiveness of children (Bugental et al., 1999). For example, children who interacted with women who communicated in the ambiguous pattern employed by low power mothers were negatively affected in their performance on a test of mental arithmetic and were less likely to show an autonomic orienting response to these women. Bugental et al. (1999) depict this as children's way of dealing with distress by disengaging their attention from the source of the distress, although this is a tactic that ultimately has negative consequences for cognitive achievement.

Perspective-Taking and Knowledge of the Child

The ability to understand and/or take the perspective of the child is a cognitive activity that seems particularly important in effective parenting. We discuss research from the social cognitive tradition that speaks to this activity, in part at least because of its overlap with the emphasis of attachment theorists on the centrality of parental sensitivity to the feelings of the child. Research on the role of perspective-taking, however, includes but also moves beyond sensitivity to those feelings. It is not just accurate comprehension of children's feelings, but also accurate knowledge of how children are thinking about and evaluating events in their environment that must be part of parenting activity. This conclusion stems from the fact that, although specific parenting practices such as reasoning and power assertion and parenting styles such as authoritarianism and authoritativeness have, on average, a particular impact on children, there is tremendous variability in how a particular child at a particular point in time and in a particular context responds to them. Variables such as the child's temperament, sex, developmental status, mood, and attachment status, as well as contextual factors such as class and culture and, in the case of misbehavior, the nature of the misdeed, all have an impact on how children respond to a given practice or a given style. (The relevant research is reviewed in Collins et al., 2000.) This observation of the complexity of interactions involved in the parenting process has led to the suggestion that effective parenting is a matter of appraisal and flexible action in the face of constantly changing features of children and of situations and that parents must know their children in order to achieve desired outcomes (Grusec, Goodnow, & Kuczynski, 2000). Thus, parents who know how their children are thinking and feeling (and who take those thoughts and feelings into account when interacting with them) should be better able to achieve their childrearing goals.

The negative impact of not understanding a child appears in early work on abusive parenting with the suggestion that parents who maltreat their children do so because they have unrealistically high expectations of those children and thus view the child's failure to live up to their expectations to be the result of intentional and spiteful predispositions. This attribution results in anger and coercive and abusive tactics on the part of the parent (Twentyman, Rohrbeck, & Amish, 1984). In the domain of cognitive development, the evidence indicates that children of parents who can accurately predict their children's cognitive performance perform better, possibly because these parents are better able to match their teaching efforts to their children's developmental level (Hunt & Paraskevopoulous, 1980; Miller, 1988; Miller, Mondal, & Mee, 1991). In a similar manner, Hastings and Grusec (1997) report that parents who were able to accurately identify the thoughts and feelings of their adolescents during conflicts (e.g., how much adolescents blamed themselves and/or their parents for the disagreement, how angry the adolescents were during the disagreement) were better able to achieve satisfactory conflict outcomes.

The importance of accurate perception of children's thoughts and feelings also emerges in recent work by Grusec, Wolfe, and Davidov (2003). They asked children to evaluate different parenting interventions on a variety of dimensions including perceived fairness of the parent using the intervention, quality of the parent–child relationship, and reasons for why children might comply with parental directives in response to the different interventions. Mothers were asked to predict how their children would respond. Their accuracy was predictive of their children's compliance with the mothers' request to clean up the room in which they were playing. The data suggested that more accurate mothers used different approaches suited to their child's perceptions of the situation when the children protested, whereas less accurate mothers simply repeated their direction in response to protest.

A similar picture emerges in studies in which maternal perspective-taking has been assessed. Some studies, for example, have related mothers' reports of the extent to which they try to understand the point of view of their child to child outcomes. Thus, Gondoli and Silverberg (1977) report that mothers who scored high on dyadic perspective-taking with respect to their adolescent children had better relationships with them. Lundell and colleagues (2003) considered maternal perspective-taking in the context of parent–adolescent conflict and the goals that adolescents have during the conflict. They were specifically interested in dominance goals expressed by adolescents, that is, their desire to alter the mother's behavior in a forceful and angry way. Adolescent dominance goals, maternal perspective-taking, and conflict intensity (a marker of a negative dyadic relationship and poor adolescent outcomes) were all intercorrelated. Analyses indicated that maternal dominance goals mediated the relationship between perspective-taking and conflict intensity: Mothers who had high scores on perspective-taking had adolescents who endorsed fewer dominance goals, and the dyad reported less intense conflict. The suggestion is that mothers use their perspective-taking skills to manage conflicts so that adolescents do not become angry and hostile and that, as a result, the dyad experiences more positive interaction.

Controlled and Automatic Cognition

Much of the research we have reviewed thus far focuses on conscious, explicit processes rather than automatic (and potentially unconscious) processes. Bugental's work on power schemas is unique in that it stresses the automatic processes at work in parents' interpreting difficult interactions with children as a threat to their power (Bugental et al., 1997). Of course, automatic processes may also play a role in goals, attributions, perspective taking, and so on, but such processes have not been explored. We now turn to a discussion of controlled and automatic cognition and its role in parenting cognitions.

Bugental and Happaney (2002), reviewing the work on parental attributions, discuss the differences between controlled and automatic processes. They state that explicit, controlled, processes are voluntary and require the active attention of the individual. They necessitate mental effort, are flexible, and only one cognitive task may be performed at one time. Implicit, automatic, processes are relatively inflexible, and do not require volition. Parents may or may not be aware of their automatic attributions; the crucial point is that volition is not involved. Automatic attributions may be influenced by implicit schemas, extraneous factors such as mood, and past experiences. When automatic attributions are in accord with reality, they may lead to appropriate parental behavior. When they are not in accord with reality, it may be less easy for parents to behave appropriately, and difficulties in the parent–child relationship may ensue. If automatic inferences are chronically at odds with reality, these difficulties may be amplified.

Automatic processes can play an important role in effective parenting. Conscious self-regulation requires mental resources, and self-regulation in one area leaves fewer mental resources for self-regulation in other areas (Bargh & Chartrand, 1999; Higgins & Bargh, 1992). Parents cannot consciously deliberate over every action of their children and effectively perform household chores, attend to other children, or engage in leisure activities. Often, then, automatic parenting processes are adaptive. Papousek argues that evolution has caused parents to be automatically sensitive and responsive to children, and that parents often are not aware of these processes. For example, parents will respond appropriately to cues in infant hand gestures, but afterward will report that they were influenced by the infant's facial expressions (Papousek & Papousek, 1987).

In the following section, we move to a more detailed consideration of automatic processes of emotion regulation, contrasting different ways in which individuals engage in this processing. We make inferences about the impact of these different forms of processing on parenting processes and child outcomes. We argue that when a person is faced with negative events (as, for example, in dealing with a noncompliant child), effective emotion regulation requires a balance and flexibility of movement between mobilizing and then minimizing cognitive activity regarding the event. Whereas most parents automatically engage in both activities, we argue that some parents consistently engage in only one strategy – some parents consistently mobilize; others consistently minimize. We discuss the implications of these patterns of emotion regulation for parental cognition.

*Automatic Processes of Emotion Regulation and Their Links
to Parenting Cognitions*

Taylor (1991) argues that, when negative events occur, individuals initially mobilize their cognitive processes around the negative event. More than with positive events, they focus on and analyze associated stimuli, gather more diagnostic information, engage in greater attributional activity, and more systematically elaborate their thoughts. However, as the event recedes in time, they automatically minimize, or engage in activity that limits the effects of the event on their mood. As positive and negative events regress, negative ones are recalled less strongly than are positive ones and are interpreted in ways that limit their importance. Following positive events, thought processes are simpler. Individuals ". . . use intuitive simple solutions to problems, make greater use of judgmental heuristics, use broad and inclusive categories rather than specific categories in classification tasks, and use less information" (Taylor, 1991; p. 71). Broad, heuristic thinking, in fact, is important in the case of both positive and negative events because it allows relatively quick processing and enables the individual to reflect on experiences and integrate thoughts about them into organized schemas. These processes are generally adaptive: If there is a problem with a child, it is important that the parent attend to and consider the problem. However, in most cases it would not be adaptive for parents to constantly ruminate about problems with children that have occurred in the past, or may occur in the future. Thus, adaptive parenting involves flexible movement between mobilization and minimization.

There are, however, individuals who consistently minimize, as well as individuals who consistently mobilize, when faced with negative events. Within the social-psychological literature, they are referred to as repressive and sensitizing (or high-anxious) individuals. These groups are often studied, along with low-anxious individuals, using a method developed by Weinberger, Schwartz, and Davidson (1979). This method requires that individuals respond to measures of anxiety and defensiveness. Sensitizers, or high-anxious individuals, score high on anxiety and low on defensiveness. Repressors report low levels of anxiety but score high on defensiveness. Low-anxious individuals score low on both measures (a fourth group, defensive high-anxious, scores high on both measures, but is less frequently studied). We now consider the implications of repressive and sensitizing anxious styles for parents' processing of information, their ability to consider the child's perspective, the emotions they experience, and the responses they generate.

Repressors. Repressors deny experiencing negative affect but, when presented with sexual and aggressive stimuli, they show facial and physiological signs of high anxiety, higher than low-anxious participants, and – depending upon the measure in question – somewhat higher than high-anxious participants (Asendorpf & Scherer, 1983; Weinberger et al., 1979). Consistent with their defensiveness, repressors engage in limited thought regarding aversive events and display more defensive attributions about the self. For example, research conducted by Tublin and Weinberger and cited by Weinberger (1990) found that, in contrast to nonrepressors, repressors, when asked to report their thoughts about an audiotape containing expressions of intense interpersonal anger, focused on external factors, judging the quality of the tape and the actors, and did not discuss internal processes and self-relevant thoughts such as what they would feel or think in such a situation. Repressors also have fewer memories of negative emotions than non-repressors, attend less to emotionally upsetting material, and encode negative emotions more simply. For example, they notice dominant emotions but are less likely to notice other emotions that co-occur with the dominant emotion, such as sadness occurring with the dominant emotion of anger, or fear occurring with the dominant emotion of sadness (Davis & Schwartz, 1987; Hansen, Hansen, & Shantz, 1992). Weinberger states that repressors rigidly maintain self-esteem by attributing their own failures to external causes not under their control. Thus, the defensive attributional patterns of repressors, their "leakage" of anxiety, and their physiological responses to threat resemble the patterns of Bugental's low power mothers. Weinberger also describes repressors as being less socially astute and empathic. They appear to have difficulties in perspective taking and social understanding, difficulties associated with problematic parenting that we have discussed above.

If parents automatically minimize information regarding negative events in parent–child interactions, a number of consequences might follow. In terms of processing, repressive parents might be slow to notice negative affect on the part of their children. They might also be less likely to take their children's perspective, since this involves mobilization. They might feel more hostility in difficult interactions with children, given their defensive attributional biases. If they limit their processing of aversive events in difficult parent–child interactions, they might respond to children with simple, facile solutions that ignore their children's internal emotional states. They might use low-level reasoning (e.g., "Because I said so") or normative statements ("Good girls listen to their parents"), rather than reasoning that addresses their children's perspective. They might also strictly demand compliance as a simple way of achieving their aims. All this fits with our description above of parents who are primarily parent-centered in their goals as well as distorted in their attributional processes. Little empirical work has examined the repressive style of coping and parent–child interactions although one study by Atkinson et al. (1995) found that mothers who reported avoiding upsetting information as a coping strategy were less sensitive in their interactions with toddlers with Down syndrome.

Sensitizers, or Anxious Individuals. The research examining the social-cognitive processes of anxious individuals tends to be heterogeneous, in that it examines different types of anxiety such as test and social anxiety. Generally, however, it can be said that anxious individuals are vigilant for, and allocate attention more quickly to, threatening information (MacLeod & Mathews, 1991; Mathews, 1990). Borkovec suggests that anxious, worrisome thinking, characterized by a lack of organization and tendency to move from one negative thought to another, functions to inhibit in-depth thought about the perceived threat, which reduces the intensity of emotional arousal (Borkovec & Hu, 1990; Borkovec, Lyonfields, Wiser, & Deihl, 1993). Anxious individuals are also more likely to experience thoughts (threatening and non-threatening) irrelevant to stressful tasks on which they are focused, and appear to have difficulty relating information from the current situation to information stored in memory (Darke, 1988; Ingram, Kendall, Smith, Donnell, & Ronan, 1987).

If parents consistently mobilize, this may also have certain consequences. Regarding processing of information, if parents move from one negative thought to another, they will be less likely to notice their children's cues. Regarding perspective-taking, mentally entangled parents who are focused on problems might have difficulties maintaining a distinction between their own and their children's perspectives, for example, a parent might be overly concerned that a child has eaten enough even though the child shows no sign of being hungry. Regarding emotions, their focus on potential problems might result in less parental warmth. Regarding behavior, if they have difficulty coordinating their thoughts about the current situation with information stored in memory, they might be less likely to be able to generate effective responses to their children, whether the task is to deal with a difficult child or assuage a child's distress. A few studies have examined the association between parental anxiety and behavior toward children. Whaley, Pinto and Sigman (1999) observed anxious mothers discussing issues with their children, and found them to be less warm, less supportive of their children's autonomy, more likely to catastrophize, and more critical and less positive with their children. Similarly, Hirshfeld and colleagues (1997) found anxious mothers, when asked to describe their children, to be more critical of them. Atkinson et al. (1995), however, found the tendency of mothers to mobilize toward aversive events to be unrelated to maternal sensitivity with toddlers.

In summary, in negative interactions with children, adaptive parenting may require the flexibility of movement from mobilization to minimization. Repressive parents, who consistently minimize, may defend themselves by avoiding threatening information whereas anxious parents, who consistently mobilize, may move from one negative thought to another, without mentally "backing off" from threatening cognition and organizing their thoughts. In problematic parent–child interactions, these patterns may create difficulties in the processing of information, the consideration of the child's perspective, the emotions parents experience, the attributions they make, and the responses they generate. Research connects mobilizing and minimizing patterns of affect regulation to less adaptive parenting behavior; presumably parental cognitions mediate this relationship, although the specific associations have yet to be empirically established.

Links between Mobilization and Minimization and Events
in the Attachment Domain

We have noted links between mobilizing and minimizing processes and parenting cognitions described by social cognitive researchers. In this section we note parallel similarities between mobilizing and minimizing processes and individual differences in caregiving representations as described by attachment researchers. We discuss similarities first with respect to adult attachment classifications, because an empirical link has been established between these classifications and mobilizing and minimizing processes. We then discuss similarities between mobilization and minimization and categories of caregiving representations themselves, as measured by George and Solomon (1996) and Zeanah and colleagues (e.g., Zeanah & Benoit, 1995).

Caregiving representations and representations of children have been linked to patterns of adults' representations of their own attachment relationships, as assessed by the Adult Attachment Interview (AAI) (George, Kaplan & Main, 1984). On the AAI, adults discuss issues concerning attachment in their own childhood. Those classified as secure are open, coherent, and reflective in discussing their attachment relationships. Dismissive adults minimize discussion of attachment-related themes, portray negative events in a falsely positive light, and depict themselves as strong and independent. Preoccupied adults are preoccupied with the attachment relationship, and their discourse is mentally entangled and rambling in nature. There are obvious similarities between repression-sensitization and attachment classifications: Dismissive and repressive individuals both minimize reports of distress and anxiety, preoccupied and high-anxious individuals dwell upon negative events, and low-anxious and secure individuals seem well-adjusted. There is also empirical evidence that dismissive individuals tend to be classified as repressors, and that preoccupied individuals score higher on measures of anxiety (Mikulincer & Orbach, 1995; Weems et al., 2002).

There are a number of similarities between repressors and dismissive mothers. First, both repressors and dismissive mothers focus on external rather than internal factors. In laboratory observations, Crowell and Feldman (1988) found dismissive mothers to be strict, controlling, task-focused, and emotionally remote. Second, just as repressors ignore upsetting information, dismissive mothers tend not to be attuned to their infants' affect specifically when it is negative – in this case, they either misread their infants' negative affect and do not respond, or, if it continues, respond inappropriately (Haft & Slade, 1989). Third, we speculate that repressors might be less likely to consider their children's perspective. George and Solomon found that dismissive mothers in fact do this – they emphasize their own perspective and needs and do not integrate these considerations with the needs and wants of their children. Also, their descriptions of self and child tend to be stereotyped and role-focused (George & Solomon, 1996). Finally, repressors defend the self, and we speculated that their defensiveness might lead to hostility in problematic interactions with children. Dismissive mothers do display hostility, representing their relationships with their children as having higher levels of anger than do secure and preoccupied mothers (Slade et al., 1999). Also, when observing a videotape of a difficult infant, they describe the infant in more negative and less positive terms than secure mothers (Zeanah et al., 1993). They also show low feelings of power on Bugental's Parent Attribution test, which of course is linked with defensive arousal and coerciveness during difficult interactions with children (Grusec & Mammone, 1994).

Preoccupied individuals, on the other hand, exhibit many of the qualities of an anxious processing style. These similarities include the lack of cognitive organization as well as movement from topic to topic typical of anxious individuals. Preoccupied mothers do not consistently ignore their child's negative emotions, but respond inconsistently to the positive and the negative emotions of their children (Haft & Slade, 1989). In addition, their representations of their parenting role tend to be uncertain and their affect is poorly integrated with the situation or person who elicits it (George & Solomon, 1996). Finally, Crowell and Feldman (1988) observed preoccupied mothers to be inconsistent with their children. At times they were warm, but at other times they were angry, coercive, or puzzled. They also presented the goal of and instructions for the tasks in which parent and child were involved in a manner that was confusing and not well coordinated with the child's perspective (Crowell & Feldman, 1991).

Preoccupied and dismissive parents' habits of emotion regulation, then, are related to less adaptive methods of processing information and less adaptive representations of the caregiving relationship. Dismissive mothers attempt to defend against negative emotions by avoiding them, but report higher levels of hostility in the parent–child relationship. Preoccupied mothers are entangled in their negative emotions so that their thoughts and behavior are uncertain and poorly integrated with the demands of the caregiving situation.

We move now from a consideration of the similarities in caregiving representations between repression-sensitization and typologies of discourse in the AAI to a consideration of the similarities between repression-sensitization and typologies of caregiving representations themselves. Caregiving representations are assessed by having mothers talk about their children (see Steinberg & Pianta, this volume). To accomplish this, George and Solomon (1996) have used the Parent Development Interview (Aber et al., 1985). Mothers are asked to describe themselves as parents, the nature of the mother–child relationship, and how they manage attachment-related situations. George and Solomon (1996) rate maternal responses on four scales, three of which are pertinent to our discussion of mobilization and minimization: the secure base, rejection, and uncertainty scales. The secure base scale assesses mothers' ability to provide protection for the child and is characterized by positive thoughts about caregiving and "flexible integration of thought regarding the self, child, and relationship" (p. 204). The rejection scale assesses the extent to which the mother emphasizes her own perspective, sees herself and the child as unwilling to participate in the caregiving relationship, and does not recognize the child's need to be comforted when distressed. The uncertainty scale assesses the extent to which the mother is confused and vacillates in her opinions of herself, the child, and the mother–child relationship. Mothers are assigned a typology based on the scale on which they score highest.

Zeanah and colleagues (Zeanah & Benoit, 1995) assess caregiving representations with the Working Model of the Child Interview (WMCI). Mothers are asked to describe the history of their experience of the child, beginning with events during pregnancy, as well as their ideas about the child's characteristics. Balanced, disengaged, and distorted mothers are identified from the interview. Balanced mothers are clear and straightforward, and show empathy for the child's perspective. Disengaged mothers display an emotional distance toward their infants and describe their children in generic ways.

Distorted mothers are inconsistent, confused, and unrealistic, and appear to be struggling to be emotionally close to their infants without success.

In these lines of research, secure base and balanced mothers are similar to low anxious individuals, in that their thought is flexible and coherent. Rejecting and disengaged mothers have minimizing characteristics. They avoid thinking about negative events by ignoring their children's needs for comfort when distressed, and their generic descriptions of their children resemble the simple, heuristic thought typical of minimization. Uncertain and distorted mothers have mobilizing characteristics, with their confusion, vacillation, and inconsistency similar to the mental entanglement of anxious individuals. Little work has examined the relationship between these typologies and maternal behavior. However, Rosenblum, Dayton, and McDonough (this volume) observed mothers interacting with children and describe disengaged and distorted mothers as having deactivating and heightened strategies, respectively, in response to infant distress.

Similarities between Attachment and Social Cognitive Approaches

As we have just argued, social cognitive and attachment approaches are linked in terms of their associations with features of automatic cognition. We turn now to some more general similarities (Grusec & Ungerer, 2003). First, attachment and social cognitive approaches both describe maladaptive parenting as reflecting problematic mental representations. Feelings of parental inefficacy reflect maladaptive self-schemas and are associated with emotional disengagement, less responsive behavior, higher levels of hostility, and lower levels of aspirations for children. Similarly, mothers high in illusory feelings of control show physiological signs of defensive arousal that are related to decrements in information processing abilities in interactions with children. They also have more negative, hostile interactions with their children. Likewise, mothers who feel they have low levels of power relative to their children have threat-based schemas (Bugental, 1992), and demonstrate physiological signs of defensive arousal, impaired information processing abilities, and less adaptive behavior with difficult children. Similarly, attachment theorists state that parental mental models of relationships affect parental perception and responses to children. Attachment and social cognitive approaches also both discuss the importance of emotions and the regulation of emotions (including defensive processes) in influencing parental cognitions and responses toward children (Bugental et al., 1993; Dix, 1991; George & Solomon, 1996).

Attachment and social cognitive theories are also similar in that they emphasize that parents' inaccurate perceptions of and responses to children's cues will lead to more maladaptive outcomes in their children. Attachment theorists have examined such constructs as parental awareness and interpretation of children's emotional cues, perspective taking, and parental attributions (e.g., Bretherton et al., 1989; Rosenblum et al., this volume; Steinberg & Pianta, this volume). Similarly, social cognitive approaches examine the role of parental attributions and perspective-taking in child outcomes (e.g., MacKinnon-Lewis et al., 1994).

Attachment and social cognitive theories also both assume that internal processes provide the meaning for specific behaviors. Darling and Steinberg (1993), for example, state that the meaning of any particular parental behavior is constructed in light of the attitudinal "style" of the parent. Thus, a warm parent and a hostile parent might both express displeasure toward a child for being dishonest, but their behavior will be interpreted differently by their children. Similarly, secure children are not upset by minor separations from their parents, whereas ambivalent children are (Ainsworth et al., 1978), because the meaning of the separation is constructed in light of the ongoing parent–child relationship.

Finally, attachment and social cognitive approaches both acknowledge that less adaptive child outcomes in turn affect subsequent parental behavior. For example, children of Bugental's low power mothers become increasingly noncompliant with their parents over time, causing parents in turn to become more coercive in their actions. Similarly, children of preoccupied parents often display poorly controlled and exaggerated affect that makes it difficult for mothers to correctly "read" and respond to their child.

Differences between Attachment and Social Cognitive Approaches

Attachment and social cognitive approaches do have different emphases, however, that make distinct contributions to the parenting literature. Attachment theory stresses the fact that mental representations are not necessarily conscious; thus, mental representations are assessed through the analysis of discourse (one method of assessing non-conscious representations). Social cognitive researchers, on the other hand, have placed less emphasis on non-conscious, automatic processes, and frequently use explicit, self-report measures. Their heavy reliance on such measures, however, creates problems when they are dealing with automatic processes, given that parents may inaccurately report their cognitions because of lack of awareness and self-presentation concerns (Bugental et al., 1998). Thus, it is important that other less transparent methods be used to assess parenting cognitions. These include the measurement of response latencies, assessing attributions while parents are under cognitive load, word fragment completions, and analysis of discourse (Bugental et al., 1997; Fazio, Jackson, Dunton, & Williams, 1995; Greenwald, McGhee, & Schwarz, 1998; Hetts, Sakuma, & Pelham, 1999; Newberger, 1980). Attachment researchers have contributed to the use of the latter method, and it would be fruitful to use this approach more frequently to assess parental cognitions.

Attachment and social cognitive theories also have focused on different areas of the parent–child relationship. Attachment theory has emphasized the issue of the parent as a source of protection and security for children in distress. Social cognitive theory, on the other hand, has emphasized parental control and the socialization of children. For example, it has examined issues such as children's internalization of parental values, and how parental control and acceptance combine to influence children's outcomes (e.g., Maccoby & Martin, 1983).

Attachment theory also places greater emphasis on typological processes of emotion regulation, and considers these processes developmentally and intergenerationally (Thompson, 1999; Van-Ijzendoorn, 1995). Its typological approach means that it can capture a number of variables that co-occur in real life (mental models of self and other, attentional processes, affect regulation, and behavior), and examine the effects of different constellations of these variables (i.e., the different patterns of adult attachment).

However, social cognitive approaches have examined in more depth the specific aspects of parental cognitions, their interrelationships, and the mediating and moderating role of specific variables. As one example, Bugental (Bugental, 1992) considers how the threat-based schemas of low power mothers cause them to become defensively aroused when children are difficult, and considers the effect that this arousal has on mothers' ability to attend to ongoing interactions with children. She has observed in detail indications of maternal affect in ongoing interactions, such as facial expressions and prosody, and has examined children's responses to these cues. Also, she has also examined the moderating role of child temperament. With easy children, the deficits of low-power mothers do not manifest themselves; it is only with children who are difficult that the problem occurs. A recent meta-analysis by Bakermans-Kranenburg, van Ijzendoorn, and Juffer (2003) of attachment research suggests that it is important to consider specific cognitions in that domain as well: Bakermans-Kranenburg and colleagues (2003) found that interventions that targeted parental sensitivity by focusing primarily on enhancing parental awareness of children's signals and interpreting them properly (Egeland et al., 2000) were more effective than those that only targeted parents' attachment representations and/or social support.

The two approaches, then, complement each other. Social cognitive approaches examine specific aspects of cognition and affect, their relationship to parenting behavior, and their effects on children. Attachment approaches describe powerfully how the constellations of affect, cognition, and behavior in secure, dismissive, and preoccupied individuals develop, are transmitted from parent to child, and change over time. This is not to say that attachment and social cognitive theorists never utilize typological and more specific approaches, respectively, but that they differ in emphasis. Social cognitive researchers have often used Baumrind's typologies of parenting style as a means of organizing their ideas and research approaches, and attachment researchers often examine specific aspects of parental awareness and interpretation of emotion (e.g., Bretherton et al., 1989; Rosenblum et al., this volume; Steinberg & Pianta, this volume).

Summary and Future Directions

In this chapter we have considered social cognitive approaches to parent–child relationships, especially aspects of parental cognition that are related to individual differences in adaptive and maladaptive parenting. Good parenting is parenting that has the child's well-being as a goal, that is flexible in pursuit of this goal, considers the child's perspective, and is benign in the attributions offered for children's behavior. It is associated with higher levels of parental efficacy, the absence of feelings of powerlessness with children, and a lack of overestimation of the amount of control a parent has. There is evidence that these attributes are interrelated and sustain each other. The attributions one makes about children, for example, may affect the goals one has in interactions with children and one's goals, in turn, will influence the degree to which one engages in perspective-taking and the attributions one makes (Dix, 1992). The schemas one has about the self and self-in-relation-to-child, such as self-efficacy, illusory control over children, power relative to children, and a parent's style of emotional regulation, may serve as a basis for individual differences, influencing parental goals, perspective taking, and attributions about children.

Some of the ideas presented in this chapter remain to be tested. Little research has examined the effects of anxious and repressive styles of emotion regulation on parental cognition. And while attachment researchers have assessed implicit representations of relationships, with the exception of perspective-taking (Newberger, 1980) and feelings of control (Bugental et al., 1989), much of the social-cognitive work in the area of parent–child relationships assesses constructs explicitly. Thus, there is a need to assess constructs such as goals, attributions, and evaluations of children in less explicit ways.

In the future, it will also be important to consider the role of culture in parenting processes and cognitions. We have found that strict parenting is more strongly associated with maladaptive parental cognitions in Anglo-European groups, which emphasize independence, than in cultural groups which emphasize interdependence (Rudy & Grusec, 2001). It is possible that these associations in Anglo-European groups exist because of automatic processes, as discussed previously. However, there is evidence that suggests that in more interdependent cultural groups, strict parenting may be influenced by controlled cognitive processes. In cases where parental strictness reflects conscious processes, strict parents should have less difficulty in perceiving and responding to negative emotions in children than in cases where similar levels of parental strictness reflect automatic processes. This is a proposition that remains to be tested directly.

References

Aber, J. L., Slade, A., Berger, B., Bresgi, I., & Kaplan, M. (1985). *The Parent Development Interview*. Unpublished manuscript, Barnard College, Columbia University, New York.

Ainsworth, M. D., Blehar, M., Waters, E., & Wall, S. (1978). *Patterns of Attachment: A Psychological Study of the Strange Situation*. Hillsdale, NJ: Lawrence Erlbaum Associates.

Asendorpf, J. B. & Scherer, K. R. (1983). The discrepant repressor: Differentiation between low anxiety, high anxiety, and repression of anxiety by autonomic-facial-verbal patterns of behavior. *Journal of Personality & Social Psychology, 45*, 1334–46.

Atkinson, L., Scott, B., Chisholm, V., Blackwell, J., Dickens, S., Ram, F., & Goldberg, S. (1995). Cognitive coping, affective distress, and maternal sensitivity: Mothers of children with Down syndrome. *Developmental Psychology, 31*, 668–76.

Bakermans-Kranenburg, M. J., van IJzendoorn, M. H., & Juffer, F. (2003). Less is more: Meta-analyses of sensitivity and attachment interventions in early childhood. *Psychological Bulletin, 129*, 195–215.

Bandura, A. (1977). Self-efficacy: Toward a unifying theory of behavior change. *Psychological Review, 84*, 191–215.

Bandura, A. (1986). *Social Foundations of Thought and Action: A Social Cognitive Theory*. Englewood Cliffs, NJ: Prentice Hall.

Bargh, J. A. & Chartrand, T. I. (1999). The unbearable automaticity of being. *American Psychologist, 54*, 462–79.

Bondy, E. M. & Mash, E. J. (1999). Parenting efficacy, perceived control over caregiving failure, and mothers' reactions to preschool children's misbehavior. *Child Study Journal, 29*, 157–73.

Borkovec, T. D. & Hu, S. (1990). The effect of worry on cardiovascular response to phobic imagery. *Behaviour Research & Therapy, 28*, 69–73.

Borkovec, T. D., Lyonfields, J. D., Wiser, S. L., & Deihl, L. (1993). The role of worrisome thinking in the suppression of cardiovascular response to phobic imagery. *Behaviour Research & Therapy, 31*, 321–4.

Bretherton, I., Biringen, Z., Ridgeway, D., Maslin, C., & Sherman, E. (1989). Attachment: The parental perspective. *Infant Mental Health Journal, 10*, 203–21.

Brody, G. H., Flor, D. L., & Gibson, N. M. (1999). Linking maternal self-efficacy beliefs, developmental goals, parenting practices, and child competence in rural single-parent African American families. *Child Development, 70*, 1197–208.

Bugental, D. B. (1992). Affective and cognitive processes within threat-oriented family systems. In I. E. Sigel, A. V. McGillicuddy-Delisi, & J. J. Goodnow (Eds.), *Parental Belief Systems: The Psychological Consequences for Children*. Hillsdale, NJ: Lawrence Erlbaum Associates, Inc., pp. 3–39.

Bugental, D. B., Blue, J., Cortez, V., Fleck, K., Kopeikin, H., Lewis, J., & Lyon, J. (1993). Social cognitions as organizers of autonomic and affective responses to social challenge. *Journal of Personality and Social Psychology, 64*, 94–103.

Bugental, D. B., Blue, J., & Cruzcosa, M. (1989). Perceived control over caregiving outcomes: Implications for child abuse. *Developmental Psychology, 25*, 532–9.

Bugental, D. B. & Goodnow, J. J. (1998). Socialization processes: Biological, cognitive, and social-cultural perspectives. In W. Damon (Ed.), *Handbook of Child Psychology*. New York: Wiley, pp. 389–462.

Bugental, D. B. & Happaney, K. (2001). The role of attributional bias in parenting: When are caregiving relationships transformed into power struggles? In J. R. M. Gerris (Ed.), *Dynamics of Parenting: International Perspectives on the Nature and Sources of Parenting*. Leuven, BE: Garant, pp. 17–31.

Bugental, D. B. & Happaney, K. (2002). Parental attributions. In M. H. Bornstein, (Ed). *Handbook of Parenting: Vol. 3: Being and Becoming a Parent*. Mahwah, NJ: Lawrence Erlbaum Associates, Publishers, pp. 509–35.

Bugental, D. B., Johnston, C., New, M., & Silvester, J. (1998). Measuring parental attributions: Conceptual and methodological issues. *Journal of Family Psychology, 12*, 459–80.

Bugental, D. B. & Lewis, J. C. (1999). The paradoxical misuse of power by those who see themselves as powerless: How does it happen? *Journal of Social Issues, 55*, 51–64.

Bugental, D. B., Lewis, J. C., Lin, E., Lyon, J., & Kopeikin, H. (2000). In charge but not in control: The management of authority-based relationships by those with low perceived power. *Developmental Psychology, 35*, 1367–78.

Bugental, D. B., Lyon, J. E., Krantz, J., & Cortez, V. (1997). Who's the boss? Differential accessibility of dominance ideation in parent-child relationships. *Journal of Personality & Social Psychology, 72*, 1297–309.

Bugental, D. B., Lyon, J. E., Lin, E., McGrath, E. G., & Bimbela, A. (1999). Children "tune out" in response to the ambiguous communication style of powerless adults. *Child Development, 70*, 214–30.

Bugental, D. B., Mantyla, S. M., & Lewis, J. (1989). Parental attributions as moderators of affective communication to children at risk for physical abuse. In D. Cicchetti & V. Carlson (Eds.), *Child Maltreatment: Theory and Research on the Causes and Consequences of Child Abuse and Neglect*. New York: Cambridge University Press, pp. 254–79.

Collins, W. A., Maccoby, E. E., Steinberg, L., Hetherington, E. M., & Bornstein, M. H. (2000). Contemporary research on parenting: The case for nature and nurture. *American Psychologist, 55*, 218–32.

Crowell, J. A. & Feldman, S. S. (1988). Mothers' internal models of relationships and children's behavioral and developmental status: A study of mother-child interaction. *Child Development, 59*, 1273–85.

Crowell J. A. & Feldman, S. S. (1991). Mothers' working models of attachment relationships and mother and child behavior during separation and reunion. *Developmental Psychology, 27*, 597–605.

Darke, S. (1988). Effects of anxiety on inferential reasoning task performance. *Journal of Personality & Social Psychology, 55*, 499–505.

Darling, N. & Steinberg, L. (1993). Parenting style as context: An integrative model. *Psychological Bulletin, 113*, 487–96.

Davis, P. J. & Schwartz, G. E. (1987). Repression and the inaccessibility of affective memories. *Journal of Personality & Social Psychology, 52*, 155–62.

Dix, T. (1991). The affective organization of parenting: Adaptive and maladaptive processes. *Psychological Bulletin, 110*, 3–25.

Dix, T. (1992). Parenting on behalf of the child: Empathic goals in the regulation of responsive parenting. In I. E. Sigel, A. V. McGillicuddy-DeLisi, & J. Goodnow (Eds.), *Parental Belief Systems: The Psychological Consequences for Children.* Hillsdale, NJ: Lawrence Erlbaum Associates, Inc., pp. 319–46.

Dix, T. H. & Grusec, J. E. (1985). Parent attribution processes in child socialization. In I. E. Sigel (Ed.), *Parent Belief Systems: Their Psychological Consequences for Children.* Hillsdale, NJ: Erlbaum, pp. 201–33.

Dix, T. H., Reinhold, D. A., & Zambarano, R. J. (1990). Mothers' judgments in moments of anger. *Merrill-Palmer Quarterly, 36*, 465–86.

Dix, T., Ruble, D. N., & Zambarano, R. J. (1989). Mothers' implicit theories of discipline: Child effects, parent effects, and the attribution process. *Child Development, 60*, 1373–91.

Donovan, W. L., Leavitt, L. A., & Walsh, R. O. (1990). Maternal self-efficacy: illusory control and its effect on susceptibility to learned helplessness. *Child Development, 61*, 1638–47.

Donovan, W. L, Leavitt, L. A., & Walsh, R. O. (1997). Cognitive set and coping strategy affect mother's sensitivity to infant cries: A signal-processing approach. *Child Development, 68*, 760–2.

Donovan, W. L., Leavitt, L. A., & Walsh, R. O. (2000). Maternal illusory control predicts socialization strategies and toddler compliance. *Developmental Psychology, 36*, 402–11.

Egeland, B., Weinfield, N. S., Bosquet, M., & Cheng, V. K. (2000). Remembering, repeating, and working through: Lessons from attachment-based interventions. In J. D. Osofsky & H. E. Fitzgerald (Eds.), *Handbook of Infant Mental Health. Infant Mental Health in Groups at High Risk.* New York: Wiley, pp. 35–89.

Fazio, R. H., Jackson, J. R., Dunton, B. C., & Williams, C. J. (1995). Variability in automatic activation as an unobstrusive measure of racial attitudes: A bona fide pipeline? *Journal of Personality & Social Psychology, 69*, 1013–27.

George, C., Kaplan, N., & Main, M. (1984). *Adult Attachment Interview.* Unpublished manuscript, University of California at Berkeley.

George, C. & Solomon, J. (1996). Representational models of relationships: Links between caregiving and attachment. *Infant Mental Health Journal, 17*, 198–216.

Gondoli, D. M. & Silverberg, S. B. (1997). Maternal emotional distress and diminished responsiveness: The mediating role of parenting efficacy and parental perspective taking. *Developmental Psychology, 33*, 861–8.

Greenwald, A. G., McGhee, D. E., & Schwartz, J. L. (1998). Measuring individual differences in implicit cognition: The implicit association test. *Journal of Personality & Social Psychology, 74*, 1464–80.

Grusec, J. E., & Mammone, N. (1994). The sources of parent belief systems. In N. Eisenberg (Ed.), *Review of Personality and Social Psychology.* New York: Sage, pp. 49–73.

Grusec, J. E., Goodnow, J. J., & Kuczynski, L. (2000). New directions in analyses of parenting contributions to children's internalization of values. *Child Development, 71*, 205–11.

Grusec, J. E. & Ungerer, J. (2003). Parent-child interaction and the role of parenting cognitions in children's socialization. In L. Kuczynski (Ed.), *Handbook of Dynamics in Parent-Child Relationships.* Thousand Oaks, CA: Sage, pp. 211–28.

Grusec, J. E., Wolfe, J., & Davidov, M. (2003). Children's evaluations of parental discipline strategies and the role of mothers' knowledge of those evaluations in achieving compliance. Unpublished manuscript, University of Toronto.

Haft, W. L. & Slade, A. (1989). Affect attunement and maternal attachment: A pilot study. *Infant Mental Health Journal, 10*, 157–72.

Hansen, C. H., Hansen, R. D., & Shantz, D. W. (1992). Repression at encoding: Discrete appraisals of emotional stimuli. *Journal of Personality & Social Psychology, 63*, 1026–35.

Hastings, P. & Grusec, J. E. (1997). Conflict outcomes as a function of parental accuracy in perceiving child cognitions and affect. *Social Development, 6*, 76–90.

Hastings, P. & Grusec, J. E. (1998). Parenting goals as organizers of responses to parent-child disagreement. *Developmental Psychology, 34*, 465–79.

Hetts, J. J., Sakuma, M., & Pelham, B. W. (1999). Two roads to positive regard: Implicit and explicit self-evaluation and culture. *Journal of Experimental Social Psychology, 35*, 512–59.

Higgins, E. T. & Bargh, J. A. (1992). Unconscious sources of subjectivity and suffering: Is consciousness the solution? In L. L. Martin & A. Tesser (Eds.), *The Construction of Social Judgments.* Hillsdale, NJ: Lawrence Erlbaum Associates, Inc., pp. 67–103.

Hirshfeld, D. R., Biederman, J., Brody, L., Faraone, S. V., & Rosenbaum, J. (1997). Expressed emotion toward children with behavioral inhibition: Associations with maternal anxiety disorder. *Journal of the American Academy of Child & Adolescent Psychiatry. 36*, 910–17.

Holden, G. W. & Buck, M. J. (2002). Parent attitudes toward childrearing. In M. Bornstein (Ed.), *Handbook of Parenting.* Mahwah, NJ: Lawrence Erlbaum Associates, Inc., pp. 537–62.

Holden, G. W. & Edwards, J. (1989). Parental attitudes toward child rearing: Instruments, issues, and implications. *Psychological Bulletin, 106*, 29–58.

Horney, K. (1933). Maternal conflicts. *American Journal of Orthopsychiatry, 3*, 445–63.

Hunt, J. M. & Paraskevopoulous, J. (1980). Children's psychological development as a function of the inaccuracy of their mothers' knowledge of their abilities. *Journal of Genetic Psychology, 136*, 285–98.

Ingram, R. E., Kendall, P. C., Smith, T. W., Donnell, C., & et al. (1987). Cognitive specificity in emotional distress. *Journal of Personality & Social Psychology, 53*, 734–42.

Levy, D. (1943). *Maternal Overprotection.* New York: Columbia University Press.

Lundell, L., Grusec, J. E., McShane, K., & Davidov, M. (2003). Adolescents' goals in conflicts with their mothers. Unpublished manuscript, University of Toronto.

Maccoby, E. E. & Martin, J. A. (1983). Socialization in the context of the family: Parent-child interaction. In E. M. Hetherington (Ed.), *Handbook of Child Psychology. Socialization, Personality and Social Development.* New York: Wiley, pp. 1–102.

MacKinnon-Lewis, C., Lamb, M. E., Arbuckle, B., Baradaran, L. P., & Volling, B. L. (1992). The relationship between biased maternal and filial attributions and the aggressiveness of their interactions. *Development & Psychopathology, 4*, 403–15.

MacKinnon-Lewis, C., Volling, B. L., Lamb, M. E., Dechman, K., Rabiner, D., & Curtner, M. E. (1994). A cross-contextual analysis of boys' social competence: From family to school. *Developmental Psychology, 30*, 325–33.

MacLeod, C. & Mathews, A. (1991). Biased cognitive operations in anxiety: Accessibility of information or assignment of processing priorities. *Behaviour Research & Therapy, 29*, 599–610.

Mathews, A. (1990). Why worry? The cognitive function of anxiety. *Behaviour Research & Therapy, 28*, 455–68.

Mikulincer, M. & Orbach, I. (1995). Attachment styles and repressive defensiveness: The accessibility and architecture of affective memories. *Journal of Personality & Social Psychology, 68*, 917–25.

Miller, S. A. (1988). Parents' beliefs about children's cognitive development. *Child Development, 59*, 259–95.

Miller, S. A. (1995). Parents' attributions for their children's behavior. *Child Development, 66*, 1557–84.

Miller, S. A., Mondal, M., & Mee, L. L. (1991). Parental beliefs, parental accuracy, and children's cognitive performance: A search for causal relations. *Developmental Psychology, 27*, 267–76.

Newberger, C. M. (1980). The cognitive strructure of parenthood: Designing a descriptive measure. In R. L. Selman & R. Yando (Eds.), *Clinical-Developmental Psychology: New Directions for Child Development.* San Francisco: Jossey-Bass, pp. 45–67.

Nix, R. L., Pinderhughes, E. E., Dodge, K. A., Bates, J. E., Pettit, G. S., & McFadyen-Ketchum, S. A. (1999). The relation between mothers' hostile attribution tendencies and children's externalizing behavior problems: The mediating role of mothers' harsh discipline practices. *Child Development, 70*, 896–909.

Papousek, H. & Papousek, M. (1987). Intuitive parenting: A dialectic counterpart to the infant's integrative competence. In J. D. Osofsky (Ed.), *Handbook of Infant Development. Wiley Series on Personality Processes,* Oxford, England: John Wiley & Sons, pp. 669–720.

Rosenblum, K. L., Dayton, C. J., & McDonough, S. (this volume). Communicating feelings: links between mothers' representations of their infants, parenting and infant emotional development.

Rudy, D. & Grusec, J. E. (2001). Correlates of authoritarian parenting in individualist and collectivist cultures and implications for understanding the transmission of values. *Journal of Cross-Cultural Psychology, 32*, 202–12.

Sameroff, A. J., Seifer, R., & Elias, P. K. (1982). Sociocultural variability in infant temperament ratings. *Child Development, 53*, 164–73.

Slade, A., Belsky, J., Aber, J. L., & Phelps, J. L. (1999). Mothers' representations of their relationships with their toddlers: Links to adult attachment and observed mothering. *Developmental Psychology, 35*, 611–19.

Taylor, S. E. (1991). Asymmetrical effects of positive and negative events: The mobilization-minimization hypothesis. *Psychological Bulletin, 110*, 67–85.

Teti, D. M. & Gelfand, D. M. (1991). Behavioral competence among mothers of infants in the first year: The mediational role of maternal self-efficacy. *Child Development, 62*, 918–29.

Teti, D. M., Gelfand, D. M., & Pompa, J. (1990). Depressed mothers' behavioral competence with their infants: Demographic and psychosocial correlates. *Development and Psychopathology, 2*, 259–70.

Thompson, R. A. (1999). Early attachment and later development. In J. Cassidy & P. R. Shaver (Eds.), *Handbook of Attachment: Theory, Research, and Clinical Applications.* New York: Guilford Press, pp. 265–86.

Twentyman, C. T., Rohrbeck, C. A., & Amish, P. L. (1984). A cognitive-behavioral model of child abuse. In S. Saunders (Ed.), *Violent Individuals and Families: A Practitioner's Handbook.* Springfield, IL: Thomas, pp. 86–111.

van IJzendoorn, M. (1995). Adult attachment representations, parental responsiveness, and infant attachment: A meta-analysis on the predictive validity of the Adult Attachment Interview. *Psychological Bulletin, 117*, 387–403.

Weems, C. F., Berman, S. L., Silverman, W. K., & Rodriguez, E. T. (2002). The relation between anxiety sensitivity and attachment style in adolescence and early adulthood. *Journal of Psychopathology & Behavioral Assessment, 24*, 159–68.

Weinberger, D. A. (1990). The construct validity of the repressing coping style. In J. L. Singer (Ed.), *Repression and Dissociation: Implications for Personality Theory, Psychopathology, and Health.* Chicago: University of Chicago Press, pp. 337–86.

Weinberger, D. A., Schwartz, G. E., & Davidson, R. J. (1979). Low-anxious, high-anxious, and repressive coping styles: Psychometric patterns and behavioral and physiological responses to stress. *Journal of Abnormal Psychology, 88*, 369–80.

Weiner, B. (1985). A cognitive (attribution)-emotion-action model of motivated behavior: An analysis of judgments of help-giving. *Journal of Personality and Social Psychology, 39*, 186–200.

Whaley, S. E., Pinto, A., & Sigman, M. (1999). Characterizing interactions between anxious mothers and their children. *Journal of Consulting & Clinical Psychology, 67*, 826–36.

Zeanah, C. H. & Benoit, D. (1995). Clinical applications of a parent perception interview. In K. Minde (Ed.), *Infant Psychiatry, Child Psychiatric Clinics of North America.* Philadelphia: W. B. Saunders, pp. 539–54.

Zeanah, C. H., Benoit, D., Barton, M., Regan, C., Hirshberg, L. M., & Lipsitt, L. P. (1993). Representations of attachment in mothers and their one-year-old infants. *Journal of the American Academy of Child & Adolescent Psychiatry, 32*, 278–86.

PART II

Research Applications

4 Communicating Feelings

Links Between Mothers' Representations of Their Infants, Parenting, and Infant Emotional Development

Katherine L. Rosenblum, Carolyn J. Dayton, and Susan McDonough

Abstract

In the present chapter we explore how mothers' internal working models of their seven-month-old infants organize emotions in the parenting context, and ultimately, influence infant emotion regulation. We propose that mothers' internal working models of their infants function as emotion regulators, and influence a variety of components of the affective organization of parenting, including a) maternal emotion activation, b) qualities of maternal emotional engagement with their infants, and c) emotion regulation strategies mothers employ during emotionally challenging interactions. Results underscore the important role played by emotional processes in explaining the correspondence between maternal and infant emotion regulation strategies.

The relationship with a primary caregiver is the emotional cocoon from which the infant's social and emotional self develops and emerges. Developmentalists from a range of theoretical perspectives have underscored the centrality of the parent–infant relationship for early infant emotional development and emphasize the belief that parent–infant interaction during the earliest months may serve as the foundation for the differentiation of the self (Fonagy, 1999; Mahler, Pine, & Bergman, 1975; Sameroff & Emde, 1989; Winnicott, 1965). In other words, the self is born out of relationships and develops as part of, and within, a specific relational context.

Relationships are inherently affective bonds between individuals, and thus, not surprisingly, affective processes play a central role in the attachment and caregiving behavioral systems. For example, during infancy emotional stimuli (e.g., fear reactions/distress) trigger the need for proximity seeking, and infant attachment security reflects, at least in part, the ability to express both positive and negative emotion in the presence of the primary attachment figure with the (assumed) expectation that emotional and safety needs will be met (Bowlby, 1969; Thompson & Lamb, 1984). Parenting is also an inherently emotion-laden process (Dix, 1991), and the caregiving system is similarly activated by emotion (e.g., infant distress promotes parent emotional response that, in turn, triggers caregiving behavior) (Solomon & George, 1996).

From an attachment perspective, early day-to-day relational experiences have a central role in shaping the infant's social and emotional expectations, eventually generalizing into internal "templates," or "working models," of relationships (Bowlby, 1969; Stern, 1989). There are a variety of factors that may influence the quality of the behavioral level of this interaction, including the manner in which the caregiver perceives and experiences the infant's needs, demands, emerging personality, and future potential. How the parent represents the child and his or her relationship with the child is likely to shape the quality of his or her interpretation of the infant's signals and cues, and thereby guides the caregiving response. This in turn is likely to hold consequences for the emotional tone of the daily "lived moments," and ultimately, the child's emotional security (Cummings & Davies, 1996; Gergely & Watson, 1996; Goldberg, MacKay-Soroka, & Rochester, 1994; Sroufe, 1995).

While much of the extant attachment-based research has focused on parents' representations of their own early relationships and consequences for child attachment security at one year and beyond (e.g., Benoit & Parker, 1994; Fonagy, Steele, & Steele, 1991), in this chapter we will explore the role of parents' representations of their infants on parenting and infant emotional development *during* the first year of life. Our emphasis will be on the role of parenting representations in both reflecting and shaping parents' emotional experience of the child, and subsequent links to caregiving and child emotional development. As reflected in this volume, there are a number of interviews designed to assess parents' representations; in this chapter we focus on one specific interview designed to assess parents' representations of their infant and their relationship with their infant: the "Working Model of the Child Interview" (Zeanah & Benoit, 1995), and present data from our own work that highlight the important role that may be played by such representations on early infant emotional development.

Infant Emotional Development: The "Relational Cocoon"

There is a significant and growing literature regarding the importance of the parent–infant relationship for early social-emotional development (Sroufe, 1995). During earliest infancy, the regulation of many of the infant's interoceptive states depends upon the behavior of the caregiver. As the infant develops, the repertoire of self-regulating behaviors increases. Emotional development during the first year also reflects this progression, with optimal development moving from the pleasurable feelings associated with the caregiver-assisted regulation of physiological needs to the positive self-feelings and emergent autonomy made possible through the establishment of a secure base with a trusted attachment figure. At each stage in early development, the caregiver is critical in helping the infant successfully negotiate age-salient emotional tasks (Erikson, 1985; Sroufe, 1995). The infant's capacity to signal the caregiver to respond to internal feeling states reflects early infant emotional self-regulation, and success in the use of such signals is likely to lead to feelings of positive affect and efficacy in the modulation of feeling states (Derryberry & Reed, 1996).

Given the critical role played by the primary caregiver in helping to shape the infants' early emotion-regulation strategies, factors that influence the caregiver's ability to accurately and sensitively identify and respond to infant emotion-cues takes on a particularly important role. Indeed, the impact of parents' affective processes on infant emotional development has been studied from a number of different perspectives (see Rudy & Grusec, this volume). Multiple aspects of infant emotional behavior, including expressiveness, self- and other-directed emotion regulatory behaviors, and soothability, have been linked, for example, to the parent's own emotional expressiveness (e.g., Garner, 1995), awareness of emotional states (e.g., Gergely & Watson, 1996), and parental emotional dysregulation (e.g., depression; Field, 1994). We propose that parents' representations of their infants are also important influences on their emotional engagement with their infants, as they reflect and guide parents' emotional responses to their infants (Milligan et al., 2003; Goldberg et al., 1994), and consequently, are likely to provide a critical context for infant emotional development.

Internal Working Models: Organizing and Reflecting the Emotional Experience of Relationships

Internal working models are mental templates that shape and guide the individuals processing of relational experience. They are organizational constructs, built over time on the basis of lived interactive experience, and are composed of both cognitive and affective elements. Typically internal working models operate outside of conscious awareness (Zimmermann, 1999). Research on adult attachment representations have focused primarily on the individual's current state of mind with respect to early attachment relationships assessed via the Adult Attachment Interview (AAI) (George, Kaplan, & Main, 1985). Responses to the AAI are thought to yield important information about current internal working models of early relationships to primary care-givers. Attachment researchers have proposed that access to relevant emotional experience, without the need to minimize or distort emotional material, distinguishes the secure (autonomous) working model category from other insecure patterns of representation (Main, Kaplan, & Cassidy, 1985; Zimmermann, 1999). Significant intergenerational correspondence in parent AAI classifications and infant internal working models has been well established (e.g., Benoit & Parker, 1994; Fonagy, Steele, & Steele, 1991; van IJzendoorn, 1995).

As reflected in the current volume, however, an area that has been receiving increased attention over recent years is the role of parents' internal working models of parenting, or of their child and relationship with their child, as predictors of parental behavior with the child (Biringen, Matheny, Bretherton, Renouf, & Sherman, 2000; Slade, Belsky, Aber, & Phelps, 1999; Solomon & George, 1996). Researchers have argued for the importance of considering the unique role of the caregiving system, a complementary behavioral system to the infants' attachment system (Solomon & George, 1996). While research evidence does support the influence of the parent's representation of early caregiving experiences on infant attachment security, these representations are more distal to the parent–child relationship than the caregiver's representation of his or her own child or of parenting. George and Solomon (1996) suggest that during adolescence the individual begins to develop a representation of self as caregiver that is rooted in, or influenced by, the internal working model of early relationships (i.e., their AAI classifications). Evidence suggests that these working models are not redundant, but rather that attachment and caregiving reflect parallel yet distinct behavioral systems. For example, Slade and colleagues (1999) examined whether mothers' representations of parenting mediated the association between AAI classifications and parenting behavior. They found that both AAI classifications and parenting representations were associated with quality of behavioral interaction. Mothers who were more joyful and coherent in their parenting representations were more positive and less negative while interacting with their toddlers. However, the parenting representations did not mediate the link between AAI classifications and behavior, suggesting parenting and representations contribute uniquely to the quality of caregiving and parental emotional displays.

What other evidence supports the conclusion that parents' internal working models of parenting influence their emotional interaction with their infants? To date, there are only a handful of studies directly assessing parents' representations of their infant or of parenting and observations of parent–infant interactive behavior. These include the work by Slade and colleagues (1999) described earlier, and the work of Biringen and colleagues (2000), who found that levels of emotional availability in interaction evident when the infant was 18 months of age predicted subsequent maternal sensitivity/insight in the parenting representation when infants were 39 months of age. In our own work we have also examined the link between parents' working models and emotions during parent–child interaction, extending prior work by examining these links when infants were under one year of age. But before we discuss these results, we will turn our attention to providing a more sophisticated model of emotions in parenting.

The Affective Organization of Parenting: Links with Parents' Representations of Their Children

Psychological research on emotion processes has made significant advances in recent years, providing a more sophisticated conceptualization of affective processes. This work has, however, had relatively little impact on research regarding affective processes in parenting (Dix, 1991), despite the fact that parenting is clearly an emotional (both challenging and pleasing) task. In his review article on the affective organization of parenting, Dix (1991) presents a model of parenting that highlights the central role of affective processes. The three elements of affective organization emphasized are: a) factors that activate particular emotional responses in the parent, b) the role of emotions in orienting, organizing, and/or motivating the parents' behavioral responses to the child, and c) the processes by which parents might control or regulate their emotional responses. To illustrate each of these components, mothers vary in terms of a) how negatively they experience their child's cries, b) how behaviorally sensitive they are in responding to their distressed child, and c) how well they are able to control their displays of distress. In this chapter, we propose an extension of this model, illustrating how parents' working models of their children or of caregiving influence or reflect emotional processes at each of these three levels.

Our perspective on the role of working models as regulators of the affective organization of parenting is consistent with current research and theory in the attachment literature. For example, Zimmermann (1999) has argued that one of the primary functions of internal working models of attachment relationships (i.e., assessed via the AAI) is the "adaptive regulation of negative arousal when feeling insecure" (p. 295), and thus internal working models have a central role in the regulation of emotion in a relational context. We propose that parents' representations of their children and of parenting are important regulators of the emotion experienced by the parent in relation to the child, and subsequently serve as motivational factors for parental behavioral responses.

Consider the following two vignettes; both are mothers of seven-month-old infants responding to a series of questions regarding aspects of parenting that may be experienced as challenging or difficult.

Vignette #1

Interviewer:	*What about when your child is emotionally upset? Can you recall a specific example?*
Mother:	Um, usually, I, you know, I told you I suffer from depression and he usually gets upset when I get upset. If he sees me cry, or if he knows that I am crying he usually starts to cry, too.
I:	*What do you do, at that specific time what did you do with him?*
M:	Um, try and talk to him and hold him and pull myself together, so that way I can help him ... get, you know, back together with himself.
I:	*And what did you feel like doing?*
M:	Um, ... more, more, leaving the room, ... I would rather leave the room and cry than for him to have to see me.
I:	*What do you feel like?*
M:	Um, probably embarrassed.

Vignette #2

Interviewer:	*What about your child's behavior now is the most difficult for you to handle?*
Mother:	... OK, the most difficult to handle ... is when she's overly tired and. ... When she goes through her fussiness where, it's just crying and nothing relaxes her. Even a bath. And whatnot – so it's w-when she's really overly tired. Then I have a hard time cause I'm tired at the end of the day, and then I have a hard time with patience. Like, "I've done everything to make you happy – we're on the same routine," you know? That's when it bothers me.
I:	*And how often does this occur?*
M:	At most two to three times a week – usually she's very easy. ... Put her down she goes out.
I:	*And what do you feel like doing when your child reacts this way?*
M:	Call her father (laughs). "Come put your kid down she won't go down for me!"

I:	*And how do you feel when she reacts this way?*
M:	It bothers me when she starts getting more and more upset and I can't ... control it. But I also know I'm tired. It usually is when I'm really tired that the little things ... that I wanna sit down and relax and I haven't been able to. ... So that's the conflict. So I just have to take a deep breath and say ... "It's not gonna be much longer, til I can lay down."
I:	*And what do you actually do?*
M:	I'll either – it's come down to where she either ... recently she likes to sit up on my lap, or lay down with me. And I grab her big comforter from her bed. And that seems just to soothe her. It's like, she doesn't wanna lay down by herself, so by doing it together we calm down together.

There are several notable aspects of these vignettes with respect to understanding parents' emotion regulation strategies in the context of parenting. Both mothers describe situations that *activate*, or give rise to negative emotions experienced internally. How the mother actually emotionally *engages* with her infant appears to differ, and this is likely due, in part, to differences in the effectiveness of their emotion *regulation* efforts.

In the second vignette, the mother has an open regulation strategy, acknowledging the conflict she experiences and fairly directly describing her frustration and anger (e.g., "that's when it bothers me"). These feelings are not overwhelming, however, and she shows us that she can formulate her actual response in terms of the infant's needs, thus protecting her child from having to face the burden of her internal emotional reaction. Indeed, her behavioral engagement strategy has the dual effect of helping both her infant and herself ("by doing it together we calm down together"). The first vignette is somewhat more problematic. At the level of emotion activation, the mother is quite distressed by her own feelings (e.g., "embarrassed"), and her attempts to keep the depression from directly impacting the child are unconvincing (e.g., note that the child is crying because she is crying). Both of these mothers differ in the level of negative emotion that is activated by their infants' behavior, and their ability to successfully regulate their difficult emotions leads to differences in the quality of emotional engagement with their infants. These two mothers also differ in their working models of their children and the quality of their emotion regulation is consistent with these working model classification differences, an issue we will take up later in this chapter.

Let us now explore the particular ways in which parents' representations of their infants may serve a regulatory role in the activation of emotion, the parents' behavioral engagement, or displays of emotion, and in the strategies that parents may consciously or unconsciously use to regulate these emotion displays. We propose that parents' representations are linked to caregiving sensitivity via their influence on multiple elements of affective organization in the parent; parents representations influence the *activation* of emotion, the *engagement* of emotional processes, and emotion *regulation*. We provide a brief summary of current research on working model influences on each of these aspects of the affective organization of parenting before returning to our own research on this topic.

Activation of Emotion

Activation processes precede, or precipitate, emotion. They reflect the inner subjective qualities that will, in part, determine the emotional response to some external or more objective event. Dix (1991) identifies a number of activation-relevant factors that may predispose a person to experience negative affect in the context of parenting. These include inappropriate developmental expectations, a failure to adopt an empathic or child-focused perspective with the child, malevolent attributions regarding the infant's behavior, feelings of helplessness or lower efficacy, and the lack of effective strategies for eliciting desired child behaviors.

It is likely that parents' internal working models of their relationship with their infant reflect these types of "predisposing" or "subjective" factors, and may increase the likelihood that the parent will experience more negative affect in interaction with the infant. Evidence for this comes from research linking working models with biases in the experience of other emotions. For example, Zeanah and colleagues (1993) demonstrated that mothers AAI classifications were associated with their ratings of infant distress, such that dismissive mothers reported more negative affect in response to the emotionality of distressed infants than other mothers.

Engagement Processes

Once activated, emotions influence cognitive (e.g., expectations, appraisals) and behavioral (e.g., response tendencies, emotion display) processes (Dix, 1991). Emotion-triggered cognitive processes may alert the person to perceive and evaluate particular features of an event, motivate the person to seek particular outcomes, and/or influence the likelihood of certain behavioral responses. It is generally assumed that parents engage in "emotion-consistent" behavior, and that the link between negative emotion and negative behavior is likely to be stronger than that between positive emotion and behavior (Fredrickson,

1998; Frijda, 1986). For example, Frijda suggests that emotions are, by definition, associations with urges to act in particular ways, called "specific action tendencies." Extant research on several negative emotions supports this notion, for example, a large body of research revealing that anger is associated with blocked goals, and an accompanying motivation to act to remove the offending "barrier." Similarly, when experiencing fear, the body reacts by mobilizing appropriate autonomic support for the possibility of running (Lazarus, 1991). In other words, through specific action tendencies emotions prepare or mobilize both the body and mind to act in specific ways. Fredrickson (1998), however, has proposed that positive emotions operate differently. While positive emotions do often produce urges to act, they appear to be less prescriptive than negative emotions about the specific nature of the behavior to be enacted. Fredrickson proposes that positive emotions may yield *nonspecific* action tendencies, and in reviewing extant research, she highlights a "broaden and build" theory of positive emotion, such that positive emotions help the person to broaden cognition (e.g., research linking positive emotion with creative thinking) and build resources (e.g., research linking play with positive emotion and intellectual processes). In sum, research on negative emotions supports the notion of a priming effect, such that negative emotions increase negative expectations, which in turn may increase the likelihood that a parent will behave more negatively than if s/he were not negatively aroused. It is possible that parents' positive emotions help to create an environment that optimizes developmental processes, but in a less isomorphic, direct manner than observed with negative emotion.

The internal working model of the child and the relationship with the child may influence this level of engagement by filtering the degree to which parents identify and orient to emotions in the child, as well as by influencing behavior towards the child. There is some data supporting these hypotheses. Goldberg, MacKay, and Rochester (1994) found that infant attachment classifications were associated with unique patterns of maternal emotion socialization. Specifically, they found that mothers of secure infants attended to the full range of infant affective expressions and responded more often than other mothers, while mothers of avoidant infants were less responsive, particularly to infant negative emotion. Mothers of resistant infants were especially responsive to negative affect, but did show some response to positive affect as well. Milligan et al. (2003) found that maternal attachment classifications were related to the communication of emotion through the manner in which mothers sang songs to their infants. Mothers with dismissive classifications did not modify the playfulness of their singing to adjust to infant distress. Haft and Slade (1989) examined differences in affective attunement (i.e., the mother's ability to match the infant's affective state in contour, intensity, and temporal features), and found that mothers with autonomous AAI classifications were more attuned to a wider range of infant affect.

Results from these studies are consistent with current theoretical propositions from both the attachment and the emotion literature. Cassidy (1994) has described three patterns of maternal affective communication that correspond to maternal AAI classifications (open, minimized, and heightened); these patterns have parallels in the two patterns of problematic emotional engagement in the parenting context identified by Dix (1991). For one group of individuals, emotion is deactivated, and the parent is unavailable because she or he does not experience emotion in a manner that motivates empathic responding. For another group, emotions may be too strong, and promote a focus on short-term goals versus long-term motivational strategies. For example, imagine a parent who "sneaks" away quickly without saying good-bye in order to avoid child crying versus a parent who thinks about how to anticipate and signal departures in order to build a sense of security to handle separations with trust in the parent's eventual return. The research evidence described above generally supports the proposition that dismissive mothers are likely to ignore or reject the infant's emotional cues, while the preoccupied group responds inconsistently, which may reflect, in part, the uncertainty associated with identifying appropriate goals, and responding to short- versus- long-term agendas.

Emotion Regulation Processes

Consistent with Zimmerman (1999), we suggest that internal working models are themselves emotion regulators that influence the activation and attribution of emotion as well as the manner of behaviorally responding. Thompson (1990) has defined emotion regulation as the acquired strategies of emotion self-management, as well as the variety of external influences by which emotion is regulated. Attachment plays a role at both levels of this process; internal working models may shape the "emotion self-management" process, and attachment figures are likely to be significant external influences on the regulation of emotion. Regarding internal working models, Cassidy (1994) describes the emotion regulation strategies employed by infants with different types of attachment classifications; specifically, avoidant working models employ a deactivating attentional strategy, characterized by affect inhibition or minimization, whereas ambivalent strategies are characterized by affect heightening or enhancement.

Emotion regulation strategies help the individual parent to suppress or cope with negative emotion aroused in the context of caregiving (Dix, 1991).

For example, once the parent is distressed, how does she or he manage these feelings? Are these feelings displayed? What cognitive, behavioral, and social processes might influence the decision to display, or keep hidden, particular emotional reactions? In order to behave sensitively in challenging situations, the parent must be able to tolerate his or her negative emotions, recognize that they pose a threat to the infant, and employ effective control strategies to regulate the show of distress. Individuals may or may not be consciously aware of these emotion regulation strategies, and may or may not be aware of their effectiveness or lack thereof.

Returning to our two vignettes, recall how differently the mothers responded to a question regarding infant behavior they found difficult or challenging. In the first case the emotions the mother describes are strong, flooding her ability to successfully impose cognitive controls to regulate her behavioral response to the infant. Her working model of the child classi-fication reflects this affect-heightening emotion regulation strategy. In the second vignette, the mother's emotions are accessible, that is, she does not deactivate or dismiss their importance. Nor are these emotions overwhelm-ing, flooding her capacity to regulate her behavioral response to the infant. Rather, she can both acknowledge and display her feelings, and regulate using cognitive controls her behavioral response to the infant. Her working model of the infant classification reflects this open, balanced emotion regulation strategy.

Rethinking Sensitivity: The Role of Emotional Processes

An abundance of literature has established the importance of interactive pat-terns and parental behavioral sensitivity as a precursor to infant and child attachment security at one year of age and beyond. In the early and pio-neering study on infant attachment relationships, the Baltimore study, Mary Ainsworth and her colleagues (1978) identified parental sensitivity as the primary and significant contributor to the ontogeny of individual differences in infant quality of attachment. On the basis of extensive home visit obser-vations, they determined that parental sensitivity towards the infant was very highly correlated to the infant's attachment classification. While the emphasis Ainsworth and other attachment researchers have placed on sensitive response to the infant is consistent with more current work identifying parental sensi-tivity as an important predictor of infant and child attachment security, cur-rent studies have failed to obtain effect sizes as large as the Baltimore study (Egeland & Farber, 1984; Grossman et al., 1985; DeWolff & van IJzendoorn, 1997).

In response to these concerns, DeWolff and van IJzendoorn (1997) under-took a large meta-analysis examining how maternal sensitivity may be related to infant attachment security. Their results confirmed that parental sensitivity is indeed related to attachment security; however, they observed that the effect size of this association is only in the moderate range.

In the context of this current research, it seems important to ask again – What is parental sensitivity? In the Ainsworth system, sensitivity was a higher-level category, subsuming many qualities of the infants' relational environ-ment (Bretherton, 2000). At a basic level, parental sensitivity reflects the quality of caregiving. Sensitive parents provide adequate, responsive, con-tingent care to the infant. They create a safe atmosphere that potentiates the optimal development of the child – room to explore safely, learn, play, and seek safety when danger or threat is imminent. However, in addition to the behavioral-specific (responding to child distress with physical action, or non-intrusive engagement) and physical (e.g., setting up a "baby-proof" home environment) qualities, sensitivity incorporates a number of emotion-salient components (Bretherton, 2000). Sensitive parents have an empathic stance towards the infant, such that they are able to identify when the infant needs comfort, and are able to provide assistance as needed, thus helping the infant with the regulation of emotion.

Consistent with current conceptualizations, we propose that sensitivity reflects, in large part, the quality of emotional connection to the child that allows for optimal parenting (Biringen et al., 2000; Emde, 2000). While vir-tually all parents experience an emotional bond with their infants, the quality of their emotional responses may vary. For example, a sensitive parent likely experiences an empathic response, and is emotionally available to the infant. The ability to identify and tolerate the infant's emotional needs allows for responding accurately, empathically, and in a manner that is "in-tune" with the infant's needs and experiences. This makes possible pleasurable, playful interaction. Insensitive parenting occurs when a parent is emotionally unavail-able, either because s/he is detached and uninvolved, or because the emotional response is so strong it floods the parent and overwhelms appropriate, sensi-tive behavior.

Assessing the "Emotional Dance" between Parents and Infants

Individual differences with respect to the qualities of the emotional engage-ment exist from very early on, reflected as differences in the type of "emotional dance" conducted by parent and child. Parents' emotional exchanges with infants tend to follow meaningful patterns of interaction. Stern (1985), for example, has written extensively about his observation of mother–infant emotional exchange, noting that the affective interactions have a dynamic "shape" to them, and that patterns of affective engagement vary across mother–infant dyads. The mental health of the infant, Stern suggests, is strongly affected by the synchrony of the interaction.

Emotional exchange has also been proposed to play a central role in the infant's emerging ability to recognize his or her own emotional states, and regulate his or her own emotional arousal (Sroufe, 1995). Gergely and Watson (1996), for example, provide a compelling account of how maternal "affective mirroring" behavior helps infants to develop emotional self-awareness and a capacity for self-regulation of emotion. They propose a model in which the mother's ability to activate, regulate, and engage emotionally is related to the infant's own ability to internalize an understanding of emotional experience. At the level of activation, the mother must accurately perceive the infant's emotions. At the level of regulation, the mother must mentally process and transform the emotion, and subsequently, at the level of engagement, display a "marked" exaggerated response to the infant's emotional displays. The authors speculate regarding the impact of deviant "affect-mirroring" styles, suggesting that parents' own intrapsychic conflicts are likely to impact their ability to respond appropriately to the infant's affective displays. The authors further speculate that parents' own representations of attachment relationships may contribute to their ability to sensitively and appropriately engage in this process. For example, they suggest that mothers whose internal representations of relationships reflect a tendency to over-activate emotional arousal, and whose cognitive controls are flooded by emotional/relational experience, may tend to simply mimic their infants' emotional expression, without processing and transforming the emotion. This "pure mirroring" may consequently escalate the infant's emotional state, having failed to provide the necessary containment and assistance in coping with the experienced emotion.

Assessment of the parent–infant emotional "dance" is made possible via the Still Face procedure. Like the Strange Situation, the Still Face allows for the examination of dyadic interaction in the context of low and high stress, as well as the processes by which parents and infants return to a positive affective state following a brief period of maternal unavailability (i.e., interactive repair). In the Still Face maternal unavailability is simulated by having the parent hold a flat, unresponsive expression for a brief period of time; this is preceded and followed by short episodes of normal face-to-face interaction. The temporary maternal unavailability and lack of responsiveness during this procedure is a reliable stress inducer, even for very young infants (Field et al., 1986; Weinberg & Tronick, 1996). Many mothers also report feeling distressed by the experience of holding a still, unresponsive, expression while their infants are upset, and as an illustration of the motivational function of emotions, research has shown that differences in report of maternal distress during the Still Face correspond to different parenting behaviors during the period following the procedure (Mayes et al., 1991).

There is accumulating evidence that infant response to the Still Face during the first half of the first year of life is associated with attachment security at one year of age (Braungart-Reiker et al., 2001; Cohn et al., 1991; Kogan & Carter, 1996). For example, Cohn and colleagues (1991) report that six-month-old infants who demonstrated any attempt at positive eliciting behaviors (e.g., smiling, play-face expressions) during the Still Face were more likely to be securely attached at 12 months. Similarly, Kogan and Carter (1996) found that four-month-old infants who displayed more resistance (e.g., crying, lack of soothability) and avoidance (e.g., gaze aversion, turning away from mother) during the period immediately following the Still Face were less likely to demonstrate contact-maintenance, a common feature of secure attachment, during the Strange Situation at 12 months. Finally, Braungart-Reiker and colleagues (2001) found that both maternal sensitivity and infant affect regulation during the Still Face procedure when infants were four months of age predicted infant–maternal attachment classifications at one year. Taken together, these results appear to demonstrate some stability in the emotional precursors of subsequent attachment-related behavior.

We now turn to a presentation of our own work examining how mothers' working models of their seven-month-old infants influence the affective organization of their parenting and the quality of the emotional dance between mother and child.

Representations of the Infant, Maternal Emotion Activation and Expression, and Infant Emotion Regulation: Results from the Michigan Family Study

In our own work on the Michigan Family Study (MFS) (McDonough, 1994; Rosenblum et al., 2002) we have examined the role of mothers' representations of their infants on maternal behavior and infant emotion regulation. We present here our work examining the links between mothers' representations of their infants and two aspects of emotion in parenting: maternal emotion *activation* and emotional *engagement* with their infants, as well as the consequences for early infant emotion regulation.

The Michigan Family Study

The MFS is a longitudinal study focused on the role played by primary relationships and other contexts in shaping the trajectories of infant behavioral regulation from infancy to early childhood. We will report here on data from the first wave of data collection, when infants were seven months of age. The MFS sample includes 258 mothers and infants; however, maternal representational data are available only for the first 100 participants ($N = 100$). Mothers of six-month-old infants were recruited from routine "well-baby" pediatric appointments, and study participants comprised a wide range of demographic and socio-economic circumstances (for more details, see Rosenblum et al., 2002).

The MFS protocol involved a home and laboratory visit when the infants were seven months of age. During the home visit, a trained graduate student assistant interviewed the mother with regard to demographic information and her perceptions of her infant's behavior and development. She also administered a projective test requiring the mother to interpret the emotion being displayed in a series of photographs of infants displaying ambiguous facial expressions, the IFEEL task (Butterfield, Emde, & Osofsky, 1987).

During the laboratory visit, mothers and infants engaged in a series of videotaped interactive tasks, including the Still Face procedure (Rosenblum et al., 2002; Tronick, 1989). For this procedure the infant was placed in a highchair and his or her mother sat in a swivel chair in front of the highchair. Both maternal and infant behaviors were recorded using separate cameras and split-screen technology. The experimenter was not in the room and gave instructions to the mother through a microphone from behind a one-way mirror. The Still Face was cut short if the infant demonstrated high levels of distress and cried continuously for more than 30 seconds. Four mother–infant dyads did not complete the Still Face procedure, either because the infant was excessively distressed at the outset of the procedure, or because the mother took the infant out of the highchair during the task. Therefore, analyses involving mothers' representations and Still Face behavior data are presented for 96 mother–infant dyads ($n = 96$).

Following all interactive tasks, the mothers were interviewed using a modified version of the Working Model of the Child Interview (Rosenblum, Muzik, & Dayton, 2002; Zeanah & Benoit, 1995). Infants were cared for in an adjacent room while mothers were interviewed by a trained graduate student research assistant.

Maternal Representations of the Infant: The "Working Model of the Child Interview"

As noted previously, a number of interviews exist designed to assess parents' representations of parenting. On the MFS we employed an interview designed to assess the parents' representation of the child and the relationship with

Table 4.1. *Representational Typology Categories for the WMCI*

	Balanced	Disengaged	Distorted
Emotion Regulation Strategy	Flexible, balanced integration of positive and negative affect.	Emotion deactivation. Cognitively driven responses with low levels of emotional involvement.	Heightened emotion. Strong feelings pervade the interview. Emotionally driven, with low levels of cognitive control.
Representation of Infant	Infant perceived as easy or challenging, but caregiver is generally accepting of and enjoys the infant, and views challenges as understandable, normal perturbations that will change.	Infant is either idealized or rejected. Caregiver often emphasizes infant independence, and caregiving sensitivity and acceptance of the infant's needs tend to be low.	Caregiver typically emphasizes infant's dependence. Narratives often characterized as role-reversed, self-involved, confused, distracted, uncertain, or overwhelmed.
Coherence	Narrative is high in internal consistency and well-organized.	Low coherence, often manifested in contradictions, failure to support generalized descriptions with memories of specific events, and sparse recall.	Low coherence, often manifested as a wandering narrative, low in organization, insuccinct, with many unexplained referents and multiple unrecognized contradictions.

the child: The Working Model of the Child Interview (WMCI) (Zeanah & Benoit, 1995). The WMCI is a semi-structured interview designed to capture a parent's internalized perceptions and subjective experience of their child's personality and relationship with their child.

The interview yields both dimensional and categorical data, with ratings on multiple scales reflecting specific qualities of the narrative, and assignment to one main typology classification that reflects both content and process features of the narrative. The three representational typology categories are: balanced, disengaged, and distorted (see Table 4.1). Balanced representations were characterized by emotional warmth and acceptance; sensitive responsiveness to infant needs; coherence, and richly detailed, accessible descriptions. Parents in this category provided convincing details and experiences that conveyed their involvement and delight in their relationship with their infant. Disengaged representations were characterized by an emotional aloofness and distance from the infant. Parents in this category were likely to describe their infants in a manner that minimized affective involvement, revealing their tendency to reject their infants' emotional and dependency needs. When expressed, anger was "cool" and rejecting; for example, sarcastic comments or emotionally distancing rejection of the infant's needs for closeness, such as, "he just cries because he's spoiled." Distorted representations were characterized broadly by a distortion imposed on the image of the infant and/or the relationship with the infant. As described by Zeanah and Benoit (1995), distortion refers to an internal inconsistency in the narrative rather than necessarily reflecting a contradiction with putative "objective" reality. Parents in this category were often incoherent, and provided confused, contradictory, bizarre, or "unresolved" descriptions of their infant and their relationship. Unlike their disengaging counterparts, parents in this category tended to express a great deal of "hot" emotional experience, which interfered with their ability to provide a coherent, organized narrative. For example, a parent might describe at great length and with angry intensity their annoyance with the child's sleep problems. Sample WMCI questions, as well as more details regarding the scoring system, are included in Appendix 4.1.

The majority of the mothers met criteria for balanced typology classification ($n = 55$), while the remainder were fairly evenly distributed between the disengaged ($n = 22$) and distorted ($n = 23$) categories. In addition, a subset of the WMCI scores were examined, specifically, those scales assessing the affective tone of the representation of the infant (that is, the "emotional coloring" of the parents' representation of the infant). Only affective tone scales with sufficient variability were included in these analyses, specifically, the joy, anger, indifference, anxiety, and sadness scales.

Mothers' Attributions Regarding Infant Emotion: The IFEEL Task

Mothers completed the Infant Facial Expressions of Emotions from Looking at Pictures task (IFEEL) (Butterfield, Emde, & Osofsky, 1987) during the home visit. The IFEEL is a projective test designed to pull for individual differences in verbal responses about emotions seen in babies. The test consists of a set of 30 pictures of infants, and parents are asked to describe in one word the emotion the infant is expressing. Maternal responses were scored according the categorical method, which classifies each response as belonging to one of 12 specific emotion categories (e.g., joy, sad, anger, surprise, content, passive, shame, disgust, distress, cautious, interest, and fear). Examination of the psychometric properties of the IFEEL using these scoring techniques was conducted with a sample of mothers of infants between the ages of 3 and 12 months, and results confirmed the adequacy of the psychometric properties of the instrument for use with this population (Appelbaum, Butterfield, & Culp, 1993).

Maternal and Infant Affective Behavior During the Still Face

The Still Face has been widely used to examine infant emotion regulation in response to temporary maternal unavailability with infants between two and seven months of age (Rosenblum et al., 2002; Tronick, 1989; Weinberg & Tronick, 1996). The procedure itself is composed of three brief segments that challenge infant, and presumably parent, affective self-regulation: a first "Free Play" segment during which the mother and infant interact in face-to-face play; a second period, the "Still Face," during which the mother holds a still face and is unresponsive to the infant; and a final "Reengagement" episode, during which the mother again interacts in face-to-face play with the infant.

Maternal and infant affective behavior was scored during both the Free Play and Reengagement episodes of the Still Face procedure using a system developed by Miller et al. (2002). Each dimension of infant and maternal interactive behavior was given a global score along a four-point scale from 0 (absent) to 3 (high levels present). Maternal positive affect reflected the degree of positive affect displayed by mothers during interaction with their infants, whereas the anger/hostility score reflected the degree to which mothers rejected their infants' bids or made negative comments directly to or about their infants. The resignation/anxiety scale assessed mothers' apparent tendencies to express negative feelings or anxiety by fidgeting, sighing, retreating from interaction, looking worried, or using a high-pitched tone of voice. Infant affective expression was assessed on two scales: infant negative and infant positive affect. Coders were trained extensively, and efforts were taken to ensure that the same coder did not code both mother and infant behavior. For the initial reliability sample ($n = 20$) there was greater than 80% exact agreement, and continued double coding at regular intervals was conducted to minimize rater drift. Weighted kappa coefficients for the mother and infant behavior scales on a subset of 50 segments ranged from 0.61 to 0.87.

Table 4.2. *Conceptual Grid Linking Elements of the Affective Organization of Parenting with Assessment Measures Employed in the Michigan Family Study*

	Emotion Activation	Emotion Regulation	Emotion Engagement
Illustration in Parenting: "When I hear the baby cry…"	"How does it make me feel?"	"Am I overwhelmed by feeling?" "Do I distance or deactivate my feelings?" "Am I open to experiencing the feelings without being overwhelmed?"	"What feelings do I assume the baby has?" and "What feelings do I show?"
Assessment in the Parent	Content features of the WMCI: *Affective Tone Scales*	Process features of the WMCI: *Typology Categories*	Projection of infant emotional experience: Attributions on the IFEEL task
		Emotional Displays during Interaction: *The Still Face Procedure*	Emotional Displays during Interaction: *The Still Face Procedure*
Assessment in the Infant		Emotional Displays during interaction with mother: *The Still Face Procedure*	Emotional Displays during interaction with mother: *The Still Face Procedure*

Linking Working Models of the Child with Maternal Emotion Activation and Engagement

We now turn to the results of our analyses linking mothers' working model of the child typology classifications to aspects of maternal emotion activation and engagement. Table 4.2 provides a conceptual grid identifying the elements of affective organization captured by each of our assessment methods. We begin with links between working models and emotion activation, then turn to links between working models and cognitive and behavioral engagement processes, and conclude by linking maternal working models to infant emotion regulation.

Emotion Activation: Associations between the WMCI and the Affective Tone of the Representation

Activation processes precipitate emotion and are determinative of which emotion will be experienced, when it will occur, and how strongly it will be activated. We assume that representations of relationships, as mental templates through which relational information is processed, will prime mothers to experience certain types of emotion in relation to thinking about infant behavior and emotional expression. Although the WMCI typology classifications may reflect general cognitive disconnection or deactivating emotional strategies, the specific emotional coloring of the representation may be considered, at least in part, to be independent of these process features of the narrative. For example, mothers may express anger/frustration in a cold, sarcastic (deactivated) manner, in a "hot" over-involved (heightened) manner, or in a well-regulated, coherent and contained (open) manner. In all cases, anger/frustration is manifest, but the regulation strategy varies. Our specific hypotheses were that mothers with balanced representations would be most highly colored by intense feelings of joy, whereas disengaged representations would be associated with lower intensity of positive emotion ratings, coupled with a propensity towards higher levels of (cold) anger. We expected that distorted mothers would show high levels of all emotion, but that they would be higher than the other two groups in their negative affective coloring (i.e., anger and anxiety).

In order to test these hypotheses, we analyzed a subset of the data ($n = 35$) for which there were independent raters for the typology classification versus the affective tone scales. Although separate coders were used for this analysis, it is nonetheless important to note that scores on any particular affective tone dimension did not determine the overall typology classification that parent was assigned. For analyses involving this subset, there were 17 balanced, 10 disengaged, and 8 distorted narratives.

Results indicated differences between the three typology groups both in terms of the valence and the intensity of the affective coloring of the representation in the expected direction (see Figure 4.1).

One-way ANOVAs followed by post hoc comparisons (Bonferonni corrections) revealed that mothers with balanced representations demonstrated higher levels of joy than mothers in either of the other two categories, $F(2, 33) = 12.86$, $p < 0.01$, and lower levels of anger than mothers in the disengaged categories, $F(2, 33) = 3.93, p < 0.05$. There were no differences between the two non-balanced categories with respect to anger; however, mothers with disengaged representations had representations characterized by more indifference than mothers in either of the other two categories, $F(2, 33) = 17.65, p < 0.01$. Mothers in the distorted category had representations that were colored by the highest levels of internalizing affect; specifically, they had higher levels of anxiety, $F(2, 23) = 6.69, p < 0.01$ and sadness, $F(2, 23) = 3.77, p < 0.05$.

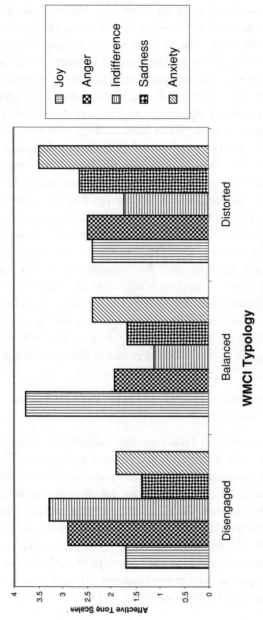

Figure 4.1. The affective tone of mothers' representations of their infants by WMCI typology classifications.

129

These results indicated support for our hypotheses. Mothers in the balanced category had representations colored by joy, but on average their representations also included mild levels of anger, sadness, and anxiety. The representations of both non-balanced groups were colored by anger, but in contrast to the indifference evident in the disengaged representations, distorted mothers' representations revealed feelings of anxiety and sadness. Unexpectedly, only the disengaged group had representations that were significantly angrier than the balanced representations. While these findings were generally consistent with Cassidy's (1994) description of open versus deactivated versus heightened affective styles, they diverge from the typical portrayal of disengaged or dismissing mothers as inhibiting affect in general. Rather, these findings appear more consistent with a depiction of disengaged mothers as perhaps experiencing higher levels of internal anger and frustration, which may result from personal feelings of rejection or loneliness. It is possible that, in contrast to distorted mothers, disengaged mothers may be more likely to manifest "cool" anger in their narratives, for example, in the form of sarcasm directed towards the infant, as well as to behave in an emotionally "cool" form of anger during interaction, that is, forms of rejection versus hot angry exchanges. In sum, it was generally apparent that the emotions activated in the context of describing the baby and the relationship with the baby varied according to the mother's internal working model of this relationship.

Emotional Engagement: Associations between the WMCI, Emotion Attributions, and Behavioral Displays

Our next set of analyses extended this issue by examining the links between mothers working models of their infants and engagement processes. Engagement processes orient, organize, and/or motivate parental emotional behavior in response to the child. Once activated, parental emotions influence cognition (e.g., appraisals) and behavioral (response tendencies) processes. We examined influences on both cognitive and behavioral engagement processes. At the cognitive level, we explored links between mothers' working models of their infants and mothers' emotion attributions on the IFEEL task; at the behavioral level we explored links beween mothers' working models of their infants and their emotional displays during the Still Face.

Working Models of the Infant and Maternal Emotion Attributions on the IFEEL. Our next set of analyses examined whether mothers' representations of their infants also influenced the types of attributions they made regarding the emotion displayed by an unknown infant. Our prediction was that mothers with balanced representations would attribute more positive valence emotions, while mothers with distorted or disengaged representations would attribute more negative emotions.

In order to test this hypothesis, we conducted a series of one-way analyses of variance with the IFEEL categories as a dependent variable, and mothers' WMCI classifications as the independent variable. Significant WMCI typology differences were observed for three of the IFEEL categories: interest, $F (2, 97) = 8.50$, $p < 0.01$, cautious, $F (2, 97) = 4.18$, $p < 0.05$, and anger, $F (2, 97) = 11.12$, $p < 0.01$. Post hoc comparisons revealed that mothers in the balanced category were more likely to interpret interest ($M = 8.13$, $SD = 3.37$) than mothers in the distorted ($M = 4.91$, $SD = 2.66$) category. Similarly, balanced mothers perceived more caution ($M = 2.31$, $SD = 1.94$) than mothers in the disengaged ($M = 1.23$, $SD = 1.11$) or distorted ($M = 1.43$, $SD = 1.50$) categories. Finally, mothers in the disengaged ($M = 2.05$, $SD = 1.59$) and distorted ($M = 1.75$, $SD = 1.47$) categories attributed more anger than mothers in the balanced category ($M = 0.96$, $SD = 1.10$).

We also examined the intercorrelations between working model affective tone scales and IFEEL categories, and results indicated a number of significant associations. Joy in the maternal working model of the child was associated with fewer attributions of anger ($r = -0.39$) and distress ($r = 0.20$) on the IFEEL. Anger in the maternal narrative was associated with more attributions of anger ($r = 0.29$) and passivity ($r = 0.20$), and fewer attributions of interest ($r = -0.28$) and cautiousness ($r = -0.27$) on the IFEEL. Indifference in the maternal narrative was associated with more anger attributions ($r = 0.32$) and sadness in the maternal narrative with more sad attributions ($r = 0.21$) on the IFEEL.

Thus, there was mixed support for our hypotheses. Mothers with balanced representations did not make more positive attributions as expected, but they did make more benign attributions regarding ambiguous infant affective displays (i.e., interest). On the other hand, consistent with their tendency to have representations of their own infants that were colored by anger, mothers in the disengaged category attributed more anger to the ambiguous emotion displayed by an unknown infant. Similarly, anger and sadness in the maternal narratives were associated with anger and sadness, respectively, in maternal attributions on the IFEEL. These results are consistent with the notion that links between emotion activation (in this case, the affective tone of the representation) and engagement processes (in this case, attributions) are strongest for negative, as opposed to positive, emotion. Given that the emotion expressions were designed to be "ambiguous," the benign attributions made by mothers in the balanced category may reflect more accurate attributions, while the disengaged mothers' projections of anger may reflect more strongly their own negative perceptual biases. It is also possible that disengaged mothers actually experience more "angry" interactions with their infants, in which case these results might be understood not as reflecting projections of internal feeling states per se, but rather, as Magai (1999) has suggested, actual differences in the dyads' prior interactive history.

Working Models of the Infant and Maternal Emotional Display during the Still Face. We next turned our attention to the question of behavioral engagement, or how mothers communicate their internal feelings to their infants. We were interested in the extent to which mothers might show emotion-consistent parenting behaviors with their own child, and the ways in which these displays might be influenced by infant distress. Our hypotheses were that mothers with balanced representations would demonstrate the highest levels of positive affect in interaction with their infants, while mothers with non-balanced representations would show more negative (angry/hostile and anxious/resigned) emotion during interaction. Because both disengaged and distorted mothers were not differentiated in their levels of anger in the affective tone of the representation, we did not predict differences between these groups in their angry behavior. However, given higher levels of sadness and anxiety in their representations, we expected mothers in the distorted category to display more behavioral level anxiety/resignation. Finally, we anticipated that these differences would be most pronounced following the Still Face during Reengagement, which prior research has demonstrated is a context of heightened infant distress.

In order to test these hypotheses we examined links between mothers' representation (both typology classifications and affective tone scores) and mothers' emotion expression (i.e., joy, hostility/rejection, and resignation/anxiety) during the Still Face procedure, both during the Free Play that precedes the Still Face, and the Reengagement episode following the Still Face ($n = 96$). Results indicated that differences existed in the types of emotions displayed by mothers in each of the representational classification typologies, but that the nature of these associations varied according to the situational context.

Correlational analyses between the WMCI affective tone scales (i.e., joy, anger, indifference, anxiety, and sadness) and maternal affective behavior during the Still Face procedure (i.e., positive affect, anger/hostility, and resignation/anxiety) revealed several significant associations, with patterns varying according to the specific Still Face episode (see Table 4.3). In general, mothers with joyful representations of their infant demonstrated lower levels of anger/hostility, while mothers with representations colored by anger

Table 4.3. *Correlations between Affective Tone Scales and Maternal Affective Behavior during the Still Face Procedure*

	Maternal Positive Affect Free Play	Maternal Positive Affect Reengagement	Maternal Anger/ Hostility Free Play	Maternal Anger/ Hostility Reengagement	Maternal Anxious/ Resigned Free Play	Maternal Anxious/ Resigned Reengagement
Affective Tone						
Joy	.19	.19	−.30**	−.02	−.05	−.15
Anger	−.02	−.30**	.14	.10	−.09	.09
Indifference	−.17	−.27*	.31**	−.08	.11	.10
Anxiety	−.03	.11	−.10	.11	.09	.11
Sadness	.03	.11	−.10	.10	.18	.20*

$^*p < .05; ^{**}p < .01$

demonstrated less positive affect. Indifference in the representation was associated with both lower positive affect and higher levels of angry/hostile behavior. Finally, representations colored by sadness were associated with higher levels of resignation/anxiety.

In order to examine the association between mothers representational typologies and maternal behavior across the Still Face procedure, a series of repeated measures analysis of variance models were conducted, with maternal behavior codes across the two episodes of the Still Face procedure (i.e., Free Play and Reengagement) as the within subjects factor and maternal WMCI typology category as the between subjects factor.

We began with an analysis of maternal positive affect across the Still Face, and results indicated a significant main effect for positive affect, $F(1, 93) = 24.64, p < 0.001$, although the interaction between WMCI classification and Still Face episode was not significant (see Figure 4.2).

Overall, positive affect decreased for the entire sample from Free Play to Reengagement, with a similar pattern observed for mothers with balanced, disengaged, and distorted WMCI classifications. Notably, the trend was for mothers in the balanced category to show the highest level of positive affect. While a one-way analysis of variance did not yield significant typology group differences in positive affect during the Free Play, at Reengagement mothers with balanced representations showed significantly more positive affect ($M = 2.02, SD = 0.72$) than mothers in the disengaged group ($M = 1.33, SD = 0.73$), $F(2, 93) = 6.58, p < 0.01$.

Our second repeated measures analysis was for maternal anger/hostility across the Still Face procedure, and this time results yielded no main effect. However, results did reveal a significant typology × episode interaction, $F(2, 93) = 6.40, p < 0.01$ (see Figure 4.3). Post hoc one-way

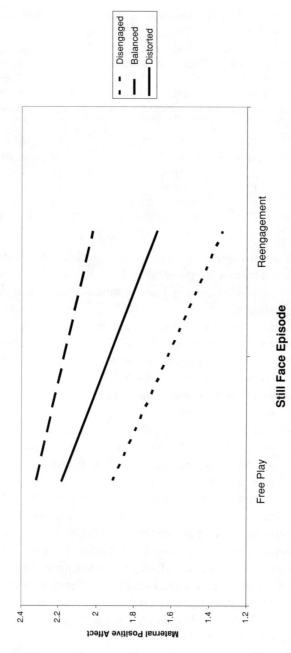

Figure 4.2. Mothers' emotion displays across the Still Face procedure, from the initial Free Play episode to Reengagement following the Still Face: Maternal positive affect.

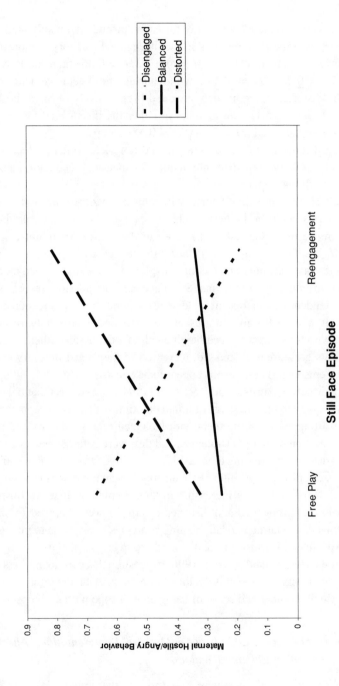

Figure 4.3. Mothers' emotion displays across the Still Face procedure, from the initial Free Play episode to Reengagement following the Still Face: Maternal hostile/angry behavior.

ANOVAs were conducted separately for each episode, and results indicated that during the Free Play mothers in the disengaged category demonstrated higher levels of anger/hostility ($M = 0.67$, $SD = 0.86$) than the balanced group ($M = 0.26$, $SD = 0.44$), while during the Reengagement mothers in the distorted category demonstrated higher levels of anger/hostility ($M = 0.82$, $SD = 1.01$) than mothers in either the disengaged ($M = 0.19$, $SD = 0.40$) or balanced ($M = 0.34$, $SD = 0.68$) groups.

Our third repeated measures analysis did not yield a main effect, nor a significant typology x episode interaction, for maternal resignation/anxiety across the Still Face episodes.

There was general support for our hypotheses. Mothers in the balanced group demonstrated the highest levels of positive affect, and as predicted, this difference only reached significance in the context of infant distress. Results for displays of angry/hostile behavior yielded a very interesting interaction, such that the anger and hostility displayed by the disengaged mothers decreased from the first to the final Still Face episode, possibly revealing the mothers' tendency to increasingly "disengage" and grow less responsive to their children as their children grew more distressed. Conversely, distorted mothers, who likely experienced heightened affective arousal themselves as their infants grew more distressed, increased in their level of angry/hostile across the episodes. These results appear to be consistent with the findings of Goldberg, MacKay-Soroka, and Rochester (1994), and suggest that balanced mothers respond to the full range of infant emotion with more acceptance and optimism. It appears that mothers with balanced representations had more effective emotion regulation strategies, and thus were better able to cope with their own distress, decreasing their display of positive affect over the course of the Still Face episodes (presumably in an appropriate response to the infants' increased distress), but not increasing in their display of anger or hostility. Mothers in the disengaged and distorted groups, however, appear to utilize less optimal deactivating and heightening strategies in response to infant distress, respectively. Results for the distorted group are particularly interesting in light of the Gergely and Watson (1996) suggestion that certain mothers may "mirror" infant distress too closely, thus failing to provide the infant with the necessary containment and sense of being able to cope with such upset.

"Getting the Message": Links between Mothers' Representations, Affective Displays, and Infant Emotion Regulation

Were these emotional messages received by the infant? We expected that the affective tone of mothers' representations would be linked with infant emotion expression during the Still Face procedure. Specifically, we expected higher levels of joy in the mothers' WMCI narrative to be linked with higher levels of infant positive affect, and higher levels of anger/hostility or resignation/anxiety in the mothers' representations to be linked with more infant negative affect. Results of correlational analyses, however, did not support this assumption; there were no significant correlations between mothers' affective tone in the representation and infant emotion displayed during the Still Face procedure.

Elsewhere, we have published data regarding links between the mothers' representational typology classification and infant emotion regulation strategies across the Still Face procedure (see Rosenblum et al., 2002). In contrast to the results for affective tone, we found mothers' representation typologies were indeed associated with differences in infant emotion displayed during the Still Face procedure. Most notably, during the Reengagement infants of mothers with balanced representations demonstrated more positive affect than infants of mothers in either of the other two categories. There was a significant typology x Still Face episode interaction, such that while all infants displayed lower levels of positive affect during the Still Face, only infants of mothers in the balanced representation category returned to high levels of positive affect upon resuming interaction. Maternal positive affect during the Reengagement mediated the association between mothers' representations and infant positive affect during the Still Face Reengagement.

There is, therefore, some support for the notion that mothers representations and infant emotion regulation strategies are linked, and that maternal emotion displays mediate these associations. However, these results were obtained only for mothers' internal working models of the relationship assessed via the typology score, and not for solitary indicators of the affective tone of the representation. This finding underscores the importance of assessing both the affective and cognitive elements of the working model in order to fully understand how they function together to regulate maternal affective behavior and influence the infants' emotional development. These results also highlight the important and unique role played by positive emotions in developing effective self-regulation strategies.

Conclusions

Relationships are affective bonds and parenting is an emotionally rich experience. In this chapter we have presented evidence from our own work that suggests that parents' working models of their infants serve as emotion regulators, influencing several aspects of parenting, in particular, emotion activation and engagement processes. Our data indicate that parents' representations of their infants, coupled with the emotion-communications that infants experience on a day-to-day basis, influence the infants' emerging self-regulatory capacities. It appears likely that parents' representations underlie this process, influencing not only the way the parent responds at the internal level to the infants' behavioral cues, but also the manner in which the parent responds at the behavioral level to the child during interaction.

Consistent with the work of others who have identified infants' display of positive affect during the Still Face as a predictor of subsequent social-emotional adjustment, our data underscore the importance of parents' positive emotions, both at the level of representation and during interaction with the infant. While a great deal of research has identified problematic or worrisome parenting behaviors defined in terms of the presence of negative, hostile, or rejecting communications, it may be equally important to identify the parents' capacity to experience joy or express positive emotions during interaction with the infant. Parents' parenting representations appear to reflect their ability to contain anxiety and use positive emotion to help their infants regulate distress during a challenging interactive task. Parents' success in using positive emotions to self-regulate is likely to influence their infants' capacity to tolerate expression of both positive and negative emotions, as well as the likelihood that they will use the caregiver to help down-regulate feelings of distress during separation.

The Still Face procedure provides a unique opportunity to observe individual differences in mother–infant interaction in a structured, standardized context. Both the Strange Situation and the Still Face procedure allow examination of the dyads capacity to engage in the process of interactive repair, that is, how the mother and infant negotiate reengagement following a temporary disruption and imposed maternal unavailability. Furthermore, the Still Face allows for observation of interaction during both low and high challenge situations. In our research, we have found that mothers' internal working models of the infant and of the relationship interact with qualities of the task demands, such that low and high challenge situations pull differently for affective displays depending on the quality of the representation.

Given the vast number of expressive interchanges that occur between mother and infant during the first months of life (Magai, 1999), the influence of mothers' working models of their infants as emotion regulators during early interactive episodes is likely to hold significant consequences for infant emotional development, in particular, the development of the infants' own internal working models of relationships. How the mother internally represents the infant and the relationship with the infant thus constitutes an integral part of the complex web of relational experience from which the infant develops his or her own social-emotional self.

Appendix 4.1
The Working Model of the Child Interview

The interview used for research described in the present chapter is a modified version (Rosenblum, Muzik, & Dayton, 2002) of the "Working Model of the Child Interview" (WMCI; Zeanah & Benoit, 1995). The WMCI is a semi-structured interview designed to capture a parent's internalized perceptions and subjective experience of their child's personality and relationship with their child. A number of adaptations to the Zeanah and Benoit (1995) interview were made, including omitting questions regarding early infant development, and inserting questions regarding current family experiences that the parent perceives as particularly stressful or difficult. The WMCI requires an average of one hour to complete and interviews are audio-taped and transcribed for coding purposes.

Validity

Extant research on the WMCI indicates good external validity, with links to infant attachment classification and clinical status. For example, Benoit, Parker, and Zeanah (1997) found high degrees of correspondence between WMCI classifications and 12-month-old Strange Situation attachment classifications, both for prenatal WMCI classifications (reported concordance 74% compared to 54% expected by chance) and WMCI classifications based on interviews conducted when infants were 11 months old (reported concordance 73% compared to 55% expected by chance). Similarly, Sims, Hans, and Bernstein (1996) examined correspondence between WMCI ratings and 18-month-old attachment status among a sample of high-risk, inner city African American mothers, and found significant associations between WMCI ratings and infant attachment security. Specifically, mothers whose WMCI classification was "balanced" (corresponding to the AAI autonomous pattern) were more likely to have infants classified as secure on the Strange Situation (reported concordance 64%). The degree of correspondence between WMCI and SS classifications reported by Sims et al. (1996) is somewhat lower than reported by Benoit, Parker, and Zeanah (1997); this may be in part due to the lower number of "balanced" mothers and "secure" infants in the former, high-risk study sample.

The WMCI has also been found to reliably discriminate clinical versus non-clinical samples of infants (e.g., Coolbear & Benoit, 1999; Benoit, Zeanah,

Parker, Nicholson, & Coolbear, 1997). For example, Benoit et al. (1997) reviewed results from a series of studies comparing the WMCI classifications of a sample of mothers of infants with sleep disorders, failure-to-thrive, or mothers of infants being seen in a general psychiatric clinic to the WMCI classifications of a matched, non-psychiatric control group. Clinical subjects were more likely to have non-balanced representations of the infant; however, the authors did not observe group differences between the two subtypes of non-balanced classifications.

Sample WMCI Questions

Parents are asked to describe in detail their child's individual characteristics, personality and development, as well as characteristics of their relationship with their child. They are also asked to describe their own emotional reactions and behavior in response to their child in a variety of pleasurable and challenging contexts. The interview is designed to activate both semantic and episodic memory systems in addition to eliciting a wide range of potentially emotionally laden reactions and experiences. Following are some sample questions from the WMCI, selected to illustrate questions focused on the child's personality and behavior, the relationship with the child, the parents' openness to change and future expectations, and integrative questions.

Child's personality and behavior
- Describe what you think of your child's personality now. What is s/he like?
- I'd like you to pick five words or phrases to describe your child's personality. *Followed by*:
  - What is it about [your child] that makes you say that?
  - Now can you please give me a specific example that would illustrate what you mean by [word/phrase]?
- What about your child's behavior now is the most difficult for you to handle? Can you give me a typical example? *Followed by*:
- What do you feel like doing when your child reacts this way?
- How do you feel when your child reacts this way?
- What do you actually do?

Future expectations

- When you worry about [your child] what do you worry most about?
- As you look ahead, what will be the most difficult time in your child's development?

Integrative questions

- How do you feel your relationship with your child has affected your child's personality?
- Knowing what you know now, if you started all over again with your child, what would you do differently?

Coding

The coding scheme presented here is drawn largely from the system developed by Zeanah and Benoit (1995) for use with the WMCI. While Zeanah and Benoit have developed a "coherence" scale for use with the WMCI, in our work we have assessed the parent's narrative coherence using scales drawn from the Family Story Collaborative Project (FSCP; Fiese et al., 1999). Additional scales were developed by the present authors for use on the Michigan Family Study (Rosenblum, Muzik, & Dayton, 2002).

All of the dimensions coded from the narrative transcripts were scored along a five-point scale reflecting the characteristic level of each quality across the entire interview; thus, each parent received only one score for each scale. Each dimension is scored such that higher values reflect the greater presence of the quality reflected in the scale title. Following is a brief description of each of the WMCI scales being used for the present investigation.

Eighteen scales were scored, each falling into one of three broad categories. 1) *Infant- and relationship-salient codes* capture specific aspects (both manifest and latent) of the parent/infant relationship; 2) *Narrative coherence codes* assess the organization and internal consistency of the narrative; and 3) *Affective tone codes* reflect the differential "affective coloring" of the representation.

I. Infant- and Relationship-Dimensions of the Representation

Richness of Perception (Zeanah & Benoit, 1995)

Assesses how richly elaborated the descriptions of the infant are, with higher scores reflecting the parent's greater sense of "knowing" and "being able to describe" the infant.

Caregiving Sensitivity (Zeanah & Benoit, 1995)

Reflects the parent's ability to recognize and respond to the infant's emotional and physical needs and experiences. High scores reflect the parent's recognition of the infant as experiencing a range of emotional states and biological needs, and a consistent, convincing willingness to respond to these needs.

Acceptance of the Infant (Zeanah & Benoit, 1995)

Captures the degree to which the parent's representation of the infant is colored by rejection (low ratings) or acceptance and genuine delight in the infant (high ratings).

Resentment of the Parenting Role (Rosenblum, Muzik, & Dayton, 2002)

Indicates the degree to which the parent feels overburdened by and resentful of the parenting role, with high scores reflecting greater resentment and low scores reflecting acceptance and enjoyment of the parenting process.

Intensity of Involvement (Zeanah & Benoit, 1995)

Assesses the caregiver's psychological preoccupation with the infant and/or the caregiver's psychological immersion in the relationship and in parenting. High scores reflect clear, consistent, and striking affective engrossment, while low scores reflect a lack of psychological involvement with the infant.

Infant Difficulty (Zeanah & Benoit, 1995)

Reflects the caregiver's perception of the infant as difficult to care for and understand. Scores reflect both direct statements made by the caregiver, as well as indirect indications (e.g., sarcasm, hostility) that the caregiver experiences the infant as difficult.

Openness to Change (Zeanah & Benoit, 1995)

Reflects the flexibility of the representation to accommodate new information about the infant. Scores at the low end of the scale reflect rigidity of the caregiver's perceptions, and a sense that the caregiver would resist incorporating new information in order to maintain a particular point of view.

Helplessness in Parenting (Rosenblum, Muzik, & Dayton, 2002)

Captures the degree to which the parent experiences herself as being vulnerable or helpless. Parents with high scores tend to describe themselves as inadequate, lacking resources, or powerless in response to the infant and parenting demands. On the low end of this scale, parents appear highly effi-cacious and able to cope with almost all situations.

Impact of Regulatory Processes on Parental Functioning (Rosenblum, Muzik, & Dayton, 2002)

Indicates whether the mother has explicitly reported concern regarding her infant's crying, sleeping, or feeding behavior, with high scores reflecting the degree to which concerns about the infant's behavior have begun to affect the parent's feelings about the infant, or the relationship between the parent and infant.

II. Narrative Coherence

Internal Consistency (Fiese et al., 1999)

Refers to the presence or absence of contradictions in the parent's narrative. Narratives rich in uncontradicted detail that include synthesizing statements regarding the parent's perception and experience of the infant score at the high end, while parents who make contradictory statements regarding their perceptions of the infant, or who fail to support their generalizations with convincing evidence receive low scores.

Organization (Fiese et al., 1999)

Refers to the structure and "understandability" of the narrative. Organized narratives are concise, on-topic, and the story being told is easily understood. Indices of low organization include the tendency to wander off topic, make unexplained references, and provide too much information. The subject may need the assistance of the interviewer in order to make the narrative understandable.

III. Affective Tone of the Representation of the Child (Zeanah & Benoit, 1995)

A series of scales are scored in order to assess the affective tone of the care-giver's representation of the infant, or the degree to which the rater perceives the particular affective tone "colors" the caregiver's representation of the infant. Low scores reflect the absence of the affective quality in the narrative, while high scores reflect extreme coloring of the representation by the partic-ular affective quality. Note that these scores are not based on what the parent says per se, but rather, the rater's perception that the representation is characterized by each particular affective quality. The following affective scales were scored: *Joy, Anger, Anxiety, Indifference, Sadness, Guilt,* and *Fear for Infant's Safety.*

WMCI Typology Classifications (Zeanah & Benoit, 1995)

In addition to the 18 individual scale dimensions, each narrative was assigned to one of three categories, which represent different representational typologies.

Balanced

Balanced representations are characterized by emotional warmth and acceptance, sensitive responsiveness to infant needs, coherence, and richly detailed, accessible descriptions. These parents seem to "know" their infant in an essential way, and provide convincing details and experiences that convey their involvement in the relationship and delight in the infant. Although parents in the balanced category may experience feelings of challenge or difficulty in parenting the infant, such issues and concerns do not overwhelm the parents' ability to cope, and have not come to dominate the parents' perception of the infant. Characteristic of this group of parents is the accessibility of a range of emotions, without the need to minimize or the tendency to be overwhelmed by the experience of feelings regarding the infant and the relationship.

Disengaged

Disengaged representations are characterized by an emotional aloofness and distance from the infant. Parents in this category are likely to describe their infant in a manner that minimizes psychological involvement, and may reveal the parents' rejection of the infant's emotional and dependency needs. They may idealize the relationship with the infant, but are often unable to support these idealizations with specific episodic memory accounts. Repressed hostility and anger are frequent, manifesting in the form of cool distancing and rejection of the infant.

Distorted

Distorted representations are characterized broadly by a distortion imposed on the representation of the infant and/or the relationship with the infant. Parents in this category are often very incoherent, in the sense of providing confused, contradictory, or bizarre descriptions of the infant and the relationship. Parents in the distorted category may be confused and unsure about their relationship with the infant, or anxiously overwhelmed by the infant's perceived needs and experiences. They may be role-reversed in the relationship with the infant, describing the young baby as a "buddy" and "confidant," thus revealing a tendency to place the emotional burden of the relationship on the infant.

References

Ainsworth, M. D. S., Blehar, M. C., Waters, E., & Wall, S. (1978). *Patterns of Attachment: A Psychological Study of the Strange Situation*. Hillsdale, NJ: Erlbaum.

Appelbaum, M. I., Butterfield, P. M., & Culp, R. E. (1993). Operating characteristics and psychometric properties of the IFEEL pictures. In Emde, Osofsky, & Butterfield (Eds.), *The IFEEL Pictures: A New Instrument for Interpreting Emotions*. Madison, CT: International Universities Press, pp. 97–126.

Benoit, D. & Parker, K. C. H. (1994). Stability and transmission of attachment across three generations. *Child Development, 65*, 1444–56.

Benoit, D., Parker, K. C. H., & Zeanah, C. H. (1997). Mothers' representations of their infants assessed prenatally: Stability and association with infants' attachment classifications. *Journal of Child Psychology and Psychiatry and Allied Disciplines, 38*, 307–13.

Benoit, D., Zeanah, C. H., Parker, K. C. H., Nicholoson, E., & Coolbear, J. (1997). "Working Model of the Child Interview": Infant clinical status related to maternal perceptions. *Infant Mental Health Journal, 18*, 107–21.

Biringen, Z. Matheny, A., Bretherton, I., Renouf, A., & Sherman, M. (2000). Maternal representation of the self as parent: Connections with maternal sensitivity and maternal structuring. *Attachment & Human Development, 2*, 218–32.

Bowlby, J. ({1969} 1982). *Attachment and Loss. Vol. I. Attachment*. New York: Basic Books.

Braungart-Rieker, J. M., Garwood, M. M., Powers, B. P., & Wang, X. (2001). Parental sensitivity, infant affect, and affect regulation: Predictors of later attachment. *Child Development, 72*, 252–70.

Bretherton, I. (2000). Emotional availability: An attachment perspective. *Attachment & Human Development, 2*, 233–41.

Butterfield, P. M., Emde, R. N., & Osofsky, J. D. (1987). *IFEEL Pictures Manual*. The Regents of the University of Colorado.

Cassidy, J. (1994). Emotion regulation: Influences of attachment relationships. In N. Fox (Ed.), *Biological and Behavioral Foundations of Emotion Regulation. Monographs of the Society for Research in Child Development, 59*, 228–49.

Cohn, J. F., Campbell, S. B., & Ross, S. (1991) Infant response in the still-face paradigm at 6 months predicts avoidant and secure attachment at 12 months. *Development and Psychopathology, 3*, 367–76.

Coolbear, J. & Benoit, D. (1999). Failure to thrive: Risk for clinical disturbance of attachment. *Infant Mental Health, 20*, 87–104.

Cummings, E. M. & Davies, P. (1996). Emotional security as a regulatory process in normal development and the development of psychopathology. *Development and Psychopathology, 8*, 123–39.

Derryberry, D. & Reed, M. A. (1996). Regulatory processes and the development of cognitive representations. *Development and Psychopathology, 8*, 215–34.

DeWolff, M. & van IJzendoorn, M. H. (1997). Sensitivity and attachment: A metaanalysis on parental antecedents of infant attachment. *Child Development, 68*, 571–91.

Dix, T. (1991). The affective organization of parenting: Adaptive and maladaptive processes. *Psychological Bulletin, 110*, 3–25.

Egeland, B. & Farber, E. A. (1984). Infant-mother attachment: Factors related to its development and changes over time. *Child Development, 55*, 753–71.

Emde, R. N. (2000). Next steps in emotional availability research. *Attachment & Human Development, 2*, 242–8.

Erikson, E. (1985). *Childhood and Society, 35th Anniversary Edition*. New York: W.W. Norton.

Field, T. (1994). The effects of mother's physical and emotional unavailability on emotion regulation. In N. A. Fox (Ed.), *The Development of Emotion Regulation: Biological and Behavioral Considerations. Monographs of the Society for Research in Child Development, 59* (2–3, Serial No. 240), 208–27.

Field, T., Vega-Lahr, N., Scafidi, F., & Goldstein, S. (1986). Effects of maternal unavailability on mother-infant interactions. *Infant Behavior and Development, 9*, 473–8.

Fiese, B. H., Sameroff, A. J., Grotevant, H. D., Wamboldt, F. S., Dickstein, S., & Fravel, D. L. (1999). The stories that families tell: Narrative coherence, narrative interaction, and relationship beliefs. *Monographs of the Society for Research in Child Development, 64* (2, serial no. 257).

Fonagy, P. (1999). Psychoanalytic theory from the viewpoint of attachment theory and research. In J. Cassidy & P. Shaver (Eds.), *Handbook of Attachment: Theory, Research, and Clinical Applications*. New York: Guilford Press, pp. 595–624.

Fonagy, P., Steele, H., & Steele, M. (1991). Maternal representations of attachment during pregnancy predict the organization of infant-mother attachment at one year of age. *Child Development, 62*, 891–905.

Fredrickson, B. (1998). What good are positive emotions? *Review of General Psychology, 2*, 300–19.

Frijda, N. H. (1986). *The Emotions*. Cambridge: Cambridge University Press.

Garner, P. W. (1995). Toddlers' emotion regulation behaviors: The roles of social context and family expressiveness. *The Journal of Genetic Psychology, 156*, 417–30.

George, C., Kaplan, N., & Main, M. (1985). *Adult Attachment Interview*. Unpublished manuscript, University of California, Berkeley.

Gergely, G. & Watson, J. S. (1996). The social biofeedback theory of parental affect-mirroring: The development of emotional self-awareness and self-control in infancy. *International Journal of Psychoanalysis, 77*, 1181–212.

Goldberg, S., MacKay-Soroka, S., & Rochester, M. (1994). Affect, attachment, and maternal responsiveness. *Infant Behavior and Development, 17*, 335–9.

Grossman, K., Grossman, K. E., Spangler, G., Suess, G., & Unzer, L. (1985). Maternal sensitivity and newborns' orientation responses as related to quality of attachment in northern Germany. In I. Bretherton & E. Waters (Eds.), Growing points of attachment theory and research. *Monographs of the Society for Research in Child Development, 50* (1–2, Serial No. 209), 233–57.

Haft, W. L. & Slade, A. (1989). Affect attunement and maternal attachment: A pilot study. *Infant Mental Health Journal, 10*, 157–72.

Kogan, N. & Carter, A. S. (1996). Mother-infant reengagement following the Still-Face: The role of maternal emotional availability in infant affect regulation. *Infant Behavior and Development, 19*, 359–70.

Lazarus, R. S. (1991). *Emotion and Adaptation*. New York: Oxford University Press.

Magai, C. (1999). Affect, imagery, and attachment: Working models of interpersonal affect and the socialization of emotion. In J. Cassidy & P. Shaver (Eds.), *Handbook of Attachment: Theory, Research, and Clinical Applications*. New York: Guilford Press, pp. 787–802.

Mahler, M. S., Pine, F., & Bergman, A. (1975). *The Psychological Birth of the Human Infant: Symbiosis and Individuation*. New York: Basic Books.

Main, M., Kaplan, N., & Cassidy, J. (1985). Security in infancy, childhood, and adulthood: A move to the level of representation. In I. Bretherton & E. Waters (Eds.), Growing points of attachment theory and research. *Monographs of the Society for Research in Child Development, 50* (1–1, Serial No. 209), 66–106.

Mayes, L. C., Carter, A. S., Egger, H. L., & Pajer, K. A. (1991). Reflections on stillness: Mothers' reactions to the still-face situation. *Journal of the American Academy of Child and Adolesecent Psychiatry, 30*, 22–8.

McDonough, S. C. (1994). *Preventing mental health problems in multirisk infants*. National Institute of Mental Health RO1 Grant Proposal, University of Michigan.

Miller, A., McDonough, S., Rosenblum, K. L., & Sameroff, A. J. (2002). Emotion regulation in context: Situational effects on infant and caregiver behavior. *Infancy, 3*, 403–33.

Milligan, K., Atkinson, L., Trehub, S. E., Benoit, D., & Poulton, L. (2003). Maternal attachment and the communication of emotion through song. *Infant Behavior and Development, 26*, 1–13.

Rosenblum, K. L., McDonough, S., Muzik, M., Miller, A., & Sameroff, A. (2002). Maternal representations of the infant: Associations with infant response to the Still Face. *Child Development, 73*, 999–1015.

Rosenblum, K. L., Muzik, M., & Dayton, C. A. (2002). *Working Model of the Infant Interview: 7-Month Version – Revised*. Unpublished manuscript: University of Michigan, Ann Arbor.

Sameroff, A. J. & Emde, R. (1989). *Relationship Disturbances in Early Childhood: A Developmental Approach*. New York: Basic Books.

Sims, B. E., Hans, S. L., & Bernstein, V. (1996, April). *Inner City Mothers' Working Models of Their Toddlers*. Paper presented at the 10th biennial meetings of the International Conference on Infant Studies, Providence, Rhode Island.

Slade, A., Belsky, J., Aber, J. L., & Phelps, J. L. (1999). Mothers' representations of their relationships with their toddlers: Links to adult attachment and observed mothering. *Developmental Psychology, 35*, 611–19.

Solomon, J. & George, C. (1996). Defining the caregiving system: Toward a theory of caregiving. *Infant Mental Health Journal, 17*, 183–97.

Sroufe, L. A. (1995). *Emotional Development: The Organization of Emotional Life in the Early Years*. Cambridge, UK: Cambridge University Press.

Stern, D. N. (1985). *The Interpersonal World of the Infant: A View from Psychoanalysis and Developmental Psychology*. New York: Basic Books.

Stern, D. N. (1989). The representation of relational patterns: Developmental considerations. In A. J. Sameroff & R. N. Emde (Eds.), *Relationship Disturbances in Early Childhood*. New York: Basic Books, pp. 52–69.

Thompson, R. (1990). Emotion and self-regulation. In R. A. Thompson (Ed.), *Nebraska Symposium on Motivation, 1988: Socioemotional Development*. Lincoln: University of Nebraska Press, pp. 367–467.

Thompson, R. & Lamb, M. E. (1984). Assessing qualitative dimensions of emotional responsiveness in infants: Separation reactions in the Strange Situation. *Infant Behavior and Development, 7*, 423–45.

Tronick, E. Z. (1989). Emotions and emotional communication in infants. *American Psychologist, 44*, 112–19.

van IJzendoorn, M. H. (1995). Adult attachment representations, parental responsiveness, and infant attachment: A meta-analysis on the predictive validity of the Adult Attachment Interview. *Psychological Bulletin, 117*, 387–403.

Weinberg, K. M. & Tronick, E. Z. (1996). Infant affective reactions to the resumption of maternal interaction after the still-face. *Child Development, 67*, 905–14.

Winnicott, D. (1965). *The Maturational Processes and the Facilitating Environment*. New York: International Universities Press.

Zeanah, C. H. & Benoit, D. (1995). Clinical applications of a parent perception interview in infant mental health. *Infant Psychiatry, 4*, 539–54.

Zeanah, C. H., Benoit, D., Barton, M., Regan, C., Hirschberg, L. M., & Lipsitt, L. (1993). Representations of attachment in mothers and their one-year-old infants. *Journal of the American Academy of Child and Adolescent Psychiatry, 32*, 278–86.

Zimmermann, P. (1999). Structure and functions of internal working models of attachment and their role for emotion regulation. *Attachment and Human Development, 3*, 291–306.

5 The Dual Viewpoints of Mother and Child on Their Relationship

A Longitudinal Study of Interaction and Representation

Anat Scher, Judith Harel, Miri Scharf, and Liora Klein

Abstract

This chapter addresses behavioral and representational facets of the mother–child emotional tie at two developmental periods: towards the end of infancy and towards school entry. Using data from a longitudinal study with low-risk mothers and infants (Scher, 1991), we examined the predictive validity of mothers' sensitivity when playing with their 12-month-olds to parenting representations at age six years. The Attachment Story Completion Task (Bretherton, Ridgeway, & Cassidy, 1990) was administered to 42 children; their mothers ($n = 26$) participated in the Parent Development Interview (Aber et al., 1985). It was found that high maternal sensitivity during infancy was a precursor of mother's representations of her parenting competency, provision of secure base, and low levels of negative emotionality. Higher levels of negative emotionality, described by the mothers, correlated concurrently with more negative representations of the maternal figure in the narratives of the children. Mothers' sensitivity to the child's feelings correlated with more frequent representations of the mother as a protective figure in the children's stories. The links over time and across domains and perspectives are considered within the frameworks of attachment theory and psychoanalytic approaches.

The study of parenting is a fast-growing field that has yielded a comprehensive body of knowledge, with diverse perspectives (see Bornstein, 2002). Yet many questions remain unanswered on the interplay between the behavioral and representational levels in parent–child relationships. Two areas that require further research are (a) the extent to which parent–child interactions during infancy are precursors of later parent–child relationships and their representations, and (b) the contribution of parenting behavior and representations to the child's mental representation of the relationships.

149

This chapter sets out to address these aspects concurrently, as well as across time. Findings are presented from a longitudinal study, a major feature of which was the inclusion of the perspective of the child and the parent, in this case – the mother.

The study focused on behavioral and representational facets of the mother–child emotional tie at two developmental periods: towards the end of infancy and toward school entry. Two main issues were addressed. The first concerned the predictive validity of the early mother–infant interaction at 12 months for mother's and child's later representations of the relationship. The relational constructs included the views of mothers and children. The second issue was the convergence between the mother's and the child's representations of the caregiving tie. To elucidate these matters, we first frame the research within a broad theoretical perspective, based on psychoanalytic and attachment theories of relationships and their mental representations, and discuss previous research that shaped our investigation.

Representations of Parent–Child Relationships, Their Function and Development

Representations of self, other, and their relationship emerge from the interaction between self and other, as described in attachment theories and object-relations psychoanalytic theories of development (Blatt & Lerner, 1983; Bowlby, 1988; Bretherton, 1985; Sandler & Sandler, 1998; Stern, 1985; Main, Kaplan, & Cassidy, 1985). The notion of "representations" was introduced into the psychoanalytic literature by Edith Jacobson (1964). She discussed self and other representations, based on the child's experience with the caregiver, as key determinants of mental functioning. The "representation" as conceptualized by Jacobson is the experiential impact of external and internal worlds, and is subject to distortions. Her "representation" is close to Bowlby's (1973) concept of Internal Working Models of Relationships. An important difference is Jacobson's emphasis on the influence of the "internal world" on representations. Generally, psychoanalytic theories and attachment theories differ as to the relative importance of actual, observable interaction vs. fantasized interactions in regard to the development of relational representations (Fonagy, 2001; Stern, 1989). Psychoanalytic theories, following Jacobson, emphasize the influence of fantasy, whereas attachment theory underscores the influence of real interactions.

Representations affect and shape the child's developing personality, and serve as guidelines for future interactions and future representations. Stern

(1985; 1995) described a system in which interaction and representation influence each other, and characterized the mother–infant interaction as "the meeting ground" between the mother's and the infant's representations. Representations guide their everyday interactions by giving meaning to their behavior; further, according to the behaviors of the two, existing representations are updated, or new ones are created. Representations and interactions are mutually influenced and changed, in well-adjusted dyads. A degree of compatibility between them is expected, as well as between the child's and the mother's representations of their relationship. The child's earliest representations are pre-symbolic in form and represent the mother–baby *relationship*. From these the child builds the representations of self and of the mother. Studies of the earliest representations show that the infant is able to represent expected, characteristic interaction structures, including their temporal, spatial, and affective features (Beebe, Lachman, & Jaffe, 1997). Later representations become also symbolic (such as drawings) and/or verbal (Stern, 1985). The developmentally most advanced representation was described by Stern (1989) as "the narrative model," emerging in the third year of life. While the first models are non-conscious, non-verbal, private, and made up of subjectively experienced events, the narrative model is conscious, verbal, narratable, social, and made up of referents experienced via words.

Early studies of attachment patterns dealt mainly with the representations that the child was building, their antecedents, and their sequelae (Belsky & Cassidy, 1994; Cassidy, 1988). But the representation building process, during mother–child interactions, goes on for both participants. Thus, in mother–child interactions, two representational systems are created and recreated, the mother's and the child's (Bowlby, 1969; Bretherton & Munholland, 1999). Moreover, adults, even before they have a child, develop representations of one, which influence their child's representations of self, other, and their relationship (Ammaniti, 1991; Benoit et al., 1997b; Stern, 1991). With the accumulation of more studies that point to links between parental representations and psychopathology in children (e.g., Bornstein, 1993; Solomon & George, 2000), understanding maternal representations becomes a task shared by developmentalists and clinicians alike.

Maternal Representations

Mothers create rich and complex representations of the child, and as Stern (1991) suggests these include several "sets of representations": concerning the baby, concerning the mother, concerning the father, and many more. The most influential representational set in the first months of the baby's life, according to Stern (1995), is the mother's representation of her own mother. Indeed, maternal representations of relations were initially studied by the Adult Attachment Interview (AAI) (Main & Goldwyn, 1985) focusing on mother's representation of her relationship with her caregiver, and showing strong relations between mother's state of mind with regard to attachment (measured by the AAI) and the child's attachment pattern (van IJzendoorn, 1995). This focus on mothers' past as a potential factor in present mothering was compatible with the psychoanalytic view of object-relations, as clinically demonstrated in the work of Selma Fraiberg on "ghosts in the nursery" (Fraiberg, Adelson, & Shapiro, 1975). Her clinical studies powerfully showed the pathological influence of relations from the mother's past, interfering with the mother's capacity to know her baby, and causing her to repeat problematic past relations in her present interactions.

The importance of studying the mother's *present* subjective experience with her own child came to the fore only later, possibly because of the belated recognition of the influence of the infant on the mother–child relationship, and the conceptualization of this relationship as two-way. This view is a fundamental tenet of the more recent "relational perspective" in psychoanalysis (Mitchell, 2000), and is supported by research on normal (Stern, 1985) and pathological development (Sameroff & Emde, 1989). Still, relatively few studies have linked the child's development with the mother's subjective experiences, goals, and internal representations of her relationship with her child (Solomon & George, 2000), perhaps reflecting the view of the mother as an object for the child rather than a subject in her own right (Benjamin, 1995).

Subjective aspects of maternal representations, those more conscious (Raphael-Leff, 1983; 1993; Stern, 1995) and those less so (Brazelton & Cramer, 1991; Fraiberg et al., 1975; Lebovici, 1983), were discussed in object-relations theories as important antecedents of maternal behavior. Psychoanalytic theories of mother–child relationships assume that representations (conscious and unconscious) related to motherhood guide maternal behavior in interactions with the infant (Fraiberg et al., 1975; Lieberman & Pawl, 1993; Stern, 1985; 1995) and contribute to the infant's building of self, other, and self-with-other representations. Unlike attachment theory, the psychoanalytic perspective views representations as related to a wide array of maternal and child behaviors, beyond security/attachment issues.

As demonstrated in this volume and in previous studies (see a review by Mayseless, this volume), various groups found that parenting representations are associated with mothers' state of mind with regard to attachment

(Slade et al., 1999), with mothers' personality and behavior (Button, Pianta, & Marvin, 2001; Bretherton et al., 1989; George & Solomon, 1999), with mother–child interactions and child's attachment behavior (Aber et al., 1999; George & Solomon, 1999; Zeanah et al., 1993), as well as with the child's own representations (Bretherton et al., 1989).

Attachment and psychoanalytic theories similarly describe representations as *relatively* stable. They guide the interpretation of interpersonal situations and behavior in the present and influence future interactions, but they are also dynamic, changeable, and updated in accordance with development and altering circumstances (at least in individuals with flexible/coherent representations). This complex feature of representations calls for longitudinal studies to examine the links between representations and behavior at different time intervals, as well as the links between the representations of the two partners, the mother and the child. Clearly, the study of the match between mothers' representations of their relationship with their child and the ways the latter views this relationship is of utmost theoretical and clinical significance.

Child's Representations of Close Relationships

The child's representations were initially studied by the Strange Situation paradigm (Ainsworth et al., 1978), on the assumption that the child's behavior in the reunion episodes reflects her/his attachment pattern and thus the representation of the parent–child relationship. A vast body of research pointed to the importance of the infant's attachment pattern for a variety of developmental outcomes, (e.g., Cassidy & Shaver, 1999; Fonagy, 2001). To study relationship representations of children beyond infancy, narrative methods were developed (e.g., Fivush & Reese, 2001; Main et al., 1985). Pre-school children are already able to tell meaningful narratives about themselves and their relationships (Buchsbaum & Emde, 1990; Oppenheim, Emde, & Warren, 1997). The study of children's narratives as a window to their inner world has a long tradition in clinical practice, mainly through the stories told by children to the Children's Apperception Test pictures (CAT) (Bellak, 1954). The empirical study of narratives of young children uses a somewhat different technique, namely the child has to complete a story stem introduced by the experimenter and dramatized with the use of dolls and small props to enhance the child's motivation to participate (Bretherton, Ridgeway, & Cassidy, 1990; Buchsbaum & Emde, 1990; Woolgar, 1999).

Studies using children's narratives showed that these contain mainly positive themes and are relatively stable from three to five years of age (Luborsky, Luborsky, Diguer, et al., 1998); narratives of abused children contained more conflictual themes than those of children who had not suffered abuse (Toth et al., 2000); they also showed more negative representations of self and parent (Toth, Cicchetti, Macfie, Maughan, & Vanmeene, 2000). The child's representations have been linked to behavioral aspects too. Von Klitzing and colleagues (2000) showed that aggressive themes in children's narratives were correlated with behavior problems reported by parents and teachers in a large sample of twins. Oppenheim et al. (1997) reported a link between children's narratives and social-emotional adaptation. This link has been also demonstrated with older children. For example, Granot and Mayseless (2001) documented that secure children, aged nine to 11, showed better adjustment to school as reflected in teachers' reports of scholastic, emotional, social, and behavioral adjustment, as well as in peer-rated social status. These studies all support Stern's claims about the development of the "narrated self" in early childhood (1989), and point to the validity of children's narratives as a measure of the child's representation of self and other, and the links of these representations to the child's functioning.

Links Between the Mother's and the Child's Representations of Relationships

Bowlby (1973) postulated that representations of self and mother are complementary: a child who represents the self as loveable represents the mother as loving; one who represents the self as rejected and flawed represents the mother as rejecting. The models of self and other are transactional and dynamic, changing along with the child's development and transformations that the parent might experience. Since representations are built within mother–child interactions and are the basis for interpreting, experiencing, and anticipating interpersonal events, a certain degree of fit between the child's and the parent's representations of their relationship is important for a smooth interaction (Bretherton et al., 1989). Maternal representations of attachment are linked to the child's attachment, but only part of this link is transmitted via maternal behavior, for example, maternal sensitivity/responsiveness to the child (DeWolff & van IJzendoorn, 1997; Raval et al., 2001). Looking for alternative ways to explain the link between representations, and between representations of attachment and behavior, the concept of "metacognitive monitoring" or "reflective functioning" proved useful, as described below.

Moving from behaviors to representations, Main (1991) used the concept of "metacognitive monitoring" to explain the links between attachment representations of mother and child. This capacity enables the individual to "step back and consider his or her own cognitive processes as objects of thought or reflection" (1991; p. 35). The mother's metacognitive capacity is related to her attachment representation: a secure model is based on a higher metacognitive capacity than an insecure one. Mothers with more advanced metacognitive capacities are able to respond more adaptively to their children's attachment needs, promoting secure attachment in the child. Bridging psychoanalytic and attachment theories, Fonagy (2001) looked beyond metacognitive monitoring as a cognitive capacity and described the "reflective function" as the ability to regard oneself and the child as motivated by internal mental states (intentions, feelings, goals, memories, etc.). Analyzing responses to the AAI, Fonagy et al. (1991b) concluded that it was the caregivers' "reflective functioning" that explained the major part of the link between maternal and child attachment and, as they said later, also between attachment and sensitivity. Subsequent research demonstrated an association between the parent's capacity for reflective functioning and the caregiver's and the child's attachment pattern (Slade, Grienenberger, Bernbach, Levy, & Locker, 2001).

Parental representations of the child are an important factor in the child's developing representations of the self. Fonagy and Target (2003a) proposed that a child would develop a "theory of mind," the ability to understand the other and the self in mental terms, provided that the parent represented the child as having a mind. The child would identify with the parent's representation of him/her as a psychological (not just a physical) being and develop a mind of its own. Fonagy and Target (2003a) claim that this crucial developmental achievement is reached in the context of a secure attachment relationship; research has demonstrated a significant association between secure attachment of the mother and the child and the mother's capacity for "mind reading," operationalized as "reflective function" (Fonagy et al., 1991b; Fonagy et al., 2002).

Following the premise that interactions are the "meeting ground" between maternal and child's representations of the relationship, and that mothers bring to the interaction a richer repertoire of representations than the infant (Stern, 1985), studies searching for the antecedents of representations activated in the present mother–child dyad, looked in two main directions: a) earlier maternal representations, such as mother's representations of her relationship with her mother (van IJzendoorn, 1995), mother's prenatal representation of the infant (Ammaniti, 1991; Benoit, Parker, & Zeanah, 1997; Fonagy, Steele, & Steele, 1991), and b) the behavior of the mother in the context of dyadic interaction with her child (Biringen et al., 2000; Button, Pianta, & Marvin, 2001).

To recap, an extensive theoretical base, namely attachment and psychoanalytical theories, suggest a link between parental behavior and the representations that parents and children develop of their relationship. These theories also suggest a link between the mother's and the child's representations of the relationship. Only a handful of studies have addressed these issues and examined them across time, and only a few include the dual viewpoints of parent and child. Our study set out to address the predictive validity of early mother–child quality of interaction to later mental representations of the relationship by mothers and children.

The Study

In line with the themes just presented, two hypotheses were formulated: (a) maternal sensitivity during infancy will predict mothers' parenting representations as the child approaches school age, and (b) the child's representation of the mother–child relationship will be associated with early maternal sensitivity as well as with the concurrent maternal parenting representations. To address these hypotheses, we present data from a longitudinal study with low-risk Israeli mothers and their children. The first data wave was of observations of mothers' behavior when playing with their 12-month-olds, gathered in the course of an investigation that focused on sleep in the first year (Scher, 1991). The second data collection, assembled when the children were aged six, consisted of interviews with the mothers that focused on parenting representations (Aber et al., 1985). At age six, the children were screened developmentally (WIPPSI), and their mental representation of the caregiving tie was assessed by means of the Attachment Story Completion Task (Bretherton, Ridgeway, & Cassidy, 1990).

Research Design and Participants

The original sample included 118 low-risk mothers and their healthy infants (49% boys, 39% first-born) recruited in the maternity ward of a general hospital in Israel. Mothers' mean age was 29 ($SD = 4.6$), and the mean education level was 14 ($SD = 2.5$) years. Forty-two of the children (20 boys and 22 girls) participated in a developmental assessment, at the age of six. A comparison of the latter group with the children who did not take part in the session at age six showed that the two groups were alike in terms of demographic and child factors. As to maternal variables, the mothers who participated the second time tended to show higher sensitivity when interacting with their infants ($t = 1.91$, $p = 0.06$); otherwise the two groups were not different.

The first-year data included various measures that were collected at home and in the laboratory. For the purpose of the present chapter, play observations, conducted in the laboratory at 12 months, and temperament data were examined. The assessment at age six was in two sessions. The first, held in the laboratory and included, among other procedures, a developmental test (WIPPSI) and the Attachment Story Completion Task. About a month later, the mothers were contacted by phone and were asked to take part in an interview. A home visit was then arranged. Thirty-two mothers were administered the Parenting Development Interview (Aber et al., 1985). To enhance reliability, the play observations in the first year, the child's developmental assessment, the Attachment Story Completion Task, and the parenting interview at six years were carried out by independent examiners who had no access to the records. To control for child's variables, infants' fussy temperament, rated by the mothers at nine months (ICQ) (Bates, Freeland, & Lounsbury, 1979), and the child's IQ at six years (WIPPSI-short version, Israeli norms) were included in the analyses. Overall, gender was not associated with the study's variables and thus, was not included in further analyses.

Mother–Infant Interaction at 12 Months

Mother–child interaction during play was coded using the *Parent-Child Early Relational Assessment* (PCERA) (Clark, 1985). A subset of 11 variables describing aspects of mother's behavior when interacting with her child was selected (for procedure and reliability, see Harel, Oppenheim, Tirosh, & Gini, 1999). The items (scored from 1-poor to 5-optimal) were grouped in two scales: *Maternal affect* measured the affective aspect of mother's behavior (enthusiastic, apathetic, anxious, angry; $\alpha = 0.66$); *Maternal sensitivity* scale measured mother's sensitive responsiveness and attunement to her child's behavior (flexible, non-intrusive, consistent, mirroring of positive behavior, contingent responsiveness, structuring and mediating, reading and appropriately responding to cues; $\alpha = 0.88$). The correlation between *sensitivity* and *affect* was $r = 0.58$, $p < 0.001$. These two maternal constructs were not correlated with the child's level of fussiness, as assessed by the ICQ.

Parenting Representations at Six Years

The Parent Development Interview (PDI) (Aber et al., 1985) is a 1.5-hour semi-structured interview in which parents are asked to describe their relationships with their child and themselves as parents. Questions center on pleasurable and difficult times with the child, and on the child's reactions to separations and routine upsets (for a more detailed description, see Steinberg & Pianta, this volume). The interviews were audiotaped and then transcribed verbatim. The coding system that was used is based on an adaptation previously presented by Scharf, Mayseless, and Kivenson-Baron (1998, 2000). As described, the coding had the benefit of several sources: primarily the seminal development of the AAI (Main & Goldwyn, 1985, 1998) and the works on parenting representations of parents to young children, in particular those by (alphabetically ordered) Aber, Benoit, Bretherton, George and Solomon, Marvin, Pianta, Slade, Zeanah, and their colleagues. In addition, the coding system relied on by Westen et al. (1991) and Fonagy et al. (1997) with regard to self-reflection and reflection about the child was used. Insights from the works of Coleman and Karraker (1998) with regard to parental competence and self-efficacy were also incorporated (Scharf, Mayseless, & Kivenson-Baron, 1998, 2000).

Based on the transcripts, the following domains were addressed: *representations of the self as a parent* (parental competence, self-understanding), *representations of the child* (trust, child's understanding, and richness of perception), *representations of the relationship* (sensitivity, positive feelings, autonomy, goal-directed partnership). The affective component of parents' representations of their caregiving was assessed, too. The *negative emotionality* scale consisted of a composite score of pain, anger, fear, and guilt feelings (each scored separately) in the representations of the relationship. Another construct that was operationally defined was mothers' *reflective capacity*, as measured by mothers' self-understanding and their understanding of the child (see Appendix 5.1). The cognitive and emotional narrative style (i.e., adequate, flooded, restricted) was also scored. Ten interviews were double coded. Inter-judge reliability of the scales (intra-class correlations between the two coders) ranged from 0.84 to 0.97. Agreement between coders on the profile classifications was 91.7% ($\chi^2 = 17.25$; $p = 0.002$; $\kappa = 0.84$). The narratives of 38% of the mothers were balanced ($n = 10$), 27% flooded ($n = 7$), and 35% restricted ($n = 9$).

To assess the associations among the different domains of mothers' parenting representations, we first examined the domains' internal consistency (see Table 5.1) and confirmed the reliability of the aggregated scales. The strong inter-correlations of the three parenting representation domains (parent, child, and relationships) indicated that mothers who expressed confidence in their parenting and were able to reflect on their actions/thoughts were also highly confident of the child's capacities, and were also high in the attribution of positive qualities of their relationship with the child (e.g., sensitivity, positive feelings, partnership). In accord with George and Solomon (1999), our dataset showed that competence in the parenting role and the provision of secure base overlapped. The negative emotionality index (consisting of pain, anger, fear, guilt) was only moderately correlated with the representation of

Table 5.1. *Reliability Coefficients, Inter-correlations among the Parenting Representation Scales, and Correlations with Child Variables*

	Parent ($\alpha = 0.83$)	Child ($\alpha = 0.94$)	Relationship ($\alpha = 0.90$)	Negative Emotionality ($\alpha = 0.73$)	Fussy ($n = 24$)	IQ ($n = 17$)
Parent's representations of herself		0.95***	0.92***	−0.34+	−0.01	0.26
Child's representations			0.92***	−0.28	−0.06	0.16
Relationships' representations				−0.41*	−0.04	0.21
Negative emotionality					0.07	−0.14
Balanced description	0.94***	0.95***	0.91***	−0.25	−0.02	0.11
Flooded description	−0.37+	−0.28	−0.36+	0.76***	−0.20	−0.16
Restricted description	−0.40*	−0.48**	−0.40*	−0.46*	0.12	0.03

$^+ p < 0.10$, $^* p < 0.05$, $^{***} p < 0.001$; $n = 26$

relationships ($r = -0.41, p < 0.05$). The associations between negative emotionality and mothers' representations of themselves, and between negative emotionality and the representations of the relationship, were not significant. Mothers' representations of themselves were positively associated with balanced description and negatively with restricted description; child and relationship representations were negatively associated with restricted description. Negative emotionality was associated positively with flooded description and negatively with restricted description.

Table 5.1 also presents Pearson correlation coefficients between the parenting representation domains and the child variables. As indicated, the temperament rating (fussiness: ICQ) was not associated with later maternal representations; similarly, the child's IQ at age six was not significantly related to mothers' parenting representations.

Mother–Infant Interaction and Parenting Representations

Table 5.2 presents the association between mothers' behavior in the play interaction at 12 months, as measured by the PCERA, and subsequent parenting representations. The table includes Pearson correlation coefficients of

Table 5.2. *Spearman Correlation Coefficients of Mother's Parenting Representations with Early Mother–Infant Interaction and with Child's Representations of the Mother Figure*

	Mother's Behavior		Child's Representations of the Mother			
	Sensitivity	Affect	Protector	Regulator	Positive	Negative
Parent's representations of herself						
Maternal competence	0.60***	0.03	0.38$^+$	0.09	0.07	−0.11
Self-understanding	0.43*	0.12	0.57**	0.13	0.05	0.03
Child's representations						
Richness of child's description	0.43*	0.13	0.69***	0.19$^+$	0.18	0.10
Confidence	0.48*	−0.05	0.54**	0.25	0.31	−0.07
Child's understanding	0.48**	0.04	0.58**	0.10	0.06	0.08
Relationships' representations						
Sensitivity	0.52**	0.10	0.55**	0.21	0.09	0.09
Positive feelings	0.57**	0.02	0.69***	0.28	0.33	0.02
Partnership	0.70***	0.24	0.50**	0.30	0.26	0.09
Autonomy encouragement	0.37$^+$	0.19	0.22	0.12	0.14	−0.27
Negative emotionality						
Pain	−0.28	−0.19	0.15	−0.09	−0.22	0.44*
Worry	−0.15	−0.01	−0.04	−0.29	−0.30	0.23
Anger	−0.32	−0.03	0.12	−0.06	0.02	0.40*
Guilt	−0.23	0.06	0.32	0.03	0.11	0.35$^+$
Aggregate scales						
Parent's representations	0.56**	0.09	0.51**	0.12	0.06	−0.04
Child's representations	0.49**	0.05	0.64***	0.19	0.20	0.04
Relationships' representations	0.61***	0.16	0.54**	0.25	0.23	−0.04
Negative emotionality	−0.31	−0.05	0.17	−0.13	−0.12	0.45*
Balanced description	0.45*	0.07	0.57**	0.21	0.09	0.07
Flooded description	−0.19	0.08	0.23	0.17	0.19	0.36$^+$
Restricted description	−0.24	−0.13	−0.65***	−0.36$^+$	−0.27	−0.41*

$^+ p < 0.10$, $^* p < 0.05$, $^{**} p < 0.01$, $^{***} p < 0.001$; $n = 26$

the maternal *sensitivity* and *affect* constructs with the 13 representation variables, with three process scales, and with the aggregated scales.

Higher sensitivity, observed during mother-infant interaction in infancy, showed moderate to strong association with parenting representation (mother, child, relationship). In contrast to the predictive validity of mothers' sensitivity, maternal affect was not correlated with the parenting representation variables. This result may be partially due to the positively skewed distribution and the low variability of maternal affect ($M = 4.54$; $SD = 0.32$; range 3.88–5.00; skewness $= −0.13$), as measured in the play context.

Representation of the Mother Figure by the Child

The Attachment Story Completion Task (Bretherton et al., 1990) was administered when the children were six years of age. The procedure consists of five
story beginnings that are narrated and acted out for the child (by the tester)
using small family figures (mother, father, two child figures, and grandmother)
and props, which the child is free to use as he/she chooses to complete the
story. The story-stems aim to provoke relationship themes: the spilled juice
story (authority), hurt knee (pain-protective behavior), monster in the bedroom (fear-protective behavior), parents go away (separation), parents return
(reunion). In our study, a female examiner introduced the story-stems and
then asked the child to "show what happens next." The task was administered
according to the standard protocol (Bretherton et al., 1990; pp. 300–5). It was
videotaped and transcribed for scoring (transcriptions included the narrated
story as well as non-verbal actions describing the behavior of the mother
figure, such as spanking or kissing). The enacted narratives were coded by
the guidelines developed by Oppenheim et al. (1997) for scoring children's
representations of maternal figures. All instances of children's descriptions
of maternal behaviors were listed and subsequently grouped according to
the emotional meaning of the behavior. When scoring the four story-stems
(the separation and reunion stories were scored as one story) with respect to
the child's representations of the mother figure, we first examined whether
or not the mother figure appeared in the child's story. Twenty-eight of the
42 children (67%) mentioned the mother in all four stories, 11 children (26%)
spoke about the mother in three of them, two (5%) did so in two of them, and
one child mentioned the mother in only one story.

Two coders scored all the transcribed narratives; inter-rater agreement was
0.93. In line with Oppenheim et al. (1997), we also differentiated positive
and negative representations of the mother figure. The *positive* representations included descriptions of the mother as a *protective, caring, regulating, affectionate, considerate, helpful, supportive,* and *forgiving* figure. The
negative representations showed her as *physically abusive, verbally abusive,
bizarre, inconsiderate,* and *ignoring.* For each story the number of positive
and of negative representations played by the mother figure was noted. The
representation scores consisted of the average number of roles played by
the mother per story. The positive score ranged from 0 to 2.50 ($M = 0.97$,
$SD = 0.55$), the negative from 0 to 0.75 ($M = 2$, $SD = 0.19$). The number
of positive roles assigned to the mother significantly exceeded the number
of negative representations ($t = 8.12, p < 0.001$). The positive and negative
representation scores did not correlate.

We were specifically interested in the depiction of the mother in the protective and regulating roles, as these pertain directly to the major function of caregiving according to some of the current conceptualizations of attachment theory (George & Solomon, 1999). Protection is related to mother protecting child from real or imagined dangers by removing the frightening stimulus or warning the child, and regulating concerns mothers' regulation of intense emotion, such as "go to bed – there's nothing here."

The mother as a protective figure appeared in the narratives of 69% of the children, and 45% of them attributed regulating qualities to the mother figure. Each child received scores pertaining to the representation of the mother as a *protector* and as a *regulator*, ranging from 0 (none of the stories) to 1 (the theme appeared in all stories – 0.25 for each story). The mean protector score was 0.20 ($SD = 0.17$, range 0–0.50) and the mean regulator score was 0.14 ($SD = 0.17$, range 0–0.50). The representation of the mother figure as a source of protection and regulation was particularly prevalent in the children's narrative about the "monster in the bedroom." The correlation between the two roles was $r = 0.47$, $p < 0.05$).

The Maternal Figure and Mothers' Parenting Variables

Table 5.2 presents the associations between early mother–infant interaction and subsequent children's representation of the mother figure. The concurrent association between mothers' own representations of their parenting and the child's representations are also shown. Mothers' sensitivity and affective tone when playing with their infants were not significantly associated with the way the child, at age six, represented the mother doll figure. Examination of mothers' and children's representations at six years showed no concordance between the overall prevalence of positive representations of the mother figure in the children's enacted stories and mothers' view of their own parenting. But the theme of the mother as *protective* figure appeared more often in the narratives of children of mothers whose parenting representations were more positive. Higher scores on children's protective representations of the mother figure were significantly correlated with mothers' representations of self as a parent, of the child, and of the relationship. Likewise, regarding the mothers' reflective capacity, the children's representations of the mother as a protector were positively associated with mothers' self-understanding and with their ability to understand the child's behavior and emotions.

The mother's and the child's views also concurred with respect to representations that involved the mother's negative emotionality and the child's negative representations. A higher score pertaining to the child's negative representation of the mother figure was significantly associated with more negative emotionality in the mothers' representations of their relationship with the child ($r = 0.45, p < 0.05$). Balanced description was associated with mothers' sensitivity (at age one year) and with portraying the mother as protecting, while restrictive description was negatively associated with portraying the mother as protector and negatively associated with child's negative representations. The representations of mothers whose children excluded the mother figure from their narrative were characterized as less rich in child's description ($M = 1.94, SD = 0.68$ versus $M = 2.78, SD = 1.07; F = 5.09$ $p < 0.05$) and less confident in the child ($M = 2.00, SD = 0.53$ versus $M = 2.75, SD = 1.09; F = 9.53, p < 0.01$). They also revealed less sensitivity ($M = 1.88, SD = 0.74$ versus $M = 2.72, SD = 0.94; F = 7.27, p < 0.01$) and less positive feeling toward the child ($M = 2.38, SD = 0.52$ versus $M = 3.19, SD = 0.91; F = 7.20, p < 0.01$). Their transcripts were also less balanced ($M = 1.50, SD = 1.04$ versus $M = 2.42, SD = 1.40; F = 9.03$, $p < 0.01$) than those of mothers whose children did not exclude the mother figure from the narrative.

To examine which of the maternal parenting representation domains (i.e., parent, child, relationship) contributed most to the prediction of the child's representation of the mother as a protective figure, we conducted a multiple step-wise regression. The two significant predictors of the protective score proved to be mothers' representations of child ($\beta = 0.24, t = 2.76, p < 0.01$) and negative emotionality in the representation of mother–child relationship ($\beta = 0.07, t = 2.22, p < 0.05$).

Discussion

Mothers' Sensitivity as a Precursor of Later Parenting Representations

This study showed that mothers' behavior in the mother–infant play interaction predicted aspects of mothers' parenting characteristics when the child reached six years of age. More specifically, the level of maternal sensitivity in play strongly correlated with maternal parenting representations, so that sensitive behavior predicted more competence in the self as a parent, more trust in the child's capacities, and a higher degree of emotional availability and partnership in the representations of the dyadic relationship. These findings suggest that maternal sensitivity in the first year might be an early behavioral expression of mothers' sense of competence as a parent, their capacity to mentalize and reflect coherently on their parenting, and to represent their child's feelings and emotions sensitively. In short, this longitudinal dataset highlighted an early behavioral marker of mothers' capacity to mentally represent their parenting.

The level of mothers' sensitivity when playing with their infant correlated negatively with negative emotionality in mothers' representations of their relationship with their six-year-old child. As highlighted by Slade et al. (1999), affect is an important aspect of mental models of caregiving relationships. By including negative emotionality as a unique dimension of parenting representations, the present study illuminated a significant, albeit moderate link between the level of maternal sensitivity, as manifested in early mother–infant interaction, and the degree of anxiety, fear, and guilt in subsequent representations of the mother–child relationship. Mothers who were more sensitive when playing with their one-year-old reported less worries and frustrations with respect to this child five years later. Similarly, Button et al. (2001), studying mothers' representations and behavior when interacting with disabled compared with control children, aged one to four years, found that representations of worry about the child's future were concurrently related to insensitive and unresponsive behavior by the mother. The authors suggested that this association reflects the ways in which mother's negative affective state compromises her capacity to read and respond sensitively to the child's cues. The longitudinal paradigm of the present study allows us cautiously to suggest that low sensitivity to the child's cues at 12 months of age may serve as a risk indicator for later negative emotionality in parent–child dynamics. If replicated, this finding is important from an intervention perspective.

The unraveling of the characteristics and functions of the representational facet of parenting has been a major task in theorizing and researching the meeting points between parenting and child development. To mention a few constructs that tap this capacity: "reflective function (Fonagy & Target, 2003b), insightfulness (Koren-Karie et al., 2002), and mind-mindedness (Meins, 1997), all of which are central to enhancing the child's well-being (Bohlin & Hagekull, 2000; Zeanah & Benoit, 1995). In an attempt to account for the link between maternal sensitivity and mind-mindedness, Meins (1997) suggested that one of the most important factors in mothers' ability to interact with their children in a sensitive way is their propensity to treat their children as individuals with minds. Fonagy and Target (2003b) suggested that sensitivity in the relationship is mainly a behavioral manifestation of the mother's reflective capacity. In their words:

> the parent's capacity to adopt the intentional stance towards a not yet intentional infant, to think about the infant in terms of thoughts, feelings and desires in the infant's mind and in the parent's own mind in relation to the infant and his or her mental state is the key mediator of

the transmission of attachment and accounts for classical observations concerning the influence of caregiver sensitivity. (p. 321)

The present data showing that mothers' sensitivity at 12 months was a powerful predictor of their subsequent parenting representation are in line with Biringen et al.'s (2000) report linking mothers' sensitivity at 18 months and their parenting when the children were 39 months old. The contribution of our dataset is its extending the predictive validity of maternal sensitivity to later parenting across a longer time span: from 12 to 72 months. In attempting to explain this link, Biringen et al. (2000) suggested that early experiences within the dyadic relationship might lay the foundations for mothers' sense of self as a parent. A directional link is but one alternative. The association between early maternal sensitivity and mothers' later parenting representations could be regarded as a marker of the parent's underlying capacity to understand and to act effectively on the child's changing needs as he/she develops. George and Solomon (1989) argued that as the child becomes more able to function autonomously, the caregiver's behavior adapts to meet this developmental change. In this vein, the link between parenting variables across time merely unravels the parental capacity to be highly tuned, or not so tuned, to their growing child's changing developmental needs.

Maternal Affect During Interaction

While sensitivity in mother–infant play interaction was a strong predictor of the parenting constructs at six years, mothers' affect in the play episode at 12 months was not associated with the later parenting variables. This might have been due partially to the low-risk nature of the present sample. Indeed, the mean score of mothers' positive affect was high and the variance was rather low. From a different angle, another methodological limitation of the present dataset is that it was mothers' affective tone that we measured rather than affect regulation of the dyad (Stern, 1985). At 12 months of age, affect attunement – the domain of intersubjective relatedness (Stern, 1985) – is an important characteristic of the mother–child relationship, but our affect measure did not capture it. Sensitivity, rather than affect, may actually have tapped affect attunement in the dyad more closely.

The Mother Figure, and Her Absence, in the Child's Narratives

Overall the representations were positive, describing the mother as protective, regulating, affectionate, and dependable, and so encompassing the different facets of secure-base and goal-directed partnership (Bowlby, 1988). In line with Luborsky et al. (1998), who described the narratives produced by three-to five-year-olds as containing mainly positive themes, the positive representations in the narratives of our six-year-olds significantly outweighed the negative ones, confirming that in a low-risk sample children's internal working model of the mother–child relationship is positive. As the method of assessment includes both the parental figure and the subject of the caregiving actions, it may be concluded that children's representations incorporate both *seeking* and *receiving* protection and comfort in the mother–child relationship.

It is important to underscore that the mother figure did not take an active part in all the stories (even though her image was before the child, ready to be included in the narrative). In some cases, the mother figure was not included at all! Discussing this phenomenon is beyond the scope of the present chapter. Suffice is to say that as we did not include a measure of the father figure, it is not clear if the father figure represented aspects of the caregiving role, or alternatively, that a parent figure was absent from the child's story altogether. As our findings indicated that the mothers whose children excluded their figure from the narratives represented their child less positively and expressed less confidence in the child compared to mothers whose figure appeared in the narrative, excluding mothers from the narrative might imply difficulties in the dyad. Further research is needed in order to understand the correlates and implications of inclusion and exclusion of the caregiving figures from the construction of narratives by children at different ages.

The Trans-Generational Hypothesis: Partial Support and Applied Implications

The children's parenting representations, particularly the mother figure as a source of protection, correlated with mothers' representations of their own sensitive responding to the child's emotional needs. Several possible explanations may be posited for this trans-generational effect. First, parenting behavior may have shaped children's representations of the parental role and its characteristics. However, our data did not support transmission over the time period investigated in the present study: mothers' sensitivity when interacting with their 12-month-olds did not predict the child's mental representation of the mother figure at age six years. A second line of explanation of the association between the child's and the mother's view of parenting underscores the mother's reflective function and mentalizing capacity, rather than her behavior, as the mediating variable that accounts for the link between mothers' and children's representations. Mothers' capacity to mentalize promotes their consideration of their own actions and the child's emotional needs; this capacity molds the representations of the parenting role that the child develops over time. Interestingly, George and Solomon (1989), studying concurrently mothers' behavior in the home and their caregiving representations when interacting with their six-year-old children, found the former little related to the latter. The advantage of the parenting interview used in this study is that it provided a window for assessing mothers' representations within the context of the ongoing and current mother–child relationships.

Overall, the present findings about the link between the mothers' perspective and their children's accord with the premise that the two sets of representations are partially built-in in the dyadic tie. Yet while a certain degree of fit between these representations (e.g., mother representing the child as autonomous and the child representing mother as someone who allows the child the freedom to explore the world) may reasonably be anticipated, they are not expected to converge fully. Specific aspects of mothers' parenting representations are built even before the child is born and are influenced by many factors outside the mother–child relationship (Benoit et al., 1997b; Raphael-Leff, 1993; Stern, 1995; Solomon & George, 2000), so the perspectives of the child and the mother are by no means identical. Considering the child's developmental level (both cognitive and emotional), it is also conceivable that his or her representation will not be a complementary replica or just "the other side of the coin" of the mother's representations. Processes of projection and projective identification are described by psychodynamic theories as potential factors leading to discrepancies between actual behaviors in the relationship and its representations (Stern, 1991; Lieberman & Pawl, 1993). Finally, by employing the doll-play methodology, we did not necessarily tap the child's representation of his or her own experience of the dyadic tie, but the attribution of parenting and caregiving characteristics within a pretense play context.

From a different angle, mothers' level of negative emotionality in their parenting representations was concurrently associated with the child's negative representations of the mother figure; therefore, a possible avenue for future longitudinal investigation concerns the moderators and modulators of early negative emotionality in the dyad to later mother–child relationships. This direction is important for clarifying transgenerational effects, and might be also relevant for intervention purposes. Slade (1999) argued that since the child's representations of her or his inner experience must be seen as an outcome of the parents' capacity to represent the child's mind, understanding the interface of the child's mind and the minds of his or her significant others is central to the focus of the therapeutic processes. She adds that from a clinical perspective, understanding and transforming the parents' conception of the child and the child's own mind, and separating awareness from distortions, is essential for the child's progress in therapy. These representations may guide the mother's behavior in interactions with the child and may influence her interpretations of the child's behavior. In parallel, the children's own representations are likely to change their behavior, as well as the interpretation of mother's behavior (Ben-Aaron, Harel, Kaplan, & Avimeir-Patt, 2001).

The match between the child's and the mother's representations of the same relationship is an important topic for further research. Future investigations should strive not only to illuminate the interplay of minds within the dyadic tie, but also to guide intervention. In therapy, differences between parental and child representations might be revealed and reflected on, ultimately leading to changes in behavior and in subsequent representations. Studying the goodness of fit between mothers' and children's representations, in normal and clinical populations, across different contexts and ages, is a theoretical, methodological, and applied challenge.

Protection: A Meeting Point Between Mother's and Child's Views on Parenting

The association between mothers' representations of their relationship with the child and the child's own narratives about the mother figure showed the following pattern: The most prevalent caregiving role assigned to the mother figure in the child's narrative was protective. This is not surprising given that the story completion task 'invites' such themes and is specifically geared to assess attachment and caregiving issues. The present finding that highlights the protective function is in line with attachment theory (Bowlby, 1969; 1973) and supports George and Solomon's (1999) elaboration on the caregiving behavioral system. According to this contention, caregiving behavior is organized in a behavioral system independent from, but developmentally and behaviorally linked to, attachment (Solomon & George, 1996). This conceptualization implies that caregiving involves "a shift away from the perspective of *being protected* (the goal of the child) to the perspective of *providing protection* (the goal of the parent)" (George and Solomon, 1999; p. 650).

In our study, protection proved to be the prevalent theme in the narratives of the six-year-olds who performed the Attachment Story Completion Task, a result that supports the centrality of this aspect of parenting in the child's experiences when attachment themes are enacted. Moreover, the representations of the mother as a protective figure correlated with mothers' appraisal of their own parenting competence and sensitivity to the child's emotional needs and capacities. The contribution of the present dataset is not only its bringing together the perspective of the child and the mother, but also its addressing, theoretically and methodologically, the representation of the caregiving behavioral system from the standpoint of the mother and of the child.

Summary

The main objective of this chapter was to examine mother–child relationships and their representations across time and perspectives. Using data from a longitudinal study with low-risk mothers and infants, we found that mothers' sensitivity when playing with the infant was a significant predictor of the way mothers viewed their parenting and their relationship with their child five years later. These findings illustrate that specific aspects of mother–child interaction, at the infancy stage, may serve as markers of later parenting representations. In a low-risk sample of mothers and children, high maternal sensitivity during infancy was a precursor to effective and affective parenting, as measured by mothers' representations of competency, provision of secure base, and low levels of negative emotionality in mother–child relationships. Higher levels of negative emotionality, described by the mothers, correlated with more negative representations of the maternal figure in the children's narratives. Mothers' parenting competence and sensitivity to the child's feelings correlated with more frequent representations of the mother as a protective figure.

In conclusion, with respect to the mothers, the results point to a link over time (from age one year to age six years) and across domains (from behavioral to representational). As for the associations between the mother's and the child's views on relationships, a significant link between the two sets of representations emerged. Among the limitations of the present study are the small sample size, its low-risk nature, and the low variability, all of which restrict its generalizability. The methodology of our study did not allow us to unravel the mechanisms responsible for the convergence between the domains and the perspectives, but mothers' reflective and mentalizing capacity has been suggested as one possible mechanism of intergenerational transmission. To further illuminate the meeting points of (a) parenting behavior and its representation and (b) the perspectives of the parent and the child, and to explain their interface, more longitudinal investigations are called for. Meeting these goals require encompassing multiple levels of behavioral, representational, and contextual elements, and examining their dynamic interplay in different populations.

Appendix 5.1
The Parenting Interview: Coding Scales

(1) Representations of the Parent

Parental competence measures the extent that the parent has realistic confidence with regard to his/her capacity to handle effectively various daily demands and activities as well as difficult situations.

Self-understanding measures the extent to which attributions of the causes of the self-actions, thoughts, and feelings are logical, accurate, complex, and reflective.

(2) Representations of the Child

Trust/confidence in child's capacities measures the extent that the parent has realistic confidence with regard to the child's coping capabilities in different contexts.

Child's understanding measures the extent to which attributions of the causes of the child's actions, thoughts, and feelings are logical, accurate, complex, and reflective.

Richness of child's perception measures the richness and the elaboration in delineating who the child is. High scores are won for a detailed description of the child characteristics that reflects knowing your child thoroughly.

(3) Representations of the Parent–Child Relationships

Sensitivity measures emotional availability to the child's needs and affective responses; the extent to which the parent comforts the child when distressed, and enables the child freely to express variety of emotions, difficulties, and needs.

Positive feelings assess the extent to which the parent describes his/her relationship with the child as characterized by positive feelings, including acceptance, joy, pleasure, pride, warmth, and affection. (An exaggerated description and a tendency to idealize receive non-optimal scores.)

Autonomy assesses the extent to which the parent encourages independent activities and decisions that are appropriate to the child's capabilities and his/her developmental stage.

Goal-corrected partnership assesses mutuality and reciprocity in the relationship, joint activities, and open communication between the child and the parent.

Pain and/or Difficulty; Anger; Worry/Fear; Guilt assess the extent to which the parent describes his/her relationship with the child as characterized by the above emotions (each separately).

(4) Narrative Style (Process Scales)

Adequate/balanced description assesses the extent to which the parent presents and evaluates himself/herself and the child in a logical, consistent, understandable, and comprehensible manner that does not require extensive inferences and interpretations. The parent gives evidence and supports his/her assertions and the information given is relevant and complete.

Flooded description assesses the extent to which the parent is unable to contain his/her feeling or thoughts regarding the child, herself/himself, or the relationship. Although there is an extensive investment in the relationship, there is an obvious inability to focus or to explore the relationships objectively.

Restricted description assesses the extent to which the parent avoids answering the questions or resists them by not giving information ("that's all," "it depends," "I don't know"). The use of global or neutral language in description of the self or the child is pervasive and the parent seems somewhat uninvolved.

References

Aber, J. L., Slade, A., Berger, B., Bresgi, I., & Kaplan, M. (1985). *The Parent Development Interview*. Unpublished manuscript.

Aber, L., Belsky, J., Slade, A., & Crnick, K. (1999). Stability and change in mothers' representations of their relationship with their toddlers. *Developmental Psychology, 35*, 1038–47.

Ainsworth, M., Blehar, M. C., Waters, W., & Wall, S. (1978). *Patterns of Attachment*. Hillsdale, NJ: Erlbaum.

Ammaniti, M. (1991). Maternal representations during pregnancy and early infant-mother interactions. *Infant Mental Health Journal, 12*, 246–55.

Bates, J., Freeland, C., & Lounsbury, M. (1979). Measurement of infant difficultness. *Child Development, 50*, 794–803.

Beebe, E., Lachman, F., & Jaffe, J. (1997). Mother-infant interaction structures and presymbolic self and object representations. *Psychoanalytic Dialogues, 7*, 113–82.

Bellak, L. (1954). *The Thematic Apperception Test and the Children's Apperception Test in Clinical Use*. New York: Grune and Stratton.

Belsky, J. & Cassidy, J. (1994). Attachment: Theory and evidence. In M. Rutter & D. Hayes (Eds.), *Development through Life: A Handbook for Clinicians*. Oxford: Blackwell, pp. 373–402.

Ben-Aaron, M., Harel, I., Kaplan, H., & Avimeir-Patt, R. (2001). *Mother-child and Father-child Psychotherapy: A Manual for the Treatment of Relational Disturbances in Childhood*. London and Philadelphia: Whurr Publishers.

Benjamin, J. (1995). *Like Subjects, Love Objects*. New Haven, CT: Yale University Press.

Benoit, D., Parker, K. C., & Zeanah, C. H. (1997a). Mothers' representations of their infants assessed prenatally: Stability and association with infants' attachment classifications. *Child Psychology and Psychiatry, 38*, 307–13.

Benoit, D., Zeanah, C. H., Parker, K. C., Nicholson, E., & Coolbear, J. (1997b). "Working Model of the Child Interview": Infant clinical status related to maternal perceptions. *Infant Mental Health Journal, 18*, 107–21.

Biringen, Z., Matheny, A., Bretherton, I., Renouf, A., & Sherman, M. (2000). Maternal representation of the self as a parent: Connections with maternal sensitivity and structuring. *Attachment & Human Development, 2*, 218–32.

Blatt, S. J. & Lerner, H. (1983). Investigations in the psychoanalytic theory of object relations and object representations. In J. Masling (Ed.), *Empirical Studies of Psychoanalytic Theories*. Hillsdale, NJ: Erlbaum, pp. 189–249.

Bohlin, G. & Hagekull, B. (2000). Behavior problems in Swedish four-year-olds. In P. M. Crittenden & A. H. Claussen (Eds.), *The Organization of Attachment Relationships: Maturation, Culture, and Context*. Cambridge, UK: Cambridge University Press, pp. 75–96.

Bornstein, M. H. (Ed.). (2002). *Handbook of Parenting*. Mahwah, NJ: Erlbaum.

Bornstein, R. F. (1993). Parental representations and psychopathology: A critical review of the empirical literature. In J. M. Masling & R. F. Bornstein (Eds.), *Psychoanalytic Perspectives on Psychopathology*. Washington, DC: American Psychological Association, pp. 1–41.

Bowlby, J. (1969). *Attachment and Loss: Volume 1. Attachment*. London: Hogarth Press and Institute of Psychoanalysis.

Bowlby, J. (1973). *Attachment and Loss: Volume 2. Separation: Anxiety and Anger*. London: Hogarth Press and Institute of Psychoanalysis.

Bowlby, J. (1988). *A Secure Base: Clinical Applications of Attachment Theory*. London: Routledge.

Brazelton, B. T. & Cramer, B. G. (1991). *The Earliest Relationship: Parents, Infants and the Drama of Early Attachment*. Boston, MA: Addison-Wesley.

Bretherton, I. (1985). Attachment theory: Retrospect and prospect. In I. Bretherton & E. Waters (Eds.), *Growing Points of Attachment Theory and Research. Monographs of the Society of Research in Child Development, 50* (1–2, serial No. 209), pp. 3–35.

Bretherton, I., Biringen, Z., Ridgeway, D., Maslin, C., & Sherman, M. (1989). Attachment: The parental perspective. *Infant Mental Health Journal, 10*, 203–21.

Bretherton, I. & Munholland, K. A. (1999). Internal working models in attachment relationships. A construct revisited. In J. Cassidy & P. R. Shaver (Eds.), *Handbook of Attachment: Theory, Research and Clinical Application*. New York: Guilford Press, pp. 89–111.

Bretherton, I., Ridgeway, D., & Cassidy, J. (1990). Assessing internal working models of the attachment relationship: An Attachment story completion task for 3-year-olds. In M. T. Greenberg, D. Cicchetti, & E. M. Cummings (Eds.), *Attachment in the Preschool Years: Theory, Research, and Intervention*. Chicago: University of Chicago Press, pp. 273–308.

Buchsbaum, H. & Emde, R. (1990). Play narratives in 36-month-old children's early moral development and family relationship. *The Psychoanalytic Study of the Child, 45*, 129–55.

Button, S., Pianta, R. C., & Marvin, R. S. (2001). Mothers' representations of relationships with their children: Relations with parenting behavior, mother characteristics, and child disability status. *Social Development, 10*, 455–72.

Cassidy, J. (1988). Child-mother attachment and the self in six-year-olds. *Child Development, 59*, 121–34.

Cassidy, J. & Shaver, P. R. (Eds.). (1999). *Handbook of Attachment: Theory, Research and Clinical Applications.* New York: Guilford Press.

Clark, R. (1985). *The Parent-child Early Relational Assessment. Instrument and Manual.* University of Wisconsin Medical School, Department of Psychiatry, Madison, WI.

Coleman, P. K. & Karraker, K. H. (1998). Self-efficacy and parenting quality: Findings and future applications. *Developmental Review, 18*, 47–85.

De Wolff, M. & van-IJzendoorn, M. H. (1997). Sensitivity and attachment: A meta-analysis on parental antecedents of infant attachment. *Child Development, 68*, 571–91.

Fivush, R. & Reese, E. (2001). Reminiscing and relating: Developing relations between parent-child narratives and attachment. Presented at the Biennial Meeting of the Society for Research in Child Development, Minneapolis, MN, April 22.

Fonagy, P. (2001). *Attachment Theory and Psychoanalysis.* New York: Other Press.

Fonagy, P., Gergely, G., Jurist, E., & Target, M. (2002). *Affect Regulation and Mentalization: Developmental, Clinical and Theoretical Perspectives.* New York: Other Press.

Fonagy, P., Steele, H., Moran, G., Steele, M., & Higgitt, A. (1991a). The capacity for understanding mental states: The reflective self in parent and child and its significance for security of attachment. *Infant Mental Health Journal, 13*, 200–17.

Fonagy, P., Steele, H., & Steele, M. (1991b). Maternal representations of attachment during pregnancy predict the organization of infant-mother attachment at one year of age. *Child Development, 62*, 891–905.

Fonagy, P., Steele, M., Steele, H., & Target, M. (1997). Reflective functioning manual, version 4.1, for application to Adult Attachment Interviews. London: University College.

Fonagy, P. & Target, M. (2003a). Fonagy and Target's model of mentalization. In P. Fonagy & M. Target, *Psychoanalytic Theories: Perspectives from Developmental Psychopathology.* London and Philadelphia: Whurr Publishing, pp. 270–82.

Fonagy, P. & Target, M. (2003b). Early intervention and the development of self-regulation. *Psychoanalytic Inquiry, 23*, 307–35.

Fraiberg, S. H., Adelson, E., & Shapiro, V. (1975). Ghosts in the nursery: A psychoanalytic approach to the problem of impaired infant-mother relationships. *Journal of the American Academy of Child Psychiatry, 14*, 387–422.

George C. & Solomon, J. (1989). Internal working models of caregiving and security of attachment at age six. *Infant Mental Health Journal, 10*, 222–37.

George C. & Solomon, J. (1999). Attachment and caregiving: The caregiving behavioral system. In J. Cassidy & P. R. Shaver (Eds.), *Handbook of Attachment: Theory, Research and Clinical Applications.* New York: Guilford Press, pp. 649–70.

Granot, D. & Mayseless, O. (2001). Attachment security and adjustment to school in middle childhood. *International Journal of Behavioral Development, 25*, 530–41.

Harel, J., Oppenheim, D., Tirosh, E., & Gini, M. (1999). Associations between mother-child interaction and children's later self and mother feature knowledge. *Infant Mental Health Journal, 20*, 123–37.

Jacobson, E. (1964). The self and the object world: Vicissitudes of their infantile cathexes and their influence on ideational affective development. *Psychoanalytic Study of the Child, 9,* 75–127.

Koren-Karie, N., Oppenheim, D., Dolev, S., Sher, E., & Etzion-Carasso, A. (2002). Mothers' insightfulness regarding their infants' internal experience: Relations with maternal sensitivity and infant attachment. *Developmental Psychology, 38,* 534–42.

Lebovici, S. (1983). *La mere, le nourisson et le psychoanalyste: Les interaction precoces.* Paris: Paidos/Le Centurion.

Lieberman, A. F. & Pawl, J. (1993). Infant parent psychotherapy. In Ch. Zeanah (Ed.), *Handbook of Infant Mental Health.* New York: Guilford Press, pp. 427–42.

Luborsky, L., Luborsky, E. B., Diguer, L., Schmidt, K., Dengler, D., Schaffler, P., Faude, J., Morris, M., Buchsbaum, H., & Emde, R. (1998). Stability of the CCRT from age 3 to 5. In L. Luborsky & P. Crits-Cristoph, *Understanding Transference.* Washington, DC: American Psychological Association, pp. 233–51.

Main, M. (1991). Metacognitive knowledge, metacognitive monitoring, and singular (coherent) vs. multiple (incoherent) model of attachment: Findings and directions for future research. In C. Parkes, J. Stevenson-Hinde, & P. Marris (Eds.), *Attachment Across the Life Cycle.* London: Routledge, pp. 127–60.

Main, M. & Goldwyn, R. (1985, 1998). *Adult Attachment Rating and Classification Systems.* Unpublished manuscript, Department of Psychology, University of California, Berkeley.

Main, M., Kaplan, N., & Cassidy, J. (1985). Security in infancy, childhood and adulthood: A move to the level of representation. In I. Bretherton & E. Waters (Eds.), *Growing Points in Attachment Theory and Research. Monographs of the Society for Research in Child Development, 50,* Serial No. *209,* 66–104.

Mayseless, O. (this volume). Studying Parenting Representations as a window to Parents' Internal Working Model of Caregiving.

Meins, E. (1997). *Security of Attachment and Social Development of Cognition.* Hove, UK: Psychology Press.

Mitchell, S. A. (2000). *Relationality: From Attachment to Intersubjectivity.* Hillsdale, NJ: Analytic Press.

Oppenheim, D., Emde, R., & Warren, E. (1997). Children's narrative representations of mothers: Their development and associations with child and mother adaptation. *Child Development, 68,* 127–38.

Raphael-Leff, J. (1983). Facilitators and regulators: Two approaches to mothering. *British Journal of Medical Psychology, 5,* 379–90.

Raphael-Leff, J. (1993). *Pregnancy: The Inside Story.* London: Sheldon Press.

Raval, V., Goldberg, S., Atkinson, L., Benoit, D., Myhal, N., Poulton, L., & Zwiers, M. (2001). Maternal attachment, maternal responsiveness and infant attachment. *Infant Behavior and Development, 24,* 281–304.

Sameroff, A. J. & Emde, R. (1989). *Relationship Disturbances in Early Childhood.* New York: Basic Books.

Sandler, J. & Sandler, A. (1998). *Internal Objects Revisited.* Madison, CT: International Universities Press.

Scharf, M., Mayseless, O., & Kivenson, I. (1998, 2000). *Manual for Coding Parenting Representations.* Unpublished manuscript, University of Haifa.

Scher, A. (1991). A longitudinal study of night waking in the first year. *Child: Care, Health and Development, 17*, 295–302.

Slade, A. (1999). Representations, symbolization, and affect regulation in the concomitant treatment of a mother and child: Attachment theory and child psychotherapy. *Psychoanalytic Inquiry, 91*, 797–830.

Slade, A., Belsky, J., Aber, L., & Phelps, J. (1999). Mothers' representations of their relationships with their toddlers: Links to adult attachment and observed mothering. *Developmental Psychology, 35*, 611–19.

Slade, A., Grienenberger, J., Bernbach, E., Levy, D., & Locker, A. (2001). Maternal reflective functioning and the caregiving relationship: The link between mental states and mother-infant affective communication. Paper presented at the Biennial Meeting of the Society for Research in Child Development, Minneapolis, MN, April 22.

Solomon, J. & George, C. (1996). Defining the caregiving system: Toward a theory of caregiving. *Infant Mental Health Journal, 17*, 183–97.

Solomon, J. & George, C. (2000). Toward an integrated theory of maternal caregiving. In J. D. Osofsky & H. E. Fitzgerald (Eds.), *WAIMH Handbook of Infant Mental Health.* New York: Wiley, pp. 325–67.

Steinberg, D., & Pianta R. C. (this volume). Maternal representations of relationships: Assessing multiple parenting dimensions.

Stern, D. (1985). *The Interpersonal World of the Infant.* New York: Basic Books.

Stern, D. (1989). The representation of relational patterns: Developmental considerations. In A. J. Sameroff & R. Emde (Eds.), *Relationship Disturbances in Early Childhood.* New York: Basic Books, pp. 52–69.

Stern, D. (1991). Maternal representations: A clinical and subjective phenomenological view. *Infant Mental Health Journal, 12*, 74–186.

Stern, D. (1995). *The Motherhood Constellation: A Unified View of Parent-Infant Psychotherapy.* New York: Basic Books.

Toth, S. L., Cicchetti, D., Macfie, J., Maughan, A., & Vanmeene, K. (2000). Narrative representations of caregivers and self in maltreated preschoolers. *Attachment & Human Development, 2*, 271–305.

Toth, S. L., Cicchetti, D., Macfie, J., Rogosh, F. A., & Maughan, A. (2000). Narrative representations of moral-affiliative and conflictual themes and behavioral problems in maltreated preschoolers. *Journal of Clinical and Child Psychology, 29*, 307–18.

van IJzendoorn, M. H. (1995). Adult attachment representations, parental responsiveness, and infant attachment: A meta-analysis on the predictive validity of the Adult Attachment Interview. *Psychological Bulletin, 117*, 387–403.

von Klitzing, K., Kimberly, K., Emde, R. N., Robinson, J., & Schmitz, S. (2000). Gender specific characteristics of 5-year olds' play narratives and associations with behavior ratings. *Journal of the American Academy of Child and Adolescent Psychiatry, 39*, 1017–23.

Westen, D., Huebner, D., Litton, N., & Silverman, M. (1991). Assessing complexity of representations of people and understanding of social causality: A comparison of natural science and clinical psychology graduate students. *Journal of Social and Clinical Psychology, 10*, 448–58.

Woolgar, M. (1999). Projective doll play methodologies for preschool children. *Child Psychology and Psychiatry Review, 4*, 126–34.

Zeanah, C. H. & Benoit, D. (1995). Clinical applications of a parent perception interview in infant mental health. *Child and Adolescent Psychiatric Clinics of North America, 4*, 532–54.

Zeanah, C. H., Benoit, D., Barton, M., Regan, C. Hirshberg, L. M., & Lipsitt, L. (1993). Representations of attachment in mothers and their one-year-old infants. *Journal of the American Academy of Child and Adolescent Psychiatry, 32*, 278–86.

6 Modeling and Reworking Childhood Experiences

Involved Fathers' Representations of Being Parented and of Parenting a Preschool Child

Inge Bretherton, James David Lambert,
and Barbara Golby

Abstract

We examine intergenerational parenting representations of 49 highly educated, married fathers from dual career families who shared childrearing with their wives. Responding to the Parent Attachment Interview, the men discussed similarities and differences between their remembered childhood relationships with mother and father and their current relationship with a preschool son ($N = 27$) or daughter ($N = 22$). Rather than globally identifying with one parent (whether father or mother), a relatively high percentage of the men were selective in the positive qualities they modeled and the disappointing qualities they rejected in either or both parents. Overall, they described more intergenerational differences (reworking of the remembered relationships from childhood) than similarities (modeling themselves after their parents). Concerning similarities, men in our study were much more likely to adopt their mothers than their fathers as influential models with respect to affection/ attachment/communication and, to a slightly lesser extent, discipline practices. In the domain of joint father–child activities, the percentage of men who saw themselves as similar to their fathers was higher. Findings are discussed from the perspective of attachment theory and societal change in fatherhood ideals.

The notion that parent–child relationship patterns and representations are transmitted across generations has a long history in the clinical literature on child maltreatment and parental depression. In an influential synthesis of this literature, Belsky (1984; p. 83) hypothesized that "determinants of parenting highlighted by child abuse research might also play a role influencing parenting that falls within the normal range of functioning." Most intergenerational parenting studies undertaken since then still retain a focus on negative parenting, such as the transmission of harsh discipline, although they display greater sophistication through prospective and multi-informant designs (Capaldi et al., 2003; Simons, Whitbeck, Conger, & Wu, 1991; Thornberry, Freeman-Gallant, Lizotte, Krohn, & Smith, 2003). However, an updated review by Belsky and Jaffee (in press) reveals a growing interest in the intergenerational transmission of *positive* parenting behavior such as nurturance, affection, and acceptance (e.g., Olson, Martin, & Halverson, 1999). With some exceptions (e.g., Capaldi et al., 2003 and attachment studies to be considered later), much of this intergenerational continuity research focused on mother–child relationships.

In the 1970s, fueled by societal changes in the conception of ideal father-hood as well as concerns about the effects of father-absence, a few intergen-erational fathering studies began to emerge that emphasized *discontinuity* as much as *continuity*. These studies juxtaposed what was termed the "model-ing hypothesis" according to which fathers re-enact or model the fathering patterns they experienced as children (derived from studies by Block, 1971; Cowan & Cowan, 1987; Cowan, 1988; Manion, 1977) with the "compen-satory hypothesis," according to which men make deliberate efforts not to emulate parenting practices by their own fathers that they experienced as unsatisfactory or detrimental (based on studies by Barnett & Baruch, 1988; Daly, 1993; Russell, 1982).

At first glance, the intergenerational modeling and compensatory hypothe-ses appear to be incompatible. However, in a study of married Israeli men with children aged three to six years, Sagi (1982) found evidence supporting both hypotheses. The men rated both themselves and their fathers on various facets of parenting (physical care, socialization, decision-making, availability, and warmth nurturance). Significant intergenerational correlations between these ratings supported the modeling hypothesis. However, in terms of absolute rather than relative levels of involvement in parenting, the men rated them-selves higher than their fathers in all domains. Based on these findings, Sagi proposed that intergenerational modeling and compensation can take place concurrently.

In a subsequent study, Snarey (1993) obtained further support for the simul-taneous operation of modeling and compensatory processes, the latter now conceptualized as "reworking." Snarey hypothesized that "fathers would seek to replicate what was positive in the fathering they received and also seek to make up for what was distant or negative in it" (Snarey, 1993; p. 286). Findings were gleaned from in-depth analyses of lengthy interviews conducted with over 200 participants, their parents, and children in a four-decade longitudi-nal study that began in Boston, Massachusetts. At first interview participants were young adolescents, with re-interviews scheduled when they were 25 and 31 years of age and had become parents. The participants' children were mostly born in the mid-1950s, and these children became parents in the late 1970s and 1980s.

Snarey used the initial interviews conducted in adolescence, complemented by information provided by the participants' parents, to derive retrospective ratings of participants' boyhood relationships with fathers and mothers (warmth and nurturance, supervisory style, and physical punishment). He then compared these ratings with the level of support the participants provided to their own children in the areas of socioemotional, academic, and physical-athletic development. Regression analyses revealed that participants who had a distant relationship with their fathers in childhood, but who were brought up in an overall positive family atmosphere, were later *more* supportive of their own children (reworking model).

Additional insights into the joint operation of modeling and reworking of father–son relationships across three generations emerged from Snarey's detailed accounts of intergenerational similarities and differences for four families. In one of these families, the participant reported receiving strict physical discipline from his own father, but using physical discipline with his own son much more sparingly (simultaneous modeling and reworking). In addition, this man compensated for his father's total lack of involvement in shared activities by extensively engaging his own son in play and sports. In the next generation, the son emulated his father's positive parental involvement in sports and play, but compensated by disavowing physical discipline altogether. Note that statistical analyses would obscure such findings, unless both modeling and reworking were systematically assessed.

Also supporting concurrent intergenerational modeling and "reworking" of father–child relationships, Floyd and Morman (2000) documented a (lop-sided) U-shaped correlation between the affectionate involvement participants received from fathers and provided to sons. Participants who rated their fathers highest on affection (including relational satisfaction and closeness) also gave most affection to their own sons (modeling). At the same time, men who had received the lowest levels of affection from their fathers gave more affection to their children than participants who had received intermediate levels (compensation).

In a subsequent study, Palkowitz (2002a), who conducted intensive interviews with men about what it takes to be a "good father," obtained considerably stronger evidence for reworking than modeling, possibly due to the wording of the interview question: "How has fatherhood affected your feelings about your own boyhood?" Only two of the 40 fathers in the Palkowitz study spontaneously mentioned modeling whereas the remaining 38 dwelt on fathering issues they needed to rework. Daly (1993) reported similar results from an earlier qualitative study of Canadian fathers. Men in his sample had great difficulty in specifying any individual whom they regarded as the sole role model for their parenting, and seemed to select models from "a wide purview of choices," including their mothers and wives. When speaking of their own fathers, these men portrayed them primarily as negative role models.

Attachment studies employing the Adult Attachment Interview or AAI (George, Kaplan, & Main, 1985) offer a somewhat more complex understanding of the modeling-reworking issue. Based on 15 open-ended questions, the AAI allows a parent to reflect on childhood attachment relationships with both parents. After an introductory section, interviewees are asked to provide five adjectives that characterize their childhood relationships with mother, father and other significant caregivers, followed by an invitation to support each adjective with detailed memories. Interviewees are also asked to recall what they did when physically hurt, emotionally upset or ill, and to describe notable separations, parental rejection, threats, abuse, and childhood traumas including loss. In the final section of the interview, parents are asked to discuss the effects that their childhood attachment relationships to parents may have had on their adult personality and on the relationship with their own child or children.

Close examination of the AAI transcripts as a whole revealed four major patterns of responding that predicted how interviewees' children behaved with them in the Strange Situation, a procedure used to assess the quality of parent–infant attachment (Hesse, 1999; Main, 1995; Main, Kaplan, & Cassidy, 1985). Adults whose interviews were classified as autonomous-secure produced reasonably coherent and collaborative narratives that were emotionally open, thoughtful, to the point, and neither excessively long nor excessively terse. Not all of these individuals described a secure childhood. Those who were able to give coherent accounts of very distressing attachment experiences in childhood with parents were called "earned secure." In the Strange Situation, infants of parents with autonomous-secure and earned-secure AAI classifications were highly likely to be classified as securely attached.

A second group of interviewees tended to idealize parents in general terms ("my dad was a saint"), but were unable to illustrate such general statements with specific recollections. Moreover, when negative memories emerged later in the interview, these adults did not appear to notice the contradiction with their earlier idealized characterizations of a parent. They also claimed that childhood attachment relationships had little impact on their current thoughts, feelings, or relationships. The relatively terse AAIs of these individuals were classified as dismissing. In the Strange Situation, infants of dismissing parents tended to be classified as avoidantly attached.

A third group of individuals tended to give irrelevant answers to the interviewer's questions, often becoming highly engrossed in recounting conflicted memories. Some spoke very angrily to a (nonpresent) parent; others lapsed into childlike speech. Despite the length of their interviews, preoccupied parents' statements were vague as well as wavering, and hence very hard to follow. In the Strange Situation, their infants tended to be classified as ambivalently attached.

Individuals in a fourth group showed more extreme lapses in the monitoring of reasoning and discourse than the preoccupied individuals, but only while describing bereavements or other traumatic childhood experiences. These lapses included sudden shifts into trance-like states during which the participants paid little attention to the interviewer. They sometimes adopted speech registers inappropriate to the interview situation (e.g., speaking as if delivering a eulogy at a funeral). Another common feature of these interviews was excessive attention to minute details when describing the loss or traumatic event. Their interviews were classified as Unresolved/Disorganized. Infants observed with such parents in the Strange Situation tended to be classified as disorganized.

In terms of modeling or reworking childhood attachment patterns in the next generation, parents with autonomous-secure AAI classifications seem to be modeling the supportive parenting they remember from childhood, whereas individuals with earned secure classifications seem to have reworked their memories of insecure childhood attachments and are hence able to relate to their infants in a more positive way. In contrast, individuals with dismissing AAIs seem to be emulating negative parenting practices without awareness that they are doing so, or without recognizing possible links between past experiences and their own behavior. Preoccupied individuals recall conflictual attachment relationships in childhood in considerable detail, but seem to have little insight into how these experiences might have shaped their own parenting. Finally, individuals with unresolved AAI classifications seem to parent their children in a confusing way that constitutes neither modeling nor compensating or reworking. Main and Solomon (1990) suggest that unresolved parents are either frightened of or frightening to their children in attachment situations (see Schuengel, van IJzendoorn, & Bakermans-Kranenburg, 1999, for corroboration of this claim).

Associations between parental AAI patterns and infant Strange Situation classifications have been studied in mothers and fathers but, for reasons not entirely clear, the concordances are not as consistent for fathers as for mothers (Main et al., 1985; see a meta-analysis by van IJzendoorn & DeWolff, 1997). Nevertheless, several studies have shown that fathers' AAI classifications (believed to reflect attachment quality in the family of origin) moderately predict infant behavior with them in the Strange Situation (the current attachment relationship). This was the case even when AAIs were conducted before the child's birth (Radojevic, 1994; Steele, Steele, & Fonagy, 1996). More recently, Grossmann, Grossmann, Fremmer-Bombik, Kindler, Scheuerer-Englisch, and Zimmermann (2002) have questioned whether the Strange Situation is the best assessment for studying the quality of fathers' relationships with young children. In their two-decade longitudinal study they found that it was German fathers' sensitive support during challenging play with their toddlers, rather than secure attachment in the Strange Situation, that predicted later peer competence and social adaptation. It will be interesting to see whether participants in the Grossmann et al. longitudinal study will model this aspect of the father–child relationship when they become fathers themselves (the original child participants in this longitudinal study are now young adults).

Societal Change

Whereas a father's dissatisfaction with care received in the family of origin is one possible determinant of discontinuities in parenting patterns across generations, larger-scale historical changes have also had an impact. The 1970s and 1980s produced a shift in the conception of optimal fathering in Western industrial societies that manifested itself both in the popular literature and in empirical studies conducted by sociologists and family scientists. "New fathers" were expected to be present at their child's birth, to become more involved in infant care, and show interest in both their daughters' and sons' development (Pleck, 1987). In short, fathers were encouraged to rework the fathering they had received in childhood by becoming more involved and expressive (i.e., less gendered, more androgynous). Among the various explanations offered for the emergence of the "new fatherhood" ideology were mothers' increasing participation in the work force and ideas about shared parenting promulgated by the women's movement (Benokraitis, 1985; Palkowitz, 2002b). Fathers were exhorted to "pick up the slack" in childrearing when wives worked outside the home (Atkinson & Blackwelder, 1993), and their share of involvement in caring for children did indeed consistently increase, though it still remains lower than mothers' (e.g., Barnett & Baruch, 1988; Coltrane, 1996). The most substantial increases in father involvement were noted in families where mothers were full-time employed professionals (e.g., Darling-Fisher and Tiedje, 1990) and men held more egalitarian beliefs about parenting and household tasks (e.g., Russell, 1982). Although these sociological studies attribute the emerging ideal of more involved, expressive fathering to external pressures and historical cohort effects rather than the desire to compensate for unsatisfactory childhood experiences with fathers, it is possible that both assumptions have validity.

The study presented in this chapter explores intergenerational modeling and reworking processes as narrated by a group of 49 upper middle-class fathers of preschool children married to professional wives. Based on findings by Darling-Fischer and Tiedje (1990), we expected that this group would be especially likely to practice more involved fathering.

Fathers were interviewed about specific aspects of their relationship with a preschool son or daughter, and then asked how that relationship resembled or differed from the relationship with each parent as remembered from childhood. In the tradition of other qualitative studies (e.g. Daly, 1993; Lewis, 1986; Palkowitz, 2002a; Snarey, 1993), we attempted to capture the men's representations in their own words rather than converting their responses into ratings.

Method

Sample

Forty-nine European-American, upper middle-class professional couples participated in the study (two mothers were temporarily not working outside the home, and one had not been employed since the child's birth). Fathers' mean age was 38 years and mothers' 37 years. Fathers' education averaged 17.8 years and mothers' 17.1 years. On the Hollingshead nine-point occupational scale, scores for fathers and mothers ranged from "9" for higher executives and major professionals to "6" for technicians, small business owners and semi-professionals, with a mean of 8.0 for the fathers and 7.5 for mothers. Sixty-nine percent of the fathers obtained scores of 8 and 9 on the occupational scale, while 45% of the mothers did so. Their children (27 boys, 22 girls) were three years one month to five years 11 months old and were evenly spread across the whole age range ($M =$ four years four months). Twenty-two percent of the fathers had one child, 67% had two children, and only 10% had three children. The interview focused on 51% first-borns, 47% second-borns, and one child who was third in birth-order.

The families were contacted through four local preschools that primarily served professional families. An initial letter of invitation was followed up with a telephone call. Depending on the particular preschool, between 50% and 70% of the families agreed to participate. Families received a gift certificate for a children's book or a toy as a token of appreciation.

Procedure

We interviewed fathers and mothers concurrently but separately in their own home, using the Parent Attachment Interview (Bretherton, Biringen, & Ridgeway, 1989; see also Bretherton, Biringen, Ridgeway, Maslin, & Sherman, 1989). A male researcher interviewed the fathers and a female the mothers. The 45–90-minute interviews were conducted after the children had been put to bed or during the weekend while someone else cared for the children.

Interviews were audio-recorded and transcribed verbatim, noting pauses and other audible responses such as chuckles or sighs. The current report is based on analyses of the father interviews. After completing the Parent Attachment Interview, each parent also filled out several questionnaires that are not the focus of the current report.

The Parent Attachment Interview (PAI)

The PAI was devised by Bretherton, Biringen, and Ridgeway (1989) to capture a parent's representation of the attachment-relationship with a particular child but yields information about many other salient aspects of parenting, including play and discipline. In a previous study (Bretherton, Biringen, Ridgeway, Maslin, & Sherman, 1989), sensitivity/insight ratings applied to the interview were correlated with secure mother–child attachment classifications of a separation-reunion procedure at age 3, as well as with security-ratings of children's responses to the Attachment Story Completion Task (Bretherton & Ridgeway, 1990).

The PAI consists of 21 questions. Three warm-up questions explore thoughts and feelings before, during, and after the child's birth. The interview then moves to the current father–child relationship, followed by queries about similarities and differences in the father–child and mother–child relationship. The next question deals with the issue of intergenerational transmission, specifically with similarities and differences between a parent's current relationship with a preschool child and the remembered relationships with both parents in childhood. It is on fathers' responses to the intergenerational question that this chapter is based.

Given the open-ended nature of the interview, fathers' responses to the PAI should not be regarded as exhaustive. Open-ended questions suggest general topics, but give interviewees the freedom to choose issues that are salient to them rather than to the researcher. Under these circumstances, a father's answers to our questions (including the intergenerational question) were likely to reflect what was uppermost in his mind (and what he was willing to share), rather than the full range of possible issues or topics that he could have brought up in response to the questions. Thus, if a father did not mention a particular issue in comparing himself to his father or mother, we cannot conclude that he had no opinion about it or considered it completely unimportant. To guard against social desirability bias, we tried to phrase questions in a nonjudgmental way (e.g., we asked for intergenerational similarities and differences in parent–child relationships, rather than: "Do you think your father was a good dad?"). In addition, we encouraged fathers to illustrate more general statements with specific examples if they did not do so spontaneously.

Analysis Procedures

We present our findings in terms of major themes that emerged from fathers' comparison, of parent–child relationships across generations. Themes were drawn not only from the men's responses to the direct question about intergenerational similarities and differences but also from relevant answers to other questions, such as a man's spontaneous remarks about childhood relations in the family of origin while talking about disciplining his child.

To identify themes, we first extracted and printed out all relevant statements verbatim and then used color-coding to mark provisional theme categories. The next step was to construct a series of charts in which each man's themes and sub-themes in various domains were entered in separate columns. These charts retained sufficient contextual information to allow us to verify that a statement fit the category to which it was assigned by the coder, and to create new theme categories or collapse old ones as more interviews were analyzed. Bretherton and Lambert re-examined all statements and charts for congruence with the categories and sub-categories to which they had been assigned, checking back with the original interview text if an entry seemed unclear. This procedure was an extension to that adopted in a prior PAI study of mothers (Bretherton et al., 1989). It is similar to methods used by Ainsworth (personal information) to analyze home observation narratives from the Baltimore Study (Ainsworth et al., 1978). It also resembles certain aspects of the "grounded theory approach" to qualitative data analysis as elaborated by sociologists Strauss and Corbin (1990). These approaches have the dual goals of theory verification and theory generation, a process that Kuczynski and Daly (2003; p. 383) aptly called "interpretive induction."

Findings

Because of the potential for confusion between the child's father and grandfather (the father's father), we will refer to the participant fathers as "men" in this section and to their parents as father and mother. The two men who had lost their mother and another who lost his father in early childhood were excluded from the analyses where appropriate. Although we did not formally gather information regarding the number of children in the men's families of origin, 41 of the 49 men spontaneously supplied this information in the course of the interview. Fifteen men came from families with 4–10 children, and most of the remaining families of origin had 3 children. The overall mean for the fathers' families of origin was 3.6 children.

The findings are presented in three parts. In Part I, we consider issues regarding men's lack of or uncertainly about childhood memories that arose in the course of the interview. Part II is devoted to the men's discussion of modeling and reworking, and Part III presents narrative data pertaining to the major intergenerational relationship domains fathers chose to discuss during the interview: (1) affection/attachment/ understanding, (2) discipline, and (3) shared activities and shared time.

Memory Issues

Drawing comparisons between parent–child relationships across generations makes different demands on long-term memory than the husband–wife comparison that preceded it in the interview (Bretherton, Lambert, & Golby, 2005). Presumably for that reason, 24% of the men initially stated that they lacked childhood memories, as illustrated by quotes from two fathers:

> I don't have any, I don't have any good remembrances of things when I was a kid.

> I don't have many memories, either fond or otherwise. It's just kind of a blank.

One of these fathers felt stymied by our intergenerational question, especially because he was being asked to provide specific examples of his childhood experiences:

> Okay, um, . . . God, my head's spinning at this point. I think I've gone on too long. Uh, (chuckle). If it were the last question I'd be a lot happier. Um (pause). . . . I don't know. It, I think, you know, it's hard for me to pick out something that . . . about her. These questions are all, tend to be on the very broad side. I mean you keep asking for specific, you know, give me the specifics in response to a very broad question. But um . . . let's see. I'm trying.

Despite his initial reaction, this man then provided a description of his mother's very undemonstrative behavior (ascribed to her Scandinavian ancestry), adding that he "decided quite consciously that I should not be like that." His father had quite often created family scenes of "blowing up" and "flying of the handle," a tendency this man tried to control in himself, but not always successfully.

Altogether, seven men with initial memory disclaimers went on to describe a very troubled family situation or especially negative relationship with a parent, suggesting the initial reaction may have been defensive. Two other men gave specific, but superficial answers that seemed somewhat evasive (e.g., one talked about intergenerational similarities in eating habits). A few others explained that their childhood memories only started after five to seven years of age, or that they remembered only some aspects of the relationship (e.g., attachment, but not play).

The complexity of memory-related issues was especially well illustrated by one man's reflections that we will present more extensively. After protesting that he did not have the best of memories, he recalled (as a similarity) that his mother had told him that he would always be loved, "no matter what" and that he did so with his children, but the example he gave had an ambivalent undertone:

> I tell [child] that, and both girls, and sometimes I will tease them. I did that just this evening. Uh, I told [child] that if she ate her six grapes on her plate that I would love her forever, but if she didn't eat her six grapes, that "I don't know," and then [older daughter] chimed in and said: "You would love us forever anyway." So they know that, and that is something I remember from my own mother.

When subsequently probed for perceived intergenerational differences, this man revealed doubts about what he remembered and what he had been told:

> Well it is hard for me to say that because my mother is a very strange beast, and she has been different in more recent years, I think, than she was when I was a very young child, and I can't remember so well what she was like when I was a young child. In very recent years she has expressed all kinds of feelings about maybe she wasn't cut out to be a parent and she never really liked it and so on. I never really had a sense of that as a child. As I told you I was sure she loved me. I never felt otherwise. So, but when I hear her say things like this I do see differences. I like being a parent and I like kids. Ask her now and she would say she doesn't like kids. She doesn't really like babies. She liked us when we became adolescents. Well, I like little kids. I've always liked little kids

even before I had my own. So that's a difference, if it's true. I never, I'm not quite sure to what extent she's re-written history. That is something, it is not a lot, but it is one difference.

This man went on to explain that his sister did not remember her childhood very well either, but had speculated often that "we must not have been very happy as children because we blocked it out." He himself, however, believed "that I have a faulty memory." Regarding his father, this man saw himself as much more involved and more sensitive, describing his father currently as "just not terribly effective at reading people's feelings," and inferring "so he must have been like that with his own kids."

This man's wife (during the mother-interview) expressed a different view. She ascribed her husband's difficulties in relating sensitively to his children to family of origin experiences that he was trying to overcome:

> [Husband] comes from a very different background, [husband] comes from a family which is extremely, I'd say, unusually short in their nurturing of empathetic feelings, I'd say . . . a very, very unusually short. But what I find to be amazing is that [husband] has really had to work on it and he has come a tremendous distance, and I don't think it is just being male, I think his whole, his mother and his sisters are extreme in that area, not being able to acknowledge the importance of feelings, except for "I want," the "me" type of feelings, which [husband] wasn't necessarily, but he was not really feeling the importance that you acknowledge someone else's empathy.

This woman expressed appreciation for her husband's deliberate efforts, with her encouragement, to work on being a sensitive and empathic father, but also commented that this did not yet come naturally:

> He will actively work on it, when he really needs to tackle it, he will. When it becomes the hardest is when he has been away on a trip. He enjoys the freedom, it takes him a while to click into . . . and he will need to be reminded that: "You need to work on really thinking about the girls' needs and where they are coming from," and then he will do fantastically well, he will really stimulate them and respond to them and notice them, he is very clever with them, he will find different things, um, but it's as if he has to click it on, not something he, he was raised with necessarily. He has had to really cultivate it in himself, and it can click off sometimes.

Also related to memory, 10% of the men (including the father we just cited) mentioned that they relied on observations of their parents' current behavior with grandchildren or conversations with adult siblings to infer how their parents might have treated them as preschoolers. One man believed his father must have ignored him as a child, based on the following experience:

> The kid wanted something, so I said: "Go and talk to your grandfather," and my father was ignoring him, and I said: "Well, why don't you, here's your grandkid," and he said: "No, that's all right. If you ignore him long enough, they'll go away," and boy, if that didn't summarize a whole lot!

Commenting on memory as a reconstructive process, one man acknowledged that his understanding of the mother–child relationship had changed with greater maturity and parenthood. He had gained a deeper appreciation of his mother's attentiveness to him as a child, especially in contrast with his rejecting father. In his judgment of her, he made allowances for her own difficult childhood with a stepmother and absent father:

> With my Mother when I was a kid, um (pause) well um, my thoughts of my mother have changed quite a bit since I have become a parent and actually since I've grown up, so I guess applying the standard of what I know today about my relationship then and comparing that to what I believe I know about my relationship with [child], I'd say it's pretty similar, you know, I think my mom was pretty good.

Discussion of Modeling and Reworking (General)

To make it easier for the men to address both positive and negative aspects of childhood experiences with parents, we invited them to speak about similarities and differences in parent–child relationships across generations rather than make explicit value judgments.

Modeling. A considerable number of the men nevertheless explicitly stated that they modeled themselves after one or both of their parents, either generally or with respect to a particular quality. This is how three men worded their statement about modeling:

> Maybe it's patterning myself after her.

> I'm trying to adapt my own style of child rearing very much to, not just mom, but the way they both did.

> I try to make him a role model for myself and try to pick up the positive things that he has done.

More of the men talked of emulating their mothers' (24%) than their fathers' (14%) parenting, and three expressed sentiments that were very reminiscent of Snarey's (1993) version of how the modeling and reworking hypothesis could be combined:

> I try, from my father, I remember what he didn't have time to do, and I try to do that for my kids whenever possible.

> I think you try to learn a little bit and think about the way you related, to use the good points and avoid maybe some of the things you didn't enjoy as a child.

> I think I try to bring up, I try to bring up my kids like I was brought up for the most part. There are things, obviously, that are different but it seems like, ah, I try to improve on how I was brought up, but basically, I've patterned it after how I was brought up.

Reworking. The percentage of men who reported compensating for their father's specific or overall shortcomings was substantially higher than the percentage who described modeling his desirable qualities (42% vs. 14%). For mothers, in contrast, this differential was quite small (28% vs. 24%). Many of the men emphasized that trying to parent differently from one's own parent required a conscious effort, as illustrated by three examples:

> I've decided quite consciously that I should not be like that.

> I tried to break away from that kind of role.

> That's another pattern that I have tried consciously to change.

> So I'm actually trying to make differences instead of have similarities.

However, compensating for adverse childhood relations with parents is not necessarily easy, especially when stressed or fatigued, as described by one of the men:

> Unfortunately when push comes to shove and you're tired, you always fall back on what you, you know, had as a kid . . . I try not to be that way, although deep down, that's my reflex.

One of the two men who had lost his own mother in very early childhood, and his father in adolescence had thought deeply about how to rework his experiences despite having no concrete model, saying:

> I'm patterning my parenting role on . . . you know, the way I would have liked my family life to be rather than the way it was.

Variations in Modeling and Reworking. A substantial percentage of men described their childhood relationship with a parent as similar in some regards and different in others (46% for fathers; 51% for mothers). Slightly fewer men commented only on differences (40% for fathers; 28% for mothers), and even fewer only on similarities (14% for fathers; 21% for mothers). These comparisons include instances of both modeling and reworking.

Only three men mentioned a negative quality that they shared with a father (communication difficulties, impatience, or being overly perfectionistic), and only two felt their mother had been a better parent than they were in at least one regard (supportiveness; shared time). Several other men (19%) started out by admitting that they resembled their father or mother in terms of a negative quality (e.g., lacking patience in respect to discipline; inability to devote enough time to the child), but followed this up by explaining that their own "flashpoint was higher"; or that they were more willing to make themselves available to their children whenever possible. The differences described in these instances were small, but in the men's favor.

Two interviews seemed initially to give the false impression that a father saw himself in a less favorable light than his mother. One said he was less "lovey-dovey" (affectionate) than his mother, but he regarded this as a positive masculine quality. The other noted that he supervised his child less than his mother, but regarded this as a positive change from her overprotectiveness. In sum, when the men admired their parents, they tended to see themselves as similar and when they felt negatively about how they had been parented, they saw themselves as doing better.

Societal Change. In discussing intergenerational differences in parenting, a number of the men made reference to societal changes in the roles of husband–fathers and wife–mothers to explain differences between their own parenting and their parents' practices. With few exceptions, their fathers had played the breadwinner role while the task of childrearing had fallen mostly to their mothers. As two of these men put it:

> It was a different style of parenting then, . . . a lot of parenting got left to my mother.

> At that age, men were working and the wife stayed home and they (fathers) didn't interact much with the kids or have much to do with childrearing.

In relation to their mothers, many men commented that family size alone was responsible for intergenerational differences in parenting. As already noted, some of these men grew up in large families with up to 10 children.

Table 6.1. *Percentages and Frequencies of Men Who Mentioned Specific Topics When Comparing Themselves to Their Mothers and Fathers in Terms of Similarities and Differences*

Topic Mentioned	Comparison with own Mother (N = 47)		Comparison with own Father (N = 48)	
Attachment/Closeness/ Affection	P* mentioned	55% (n = 26)	P mentioned	33% (n = 16)
	P similar	50% (n = 13)	P similar	13% (n = 2)
	P more	50% (n = 13)	P more	87% (n = 14)
Discipline	P mentioned	45% (n = 21)	P mentioned	50% (n = 24)
	P similar	24% (n = 5)	P similar	8% (n = 2)
	P more lenient	67% (n = 14)	P more lenient	58% (n = 14)
	P stricter	9% (n = 2)	P stricter	13% (n = 3)
			P role different	21% (n = 5)
SharedActivities/Time	P mentioned	47% (n = 22)	P mentioned	73% (n = 35)
	P similar	48% (n = 10)	P similar	38% (n = 13)
	P more	50% (n = 11	P more	62% (n = 22)
	P less	2% (n = 1)		

* *P* = Participants (men in study)

Discussion of Intergenerational Reworking and Modeling in Specific Parenting Domains

As already noted, the men addressed three major relationship domains when comparing themselves to their parents. These were (1) affection, love, understanding, and communication, (2) discipline, and (3) joint activities and shared time. The percentages as well as the number of men who discussed each of these topics with respect to a father or mother are listed in Table 6.1. Within each of the three domains, percentages refer to the subgroup of fathers who touched on the specific sub-topic, not to the sample as a whole.

Affection, Love, Understanding, Communication. Over half of the men raised issues of affection, love, understanding, and communication when comparing themselves to mothers, but only a third did so in the comparison with fathers.

Comparison with Mothers. Half of the men who mentioned these topics felt that they resembled their mothers:

> I can remember my mother being affectionate with me when I was small, put me to bed most nights, you know, in a very affectionate, warm, and loving way, um that, that's similar to the way I do for [daughter].

The physical touch and hugging is very comforting, very reassuring. I'm sure I clung to her leg as much as he clings to mine, and wants to be held. Actually, he doesn't cling to my leg much, but he's quite pleased to sit on your lap for periods of time.

The remainder of the men who commented on affection-related topics felt they were more affectionate, expressive, loving or understanding than their mothers, and in the following two cases, much more so:

I have really let go of that pattern or modeling, and try and be affectionate and demonstrative, so that's a major difference.

My mother was not a physical [meaning physically affectionate] person, and that's one thing that, I think, that we've made some strong efforts with my wife's family being very "touching"... "I love you,"... We never hold back on that, we say it to each other regularly. It's not bantered around meaninglessly, it is carefully chosen; so it's something we're not afraid of to say, and we're not afraid to touch and hug one another.

One of these men felt his mother had never been there for him:

I mean I can't relate to anything my mother has every done for me... when I was younger it was nonexistent... If I was lonely or if I was sad, I couldn't talk to my father because he wouldn't understand, I mean he was the big macho worker, and my mother was just too tired, so we "deal with it yourself."

Another man concluded that his mother's lack of availability might be the reason why he wanted to compensate by being as available as possible to his own child. Noting that he had not reflected on this possibility before, he added pensively: "Subconsciously, it's got to be there."

One father, an exception in our study, spoke about affection (and parenting in general) in a highly gendered way. Although he had appreciated his mother's affection as a child, this is not a quality he wanted to emulate as parent. "I'm not inclined to be real lovey-dovey," he said, "but my mother was."

Comparison with Fathers. In contrast to what they had said about their mothers, few men saw themselves as similar to their fathers in affection and understanding, and their descriptions of paternal affection were relatively unelaborated. One of these men said: "I felt he loved me and paid me attention, and I love and pay lots of attention to [child]."

The great majority of men who mentioned this topic, believed themselves to be more affectionate and/or expressive than their fathers, as illustrated by two examples, including one father who seemed to be consciously reworking the messages of traditional masculinity he received from his father:

> Mostly, very different...I can remember very few instances where he ever touched me or picked me up.

> My father was very hard, is still very hard, is very prejudiced, very macho...You were always strong, men didn't show pain, men don't cry. I cry and I show pain. I think it's stupid not to. I try and teach that to the other two boys that I had and [child], especially [child]. It's o.k. to cry, it's o.k. to be sad...I try to instill that, so I'm a million times different from my father.

Discipline. Just under half of the men brought the topic of discipline into the intergenerational comparison with mothers, and just over half did so in relation to their fathers (see Table 6.1).

Comparison with Mothers. Of the men who mentioned their mothers' disciplinary practices, about a quarter perceived themselves to be following in their mother's footsteps:

> I'm sure we have discipline in common...Go there for justice and for dealing with your siblings. You hear uproar, and then you become the arbitrator.

> My mother was also...the sort of person who would lay down the rules and enforce them. I think I'm acting the same way my mother acted with me.

Only one man thought he was stricter than his mother had been with him (though he did not regard this as negative). Another admired his mother's patience, but felt unable to emulate it. The remainder of the men – about two-thirds – perceived themselves as more lenient than their mothers had been with them. Whereas these men had hardly ever used the term "authoritarian" when speaking of themselves or their wives in the earlier part of the interview (see Bretherton, Lambert, & Golby, 2005), a number did apply it (or very authoritarian metaphors) to their own mothers:

> I'm not as authoritarian as my mother. My mother had 5 kids, and my mother was one of those persons who probably shouldn't have had children.

> You know my impressions of my mom were . . . not that she ruled with an iron fist, but ah, you know, she laid down the law, and that was followed, and I tried not to cross it . . . and it's hard to deal with [son].

> My mother had 6 kids . . . She was like a platoon sergeant . . . I kind of let them go, let [daughter] do whatever it is that she wants to do and try and encourage that rather than MAKING her do things.

As noted earlier, the men frequently attributed the difference in disciplinary styles to generational differences in family size.

Comparison with Fathers. A small group of men only mentioned that their fathers opted out of the role of authority figure in the family of origin whereas they did not. The other 19 men discussed similarities and differences in disciplinary styles.

Only two men felt that they resembled their father in the practice of discipline. Both said they, like their fathers, lacked patience, but one of them was also trying to change his behavior with his wife's help:

> Impatience is similar . . . if she's [child] doing something that irritates me . . . instead of trying to explain it to her, I'll yell at her or raise my voice quicker than I should.

> I find myself doing things that my dad would do in his dealings with me, and [wife] is very good at pointing it out because my mother talks to [wife] about how my father would never let us kids do anything, [wife] is pretty good at pointing out: "Let him do this." And the joy they get from doing this is so much better . . . my dad in a situation like that . . . he would have taken it away. I'm working on it myself to overcome.

The three men who described themselves as stricter than their fathers came from families in which the father had left the disciplinary role entirely to the mother, something they regarded as undesirable.

Just over two-thirds of the of the men who broached discipline issues with respect to their fathers, believed they were more lenient or patient than their fathers had been, but their evaluations of this difference varied. A very few men were apologetic about being overly lax, and lauded their father's ability to exercise authority. One of these said:

> I'm not like my father, I can't be that way. My Dad had the knack of being able to say: "[Son], this is the way it is," and if I did it, he always stuck to the consequence. I never remember him wavering; but see, I'm not like that. I wish I was, but I waiver because I must have a soft heart for her or something . . . I find myself saying: "Here are the rules and

here are the consequences," but I still find myself wavering and saying: "Okay, well this time I'm going to let you go."

Much more commonly, however, men disapproved of their father's arbitrary authoritarian style and tried to approach discipline issues with greater understanding, as shown in statements by two fathers:

> He disciplined me a lot, but didn't (pause), I never knew why certain things happened. He didn't explain things very well to me, why things happened, and that's why she's, that's how I try to differ from them the way I was . . . he was . . . I think, you know, there's . . . that there's nothing wrong with trying to understand why things are happening and I didn't with my dad (laugh) for a long time understand why he had me do certain things. And ah, that's a big difference . . . I don't want that to be that way. And he was always right, his attitudes were right, his values were right and that was it, and he was the boss and there was no room for discussion, period. So it just whatever was deemed was deemed and that was it.

> He was more violent than I am . . . much more likely to hit a kid than I am. I'd hinted at that when I talked about consequences. We were afraid of people because he would hit us with his belt, and I don't do that.

A few men described childhood feelings of fear when their father reacted to misbehavior or failure with angry outbursts. These were feelings the men did not want their own children to experience. Here are two examples of men who described such episodes:

> My father had a very bad angry streak in him. He'd blow up a lot . . . I think I do it a lot less than my father ever did, and I don't think I cause him [child] the fear that I think we all had of my father 'cause I think he was a little bit more out of control.

> His line was a lot harder than mine, but my emotional need to be obeyed is almost as strong. He was bigger on consequences, I make as much noise but with less consequences. My father was physically threatening, . . . that's not a goal of mine. I'm pretty cowed by the idea that my kids are frightened of me.

Sometimes being shamed or ridiculed by their father led men to experience feelings of inadequacy, as illustrated by two examples:

> He is a very impatient man, I don't think I have the same degree of impatience. One of my strongest memories as a child of being about 5, 4 or 5, 6, 7 years old, he was working in the attic and wanted to change

a bulb and couldn't reach it, so he wanted me to get up on his shoulders and reach it and I was frightened to do that, and I don't know if he called me a sissy, but he made me feel inadequate or inferior, and I don't think I have ever done that with [child], and wouldn't, I would react differently, not quite as controlling.

I think that he lacked patience and maybe to some extent I may lack patience too . . . but I remember my father, I mean, I would dread playing catch with him because he'd want me to make the perfect motion, otherwise I'd be throwing like a girl or something. I mean, he'd just be worried about that stuff from the word go, and not just throw me the ball and throw it back, and "let's talk about how good the Dodgers [baseball team] are this year," you know, which is the way you're supposed to do it.

Finally, one man who saw himself as somewhat more lenient than his own father, nevertheless questioned whether changes in accepted discipline practices were really desirable. He described feeling especially uncertain about the role of spanking, and asked:

How should you discipline your children and should you spank them? When I was raised, not only could you spank and not be frowned upon, but you were supposed to, you really were. I mean, there is, was no question. The common phrase at that time was "Spare the rod, spoil the child." So, I mean, we weren't beaten but, if you did something wrong you got spanked. Now, what do you do now? . . . You don't do that kind of discipline as much as people used to, and is it right or wrong? I'm still not convinced. I know it's fashionable to not be very forceful physically but I, I'm still not sure that there shouldn't be some role for it.

Joint Activities and Shared Time. Eighty-seven percent of the men addressed the topic of joint activities. Of these, almost three-quarters compared themselves to their fathers, but only about half discussed this domain in relation to mothers (see Table 6.1).

Comparison with Mothers. Just over half of the men who compared themselves to mothers, saw intergenerational similarities in the amount of attention and time they devoted to being with or engaging in activities with their child. As one man put it, speaking of both parents:

I love my mom, and they did a lot of stuff with us. That's why I do so much with [child]. I mean we did a lot as a family . . . doing things

> during the day, doing things at night, telling stories, my mom and dad were both great storytellers.

Surprisingly, most of the other men commenting on this topic mentioned that they spent more time in joint activities with their own child than their mother had done, and this despite the fact that almost none of the mothers had been employed outside the home and had therefore, at least in theory, been more accessible. As previously noted, many men explained intergenerational differences in terms of societal changes in family size and related differences in housework:

> I grew up in a family of 7, so there were a lot more kids, and a lot more for her to do, so I don't think she had anywhere near the time that we have with [daughter].

> I came from a large family, so I think her energies were pretty limited.

> I mean, I am involved with [child] and his brother the whole time, and I think of my mother as being more distant and doing more adult activities and kind of leaving me on my own.

Only one of the men believed that he was spending less time engaged with his child than his mother had been with him.

Comparison with Fathers. Not only did a higher percentage of the men discuss joint activities and time with fathers, but this was also the domain in which a substantial percentage saw themselves as intergenerationally similar, with almost two-fifths feeling they spent as much positive time with the child as their fathers had done. Two men said:

> I admit I did everything with my dad...down in the workshop, just building things...and I just do that with [child]...I just try to do everything with him [child]. I know he loves it and I love doing it with him.

> My father was always interested in answering my questions, scientific and moral stuff, and he'd give me an explanation which I remember and carry with me today. And even the little sayings he had about how one should treat other people, and you know, I...remember them, I remember the conversation taking place. It wasn't just fast with questioning, whipped off an answer. He was really interacting with me a lot. So I'm trying to do the same thing...if he has a question, I want to discuss it and make it a learning experience for him.

Men who described father–child joint activities and shared time as similar across generations tended to emphasize parental enjoyment and the child's appreciation of one-on-one attention:

> I think he [father's father] was a person who just generally likes children. He liked being boisterous with them. He liked reading to us. I like doing these things with [child].

> I think the, the special time, you know, the weekend kind of special time thing, one-on-one is similar to what he did. He, when we were growing up, um, was forced to be gone a lot, travel a lot, but when he was home, he was home. And uh, and wasn't the kind of guy that would, you know, be working all week and then go out and golf on the weekend. I mean, he was always there for us ... and I think that's a similarity between us.

However, more than half of the men said they spent more time with their children than their fathers, whether by engaging in play, various outdoor and indoor activities, teaching a skill to the child, or working together. In the context of discussing these topics, some of these men expressed highly negative opinions about their father's unavailability:

> He basically checked out and said "it's your job" [referring to the mother].

> He wasn't there, he just plain wasn't there.

In some cases, the men attributed their father's unavailability to work:

> My dad worked incredible hours ... it really was a single parent family.

> My father was a very distant figure in my life because he worked so much out of the home ... my mother was really the dominant parental figure in my life ... my dad really wasn't around that much.

Other men intimated that, in addition to work commitments, their fathers were uninvolved by choice:

> He'd spend 18 hours a day on the job, and when he was home, he'd bring work home with him ... And when he was doing something to relax he didn't want the kids around because he was relaxing.

> He was definitely a 60 hours a week type worker. It was as if he was married to his job ... and sometimes he used it as a crutch ... He couldn't really communicate with us ... he was detached ... he had what we call a

den . . . When I talked with him, he was always polite, pleasant, but . . . he was really hiding out from the rest of us, from being part of the family.

[He] would come home, read his books, have his dinner, and have his drink, and "keep the kids out of my hair". . . he was a nonparticipatory parent.

As noted earlier, some of these men excused their own father's lack of involvement by referring to then-prevalent societal expectations: "50s behavior," "traditional," "different style."

Discussion

Memory

The topic of memory requires discussion before we consider the remainder of our findings. Unlike Snarey (1993), we did not have access to data collected while the study fathers were children. The men's narratives thus represent their retrospective understanding as informed by current adult reflections about the past and the present.

We found it interesting that some men who did not remember early childhood inferred what they might have experienced by observing their parents interact with grandchildren. That a minority of men found it initially difficult to recall specific episodes to illustrate their general descriptions of relations with parents in early childhood is perhaps not surprising, given findings on childhood amnesia that show that few adults remember more than a couple of fragments from early childhood (Bauer, Kroupina, Schwade, Dropknik, & Wewerka, 1998; Nelson, 1993). Thus, the fact that a third of the preschoolers were only three to four years old may have made it difficult for them to recall experiences at that same age.

However, more than childhood amnesia might be in play in some cases. Inability to recall childhood experiences in the Adult Attachment Interview, or contradictory statements, if pervasive, are some of the criteria for a dismissing AAI classification (Hesse, 1999), and tend to be associated with avoidant child–parent attachment. Whereas we do not feel confident in applying criteria developed for the AAI to intergenerational accounts of parent–child relations in the PAI, we were intrigued by one man's difficulty in squaring his memories of what his mother told him in childhood (that he would always be loved) with her current statements that she had not liked young children. Because this man also lacked other specific memories of interacting with his mother, he wondered whether he himself or his mother had "rewritten history." Whereas this man's sister believed that she had blocked out her early memories, he came down on the side of having "a faulty memory." It was from his wife's interview that we learn about the man's struggles to overcome his lack of spontaneous empathy and sensitivity, deficits that she (but not he) attributes to his self-centered family of origin. His teasing expression of "love forever," made conditional on his child eating six grapes, seems indicative of underlying conflicts of which he is unaware.

Bowlby (1973, 1980) attached particular significance to such discordances, linking them to difficulties in formulating integrated representations or "working models" of self and parent in attachment relationships. Given that there are now several longitudinal studies for which childhood assessments of parent–child relations, including father–child interactions and later AAIs are available, it might be possible to conduct studies in which earlier observations of father–child relationships can be compared with an individual's later difficulties in recalling specific attachment experiences during the AAI. This could provide deeper insight into the extent to which defensive processes are associated with claims of lacking childhood memories. A related study of mothers with "earned secure" AAI classifications who participated in the Minnesota Longitudinal Attachment Study from infancy has already been completed by Roisman et al. (2002). They found that individuals, defined as "earned secure" on the basis of coherently describing adverse childhoods as young adults unexpectedly did not differ from secure-autonomous individuals in terms of observations conducted in early childhood. The authors therefore warn that memories of parents as rejecting or neglecting do not necessarily imply that the individual had parents who behaved this way consistently. Based on their findings, the authors remark: "Much remains unknown about those who rise above harsh or ineffective parenting experiences" (p. 1217). Some individuals in the Roisman et al. study were given the designation of "prospectively earned secure" (insecure classification in infancy and secure-autonomous AAI classification in young adulthood). However, we do not learn to what extent these individuals described an at least somewhat distressing childhood while responding to the AAI.

Intergenerational Transmission: Compensation and Modeling

In line with Snarey's (1993) notion that individuals emulate parents' positive relationship qualities and attempt to rework unsatisfactory aspects, men in our study mentioned positive relationship qualities such as affection, more lenient discipline, and more time together when they felt themselves to be similar to one or both parents. In contrast, when commenting on intergenerational differences, the men primarily described nonaffectionate, unsupportive, authoritarian, and unengaged relationships in the family of origin.

In view of the findings by Roisman et al. (2002), we cannot assume that negative experiences these fathers remembered were necessarily typical of their parents' practices in childhood, but neither should we assume that they were nonveridical. Some of the men may have used memories of infrequent negative interactions as examples of how not to parent, even if their parents did not engage in these behaviors frequently.

Modeling Mothers and Fathers. In contrast to the majority of intergenerational father studies, the men we interviewed were asked to compare their childhood relationship with both parents to their relationship with a preschool age son or daughter. Rather than globally identifying with one parent (whether father or mother), a relatively high percentage were selective in the positive qualities they modeled and the disappointing qualities they rejected in either or both parents. Nevertheless, men in our study were much more likely to adopt their mothers than their fathers as influential models with respect to affection/attachment/communication and, to a lesser extent, discipline practices. Of the men who considered these topics, about half "patterned themselves after" their mothers in terms of attachment/affection and a quarter in terms of discipline. The percentage who described intergenerational father–child similarities in these domains was very low indeed. However, most men seemed unconcerned about identifying more with their mothers than fathers in these domains. Men with no parental model, we assume, would find it *most* difficult to change their practices. Some, as the men themselves stated, sought and received help from their wives. Some fathers mentioned seeking therapy.

Our findings differed in the domain of shared activities, play, and companionship. Not only did more men compare themselves to their fathers than mothers in this domain than when discussing affection and discipline, but the percentage of men who saw themselves as similar to their fathers was also highest here. Many men remembered this aspect of the father–son relationship in vivid detail and with enjoyment. Moreover, their accounts accord with descriptions of closeness to their own children during one-on-one companionship or play in the earlier parts of the interview (Bretherton, Lambert, & Golby, 2005). In contrast, men who wished that their fathers had spent more time with them seemed quite resentful, suggesting that positive engagement in shared activities and time with a father in childhood is an important way of experiencing connectedness with him. This is also suggested by longitudinal findings by Grossmann et al. (2002), who found that fathers' sensitive support during challenging play in toddlerhood and early childhood predicted better relationship outcomes in adolescence and early adulthood, whereas toddler–parent attachment classifications predicted positive developmental outcomes only in relation to mothers.

Societal Influences

Our study highlights men's awareness that societal standards of optimal fathering must be judged in relation to societal changes in family life. In the course of discussing reasons for intergenerational differences in parent–child relationships, many fathers mentioned large family size as reasons why their mothers had less time for them in childhood and offered the traditional gendered division of labor as a reason why their breadwinning fathers were often unavailable. However, despite the recognition that traditional family life was supported by society-wide norms, many of the men viewed their own fathers' lack of availability with anger, whether the topic came up in relation to attachment or companionship. Somewhat unfairly, they seemed to apply current "new father" ideals to father behaviors that had been commonplace in the past. A possible interpretation of these findings is that the emergence of the "new father" ideology is not due to societal changes in parenting and work roles alone. Many of the men interpreted their fathers' then normative unavailability, harshness, and lack of interest as rejection rather than accepting it without question. Not only could this explain why memories of these experiences still aroused quite negative feelings, but also why these men were receptive to new ideas about fathering that represented what they might have hoped for from their own fathers. Socialization practices, even if societally accepted or acceptable, are not always experienced as comfortable by the recipients and may induce an individual to try different approaches when becoming a parent. At the same time, the extent to which an adult who attempts to create a "corrective parenting script" succeeds in doing so varies, and as family therapist Byng-Hall (1995) stresses, clinicians frequently encounter involuntary unconscious relapses into the "replicative script" from childhood that a parent is trying to avoid. Furthermore, parents who adopt new practices do not always to so without reservation, as illustrated by the father who was unsure about the wisdom of completely renouncing spanking as a discipline practice, given that the new methods he was trying to follow seemed less effective for him than he had hoped.

How Real Is Generational Change?

Using the "the engaged father" ideal as portrayed in the literature as yard-stick, our study showed that many of the men in our study tended to work towards this image. In doing so, a majority used their mothers as a model, especially in the domains of affection/understanding and discipline. With one exception, men did not seem to feel undermined in their masculinity by emulating mothers. In the domain of play, companionship, and shared activities, however, more men modeled fathers than mothers. In sum, the men we studied seemed to rework their role as fathers by desiring the same emotional closeness with their children that they felt with their own mothers, while at the same time maintaining the traditional role of father as companion and playmate.

If not emulating a parent, most of the men believed they surpassed one or both parents in positive relationship qualities. Does this mean that self-serving bias was in play and the men were unrealistically optimistic about themselves? In an interview study of first-time fathers with one-year-olds conducted in Great Britain, Lewis (1986) obtained similarly optimistic responses. Moreover, when he compared his own findings to those from a study with mothers by Newson and Newson (1963) completed 20 years earlier, he noticed that these mothers also reported more lenient discipline and greater emotional closeness in parent–child relations than the previous generation.

Does this show that parent–child relationships are becoming steadily more affectionate and lenient? In regard to his infancy study, Lewis (1986) rejects this hypothesis, pointing out that parents of infants or very young children do not have memories that stretch that far back. For that reason, fathers of infants would be unable to make the appropriate intergenerational comparison. However, this cannot be the explanation for findings of the current study. Men in our study were experienced fathers of preschoolers, and many had more than one child. Furthermore, in the remainder of our interview, they provided detailed accounts affectionate care, authoritative discipline, and positive involvement in companionship (Bretherton, Lambert, & Golby, 2005). We suspect that, were we to have access to observations of parent–child relations across both generations, we would be able to document many of the generational differences fathers describe.

It is, however, possible that the intergenerational differences in the men's parenting representations could, in part, be explained in terms of a difference in viewpoints. A man trying to elicit cooperation from a resistant child, for example, may consider himself as quite lenient in comparison to his own father or mother. But his limit-setting, albeit democratic, may appear quite restrictive to his child. Similarly, a man who has many other work and household commitments may perceive the time devoted to parent–child companionship as more extensive than his child who does not have such obligations. Thus, the differences a man perceives between his care *of* a child and the care he received *as* a child may appear more striking to him than they might appear to an outside observer. Finally, fulfilling the simultaneously challenging and rewarding task of parenting reasonably well may require the optimistic belief that one can do as well, and perhaps even better than the previous generation.

Acknowledgments

This study was funded by the John D. and Catherine T. MacArthur Research Network on Early Childhood Transitions, the Research Committee of the Graduate School of the University of Wisconsin-Madison, and supported by the Waisman Center. We express our heartfelt thanks to the fathers who participated in our interviews, to Damien Doyle who interviewed them, and to Mary Copus, Janet Gehrke, Julia North, and Margaret Peterson who transcribed the interviews.

References

Ainsworth, M. D. S., Blehar, M. C., Waters, E., & Wall, S. (1978). *Patterns of Attachment: A Psychological Study of the Strange Situation*. Hillsdale, NJ.: Erlbaum Associates.

Atkinson, M. P. & Blackwelder, S. P. (1993). Fathering in the 20th century. *Journal of Marriage and the Family, 56*, 975–86.

Barnett, R. C. & Baruch, G. K. (1988). Correlates of fathers' participation in family work. In P. Bronstein & C. P. Cowan (Eds.), *Fatherhood Today: Men's Changing Role in the Family*. New York: Wiley, pp. 66–78.

Bauer, P. J., Kroupina, M. G., Schwade, J. A., Dropknik, P. L., & Wewerka, S. S. (1998). If memory serves, will language? Later verbal accessibility of early memories. *Development and Psychopathology, 10*, 655–79.

Belsky, J. (1984). The determinants of parenting: A process model. *Child Development, 55*, 83–96.

Belsky, J. & Jaffee, S. R. (in press). The multiple determinants of parenting. In D. Cicchetti & D. Cohen (Eds.), *Handbook of Developmental Psychopathology*. (Volume 3: Risk, disorder and adaptation). New York: Wiley.

Benokraitis, N. (1985). Fathers in the dual earner family. In S. Hanson and F. Bozett (Eds.), *Dimensions of Fatherhood*. Beverly Hills, CA: Sage, pp. 243–68.

Block, J. (1971). *Lives through Time*. Berkeley, CA: Bancroft.

Bowlby, J. (1973). *Attachment and Loss: Volume 2. Separation*. New York: Basic Books.

Bowlby, J. (1980). *Attachment and Loss: Volume 3. Loss*. New York: Basic Books.

Bretherton, I., Biringen, Z., & Ridgeway, D. (1989). *The Parent Attachment Interview*. Unpublished manuscript, University of Wisconsin-Madison.

Bretherton, I., Biringen, Z., Ridgeway, D., Maslin, C., & Sherman, M. (1989). Attachment: The parental perspective. *Infant Mental Health Journal, 10*, 203–21.

Bretherton, I., Lambert, J. D., & Golby, B. (2005). Involved fathers of preschool children as seen by themselves and their wives: Accounts of attachment, socialization, and companionship. *Attachment and Human Development, 7*, 229–51.

Bretherton, I. & Ridgeway, D. (1990). Attachment story completion task to assess young children's internal working models of child and parent in the attachment relationship.

In M. T. Greenberg, D. Cicchetti, & E. M. Cummings (Eds.), *Attachment in the Preschool Years: Theory, Research, and Intervention*. Chicago: University of Chicago Press, pp. 300–5.

Byng-Hall, J. (1995). *Rewriting Family Scripts*. New York: Guilford.

Capaldi, D. M., Pears, K. C., Patterson, G. R., & Owen, L. D. (2003). Continuity of parenting practices across generations in an at-risk sample: A prospective comparison of direct and mediated associations. *Journal of Abnormal Child Psychology, 31*, 127–42.

Coltrane, S. (1996). *Family Man: Fatherhood, Housework and Gender Equality*. New York: Oxford University Press.

Cowan, C. P. & Cowan, P. A. (1987). Men's involvement in parenthood: Identifying the antecedents and understanding the barriers. In P. W. Berman & F. A. Pedersen (Eds.), *Men's Transition to Parenthood: Longitudinal Studies of Early Family Experiences*. Hillsdale, NJ: Erlbaum, pp. 145–74.

Cowan, P. (1988). Becoming a father, a time of change, and opportunity for development. In P. Bronstein & C. P. Cowan (Eds.), *Fatherhood Today: Men's Changing Role in the Family*. New York: Wiley, pp. 13–35.

Daly, K. (1993). Reshaping fatherhood: Finding the models. *Journal of Family Issues, 14*, 510–30.

Darling-Fisher, C. S. & Tiedje, L. B. (1990). The impact of maternal employment characteristics on fathers' participation in child care. *Family Relations, 39*, 20–6.

Floyd, K. & Morman, M. T. (2000). Affection received from fathers as a predictor of men's affection with their own sons: Tests of the modeling and compensation hypotheses. *Communication Monographs, 67*, 347–61.

George, C., Kaplan, N., & Main, M. (1985). *Adult attachment interview for adults*. Unpublished manuscript, University of California, Berkeley.

Grossmann, K., Grossmann, K. E., Fremmer-Bombik, E., Kindler, H., Scheuerer-Englisch, H., & Zimmermann, P. (2002). The uniqueness of the child-father attachment relationship: Fathers' sensitive and challenging play as a pivotal variable in a 16-year longitudinal study. *Social Development, 11*, 307–31.

Hesse, E. (1999). The adult attachment interview: Historical and current perspectives. In J. Cassidy and P. R. Shaver (Eds.), *Handbook of Attachment: Theory, Research and Clinical Applications*. New York: Guilford, pp. 395–433.

Kuczynski, L. & Daly, K. (2003). Qualitative methods for inductive (theory-generating) research. In L. Kuczynski (Ed). *Handbook of Dynamics in Parent-Child Relations*. Thousand Oaks, CA: Sage, pp. 373–92.

Lewis, C. (1986). *Becoming a Father*. Milton Keynes: Open University Press.

Main, M. (1995). Attachment: Overview, with implications for clinical work. In S. Goldberg, R. Muir, & J. Kerr (Eds.), *Attachment Theory: Social, Developmental and Clinical Perspectives*. Hillsdale, NJ: Analytic Press, pp. 427–74.

Main, M., Kaplan, K., & Cassidy, J. (1985). Security in infancy, childhood and adulthood: A move to the level of representation. In I. Bretherton and E. Waters (Eds.), *Growing points of attachment theory and research, Monographs of the Society for Research in Child Development, 50*, Serial No. 209 (1–2), 66–104.

Main, M. & Solomon, J. (1990). Procedures for identifying infants as disorganized-disoriented during the Ainsworth Strange Situation. In M. T. Greenbert, D. Cicchetti,

& E. M. Cummings (Eds.), *Attachment in the Preschool Years: Theory, Research, and Intervention*. Chicago: University of Chicago Press, pp. 121–60.

Manion, J. (1977). A study of fathers and infant caretaking. *Birth and the Family Journal, 4*, 174–9.

Nelson, K. (1993). The psychological and social origins of autobiographical memory. *Psychological Science, 4*, 7–14.

Newson, J. & Newson, E. (1963). *Infant Care in an Urban Community*. London: Allen & Unwin.

Olson, S. F., Martin, P., & Halvorson Jr., C. F. (1999). Personality, marital relationships, and parenting in two generations of mothers. *International Journal of Behavioral Development, 23*, 457–76.

Palkowitz, R. (2002a). *Involved Fathering and Men's Adult Development: Provisional Balances*. Mahwah, NJ: Lawrence Erlbaum.

Palkowitz, R. (2002b). Involved fathering and child development: Advancing our understanding of good fathering. In C. S. Tamis-LeMonda & N. Cabrera (Eds.), *Handbook of Father Involvement: Multidisciplinary Perspectives*. Mahwah, NJ: Erlbaum, pp. 119–39.

Pleck, J. (1987). American fathering in historical perspective. In M. S. Kimmel (Ed.), *Changing Men: New Directions in Research on Men and Masculinity*. Newbury Park, CA: Sage, pp. 83–97.

Radojevic, M. (1994). Mental representations of attachment among prospective Australian fathers. *Australian and New Zealand Journal of Psychiatry, 28*, 505–11.

Roisman, G., Padron, E., Sroufe, L. A., & Egeland, B. (2002). Earned-secure attachment status in retrospect and prospect. *Child Development, 73*, 1204–19.

Russell, G. (1982). Shared-caregiving families: An Australian study. In M. E. Lamb (Ed.), *Nontraditional Families*. Hillsdale, NJ: Erlbaum Associates, pp. 139–71.

Sagi, A. (1982). Antecedents and consequences of various degrees of paternal involvement in childrearing: The Israeli project. In M. E. Lamb (Ed.), *Nontraditional Families*. Hillsdale, NJ: Erlbaum, pp. 203–32.

Schuengel, C., van IJzendoorn, M. H., & Bakermans-Kranenburg, M. J. (1999). Frightening, frightened and/or dissociated behavior, unresolved loss, and infant disorganization. *Journal of Consulting and Clinical Psychology, 67*, 54–63.

Simons, R. L., Whitbeck, L. B., Conger, R. D., & Wu, C. I. (1991). Intergenerational transmission of harsh parenting. *Developmental Psychology, 27*, 159–71.

Snarey, J. (1993). *How Fathers Care for the Next Generation: A Four-decade Study*. Cambridge, MA: Harvard University Press.

Steele, H., Steele, M., & Fonagy, P. (1996). Associations among attachment classifications of mothers, fathers, and their infants: Evidence for a relationship-specific perspective. *Child Development, 67*, 541–55.

Strauss, A. & Corbin, J. (1990). *Basics of Qualitative Research: Grounded Theory Procedures and Techniques*. Thousand Oaks, CA: Sage.

Thornberry, T , Feeeman Gallaut, A., Lizotte, A., Krohn, M., & Smith, C. (2003). Linked lives: The intergenerational transmission of antisocial behaviour. *Journal of Abnormal Child Psychology, 31*, 171–84.

van IJzendoorn, M., & DeWolff, M. (1997). In search of the absent father: Meta-analysis of infant-father attachment. *Child Development, 68*, 604–9.

7 Maternal Representations of Parenting in Adolescence and Psychosocial Functioning of Mothers and Adolescents

Ofra Mayseless and Miri Scharf

Abstract

The notion of caregiving representations was applied to assess parenting representations of mothers of adolescent sons. The association between these representations and the mothers' state of mind with respect to attachment was examined. In addition, mothers' parenting representations were examined as predictive of the coping of the sons with the developmental tasks of leaving home and individuation. Eighty-two mothers of male adolescents from middle-class intact families were administered the Parenting Representations Interview-Adolescence (PRI–A) approximately a year prior to the son's conscription to mandatory military service. The coping and adaptation to the basic training period as well as levels of individuation three years later were assessed. Mothers' parenting representations were moderately associated with their own AAI categorizations. Mothers' parenting representations were further predictive of the psychosocial developmental accomplishments of their sons. These findings attest to the significance of the mothers' parenting representations in affecting the sons' experiences as part of their developmental trajectory.

Within the paradigm of attachment theory, the interest in parents' caregiving system, namely their motivational system to give care and protection, started to rise a decade ago (George & Solomon, 1989, 1996; Bretherton et al., 1989). This interest was reflected in the study of parents' internal world, their beliefs, emotions and affects, that is, their parenting representations. Several researchers in different laboratories have suggested various ways of assessing parenting representations. They have mostly employed semi-structured interviews modeled after the Adult Attachment Interview (AAI: Main & Goldwyn, 1998), and have developed various different ways of analyzing those interviews (e.g., Aber et al., 1999; Benoit et al., 1997; Bretherton et al.,

1989; George & Solomon, 1989; see a review in Mayseless, this volume). Unlike the AAI, which mostly probes the parents' relationships with their own parents, and which serves to assess a person's general state of mind with respect to attachment, these different interviews asked about relationships with a specific child. Generally, they were analyzed in a variety of ways, some parallel to but some different from the coding scheme of the AAI. Thus, in line with AAI coding, most coding schemes of parenting interviews looked at information processing evident in the interview. In addition, they examined specific parenting aspects such as the provision of a secure base (e.g., George & Solomon, 1989), or specific emotions such as guilt and worry (e.g., Aber et al., 1999).

Through these different interview methods researchers demonstrated that mothers' conceptions and representations of their parenting and their representations of their relationships with their child are associated with their own and their child's behavior (Aber et al., 1999; Benoit et al., 1997; George & Solomon, 1989; Pianta et al., 1996; Slade et al., 1999). For example, significant associations between these representations and the child's attachment security as assessed in the Strange Situation and in other methods (such as the six-year-old reunion) were demonstrated (e.g., Bretherton et al., 1989; Huth-Bocks, Levendosky, Bogat, & von Eye, 2004; George & Solomon, 1989; Solomon & George, 1999). Similarly, significant associations were found between mothers' parenting representations and their state of mind with respect to attachment as assessed by the AAI (Slade et al., 1999; George & Solomon, 1989).

The studies that examined maternal representations of their parenting mostly investigated mothers of infants and young children (Pianta et al., 1996; Slade et al., 1999) or mothers of six-year-olds (George & Solomon, 1989). This chapter describes an attempt to assess representations of parents of adolescents, and to examine their association with psychosocial functioning of mothers and of their adolescent sons. To this end, we developed an interview which builds on interviews developed and employed by other researchers to examine parental representations of mothers of younger children. The *Parenting Representations Interview–Adolescence* (PRI–A) (Scharf & Mayseless, 1997/2000) takes into account age-related aspects that are more salient in adolescence, such as mutuality, autonomy promotion, and monitoring, as well as boundary disturbances. In the first research project conducted in 1997, we administered this interview to mothers and fathers of adolescent sons ($N = 88$). The second study conducted three years later included only adolescent daughters ($N = 120$) and their parents. In this chapter we present the results with the PRI–A of the mothers from the first project (Mayseless, Scharf, Kivenson-Baron, & Schnarch, 2005). All other PRI–As from the two research projects are currently being analyzed.

Specifically, here we examine the association between mothers' parenting representations and their attachment representations. We also examine the association between mothers' parenting representations and how their emerging adult sons coped with the developmental tasks of separation (as part of the leaving home transition) and individuation.

Current Assessment Methods of Parenting Representations With Infants and Young Children

As reviewed in Mayseless (this volume), most current assessment methods of parenting representations rely on 1 hour to 1.5 hour-long semi-structured interviews modeled after the Adult Attachment Interview (AAI). These include specific questions relating to the child, the relationship, and the mothers' various positive and negative feelings. In some interviews a detailed description of pregnancy and infancy is elicited (e.g., WMCI; Zeanah & Benoit, 1995). Interviews differ somewhat in the extent to which they focus on the child (e.g., asking the parent to provide five adjectives describing the child) or on the relationship (e.g., asking the parent to provide five adjectives describing the relationship with the child). Similarly, some interviews probe more intensely than others the mother's feelings and attitudes. In still other interviews, similarities and differences between the child and the mother or the child and the father are explored; in some cases mothers are asked about their future projection of the relationship or of the child's future. The questions are followed by requests for elaboration and concrete examples. In most cases interviews are audiotaped and transcribed, and the coding is based on the transcripts.

In terms of coding schemes, several different approaches are taken. In some cases, coding is geared eventually to classify parent's representation into three or four categories of caregiving representations corresponding to the three or four attachment categories (e.g., balanced, disengaged, and distorted categories suggested by Zeanah et al., 1994). In other cases, continuous scales are employed to capture major dimensions of the representations using the impression from the interview as a whole. Some researchers have used very few scales (e.g., the sensitivity/coherence scale of Bretherton et al., 1989). However, other researchers have spread a wider net and explored the utilization of a large number of scales focused on the mother's representations of herself (e.g., her perceived competence), of the child (e.g., infant difficulty, richness of the child's description), and of their relationship (e.g., parental acceptance). In addition, several unique scales assessing specific emotions and their modulation have been suggested (e.g., joy, guilt, anger, anxiety). Finally, scales assessing thought processes evident in the narrative (e.g., coherence) were included. In most studies this large array of scales was subjected to different forms of data reduction, resulting in a much smaller number of composite scales. However, most coding schemes retained the separate scales and suggest using them in any new coding (Zeanah et al., 1994; Aber et al., 1999).

As noted, most of these studies looked at mothers of infants or toddlers, and in only a few cases (e.g., George & Solomon, 1989), as far as is known, were older children (six-year-olds) examined (see also Scher et al., this volume). The current examination leaps to a much older age – adolescence – in an attempt to investigate the parenting representations of mothers of children at that age. To highlight the specific adjustments we made in the interview and its coding, and to underscore the outcomes that we explored, we present a brief overview of the unique characteristics of parenting adolescents.

Parenting Adolescents

The time of adolescence involves a "dramatic change in the child's physical, cognitive, emotional, and social competencies and concerns" (Steinberg & Silk, 2002; p. 103). The onset of puberty marks major hormonal changes expressed in physical change, rapid growth, and the development and maturation of sexual and emotional characteristics, mood swings, and an increase in negative affect. These changes are accompanied by alterations in the adolescents' self-image and the way they interact with others. At the cognitive level adolescents develop a more formal and efficient way of thinking, and they become more capable of thinking abstractly and viewing things in a relativistic way. They thereby become more critical of themselves and of others, including their parents.

Another major transition concerns changes in the social realm. Adolescents spend far less time with their parents and more with their peers; this developmental transition is accompanied by emotional changes as well. Adolescents, at least during puberty changes, seem to distance themselves from parents, demand more privacy, and invest more in their peers emotionally and socially. The relationships with peers become an important arena in which to seek companionship and intimacy. In relationships with parents, changes toward greater autonomy, less supervision, and more mutuality are evident.

Some researchers have argued that the main developmental task of parents of adolescents is to learn how to let go while keeping the channels open for communication and reliance in times of need (Allen & Land, 1999). The capacity to strike a balance between connectedness and individuality seems to be a major challenge of this period (Hill & Holmbeck, 1986; Allen, Moore, & Kuperminc, 1997; Kobak & Cole, 1994), and negotiations regarding changes in relative power, redefining closeness, and decreasing supervision while maintaining monitoring pervade the relationships.

In addition, as the adolescents themselves invest in self-definition and in their future goals and developmental trajectory, parents too invest in envisioning the child and their relationships in the future. In sum, adolescent-specific aspects of parenting seem to encompass autonomy promotion, monitoring, mutuality, and letting go, aspects that we specifically included in the PRI–A. This was incorporated when we devised the interview questions (e.g., asking about letting go) and when we formulated specific rating scales that capture these qualities in the parenting representations.

The Parenting Representations Interview – Adolescence (PRI–A)
(Scharf & Mayseless, 1997/2000)

The PRI–A is a semi-structured interview designed to arouse memories and emotions regarding parenting experiences with adolescent children. In this version (1997) as well as the revised (2000), parents were requested to give a general description of their relationships with their children and to support this description with specific incidents from childhood and adolescence. The interview elicited experiences and interactions involving closeness, pain/difficulty, guilt, anger, worry, discipline, children's increasing autonomy, and the way the parents dealt with these situations. Parents were also asked to describe how they saw their child in the future and to describe their imagined future relationship with him or her. Besides these questions, which are mostly used in interviews with parents of young children, the PRI–A asked about specific experiences of parents of adolescents, regarding conflicts, monitoring, mutuality, the centrality of parenthood in parent's life, similarities and differences between the parent and the adolescent, and developmental changes in the relationship. Interviews were audiotaped and then transcribed verbatim.

Coding. The construction of the interview, in particular the coding of the PRI–A (Scharf, Mayseless, & Kivenson-Baron, 1997/2000), benefited from several sources: the seminal breakthrough of the development of the AAI (Main & Goldwyn, 1998) and works on parenting representations of young children's parents, in particular those by (alphabetically ordered) Aber,

Benoit, Bretherton, George and Solomon, Marvin, Pianta, Slade, Zeanah, and their colleagues. We also had recourse to Westen and colleagues (1990) and to Fonagy and colleagues (1997) with regard to self-reflection and reflection about the child. The general theoretical framework of Steinberg and Holmbeck and their colleagues with regard to the characteristics of adolescence also guided our construction of the coding scheme (Steinberg, 2001; Holmbeck, Paikoff, & Brooks-Gunn, 1995).

Based on the transcripts, several scales were coded, relating to four basic domains: (1) representations of the parent, (2) representations of the adolescent, (3) representations of the relationships (e.g., monitoring, warmth and affection) and different emotions and feelings such as pain and guilt, and (4) the cognitive and emotional process evident in the narrative. Based on the global profile of representations evident in the transcripts and in particular based on the cognitive and emotional process scales, interviewees were assigned a best-fit classification: adequate/balanced, flooded, restricted, and confused. These corresponded to the autonomous, preoccupied, dismissing, and unresolved state of mind assessed by the AAI. Insights from use of the interview in the first sample with adolescent males led to several revisions and adjustments. In particular, several scales were added, which obviously were not included in the analyses of the first research project; these are marked with an asterisk. All the scales presented range from 1 (low end of the scale) to 5 (high end of the scale).

Coding Scales of the PRI–A

(1) Parent's Representations of Self. *Competence* measures the parent's realistic confidence in his/her capacity to handle effectively various parenting situations, including general difficulties and daily demands and activities. Claims to competence without adequate evidence in the transcript do not qualify for high scores.

Self-understanding measures how logical, accurate, complex, and reflective are parent's attributions of the causes of self-actions, thoughts, and feelings.

* Sense of Sacrifice measures the extent to which the parent feels that he or she has made a great sacrifice and has forfeited personal pleasures and self-actualization in order to care for the child.

(2) Parent's Representations of the Adolescent. *Trust/confidence in child's capacities* measures the parent's realistic confidence in the child's coping capabilities in different contexts.

Child's understanding measures how logical, accurate, complex, and reflective are the parent's attributions of the causes of the child's actions, thoughts, and feelings.

* *Elaborate perception of the child* assesses the richness and elaboration of the description of the child in the transcript. High scores are awarded for a detailed description of the child that reflects thorough knowledge of him or her.

Elaborate perception of the child in the future assesses the richness and elaboration of the description of the child *in the future*.

(3) Parent's Representations of the Parent–Child Relationship. * *Secure base/safe haven* assesses the extent that the parent is emotionally available, comforts, and helps the child when in distress. The parent allows the child freely to express emotions, needs and difficulties, reacts in a sensitive manner, and succeeds in reducing the child's distress.

* *Provision of instrumental help and pampering* assesses the extent to which the parent performs instrumental activities with and for the child and pampers and indulges the child. The parent gives the child a lift, goes with the child to buy things, cooks special food, buys special things to make the child happy.

Warmth and affection assesses the extent to which the parent describes his/her relationship with the child as positive, involving acceptance, joy, pleasure, pride, warmth, and affection. (Exaggerated description and a tendency to idealize receive non-optimal scores.)

Partnership and Mutuality assesses reciprocity in the relationship, as well as flexibility and openness, willingness to negotiate, adequate partnership in responsibility and decisions, and open communication and sharing between the child and the parent.

Emphasizing/stressing achievement assesses how much the parent refers to and stresses the child's achievements – grades, investment in academic/artistic/sports activities – when describing his relationships with the child.

Autonomy granting assesses how much the parent facilitates autonomous decision making and behavior, balanced with adequate scaffolding suited to the situation and the child's developmental stage. The scale reflects tolerance for different opinions, perceptions, and behaviors, as well as the child's privacy and encouraging independent activities and reasoning by the child.

Monitoring assesses how much the parent knows about where the child spends free time, who his/her friends are, and his/her functioning at school and in other settings; also how much behavioral control of the child the parent exercises when necessary.

The nature of the future relationship with the child assesses how positive is the parent's perception of the future relationship (high score); or how pervasively pessimistic, uncertain and filled with anxiety this perception is; if a positive picture is portrayed without adequate backing in the transcript, a low score is assigned.

Inappropriate/inadequate boundaries assesses the how far the boundaries between the child and the parent are inappropriate and exhibit lack of differentiation. The parent may try strenuously to behave like the child's friend, or his or her involvement in the child's life is exaggerated and intrusive and entails over-identification, whereby the child's life and feelings are the parent's. In the first version (Scharf et al., 1997), this scale also included the occurrence of role reversal, for which a separate scale was devised in the second version (Scharf et al., 2000).

* *Role reversal* assesses how far the roles between parent and child are reversed. The child is expected to take care of the parent in a parental role and/or the child is expected to play a spousal role vis-à-vis the parent.

Pain and/or difficulty assesses how much the parent describes his/her relationship with the child as painful, sad, or difficult. A high score denotes a sense of extreme difficulty in taking care of the child.

Anger assesses how much the parent describes his/her relationship with the child as one of anger, rage, and irritation.

Worry/fear assesses how much the parent describes his/her relationship with the child as characterized by worry, fear, and anxiety. High scores reflect worries regarding the child's health and security, affecting behavior toward the child, without the parent being able to contain and regulate these feelings.

Guilt assesses how much the parent describes his/her relationship with the child as involving guilt feelings on his or her part. High scores denote uncontained pervasive guilt.

* *Non-involvement /indifference* assesses how far the relationship with the child is characterized by indifference and lack of interest. The parent appears uninvolved.

* *Idealization* assesses the discrepancy between the general highly positive descriptions of the child as "perfect," "just great," and the relationship as "very loving" and the factual and more believable descriptions of the child and the relationship.

Conflicts and power struggles assesses how far the parent describes disagreements, conflicts, and struggles in the relationship with the child.

(4) Narrative Style (Process Scales). *Adequate/Balanced* description assesses the logic, consistency, lucidity, and cogency of the parent's presentation and evaluation of himself/herself and the child, without any need for extensive inferences and interpretations. The parent offers evidence and supports his/her assertions. and the information given is relevant and complete.

Flooded description assesses the parent' inability to contain his/her feeling or thoughts regarding the child, herself/himself, or the relationship. Although an extensive investment is made in the relationship, there is an obvious incapacity to focus and to explore it objectively.

Restricted description assesses the parent's avoidance of answering the questions or resisting them by not giving information ("That's all," "It depends," "I don't know"). The use of general or neutral language in description of the self or the child is pervasive and the parent seems somewhat uninvolved.

Confused description assesses the parent's vagueness and confusion, inability to focus responses, losing track of the questions, or making clearly erroneous or bizarre attributions.

Twenty interviews were coded by two coders. Inter-judge reliability of the scales (intra-class correlations) was high, from 0.78 to 0.96 and there was full agreement on classification of parenting representations. The classification resulted in 49 *adequate/balanced* mothers, 16 *flooded*, and 17 *restricted*. The general profile of parenting representations in each category was subjected to a MANOVA (F (40, 118) $=$ 15.59, $p < 0.001$; see Table 7.1). As shown in Table 7.1, each category had a unique profile of characteristics in the three domains of the representations (mother, child, relationship).

Specifically, adequate/balanced mothers evinced the highest competence and confidence in the child, the highest warmth and affection, partnership and mutuality, monitoring, and promotion of autonomy, the soundest attributions for self-understanding and child's understanding, as well as elaborate perception of the child and the relationship in the future. They exhibited moderate levels of guilt, anger, and worry, and along with flooded mothers the highest level of conflicts and pain. Flooded mothers were conspicuous in their highest level of inappropriate/inadequate boundaries and focus on achievement and highest levels of all negative emotions, conflicts, pain, worry, guilt, and anger. Restricted mothers showed the least sound attributions for self-understanding and child's understanding, the lowest levels of all negative emotions, the lowest level of monitoring, and intermediate levels of autonomy promotion.

Thus, flooded mothers appeared to adopt a caregiving strategy of high engagement and strong emotional involvement, high levels of negative

Table 7.1. *Caregiving Characteristics of Mothers in Adequate/Balanced, Flooded, and Restricted Categories of Parenting Representations*

Parenting Representations' Scales	F (2, 79)	Adequate/ Balanced	Flooded	Restricted
Representations of the self		Mean	Mean	Mean
Competence	45.42**	3.58a	2.25c	2.62b
Self-understanding	34.09**	3.22a	2.47b	1.88c
Representations of the adolescent				
Trust/confidence in the child's capacities	23.72**	3.68a	30.31b	29.41b
Child's understanding	53.81**	3.30a	2.44b	1.91c
Elaborate perception of the child in the future	9.65*	2.70a	2.06b	1.91b
Representations of the parent–adolescent relationships				
Warmth and affection	12.93*	3.99a	3.47b	3.32b
Partnership and mutuality	43.66**	3.45a	2.19b	2.32b
Emphasizing/stressing achievement	5.44*	1.90b	2.66a	2.00b
Autonomy granting	10.90*	3.49a	2.81c	3.18b
Monitoring	30.80**	3.43a	2.75b	2.32c
The nature of future relationships with the child	27.70**	3.64a	2.50b	2.53b
Inappropriate/inadequate boundaries	35.88**	1.49b	3.04a	1.21b
Pain and/or difficulty	17.46*	2.85a	3.21a	1.85b
Anger	28.57**	2.76b	3.50a	1.74c
Worry/fear	27.92**	3.36b	3.97a	2.50c
Guilt	13.14*	2.33b	3.03a	1.38c
Conflicts and power struggles	29.17**	2.70a	3.03a	1.59b
Narrative style (process scales)				
Adequate/balanced description	161.88***	3.72a	2.31b	1.85c
Flooded description	78.34**	1.52b	3.72a	1.24b
Restricted description	147.40***	1.44b	1.47b	4.03a

$* p < 0.01$, $** p < 0.001$; means in a row which do not share a letter are significantly different (Duncan post hoc $p < 0.05$)

emotionality, and low differentiation between themselves and the child; restricted mothers seemed less involved in monitoring the child or in being emotionally and psychologically engaged. Their low level of engagement or involvement was apparent at the behavioral level (low monitoring), at the cognitive, mental level (low levels of reflectivity on self and the child), and at the emotional level (low levels of negative emotions). Interestingly, regarding positive emotions and positive interactions, restricted and flooded mothers evinced the same low levels of these qualities as compared with adequate/balanced mothers. It is noteworthy that adequate/balanced mothers exhibited moderate levels of negative emotions in the context of high levels of positive ones, reflecting the claim that "good mothering" does not mean an all-positive idealistic relationship but a balanced emotional makeup. This combination might be especially characteristic of adolescence, when high levels of negative emotionality and felt difficulty in parenting are probably inevitable, and part and parcel of normative parent–adolescent relationships (Steinberg & Steinberg, 1994).

Issues of Data Reduction. The suggested coding scheme of the PRI–A includes a large number of scales (21 for the first version, and 26 for the second). These scales were sometimes quite highly correlated (e.g., maternal competence, and partnership and mutuality). In general, such a situation calls for data reduction and the construction of aggregate scales. However, in this presentation we have opted to retain the separate scales, for several reasons. First, this is the first study, as far as we know, in which parenting representations of mothers of adolescents were examined. Therefore, it could qualify as research into as yet uncharted or barely charted territory. Accordingly, casting a wide net is recommended. Second, the "wide net" we utilized does not reflect an inflation of identical constructs; rather, each of the constructs assessed has been underscored by numerous researchers as significant and important and as reflecting a unique aspect or facet of parents' representations. For example, maternal competence, though highly correlated with partnership and mutu-ality, reflects a quite different construct in the conceptualizations regarding parenting and parent–child relationships (De Wolff & van IJzendoorn, 1997; Bornstein et al., 1998).

Third, though in many mothers these facets are positively correlated, this may not always be the case in other mothers or in other samples. For example, though in most cases a mother who serves as a secure base also shows warmth and affection, this may not always be the case (Goldberg, Grusec, & Jenkins, 1999). Fourth, and related to the foregoing point, though the different facets or aspects are correlated, each may exert a distinct influence on the child and may be uniquely predictive of diverse outcomes. This diversity or specificity of prediction may be especially true in the examination of varied samples (e.g., risk and non-risk) and different cultures, or when using different meth-ods of assessment (e.g., self-report, observations). To collapse all the positive markers together at this early stage of the inquiry may obscure such possible unique paths of prediction. Fifth, similar diversity may apply in a probe of the antecedents of these parenting representations. Though correlated, each may be linked to a somewhat different set of antecedents and may be related to different parts of the parents' personality and experience. In sum, we decided to retain the large number of intercorrelated scales but to use other statistical precautions. In particular, to avoid capitalizing on chance and interpreting spurious results, we used an overall alpha level rather than a separate alpha level for each specific statistical examination, using MANOVAs and Bonferonni adjustments when applicable.

Developmental Tasks of Late Adolescence and Emerging Adulthood

Our study examined adolescents at the end of this period, namely during late adolescence and emerging adulthood. At this period, several specific developmental tasks have been described: (1) leaving home and coping effectively with this transition and (2) developing mature psychosocial functioning (Arnett, 2001; Gray & Steinberg, 1999).

Although these developmental achievements start evolving before late adolescence (Collins & Sroufe, 1999; Furman, Brown, & Feiring, 1999; Sullivan, 1953), in that period and in emerging adulthood these tasks are deemed more central and salient (Allen & Land, 1999; Arnett, 2001; Gray & Steinberg, 1999). First, in most Western cultures young men and women are expected to leave their parents' home (Goldscheider & Davanzo, 1986; Moore, 1987) and cope effectively with being apart from them and with the demands of the new environment. In North America, this has most often been studied in the context of the home-to-college transition (Kenny & Donaldson, 1991; Lapsley, Rice, & FitzGerald, 1990; Schultheiss & Blustein, 1994).

Second, the process of developing mature psychosocial functioning, which includes a sense of differentiation from immature dependencies and the achievement of some degree of self-definition (individuation), has also been described as an age-normative change (Blos, 1979; Hill & Holmbeck, 1986; Rice & Mulkeen, 1995). Young adults are expected to develop higher levels of individuation and differentiation of the self, evinced in the capacity to rely on oneself rather than excessively on parents and others for support and guidance, and the capacity to make independent decisions and follow them through (Arnett, 2001; Bowlby, 1973; Blos, 1967; Greenberger & Sorensen, 1974; Gray & Steinberg, 1999).

In the study described here, these processes were examined in the Israeli context. In it, the great majority of the 18-year-old cohort of Jewish men (85%) leave their parents' home for a period of three years' mandatory service in the Israel Defense Forces (IDF).

Hypotheses

1. *Associations of parenting representations with mothers' state of mind.* In general, we expected mothers' parenting representations to be associated with their state of mind with respect to attachment. Autonomous/secure state of mind of the mother was expected to be associated with positive markers of parenting representations in four domains: (a) the relationship (e.g., warmth and affection, monitoring, autonomy granting and partnership, and mutuality); (b) the child (e.g., as capable and trustworthy); (c) the mother in her parental capacity (e.g., parental competence); and (d) positive markers of thought processes (e.g., flexibility, reflectivity). In contrast, non-autonomous states of mind of mother were expected to be associated with lower levels of these positive markers of parenting representations and with negative markers of parenting representations. Negative markers included difficulties in letting go, appearing more generally as boundary disturbances, and hyperactivation, that is, heightened anxiety and guilt, or deactivation, that is, detachment and little investment in the parental role.

2. *Parenting representations and coping with separation and individuation.* We expected maternal representations of parenting to be related to their son's coping with the developmental tasks of leaving home and developing individuation. Specifically, positive markers of parenting representations in the four domains (relationship; child; mother; thought processes) were expected to be associated with success in separation and individuation. In contrast, negative markers of parenting representations such as boundary disturbances and hyperactivation – heightened anxiety and guilt – or deactivation – detachment and little investment in the parental role – were expected to be associated with lower levels of attainment of these developmental tasks.

The Study of Parenting Representations of Mothers of Adolescent Sons

Sample

The study reported here is part of a longitudinal project examining parent–adolescent son relationships in Israel during late adolescence and young adulthood (see detailed information about the sample in Scharf et al., 2004). Participants in the study were identified and recruited from published lists of high-school seniors in metropolitan middle class neighborhoods in the northern part of Israel. We limited our choice of subjects to intact families, and families who had not immigrated recently to Israel (i.e., families for whom life had been fairly stable), so as to avoid diverse sources of variation. This constraint did not result in a highly skewed sample because divorce rates in Israel are much lower than in the United States (8.5%, according to the *Statistical Abstract of Israel*, 1996) and because in these neighborhoods new immigrants comprise only 5% of the population (*Statistical Abstract of Israel*, 1996).

The final sample included 88 families, which reflected consent by 41% of eligible families. In Israel, parental level of education, density of living quarters, and neighborhoods are considered better indices of SES than income (Dar & Resh, 1991). In addition, families of Western origin (Europe or North America) are more prevalent at high SES levels. In line with the prevailing characteristics of the middle-class neighborhoods from which they were sampled, the families in our sample were primarily well-educated (80% percent of the fathers and 74% of the mothers had at least a college education), 70% of the families were of Western origin, and their living quarters were of moderately low density.

At the time of the first assessment, adolescents' ages ranged from 17 to 18 years. Mean number of children in the families was 2.93 ($SD = 0.74$), with 37% first-born. None of the background variables was associated with the variables assessed in this study. In terms of military service, 59% of the adolescents were assigned to combat units and 41% to non-combat units. Thirty percent served as officers and 70% as rank-and-file soldiers.

Procedure

Parents were administered the *Parenting Representations Interview – Adolescence* (PRI–A) and the AAI when their sons were high-school seniors, approximately a year prior to their son's conscription (Time 1 – late adolescence assessment). Halfway through the basic training period (approximately five weeks after conscription) during a weekend furlough, 84 of the adolescents filled out questionnaires regarding their coping with this transition (Time 2 – basic training assessment). In addition, they were asked to provide the names of two peers (friends from their basic training unit who knew them well). These peers were contacted by the research team, and rated the respondents' coping and adjustment by means of a phone interview. Logistic problems prevented us from gathering peers' data for more than a sub-sample of the adolescents ($n = 64$). This sub-sample did not differ from the rest, for whom peers' reports were not available, on any of the background variables or the measures employed in this study.

Finally, at the end of the adolescents' three-year mandatory military service (Time 3 – emerging adulthood assessment), 74 adolescents were able to complete questionnaires. No difference existed between participants who completed the Time 3 assessment and the others on any of the background variables or the measures employed in this study.

In this report, only mothers' parenting representations are examined. Because of technical problems, several interviews with the mothers were not available for coding. Thus, this report is based on 82 mother–son dyads.

Measures

Time 1 – Late Adolescence Assessment. At this assessment time the PRI–A (described in previous sections) and the Adult Attachment Interview (AAI) were administered to the mothers.

The AAI (Main & Goldwyn, 1998) is a structured interview designed to arouse memories and emotions regarding attachment experiences. Participants were requested to give a general description of their relationships with their parents and to support these descriptions with specific biographical incidents. The interviewees were asked to give explanations for their parents' behavior, to describe the nature of their current relationship with their parents, and to assess the influence of childhood experiences on their development and personality. Scores were assigned to inferred childhood experiences of love, rejection, involvement, inattentiveness (neglect), and pressure to achieve exerted by each parent, and to respondent's state of mind with regard to idealization, anger, derogation, insistence on inability to recall childhood, passivity, and coherence. The coding of the AAI is based on the participant's reflections and evaluations, and assigns transcripts to the following state-of-mind groups: *secure-autonomous* (F), *insecure-dismissing* (DS), *insecure-preoccupied* (E), and *unresolved trauma or loss* (U) (Main & Goldwyn, 1998). The interviews were audiotaped and transcribed verbatim. Ruth Schnarch, a reliable coder of the AAI, analyzed the mothers' AAI transcripts, identified by number only. Ten transcripts were analyzed by Miri Scharf, and inter-rater reliability was 90% (*kappa* = 0.83). Disagreements between coders were resolved by consensus.

Time 2 – Basic Training Assessment. Level of distress, coping strategies, and functioning were examined as indicators of coping with the normative Israeli leaving-home transition.
Adolescent's Report. Level of distress was assessed by nine items from the *Mental Health Inventory* (MHI: Veit & Ware, 1983; e.g., feeling depressed,

lonely, nervous, anxious, or in control). Adolescents were asked to answer each item using a 1 (never) to 6 (all the time) scale, in reference to their feelings in military service during the previous two weeks (Cronbach's $\alpha = .76$). The measure has shown high internal reliability and good test–retest reliability, as well as construct and discriminant validity (e.g., Florian & Drory, 1990).

Perceived success in functioning in the military context was assessed by six items from the *Secondary appraisal scale* developed by Folkman & Lazarus (1985). Adolescents were asked to indicate on a 1 (not at all) to 5 (to a very large extent) scale how successfully they believed they had coped with basic training and its demands, and how challenged and threatened they felt by their experiences in basic training (Cronbach's $\alpha = 0.77$). The questionnaire has shown good internal reliabilities and construct validity (e.g., Mikulincer & Florian, 1995).

Ways of Coping (Folkman & Lazarus, 1980) measures cognitive and behavioral strategies people use in coping with stressful situations. Participants were asked to indicate on a 1 (not at all) to 5 (to a very large extent) scale how much they employed each of these strategies during their basic training. We included *Problem-Focused Coping* (six items, e.g., "I concentrated only on what should be done immediately") and *Emotion-Focused Coping* (eight items, e.g., I wished that I could change what was happening or how I felt"). Cronbach's αs were 0.53 and 0.75, respectively. The problem-focused coping scale of this version (community version) has typically low internal reliabilities (Folkman & Lazarus, 1985), probably because the items reflect different coping efforts, which may be somewhat mutually exclusive. (For a similar point, see Carver, Scheier, & Weintraub, 1989.)

Peers' Report. The *Peers' appraisal of adjustment questionnaire* was designed to assess adjustment and coping by different observers (Catz & Orbach, 1990). The questionnaire included dimensions that tapped the peers' evaluations of the recruit's adjustment. Two peers from basic training were asked to answer these questions using a 1 (not at all) to 5 (very much) Likert scale. The mean of their answers on two scales was computed: *Distress*, how stressed the focal adolescent was (three items, Cronbach's $\alpha = 0.86$); and *Instrumental and social functioning*, the extent to which he successfully coped with the basic training demands, including instrumental, social, and discipline aspects (six items, Cronbach's $\alpha = 0.82$).

Time 3 – Emerging Adulthood Assessment. Two measures assessing various facets of individuation (differentiation of the self-system and individuation) were included. The *Differentiation of Self Scale* (Haber, 1990; 1993) is a 24-item uni-dimensional scale that measures intellectual and emotional differentiation of the self-system based on Bowen's conceptualization (e.g., "I will change my opinion more on the basis of new knowledge than on the basis of the opinions of others"; "My life is guided by a clear set of goals that I have established for myself"). The scale has demonstrated internal reliability and content and construct validity (Garbarino, Gaa, & Gratch, 1995; Haber, 1990). Emerging adults and each parent filled out the questionnaire pertaining to the emerging adult's differentiation. Cronbach's αs were 0.87, 0.89, and 0.85 for the emerging adults', mothers', and fathers' reports, respectively.

The *Separation-Individuation Test of Adolescence – SITA* (Levine, Green, & Millon, 1986) is a self-report measure that includes several scales assessing psychological separation and individuation from a psychoanalytic perspective based on Mahler's conceptualizations. In the present report, four scales are included: separation anxiety, engulfment anxiety, dependency denial, and healthy separation (Cronbach's αs were 0.69, 0.79, 0.72, and 0.63, respectively). All but the last one denote different problems in the process of separation and individuation during adolescence. The scale has been employed in several studies in the United States (Levine & Saintonge, 1993) and in Israel (Mazor, Alfa, & Gampel, 1993), and has good psychometric properties and construct-validity.

Results

The Association Between Mothers' State of Mind and Parenting Representations

The analyses of mothers' AAI resulted in 37 Autonomous mothers, 29 Dismissing, nine Preoccupied, and 10 Unresolved. Assignment of Unresolved mothers to the underlying category resulted in 41 Autonomous, 32 Dismissing, and 12 Preoccupied mothers. As can be seen in Table 7.2, there was a significant association in the three-way cross-tabulation of mothers' AAI and parenting categories (χ^2 (4) $= 10.86, p < 0.03; kappa = 0.21, p < .05$), with 52% correspondence. When the four-category classification for the AAI was used, the association was again significant ($\chi^2(6) = 14.77, p < 0.02$). Three of the 10 Unresolved mothers were categorized as having adequate/balanced parenting representations, five as having flooded, and two as having restricted representations. Finally, the two-way cross-tabulation was also significant ($\chi^2(1) = 3.71, p < 0.05; \kappa = 0.21, p < 0.05$) with 60% correspondence.

Table 7.2. *Cross-Tabulation of Mothers' Attachment and Parenting Representations*

Mothers' Parenting Representations	Mothers' State of Mind with Respect to Attachment			
	Autonomous	Preoccupied	Dismissing	Total
Adequate/balanced classification	26	5	16	47
Flooded classification	7	6	3	16
Restricted classification	6	1	9	16
Total	39	12	28	79

A MANOVA conducted to examine the association between mothers' state of mind with respect to attachment (three-way categorization) and the continuous scales of their parenting representations was significant ($F(40, 112) = 1.63$, $p < 0.05$) and followed by univariate ANOVAs and post-hoc Duncan tests. As can be seen in Table 7.3, autonomous mothers showed more positive qualities of the relationships (i.e., higher competence and partnership and mutuality) than preoccupied mothers, with dismissing mothers occupying an intermediate position. In addition, as expected Preoccupied mothers

Table 7.3. *Parenting Representations as a Function of Mothers' Three Categories AAI*

Parenting Representations' Scales	F (2, 79)	Autonomous	Preoccupied	Dismissing
Representations of the self		Mean	Mean	Mean
Parental competence	5.28*	3.32a	2.50b	3.09a
Representations of the parent–adolescent relationships				
Partnership and mutuality	3.10*	3.16b	2.54a	2.84ab
Autonomy granting	2.91*	3.46b	3.08a	3.18ab
Inappropriate/inadequate boundaries	7.56**	1.67a	2.70b	1.52a
Pain and/or difficulty	4.27*	2.88ab	3.13b	2.39a
Anger	7.86**	2.84a	3.33a	2.29b
Worry/fear	11.55***	3.41b	3.92a	2.88c
Guilt	6.12*	2.46a	2.83a	1.77b
Conflicts and power struggles	3.60*	2.65ab	2.27b	2.92a
Narrative style (process scales)				
Adequate/balanced description	1.51	3.24	2.75	2.96
Flooded description	7.84**	1.88b	1.54b	2.96a
Restricted description	4.13*	1.75b	2.88a	1.58b

* $p < 0.05$; ** $p < 0.01$, *** $p < 0.001$; means in a row which do not share a letter are significantly different (Duncan post hoc $p < 0.05$)

showed the highest level of uncontained negative emotions and inappropriate/inadequate boundaries, and Dismissing mothers showed the lowest. Finally, Dismissing mothers showed the highest level of restricted narrative, and Preoccupied mothers showed the highest level of flooded narrative of all.

Contrary to expectations, Autonomous mothers did not show higher reflectivity regarding themselves and the child, more elaborate future perception of the child or the relationship, or higher levels of adequate/balanced narrative. When analyses were conducted with the four-way categorization of mothers' AAI (including the Unresolved category), the MANOVA was again significant ($F(60, 164) = 1.51, p < 0.05$), reflecting the same profile of results obtained with the AAI three-category partition; the Unresolved category received the lowest score of the positive qualities of the relationships, the highest score on flooded transcripts along with the preoccupied group, and intermediate scores on inappropriate/inadequate boundaries and negative emotions (see Table 7.4).

Altogether, these analyses reveal a significant association between mothers' state of mind with respect to attachment and their parenting representations with preoccupied state of mind (in the case of the three-way classification) or unresolved state of mind (in the case of the four-way classification) demonstrating the most negative parenting representations.

The Association Between Parenting Representations and Son's Coping With Separation During the Leaving Home Transition

The MANOVA conducted with parenting representation classifications as the independent variable and self-reported adjustment and coping scales as dependent variables was significant ($F(8, 144) = 2.25, p < 0.01$). Follow-up ANOVAs indicated that sons of flooded mothers felt the highest levels of distress ($M = 2.49$). Next came sons of adequate/balanced mothers ($M = 2.24$), with sons of restricted mothers showing the lowest distress ($M = 1.96, F (2, 78) = 3.42, p < 0.05$). The MANOVA with peers' reports of the adolescents' adjustment was not significant. Pearson correlations between mothers' parenting representations and self and peers' reports of adjustment indicated several significant associations. As can be seen in Table 7.5, mothers' confidence in their child and their warmth and affection were positively associated with markers of better adjustment, that is, less distress – peers' report; more problem-focused coping, and better functioning – self and peers' report. In contrast, aspects of the representations which reflect flooded mothers (inappropriate/inadequate boundaries, stressing achievements, flooded transcript, and high levels of negative emotions) were related to lower levels of

Table 7.4. *Parenting Representations as a Function of Mothers' Four Categories AAI*

		Mothers AAI Categories			
Parenting Representations' Scales	F (3, 78)	Autonomous	Dismissing	Preoccupied	Unresolved
		Mean	Mean	Mean	Mean
Representations of the self					
Parental Competence	3.72*	3.38a	3.08ab	2.61b	2.70b
Self-understanding	2.67*	3.09a	2.62ab	2.78ab	2.40b
Representations of the adolescent					
Trust/confidence in the child's capacities	4.01**	3.56a	3.46a	3.22ab	2.85b
Representations of the parent–adolescent relationships					
Warmth and affection	3.66*	3.85a	3.84a	3.50ab	3.25b
Partnership and mutuality	4.38***	3.26a	2.86ab	2.67ab	2.35b
Monitoring	3.56**	3.29a	2.92ab	3.11a	2.55b
The nature of future relationships with the child	2.78*	3.44a	3.00ab	3.11ab	2.65b
Inappropriate/inadequate boundaries	4.83**	1.65bc	1.44c	2.61a	2.30ab
Pain and/or difficulty	2.65*	2.88ab	2.38b	3.17a	2.80ab
Anger	4.04**	2.85ab	2.28b	3.27a	2.85ab
Worry/fear	6.38***	3.46a	2.84b	3.83a	3.40a
Guilt	3.71*	2.47ab	1.74b	2.83a	2.40ab
Narrative style (process scales)					
Adequate/balanced description	2.29	3.32a	3.02ab	2.78ab	2.55b
Flooded description	5.39**	1.78b	1.50b	2.72a	2.75a
Restricted description	2.40	1.68	2.44	1.67	2.20

* $p < 0.05$, ** $p < 0.01$, *** $p < 0.001$; means in a row which do not share a letter are significantly different (Duncan post hoc $p < 0.05$)

Table 7.5. *The Association between Mothers' Parenting Representations and Their Sons' Coping with Military Service – Time 2*

Parenting Representations Scales	Adolescents' Report (N = 80)				Peers' Report (N = 64)	
	Distress	Functioning	Emotion Focused Coping	Problem Focused Coping	Distress	Functioning
Representations of the adolescent						
Trust/confidence in the child's capacities	−0.08	0.22#	−0.17	0.24*	−0.17	0.28*
Representations of the parent–adolescent relationships						
Warmth and affection	−0.12	0.27*	−0.08	0.25*	−0.26*	0.58***
Partnership and mutuality	−0.04	0.23*	−0.08	0.29*	−0.10	0.20
Stress achievement	0.25*	−0.15	0.11	−0.19#	−0.08	−0.10
The nature of future relationships with the child	−0.02	0.24*	−0.15	0.25*	−0.08	0.26*
Inappropriate/inadequate boundaries	0.36**	−0.27*	0.13	0.08	0.29*	−0.10
Pain and/or difficulty	0.36***	−0.22*	0.20#	0.01	0.26*	−0.30*
Anger	0.37***	−0.26*	0.28*	−0.03	0.32**	−0.27*
Worry/fear	0.31**	−0.15	0.02	0.16	0.28*	−0.08
Guilt	0.23*	−0.20#	0.21#	−0.01	0.36**	−0.23#
Conflicts	0.33**	−0.22*	0.19#	−0.01	0.30*	−0.25*
Narrative style (process scales)						
Adequate/balanced description	0.04	0.14	−0.04	0.21#	−0.07	0.21
Flooded description	0.24**	−0.30**	0.10	−0.02	0.34**	−0.21
Restricted description	−0.25*	0.03	−0.02	−0.13	−0.13	0.02

# $p < 0.10$, * $p < 0.05$, ** $p < 0.01$, *** $p < 0.001$

Table 7.6. *Individuation of Sons as a Function of Their Mothers' Parenting Representations Categories*

Markers of Individuation	Mothers' Parenting Representations' Categories			
	Adequate/Balanced	Flooded	Restricted	F (2, 72)
Differentiation of Self Scale	3.85	3.63	3.68	2.05
SITA				
Dependency denial	1.78b	2.14a	1.77b	3.87*
Healthy Separation	3.87	3.72	3.83	0.36
Separation Anxiety	2.01b	2.43a	1.71c	9.06***
Engulfment Anxiety	2.30b	2.98a	2.11b	6.91**

# $p < 0.10$, * $p < 0.05$, ** $p < 0.01$, *** $p < 0.001$; means in a row which do not share a letter are significantly different (Duncan post hoc $p < 0.05$)

adjustment (i.e., higher distress, lower functioning) as reflected in self and peers' reports.

When a Bonferroni adjustment was incorporated, the significant associations retained were those between warmth and affection and functioning – peers' report, and the associations between distress – self and peers' report and negative feelings, flooded descriptions, and inappropriate/inadequate boundaries. In general, it appears that parenting representations that include over-involvement and inadequate boundaries are related to lower levels of the son's coping with the leaving home transition into military service.

The Association Between Parenting Representations and the Son's Psychosocial Functioning: Time 3 Assessment

The MANOVA conducted with the parenting representation groups as the independent variable and individuation indicators assessed at the third point in time as dependent variables was significant ($F(14, 110) = 2.70, p < 0.01$). Follow-up ANOVAs indicated that sons of flooded mothers evinced the lowest levels of individuation, as reflected in their highest scores in separation anxiety, engulfment anxiety, and dependency denial (see Table 7.6). A similar profile of results was revealed when the continuous scales of mothers' parenting representations were used in computing Pearson correlations with these developmental outcomes. Specifically, as can be seen in Table 7.7, separation anxiety and engulfment anxiety were positively associated with indicators characteristic of flooded mothers – high levels of inappropriate/inadequate boundaries, negative emotions, and focusing on achievement. A sense of individuation was positively associated with markers characteristic of

Table 7.7. *The Association between Mothers' Parenting Representations and Their Sons' Individuation – Time 3*

		SITA		
Parenting Representations' Scales	Differentiation of Self Scale	Dependency Denial	Separation Anxiety	Engulfment Anxiety
Representations of the self				
Parental Competence	0.29**	−0.11	−0.06	−0.22*
Self-understanding	0.25*	−0.02	0.03	0.07
Representations of the adolescent				
Trust/confidence in the child's capacities	0.40***	−0.25*	−0.05	−0.22*
Child's understanding	0.35**	−0.06	0.04	0.04
Elaborate perception of the child in the future	0.05	0.01	0.19	−0.06
Representations of the parent–adolescent relationships				
Warmth and affection	0.24*	−0.17	−0.09	−0.14
Partnership and mutuality	0.28*	−0.16	−0.04	−0.07
Emphasizing/stressing achievement	−0.25*	0.21#	0.32**	0.33**
Autonomy granting	0.27*	−0.25*	−0.15	−0.16
Monitoring	0.29*	−0.10	−0.06	−0.05
The nature of future relationships with the child	0.30**	−0.16	−0.08	−0.11
Inappropriate/inadequate boundaries	−0.07	0.26*	0.26*	0.52***
Pain and/or difficulty	−0.17	0.15	0.30**	0.35**
Anger	−0.10	0.28**	0.34**	0.40***
Worry/fear	0.01	0.15	0.24*	0.32**
Guilt	0.10	0.16	0.21#	0.33**
Conflicts and power struggles	−0.07	0.21#	0.30**	0.31**
Narrative style (process scales)				
Adequate/balanced description	0.25*	−0.16	0.06	−0.15
Flooded description	−0.11	0.25*	0.30**	0.43***
Restricted description	−0.07	−0.12	−0.29*	−0.25*

$\# p < 0.10$, $^* p < 0.05$, $^{**} p < 0.01$, $^{***} p < 0.001$; $N = 74$

adequate/balanced mothers (e.g., mothers' competence, partnership and mutuality, and warmth and affection) and was negatively associated with some of the indicators of restricted mothers' parenting representations (e.g., low monitoring, and low reflectivity – self-understanding).

Discussion

This study, which examined parenting representations of mothers of adolescent sons, found these representations to be meaningfully associated with the mothers' own attachment representations as well as with a number of indicators of the sons' psychosocial functioning. Specifically, mothers' parenting representations were associated with the sons' functioning and coping during the leaving home transition into military service about a year later, and with their levels of individuation almost four years later still.

Specifically, mothers' warmth and affection was positively and strongly associated with markers of better functioning in basic training, and aspects of the representations which reflect flooded mothers (inappropriate/inadequate boundaries, high levels of negative emotions) were strongly related to higher distress and to problems in individuation. This prediction is impressive given the time interval (eight months to one year), the different context, and the different methods and informants employed to assess the constructs. The association between maternal representations and the peers' reports of the sons' adaptation is especially compelling because these peers were not part of the mother–son dyad.

On the whole, these findings attest to the significance of mothers' parenting representations in predicting their adolescent sons' functioning in various domains. These associations are especially noteworthy in light of the diverse areas of functioning assessed, the longitudinal predictions, and the multi-source, multi-method design.

These results accord with previous studies examining parenting representations of mothers of younger children, mostly infants, toddlers, and preschoolers (e.g., Pianta et al., 1996; Slade et al., 1999). Adolescence, however, is marked by several unique characteristics which highlight the importance of our findings. First, as discussed by George and Solomon (1996; 1999) and Allen et al. (2003), caregiving or parenting representations are expected to be conceptually and developmentally linked with attachment representations and affected by their quality. Yet other sources of influence, in particular the history of the mother's relationship with her child and the quality of her current relationship with the child, may strongly affect these representations. This is especially true when parents and children have had a long history together, as in the case of parenting representations of parents of adolescents.

The fact that we found a significant association between mothers' attachment and parenting representations attests to the importance of the mothers' state of mind with regard to attachment for their parenting even in adolescence.

Specifically, autonomous mothers were conspicuous in their positive parenting representations (i.e., higher competence and partnership and mutuality) and moderate levels of negative emotions. Preoccupied mothers showed the highest level of uncontained negative emotions and inappropriate/inadequate boundaries, whereas dismissing mothers showed the highest level of restricted narrative and lowest level of negative emotions. Yet some of the central facets of parenting representations such as reflectivity did not differentiate among the state-of-mind groups.

Thus, it is important to note that despite the similarity in method and coding scheme (i.e., in-depth structured interview, utilization of both content and information processing coding scales), the associations between mothers' AAI and parenting representations were not so strong as to suggest that the two assess the same construct. These findings are significant because they underscore the unique place of parenting representations in mothers' caregiving vis-a-vis mothers' state of mind with respect to attachment.

A distinct issue related to parents of adolescents is the importance of focusing on parents' feelings and perceptions during this period. Despite findings showing that most adolescents navigate this developmental period successfully, several recent conceptualizations suggest that for parents this period can be a very challenging and difficult experience. For parents the daily conflicts, the emotional ups and downs, the questioning of their authority, and the need to let go while continue to serve as a secure base and safe haven prove quite taxing (Steinberg, 2001). Our findings demonstrated that mothers who at this challenging developmental period are able to contain but not repress their negative emotions, and to maintain differentiated boundaries between themselves and the adolescent while providing warmth and affection, have sons who successfully cope with salient developmental tasks of late adolescence: leaving home and individuation.

In this report, we opted to retain a large number of separate yet interrelated scales to be able to examine the possibility of their distinctive predictions. Our results seem to support the choice of this strategy. Different aspects in the parenting representations of the mothers seem to play different roles with regards to various developmental outcomes. For example, in the current dataset positive feelings towards the child were strongly related to his functioning, especially during basic training as reported by peers. In contrast, maternal reflectivity, which was also seen as a positive marker of parenting representations, was not associated with coping in the military context. From the negative markers, inadequate/inappropriate boundaries proved a good predictor of distress as reported by both peers and adolescents in basic training; in addition they predicted lower levels of individuation.

In general, characteristics of flooded mothers (e.g., high levels of inappropriate/inadequate boundaries and negative emotions) were associated with the lowest levels of individuation and highest difficulty at the time of separating from the family and adjusting to the new environment. Characteristics of adequate/balanced mothers (e.g., mothers' competence, partnership and mutuality, and warmth and affection) were positively associated with coping with separation, and with individuation. In contrast, characteristics of restricted mothers (e.g., low monitoring, low reflectivity) were not associated with these outcomes. This distinct profile of association needs to be explored in future research but seems to suggest the importance of retaining, at least at this preliminary stage of research, a diversity of scales.

In this study we looked only at mothers' representations. However, the role of fathers as caregivers and their contribution to adolescent coping in general, and to coping during military service in particular, cannot be overstated. We are currently analyzing fathers' parenting representation as reflected in the PRI–A and hope to be able to explore this aspect as well. Similarly, this study examined only adolescent boys. The way girls negotiate the developmental tasks of separation and individuation might reflect a different profile of developmental processes. In addition, the role of fathers and mothers in these processes might be different for girls and boys. As the PRI–A from the girls' study are currently being analyzed, we hope to be able to shed light on gender differences in these domains in the near future.

In addition, in this study we explored the associations between mothers' parenting representations and the functioning of their adolescents during late adolescence. The experiences and feelings of parents of adolescents at other periods in adolescence (e.g., preadolescence, before and after puberty) may be somewhat different, and these periods may pose distinct challenges for the parents (Graber, Brooks-Gunn, & Petersen, 1996). Similarly, the effects of parents' representations on the adolescents may be somewhat different, depending on the period of adolescence studied. It would be the task for future research to examine these avenues.

Our study longitudinally examined developmental trajectories of male adolescents regarding two developmental tasks, across a four-year time span and during an especially malleable period. Thus, the association found between mothers' parenting representations and psychosocial developmental accomplishments of their sons is quite impressive, and attests to the significance of the mothers' parenting representations in affecting the sons' experiences as part of their developmental trajectory.

The ability to assess parenting representations has practical and clinical implications as well. Adolescence is a particularly tumultuous period in the life cycle of the family. Shedding light on the implications of various parenting representations for parents' and adolescents' psychosocial well-being could help practitioners to identify at-risk families for whom this life period is expected to be difficult and stormy for both parties. Learning about the way successful and competent parents negotiate this period, as well as learning about the deficiencies of less efficient parents may eventually help parents cope adaptively with this challenging period, and make it a less taxing and more pleasurable experience for both parties. Finally, most previous research on parents–adolescents' relationships has focused on parents' influence on their children. However, the impact of adolescents on their parents has been less explored and reflects the general focus on the child as the center of interest. This lacuna calls for systematic research and deeper understanding. The "parenting career" is demanding and lifelong, and as such it deserves more attention in itself, not only as an independent variable predicting children's functioning.

Acknowledgments

Parts of this chapter were presented in a symposium at the Biennial Meeting of the Society for Research in Child Development, Minneapolis (Mayseless, O., & Scharf, M., 2001, April). *Maternal representations of parenting, socioemotional functioning and coping of mother and adolescent sons with a stressful separation.*

References

Aber, J. L., Belsky, J., Slade, A., & Crnic, K. (1999). Stability and change in mothers' representations of their relationship with their toddlers. *Developmental Psychology, 35*, 1038–47.

Allen, J. P. & Land, D. (1999). Attachment in adolescence. In J. Cassidy & P. R. Shaver (Eds.), *Handbook of Attachment Theory and Research*. New York: Guilford Press, pp. 319–35.

Allen, J. P., McElhaney, K. B., Land, D. J., Kuperminc, G. P., Moore, C. W., O'Beirne, K. H., & Kilmer, S. L. (2003). A secure base in adolescence: Markers of attachment security in the mother-adolescent relationship. *Child Development, 74*, 292–307.

Allen, J. P., Moore, C., & Kuperminc, G. P. (1997). Developmental approaches to understanding adolescent deviance. In S. S. Luthar, J. A. Burack, D. Cichetti, & J. Weisz (Eds.), *Developmental Psychopathology: Perspectives on Adjustment, Risk, and Disorder*. Cambridge: Cambridge University Press, pp. 548–67.

Arnett, J. J. (2001). *Adolescence and Emerging Adulthood a Cultural Approach*. Upper Saddle River, NJ: Prentice Hall.

Benoit, D., Zeanah, C. H., Parker, K. C. H., Nicholson, E., & Coolbear, J. (1997). "Working Model of the Child Interview": Infant clinical status related to maternal perceptions. *Infant Mental Health Journal, 18,* 107–21.

Blos, P. (1967). The second individuation process of adolescence. *The Psychoanalytic Study of the Child, 22,* 162–86.

Blos, P. (1979). *The Adolescent Passage.* New York: International University Press.

Bornstein, M. H., Haynes, O. M., Azuma, H., Galpern, C., Maital, S., Ogino, M., Painter, K., Pascual, K., Pcheux, M. G., Rahn, C., Toda, S., Venuti, P., Vyt, A., & Wright, B. A. (1998). Cross-national study of self-evaluations and attributions in parenting: Argentina, Belgium, France, Israel, Italy, Japan, and the United States. *Developmental Psychology, 34,* 662–76.

Bowlby, J. (1973). *Attachment and Loss:* Volume 2, *Separation.* New York: Basic Books.

Bretherton, I., Biringen, Z., Ridgeway, D., Maslin, C., & Sherman, M. (1989). Attachment: The parental perspective. *Infant Mental Health Journal, 10(3),* 203–21.

Carver, C. S., Scheier, M. F., & Weintraub, J. K. (1989). Assessing coping strategies: A theoretically based approach. *Journal of Personality and Social Psychology, 56,* 267–83.

Catz, M. & Orbach, D. (1990). *Conscription of Youth from Special Backgrounds.* Tel Aviv, Israel: Israeli Defense Forces, Psychological Research Division.

Coleman, P. K. & Karraker, K. H. (1998). Self-efficacy and parenting quality: Findings and future applications. *Developmental Review, 18,* 47–85.

Collins, A. & Sroufe, A. (1999). Capacity for intimate relationships: A developmental construction. In W. Furman, B. B. Brown, & C. Feiring (Eds.), *The Development of Romantic Relationships in Adolescence.* New York: Cambridge University Press, pp. 125–48.

Dar, Y. & Resh, N. (1991). Socioeconomic and ethnic gaps in academic achievement in Israel junior high school. In N. Bleichrodt and P. J. D. Drenth (Eds.), *Contemporary Issues in Cross-cultural Psychology.* Berwyn, PA: Swets & Zeitlinger, pp. 322–33.

De Wolff, M. & van IJzendoorn, M. H. (1997). Sensitivity and attachment: A meta-analysis non parental antecedents of infant attachment. *Child Development, 68,* 571–91.

Florian, V. & Drory, Y. (1990). Mental Health Inventory (MHI) – Psychometric properties and normative data in the Israeli population. *Psychologia: Israel Journal of Psychology, 2(1),* 26–35.

Folkman, S. & Lazarus, R. S. (1980). An analysis of coping in a middle-aged community sample. *Journal of Health and Social Behavior, 21,* 219–39.

Folkman, S. & Lazarus, R. S. (1985). If it changes, it must be a process: Study of emotion and coping during three stages of a college examination. *Journal of Personality and Social Psychology, 48,* 150–70.

Fonagy, P., Steele, M., Steele, H., & Target, M. (1997). *Reflective-functioning Manual, Version 4.1.* Unpublished manuscript. Psychoanalysis Unit, University College London.

Furman, W., Brown, B. B., & Feiring, C. (Eds.). (1999). *The Development of Romantic Relationships in Adolescence.* New York: Cambridge University Press.

Garbarino, J., Gaa, J. P., & Gratch, L. V. (1995). The relation of individuation and psychosocial development. *Journal of Family Psychology, 9,* 311–18.

George, C. & Solomon, J. (l989). Internal working models of caregiving and security of attachment at age six. *Infant Mental Health Journal, 10*, 222–37.

George, C. & Solomon, J. (1996). Representational models of relationships: Links between caregiving and attachment. *Infant Mental Health Journal, 17*, 198–216.

George, C. & Solomon, J. (1999). The development of caregiving: A comparison of attachment theory and psychoanalytic approaches to mothering. *Psychoanalytic Inquiry, 19*, 618–46.

Goldberg, S., Grusec, J. E., & Jenkins, J. M. (1999). Confidence in protection: Arguments for a narrow definition of attachment. *Journal of Family Psychology, 13(4)*, 475–83.

Goldscheider, F. & Davanzo, J. (1986). Semiautonomy and leaving home during early adulthood. *Social Forces, 65*, 187–201.

Graber, J. A., Brooks-Gunn, J., & Petersen, A. C. (Eds.). (1996). *Transitions Through Adolescence: Interpersonal Domains and Context.* Hillsdale, NJ: Erlbaum.

Gray, M. R. & Steinberg, L. (1999). Unpacking authoritative parenting: Reassessing a multidimensional construct. *Journal of Marriage and the Family, 61*, 574–87.

Greenberger, E. & Sorensen, A. B. (1974). Toward a concept of psychosocial maturity. *Journal of Youth and Adolescence, 3*, 329–58.

Haber, J. (1990). The Haber Differentiation of Self scale. In C. Waltz & O. Strickland (Eds.), *The Measure of Nursing Outcomes. Measuring Client Self-care and Coping Skills.* New York: Springer, pp. 320–1.

Haber, J. (1993). A construct validity study of a differentiation of self scale. *Scholarly Inquiry for Nursing Practice, 7*, 165–78.

Hill, J. P. & Holmbeck, G. (1986). Attachment and autonomy during adolescence. In G. Whitehurst (Ed.), *Annals of Child Development.* Greenwich, CT: JAI, pp. 145–89.

Holmbeck, G. N., Paikoff, R. L., & Brooks-Gunn, J. (1995). Parenting adolescents. In M. H. Bornstein (Ed.), *Handbook of Parenting.* Vol. 1: *Children and Parenting.* Hillsdale, NJ: Erlbaum, pp. 91–118.

Huth-Bocks, A. C., Levendosky, A. A., Bogat, G. A., & von Eye, A. (2004). The impact of maternal characteristics and contextual variables on infant-mother attachment. *Child Development, 75*, 480–96.

Kenny, M. E. & Donaldson, G. A. (1991). Contributions of parental attachment and family structure to the social and psychological functioning of first-year college students. *Journal of Counseling Psychology, 38*, 479–86.

Kobak, R. & Cole, H. (1994). Attachment and meta-monitoring: Implications for adolescent autonomy and psychopathology. In D. Cicchetti & S. L. Toth (Eds.), *Rochester-symposium on Developmental Psychopathology.* Vol. 5: *Disorders and Dysfunctions of the Self.* New York: University of Rochester Press, pp. 267–97.

Lapsley, D. K., Rice, K. G., & FitzGerald, D. P. (1990). Adolescent attachment, identity, and adjustment to college: Implications for the continuity of adaptation hypothesis. *Journal of Counseling and Development, 68*, 561–5.

Levine, J. B., Green, C. J., & Millon, T. (1986). The Separation-Individuation Test of Adolescence. *Journal of Personality Assessment, 50*, 123–37.

Levine, J. B. & Saintonge, S. (1993). Psychometric properties of the Separation-Individuation Test of Adolescence. *Journal of Clinical Psychology, 49*, 492–507.

Main, M. & Goldwyn, R. (1998). *Adult Attachment Scoring and Classification Systems, Version 6.3.* Unpublished manual, University of California, Berkeley.

Mazor, A., Alfa, A., & Gampel, Y. (1993). On the thin blue line between connection and separation: The individuation process, from cognitive and object-relations perspectives, in kibbutz adolescents. *Journal of Youth and Adolescence, 22,* 641–69.

Mayseless, O., Scharf, M., Kivenson Baron, I., & Schnarch, R. (2005). Mothers' attachment and caregiving representations and their adolescent sons' functioning and state of mind with regard to attachment. Unpublished manuscript, University of Haifa.

Mikulincer, M. & Florian, V. (1995). Appraisal of and coping with a real-life stressful situation: The contribution of attachment styles. *Personality and Social Psychology Bulletin, 21,* 406–14.

Moore, D. (1987). Parent-adolescent separation: The construction of adulthood by late adolescents. *Developmental Psychology, 23,* 298–307.

Pianta, R. C., Marvin, R. S., Britner, P. A., & Borowitz, K. C. (1996). Mothers' resolution of their childrens' diagnosis: Organized patterns of caregiving representations. Special issue: The caregiving system. *Infant Mental Health Journal, 17(3),* 239–56.

Rice, K. G. & Mulkeen, P. (1995). Relationships with parents and peers: A longitudinal study of adolescent intimacy. *Journal of Adolescent Research, 10,* 338–57.

Scharf, M. & Mayseless, O. (1997/2000). *Parenting Representations Interview–Adolescence (PRI–A).* Unpublished manuscript, University of Haifa.

Scharf, M., Mayseless, O., & Kivenson-Baron, I. (1997/2000). Coding Manual of the *Parenting Representations Interview–Adolescence (PRI–A).* Unpublished manuscript, University of Haifa.

Scharf, M., Mayseless, O., & Kivenson-Baron, I. (2004). Adolescents' attachment representations and developmental tasks in emerging adulthood. *Developmental Psychology, 40,* 430–44.

Schultheiss, D. P. & Blustein, D. L. (1994). The role of adolescent-parent relationships in college student development and adjustment. *Journal of Counseling Psychology, 41,* 248–55.

Slade, A., Belsky, J., Aber, L., & Phelps, J. (1999). Maternal representations of their relationship with their toddlers: Links to adult attachment and observed mothering. *Developmental Psychology, 35,* 611–19.

Solomon, J. & George, C. (1999). The caregiving system in mothers of infants: A comparison of divorcing and married mothers. *Attachment and Human Development, 1,* 171–90.

Statistical abstract of Israel. (1996). Jerusalem: The Government of Israel, Central Bureau of Statistics.

Steinberg, L. (2001). We know some things: Parent-adolescent relationships in retrospect and prospect. *Journal of Research on Adolescence, 11,* 1–19.

Steinberg, L. & Silk, J. (2002). Parenting adolescents. In M. Bornstein (Ed.), *Handbook of Parenting: Vol. 1: Children and Parenting.* Mahwah, NJ: Erlbaum, pp. 103–33.

Steinberg, L. & Steinberg, W. (1994). *Crossing Paths: How Your Child's Adolescence Triggers Your Own Crisis.* New York: Simon & Schuster.

Sullivan, H. S. (1953). *The Interpersonal Theory of Psychiatry.* New York: Norton.

Veit, C. & Ware, J. (1983). The structure of psychological distress and well-being in general populations. *Journal of Consulting and Clinical Psychology, 51,* 730–42.

Westen, D., Lohr, N. E., Silk, K. R., Gold, L., & Kerber, K. (1990). Object relations and social cognition in borderlines, major depressives, and normals: A Thematic Apperception Test analysis. *Psychological Assessment: A Journal of Consulting and Clinical Psychology, 2*, 355–64.

Zeanah, C. H. & Benoit, D. (1995). Clinical applications of a parent perception interview in infant mental health. *Child and Adolescent Psychiatric Clinics of North America, 4*, 539–54.

Zeanah, C. H., Benoit, D., Hirshberg, L., Barton, M. L., & Regan, C. (1994). Mothers' representations of their infants are concordant with infant attachment classifications. *Developmental Issues in Psychiatry and Psychology, 1*, 1–14.

8   Like Fathers, Like Sons? Fathers' Attitudes to Childrearing in Light of Their Perceived Relationships with Own Parents, and Their Attachment Concerns

Ruth Sharabany, Anat Scher, and Judit Gal-Krauz

Abstract

How does the way parents perceive and remember their relationships with their own parents during childhood relate to their parental attitudes toward their own preschool children? A sample of 62 fathers, aged 22–40, drawn from a longitudinal study of parenthood (Scher, 1991) was used to answer this question. Four factors served to assess the fathers' childrearing attitudes with their 3.5-year-old children: control and authoritativeness; repression; encouragement of verbal and emotional expression; and promotion of autonomy (Block, 1981). The fathers' relationships with their own parents in childhood (acceptance, and encouragement of independence; Epstein, 1983) and fathers' attachment concerns (fear of abandonment and fear of dependency; Mayseless, 1995) were examined by self-reports. Perceived acceptance by fathers' own father was positively associated with rearing attitude of control and repression and negatively with autonomy promotion. A controlling rearing attitude was associated with less behavior problems. Results were discussed as supporting a "model of reference" whereby the paternal role includes reference to experiences with mother and father during childhood that indicates similarity as well as compensation and change.

Studies have documented the intergenerational transmission of risk and vulnerability between parents and their children via both mothers and fathers (e.g., Kendler, 1996). In extreme cases, instances of risk factors have been found, namely a very high likelihood that problems of mothers are transmitted to their children (Bifulco et al., 2002). Similarly, transmission of increased risk was found due to problems with the father's own father. Findings from a sample of 164 fathers from the Concordia Longitudinal Risk Project indicate inter-generational continuity, particularly for aggression (Cooperman, 2000).

We know much less about the inter-generational flow of parental, particularly paternal, relationships in a normal population not at high risk.

In this chapter, we address father's relationships with his own parents, and examine if and how they are linked to his stance and attitudes vis-à-vis his child. To this end, we examine how fathers represent and describe their parents' behavior towards themselves: the degree of acceptance and restriction, and compare father's perceived relationships with their own mother vs. father during childhood. A second focus of this chapter is on fathers' current attachment-related concerns: fear of abandonment and fear of dependence. From theory and studies, parents' attachment concerns are expected to reflect their experience with their own parents, and may underlie their tendency and ability to provide their children a sense of protection and security. To date, the perspectives of attachment theory and parental attitudes have been studied separately. Yet father's attachment concerns are expected to be related to their views on childrearing, in particular to dimensions of warmth, affect regulation (e.g., repression and expression), and independence encouragement vs. control (Rudy & Grusec, this volume). All these in turn are expected to affect the child's own adjustment. Thus, we examine the associations between representations of past relationships with the father's own parents (father and mother), his attachment orientation, his attitudes towards parenting his own child, as well as the adjustment of his child.

The Role of Fathers

The past 20 years have seen great changes in the degree of fathers' involvement and ways of participation in their children's lives in Western countries (Bornstein, 2002; Parke, 2002). Fathers are tending to assume increased responsibility, and to join more in decisions. The degree of a father's participation in childrearing depends on his motivation (Lamb & Oppenheim, 1989) and on his interaction with his spouse. Agreement with the mother on degree of involvement and her encouragement, are conducive to greater father's engagement than in cases where the mother feels threatened or disagrees with the father (Polatnick, 1973/74). Fathers whose gender identity is less stereotyped are also more likely to partake in rearing their children (Russell & Radojevic, 1992). The recognition of the role of the father comes also from ecological theory that focuses on the various persons involved in the socialization of the child, the fathers being one with most close interactions, most likely dyadic (Bronfenbrenner, 1989; 2005). For example, children of parents who are both involved in their socialization show higher cognitive abilities, less sex-stereotyped views, and more internal control (Parke, 2002).

As to the unique role of the father as distinct from the mother, two opinions are found in the literature. The traditional one expects father to socialize specific aspects of the developing personality of their offspring, so that he undertakes the role of "the other parent." He is the one who supports the sex-typed roles of the children, and reflects discipline, autonomy, and drawing away from regressive needs satisfied by the mother (Ross, 1977). Various studies document that fathers often have the role of playmates, in contrast to mothers, who concentrate on caregiving (Parke, 2002). The other opinion is that when fathers are actually involved in raising their children, the distinctive roles of parents by gender becomes blurred and individual differences prevail (Radin & Russell, 1983).

Attitudes Towards Childrearing

Childrearing attitudes include thoughts, expectations, stereotypes, beliefs, judgments, intentions, and folk-wisdom, as well as developmental models about child care (Goodnow & Collins, 1990). They are influenced by the parent's philosophy, cultural and social values, personal experience, the nature of the current relationship with the child, as well as by goals and expectations for the future (Holden & Edwards, 1989). In a comprehensive review of research, Holden and Buck (2002) identify the source of parents' attitudes to childrearing as a central question. In this chapter, we examine the link between fathers' accounts of the relationship with their own parents and their parental attitudes.

Parenting attitudes are undoubtedly an important part of the package of socialization that guides the development of the child. While the way in which attitudes on childrearing relate to values and behavior towards their children may follow a consistent pattern, this pattern may depend on the gender of the parent. For example, general attitudes of parents about childrearing (measured by the Child Rearing Practices Report, Block, 1981) were found to be correlated with behavior of the parents as observed by experimenters – degree of helping in solving problems and degree of acceptance of the children (Block, 1981). Mothers who were observed to behave in a more accepting way in collaborative problem-solving with their children displayed an attitude of encouraging emotional expression. In contrast, fathers who were also observed and rated as accepting their children, reported higher expectations regarding instrumental goals, control, and discipline. This set of findings, specifically the differences between mothers and fathers, should be underscored. The congruence between the self-reported attitudes and observed behavior of the mothers seems more understandable. By contrast, for fathers the actual observed behavior of acceptance was a reflection of higher importance of discipline, control, and specified goals.

The results of Block (1981) as well as others (e.g., Rosen & Rothbaum, 1993), show that parents' self-reported attitudes are manifested in their observed interaction with their children, although the link is not always simple. The relation of fathers' attitudes to childrearing and their actual behavior is apparent in another study (Paquet, Bolte, Turcotte, Dubeau, & Bouchard, 2000). Types of parenting were determined from self-report measures of father's involvement and parental attitudes. The study covered 468 two-parent families with at least one child aged zero to six years. The fathers, who ranged in age from 23 to 63 years, were classified into four types of parent: authoritarian, authoritative, permissive, and stimulating. The stimulating fathers proved more likely to provide emotional support to their children and be themselves more secure in their social relations, while the authoritarian and authoritative fathers were more likely to maltreat their children. A link not yet fully unraveled is the contribution of fathers' relationships with their own fathers and mothers to their own caregiving and to the emotional support they provide to their child.

*Relationship of Fathers with Their Own Mother and Father
and Their Childrearing Attitudes*

Jung and Honig (2000) suggested three different models of how father's experiences with his own father shape his attitudes to childrearing. First, when the experience was positive, using one's father as a model for one's own fatherhood applies. The second model, when the relationships were not satisfactory, implies using mechanisms of compensation. The third model highlights the notion of a cohort effect rather than interpersonal relationships. In this model, merely the generations to which the father, his own father, and his offspring belong may account for differences in attitudes and behaviors. The changes may reflect broader social economic and cultural changes reflected in more general position of society on certain socialization issues. Jung and Honig (2000) assessed grandfathers' as well as fathers' attitudes, and found that the latter were similar to the former in their position on discipline, but differed with regard to nurturance, acceptance, and flexibility, reflecting differences in cohorts.

Along similar lines, a modeling hypothesis whereby fathers imitate the involvement of their fathers, particularly when it is positive, has been suggested by Shears, Robinson, and Emde (2002). In a study on the intergenerational transmission of fathering practices, the links between men's relationship with their fathers, their attachment to their children, and their self-assessment as fathers were addressed (Shears, Robinson, & Emde, 2002). Participants were fathers and father figures (men who were significant in the child's life and participated in the child's upbringing) aged 19 and over. They were interviewed about their experiences with their two- and three-year-old children. Fathers who reported a positive relationship with their own fathers, gave better assessments of themselves as fathers. They showed similarity and continuity in their perception of the relationships with own father and with their child.

According to the second hypothesis, namely the compensation model, fathers who are currently involved with taking care of their children may be compensating for the little involvement of their own fathers in their upbringing (i.e., Belsky & Pensky, 1988; Caspi & Elder, 1988; Rutter, 1989, 1990). We propose herein that even when fathers do not emulate their own parents' attitudes and behaviors, the fathers' relationship with their own parents provides a "model of reference." This model of reference may be applied and linked to their fathering attitudes in different ways depending on different conditions, creating an intricate map. Some fathers may use their parental model for direct imitation, or modeling (Bandura, 1989; Cowan & Cowan, 1992). Other fathers may use it as something they want to repair, or to compensate for (Baruch & Barnett, 1986). Moreover, since it is a model of reference, situational factors may further determine which of these models is applied at different times and contexts. In general, what determines which path will be taken – modeling, compensating, mixture of both – may most likely be predicted from the overall nature of the relationship. Fathers who had warm and accepting fathers of their own may want to be like them, whereas fathers who felt less accepted by their parents, maybe even rejected, may wish to enjoy different relations with their own children. In addition, fathers who had negative relationships with their own fathers may repeat that pattern, harboring perhaps "implicit" attitudes, as suggested by Holden and Buck, (2002), or "automatic" attitudes, as suggested by Rudy and Grusec (this volume).

It is interesting that in a comprehensive and up-to-date review of fathering (Parke, 2002), one discovers a gap in the current knowledge about fathers' attitudes. Although continuity in behavior of fathers and their own fathers was studied in a few research projects, continuity in behaviors of fathers and their experience of their own mothers was hardly examined. In our study, we restricted ourselves to fathers' self-reported perception of their relationship with both their parents, and focused on its connection to their current childrearing attitudes.

Fathers' Relationships with Their Own Parents and Attachment Concerns

Studies of adult attachment have documented that self-report of attachment style is related to the self-reported relationship with one's own parents, and to perceiving them as having certain attitudes or behaviors towards the respondent (original study of Hazan & Shaver, 1987, and review by Shaver & Mikulincer, 2002). Adults who described their style of attachment as secure, compared to insecure, reported that their relationships with their parents were warm and accepting. In contrast, avoidant adults described their mothers as being cold and rejecting. According to attachment theory, relationships with parents are internalized and play a significant role in forming a generalized internal working model, or models, relating to both self and other. We expected that the nature of the represented relationship with parents would be reflected in these generalized internal representations, namely as attachment concerns. Thus, lower levels of attachment concerns (i.e., less fear of abandonment and less fear of dependency) were expected to be associated with perceived warm relationships with parents (Collins & Read, 1990).

Fathers' Own Attachment Concerns and Their Attitudes to Childrearing

A parent's internal working model of attachment, an umbrella of cognition, emotion, and action tendencies, guides their close relationships in general (Mayseless, Sharabany, & Sagi, 1997; Shaver & Mikulincer, 2002), and also their reactions to their children (Bowlby, 1982). In other words, the attachment system and the caregiving system are connected. For example, according to recent theoretical formulations and empirical evidence, attachment security, namely reduced anxiety and avoidance, was related to a person's capacity to give care to his or her spouse (reviewed in Shaver & Mikulincer, 2002). As highlighted by Bretherton and Munholland (1999), attachment representations are assumed to guide one's expectations, feelings, and information processing, as well as emotion regulation in situations related to attachment.

In particular, the tie with one's offspring, one of the most significant close relationships, is presumably guided by the internalized working model of closeness and caregiving, based on a parallel experience with one's own parents. According to this premise, aspects of the internal working models, dating back to the experienced and represented attachment relationship with caring figures, serve as a basis for subsequent close relationships. From this viewpoint, the attachment behavioral system (based on the relationship with one's parents) shapes the caregiving system (expressed in the relationship with one's offspring). So that, as an adult, harboring fears of being abandoned, or preoccupation with fears of being dependent may impinge on one's ability to function well as a parent. For example, fathers with greater fear of being abandoned might be more controlling and strict toward their children. In contrast, fathers with low fear of being dependent might show a more relaxed and warmer parenting style.

The association between fathers' attachment representations assessed by the Adult Attachment Interview (AAI) and the quality of the attachment formed between their child and themselves has been demonstrated by several longitudinal studies (see review by Hesse, 1999). Several other studies showed correspondence between parents' attachment representations assessed by the AAI and their relationship and behavior with their children (e.g., Cohn, Cowen, Cowen, & Pearson, 1992; Crowell & Feldman, 1991; Fonagy, Steele & Steele, 1991). Though attachment concerns assess a somewhat different facet of an individual's attachment representations, we expected them to be implicated in parenting.

In a study by Mayseless et al. (1997), children were observed in the laboratory reacting to the Strange Situation. Their mothers described their own attachment concerns, as well as their degree of intimacy with husband and friend. It has been demonstrated that children's behavior in the laboratory procedure was related to their mother's self-reported attachment concerns. Further support for the link between parents' self-reported attachment style and the nature of behavior of parent and child during leave taking in the kindergarten was provided by Sharabany and Haglili (2002). Sixty-seven children, aged three to four years, and their parents participated. Data included self-report attachment style of both mothers and fathers, and their report about leave taking in the morning from their child. The kindergarten teacher reported on three aspects of the adjustment of the child in the kindergarten: cognitive, social, and emotional. The actual leave taking in the morning was observed twice: by experimenter, and by kindergarten teachers. The results that are relevant to the present study are that the self-reported attachment style of fathers was correlated with the adjustment of the child to the kindergarten, and with the behaviors of the father–child dyad during their leave taking (as measured both by self-report and observation).

In the study reported herein, we set out to investigate the connections between fathers' attachment concerns and their parenting attitudes towards their child, in light of their representations of the parenting that they themselves received from their father as well as from their mother during childhood. Specifically we expected that representations of fathers' relationship with their own fathers and mothers would be associated with their attitudes regarding the upbringing of their children, and with their attachment concerns.

Attachment concerns were further expected to be associated with child-rearing attitudes. Finally we expected childrearing attitudes to be associated with the child's adjustment.

Method

This report is based on a larger longitudinal study (Scher, 1991) that examined patterns of sleep and their correlates during infancy. The cohort consisted of 118 low-risk infants, from intact, predominantly middle class families, residing in an urban setting in Israel. The present data were collected when the children were 3.5 years of age. The fathers, who were not actively involved in the study beyond early infancy, were asked to participate in the study by responding to a set of questionnaires that had been mailed to them, along with a self-addressed envelope for returning the questionnaires.

Sixty-two of the fathers (52% response rate) returned fully answered questionnaires. The participating sub-sample, consisting of married fathers of 27 boys and 35 girls, did not differ from the original sample with respect to fathers' age and education. At the time of the study, fathers' mean age was 35.1 years ($SD = 4.1$); their mean education level was 14.2 years ($SD = 3.3$). Most fathers ($n = 42$) were born in Israel, and 20 were born in other countries.

Measures

Parental Beliefs and Attitudes: Child Rearing Practice Report – CRPR (Block, 1981)

The CRPR was used originally as a 91-item Q-sort, aimed to estimate values, philosophies, and practices in childrearing. The original scales were constructed from interactions of mothers and children, other existing socialization scales, reflecting various cultures. It has been translated into many languages and is used in many cultures. The original CRPR consists of 28–33 scales. The Q-sort technique was modified to a questionnaire by Rickel and Biasatti (1982) and has been in use since then (Steele, Steele, & Johansson 2002). These previous studies employed a version of 40 items: 18 for restriction and 22 for nurturance. Based on factor analysis, we defined four scales as follows (see Appendix 8.1): I. *Controlling* (11 items, e.g., "I do not allow my child to get angry with me," "I believe in toilet training a child as soon as possible"; Cronbach's $\alpha = 0.88$); II. *Expressive/ nurturance* – giving support and encouraging expression of emotions and experiences (11 items, e.g., "I respect my child's opinions and encourage him/her to express them," "I make sure my child knows that I appreciate what he/she tries to accomplish"; Cronbach's $\alpha = 0.78$); III. *Repression* (10 items, e.g., "I don't allow my child to say bad things about his/her teachers," "I teach my child that in one way or another punishment will find him/her when he/she is bad"; Cronbach's $\alpha = 0.70$); IV. *Autonomy promotion* (five items, e.g., "I let my child make many decisions for himself/herself," "I give my child a good many duties and family responsibilities"; Cronbach's $\alpha = 0.65$). Overall, the scales were independent of each other (range of inter-correlations $r = -0.09$ to $r = 0.18$, n.s.) with the exception of Controlling and Repression ($r = 0.50, p < 0.01$).

Relationships with Parent in Childhood (MFP – Epstein, 1983)

The original Mother Father Peers (MFP) questionnaire contains scales depicting relationships with mother, father, and peers. Reliability of the scales has been documented (Ricks, 1985; Catlin & Epstein, 1992), and the validity of the questionnaire is based on correlations of perceived "acceptance" in childhood with being "worthy of love" in adulthood, as measured by a self-report inventory by Epstein (Epstein, 1983). It also has been validated against several other measures of parenting (Crowell, Treboux, & Waters, 1999).

In the present study we used only the mother and father forms (MF), each containing two scales: I. *Acceptance* (nine items, e.g., "He/she enjoyed being with me"; Cronbach's $\alpha = 0.80$, 0.77, respectively, for mothers and fathers); II. *Independence encouragement* (13 items, e.g., "He/she helped me learn to be independent"; Cronbach's α for mothers = 0.81, for fathers = 0.75).

Attachment Concerns: Attachment Concerns and Close-Relationships Questionnaire *(Hazan & Shaver, 1987; adapted by Mayseless, 1995)*

This is a measure of attachment-related concerns, and also a measure of willingness to give care. The instrument is based on the questionnaire developed by Hazan and Shaver (1987) that consisted of a three-division measure of styles of attachment, and on that of Collins and Read (1990), and Bartholomew (1990). The present version, based on the responses of 296 participants, and Principle Component factor analysis with Varimax rotations (Mayseless 1995), consists of 12 statements to be endorsed on a six-point Likert scale. This adaptation has been used in several studies with minor changes (e.g., Scher & Mayseless, 1994; Mayseless et al., 1996; 1997).

The measure yields components of attachment and of caregiving, as follows: *Fear of abandonment* (four items, e.g., "Usually I am not worried that I may be abandoned" (reversed item); Cronbach's $\alpha = 0.65$); *Fear of dependency* (five items, e.g., "I feel uncomfortable depending on others";

Cronbach's $\alpha = 0.70$); *Fear of Closeness* was not used, since its reliability did not reach a minimum of Cronbach's $\alpha = 0.50$. A generalized attitude about caregiving included three items (e.g., "I usually feel comfortable with people who need my help and are open to me"; Cronbach's $\alpha = 0.65$). The three measures were relatively independent (Pearson correlations ranging from -0.15 to 0.15, n.s.).

The validity of the tool was demonstrated in several studies related to parental behaviors. For example, fear of abandonment expressed by mothers was related to the assignment of limited developmental goals (Scher & Mayseless, 1994). Also, self-reported attachment concerns of mothers were related to actual attachment behavior of their child, as measured in the Strange Situation, and to intimacy with husband and friend (Mayseless, Sharabany, & Sagi, 1997). In another study, it has been demonstrated that self-reported attachment concerns were related to evaluation of narrated situations of separations, varying in their degree of severity (Mayseless, Danieli, & Sharabany, 1996).

Child Behavior and Adjustment: The Child Behavior Checklist (CBCL/2–3: Achenbach, Edelbrock, & Howell, 1987) is a widely used measure of children's competencies and problems as reported by their parents or caregivers. The CBCL/2–3 is a 99-item checklist that provides an empirically based procedure for assessing behavioral/emotional problems of two- and three-year-olds. Examples of items include: upset by separation, disturbed by change, resists bed, refuses to eat, cries much, and destroys others' things. Respondents rate the items as follows: 2 – if the item is very true or often true, 1 – if the item is somewhat or sometimes true of the child, and 0 – if the item is not true of the child. The instrument provides a number of scores including six syndrome scales (e.g., Social Withdrawal, Depressed, Aggressive, Sleep Problems), two broad-band groupings (i.e., externalizing and internalizing), and a total problem score. For the purpose of the present report, the total problem score (CBCL), which is the sum of all items scored "0," "1," and "2," served as the overall measure of the child's adjustment. The CBCL was completed by the mothers. While fathers completed the previous measures, mothers were the source for information about the well-being and adaptation, measured as lack of problems, of their child, using the CBCL/2–3.

Results

First, to compare fathers' attitudes to girls and to boys, t-tests for independent samples were carried out on the three measures: childrearing attitudes

Table 8.1. *Fathers' Attitudes to Childrearing and Their Perceived Relationships with Own Mother and Father*

Relationships with Own Parents	Childrearing Attitudes			
	Control	Expression	Repression	Autonomy Promotion
Mother Acceptance	0.11	0.17	0.15	0.11
Independence encouragement	−0.10	0.19	0.14	−0.02
Father Acceptance	0.30**	0.07	0.23*	−0.24*
Independence encouragement	0.16	−0.12	0.16	−0.24*

*$p < 0.05$,** $p < 0.01$

(CRPR), relationships with own parents (MF), and attachment concerns. No significant differences were found, therefore, on subsequent analyses data for boys and girls were combined. As for the children's behavior and adjustment, the CBCL scores of the girls ($M = 23$, $SD = 15.8$) indicated that they had less behavioral problems as compared to the boys ($M = 34$, $SD = 19.1$; $t = 2.16$, $p < 0.05$). Accordingly, the analysis pertaining to this variable will take into account the child's gender.

How Do Fathers Perceive Relationships with Their Own Mother and Father?

Fathers' accounts of their relationships with their mother and father, during childhood, were associated with each other. The correlations were statistically significantly, albeit not high, as follows: $r = 0.27$, $p < 0.05$ on acceptance and $r = 0.33$, $p < 0.01$ on encouraging independence. Acceptance correlated mildly with encouraging independence by mother ($r = 0.36$, $p < 0.01$) and more so by father ($r = 0.60$, $p < 0.001$). The mothers were perceived as more accepting than the fathers ($M = 3.15$, $SD = 0.34$ compared to $M = 2.96$, $SD = 0.34$; $t = 3.69$, $p < 0.001$); there was no difference between mothers and fathers concerning encouragement of independence ($M = 3.23$, $SD = 0.44$ and $M = 3.29$, $SD = 0.52$, respectively; $t = 0.81$, ns).

How Do Fathers' Perceived Relationships with Their Own Parents Relate to Their Childrearing Attitudes?

With respect to the relationship with father, perceiving him as accepting during childhood correlated with attitudes of expecting more control in their child's behavior, greater repression, and less autonomy promotion ($r = 0.30$, $p < 0.01$; $r = 0.23$, $p < 0.05$; $r = -0.24$, $p < 0.05$ respectively; see Table 8.1). Surprisingly, the more fathers perceived their own fathers as encouraging

Table 8.2. *Fathers' Attachment-Related Concerns, Perceived Relationships with Own Mother and Father, and Their Childrearing Attitudes: Pearson Correlations*

Relationships with Own Parents	Fear of Dependency	Fear of Abandonment	Caregiving
Mother Acceptance	−0.06	−0.15	−0.09
Independence encouragement	−0.32**	0.03	0.11
Father Acceptance	−0.15	−0.37**	−0.14
Independence encouragement	−0.09	−0.25*	0.22#
Childrearing Attitudes			
Control	−0.11	−0.21	−0.28**
Expression	−0.34**	0.21#	−0.21#
Repression	−0.15	0.02	−0.09
Autonomy Promotion	−0.06	0.03	−0.07

$\#p < 0.10, * p < 0.05, ** p < 0.01$

independence, the more their own attitude was one of granting less autonomy to their child ($r = -0.24$, $p < 0.05$, respectively). Perceived quality of relationships with mother was not related significantly to the father's childrearing attitudes. Interestingly similar aspects of perceived relationship with parent carried different implications when attributed to the father's mother vs. the father's father. This point will be discussed later.

How Do Fathers' Perceived Relationships with their Own Parents Relate to Their Attachment Concerns?

Fathers who perceived their own mothers as encouraging independence expressed less fear of being dependent in their close relationships ($r = -0.32$, $p < 0.01$, see Table 8.2). Perceiving their fathers as more accepting and granting independence during childhood correlated with being less afraid of being abandoned ($r = -0.37$, $p < 0.01$ and $r = -0.25$, $p < 0.05$, respectively). Finally, the level of independence encouragement assigned to the father showed a tendency to be correlated with an attitude of caregiving reported by the father ($r = 0.22$, $p < 0.10$).

How are Fathers' Attachment Concerns Reflected in Their Parental Attitudes?

Pearson correlations showed that the less the father feared being dependent himself, the more he encouraged his child to express his or her emotions and thoughts ($r = -0.34$, p < 0.01: see Table 8.2). The more fathers were willing to give care, the less they expected controlled behavior from their children $(r = -0.28, p < 0.01)$.

How Do Fathers' Parental Attitudes and Practices Relate to the Child's Behavior and Adjustment?

Of the four parenting scales, only controlling showed significant association with the CBCL scores. Overall, it was found that more control by the fathers was associated with less behavioral problems by the children $(r = -0.40, p < 0.01)$. This association was particularly strong for boys $(r = -0.52, p < 0.01)$ as compared to girls $(r = -0.25,$ n.s.$)$.

Discussion

Fathers' Parenting Attitudes and Their Perceived Relationships with Their Own Parents

Overall, fathers' self-reports of the relationships with their own mothers and fathers showed significant correlations, and were consistent with previous studies. Fathers' reports on their parents' acceptance and independence encouragement during childhood were rather similar. However, the pattern of associations among the various aspects attributed to mothers and to fathers differed. For example, acceptance by the father was highly correlated with granting independence by his own father, whereas with respect to mothers, this connection was much weaker.

In the present study, fathers' perception of the relationship with their own father showed a significant link with attitudes toward their child. At first sight, the connections seem rather perplexing. Fathers perceiving their own father as more *accepting* of them reported attitudes of expecting more *control* in their child's behavior, greater *repression*, and *less autonomy*. Second, experiencing their own fathers as supporting independence was associated with being more over-protective of their child. Two lines of interpretation may be offered to this pattern of results; the first underscores compensation, or "re-working," to use the expression of Bretherton, Lambert, and Golby (this volume). According to this interpretation, perceiving father as low in acceptance and independence granting yields a compensating attitude of higher autonomy promotion and lower repression. Another possibility is that fathers who had positive relationships with their own fathers transmit attitudes of more control, repression, and overprotection as part of what they see as positive fathering. Having positive memories about the parenting they received from their fathers (acceptance and independence granting), they invest more in their children by being overprotective and granting less autonomy.

In line with the second interpretation, it is important to note that in this sample an attitude of "control" by fathers was associated with *better* adjustment of the child, as reported by the mother. Thus, fathers who report more acceptance by their own fathers tend to adopt stronger controlling childrearing attitudes, which in turn are associated with better adjustment and less problems of the child as reported by the mother – a different observer. The interpretation that positive fathering is related to a more controlling attitude towards childrearing seems to also be in accord with the original Block (1981) report. In the Block studies, fathers interacting with their children were observed by independent observers in the laboratory. Those rated as behaving in an "accepting" way towards their children, were fathers who self-reported that their attitude was to expect from their offspring more instrumental goals, more control, and more discipline. This perhaps indicates a combination of a positive interaction with a demanding attitude, pointing to a complex link between attitude and behavior. The connection between one's perception of the relationship with one's own parents and one's attitudes is also complex, perhaps having to do with gender role of the parent. For example, fathers who perceive their own fathers in positive terms might be the ones who fulfill a genderized paternal role of a strict father, and this highly schematic gender role may be beneficial for the child, especially for boys, in preventing behavior problems, at least at that age group – preschoolers. Future research may need to address these notions.

Turning to the relationships with mothers and childrearing attitudes, the results obtained with the present sample of fathers, indicated that there were no significant associations. One possibility is that fathers' attitudes are related to their relationships with their fathers but other caregiving aspects, such as their actual behavior, might be emulated based on their experience with their primary caregiver – most probably their mother. Had we used observations of caregiving behaviors, we might have seen these associations. Another possibility is that experiences of being parented by their own fathers are more relevant to fathers' childrearing attitudes than experiences with their own mothers. These results accord with the notion regarding the higher importance of the same gender parent to one's functioning.

*Fathers' Attachment Concerns and Their Relationships
with Their Own Parents*

It is broadly accepted that people with positive self-esteem are those who had parents who loved them, were proud of their success, and accepted their failures (Epstein, 1983). Conversely, people with low self-esteem most likely have internalized a model of a parent who was not satisfied and was critical about their failures. Consistent with this view, the present findings indicated that fathers who reported having low "fear of abandonment" experienced their own fathers as both more accepting and encouraging independence. Conversely, fathers who currently harbor fears of abandonment reported that their fathers were more rejecting and overprotective/controlling during their childhood. With respect to representations of the relationships of their mothers, encouraging independence was associated with lower levels of fear of dependency. The feeling that their mothers granted them space for growth without menace and worry may have been contributing to their current low anxiety about being dependent themselves. It may be argued that as these fathers were confident about being supported, they did not feel that their independence was being challenged. Thus, notwithstanding the concurrent measurement, perceptions of their relationships both with their fathers and their mothers proved to be related to the general attachment concerns. Interestingly, the specific pattern of associations was dependent on the parent gender.

Childrearing Attitudes in Light of Attachment Concern

Attachment concerns of the father were reflected in his attitudes to childrearing. The less father feared being dependent himself, the more he encouraged his child to express his or her emotions and thoughts. Fathers who did not greatly fear being dependent endorsed statements reflecting being warm and at ease with closeness: "I am easy going and relaxed with my child; I respect my child's opinion and encourage him/her to express it. I feel that a child should be given comfort and understanding when he/she is scared or upset. I joke and play with my child," etc. This is an important finding in two ways. First, the connection between feeling more secure as a father (not fearing dependency) and being able to provide warmth and encourage expression of emotions is of significance from both theoretical and clinical perspectives. Second, given that attachment concerns were measured and defined in the present study as a generalized and internalized model, documenting the expected link between fathers' attachment and parenting is of methodological relevance.

Fathers whose close relationships with significant others are characterized by lower fear of dependency scores, feeling no unease at having to turn to others for help, and trusting others, encouraged their own children to express their thoughts and feelings, and to develop their individual interests. As fathers, they expressed their concern about their children, and at the same time reported enjoying their role as fathers.

Focusing on caregiving in close relationships, it may be speculated that high levels of willingness to care for others may be a compensatory sign for one's own need of dependency, namely projecting the need onto those of others. These fathers are likely to feel more confident, effective and rewarded, when they could care for others, and take charge of others' emotional and psychological needs (Mayseless, 1995). In the context of the present study, the more general attitude of willingness to take care of others expressed by fathers, the less controlled behavior they expected from their own children. In a way, this pattern of results points to the interplay between implicit (attachment concerns) and explicit (parental attitudes) cognitions.

Limitations of the Study

The measures used for the study rely mostly upon self reports of fathers both about their relationships with their parents, their general attachment styles, and their attitudes about childrearing. Often, this is considered a weakness in the study. However, there are two aspects that provide some support to this method. First, it has been documented repeatedly that adolescent outcomes are explained by experienced, and hence self-reported, parental behavior, and it has become an acceptable approach in adolescent research (Seginer, Vermulst, & Shoyer, 2004). Our extrapolation is that the description of fathers of their own experience of their relationships with their parents has similar merit. Second, we have a measure of the adjustment of the child as reported by an independent source, the mother. Accordingly, we find that the report of fathers having a controlling attitude toward their children is associated with less problem behavior of the child. This lends validity as well as meaning to the pattern of results, and it is discussed below.

According to Parke (2002), the nature of the father–child relationship alters as the child develops. Moreover, the father's involvement is influenced by the marital relationship, by cohort effects such as historical changes that determine the work patterns of family members, and by the timing of the onset of parenthood. Our study was limited to fathers of children at a specific age, namely, 3.5 years. It makes sense to expect that not only attitudes change with age but also that the correlates of these attitudes change across time. For example, granting independence to children aged three may mean something very different from granting it at age 14. An interesting expansion of the study would be to repeat it, comparing fathering of children in different age groups, and across time, so to unravel continuity and change across ages and time.

In line with Jung and Honig (2000), emphasis on cohort effect, another extension of the study is to consider the impact of context on fathering.

Perhaps there are features unique to Israeli society (Radin & Sagi, 1982; Sagi, 1982). For example, at present, in Israel, individual fathers who take their new fatherhood role more seriously, as requiring more nurturing, being involved in daily caregiving, and so on, face resistance from their social context (e.g., nurses at "Well-Baby" clinics, wives, employers), who are resistant to the change and its ramifications, as apparent in media reports (e.g., the daily Israeli newspaper, *Yediot Acharonot*, 13 Feb. 2004).

One of the shortcomings of the present study is the reliance on measuring parental attitudes by self-report (Holden & Buck, 2002). Attitudes about parenting, like other social attitudes, are a complex concept. They are product of the history of interactions with one's own socializing agents (parents, cultural norms, etc.). They are also a product of interaction within a specific family. Although attitudes to parenting do not correspond precisely with particular behaviors, studies have shown that parental attitudes do have their correlates in the actual parent–child relationships (Block, 1981; Goodnow & Collins, 1990). The attitudes we measured here were explicit. We acknowledge that there are also attitudes that are implicit, perhaps less conscious (Holden & Buck, 2002), or, to use parallel concepts, there are parenting cognitions that are "controlled," and ones that are "automatic" (Rudy & Grusec, this volume). Here we focused on the former, not the latter. We assume that by assessing attachment concerns, and how past experiences with parents are perceived, we tapped into the potentially less conscious attitudes. Finally, due to the relatively homogeneous middle class nature of the sample, generalization is compromised. Studying a wider range of social classes is not only necessary for supporting statements about fathers in general but also may well show firmer connections among the aspects studied, because of greater variance in attitudes and experiences that are often social class-bound.

Notwithstanding the above limitations, it is worth noting that in Bretherton et al. chapter (this volume), which relies on transcribed interviews with U.S. fathers to four-year-olds, there is a general tendency in the sample, which is highly educated, to describe their parenting as affectionate, lenient, and highly involved. This pattern is congruent with societal changes in Western cultures: being more supportive of expressions of emotions and closeness, and having an ideology of less gender-typed behaviors, and having "new fathers," who are more involved. This may appear to be in contrast with the study of Jung and Honig (2000), who documented social change towards more leniency but not in increased expressions of closeness and affection. Yet the two studies may be consistent, having been conducted in different cultures. This would underscore that while change and its reflection in cohort differences may be a universal finding, the specific content is culture-bound, as well as having cohort differences within each culture.

Models and Research Agenda

Given the focus of the present chapter on fathers, it is important to stress the different inputs of their own mothers and of their own fathers. It has been conventionally accepted that mothers provide trust and closeness while fathers are the disciplinary "others." Indeed, in our sample, the mothers of our participating fathers were described as more accepting than the fathers, although fathers were not described as granting more independence. However, the present findings suggest a more complex model. It seems that the degree to which each parent is perceived to offer, in addition to the expected gender related aspect (i.e., mother–warmth, father–discipline), an interpersonal dimension that is normatively attributed to the other gender, makes for a complementary, internalized model of parenting that is more balanced. Accordingly, a conclusion of the present study that merits further examination is the following: might it be that a combination of relatively high independence that mothers grant with the relatively high level of acceptance that fathers bestow, will enable a person to develop a more balanced parenting strategy? Alternatively, regardless of gender: how important is it that the same person who is the main giver of closeness equally respects space and autonomy? How important is it that the person who is the main provider of boundaries and control be warm?

In sum, the model that we propose is one of a person's own perceived and received parenting as a *reference model*. Parents do behave in reference to and in dialogue with their own internalized models of relationships with their parents; so that the perceived relationship with their parents correlates with their stated childrearing attitudes. Likewise, the generalized model of attachment, of which attachment concerns are one part, also has relevance to parenting attitudes. Two models are applicable: modeling and compensating (or "reworking," the term used by Bretherton and colleagues, see this volume); each of these models may characterize unique aspects of socializing offspring.

A task for the future is to register when modeling occurs and to signify the circumstances under which compensation comes about. The present study has contributed the notion that fathers' attitudes, and possibly behaviors, toward their children depend not only on the content of the represented relationships with the parents (e.g. acceptance), but more on whether it was attributed to relationships with mother or father. In other words, similar relationships experienced with mother and father translate differently into attitudes on raising one's children. Mothers' granting of independence perhaps carries a different meaning from fathers'. To follow up on this speculation, direct interviewing of parents, focusing on how they *experience* their own reference model, what they think they are choosing to do, and what they actually practice, may prove to be a fruitful endeavor. One possibility is that their attitudes reflect choices, while their actual behavior reflects continuity. The notion of "reworking" the model (Bretherton et al., this volume) seems to be a more suitable term than "compensating" in its connotation of a potential change rather than a specific direction of change.

Appendix 8.1
The Items Used from the CRPR (Block, 1981)
and the Relationship Scales

I. Restriction/Control

28. I worry about the bad and sad things that can happen to a child as he/she grows up.
31. I do not allow my child to get angry with me.
47. I expected my child to be grateful and appreciate all the advantages he/she has.
49. I believe in toilet training a child as soon as possible.
55. I teach my child to keep control of his/her feelings at all times.
59. I think a child should be encouraged to do things better than others.
63. I believe that too much affection and tenderness can harm or weaken a child.
65. I believe my child should be aware of how much I sacrifice for him/her.
73. I let my child know how ashamed and disappointed I am when he/she misbehaves.
82. I think children must learn early not to cry.
83. I control my child by warning him/her about the bad things that can happen to him/her.

II. Expressive/Nurturance

1. I respect my child's opinions and encourage him/her to express them.
11. I feel that a child should be given comfort and understanding when he/she is scared or upset.
34. I am easygoing and relaxed with my child.
40. I joke and play with my child.
51. I believe in praising a child when he/she is good and think it gets better results than punishing him/her when he/she is bad.
52. I make sure my child knows that I appreciate what he/she tries to accomplish.

53. I encourage my child to talk about his/her troubles.
76. I make sure I know where my child is and what he/she is doing.
77. I find it interesting and educational to be with my child for long periods.
87. I believe it is very important for a child to play outside and get plenty of fresh air.
88. I get pleasure from seeing my child eating well and enjoying his/her food.

III. Repression

15. I believe that a child should be seen and not heard.
23. I wish my child did not have to grow up so fast.
27. I do not allow my child to say bad things about his/her teacher.
29. I teach my child that in one way or another punishment will find him/her when he/she is bad.
33. I expect a great deal of my child.
56. I try to keep my child from fighting.
57. I dread answering my child's questions about sex.
58. When I am angry with my child I let him/her know it.
64. I believe that scolding and criticism make a child improve.
86. I don't think children should be given sexual information.

IV. Independence Encouragement

21. I encourage my child to wonder and think about life.
26. I let my child make many decisions for himself/herself.
38. I talk it over and reason with my child when he/she misbehaves.
41. I give my child a good many duties and family responsibilities.
67. I teach my child that he/she is responsible for what happens to him/her.

References

Achenbach, T. M., Edelbrock, C., & Howell, C. T. (1987). Empirically based assessment of the behavioral/emotional problems of 2- and 3-year-old children. *Journal of Abnormal Child Psychology, 15*, 629–50.

Bandura, A. (1989). Cognitive social learning theory. In R. Vasta (Ed.), *Six Theories of Child Development*. Greenwich, CT: JAI Press, pp. 1–60.

Bartholomew, K. (1990). Avoidance of intimacy: An attachment perspective. *Journal of Social and Personal Relationships, 7*, 147–78.

Baruch, G. K. & Barnett, R. C. (1986). Fathers' participation in family work and children's sex-role attitudes. *Child Development, 57*, 1210–23.

Belsky, J. & Pensky, E. (1988). Developmental history, personality and family relationships: Toward an emergent family system. In R. Hinde & J. Stevenson-Hinde (Eds.), *Relationships within Families: Mutual Influences*. Oxford: Oxford University Press, pp. 193–217.

Bifulco, A., Moran, P. M., Ball, C., Jacobs, C., Baines, R., Bunn, A., & Cavagin, J. (2002). Childhood adversity, parental vulnerability and disorder: Examining inter-generational transmission of risk. *Journal of Child Psychology and Psychiatry and Allied Disciplines, 43(8)*, 1075–86.

Block, J. H. (1981). *The Child Rearing Practices Report (CRPR): A set of Q-items for the description of parental socialization attitudes and values*. Unpublished manuscript. University of California, Berkeley, Institute of Human Development.

Bornstein, M. H. (Ed.) (2002). *Handbook of Parenting: Being and Becoming a Parent*. Mahwah, NJ: Erlbaum, pp. 27–73.

Bowlby, J. (1982). Attachment and loss: Retrospect and prospect. *The American Journal of Orthopsychiatry, 52*, 664–78.

Bretherton, I. & Munholland, K. A. (1999). Internal working models in attachment relationships: A construct revisited. In J. Cassidy & P. R. Shaver (Eds.), *Handbook of Attachment: Theory, Research and Clinical Applications*. New York: Guilford, pp. 89–111.

Bronfenbrenner, U. (1989). Ecological systems theory. In R. Vasta (Ed.), *Six Theories of Child Development*. Greenwich, CT: JAI, pp. 187–250.

Bronfenbrenner, U. (2005). *Making Human Being Human*. Thousand Oaks, CA: Sage Publications.

Caspi, A. & Elder, G. H. (1988). Emergent family patterns: The intergenerational construction of problem behavior and relationships. In R. Hinde & J. Stevenson-Hinde (Eds.), *Relationships within Families: Mutual Influences*. Oxford: Oxford University Press, pp. 218–40.

Catlin, G. & Epstein, S. (1992). Unforgettable experience: The relation of life events to basic beliefs about self and world. *Social Cognition, 10(2)*, 189–209.

Cohn, D. A., Cowan, F. A., Cowan, C. P., & Pearson, J. (1992). Mothers' and fathers' working models of childhood attachment relationships, parenting styles, and child behavior. *Development and Psychopathology, 4(3)*, 417–31.

Collins, N. I. & Read, S. J. (1990). Adult attachment working models and relationship quality in dating couples. *Journal of Personal and Social Psychology, 58*, 644–63.

Cooperman, J. M. (2000). From childhood to parenthood: Continuity of risk over time and contextual factors perpetuating the inter-generational transfer of risk. *Dissertation Abstracts International: Section B: The Sciences and Engineering, 61* (3-B), 1669.

Cowan, C. P. & Cowan, P. A. (1992). *When Partners Become Parents*. New York: Basic Books.

Crowell, J. A. & Feldman, S. S. (1991). Mothers' working models of attachment relationships and mother and child behavior during separation and reunion. *Developmental Psychology, 27*, 597–605.

Crowell, J. A., Treboux, D., & Waters, E. (1999). The Adult Attachment Interview and the Relationship Questionnaire: Relations to reports of mothers and partners. *Personal Relationships, 6*, 1–18.

Epstein, S. (1983). *The Mother-Father-Peer Scale*. Unpublished manuscript, University of Massachusetts, Amherst.

Fonagy, P., Steele, H., & Steele, M. (1991). Maternal representations of attachment during pregnancy predict the organization of infant-mother attachment, at one year of age. *Child Development, 62(5),* 891–905.

Goodnow, J. J. & Collins, W. A. (1990). *Development According to Parents: The Nature, Sources and Consequences of Parents' Ideas.* Hillsdale, NJ: Erlbaum.

Hazan, C. & Shaver, P. R. (1987). Romantic love conceptualized as an attachment process. *Journal of Personality and Social Psychology, 52,* 511–24.

Hesse, E. (1999). The adult attachment interview: Historical and current perspectives. In P. R. Shaver & J. Cassidy (Eds.), *Handbook of Attachment: Theory, Research, and Clinical Applications.* New York: Guilford Press, pp. 395–433.

Holden, G. W. & Buck, M. J. (2002). Parental attitudes toward childrearing. In M. H. Bornstein (Ed.), *Handbook of Parenting,* Vol. 3: *Being and Becoming a Parent.* Mahwah, NJ: Erlbaum, pp. 537–62.

Holden, G. W. & Edwards, L. A. (1989). Parental attitudes towards child rearing: Instructions, issues and implications. *Psychology Bulletin, 106(1),* 29–58.

Jung, K. & Honig, A. S. (2000). Intergenerational comparisons of paternal Korean child-rearing practices and attitudes. *Early Child Development and Care, 165,* 59–84.

Kendler, K. S. (1996). Parenting: A genetic-epidemiologic perspective. *American Journal of Psychiatry, 153,* 11–20.

Lamb, M. E. & Oppenheim, D. (1989). Fatherhood and father-child relationships. In S. H. Cath, A. Gurwin, & L. Gunsberg (Eds.), *Fathers and Their Families.* Hillsdale, NJ: The Analytic Press, pp. 11–25.

Mayseless, O. (1995). Attachment patterns and marital relationships. In Shulman, (Ed.), *Close Relationships and Socioemotional Development. Human Development.* Westport, CT: Ablex Publishing, pp. 185–202.

Mayseless, O., Danielli, R., & Sharabany, R. (1996). Adults' attachment patterns: Coping with separations. *Journal of Youth and Adolescence, 25,* 667–90.

Mayseless, O., Sharabany, R., & Sagi, A. (1997). Attachment concerns of mothers as manifested in parental, spousal, and friendship relationships. *Personal Relationships, 4,* 255–69.

Paquet, D., Bolte, C., Turcotte, G., Dubeau, D., & Bouchard, C. (2000). A new typology of fathering: Defining and associated variables. *Infant and Child Development, 9(4),* 213–30.

Parke, R. D. (2002). Fathers and families. In M. H. Bornstein (Ed.), *Handbook of Parenting,* Vol. 3: *Being and Becoming a Parent.* Mahwah, NJ: Erlbaum, pp. 27–73.

Polatnick, M. (1973–74). Why men don't rear children: A power analysis. *Berkeley Journal of Sociology, 18,* 44–86.

Radin, N. & Russell, G. (1983). Increased father participation and child development outcomes. In M. E. Lamb & A. Sagi (Eds.), *Fatherhood and Family Policy.* Hillsdale, NJ: Erlbaum, pp. 191–218.

Radin, N. & Sagi, A. (1982). Childrearing fathers in intact families in Israel and the U.S.A. *Merrill–Palmer Quarerly, 28,* 111–36.

Rickel, A. U. & Biasatti, L. L. (1982). Modification of the Block Child Rearing Practices Report. *Journal of Clinical Psychology, 38,* 129–34.

Ricks, M. R. (1985). The social transmission of parental behavior. Attachment across generations. In I. Bretherton & E. Waters (Eds.), *Growing points of attachment theory and research. Monographs of the Society for Research in Child Development, 50,* 211–27.

Rosen, K. S. & Rothbaum, F. (1993). Quality of parental caregiving and security of attachment. *Developmental Psychology, 29 (2),* 358–67.

Ross, J. M. (1977). Towards fatherhood: The epigenesis of paternal identity during a boy's first decade. *International Review of Psychoanalysis, 4,* 327–47.

Russell, G. & Radojevic, M. (1992). The changing role of fathers? Current understanding and future directions for research and practice. *Infant Mental Health Journal, 13(4),* 296–311.

Rutter, M. (1989). Intergenerational continuities and discontinuities in serious parenting difficulties. In D. Cicchetti & V. Carlson (Eds.), *Child Maltreatment: Theory and Research on the Causes and Consequences of Child Abuse and Neglect.* New York: Cambridge University Press, pp. 317–48.

Rutter, M. (1990). Psychosocial resilience and protective mechanisms. In J. Rolf, A. Masten, D. Cicchetti, K. Nuechterlien, & S. Wientraub (Eds.), *Risk and Protective Factors in the Development of Psychopathology.* New York: Cambridge University Press, pp. 181–214.

Sagi, A. (1982). Antecedents and consequences of various degrees of paternal involvement in child rearing: The Israeli Project. In M. E. Lamb (Ed.), *Non-traditional Families.* Hillsdale, NJ: Erlbaum, pp. 205–32.

Scher, A. (1991). A longitudinal study of night waking in the first year. *Child: Care, Health and Development, 17,* 295–302.

Scher, A. & Mayseless, O. (1994). Mother's attachment with spouse, and parenting in the first year. *Journal of Social and Personal Relationships, 11,* 601–9.

Seginer, R. Vermulst, A. Shoyer, S. (2004). The indirect link between perceived parenting and adolescent future orientation: A multiple step model. *International Journal of Behavioral Development, 28 (4),* 365–78.

Sharabany, R. & Haglili, E. (2002). Does parental attachment style show in the morning separation in the kindergarten? Paper presented at the biennial meeting of the International Association of Relationship Research, July 2002, Halifax Canada.

Shaver, P. & Mikulincer, M. (2002). Attachment-related psychodynamics. *Attachment & Human Behavior, 4 (2),* 133–61.

Shears, J., Robinson, J., & Emde, R. N. (2002). Fathering relationships and their associations with juvenile delinquency. *Infant Mental Health Journal, 23(1–2),* 79–87.

Steele, M., Steele, H., & Johansson, M. (2002). Maternal predictors of children's social cognition: An attachment perspective. *Journal of Child Psychology and Psychiatry, 43(7),* 861–72.

Yediot Acharonot [Hebrew]. 13 Feb. 2004.

PART III

Clinical Implications

9 Intergenerational Transmission of Dysregulated Maternal Caregiving

Mothers Describe Their Upbringing and Childrearing

Judith Solomon and Carol George

Abstract

We present quantitative findings and detailed case histories that reveal the links between mothers' representations of their own attachment relationships (assessed in the Adult Attachment Interview (AAI)) and their representations of themselves as caregivers (Caregiving Interview). The sample comprised 57 middle-class mother–kindergarten-age child dyads. The children's attachment classification with mother was assessed in a laboratory reunion. Mothers' description of one or more elements of a "rage pattern," defined as physical or verbal abuse, unpredictable rage, and/or substance abuse on the part of their own parents, was coded from the AAI in addition to their state of mind. Results showed that 87% of mothers of disorganized-controlling children reported elements of the "rage pattern" in their upbringing while only 20% of such mothers were classified as Unresolved with respect to mourning or trauma. Three case summaries show clear parallels between the mothers' descriptions of their upbringing, their own childrearing representations, and the type of controlling (role-reversed) behavior shown by their child during reunion. The findings suggest that mothers' representations of threat and helplessness, past and present, provide a powerful and parsimonious approach to understanding intergenerational transmission of disorganized caregiving and attachment patterns.

In this chapter, we explore the links between dysregulation of the caregiving system across two generations and the development of disorganized and controlling attachments in early childhood. The findings bear directly on a growing literature in the field of attachment regarding the second-generation effects of a mother's own childrearing and attachment history. Of particular interest to us in this report are the effects of the mother's childhood experiences of helplessness in the face of unpredictable and uncontrollable fear on her capacity to facilitate organized attachment in her child. The impetus for this study was our research on mothers' caregiving representations (George & Solomon, 1989, 1996, 1999a, b; Solomon & George, 1996; 1999a, 2000). We have conceptualized caregiving representations as both the product of the current relationship with the child and a mediating mechanism through which the mother's own upbringing comes to influence her care for her child. In our past work, through careful assessment of mothers' descriptions of themselves and their children in a semi-structured interview about that relationship, we found a salient, common theme in the interviews of mothers whose children were classified as disorganized/controlling (D). These mothers described themselves as struggling and ultimately helpless to control the child and/or their own overpowering negative affect in relation to the child. We wondered if these mothers would describe their relationships with their own attachment figures in similar terms.

In what follows, we compare middle-class mothers of kindergarten-age children who have been classified as disorganized-controlling to mothers whose children display an organized attachment classification on two different measures of their representation of experiences in their own upbringing. The first measure is the now well-accepted classification system of the mother's "state of mind" with respect to attachment (George, Kaplan, & Main, 1984;1985;1996; Main & Goldwyn, 1985/1991;1994;1998). The second is a new coding system designed to capture the mother's experiences of unpredictable and out-of-control behavior on the part of parental figures. We found that the latter measure corresponds more closely to whether or not the mother's child is classified as disorganized-controlling than her adult attachment classification, that is, her "state of mind" with respect to attachment. We begin this chapter by providing the theoretical context for the questions addressed in this study. Following presentation of the quantitative findings, we provide summaries of mothers' descriptions of both their upbringing and caregiving experiences to illustrate the relationships between these representational models. We conclude by considering the implication of these findings for understanding intergenerational transmission of caregiving patterns and the development of attachment.

Lack of Resolution of Loss and Trauma and the Development of Disorganized Attachment

In the last two decades, attachment research has made a large contribution to our understanding of the intergenerational transmission of attachment patterns. The generally accepted finding has been that *what* has happened in the past is less important than the woman's current "state of mind" with respect to attachment in predicting her child's security of attachment with her (Main, Kaplan, & Cassidy, 1985; van IJzendoorn, 1995). "State of mind" typically refers to the mother's tendency to fully integrate thoughts and feelings about past attachments, or, in contrast, show evidence of defensive exclusion in reporting key events and feelings from the past. Main and her colleagues developed a classification system to capture individual differences in mothers' state of mind corresponding to each of the standard Ainsworth categories of infant attachment. Classification is based on the mother's responses to a semi-structured interview about childhood attachment relationships (The Adult Attachment Interview (AAI)) (George, Kaplan, & Main, 1984/1985/1996). Main's original work has been replicated in numerous studies and is now so well assimilated, that mothers' AAI classifications are sometimes used to represent the *current* mother–child relationship when direct measures of child attachment security are unavailable (e.g., Hodges et al., 2003).

The historical link between studies of adult attachment representations and disorganized-controlling attachments is a particularly close one. At around the same time that Main and Goldwyn (1985/1991/1994/1998) began to develop the classification system for the AAI, Main and Solomon were engaged in the process of identifying and describing the insecure-disorganized patterns of infant attachment (Main & Solomon, 1986; 1990). The hallmarks of disorganized attachment behavior are contradictory, disordered, misdirected, fearful, or disoriented behavior on reunion with the mother. Disorganized infant attachments are defined by disorganization upon reunion with mother in Ainsworth's Strange Situation (Ainsworth et al., 1978), especially when it is marked and persistent and/or occurs at the critical first moments of reunion, making it difficult to perceive the infant's underlying attachment strategy. The most common sequel in the preschool and early middle-childhood periods to an earlier disorganized classification is the appearance of role-reversal in mother–child interaction during laboratory reunions (Main & Cassidy, 1988). These relationships have been termed "controlling" by Main and Cassidy and are frequently further subdivided into relationships in which the child is punitive and hostile to the mother and those in which the child is caregiving or solicitous.

"D" classifications are found in both normative and extremely high-risk childrearing situations such as maltreatment, though they are considerably more prevalent in the latter (Cicchetti & Barnett, 1991; Lyons-Ruth et al., 1990; van IJzendoorn, 1995). This raised what seemed at the time to be a very puzzling question: What was the common interactive experience of babies in both kinds of samples? Ainsworth validated her three infant attachment classification groups against her year-long observational study of patterns of mother–infant interaction. There were no observational studies to rely on, however, to validate and explain the etiology of the disorganized-disoriented (D) group at the time it was first described.

Main's work on the AAI uncovered what appeared to be one of the missing pieces to this puzzle. She found that the majority of mothers in her sample who displayed in the AAI a "Lack of Resolution" with respect to loss (through death) of attachment figures had infants whose attachment to mother was disorganized. In Main's highly selected sample, loss of an adult in the household before age 18 was associated with infant disorganized attachment. This correspondence was not replicated in an independent study by Ainsworth and Eichberg (1991), but the link between infant disorganization and maternal Lack of Resolution was. Exposure to the data of other investigators working with higher risk samples than these (Levine, Ward, & Carlson, 1989, cited in Main & Hesse, 1990), suggested to Main that the common interactive experience underlying disorganized attachment must be associated in some way with the mother's unresolved state of mind with respect to loss or trauma (Main & Hesse, 1990).

Main's scale for Lack of Resolution of Mourning (LRM) rates evidence of a loss of monitoring of discourse or reasoning when the parent discusses loss. Examples include extreme attention to the details of the loss or evidence that the individual felt an enduring sense of guilt for the event. A separate scale, Lack of Resolution of Trauma (LRT), rates similar indices (i.e., lack of monitoring) as they emerge in the mother's discussion of attachment-related trauma such as physical or sexual abuse. High scores on either scale can result in an Unresolved classification. Main and Hesse (1990) proposed that evidence of lack of resolution of loss or trauma was indicative of dissociative processes on the part of the mother. This formed the basis for Main's hypothesis about the etiology of disorganized attachment: Maternal fear related to loss or trauma, activated by the infant or external circumstances, led the mother to behave in a subtly frightening or frightened manner toward the infant. This resulted in a breakdown in the organization of the infant's attachment behavior, because the infant's source of security (mother) was also a source of alarm.

Although Main's hypothesis is widely cited, it has received only partial empirical support. In two observational studies, only infants whose "forced" or underlying attachment classification was insecure had mothers who behaved in frightening ways (Lyons-Ruth, Bronfman, & Parsons, 1999; Schuengel, Bakermans-Kranenburg, & van IJzendoorn, 1999). Examples of such behaviors include the mother making sudden, looming movements toward the child or seeming to be lost in a trance. Recently, Lyons-Ruth (Lyons-Ruth, Yellin, Melnick, & Atwood, 2003) reported a link between

LRM and disorganization for infants classified at 12 months of age, but not when classifications at 18 months of age were examined. Van IJzendoorn, Schuengel, and Bakermans-Kranenburg (1999), using meta-analysis, reported that only 53% of disorganized infants had mothers classified as Unresolved on the AAI, indicating that there is quite a large "transmission gap" with respect to this classification.

Differentiating the Attachment and Caregiving Systems

In addition to the empirical questions raised about the place of lack of resolution of loss and/or trauma in the etiology of attachment disorganization, there are important theoretical ones. In a set of papers over the last decade, we have emphasized the differences between the attachment and caregiving systems. These tend to be confounded when the AAI is used as an "alternate" measure of child attachment (George & Solomon, 1999a,b; Solomon & George, 1996, 1999a,b). That there exists a behavioral system separate and unique from that of attachment was proposed originally by Bowlby (1969/1982; 1984) and brought to more general attention in the field by Bretherton et al. (1989).

The caregiving system is the reciprocal to attachment. Like the attachment system, it too is organized around providing security and/or protection, but from the point of view of the caregiver rather than the attached. The caregiving system is activated by the infant or child's distress or the caregiver's perception of danger or threat to the child. When strongly activated, it is terminated by proximity to the child and the assuagement of distress. An essential feature of the caregiving system, once it is consolidated, is that situations of danger and threat should activate caregiving and protection toward the child, while the caregiver's own attachment needs become subsumed to those of the child and/or directed away from the child.

Although there has been little explicit study of the development of caregiving in humans, what information there is indicates that its development begins in the toddler period and has its roots in the child's experience of being cared for. Potentially, the attachment and caregiving systems become increasingly differentiated in adolescence, through pregnancy, and the birth of the child. West and Sheldon-Keller (1994) has emphasized that representational models should not be understood as residing in the mind either as fixed mental structures or even as information processing rules (Main, Kaplan, & Cassidy, 1985). Rather, they are best understood as a "retranscription of memory in a new context ... constantly recreated as a synthesis of old categories [of experience] and new experience" (p. 63). Thus, although we can expect independent assessments of mothers' representations of both their upbringing and their childrearing to share important qualitative features, they are also potentially quite distinct, reflecting the mother's "retranscription" or reworking of her past experiences in the light of her relationship with her child.

Mothers' and Children's Representations of Their Relationship

Over the last several years, we have been studying mothers' and children's representations of their mutual relationship in relation to both the caregiving and the attachment systems. We explore kindergarten-age children's representations through analysis of their doll-play on attachment-related themes (the Attachment Doll-Play Assessment, George & Solomon, 2000; Solomon, George, & DeJung, 1995; Solomon & George, 2002). We explore mothers' caregiving representations through analysis of their responses to an hourlong interview (the Caregiving Interview (CI)) (George & Solomon, 1996, 2002). Throughout this research program, we have had particular interest in the D-controlling children and their mothers.

In the doll play assessment, children are asked to complete three story stems, the most important of which is an overnight separation between child and parents using family dolls and a "doll house." The doll play is then coded and a single classification is assigned to one of four groups corresponding to the well-known reunion-behavior based attachment groups (Secure, Avoidant, Ambivalent, or Disorganized). Classifications are based on evidence of secure story conclusions or, alternatively, features of the children's stories that indicate defensive exclusion of attachment related feelings or thoughts (shown by avoidant or ambivalent children) or dysregulation of attachment feelings or thoughts. Dysregulated story features are characteristic of children judged disorganized or controlling. These stories typically take one of two forms: *Flooded*, in which themes of family violence or catastrophe result in death and the disintegration of the family, or *Constricted*, in which the child refuses, more or less entirely, to enact a story.

In our analysis of mothers' caregiving interviews, the mother is asked to reflect on her relationship with the child in terms of the feelings these interactions engender (e.g., "What gives you the most pain or difficulty as '*child's*' mother?"; "What five words or phrases best describe your relationship with '*child*'?"). Interviewing technique, as well as the codes, and rating scales upon which caregiving classification rests, rely heavily on drawing mothers out on particular episodes that illustrate mother–child interaction. In our first reports on this research, we emphasized the relation between the child's reunion-based attachment classification and qualitative differences in the narrative content and structure of mothers' representational material. More recently, paralleling our work with children's doll play, our interest and method of analyzing mothers' representations have shifted to emphasize more directly the differences among classification groups in the way in which mothers integrate, exclude, or seem to be dysregulated with respect to attachment-related content (George & Solomon, 2002).

We have found striking parallels between mothers' descriptions of their experience of interacting with their child and their children's doll play content for all the classification groups. In particular, the mothers of children classified as disorganized or controlling in laboratory-based reunions describe sudden, out-of-control rage, threatening behaviors and interactions, and failures to repair relationships once the "storm" of anger has subsided. Mothers often explicitly describe themselves as helpless to control their reactions to their child and helpless to control the behavior of the child him or herself.

Some mothers depict intensely angry confrontations and battles of will with the child in which the mother, in desperation, can become quite punitive. This group parallels the "flooded" doll play of the children, described above. Other mothers depict themselves as retreating from their sudden and overwhelming rage by withdrawing from the child. That is, the mother constricts her behavior. Such mothers sometimes manifest a constriction of thought during the interview itself, for example by becoming suddenly unable to think or produce responses to questions. It is also typical for this group of "constricting" mothers to describe the child as precocious and caregiving toward them (role-reversal) and to show some evidence of identity-merging or possibly dissociative processes when describing their relationship with the child. From our earliest work on these representational materials, we have been struck by the fact that the subjective experience of mothers and children is one of helplessness – to control events, one another, or their own feelings and behavior– in the face of threatening or dangerous events. The experience of helplessness is at the root of trauma (Herman, 1992), and indeed may be a more reliable index of whether trauma has occurred than objective assessments of either acute or chronic assaults. We have proposed (George & Solomon, 1994) that it is the activation of the experience of helplessness in the face of perceived threat that leads to punitive and and/or role-reversing behavior on the part of the mother toward her child. The caregiving and doll play assessments raise the question whether mothers of disorganized children would describe their experiences with their own attachment figures as having engendered feelings of helplessness, or, in Main's terms (Main & Hesse, 1992), fear without resolution. Such a finding would suggest a mechanism for the intergenerational transmission of dysregulated caregiving.

Focus of This Chapter

This chapter represents a preliminary attempt to explore the links between maternal experiences of helplessness with their own attachment figures and disorganized/controlling (D) attachment in their children. We present both quantitative and qualitative data. The quantitative analysis is organized around the question of which is the better predictor of the child's disorganized/controlling attachment to mother: the mother's "state of mind with respect to attachment" or her description of childhood experiences of threatening, unpredictable, and out-of-control behavior on the part of her attachment figures? To answer this question, we compare mothers of disorganized/controlling kindergartners with mothers of children classified as organized (child attachment classification groups B, A, or C) with respect to two maternal, representational measures: the mother's AAI classification and a second measure, recently developed by us, called the "Life Events Coding." The latter is also coded from the Adult Attachment Interview and focuses on the mother's report of threatening and out-of-control events in her childhood. As discussed previously, the theoretical prediction derived from Main's hypotheses, is that Lack of Resolution of loss or trauma (the Unresolved classification) on the AAI will differentiate between these two groups of mothers. Our prediction is that the Life Events Coding will provide better discrimination between maternal groups than the mother's AAI classification.

In the qualitative section of this chapter, we describe our ongoing efforts to develop a multidimensional rating of maternal (AAI) interviews to differentiate between those mothers who describe themselves as helpless with respect to threatening and out-of-control events in childhood and go on to engender disorganized attachment in their child and those who, despite similar experiences, do not describe themselves as helpless, and whose child develops an organized attachment. This section will include summaries of AAI and caregiving interview material of a subset of cases to illustrate the links between mothers' descriptions of their upbringing and caregiving experiences. Themes within the AAI that we believe represent risks and buffers in representational processes for dysregulated caregiving are highlighted within the case summaries.

Overview of Sample, Procedures, and Measures

The sample for this report comprises 57 middle-class mothers and their kindergarten children (ages four to seven) who participated in a study of mother–child relationships in the transition to middle-childhood period. The 57 cases were drawn from a larger sample of 69 cases. Twelve families were excluded due to missing AAIs (mother declined to participate or the interview was not usable because of technical difficulties with the recording). Recruitment procedures, demographic characteristics, and child attachment classification procedures for the entire sample are described fully in Solomon et al. (1995).

Mother and child engaged in a semi-structured dyadic task and were then separated for approximately one hour while the mother was administered the Caregiving Interview (George & Solomon, 1996; 2002, adapted with permission from Slade, A. and Aber, L., 1989, personal communication). The child remained with an administrator to complete other tasks and free play. The first five minutes of the subsequent mother–child reunion were used to derive the child's attachment classification, using the validated system of Main and Cassidy (1988). These classifications were completed by the first author, who was blind to all other assessments (Solomon et al., 1995).

One to two weeks after this session, mothers were administered the AAI (George, Kaplan, & Main, 1984/1985/1996) in their homes. The AAI consists of questions about childhood experiences with parents, including experiences of support, rejection, separation, loss, and trauma, and the individual's thinking about the effects of these experiences in the present. The interview is rated for a variety of attachment-related experiences as well as aspects of the individual's discourse. These ratings are used to generate classifications of the mother's current state of mind with respect to attachment: secure (F); insecure/dismissing (Ds); insecure/preoccupied (E); or insecure/unresolved with respect to loss or trauma (U). Classification of an interview as unresolved (U) is based only on the quality of the individual's comments with respect to a particular loss or trauma. For a full description of this system, see Main and Goldwyn (1994). All of the AAI classifications were completed by the second author, who helped develop the classification system and has established reliability of 80% on previous samples with trained classifiers who completed the Main Adult Attachment Workshop and reached the pre-established level of classification reliability (George & West, submitted). She was blind to the child's attachment classification and all other information about the family.

Results

The results of this study are summarized in Table 9.1 in qualitative form, that is, on a case-by-case basis. The cases included in the table comprise all of those in which the child's reunion-based classification was disorganized/controlling. In addition, for purposes of comparison, the additional nine cases in which the Life Events Coding reflected the mother's report of

Table 9.1. *Life Events Summary*

AAI Class	Key Losses[1,2]	Family Violence[2] (P: T)[3,4]	Parent Unpredictable Anger[2]	Parent Substance Abuse[2] (alcohol)
Concordant: Mother Unresolved on AAI; Child Controlling (D)				
U/F4	F < 18	M: self[b]	M	M
CC/Ds3	F, CS < 18		F	F
CC/E1	*M = 3yrs[a]*			M, F
Non-Concordant: Mother Unresolved on AAI: Child Organized (B, secure)				
U/F2	F >18	F: self[b]		
Non-Concordant: Mother Organized on AAI; Child Controlling (D)				
E3		S-F: M, self[b]	SF	S-F
E2		M: self[b]	M	
E1	F >18	M: self[b]	M	F
E1	*C < 2 yrs[a]*			F
E2			M	
E1	Sib < 18		M	M, F
E1		M: self		M[5]
Ds4		M: S-F: self[b,c]		
E1	*F, at time of C's birth*	–	–	–
F2	F > 18	F,Sib: M, self[b]	F	F
E1	–	–	–	–
Ds3		F: sib[b]	F, M	
Concordant: Mother Organized on AAI; Child Organized Attachment (B)				
F2			M: sib[b]	M
Concordant: Mother Organized on AAI; Child Organized Attachment (C)				
E2			S-F: M, self[b]	S-F
E1			F: self[b,c]	F
Ds3	*F = 3yrs[a]*	M: self[b]	M	
Concordant: Mother Organized on AAI; Child Organized Attachment (A)				
Ds3	F > 18		M	
Ds3		F: M, sibs[b]		
Ds3	*C < 1 yr[a]*		M	
Ds2	F < 18	M: self[b]	M	

Notes:

[1] Death of nuclear family members or own child or death for which parent was rated "Unresolved" on AAI

[2] M = mother; F = father; S-F = step-father; Sib = sibling (s); CS = cousin; C = stillbirth, late miscarriage of Self's child; H = husband

[3] P: T = Perpetrator: Target

[4] For denotation of "Self" (subject): siblings may also have been a target; for "Sib(s)": Self (subject) was not a target but siblings were

[5] Mother anger/abuse increased with medication for chronic medical condition

[a] Recent loss, noted in italics

[b] Physical abuse, harsh physical treatment, verbal threats, intimidation, humiliation

[c] Sexual abuse, molestation

some or all of the elements of the "Rage Pattern" (described in the following section) are also included. (Thirty-three cases are not shown in Table 9.1.) Based on the foregoing criteria, all of the cases in the sample in which the mother's AAI was classified U (or Can't Classify, CC, which typically are included in the U category) are listed in the table as well.

Correspondence Between Adult AAI and Child Reunion-Based Attachment Classifications

The distribution of adult attachment classifications for the sample as a whole was as follows: F (autonomous) = 16 (28%); Ds (dismissive) = 18 (32%); E (preoccupied) = 19 (33%); U (unresolved + cannot classify) = 4 (7%). The distribution of child attachment classifications was as follows: B (secure) = 16 (28%); A (avoidant) = 13 (23%); C (preoccupied) = 13 (23%); D/U (disorganized-controlling/unclassifiable) = 15 (26%). AAI classifications for mothers of children classified as disorganized-controlling are also shown in Table 9.1. Although three of four U mothers had children who were classified as disorganized/controlling, 80% of children classified D had mothers whose "state of mind" with respect to attachment was judged to be organized (F, Ds, or E). That is, only three of 15 mothers of D children (disorganized, controlling, and unclassifiable) were classified as Unresolved/Can't Classify (CC). The four U/CC mothers were unresolved regarding loss rather than trauma. Of the remaining 12 mothers of D children, 9 received an adult attachment classification of E (preoccupied). Based on Main's original study, E (preoccupied) mothers would be expected to have children who were classified as C (ambivalent). That mothers of disorganized-controlling children were disproportionately drawn from the preoccupied AAI group is consistent with the meta-analysis results of van IJzendoorn (1995), who found that the Preoccupied AAI classification does not predict infant ambivalence when the disorganized group is included in the analysis. Thus, for this sample, the adult U classification appears to have only limited predictive value with respect to child classification.

Life Events Coding from the AAI and Child Reunion-Based Attachment Classifications

Ten categories of life experience were captured in the Life Events Coding system, but only four were selected as representing the experiences of interest in the current study. Our goal here was to be able to distinguish family behaviors that might parallel the out-of-control behavior and rages and the verbal and physical confrontations that appear in the symbolic representations of D children and their mothers. We also hypothesized that substance abuse in the family of origin might increase S's experience of unpredictable moods and rages in the home. In addition, given the central role of loss through death in the literature in disorganized attachment, we wanted to collect systematic information on these events as well. Life Events were coded in terms of presence/absence. No attempt was made to differentiate as to severity or frequency in this system. In summary, the following coding categories with brief definitions are analyzed in the present chapter: **Family violence** (including all forms of harsh physical or verbal treatment, or behavior leading to physical or verbal harm, intimidation, or humiliation). The target(s) as well as the victims were noted; **Affect dysregulation:** behavior (and identity) of any household member that reflects unpredictable, uncontrollable, and/or intense anger or other negative affect. Language was an important feature for coding of this category, for example, phrases such as sudden or hot temper, uncontrollable anger, rage, snaps, explodes, "loses it," "ranting and raving," etc. resulted in coding for this category; **Substance abuse**: any household member described as abusing a drug or alcohol.[1] In what follows, these three categories – family violence, affect dysregulation, and substance abuse – are referred to as elements of a "Rage Pattern." **Loss through death:** any losses in the immediate or extended family or individuals identified by S as important; the subject's miscarriages or loss of children through death were also coded.

Although the Life Events measure focuses on discrete events or descriptors of the mother's history, it is important to emphasize that it also should be viewed as a representational measure rather than an estimate of "true" events. This is because the Life Events measure is based on mothers' spontaneous answers to the questions of the AAI. As is typical in a semi-structured interview, no attempt was made to ensure that the information provided by mothers was thorough or verifiable. What mothers chose to describe and the qualities of these descriptions were entirely self-selected, and therefore can be presumed to reflect a synthesis of internal representational processes and "objective" experience.

---

[1] Additional categories coded but not included in this study were: **Household members:** who lived in the home when mother (from here on denoted as Self (S)) was growing up; **Parental divorce/separation/abandonment**; **Other attachment assaults or threats**: major separations; hospitalizations, traumatic events and catastrophes, life-threatening or chronic illness in the household; **Self's marriage history**: partners, divorces, the fathers of S's children were noted; and **Self's psychotherapy experience**: descriptions of past or current psychotherapy experience (coded separately).

Life Events coding was completed by two-person teams (four coders in all) who had no additional knowledge of the subjects or the hypotheses under study. Event categories were defined a priori and refined with the assistance of the coders on a set of six training interviews. Events were noted along with the approximate age of the subject at the time of occurrence, if relevant. Qualitative notes were also provided by the coder. Inter-team reliability on a sample of 19 interviews on events and age at which event occurred (agreements/agreements + disagreements) ranged from 87% to 100% across all categories.

Table 9.1 summarizes the results of the Life Events Coding for the above four event categories. Note that the data are displayed in four sections reflecting theoretical concordance or failure to display concordance between maternal and child attachment classifications (e.g., mother Unresolved and child Disorganized-controlling; mother Not Unresolved and child Organized (A, B, C)). As shown in Table 9.1, independent of mother AAI classification, 13 of the 15 mothers of disorganized-controlling children (87%) described one or more elements of the rage pattern in their families of origin. Indeed, all four of the Unresolved mothers (all unresolved for loss), including the one mother who was classified as Unresolved on the AAI but whose child was classified as Organized (Secure), also described one or more elements of the rage pattern in their upbringing.

These data support our hypothesis that mothers of disorganized-controlling children describe their relationships with family members (parents or siblings) in ways that are strikingly similar to the manner in which they describe their relationships to their children – these relationships were frightening and out of control. In the majority of cases, parents' affect, particularly their anger, was expressed in intense, frightening, and unpredictable ways. In some cases, parents were intermittently or chronically frankly abusive. Furthermore, family violence and rage was experienced as sudden, unmodulated, and unpredictable. Substance abuse in the form of alcoholism was common in these families and undoubtedly contributed to the unpredictable nature of family relationships. It is important to note that not all families of the mothers whose children were classified as disorganized were characterized by clear abuse. Main and Hesse (1990, 1992) have focused on mothers' responses to traumatic events (loss, abuse) and Lyons-Ruth has also focused on maltreatment history as a specific cause of dysregulated parenting (Lyons- Ruth et al., 2003). Our data indicate that maternal experiences were somewhat broader. In some cases mothers witnessed but did not report experiencing abuse themselves; in others, there appears to have been no violence at all; however, parents displayed explosive rage that appeared to "come out of nowhere" or alcohol-induced bellicosity. In the one case that stood outside the common "rage reaction" pattern, grandmother (i.e., mother's mother) was incapacitated with an organic (neurological) disease that led her to be moody, depressed, and suicidal. This behavior was undoubtedly both frightening and unpredictable to mother as a young child, but there is no evidence in the interview of either abuse or rage directed at the subject or others.

The sections of Table 9.1 labeled *Concordant: Mother Organized and Child Organized* (B, C, or A) comprise the 8 out of 42 cases (21%) in which both mother and child received an organized (F, Ds, E) classification and the Life Events coding showed one or more elements of the "Rage Pattern" defined above. Abuse, family violence, and rage were clearly uncommon overall in the histories of the mothers whose children had organized (secure and insecure) attachments to them at age five. Qualitatively, several of the "organized" mothers experienced less intense and/or less unpredictable rage and family violence. The almost complete absence of reports of substance abuse in these families may also imply that family life was less chaotic overall and that confrontations with a raging parent were more a predictable event for the mothers in this group. Nevertheless, at least three of the mothers experienced treatment from parents that seemed quite similar to what some of the D mothers reported and undoubtedly would qualify as abusive.

It is unclear from the data as coded how the experience of mothers who reported only one element of the rage pattern vs. two or more may differ. Indeed, it is difficult to imagine that family violence erupted without affect dysregulation also having been coded, although the reverse is plausible. These differences may reflect individual variation in representational processes and verbal descriptions. It is interesting, however, that none of the nine mothers whose children were classified as organized reported substance abuse in their families of origin. No relation between loss through death of a family member before age 18 or later is apparent in the data.

Qualitative Analyses: Capturing Dysregulated Representation and Behavior in Adult Attachment

The experiences of harsh, abusive, and unpredictable treatment reported by the women in these groups (disorganized and organized) were described in convincing detail. Although there is reason to think that interviewees may under-report events (Hill, Byatt, & Burnside, 2003), there is no reason to doubt the essential veracity of the accounts. By its very nature, however, the Life Events Coding scheme causes us to focus on whether or not various traumas and life challenges occurred. It obscures the representational nature of even these seemingly "objective" reports of events. Furthermore, it fails to capture the quality and patterning of events and the rich, qualitative details, including the subject's reconstruction of her own behavior, thoughts, and feelings of the moment and in retrospect.

Earlier, we suggested that a potential key to understanding the link between mothers' experiences and their own caregiving lies in the experience of *helplessness*. Harsh or even frightening treatment that has been prevented or ameliorated through the interventions of other caregivers or one's own efforts is less likely to be experienced as traumatic. Therefore, frightening events are less likely to remain psychologically segregated or unintegrated, leading to dysregulation at the level of representation and behavior (Solomon & George, 1999b). In order to evaluate the proposition that mothers' experience of themselves as helpless in the face of threat is linked to their caregiving behavior, it is obviously necessary to go beyond mothers' report of "objective" life events.

Our goal is to develop an approach to analysis of mothers' AAI that parallels our previous work with children's attachment and mother's caregiving representations. When classifying children's symbolic representations of their attachment to mother and mother's caregiving representations, we endeavor to construct coding and rating schemes that are conceptually parallel and theoretically driven. Especially with regard to capturing aspects of insecurity, this has led us to "read" content (whether of interview or doll play) in terms of its correspondence to the distinctly different defensive processes that we propose underlie the different insecure patterns (George & Solomon, 1996; 2002). Thus, although mothers of secure and insecure children all describe loving feelings, conflict with their children, and pressures relating to balancing caregiving and other obligations in the CI, the interactions mothers describe and the manner of describing them reflect important qualitative differences. These differences, we have proposed, correspond to different mechanisms of defensive exclusion from awareness of certain memories, feelings, and thoughts that mothers find disturbing. A full description of these processes and their manifestations would be too lengthy to include in the present report. Here we would like to focus on the indices of dysregulated, or, as we have sometimes described them, segregated systems (Solomon & George, 1999b; Solomon et al., 1995) that we have found to distinguish mothers whose children are classified as disorganized or controlling in reunion from other mothers on the CI.

As we discussed earlier, in the CI, mothers of children classified as D typically provide evidence of *dysregulated* emotions, thoughts, or behaviors when describing interaction with their child. Dysregulation implies that attachment or caregiving-related feelings or defenses are being overwhelmed by strong emotion, usually of a negative kind. As we have argued elsewhere

(Solomon & George, 1999b), dysregulated internal working models can be inferred when representational processes or behavior are manifestly out-of-control, or rigidly controlled leading to a striking absence or constriction of feeling, thought, or behavior, or alternations between these two extremes.

Within the CI, our coding system identifies four main kinds of evidence for dysregulation, which are coded from descriptions of the mother's experience and behavior or from features of discourse. These indices are: 1) *Flooded/Out of control* (experiences or behaviors reflective of extreme emotions, such as angry confrontation, fear, rage, or a desire to defy or punish); 2) *Constricted* (discourse or descriptions of behavior designed to suppress or deny powerful emotions, such as biting one's tongue when angry, blocking out unpleasant or frightening thoughts, "blanking out"; 3) *Abdication of care/Helplessness* (evidence of maternal thinking or behavior that endangers child, permits the child to engage in/be exposed to threats, or reflects the mother's passivity or resignation in the face of threat); 4) *Role-reversed/Merged* (experiences or descriptions of mother as merged with child or child as caring for and cheering the parent). In our analysis of the caregiving interview, evidence for dysregulation is summarized in a final rating based on the number of issues or episodes of mother–child interaction in which dysregulation is manifest and not contained by constructive action or defensive processes that contain mother and child distress. Our goal with respect to coding maternal AAIs, is to adapt this system for mothers' descriptions of interactions with parents.

As a first step toward developing a parallel system to capture these more qualitative aspects of maternal discourse about the past, we undertook a close reading of the AAIs of mothers who reported some or all of the elements of the "rage pattern." This included mothers whose children were classified as disorganized and mothers whose children were classified into one of the organized groups. As is always the case when developing measures using the "inductive method" (see Main & Cassidy, 1988), our analysis was done with full information about the AAI and other parent–child measures. Below, we describe briefly the kinds of statements that arise in the AAI that we believe will differentiate between mothers of disorganized children and mothers of children with organized attachments. These are arranged in categories paralleling the four coding categories described above for dysregulation in the Caregiving Interview. We have added a fifth category to capture elements of the mother's AAI (i.e., representation of events) that we hypothesize to be protective against the tendency to promote disorganized attachment in the child. In future work we hope to validate these features using blind coding on this and additional samples.

Flooded, Out-of-Control Experiences and Interactions

- Parent or child behavior indicative of the elements of the "rage pattern" described earlier; the parent's behavior is described as unpredictable or out-of-control;
- Other experiences or events are described using affectively extreme language.

Abdication of Care/Helplessness

- The non-threatening parent is described as failing to protect the subject, as abandoning the subject to threat or risk, or helpless or resigned to threat.
- Alternative caregiving figures described as failing to notice the problem or to intervene; the subject perceives the family as isolated.
- The subject describes herself as without active coping behavior or strategies.

Constriction

- The subject received prohibitions against revealing harsh treatment or loss; evidence of constriction of thought or behavior due to the necessity to hold threats or assaults in secret.
- Other evidence of constriction in discourse, thought, or feeling.

Role-Reversed/Merged

- The subject describes herself as taking over aspects of the parental role, for example, protecting or caring for parent; cheering a parent or showing special sensitivity to the needs and feelings of a threatening parent; (spontaneously) taking over care and concern for siblings.
- The subject experienced her identity as merged with that of parent.

Protective Representational Elements

- Predictability: Threats or assaults are described as predictable or resulting from principled parent childrearing strategy.
- Agency: The subject describes herself as active and effective in protecting herself in avoiding or minimizing threats or assaults.
- Buffering parent figure: The subject describes others (another parent, alternative caregiver) as effectively intervening or buffering the self.

Case Histories

In the following section we provide summaries of the AAI and Caregiving Interview material of three mothers. The summaries are annotated in bold to illustrate how elements of the narratives would be coded using the system described earlier (for the AAI) or were coded (for the CI). Two cases in which the mother did not receive Lack of Resolution scores sufficient for classification as Unresolved on the AAI but the child's relationship with mother was classified as disorganized/controlling are presented first. The third case presents material from a mother who experienced comparable elements of the "rage pattern" and yet whose relationship with her child was classified as organized (insecure-ambivalent). This approach allows the reader to see quite vividly the continuities and discontinuities between mothers' representations of the past and present. In addition to coding annotations, each case is followed by a brief commentary to clarify the links between the mother's representation of the past and the present. All identifying information from the cases has been deleted or substantially modified to protect the subjects. Mothers are assigned arbitrary names and their kindergarten-age child is identified as "C."

I. Mother: Sara (Mother Classified E3, Child Classified Controlling-Punitive (D1) in Reunion)

Sara's representation of attachment: *Sara remembers a great deal of closeness to mother in her early years, including her mother dressing them as twins (**Role-reversed/Merged**). She had no relationship with her biological father. In middle childhood, her mother remarried. Even during the courtship, the behavior of her step-father was out-of-control and unpredictably frightening: "He was drinking and so his personality, the swings of his personality was something that he would be just uncontrollably violent." (**Out-of-control/Flooded**) She recalled many occasions on which he went on a rampage and remembers her terror, thinking, "We're going to die" as he raged through the house. (**Out of control/Flooded**) Although Sara's mother protected her physically on this and other occasions, she continued to date and fawn over him. When Sara questioned her mother about this, mother made excuses for him, refused to speak further about it, and withdrew from Sara emotionally. (**Abdication**) The step-father's violence and verbal abuse toward Sara continued for many years. Sara developed the habit of daydreaming, watching other children from afar and wishing she could be them. She says of herself, "I learned to be invisible."*

(Abdication/Helplessness) Interestingly, Sara recounts how she would attempt to intervene directly in the step-father's attacks on the mother *(Role-reversal)* but apparently was entirely passive in trying to protect herself against his drunken attacks *(Abdication/Helplessness)*. Sara also felt abandoned by her grandmother, who had been a nurturing figure in early childhood but later lived at some distance and did not call or visit. Even when Sara came to live with grandmother, in adolescence, Sara did not share the truth because *"she (grandmother) never wanted to know anything."* *(Abdication: alternate caregiver failed to intervene)* As a teen, Sara became wild and promiscuous in her behavior, and married and divorced early. *(Flooded/Out of Control)*.

Sara's caregiving representation: Sara, a single mother, is busy with work and school as well as parenting, and describes herself as a *"chaotic mother."* *(Flooded/Out of control)* She travels a great deal for her work. Sara did not realize this was troubling C, who was cared for by his grandparents during S's absences. Only recently had C opened up to her, *"you know, I know that all your clothes are in the house and furniture's in the house, so then I think, well then you probably will come back, but, I'm afraid you might go away and leave me."* Sara describes their relationship as one of *"friends"*: *"... In some ways he's very grown up ... I mean ... in some ways I'm not so grown up."* *(Role-reversal)* Sara feels that the greatest difficulty she has as a mother is disciplining C. She perceives C as disobedient and directly challenging her authority. Sara describes a typical incident, where C wants to go outside, though it will soon be dinnertime. Sara forbids this but he runs out when her back is turned. *"Well, I have to chasing after him, and umm, I'm very angry, you know."* Eventually, she puts him in his room, but she feels this is no longer effective with C: *"I'm running out of possibilities as far as disciplining him... I'll take away your truck."* *"Go ahead, take away my truck."* Sometimes this scenario ends in Sara becoming *"furious"* and in a spanking. *(Flooded/Out of control)* Sara does not feel in control of this. *"I wish I wasn't this angry,"* she says repeatedly. *(Out of control)* Sara worries incessantly, she says, about C's future, *"I just hope he grows up to be responsible. ... I mean maybe he'll grow up to be hateful."* *(Flooded/Out of control)* Sara feels that she has no way to handle these worries. She describes herself as *"scared"* because if he continues absolutely to refuse her authority, she feels she will desperate: *"What do I do? I'll become out of control... I won't have any control... I'll lose all control... He'll be ... you know, I'm scared of that."* *(Flooded/Out of control & Abdication/ Helpless)*.

Commentary: Sara's discussion of her upbringing and childrearing show clear parallels. She depicts extremely frightening experiences at the hands of her step-father, her mother's psychological withdrawal and failure to intervene definitively, and her own passivity and helplessness over many years of abuse. This is the constellation of representational elements that we described as "helplessness" and which we propose is linked to disorganized/controlling attachment in her child. Sara's AAI was classified "E3," a category that designates individuals "living in the war zone" (George & West, in press). These individuals are preoccupied with the details of their experiences and their memories are organized around fear. They do not typically receive a designation as Unresolved because of a lack of evidence for dissociation and disorientation in the AAI. Rather, individuals judged E3 know exactly what happened and cannot shift their present attention away from details of the past. From the caregiving interview, it is clear that Sara is quite punitive with her own child. She seems to be both frightened of him and enraged. Sara not only experiences her child as out-of-control, but she experiences her anger as out-of-control as well. She wishes she could find another way, but it is as though she is compelled to confront him and become enraged. Sara's statement about her fears that her child may grow up to be "hateful" potentially has multiple meanings. It is not clear whether she fears that her child will be full of hate (perhaps like step-father); will hate her (as she did her step-father and mother); or whether she will hate him because of his bad and frightening behavior (as she did her step-father). Whatever the inner ramifications of this statement, it echoes, and presumably reflects, the current activation of Sara's experience of the past. Furthermore, we note that Sara responds to the provocations of her angry child (one whom she has made very insecure by frequent separations) with the rage that must have been necessary to physically defend her mother, and which, ultimately, was her only defense against total helplessness.

II. Mother: Simone (Mother Classified as E1 on the AAI; Child Classified as Controlling-Caregiving (D2))

Simone's attachment representation: Simone grew up in an intact family. She remembered very warm feelings toward her father when quite young and remembered her mother as involved with the children, both as a caregiver and a companion. In middle childhood, however, the family suffered the death of Simone's younger sibling. Simone describes learning as an adult of her mother's irrational and constricted response to the death of this child: she let the dead child remain in bed without remarking on what had happened, while carrying on with the day's routine and getting the older children off to school (Constriction). Simone was not told of the death until later, but remembers her sadness and *"just crying and feeling really, really bad"* **(Flooded/ Out-of-control)**. *Even now, she sometimes feels bad about this death and wonders what the sibling would have been like if she had survived. (Despite lingering thoughts of this death, the AAI discourse revealed only limited evidence of lack of resolution of mourning.) Shortly after the death, Simone's mother had a breakdown of sorts* **(Flooded/Out-of-control)**. *She was hospitalized about a year later for a serious medical condition and began to abuse alcohol and painkillers. Simone describes her mother as "rant[ing] and rav[ing]" and as a "mean drunk"* **(Out of control)**. *Mother had the habit of threatening the children with what would happen when father got home. Father responded by unbuckling his belt and that was enough, apparently, to terrorize them ("... and we'd all start screaming. And then, if he was really angry, he'd pull it out and slap it against the counter and we would like dissolve into the corner." Simone did not remember her father beating her, but a sibling was treated more harshly.* **(Flooded/out of control + Abdication (father failed to protect from mother and the reverse))** *Simone came to feel that her mother "wasn't able to cope... and that I had to be good to help that out."* **(Role-reversal)** *In addition to "being good," Simone remembered withdrawing to her room whenever she was upset.* **(Abdication/Helplessness)** *Simone did not remember other protective figures in whom she could confide, but recalled her aunt comforting her after Simone overheard her mother admit to sometimes hating her children. Simone comments on the fact that she never actually confronted her mother with the fact of having overheard this statement, suggesting both a keeping of secrets and a lack of agency* **(Constriction + Helplessness)**.

*   **Simone's caregiving representation**: *Simone describes an intense and passionate love for her child, including times when she feels so much love she could burst, or feels overpowering panic when she feels C is in some danger* **(Flooded/Out of control)**. *Simone's examples of enjoyable times focus on relaxed and intimate moments, when C shares thoughts and impressions or Simone shares her own concerns with C* **(Role-reversal)**. *Simone is clearly tickled by several examples of C's precocious discernment or behavior, for example, when mother admitted to C that she sometimes worries about how C feels at the babysitter's, C pooh-poohed these concerns with an affectionate but saucy "Well, mom, I'm five years old!"* **(Role-reversal)**. *At the same time, Simone uses the word "enemies"* **(Flooded/Out of Control)** *as one of five descriptors of the relationship with her child. She feels sharp disapproval of C's tendency to respond with strong emotion to fears and upsets. Simone has come to think that this is an aspect of C's temperament that C must learn to cope with alone, rather than thinking that she herself can take an active role*

*fostering self-regulation (**Abdication/Helplessness**). She is similarly passive about an incident where C "got lost" at school. Simone heard about this from others and failed to address the problem with school personnel (**Abdication/ Helplessness**). Simone also describes a number of incidents when C's anger toward mother erupted into direct aggression. When this happens, mother admits to feeling very angry but "I really get upset with myself when I lose patience." (**Out-of control (fears losing control)**) She struggles to "analyze" the situation, reads books of advice, and resorts to lengthy explanations to C. Nevertheless, occasionally, she says she can't help herself and loses her temper, and grabs or "swats" C. Sometimes, when C gets "wound up," Simone feels "... like I don't have the resources necessary to ... bring her down ... or channel them [C's feelings} in a different way...." (**Flooded/Out of control**). Simone seems most disturbed by the aggression or natural hostility that C shows toward a younger sibling (pulling him away from a toy or swatting him on the bottom). She associates this behavior in C to her own unpredictable sadistic feelings toward younger children when she was a child. She remembers being disturbed by these feelings as a child, to the point that she avoided spending time with younger children (**Constriction: mother withdraws from children**) and is still puzzled by these feelings at present.*

Commentary: Simone's representation of her attachment to parents and her caregiving show correspondences. There are also strong parallels to Sara's case, but with important qualitative differences. Simone, like Sara, was the victim of out-of-control and unpredictable rages, mainly in relationship with her mother, but her father was involved in these scenes as well. Clearly, neither parent protected her from the frightening behavior of the other parent. Simone, herself, did not have active strategies for dealing with parental rage and threats, but primarily simply withdrew. Again, like Sara, Simone is sometimes flooded with rage toward her child. It would seem that she also experiences intense, dysregulating anger toward her child that mirrors her parents' behavior and the inevitable fear and rage she must have experienced toward them in return. A key difference between these caregiving interviews, however, is that Simone struggles to suppress the rage she sometimes feels toward her child and avoids confrontation. As a result of this struggle, Simone withdraws emotionally, and, we presume, behaviorally from her child as well. Simone is resigned, that is to say, both passive and constricted, with respect to her child's outbursts. She is passive as well about her child's safety at school. As we typically find with mothers of children who show controlling-caregiving behavior toward the mother on reunion, Simone's constriction of thought and behavior is associated with a perception of her child as precociously mature and with heightened positive feelings that we have elsewhere described as "glorification." We might describe Simone as being flooded by love, as opposed to being flooded by negative feelings.

How are past and present linked in this case? In the present, it seems to us that Simone's view of her child as precociously mature invites her child to take the complementary stance. Furthermore, we speculate that Simone's strong disapproval of and withdrawal from her child's aggression creates pressure for her child to exert *self*-control (constrict) while also signaling Simone's vulnerability. Looking toward the past, we note that Simone felt the need to "be good" to protect her parents. Thus, it seems that we are seeing here an intergenerational pattern of *constricting rage* while manifesting caregiving role-reversal.

Especially fascinating in this case are the links between a dysregulated caregiving pattern and loss. Though Simone's discourse in the AAI did not merit a high score for lack of resolution of mourning, it seems fair to say that both she and her parents failed to fully integrate the loss of her younger sibling. Simone's mother constricted and "blanked out" for some time after the child's death. This was followed by a clear mental breakdown. Failure to fully integrate (and differentiate) the causes of her sibling's death and its consequences may also be at the root of Simone's childhood sense that she had dangerously sadistic feelings toward younger children and her current sense of strong disapproval of her own child's aggression.

III. Mother: Rachel (Mother Classified as E1 (Preoccupied) on the AAI; Child Classified as Ambivalent (C))

Rachel's attachment representation: *Rachel's parents were divorced when she was very young and mother remarried when Rachel was a preschooler. Rachel describes this relationship as "turbulent, rocky"* **(Flooded/Out of control)** *over the years. Rachel's home was "scary and not a happy place . . . basically I just stayed in my room and hid* **(Abdication/Helplessness)**. *Rachel felt that mother was psychologically absent for most of her childhood and often was physically out of the home. Rachel says of this, "She sold me. She wanted this relationship and it, it was at the cost of me."* **(Abdication)** *Rachel was often left in charge of the household* **(Role-reversal)** *and during those times Step-father was liable to create "a big blowout over something . . . He hurt me many times," Rachel said, ". . . we were all really terrified of him."* **(Flooded/Out of control)**. *When Rachel was five, Step-father molested her, but even at that age, Rachel remembers that she protested and cried and he apologized and backed off* **(Protective element: Agency)**. *Rachel described another memory of being effective in* *standing up to her step-father. Her step-father "came after her" because she had defied his rule against keeping a pet. On this occasion, she spoke back to him and ran to the neighbors', yelling, "Don't let him hurt me." She was allowed to stay there overnight. Nevertheless, "Everybody knew ... what was happening to me, and no one thought to ... make him quit." (**Protective element: Agency + Alternative caregivers failed to intervene**) When Rachel was much older, Step-father again, more forcefully, accosted her. Again, she protested vigorously, and eventually he let her go (**Protective element: Agency**). As a young adult and continuing into the present, Rachel has made use of friends and extended family to provide the advice and counseling she wishes she had had as a child (**Protective element: Buffering parent figures**).*

*Rachel's caregiving representation: Like most other mothers in our sample, Rachel highlights her pleasure in her relationship with C, though she describes it in a way that is somewhat undifferentiated and sentimental. For example, in describing herself as a mother, Rachel says "... it's fun ... it's very fun ... just a joy to be around her, she's just a ... you know, a fun ... wonderful little person." Rachel's example of the joy of being a mother focuses on watching C overcome her fear of playground equipment, and shows some blurring in perception of C and herself: "... seeing myself, in a way, as a little child and learning the [monkey] bar." Rachel's past, and her desire to overcome it in her parenting is a topic that runs constantly throughout the Caregiving Interview. For example, in discussing her worries, Rachel says that she worries "... if I'll do a good job. If she'll be ... a person without too many problems as an adult." (**Flooded/ Out-of- control**) In discussing C's sunny personality, Rachel comments, however, "It makes me feel good because it makes me feel like ... like she's benefiting from ... the better person I'm becoming. From what my childhood was like ... I'm not passing on things as much as I could. ... [I feel] Successful and proud." Like many mothers, Rachel pinpoints two issues as frustrations that can lead to anger: C's "dawdling" about getting dressed and ready to go out and wishing for time to herself to pursue solitary activities. Rachel does not depict these events as leading to uncontrollable anger or a feeling of being helpless to control C, however. She says, "... We have a rule ... any time that I feel like I'm going to raise my voice, then ... she gets a time out." Rachel also expresses frustration at C not sleeping consistently in her own bed yet. Sounding, to a degree, like Sara, Rachel describes herself as having run through her strategies, "... we tried all the things that you can try to get her out of your ... [bed]." But Rachel ultimately does not depict herself as desperate; rather she has come up with a strategy that she seems confident about: "And we have set up a thing that when she turns six, that's ... She knows, we've negotiated. ... " Rachel is divorced from*

C's father and describes C as having a great deal of trouble accommodating to changes of schedule. Rachel also describes an incident in which C "freaked out" **(Flooded/Out of control)** *after having been left for a time in the house by herself* **(Abdication)**. *Rachel's descriptions of her reactions to these events suggest that she is capable of providing protection and repair, however. With regard to the first problem, Rachel is peremptory with C's father, telling him how he must care for C in order for C to have consistency in her schedule. In responding to the second incident, she is somewhat reflective about her mistake and she is unambiguous in telling C that she will never be left alone again.*

Commentary: Rachel's AAI shows strong parallels to the first case, that of Sara. Her step-father was out-of-control, vicious, unpredictable. Rachel clearly sees her mother as having abdicated, thus leaving her helpless to the behavior of the step-father. In this case, however, molestation was a disturbing, additional element. What is distinctive in Rachel's representation of the past, however, is her description of herself as having been active and successful in defending herself (with regard to the molestation), and in having found alternative caregivers who were emotionally supportive with respect to the abuse. We propose that these differences in the representation of the past are linked, and perhaps causally so, to the discontinuities between Rachel's experiences in the past and her current caregiving representation. Rachel is sentimental about her child and somewhat given to blurring past and present in thinking about her child. These may be milder "versions" of the glorification and role-reversal we observed in Simone's caregiving representation, and yet they are qualitatively different and indeed are coded as defensive processes characteristic of mothers of ambivalent children (termed "cognitive disconnection). A striking aspect of Rachel's description of caregiving is that she explicitly feels delighted with the success of overcoming her past with her child. Furthermore, although there are problems in relationship to her child, Rachel does not describe herself as helpless, desperate, or out-of-control. Rather, she appears to come up with adequate, active strategies for repair, which we propose are both the signs and a cause of the fact that her daughter's attachment to her, though insecure, is organized. Neither Rachel nor her child is characteristically dysregulated at the representational nor the behavioral levels.

Conclusions

We have shown in this chapter that a mother's Lack of Resolution with respect to loss and maltreatment in the Adult Attachment Interview fails to predict the majority of cases of disorganized-controlling attachment in a normative sample of kindergarten age children. Only four mothers in this sample were classified as Unresolved on the AAI; three of these cases were associated with the disorganized child attachment classification. However, over 85% of the mothers of children classified as disorganized-controlling based on interaction in a laboratory reunion, were judged to be "Not Unresolved" and received adult attachment classifications which are usually associated with organized secure and insecure child attachment. Most commonly, mothers of controlling children were assigned to the E (Preoccupied) adult attachment category. The ratio of disorganized children whose mothers are unresolved for loss or trauma to those whose mothers are not unresolved may differ from sample to sample. The present finding indicates, nevertheless, that an expanded view of the intergenerational pathway leading to attachment disorganization and child controlling behavior is necessary. Future studies are also needed to determine intergenerational pathways among fathers.

A stronger predictor of disorganized-controlling attachment was the mother's report of one or more elements of what we have termed a "rage pattern" on the part of primary caregivers – the display of out-of-control and unpredictable anger, rage, and in, some cases, abuse. A common element in this pattern was substance abuse on the part of one or both parents. Notably, elements of the "rage pattern" were also associated with disorganized-controlling child attachment even when mothers were classified as Unresolved for loss. A similar pattern of findings has recently been reported by Lyons-Ruth et al. (2003) for children classified as insecure-disorganized at 18 months of age, but not for those classified as disorganized at 12 months. They found that while maternal loss predicted infant disorganization at 12 months, by the 18-month attachment assessment, maternal experiences of maltreatment, but not loss, were most predictive of infant attachment disorganization.

One implication of the present findings is that an assessment of the mother's adult attachment classification, including the Unresolved adult attachment classification status, is not equivalent to assessing her child's current attachment classification. That is, adult and child measures are not interchangeable. This is consistent with our suggestion, here and elsewhere (George & Solomon, 1996; 1999a, b; Solomon & George, 1996; 1999a), that although a mother's caregiving representation mediates the effect of her past on the present, it is a product of her accommodation to the current relationship with her child.

The data raise important theoretical questions relating to the intergenerational transmission of attachment patterns, the development of the caregiving system, and the meaning and uses of measures of mothers' representations of themselves as caregivers. In this chapter we used three cases to demonstrate how the mother's manner of describing her relationship with her child has strong parallels to her description of interaction with her own caregivers. Mothers whose children are classified as disorganized/controlling describe themselves as out-of-control and/or constricted and role-reversed with their child. We have characterized both of these patterns as reflecting the dysregulation of maternal caregiving. These same mothers describe past relationships with their own caregivers (in the AAI) in parallel ways. Childhood caregivers are described as out-of-control and threatening, alternative caregivers failed to protect, and the individual experienced herself as helpless in the face of such threats, that is, without active and effective strategies to prevent being threatened and overwhelmed. We noted a correspondence as well between mothers' ineffective strategies for coping with their parents – enraged or caregiving – and the type of controlling strategy shown by their children toward them upon reunion. In contrast, we demonstrated that mothers who experienced threat or abuse but who also described alternative caregivers as protective or themselves as effective agencies of self-protection, depict themselves in the Caregiving Interview as having effective strategies for coping with conflict and negative affect in relation to their children. In turn, the children of these mothers show organized attachment patterns.

Our study captures mothers and children at a single moment in time. Therefore, we cannot determine whether representations of the past influence the present, or the reverse. There is now growing evidence in the empirical literature of changes in an individual's attachment classification from infancy to adulthood (Thompson, 1999; Sampson & Carlson, 2005), and changes in mothers' "state of mind with respect to attachment" during the transition to parenthood and from infancy to the preschool period (Slade et al., 1995; Speiker et al., in press). Those aspects of the mother's past that are temporarily activated and contained in relation to her child, may change as the child matures. Correlatively, the maternal attachment variables that predict attachment disorganization may vary over the course of the child's development as well. Thus, lack of resolution of mourning may be a strong predictor of child attachment when mothers are less experienced and have greater concerns about their infant's survival and ability to become attached to them, while mothers' experiences regarding conflict and violence become more salient as the child matures.

Representational models of attachment and caregiving should not be viewed as having a structural reality. Rather, what we capture with representational measures such as the AAI or Caregiving Interview is the individual's immediate "retranscription" (West & Sheldon-Keller, 1994) or reconstruction of the past in terms of current experiences. Just as a woman's mental organization with respect to the past may drive her perception of her current relationship with her child, the reverse is also true. The mother's feeling of effectiveness and enjoyment of her socially responsive child might lead her to remember and represent herself and her parents in the past in a more positive way than she did before. The existence of other supportive or threatening relationships, such as that with the spouse, in a similar manner may influence the organization of representational models.

Acknowledgments

We are grateful to all of the Mills students who have donated their assistance to this research over the years. Special thanks are due to Paloma Hesemeyer, Bianca Hovda, Rebecca Jackl, and Megan McConnel who helped in the development of the Life Events Coding system and completed the coding.

References

Ainsworth, M. D. S., Blehar, M. C., Waters, E., & Wall., S. (1978). *Patterns of Attachment: A Psychological Study of the Strange Situation.* Hillsdale, NJ: Erlbaum.

Ainsworth, M. D. S. & Eichberg, C. (1991). Effects on infant-mother attachment of mother's unresolved loss of an attachment figure, or other traumatic experience. In C. M. Parkes, J. Stevenson-Hinde, & P. Marris (Eds.), *Attachment Across the Life Cycle.* New York: Routledge, pp. 160–86.

Bowlby, J. (1969/1982). *Attachment and Loss. Volume I: Attachment.* New York: Basic Books.

Bowlby, J. (1984). Caring for the young: Influences on development. In R. S. Cohen, B. J. Cohler, & S. H. Weissman, (Eds.), *Parenthood: A Psychodynamic Perspective.* New York: Guilford, pp. 269–84.

Bretherton, I., Biringen, Z., Ridgeway, D., Maslin, D., & Sherman, M. (1989). Attachment: The parental perspective. *Infant Mental Health Journal, 10,* 203–21.

Cicchetti, D. & Barnett, D. (1991). Attachment organization in maltreated preschoolers. *Development and Psychopathology, 3,* 397–411.

George, C., Kaplan, N., & Main, M. (1984/1985/1996). Adult attachment interview. Unpublished manuscript, University of California, Berkeley.

George, C. & Solomon, J. (1989). Internal working models of parenting and security of attachment at age six. *Infant Mental Health Journal, 10,* 222–37.

George, C. & Solomon, J. (1994). Disorganization of maternal caregiving strategies: An attachment approach to role reversal. Paper presented at the meetings of the American Psychological Association. August, Los Angeles, CA.

George, C. & Solomon, J. (1996). Representational models of relationships: Links between caregiving and attachment. *Infant Mental Health Journal, 17,* 198–216. Special Issue: Defining the Caregiving System. Carol George & Judith Solomon (Eds.).

George, C. & Solomon, J. (1999a). The development of caregiving: An attachment theory approach. In J. Cassidy & P. Shaver (Eds.), *Handbook of Attachment Theory and Research*. New York: Guilford Press, pp. 649–70.

George, C. & Solomon, J. (1999b). The development of caregiving: A comparison of attachment and psychoanalytic approaches to mothering. *Psychoanalytic Inquiry*, 19, 618–46 (*Attachment Research and Psychoanalysis, Volume 1: Theoretical Considerations*). D. Diamond, S. Blatt, & D. Silver (Eds.). Hillsdale, NJ: The Analytic Press.

George, C. & Solomon, J. (2000). Six-year attachment doll play classification system. (Version 00.1). Unpublished.

George, C. & Solomon, J. (2002). Internal working models of caregiving rating manual. (Version 02.1). Unpublished coding manual. Oakland, CA: Mills College.

George, C. & West, M. L. (in press). *The Adult Attachment Projective: A New Assessment of Adult Attachment*. New York: Guilford Publications.

Herman, J. L. (1992). *Trauma and Recovery*. New York: Basic Books.

Hill, J., Byatt, M., & Burnside, E. (2003). Unresolved trauma and unresolved loss in childhood may have different implications for adult depression. Presented as part of a symposium, *Trauma-related adult states of mind: Are they captured by the adult attachment interview?* K. Lyons-Ruth, Chair, biennial meetings of the Society for Research in Child Development, Tampa, FL.

Hodges, J., Steele, M., Hillman, S., Henderson, K., & Kaniuk, J. (2003). Changes in attachment representations over the first year of adoptive placement: Narratives of maltreated children. *Clinical Child Psychology and Psychiatry*, 8, 351–67.

Levine, L., Ward, M., & Carlson, B. (1989, September). Attachment across three generations: Grandmother, mother and infants. Paper presented at World Association of Infant Psychiatry and Allied Disciplines, Lugarno, Switzerland.

Lyons-Ruth, K., Bronfman, E., & Parsons, E. (1999). Atypical maternal behavior and disorganized infant attachment strategies. Frightened, frightening, and atypical maternal behavior and disorganized infant attachment strategies. In J. Vondra and D. Barnett (Eds.), *Atypical Patterns of Infant Attachment: Theory, Research, and Current Directions. Monographs of the Society for Research in Child Development*, *64* (3, Serial No. 258).

Lyons-Ruth, K., Connell, D. B., Grunebaum, H., & Botein, S. (1990). Infants at social risk: Maternal depression and family support services as mediators of infant development and security of attachment. *Child Development*, *61*, 85–98.

Lyons-Ruth, K., Yellink C., Melnick, S., & Atwood, G. (2003). Childhood experiences of trauma and loss have different relations to maternal unresolved and Hostile-Helpless states of mind on the AAI. *Attachment & Human Development*, *5*, 330–52.

Main, M. & Cassidy, J. (1988). Categories of response to reunion with the parent at age 6: Predictable from infant attachment classifications and stable over a 1-month period. *Developmental Psychology*, *24*, 1–12.

Main, M. & Goldwyn, R. (1985/1991/1994/1998). *Adult Attachment Scoring & Classificatioin Systems*. Unpublished classification manual, University of California, Berkeley.

Main, M. & Hesse, E. (1990). Parents' unresolved traumatic experiences are related to infant disorganized attachment status: Is frightened and/or frightening parental behavior the linking mechanism? In M. T. Greenberg, D. Cicchetti, & E. M. Cummings

(Eds.), *Attachment in the Preschool Years*. Chicago: University of Chicago Press, pp. 161–82.

Main, M. & Hesse, E. (1992). Disorganized/disoriented infant behavior in the Strange Situation, lapses in the monitoring of reasoning and discourse in the parent's Adult Attachment Interview, and dissociative states. In M. Ammaniti and D. Stern, *Attachment and Psychoanalysis*. Rome: Gius, Laterza, and Figli, pp. 80–140.

Main, M., Kaplan, N., & Cassidy, J. (1985). Security in infancy, childhood, and adulthood: A move to the level of representation. In I. Bretherton & E. Waters (Eds.), Growing points in attachment theory and research. *Monographs of the Society for Research in Child Development, 50* (1–2, Serial No. 209), 66–104.

Main, M. & Solomon, J. (1986). Discovery of an insecure-disorganized/disoriented attachment pattern. In M. W. Yogman & T. B. Brazelton (Eds.), *Affective Development in Infancy*. Westport, CT: Ablex Publishing, pp. 95–124.

Main, M. & Solomon, J. (1990). Procedures for identifying infants as disorganized/disoriented during the Ainsworth Strange Situation. In D. Cicchetti & M. T. Greenberg (Eds.), *Attachment in the Preschool Years: Theory, Research, and Intervention*. Chicago: University of Chicago Press, pp. 121–60.

Sampson, M. C. & Carlson, E. A. (2005). Prospective and concurrent correlates of attachment insecurity in young adulthood in a high risk sample. Biennial meetings of the Society for Research in Child Development, Atlanta, Georgia.

Schuengel, C., Bakermans-Kranenburg, M. H., & van IJzendoorn, M. H. (1999). Frightening maternal behavior linking unresolved loss and disorganized infant attachment. *Journal of Consulting and Clinical Psychology, 67*, 54–63.

Slade, A., Dermer, M., Gerber, J., Gibson, L., Graf, F., Siegal, N., & Tobias, K. (1995, March). *Prenatal representation, dyadic interaction, and the quality of attachment*. Paper presented at the biennial meetings of the Society for Research in Child Development, Indianapolis, IN.

Spieker, S., Deklyen, M., Nelson, D. C., Jolley, S., & Mennet, L. (in press). Instability of caregiver AAI classifications in a low-income sample: A focus on lack of resolution of loss and trauma. In J. Solomon and C. George (Eds.), *Disorganized Attachment and Caregiving: Research and Clinical Advances*. New York: Guilford Publications.

Solomon, J., George, C., & De Jong, A. (1995). Children classified as controlling at age six: Evidence of disorganized representational strategies and aggression at home and at school. *Development & Psychopathology, 7*, 447–63.

Solomon, J. & George, C. (1996). Defining the caregiving system: Toward a theory of caregiving. *Infant Mental Health Journal, 17*, 183–97. Special Issue: Defining the Caregiving System. Carol George & Judith Solomon (Eds.).

Solomon, J. & George, C. (1999a). The caregiving system in mothers of infants: A comparison of divorcing and married mothers. *Attachment and Human Development, 1*, 171–90.

Solomon, J. & George, C. (1999b). The place of disorganization in attachment theory: Linking classic observations with contemporary findings. In J. Solomon & C. George (Eds.), *Attachment Disorganization*. New York: Guilford Publications, pp. 3–32.

Solomon, J. & George, C. (2000). Toward an integrated theory of maternal caregiving. In J. Osofsky & H. E. Fitzgerald (Eds.), *WAIMH Handbook of Infant Mental*

Health, Vol. III: Parenting and Child Care. New York: John Wiley & Son, Publishers, pp. 323–68.

Solomon, J. & George, C. (2002, April). Understanding children's attachment representations in terms of defensive process. Paper presented at 4th Conference of the International Academy of Family Psychology. Heidelberg, Germany.

Thompson, R. (1999). Early attachment and later development. In J. Cassidy and P. Shaver (Eds.), *Handbook of Attachment: Theory, Research, and Clinical Applications*. New York: Guilford Publications, pp. 265–86.

van IJzendoorn, M. H. (1995). Adult attachment representations, parental responsiveness, and infant attachment: A meta-analysis on the predictive validity of the Adult Attachment Interview. *Psychological Bulletin, 117*, 387–403.

van IJzendoorn, M. H., Schuengel, C., & Bakermans-Kranenburg, M. J. (1999). Disorganized attachment in early childhood: Meta-analysis of precursors, concomitants, and sequelae. *Development and Psychopathology, 11*, 225–49.

West, M. L. & Sheldon–Keller, A. E. (1994). *Patterns of Relating: An Adult Attachment Perspective*. New York: Guilford Press.

10 Good Investments

Foster Parent Representations of Their Foster Children

John P. Ackerman and Mary Dozier

Abstract

This chapter explores the role of foster parent investment in forming parenting representations of foster children. Factors that influence foster parent investment are considered including biological unrelatedness, early emotional and physiological dysregulation, caregiving motives, and child effects. This chapter suggests that highly invested foster parenting may serve as a protective factor for children who have experienced disruptions in care. Empirical evidence is provided from several recent studies examining biologically unrelated caregivers and the importance of caregiver investment to the psychosocial development of children placed with alternative caregivers. A method for assessing foster parent investment is described. Lastly, clinical implications drawing from extant research on caregiver investment and the attachment needs of young foster children are discussed.

Foster parents become surrogate caregivers for children who have experienced disruptions in care and early inadequate care. The foster parent is not the birth parent of a foster child and therefore, may experience the internalization of the parent–child relationship differently from a biological parent. Additionally, the foster parent faces a number of potential barriers in forming optimal representations of a foster child. In this chapter, we highlight the unique contribution of foster parent investment to a foster child's emotional security and emerging sense of self. Foster parents provide care for high-risk children who may need high levels of acceptance and commitment to adjust to early caregiving failures. These caregivers face the task of becoming invested in children to whom they did not give birth and who often have uncertain placement futures. Though the most effective foster parent–foster child relationships are likely the ones in which caregivers are able to accept foster children as their own, there are a host of factors that impede foster

296

parent investment. We will examine these factors and their effects on foster children's development.

This chapter examines caregiver investment, which we consider to be a critical component in foster parents' representations of their children. Caregiver investment will be defined in terms of two related constructs: caregiver acceptance and a psychological commitment to raising the foster child. It is important to clarify how the term "representations" will be used because it has been used to refer to a number of concepts such as internal working models (Bowlby, 1982), parental projection and fantasy (Fraiberg, Adelson, & Shapiro, 1975), and parental state of mind with regard to one's own early attachment experiences (Main, Kaplan, & Cassidy, 1985). However, because caregiver investment is central to the developing relationship between a foster parent and child, we will focus primarily on this aspect of the foster parent's representation of the child.

Before considering how parental representations influence the developing foster child, we will first outline how foster caregivers form and maintain representations of their foster children and how this process may be different from the process by which birth parents develop representations of their children. Biological as well as social-cognitive contributions to caregiver representations will be highlighted. It is hoped that these distinctions will shed light on why many foster children face enduring challenges in new placements and alternatively, why positive outcomes can result when foster children are placed with caregivers who consistently demonstrate optimal levels of parental investment.

Caregiver Representations in the Context of Foster Care

A unique set of conditions differentiates foster parents from biological parents. We will view these differences first from an evolutionary perspective before highlighting specific biological differences that may shape parenting representations. We hypothesize that several of these conditions affect the way that parenting representations of foster children are formed. First, foster and biological mothers differ in their experience of neurochemical and psychological aspects of pregnancy. The absence of this period for foster mothers may contribute to variable levels of investment or motivation for caregiving. Second, the instability of a foster placement may enter into the way foster parents represent foster children as their own. It may be difficult to provide high levels of commitment and sensitive care for a child who may be removed from the home with little warning. Additionally, instability in care may contribute to a foster child's characteristic style of interacting with others. Third, foster parents typically assume the role of caregiver for a child who has experienced an inadequate home environment (e.g. abuse, neglect, prenatal drug exposure, etc.) for variable lengths of time. Foster children who have experienced unsatisfactory caregiving or deprivation for longer periods of time may be more likely to push away new caregivers than children who have not experienced extensive deprivation (Stovall & Dozier, 2000).

An Evolutionary Perspective on Caregiver Investment

From an evolutionary perspective of parental investment, biologically rooted adaptations serve to maximize efficient and effective caregiving. Biological parents are motivated to invest in their offspring to advance biological fitness and to ensure a genetic legacy (Belsky, 1997). Humans place a premium on intimate relationships throughout the lifespan and must be highly invested for a sustained period of time to raise their offspring. An adaptive infant–caregiver attachment is therefore of particular importance. In the most basic sense, children must be physically provided for in order to sustain life. This requires a minimal level of commitment to the parenting role. Moreover, if they are to develop into competently functioning adults, psychological elements of the parent–child relationship such as emotional support and availability play an important role. If a child is able to internalize felt security established in the context of invested caregiving, he or she may be more skilled at exploring, interacting with the physical world, and engaging in new relationships (see Bradley, 1998). Thus, emotional investment in the form of acceptance and commitment seems to be an extremely important component of all caregiver–child relationships. Often, emotional investment is an aspect of parental representations that is taken for granted in normally functioning parent–child dyads; yet in cases of abandonment, maltreatment, or disrupted care, it is clear that all caregivers are not equally invested and the consequences are often quite problematic for a child's emotional and behavioral development.

It should be emphasized that the effects of caregiver investment are not limited to the special case of foster care. Variations in caregiver investment occur in all caregiving arrangements. In fact, Bradley and colleagues (see Bradley et al., 1997) have documented a number of factors associated with variable levels of parental investment among biologically intact dyads. Additionally, foster parent investment is not limited to foster *mother* investment. However, despite increasing efforts to collect data from foster fathers, to date most data from our longitudinal project come from information obtained from foster mothers. Therefore, findings at this time can only be generalized to foster mother–foster child relationships. The assertion made in this chapter is that caregiver investment is a key protective factor for children in the high-risk population of foster care – its influence magnified by the child's experience of early disruption in the caregiving system.

Biological Adaptations Associated with Pregnancy

A key difference between foster and birth mothers is that foster mothers did not give birth to the child for whom they care. A biological mother seems to have advantages over a surrogate caregiver in terms of preparedness for the role of caregiver: a maternal biology that favors caregiving, a prenatal and perinatal period of co-regulation, and a period of bonding that promotes caregiving in infancy (Boyce et al., 1995; Carter & Altemus, 1999; Fifer, 1987; Hofer, 1984; Insel, 1997; Levine, 1983; Smotherman, Brown, & Levine, 1977).

Foster mothers do not undergo the same physiological and hormonal changes as birth mothers. Thus, there are differences in the biological preparedness of foster mothers who do not experience pregnancy. Examples of biological changes such as an increased sensitivity and responsiveness to one's own child, tolerance for outside stress, and a tendency to engage in caregiving behavior have evolved to maximize the likelihood that new mothers meet an infant's needs (see Dozier, 2000). Such responses appear to be regulated in part by hormonal changes occurring during pregnancy and in the perinatal period.

Data from both animal and human studies suggest that biological adaptations yield certain advantages to birth mothers in providing care for their young. One adaptation involves an increased production of the hormone oxytocin during pregnancy and infancy. An increased circulation of oxytocin serves to promote calmness and tolerance for stress during maternal care (Carter & Altemus, 1999) as well as tolerance for monotony and unusual sensory experiences (Levine, 1983). Elevated levels of oxytocin among rodent mothers promote an increased sensitivity to pups' cues and an enhanced tendency to engage in caregiving activities (Smotherman, Brown, & Levine, 1977). Studies with rhesus monkeys indicate that mothers show elevations in cortisol, a hormone associated with stress, when separated from their infants (Coe et al., 1978; Levine, 1983). Research on the neurobiology of attachment by Insel (1997) provides additional evidence that there are neurochemical underpinnings of early social behaviors associated with pregnancy and the perinatal period. These findings suggest that foster mothers may be at a disadvantage in terms of the biological preparedness to care for children relative to biological mothers.

Dysregulation Associated with Disruptions in Care

Foster and biological dyads also differ in that foster infants do not have the same experience of co-regulation with a foster mother that a biological child has with his or her mother. The mother plays a role as an external regulator for the child helping him or her to modulate early physiological responses (Hofer, 1984). In many primates, biological mothers communicate internal circadian and other biological rhythms to offspring through extended ventral–ventral contact, and their offspring develop synchronous parallel rhythms early in infancy (Boyce et al., 1995). Some forms of communication emerge between the mother and fetus in nearly all mammalian species, helping offspring to familiarize themselves with the mother (Fifer, 1987). These studies indicate that the parenting role may begin in the prenatal period, fostering the development of early self-regulatory abilities.

In the presence of early attachment disruption, dysregulation between mother and infant is likely to occur in a number of different systems (i.e., stress response, attachment organization). Studies looking at neuroendocrine functioning of foster children following separations from caregivers have found that foster children tend to develop more atypical diurnal patterns of cortisol production in comparison to children who have not experienced attachment disruptions (Dozier et al., in press). Even when foster children were placed with new caregivers as young infants, dysregulation was apparent in levels of cortisol produced across the day. Fisher and colleagues (Fisher et al., 2000) have demonstrated that cortisol production in preschool-age foster children is also atypical, suggesting that the effects of early adverse caregiving experiences on foster children's regulatory systems are not isolated to the first few years of life. Thus, the children that foster parents take care of may be dysregulated physiologically and behaviorally, making the task of providing care for them more challenging.

Comparing Parenting Representations of Maternal and Non-Maternal Caregivers

Compelling research suggests that biological parents not only undergo biological changes during pregnancy, but also experience significant psychological changes that allow them to form and maintain positive representations of their children in ways that foster parents may not experience. Stern (1991) has suggested that biological caregivers often show a "positive distortion" when describing their children. He suggests that mothers often demonstrate high levels of emotional involvement, resulting in positively biased representations of their child. Positive distortion, as Stern describes it, refers to the powerful subjective reality shaping a parent's belief that his or her baby is the most beautiful, special, fascinating, or loveable child. This "unrealistic" but adaptive perspective is experienced as an emotional reality for many parents. These feelings are believed to facilitate a parent's ability to make many necessary sacrifices for a child.

It seems that foster parents who come to see a foster child as their own child develop a similar perspective. Indeed, a great number of foster parents who have been interviewed about their relationship with their foster children talk about making enormous sacrifices to raise foster children. In contrast, there are caregivers who do not become highly emotionally invested in caring for a foster child. It is expected that these foster parents may be less likely to develop positive representations of their foster children and fail to interact in highly attuned ways.

The representations of mothers and non-maternal caregivers have been observed in a kibbutz setting (Ben-Aaron, Eshel, & Yaari, 1999; Eshel, Landau, Daniely, & Ben-Aaron, 2000). In this dual system of caregivers, a child's biological mother is intended to fulfill a child's emotional needs and the metapelet (non-maternal caregiver) is responsible for the social education of the child. Interestingly, findings suggest that both biological mothers and non-maternal caregivers become attachment figures for infants in a kibbutz setting (Van IJzendoorn, Sagi, & Lambermon, 1992). Thus, this arrangement of multiple caregivers has allowed investigators to explore how two adult caregivers who serve as attachment figures for a child represent the child distinctly. There are clearly differences in the role of the metapelet and a foster caregiver, but comparisons prove useful because they permit an examination of parenting representations among biologically related and unrelated attachment figures holding the child constant.

Ben-Aaron and colleagues (Ben-Aaron et al., 1999) examined maternal and non-maternal caregiver representations of children. First, biological mothers' representations were more positive and less objective than those of the metapelet, supporting Stern's (1991) notion that it is typical for mothers to positively distort views of biological children. Non-maternal caregivers, on the other hand, seem to perceive the same children in emotionally detached and objective terms. Second, mothers' descriptions of their children were more detailed, indicating high levels of maternal involvement in comparison to non-maternal caregivers. Lastly, biological mothers tended to be more concerned and anxious about their children's welfare, suggesting higher levels of emotional investment than the metapelet. Therefore, even though both caregivers served as attachment figures for the kibbutz infant, the representation of the

child formed by each caregiver varied significantly. Moreover, this variation in emotional investment was associated with different patterns of child–
caregiver interactions and attunement to child signals (Eshel et al., 2000).

Thus, in the absence of high levels of emotional investment, a non-maternal
caregiver's experience of a child may be more realistic and less emotionally
charged. However, *realistic* in this context does not carry its usual positive
connotation. The results bring to mind studies of depressed individuals who
tend to offer a somewhat more objective and realistic account of reality as
compared to normally functioning individuals who tend to distort appraisals
in a positively biased manner (Taylor & Brown, 1988). Individuals suffering
from depression appear to have what has been coined *depressive realism* or
an inability to positively distort their perceptions. This lack of defensiveness,
or positive distortion, in depressed individuals is believed to be maladaptive
for an individual's psychological well-being. Likewise, we argue that when a
foster child does not have a caregiver who is emotionally invested in their lives,
they do not have someone who believes that they are the most wonderful child
in the world. Interactions are not likely to be as rich or mutually rewarding
for the caregiver or child, and the foster child may be less likely to develop
competent strategies of social interaction.

Optimal Investment Among Foster Parents

In previous sections, we discussed biological obstacles that face surrogate
parents as they begin to develop relationships with children to whom they did
not give birth. We conceptualize these potential barriers as advantages not
afforded most surrogate caregivers, thus reducing the likelihood of developing
optimal levels of emotional investment in foster children. If, however, a foster
parent is able to generate high levels of commitment and acceptance toward
her foster child, we believe that these caregivers can function as effectively
as a biological parent in the parenting role. This is *not* to suggest that their
role will not be complicated or influenced by numerous child effects; but it
is to say that they are quite capable of providing the nurturance and support
necessary for the development of a secure parent–child attachment (Dozier
et al., 2001; Singer et al., 1985).

Caregiver investment also incorporates a strong motivational component
that will likely influence both the caregiver's representations as well as the
quality of child–caregiver interactions. Clearly, there is a range of potential
motives to engage in parenting a foster child and some motives appear to be
associated with positive foster child outcomes. The limited research available suggests that foster parent motivations such as altruism, childlessness,

and personal identification are associated with the most positive outcomes (Dando & Minty, 1987). On the other hand, caregiving motivations that were negatively associated with child developmental outcomes included monetary incentive and caring for the child of a relative. These findings may not be surprising insofar as motivations associated with being in a mutually beneficial caregiving relationship will positively influence the representation that a foster mother develops of a new foster child. Foster mothers motivated by the relationship itself rather than personal needs or constraints may be able to more readily identify infant needs and respond to them with greater sensitivity. Motives that inhibit the formation of a close attachment relationship or lead a caregiver to withhold affection or other parenting resources are likely to be detrimental to young children, especially those who are already at-risk due to previous disruptions in care.

Existing research on investment with intact parent–child dyads suggests that other relevant moderators of caregiver investment include parental depression, neuroticism, agreeableness, marital discord (Conger et al., 1994), ability to cope with stress (Lazarus, 1993), social support (Belsky, 1984), and child "difficulty" (Corwyn & Bradley, 1999). Personality variables such as agreeableness and warmth may facilitate investment whereas neuroticism may detract from it. Moreover, emotional investment is not generated in a vacuum; social context influences a foster parent's willingness to commit to caring for a foster child. Various forms of stress such as marital conflict or financial strain may diminish emotional investment in the parent–child relationship. Lastly, child effects factor into a caregiver's willingness to invest in the relationship. Corwyn and Bradley (1999) determined that child temperamental difficulty negatively influenced maternal acceptance and responsivity in biological dyads. Therefore, one must entertain the idea that within the foster mother–foster child relationship, child factors can exert an equally strong if not more powerful influence on the course of the developing relationship.

Child Effects on Caregiver Investment

Foster parents attempt to meet the needs of children placed in foster care, many of whom have been exposed to abuse or neglect, prenatal substance abuse, and other risk factors. These factors may interfere with foster parent investment in a foster child. Several factors thought to be associated with caregiver investment including child's age of placement, attachment-related problems, placement instability, and early behavioral difficulties have been examined.

Age of placement is a particularly relevant child characteristic in terms of caregiver investment. Early placed infants appear to be in a more developmentally favorable position than later placed children to reorganize attachment strategies (Chisholm et al., 1995; Stovall & Dozier, 2000; Yarrow & Goodwin, 1973). A separation from a caregiver after the first year of life is thought to be more traumatic since the disruption coincides with a sensitive period in the development of the attachment relationship (Bowlby, 1982). Thus, infants may be able to adapt more readily to a new caregiver than toddlers (Stovall & Dozier, 2000).

It may also be the case that surrogate caregivers are able to identify with the role of "parent" with younger foster children more readily than with older foster children. Infants possess physical characteristics such as large eyes, pupils, and foreheads that increase their attractiveness and encourage attachment behaviors (Hildebrandt & Fitzgerald, 1983). Furthermore, it is the youngest foster babies who inspire the greatest level of satisfaction and the most difficulty in later separation with foster mothers (Fanshel, 1966). Foster mothers who raise infants from birth rarely see themselves as merely temporary caregivers (Adamson, 1973). Foster children are often viewed as *their children* as foster mothers become emotionally involved in raising these children.

In addition to eliciting more responsive caregiving behaviors, the neediness of the newborn foster child likely activates attachment feelings that increase parental investment. Furthermore, an infant may be more capable of assimilating new patterns of caregiving responses as compared to an older child, more readily allowing for a change in expectations associated with the primary attachment figure. The caregiver, in turn, would be encouraged by the change in the child's behavior and reinforced by improvements in the developing attachment relationship. As such, the foster mother of an infant is able to internalize her role as "mother" and feel like an integral part of the ongoing development of her foster child. Thus, the effects of child age may be bi-directional in that infants may be more receptive to new caregivers and new caregivers may be more responsive to infant cues and characteristics.

Caregivers of early-placed infants often report high levels of emotional investment in their foster child (Ackerman & Dozier, 2005; Bates, 2001). This point is illustrated by the case of James, a two-year-old African American male placed with his foster mother in the first year of life. Records reveal that the cause of his placement into foster care was neglect. The following excerpt is taken from his caregiver's investment interview that is administered to all foster parents enrolled in our longitudinal foster care study. The interview is called the "This is My Baby" Interview, and it captures several aspects of a caregiver's level of emotional investment including commitment to foster child, acceptance of the child and the relationship, and a belief in one's ability to influence child's development (Bates & Dozier, 1998; 2002; see Appendix 10.1 for details). It is conducted when foster children are approximately two to three years old after they have been placed with the caregiver continuously for at least two months.

Interview Reflecting High Levels of Emotional Investment

Interviewer: I'd like to begin, Ms. S, by asking you to describe James. What is he like?

Ms. S: Oh, that's not hard. He's just a charming little boy. (Uh-huh). Very intelligent. I would say considerate. He's helpful, a concerned type person, concerned of others. Like if I bumped my toe or something or other, he'll say, "You alright mom?" You know, stuff like that. (Uh-huh). And, um, if one of the other children are crying, he wants to know they're okay and why they're crying or what have you. He's a lovely little child.

Interviewer: Do you ever wish you could raise James?

Ms. S: Yes. Yes.

Interviewer: Can you tell me a bit about that?

Ms. S: I feel as though I know James very well, and his little ideas and his way of thinking–what he likes to do, just always likes to be around you . . .

Interviewer: How much would you miss James if he had to leave?

Ms. S: Oh God, I wouldn't be able to imagine that. (Uh-huh). Um, he's been with me for two years now. And for all, eh, as far as I'm concerned, he is my son and, as far as he's concerned, I am his mother. (Uh-huh). I mean, he's never known, not really known any other mother, and he's not really known any other family other than this family. I would miss him dearly so much. That's why we want to keep him in our home.

Interviewer: What is it that you would like for James in the future?

Ms. S: I would like for him to be in a home with love and stability (Uh-huh), and being able to carry on with his ideas as he gets older and that he can think of things he wants for himself (okay), and be able to fulfill his dreams (Uh-huh) and be happy.

Interviewer: And be happy. (Um-hum). We've been talking for a few
                minutes about your relationship with James. Is there anything
                that we have not touched on that you'd like to bring up?

Ms. S: I think really the relationship with James and myself is, is
                like if he was my own child, you know, like if he was born
                into me, to me (Uh-huh), and the only difference is that I
                didn't have him, but I don't feel like I didn't, it's still the
                same, because we're close just like his mom.

The previous interview incorporates a number of the key elements associated with our operational definition of caregiver investment. Briefly, this excerpt from Ms. S's interview reflects a high degree of acceptance of the child marked by consistently positive descriptions, joy in caring for the child, and respect for the child's individuality. Similarly, there is a high degree of psychological commitment to this child as revealed in the foster mother's difficulty in considering a permanent separation and a desire to provide meaningful care for as long as James remains in her home. This is reinforced by her final comments regarding her deep connection to her foster child, which she describes as no different than a biological parent and child. Her desire to be involved in the development of her foster child is striking, and the tone of the interview is marked by the warmth of her descriptions.

In contrast to the previous example, some children do not have foster parents who view them as "their own." As discussed previously, some of the factors affecting caregiver commitment are related to what the child brings to the new relationship. For example, some foster children who are placed later in life have already developed maladaptive behavioral strategies that alienate new caregivers and cause them to respond less sensitively than they would to early-placed infants. Many foster children enter new caregiving relationships with a history of problematic care marked by neglect, emotional unavailability, or maltreatment. In the context of neglect and maltreatment, children tend to form insecure or disorganized attachment relationships (Carlson et al., 1989). Thus, when these children enter a new relationship with a foster caregiver, it is not surprising that they tend to push away new caregivers because they have expectations that their needs will not be met (Stovall & Dozier, 2000).

Children coping with disruptions in care have had experiences that reinforce expectations of others as unreliable and untrustworthy (Milan & Pinderhughes, 2000). They may be sensitized to negative aspects of social relationships leading to problematic behavioral responses. Foster children's behavioral problems and relational difficulties likely make caregiver investment particularly challenging. In fact, findings from our lab suggest that even autonomous mothers, who would be expected to respond sensitively to their foster children, respond in kind to foster children's insecure strategies (Stovall & Dozier, 2000). For example, when foster children avoid their caregivers when they are distressed, foster mothers often react in a complementary way by not attending to that child. The implication is that foster children's attachment strategies and behavioral style can influence the responsiveness of a caregiver. Behaviors that reinforce the caregiver's view of the child as "difficult" or unresponsive to bids of nurturance may ultimately lessen a foster parent's emotional investment. The alienating behaviors of late-placed foster children in conjunction with their negative caregiving expectations challenge the attachment relationship with the foster parent. Moreover, a failure to establish trusting relationships in early childhood increases the risk for developing behavioral, social, and emotional problems (Erickson, Sroufe, & Egeland, 1985; Elicker, Englund, & Sroufe, 1992; Sroufe, 1983; Sroufe, 1988).

The following except from a foster mother's "This is My Baby" Interview reflects a low level of emotional investment in her foster child who we will call Anthony. Anthony is a two-year-old African American male who was placed with his foster mother when he was 19 months old. Both he and a sibling were removed from biological caregivers after substantiated claims of physical abuse and neglect. Over the course of the interview, not only is there a marked contrast in content quality compared with the interview with James' caregiver, but the emotional tone of the interview is also different. Additionally, the foster mother indicates that she can only function as a temporary caregiver and this likely influences her ability to commit to her foster child.

Interview Reflecting Low Levels of Emotional Investment

Interviewer: I'd like to begin by asking you to describe Anthony, what he's like.

Ms. M: Well, Anthony is the type of child who is very strong-willed. (Uh-huh). He likes to have his way. If he can't, he throws a tantrum. (Oh, okay). He doesn't like to be left alone and likes a lot of activity. (Uh-huh). He's very excitable. When a lot of people come in, he likes crowds, music, and loudness. (Uh-huh). So, I don't know whether that's his background, you know, his environment he came from, or what. But other than that he is a precious little boy.

Interviewer: Do you ever wish you could raise Anthony?

Ms. M:	I don't think I have the stamina to–I really don't. (Uh-huh). He's a very active child (okay), and needs a lot of attention. And by me having two more children, it's hard. (Uh-huh). I think Anthony, Anthony just needs one-on-one. (Yeah). He needs to be in a family environment that can devote the majority of their attention to him. (Uh-huh). Because that's what he really needs. Lots of love. (Yeah).
Interviewer:	How much would you miss Anthony if he had to leave?
Ms. M:	Oh, I would miss him a great deal. He's gone through, um, a lot of changes in his personality since I've had him.
Interviewer:	That sort of leads to my next question. How do you think your relationship has affected him?
Ms. M:	I think it has helped him a great deal. (In what ways?). He's a little more settle-minded. And, he's, he listens a little better now. He understands things better than when I first received him in June.
Interviewer:	How do you think your relationship will affect him in the long term?
Ms. M:	I don't know. (Uh-huh). That I can't answer. (Okay). I just hope it would be a launching pad for him to receive, to know how to react to attention and love. (Uh-huh). I hope he would remember that. I hope it would crowd the other, the negative out, you know. (Uh-huh).
Interviewer:	And what do you want for Anthony right now?
Ms. M:	To see him function at his age level. (Okay. Yeah.). Uh-huh.
Interviewer:	And what do you want for him in the future?
Ms. M:	To see him progress–for him to exceed the development level that he's at. (Okay). And to find a permanent home that, that he could be raised in.
Interviewer:	Is there anything else about him, or your relationship with him, that you'd like to mention?
Ms. M:	Uh, no–not too much. (Okay). I can't think of anything right offhand.

This interview presents a different level of investment than was the case in the previous interview in spite of this foster mother's realistic approach and good intentions. The experience of caring for this child is not expressed in the same positive and accepting terms as was the case in Ms. S's descriptions of caring for James. Ms. M's interview generally reflects a low level of investment based on few positive and several negative descriptions of Anthony, as well as minimal emotional commitment, especially in terms of his future care. Additionally, Ms. M's goals for Anthony are very concrete and she indicates that her relationship with him may not have a lasting impact.

Effects of Foster Parent Investment on Foster Children's Socio-Emotional Development

The emotional investment of a foster parent is thought to be critical if the relationship is to compensate for the effects of early adverse experience. We expect that a relationship characterized by high levels of child acceptance and commitment to the relationship not only leads to warmer and sensitive responses by a caregiver, but also helps instill a template for trusting interpersonal relationships. In our lab we have explored foster mothers' emotional investment in their foster child and how this is reflected in concurrent and subsequent measures of foster child development. We administered the "This is My Baby" Interview to examine foster parents' level of acceptance and commitment to a foster child while in their care. From the age of two to six, foster children participated in a number of tasks examining relationship quality and socioemotional functioning.

Preliminary findings suggest that foster mother investment is associated with foster children's emotional regulation and their representations of self and others. Bates (2001) studied the effects of foster mother state of mind regarding attachment and caregiver investment on foster children's expression of negative affect in joint and independent problem-solving tasks when children were two and three years old. He found that children of less invested autonomous foster mothers displayed more negative affect during independent problem-solving tasks than children of more invested autonomous foster mothers. Interestingly, significant differences were not found among non-autonomous foster mothers. Overall, caregiver investment appears to be associated with foster children's ability to manage feelings of frustration during problem-solving tasks. The emotional regulation problems seen in foster children of caregivers who are not highly invested may be problematic later in childhood, especially at school age when children must negotiate a number of novel and potentially frustrating situations (Blair, 2002).

Ackerman and Dozier (2005) examined the influence of foster mothers' investment measured when foster children were approximately two years of age on foster children's mental representations of self and others between the ages of five and six. Foster mothers who reported higher levels of caregiver investment were found to have school-age foster children who evaluated themselves more positively. Consistent with findings regarding maltreated and neglected pre-schoolers (Toth, Cicchetti, Macfie, Maughan, & Vanmeenan, 2000; Toth, Cicchetti, Macfie, & Emde, 1997), most foster children developed a globally negative view of the self. However, more children placed with highly invested foster mothers developed positive self-representations than children placed with minimally invested foster mothers. Thus, caregiver investment may serve as a protective factor in foster children's development of the self-system.

Foster mothers who were rated low on investment of their foster children also had school-aged foster children who had more aggressive response biases towards peers compared with children of foster mothers who were highly invested in their children (Ackerman & Dozier, 2005). This bias towards aggressive responding is linked with aggressive behaviors toward peers and with peer rejection (Coie, Dodge, Terry, & Wright, 1991; Pope & Bierman, 1999; Price & Dodge, 1989).

Clinical Implications

This chapter has highlighted the importance of emotional investment in foster parents' representation of their foster children. We have argued that there are some biologically based differences between foster and biological parents that place foster parents at a relative disadvantage. Indeed, both animal and human studies suggest that biological mothers may be more prepared to be attuned and emotionally invested in their offspring than are surrogate caregivers (Ben-Aaron et al., 1999; Boyce et al., 1995; Carter & Altemus, 1999; Eshel et al., 2000; Fifer, 1987; Hofer, 1984; Insel, 1997; Levine, 1983; Smotherman et al., 1977). Foster parents, therefore, are likely to encounter obstacles in the parenting of foster children. Additionally, foster children who enter into the new relationship with problematic caregiving experiences may contribute to difficulties in parenting.

We hypothesized that children who have experienced disruptions in care and other psychosocial insults require an emotionally invested caregiver to develop optimally. Studies from our lab have demonstrated that foster parents who report high levels of emotional investment in their foster children early in the relationship have children who show a greater capacity to regulate negative emotions in toddlerhood (Bates, 2001) and represent the self and others positively at ages five and six (Ackerman & Dozier, 2005). Thus, foster mother emotional investment may be a protective factor for this particular group of at-risk children. It makes sense that children who have been separated from a caregiver and who may be coping with that loss benefit from the experience of an accepting and committed foster parent. Furthermore, it seems that a foster parent's ability to form and maintain consistent positive representations of a foster child likely depends on the degree of emotional investment established within the child–caregiver relationship.

We also discussed numerous motivational, social, and behavioral characteristics of the caregiver–child relationship that influence parenting representations. We would like to end by outlining certain clinical implications, paying special attention to the interplay between caregiver investment and the development of an effective attachment relationship. Targeting the parenting representations of foster parents is a critical component in any intervention that seeks to enhance caregiver sensitivity and promote secure attachment relationships. A foster mother who is highly invested in her foster child will be more likely to support her child's development while strengthening an attachment bond. The quality of the relationship may be heavily influenced by the foster mother's ability to interact flexibly and with a high degree of acceptance of her foster child. However, this is a difficult task when caregivers are confronted with disorganized responses from foster children or other strategies that serve to distance the child from the caregiver. Especially for foster parents who are not highly invested, an erosion of investment may occur as the child rejects attempts to provide care or support. These children, unfortunately, place themselves at greater risk to perpetuate early maladaptive interactions with others.

One primary goal of our current foster parent intervention is to generate awareness regarding foster children's behavioral and attachment strategies that often contradict the underlying needs of the child (Dozier, Higley, Albus, & Nutter, 2002). If a foster mother does not gain an understanding of the child's attachment strategies, she could very easily develop a pervasive, negative parenting representation based on unfulfilling and rejecting interactions. This could reduce the child's chances of forming an effective reliance on his or her foster parents by causing foster parents to respond to infant cues in less nurturant ways. The development of a secure attachment relationship is already made more complicated by difficult and unstable family environments (e.g., Egeland & Farber, 1984). Those infants who are maltreated or neglected by a primary caregiver and then separated and placed into foster care face even more challenging conditions.

The purpose of drawing attention to the sequelae of maltreatment and multiple disruptions in care is not to paint a portrait of a child irreversibly destined for problematic relationships. It seems reasonable to believe that for many children there is an opportunity to ameliorate many of the negative consequences of early disruptions when a loving and expectation-altering environment is provided for the child (Chisholm et al., 1995; Juffer & Rosenboom, 1997; Robertson & Robertson, 1989). If a foster mother is able to first acquire an understanding of her child's attachment strategies and underlying needs for nurturance, she may be able to offer the kind of sensitive and therapeutic home that eventually engenders trust and, in turn, a secure attachment relationship. To serve as an effective secure base, the caregiver must be able to take the baby's perspective, appreciate the child's goals, and decide how to respond accordingly. Over the course of time, the child may be capable of shifting his or her expectations, responding with behavior that matches this newly established reliability in care (Dozier et al., 2002). This kind of transactional intervention is thought to be most beneficial for foster mothers with babies who show alienating behaviors as they enter the new relationship.

An intervention aimed at modifying aspects of caregiver representations of foster children has a number of potential benefits for both the child and the caregiver. First, this intervention seeks to change caregivers' behavioral responses to their foster child's bids for nurturance. Second, the awareness gained from learning about foster children's attachment strategies may enhance parental coping and reduce the stress or anger associated with ineffective (or seemingly futile) parent–child interactions. Lastly, it is hoped that the stability of the foster placement is enhanced by foster parent interventions. Each of these benefits is hypothesized to strengthen caregiver investment, thereby increasing the probability that a given placement will facilitate a foster child's early development. Even with a highly invested caregiver who is both committed and accepting, a young foster child is still at considerable risk for later emotional and behavioral difficulties. Nevertheless, it appears that highly invested foster parents may serve to reduce that risk by providing a relationship model that engenders security and globally positive representations of the self and others.

Appendix 10.1 "This is My Baby" Interview

The "This is My Baby Interview" (TIMB; Bates & Dozier, 1998) was developed to assess a foster mothers' level of emotional investment in their infants. The interview and coding system were designed to assess whether the caregiver thinks of the foster child as her own, or whether she views the child as more of a visitor or source of income. This brief semi-structured interview is administered to a foster mother after her foster infant has lived with her for at least two months. She is asked to discuss her infant's personality, whether she has ever wished she could raise the child to adulthood, and how much she would miss the baby if he or she were to leave. The foster parent is then asked how she believes the current parent–child relationship will influence her infant now and in the future.

"This is My Baby" Interview Protocol

The interview consists of six basic questions relating to the mother–child relationship followed by a seventh question regarding the mother's experience as a foster parent. The protocol consists of the following questions:

1. I would like to begin by asking you to describe (child). What is he/she like? *Probe if necessary*: Can you tell me more about (child's) personality?
2. Do you ever wish you could raise (child)?
3. How much would you miss (child) if he/she had to leave? *Probe if necessary*: Can you tell me a little about that?
4. How do you think your relationship with (child) is affecting him/her now? In the long-term?
5. What do you want for (child) right now? What do you want for (child) in the future?
6. Is there anything about (child) that we have not touched on that you would like to tell me?
7. I would like to end by asking a few questions about your experience as a foster parent:
    a. How long have you been a foster parent?
    b. How many foster children have you cared for in all?
    c. How many foster children do you currently have?
    d. How many biological and/or adopted children are living in your home currently?

Coding System

The TIMB coding system consists of three scales: (1) acceptance of the child, (2) commitment to parenting the child, and (3) belief in her ability to influence the child's development. The three dimensions reflect how the caregiver thinks about the child and the mother–child relationship. All three scales are rated on a five-point Likert scale based on an evaluation of the audiotaped interview and verbatim transcript. Specific scores are based on the rater's weighing of positive and negative indices of the caregiver's level of acceptance, commitment, and belief in influence. Midpoint scores (e.g. 3.5) are acceptable in this coding system. Definitions of each scale are provided below, but for more detailed examples see the manual (Bates & Dozier, 1998).

Foster mother *acceptance* is operationalized as the degree to which a foster mother expresses positive feelings about her infant, a sense of pleasure or delight in caring for the child, and respect for the baby's individuality. High acceptance scores are characterized by consistent positive descriptions of the child, little evidence of annoyance with the child's personality or needs, and a clear sense of enjoying parenting the child. In contrast, low scores are characterized by extensive complaints about a child, perfunctory negative descriptions, and/or consistent anger or annoyance with a child.

Foster mother *commitment* is defined as the extent to which a foster mother views the baby as her own while in her care. Caregiver commitment refers to how much the foster parent allows herself to become emotionally invested in the child, commits physical or emotional resources to promote the child's growth or development, and gives evidence that parenting *this* child is very important to her. A high commitment score is given when a foster mother expresses a strong desire to parent the child as long as the child remains in foster care, indicates she would deeply miss the child if he or she were moved to another home, or gives evidence that she has "psychologically adopted" the foster child. Importantly, high commitment scores are not contingent on wanting to permanently adopt a child, but rather there is a strong commitment to the foster child while in her care. Low scores are given when a foster mother is indifferent to whether the child remains with her, consciously takes steps to limit her emotional connection to the child, or views the child more as an unwanted guest or source of income.

The final scale, *belief in influence*, is conceptualized as the degree to which the foster mother believes she can influence her infant's psychological development in the short term and in the future. High scores are characterized by statements indicating that the foster mother believes that her relationship with the child has both immediate and long-term influences on the child's psychological development. A foster mother scoring high on this scale tends to focus on promoting the child's sense of being loved, developing age-appropriate psychological autonomy, and being able to form and maintain stable relationships later in life. A foster mother scoring low on this scale tends to focus on helping the child obtain concrete goals such as gaining weight or helping obtain material items when the child becomes an adult.

Each interview is recorded on an audiotape and subsequently transcribed for coding purposes. Each transcript is coded by two reliable raters who use both the audio tape and transcript to determine global (1–5) scores for each of the three dimensions based on the coding manual (Bates & Dozier, 1998). Ratings are then averaged for subsequent analyses. Questions often give caregivers the opportunity to reflect on multiple dimensions in the same response, so scoring is reflective of the interview as a whole.

References

Ackerman, J. & Dozier, M. (2005). The influence of foster parent investment on children's representations of self and attachment figures. *Journal of Applied Development Psychology, 26,* 507–20.

Adamson, G. (1973). *The Care-takers.* London: Bookstall Publications.

Bates, B. (2001). Foster child autonomy during independent problem-solving: Associations with foster mother state of mind, investment, and quality of support during dyadic problem-solving. Unpublished doctoral dissertation, University of Delaware, Newark.

Bates, B. & Dozier, M. (1998). "This Is My Baby" coding manual. Unpublished manuscript, University of Delaware, Newark.

Bates, B. & Dozier, M. (2002). The importance of maternal state of mind regarding attachment and infant age at placement to foster mothers' representations of their foster infants. *Infant Mental Health Journal, 23,* 417–31.

Belsky, J. (1984). The determinants of parenting: A process model. *Child Development, 63,* 1198–208.

Belsky, J. (1997). Attachment, mating and parenting: An evolutionary interpretation. *Human Nature, 8,* 361–81.

Ben-Aaron, M., Eshel, M., & Yaari, G. (1999). Mother and caregiver representations of toddlers in a kibbutz setting. *British Journal of Medical Psychology, 72,* 189–201.

Blair, C. (2002). School readiness: Integrating cognition and emotion in a neurobiological conceptualization of children's functioning at school entry. *American Psychologist, 57,* 111–27.

Bowlby, J. (1982). *Attachment and Loss: Volume 1. Attachment.* New York: Basic Books. (Original work published 1969).

Boyce, W., Champoux, M., Suomi, S., & Gunnar, M. (1995). Salivary cortisol in nursery-reared rhesus monkeys: Reactivity to peer interactions and altered circadian activity. *Developmental Psychobiology, 28,* 257–67.

Bradley, R. (1998). In defense of parental investment. *Journal of Marriage and the Family, 60,* 791–5.

Bradley, R., Whiteside-Mansell, L., Brisby, J., & Caldwell, B. (1997). Parent's socioemotional investment in children. *Journal of Marriage and the Family, 59,* 77–90.

Carlson, V., Cicchetti, D., Barnett, D., & Braunwald, K. (1989). Disorganized/disoriented attachment relationships in maltreated infants. *Developmental Psychology, 25,* 525–31.

Carter, C. S. & Altemus, M. (1999). Integrative functions of lactational hormonus in social behavior and stress management. In C. S. Carter, I. L. Lederhendler, & B. Kirkpatrick (Eds.), *The Integrative Neurobiology of Affiliation.* Cambridge, MA: MIT press, pp. 361–71.

Chisholm, K., Carter, M. C., Ames, E. W., & Morrison, S. J. (1995). Attachment security and indiscriminately friendly behavior in children adopted from Romanian orphanages. *Development and Psychopathology, 7*, 283–94.

Coe, C. L., Mendoza, S. P., Smotherman, W. P., & Levine, S. (1978). Mother-infant attachment in the squirrel monkey: Adrenal response to separation. *Behavioral Biology, 22*, 236–63.

Coie, J. D., Dodge, K. A., Terry, R., & Wright, V. (1991). The role of aggression in peer relations: An analysis of aggression episodes in boys' play groups. *Child Development, 62*, 812–26.

Conger, R., Ge, X., Elder, G., Lorenz, F., & Simons, R. (1994). Economic stress, coercive family process, and developmental problems in adolescence. *Child Development, 65*, 541–61.

Corwyn, R. & Bradley, R. (1999). Determinants of paternal and maternal investment in children. *Infant Mental Health Journal, 20*, 238–56.

Dando, I. & Minty, B. (1987). What makes a good foster parent? *British Journal of Social Work, 17*, 383–400.

Dozier, M. (2000). Motivation for caregiving from an ethological perspective. *Psychological Inquiry, 11(2)*, 133–56.

Dozier, M., Higley, E., Albus, K., & Nutter, A. (2002). Intervening with foster infants' caregivers: Targeting three critical needs. *Infant Mental Health Journal, 23*, 541–54.

Dozier, M., Manni, M., Peloso, E., Gordon, M., Gunnar, M., Stovall-McClough, K., & Levine, S. (in press). Foster children's diurnal production of cortisol: An exploratory study. *Child Maltreatment*.

Dozier, M., Stovall, K., Albus, K., & Bates, B. (2001). Attachment for infants in foster care: The role of caregiver state of mind. *Child Development, 72*, 1467–77.

Egeland, B. & Farber, E. A. (1984). Infant-mother attachment: Factors related to its development and changes over time. *Child Development, 55*, 753–71.

Elicker, J., Englund, M., & Sroufe, L. A. (1992). Predicting peer competence and peer relationships in childhood from early parent-child relationships. In R. D. Parke & G. W. Ladd (Eds.), *Family-Peer Relationships*: Modes of linkage. Hillsdale, NJ: Erlbaum, pp. 77–106.

Erickson, M. F., Sroufe, L. A., & Egeland, B. (1985). The relationship between quality of attachment and behavior problems in preschool in a high-risk sample. In I. Bretherton & E. Waters (Eds.), Growing points of attachment theory and research, *Monographs of the Society for Research in Child Development, 50* (1–2, Serial No. 209), 147–66.

Eshel, Y., Landau, R., Daniely, A., & Ben-Aaron, M. (2000). Adult attunement and child availability: Interaction of mother and caregiver with three-year-old kibbutz children. *Infant Mental Health Journal, 21*, 411–27.

Fanshel, D. (1966). *Foster Parenthood: A Role Analysis*. Minneapolis: University of Minnesota Press.

Fifer, W. P. (1987). Neonatal preference for mother's voice. In N. Krasnegor, E. Blass, & M. Hofer (Eds.), *Perinatal Development: A Psychobiological Perspective*. San Diego, CA: Academic Press, Inc., pp. 111–24.

Fisher, P., Chamberlain, P., Reid, J., & Gunnar, M. (2000). Specialized foster care for maltreated preschoolers: Impact of children's behavior, neuroendocrine activity, and foster parent functioning following placement in a new foster home. *American Academy of Child and Adolescent Psychiatry, 39*, 1356–64.

Fraiberg, S., Adelson, E., & Shapiro, V. (1975). Ghosts in the nursery: A psychoanalytic approach to the problems of impaired infant-mother relationships. *Journal of the American Academy of Child Psychiatry, 14*, 387–422.

Hildebrandt, K. & Fitzgerald, H. (1983). The infant's physical attractiveness: Its effect om bonding and attachment. *Infant Mental Health Journal, 4*, 3–12.

Hofer, M. A. (1984). Relationships as regulators: A psychobiological perspective on bereavement. *Psychosomatic Medicine, 46*, 183–97.

Insel, T. R. (1997). A neurobiological basis of social attachment. *American Journal of Psychiatry, 154*, 726–35.

Juffer, F. & Rosenboom, L. G. (1997). Infant-mother attachment of internationally adopted children in the Netherlands. *International Journal of Behavioral Development, 20*, 93–107.

Lazarus, R. (1993). From psychological stress to the emotions: A history of changing outlooks. *Annual Review of Psychology, 44*, 1–21.

Levine, S. (1983). A psychobiological approach to the ontogeny of coping. In N. Garmezy & M. Rutter (Eds.), *Stress, Coping, and Development in Children*. New York: McGraw-Hill, pp. 107–31.

Main, M., Kaplan, N., & Cassidy, J. (1985). Security in infancy, childhood and adulthood: A move to the level of representation. In I. Bretherton & E. Waters (Eds.), *Growing points in attachment theory and research. Monographs of the Society for Research in Child Development, 50* (Serial No. 209), 66–104.

Milan, S. E. & Pinderhughes, E. E. (2000). Factors influencing maltreated children's early adjustment in foster care. *Development and Psychopathology, 12*, 63–81.

Pope, A. W. & Bierman, K. L. (1999). Predicting adolescent peer problems and anti-social activities: The relative roles of aggression and dysregulation. *Developmental Psychology, 35*, 335–46.

Price, J. M. & Dodge, K. A. (1989). Reactive and proactive aggression in childhood: Relations to peer status and social context dimensions. *Journal of Abnormal Child Psychology, 17*, 455–71.

Robertson, J. & Robertson, J. (1989). *Separation and the Very Young*. London: Free Association Books.

Singer, L. M., Brodzinsky, D. M., Ramsay, D., Steir, M., & Waters, E. (1985). Mother-infant attachment in adoptive families. *Child Development, 56*, 1543–51.

Smotherman, W. P., Brown, C. P., & Levine, S. (1977). Maternal responsiveness following differential pup treatment and mother-pup interactions. *Hormone Behavior, 8*, 242–53.

Sroufe, L. A. (1983). Infant-caregiver attachment and patterns of adaptation in preschool. The roots of maladaptation and competence. In M. Perlmutter (Ed.), *Minnesota Symposium on Child Psychology*. Hillsdale, NJ: Erlbaum, pp. 41–81.

Sroufe, L. A. (1988). The role of infant-caregiver attachment in development. In J. Belsky & T. Nezworski (Eds.), *Clinical Implications of Attachment*. Hillsdale, NJ: Erlbaum, pp. 18 38.

Stern, D. (1991). Maternal representations: A clinical and subjective phenomenological view. *Infant Mental Health Journal, 12*, 174–86.

Stovall, K. & Dozier, M. (2000). The development of attachment in new relationships: Single-subject analyses for 10 foster infants. *Development and Psychopathology, 12*, 133–56.

Taylor, M. & Brown, J. (1988). Ilusion and well-being: A social psychological perspective on mental health. *Psychological Bulletin, 103*, 193–210.

Toth, S. L., Cicchetti, D., Macfie, J., & Emde, R. N. (1997). Representations of self and other in the narratives of neglected, physically abused, and sexually abused pre-schoolers. *Development and Psychopathology, 9*, 781–96.

Toth, S. L., Cicchetti, D., Macfie, J., Maughan, A., & Vanmeenen, K. (2000). Narrative representations of caregivers and self in maltreated pre-schoolers. *Attachment & Human Development, 2*, 271–305.

Van IJzendoorn, M., Sagi, A., & Lambermon, M. (1992). The multiple caretaker paradox: Some data from Holland and Israel. In R. C. Pianta (Ed.), *Beyond the Parent: The Role of Other Adults in Children's Lives. New Direction in Child Development.* San Francisco: Jossey-Bass, pp. 5–24.

Yarrow, L. J. & Goodwin, M. S. (1973). The immediate impact of separation: Reactions of infants to a change in the mother figure. In L. J. Stone, H. T. Smith, & L. B. Murphy (Eds.), *The Competent Infant: Research and Commentary.* New York: Basic, pp. 1032–40.

11 Intergenerational Transmission of Experiences in Adolescence

The Challenges in Parenting Adolescents

Miri Scharf and Shmuel Shulman

Abstract

The chapter focuses on the nature of intergenerational transmission of parenting during adolescence, namely how parents' past experiences with their own parents in adolescence are related to their parenting of their adolescents. This issue was examined in relation to attachment theory and psychoanalytic conceptualizations. Five case studies from a research project that included seventy 15-year-old adolescents (35 girls) and their parents are presented. Parents were interviewed with regard to their experiences in adolescence and their representations with regards to their relationship with their adolescent offspring. Adolescents were interviewed about their relationships with both parents. The case studies involve narratives of parents with favorable and difficult experiences and describe parents who have and have not resolved their difficult experiences. The cases presented demonstrate the powerful grip of experiences in one's family of origin, revealing that the past continues to play an active role in present life. It also demonstrates how parents try to correct and undo their past, in many cases unsuccessfully. It is argued that the ability to achieve flexible and integrative reflection of the past enables people to accept the imperfection of their parents, themselves, and their children, to relinquish the need to fulfill longed-for wishes, and paves the way to breaking the intergenerational transmission of adverse parenting.

A large body of research and theoretical conceptualizations has been devoted to the study of developmental processes in adolescence, focusing mainly on the challenges experienced by the adolescents and their social context. Yet although this period was found to be the lowest point in parents' life and marital satisfaction (Gecas & Seff, 1990; Steinberg & Steinberg, 1994), relatively less attention has been paid to the developmental needs of the parent at this stage of life (Steinberg & Silk, 2002).

319

The physical, pubertal, cognitive, and social-related changes that adolescents undergo present the parents with new challenges, as they become acquainted with a different child from the one they knew. Parents are required to change their perceptions of their children and to adapt to the new emerging adolescent (Collins, 1995). The growing concerns with their own mid-life challenges may also show up in the quality of their relationship with their children (Greenberger & O'Neil, 1990) and result in increased strain, especially around sexuality and themes related to separation and individuation.

Anna Freud (1958) pointed out that the emergence of sexual instincts may reawaken incestuous fixations among adolescents. In response, an increased distance between parents and children may be evinced. For example, previous affectionate touching between parent and child may become less acceptable (Salt, 1991). The adolescents' physical and sexual maturity might incite parents' concerns about their own bodies, their own physical attractiveness, their own sexuality and reproductive ability, and about their own sexual experiences as adolescents (Gould, 1972; Steinberg & Steinberg, 1994). Previous research suggests that self-definitions of parenthood may be transformed following a child's puberty and emerging sexuality. For example, parents (especially fathers) tend to define their relationship with their daughters in terms of increased protectiveness (Paikoff & Brooks-Gunn, 1991). Similarly, the interaction between a daughter's menarcheal timing and her mother's reproductive status has been associated with eating problems in mother and daughter, with more problems for daughters when they matured early and their mothers were no longer menstruating (Paikoff, Brooks-Gunn, & Carlton-Ford, 1991).

The adolescents' individuation process involves challenging parents' authority, de-idealization of parents, and increased emotional separation. Within the psychoanalytic framework, Blos (1962) described how the increasing sense of mastery that characterizes adolescence leads to a drastic change in the relationship with the parents. Previously the parent was overvalued and was an object of awe; now he or she becomes undervalued and is treated like a fallen idol. In addition, increased insistence on independence may be accompanied by adolescent arrogance, rebelliousness, and defiance of parental rules or expectations (Blos, 1962; p. 91). Parents, who are used to a warm and in many instances an admiring relationship with their child, undergo a process of diminishing worth and respect in the eyes of their adolescent child (de-idealization), which might be difficult for many to cope with (Steinberg & Steinberg, 1994).

Other scholars have pointed to the complementarity between experiences related to parenthood and mid-life issues. This stage of life raises new questions and calls for reflection on what has and has not been achieved (Levinson,

1978), and presents parents with the challenge of how to come to terms with choices they have made and the lives they have led so far. Adolescents' dating, educational choices, and achievements trigger parents' comparison between themselves and their child, and can intensify doubts about their own choices (Steinberg & Steinberg, 1994; Steinberg & Silk, 2002).

In sum, adolescence entails major changes for adolescents and their parents, which make this period especially challenging. For adolescents, the peer group, and in particular close friends, serve as a support system in this transition. Parents who are engulfed with additional dilemmas of life-span issues have to find their own resources, to redefine their parenthood, and adapt it to the needs of their adolescent child.

The central premise of this chapter is that parents' own experiences with their own parents may reawaken and set the stage for their current parenting. Our purpose here is to explore how parents' experiences with their own parents when they themselves were adolescents serve as model or affect the way they now parent their adolescent children. This question was examined within the broader conceptual issue of intergenerational transmission of parenting and in relation to attachment theory, as well as psychoanalytic conceptualizations.

We first discuss the issue of intergenerational transmission of parenting as discussed in the various conceptual approaches and their related research, focusing on the unique aspects specific to adolescence. Then we present five cases of parents who were interviewed about their adolescent experiences and about their current relationship with their own adolescent offspring. Based on the cases, we try to understand how models of parenting are transmitted from one generation to the next, and under what conditions parents are capable of reworking and correcting their previous experiences. In addition, we discuss the possible mechanisms related to intergenerational transmission of parenting and formulate different pathways of intergenerational transmission.

Intergenerational Transmission of Parenting: Clinical and Theoretical Perspectives

Parents commonly undergo the experience of hearing and echoing their own parents' voices when interacting with their child. These voices can be louder in times of stress or conflict, when intense emotions are evoked, or during placid encounters, when the wish to share the intimate and intense moments with their own parents may arise (Slade & Cohen, 1996). Selma Fraiberg and her coworkers were among the first to identify a number of babies who were burdened by the oppressive past of their parents. These parents had experienced events like abuse, tyranny, or desertion, and seemed to be condemned to repeat the tragedy of their childhood with their own babies (Fraiberg, Adelson, & Shapiro, 1975).

Psychodynamically Oriented Conceptualizations

Brazelton and Cramer (1990) provided an elaborate description of how parents might replay scenes from their own childhood in their interaction with their babies. According to these authors, parents' fantasies, expectations, and inner conflicts mediate the interaction between them and their infants. They suggest that *projection* is the mechanism through which parents tend to transfer their own past images or experiences onto their child, and describe three of modes of projection that may overlap to some extent. In the first scenario the child represents a *significant person* from the parent's past. The child is cast into this portrayal and his/her role is to materialize these figures. In the second scenario the relationships re-enact past *themes* of former relationships, while in the third scenario the child represents a part of the parent's *own unconscious*, frequently some of the parent's negative parts.

Brazelton and Cramer (1990) stress that in itself projection is not pathological, and even helps processes of empathic understanding of the child. However, successful parenting is a balance between finding similarities and discerning differences between oneself and one's child. When parents are sensitive enough to recognize what parts do not fit their child and "pull back," a more balanced relationship with the child can develop. Yet in several circumstances parents may not be sensitive to or aware of their own motivations and behaviors.

Parents may attempt to establish with their child the exact opposite of the relationship they had with their own parents. For example, a strict disciplinary experience may lead parents to be unwilling to impose any limits on the child or cause the child any frustration. This may result in the child's inability to delay gratification and in his or her demanding and tyrant-like behavior. The parents may not be aware that they have actually reconstructed their past relationship, and that they are re-play the same role they played in their own childhood, namely living again under an authoritarian rule. Other parents may try to repair a painful past by trying to create an ideal and "perfect" parent–child relationship, a seemingly ideal version of the past that should have been. The energy and investment in creating the ideal relationship with the child serves simultaneously for the parents' self-gratification too. A child may also realize a longed-for ideal by addressing parents' own needs for pride or achievement. By projecting onto their child their own aspirations, this can go to extremes in which parents give up their own well-being in order to gratify their child. They thus re-create a situation in which the parents might feel unhappy and deprived. In other situations, the child may be labeled, for example, lazy or excessively dependent when parents do not tolerate these characteristics in themselves.

Brazelton and Cramer's (1990) work describes mainly parents' relationships with infants or young children. However, they can clearly be applied to adolescence as well. The notion of intergenerational transmission of parents has also been discussed specifically with regard to adolescent children. Esman (1985) described how the parent's conflict with his or her adolescent child may reactivate the parent's old, unresolved adolescent conflicts: "I couldn't get away with my stuff when I was his age – why should I let him do it now?" (Esman, 1985; p. 147). Stierlin (1981) dealt extensively with this issue in his book *Separating Parents and Adolescents*, and focused specifically on intergenerational transmission in adolescence. He suggests that parents in their forties struggle with the problems of their own life phase, how close to stay and continue investing in the family, or to start investing in their own wishes and expectations. This conflict coincides with that of their adolescent offspring, leading to a variety of interactional modes – *binding, delegating, and expelling*, which may reflect the inner conflicts of the parents more than the real needs of both generations.

The *binding* mode mainly exploits parents' dependency needs, and interferes with the age-related task of adolescent individuation. By being over-gratifying, the parent enhances regressive tendencies in the adolescent, where in fact the parent may be trying to repair past losses and deprivations. Some parents may exploit the loyalty a child has for his or her parents by inducing guilt. These parents may convey, overtly but more often covertly, that they have totally sacrificed themselves for their child, that they can live only through him or her, and they expect the child to sacrifice himself or herself for the sake of the parents.

Other parents may themselves be torn between reacting to their own wishes or the needs of the family. Through their ambivalence, they may recruit their adolescent child to act out their desires. The adolescent is then *delegated* to serve parental needs; he/she is entrusted with the mission of providing the parents with experiences they missed when they were adolescents. Such parents of adolescents use their children as proxies to express their own unresolved conflicts and to enact their past experience. For example a father may, unconsciously, enjoy his son's sexual explorations, an activity that he was not allowed or able to do while he was an adolescent. However, because of his continued ambivalence the father may disown these acts and might even punish the adolescent afterwards. Finally, in the *expelling* mode parents are occupied with their own problems; they see their children as an obstacle in realizing their plans and reject or neglect them. Stierlin (1981) described how parents' and adolescents' distinctive developmental challenges might trigger projections, enactment, and undoing related to unresolved conflicts of the parent's adolescence. While Cramer and Brazelton emphasize mostly past unresolved issues that are projected to the child, Sterilin refers to current unresolved parental issues that are related to mid-life crises. These difficulties are expressed especially in the arena of separation of both parties – parents and their adolescent children.

Another perspective incorporating psychodynamic considerations is presented by Shabad (1993). This author described development as an ongoing tension between the urge to create one's own solitary path separate from one's parents, yet at the same time to adhere to the previous generation and repeat its legacy. Once a child is brought up in a mutually respecting atmosphere, the child experiences a "developmental flexibility and dynamism which enables the child to move closer to and further away from the parent" (p. 64). In this model, respect for individual growth and the next generation is integral to and balanced with the close relationship with the previous generation.

Under less favorable conditions, parents are unable to establish a give-and-take relationship with their child. Shabad (1993) claimed that repeated unfavorable experiences such as parental criticism or intrusiveness might cumulatively constitute traumatic experiences of varying severity. The children are only left with an illusionary hope to remedy the relationship with parents and to be accepted by them. When becoming a parent, such individuals may swear not to repeat the hated behavior of their own parents. Thus, like the proponents other conceptualizations (Brazelton & Cramer, 1990; Stierlin, 1981), Shabad attempts to explain intergeneration transmission focusing mainly on transmission of difficult experiences. He hints at the possible function of these processes, suggesting that "when the future is perceived, created, and delimited by the images of the past, the uncertain dangers of encountering novelty and solitude can be eliminated" (Shabad, 2001; p. 95).

In reality, in many cases the misery is transmitted to the next generation. According to Shabad, the irresistible urge to undo one's prior harsh experiences can take the form of a compulsive wish to gain mastery over one's past through some magical undoing. Parents end up having the same experiences with their children, although they proclaim that they wish to correct their parents' misdeeds and they are even not aware that they are repeating the type of parenting they experienced. Shabad explains this "unconscious" compulsive repetition as a sort of identification with the aggressor that is found in traumatic themes as a way to master the trauma. He explains: "fixation on attempted offering oneself to one's parents that was never accepted ... the chronic disillusionment becomes so unbearable that one attempts to bridge the chasm between oneself and the psychically lost parent narcissistically – by 'becoming' the parental aggressor to oneself" (p. 69).

The only way to overcome this uncontrolled repetition requires first that parents become aware of the pain they suffered and of the resentment and long-buried wishes for "what could have been" that they may still carry. It is a process of mourning for their lost childhood that parents must undergo in order to gain more awareness of their current wishes and behavior with their own children.

Intergenerational Transmission from an Attachment Theory Perspective

The most prominent model and examination of intergenerational transmission can found in attachment theory and its derivatives. Intergenerational transmission of attachment refers to the process through which parents' experiences during childhood influence the quality of the attachment relationships developed by their children (Bowlby, 1973; Main, Kaplan, & Cassidy, 1985). Based on their experiences with caregivers, children construct mental representations termed *Internal Working Models* (Bowlby, 1980). Internal working models organize emotions, cognitions, and behavioral strategies in significant relationships (Belsky & Cassidy, 1994), and these continue to be created, altered, modified, or further reinforced based on one's life experiences. Models of self and other that develop from early relationship experiences influence the nature of interaction with the environment and expectations concerning availability, responsiveness, and attitudes of others, as well as expectations about the self in relationships. Eventually, these models will also influence parents' relationships with their own children.

Main (2000) suggested that parents repeat aspects of their own childhood experiences in relation to their child as this preserves their particular state of mind with regard to attachment. State of mind is manifested in the way parents reflect and evaluate their attachment-related experiences (Main & Goldwyn, 1998). People are classified as having a secure state of mind, termed *autonomous*, if they have access to their childhood experiences and evaluate them coherently. Their state of mind is classified as *dismissing* when they tend to minimize the importance of attachment for their own lives or to idealize their childhood experiences. A *preoccupied* state of mind characterizes people who manifest angry, passive, or confused preoccupation with attachment figures.

It was suggested (Hesse, 1999; Main et al., 1985; Slade & Cohen, 1996) that autonomous/secure state of mind allows parents also to be open with their children, to accept and manage their child's affects and impulses, and provide the child with felt security. The parent's confident and flexible attitude or parenting is resilient and consistent enough to cope with difficulties that may arise from time to time. Thus, security implies the capacity (with consciousness) to regulate, integrate, and remember the negative as well as the positive aspects of previous significant relationships. As this capacity is expressed in parental caregiving, being brought up by a secure parent implies an experience of recognition and respect for one's wishes, affects, and impulses.

Insecure parents have difficulties with their past experiences. This can be revealed by their tendency to exclude, distort, or fail to present memories and affects in relation to their early relationships. They may also have difficulty presenting their childhood in a coherent manner, as conflict and pain about their early relationships may still overwhelm them. To protect themselves, these parents become insensitive to their child and act more in order to protect their own way of experiencing relationships. This may be demonstrated by either minimizing or maximizing the child's signals. For example, Lyons-Ruth and Block (1996) suggested that parents' attempts to defend themselves against re-experiencing painful fear, helplessness, and rage related to earlier traumas result in parental emotional and physical withdrawal from, or a hostile stance towards the child. Being brought up by an insecure parent implies having experiences that reflect minimization or exaggeration of the child's needs in accordance with the parents' needs (Cassidy, 1994).

It was suggested that it is metacognitive monitoring or reflective function that underlies autonomous state of mind and sensitive caregiving (Fonagy, Steele, & Steele, 1991). Reflectivity entails the ability to see oneself and significant others in those relationships, and to have a coherent awareness of own thoughts and feelings, of others' thoughts and feelings, and of the complex relationship between mental states and interpersonal behavior. Thus, having experienced a difficult or harsh childhood does not entail having an insecure state of mind or having to re-enact past experiences. One's capacity to reflect on past experiences and resolve negative feelings is the key to flexible and sensitive caregiving.

In line with this suggestion, Pearson, Cohn, Cowan, and Cowan (1994) described mothers they characterized as earned secure. These mothers' accounts contained difficult early experiences. However, as adults these mothers had the ability to reflect and to come to terms with their past, and this allowed them to present currently a coherent and flexible state of mind. Such mothers were observed to behave in a confident and flexible manner with their infants. Snarey (1993) in his study of fathers was able to show that fathering was the combined result of modeling the positive aspects of their fathers' parenting and reworking the negative aspects of the father–son relationship they had experienced. The ability to understand fathers' motivations and forgive them was affected by the quality of relationship with the mother and the degree of the warm atmosphere at home.

In sum, parents' state of mind with regard to attachment may influence their caregiving, which in turn becomes the model a child is exposed to and develops regarding self and others in close relationships. In line with this idea of intergenerational transmission of attachment security, van IJzendoorn (1995) observed in a meta-analysis an impressive correspondence between the quality of the parent's state of mind with regard to attachment and the quality of the child's attachment to the parent. Yet some discontinuity was also noted.

Byng-Hall (1995), adopting a family systems perspective and incorporating concepts from attachment theory, outlined how family behavioral patterns pass or change from one generation to the next. According to this perspective too, children inevitably take some of their family experiences and re-create them in the next generation when they are parents. Interactions between generations involve "intergenerational scripts," whereas patterns from previous generations are transferred to and *replicated* in current interactions. According to Byng-Hall, scripts are more than a general model of how to behave within a relationship. Scripts dictate how relationships will be enacted in the family, because they cast family members in roles in certain scenarios. The impact of previous family scripts is strong. Once established, these scripts (or representations) are posited to be strongly resistant to change as they operate outside the conscious awareness and new information is assimilated into the existing schema (Bretherton & Munholland, 1999). Family members sometimes come to feel that they are programmed to behave in certain ways.

An ideal script is one that includes structured predictable actions, but is also open and flexible and leaves room to incorporate new actions compatible with the script and reflecting the new circumstances. This allows for *improvisation*, which leaves room for possible variations and required adjustments in the present and the future (Byng-Hall, 1995; p. 28). Parents who experienced difficult or even intolerable experiences in their families of origin may attempt to act contrary to those experiences and to develop *corrective* scripts in their new families. In such a case there might be a gap between the overt facade and the inner embedded script. This may result in overt or covert conflicts, especially in times of stress; then the original script might, after all, be re-enacted.

Various mechanisms were suggested in attempts to clarify the working of intergenerational transmission. Rubin, Booth, Rose-Krasnor, and Mills (1995) suggested that the skills of effective interacting with others and of competent behavior are observed in the parent–child relationship; they are learned and enacted in future relationships. Here, *parental modeling* is the mediating mechanism. Similarly, *processes of identification* were also suggested as such a mechanism. Children identify with their parents, and internalize and absorb parts of their parents. In situations where children were exposed to harsh parenting, *identification with the aggressor* may come to be enacted.

Unresolved difficult past experiences of parents might carry over to the next generation in various ways. *Projective identification* refers to an unconscious process by which unbearable experience is projected onto one's child. In this way the parent can master his/her disowned parts, now felt as belonging to one's child (Silverman & Lieberman, 1999). Parents may also try to repair painful experiences through *undoing* or they may expect their children to *re-enact* their own unresolved conflicts. However, as noted, the urge to repeat the past might be curtailed through resolution of difficult experiences. Autonomous state of mind with regard to attachment, which implies reflectivity and the ability to integrate and manage even adverse experiences, indicates that even when parents experienced a difficult childhood they can modify and alter their childhood internal working models. These revised and corrected models might translate into sensitive parenting, relatively free from immersion in the distressing past experiences.

The dynamic literature suggests that continuity or discontinuity of previous relational patterns may take other forms, beyond repetition or change. Interactions may include hidden motives that actors are not fully aware of, despite declaring of their wish for change. In addition, when children grow up they become more active players in the lives of their families (Cummings & Schermerhorn, 2003), and their unique personalities, emotions, and behaviors influence their parents as well as being influenced by them.

To gain a better understanding, this chapter presents an analysis of in-depth interviews with parents of adolescents with regard to their past adolescent experiences and their current experiences in parenting their adolescent offspring. Interpretations rely on concepts from attachment theory in general, and from the psychodynamic approaches presented here. In all, we want to show the diverse ways in which parents' past experiences affect the manner in which they parent their children.

Case Examples Highlighting Diverse Modes of Intergenerational Transmission

The Sample. The cases reported here were collected as part of a large research project examining the association between parents' own experiences in adolescence and their relationships with their mid-adolescent children.

Seventy adolescents (35 girls, mean age $= 15.06$) were identified and recruited from published lists of students in the northern part of Israel. We limited our choice of subjects to intact families, and families that had not immigrated recently to Israel. The active consent of father, mother, and adolescent was required for a family to be included in the study. Adolescents and their parents were interviewed separately in their homes, with the Adolescence Experiences' Interview (Scharf & Shulman, 1998). In line with the AAI procedure (George, Kaplan & Main, 1985), parents were interviewed regarding their own experiences during adolescence, and were asked to describe their relationships with parents and substantiate their accounts with specific episodes. They were asked about other significant relationships during their own adolescence, and the importance and the significance of the adolescence period for who they are today. In the second part, they were requested to describe their current relationships with their adolescent child (using general descriptions and specific episodes), their feelings about his/her growing autonomy, and the linkage between past and current adolescence experiences. Interviews were audiotaped and then transcribed verbatim.

The families in our sample were primarily well educated (75% percent of the fathers and 70% of the mothers had at least a college education), and were sampled from middle class neighborhoods.

The Nurtured Mother Nurturing Her Son: Replication of a Flexible Script

Rona (names are fictional in all the case descriptions) was interviewed about her relationship with Gad, her oldest son, aged 15. Rona was an only child and was born many years after her parents had married. She says that it was considered a medical miracle when she was born, and she got a lot of love and attention from her parents. She remembers vividly that it was only she and her parents: "I did not have to share my parents with somebody else. My mother invested a lot in me. I remember how we used to sit and play. At that time it looked to me natural, but later on I understood that it was rare." Rona remembers that despite the fact that her parents were new immigrants to the country and had economic difficulties, she got "the maximum that you can dream about."

Her parents regularly helped her with her homework. In particular, she is still warmhearted when she thinks of how her father had the talent to present difficult material to her. Her parents were aware of her whereabouts, were interested to know whom she went out with, and insisted on setting a time she had to be home.

Yet despite the very close and monitoring parenting, her parents never prevented her from taking part in social activities and they supported her decisions. They were also supportive when Rona became an adolescent. "I remember that I had a boyfriend who lived in another town and I used to get letters from him. Every day getting home from school I would eagerly check to see if a letter had arrived. I remember that my mother was supportive of my enthusiasm. I also remember that if I returned feeling moody, after a social activity, my mother was always there for me. If I had a problem with a grade, an exam, I got support and understanding. Once I went out and stayed overnight at a boy's house. They respected what I did, with a few instructions; they had confidence in me."

Rona thinks that adolescence was a significant time in her development: "I was quite short, rather plump, and they always cheered me up. They gave me the feeling that I was fine. OK, I'm not 1.70 meter, but I have a pleasant smile, a nice face, I'm friendly. They always emphasized my positive things and took less account of the not so good things. It gave me a lot of self-confidence. I think this shaped my personality, the confidence I got through them."

Rona describes a very warm and close relationship with her son Gad. "He is the happiest child in our family. He always comes with his stories, he is open, speaks and sings loudly, he says clearly what he thinks, very communicative. It's fun with him." However, Rona does not just idealize her son; she is also aware of and ready to talk about his difficulties as well. "Too long a conversation is not for him. Everything has to be concise, he has no patience. For the first few minutes he listens and then he's not with me. So what I want to tell him I have to tell him fast. Because of his impatience, we had a fight where I had to tell him what his obligations were. I had to set limits. For example, we didn't agree with his priorities. For him, football and TV were first and then homework. And we had problems."

Rona said that these conflicts led nowhere. "At some point I realized that after all he does what he wants, and what he is capable of doing. I stopped pushing him and showed him that whatever he achieves is good for me. It's more important for me that he's happy, that we have a good relationship, than an extra point in his grades." Rona feels that changing her attitude to schooling and having confidence in the child helps him, decreases conflicts, and contributes to a better self-image of Gad. It changed the atmosphere in the family as well as Gad's attitude to school.

When comparing Gad's life and her adolescent years, Rona realized that "he has less patience for me than I would have expected. I was with my parents most of my free time. Now there are telephones, TV, Internet, and time with friends. It was different when I was a kid. But there are also similarities. Like my parents I am really interested and involved in what is going on in his life. He doesn't need me as a friend. Also he has siblings, something I did not have. My parents' genuine interest in me did me a very good service. It shaped me. What I had with my parents I have tried to accomplish with Gad as well. For example, he can tell me, 'I'm asking my girlfriend to stay over, and she'll sleep in my room.' Or 'Today I'm sleeping at a friend's place, I'll be back late.' He feels free with me."

Case Summary. Rona's relationship with her son has many of the qualities of the relationship she had with her parents, and she claimed that her parents are her models for parenting her son. The accepting and sensitive upbringing she was exposed to reflects the characteristics of a secure attachment. As an adult, this secure state of mind has allowed her to be open with her son, to provide him with the feeling that he is accepted, and to understand and manage his impulses (Slade & Cohen, 1996). It is important to remember that an important aspect of secure attachment is its flexibility in addressing the changing environment. Gad had some problems that Rona did not experience as an adolescent, but her secure model allows her to adopt a flexible attitude in dealing with her son. Thus, continuity of a secure model implies also flexibility to adapt to novel and sometimes unexpected demands of parenting an adolescent.

The Father "Eager for Openness" and His Daughter: Partial Correction

David, in his early forties, was interviewed about his relationship with Sharon, his 15-year-old daughter. David grew up in a small village where his parents ran a farm. He described his parents as hardworking people who had very little time for him due to economic constraints. When asked to refer more specifically to his adolescence, David described that his parents were very conservative and closed people, who never talked to him about his development. "They never asked me what weighed on me, what bothered me. When I was a little tense, you know boys become tense because of their hormones, there were times when I wanted someone to talk to, [but] my parents were very reserved and busy and I was lonely and miserable. I couldn't share with them what was happening to me and I wasn't open even about my sexual development. Even when I had my first girlfriend I kept it a secret. It was hard." David was asked to elaborate what exactly he meant when he described his parents as reserved. "I remember the informative books for adolescent girls that I have at home today. Not just in the bookcase. I take it to my daughter in bed. I took it to her in bed and gave it to her to read it when she was 13.

I always was open with her. My parents not only didn't bring [a book of that kind] to me in bed, they hid it in the attic. And I knew that they hid it so I searched for it." Throughout the interview, David tried to show how different he is from his parents, and raised issues related to his daughter even when he was asked to describe his parents.

David described his parents as hard workers who had no time for him, and his father's lack of harmony with him. "He took me with him everywhere and in everything he did. He always told me, 'This is the way to do it,' whether it was seeding or plowing. He insisted that studying was a waste of time. 'Be a farmer. Why else am I teaching you?' So he was concerned about my future and less about what was happening then. He had no time for asking me about my studies because he wasn't so interested in it. It was important to add a pair of hands to the farm" ... "When I was 16 I had a girlfriend, then instead of ... he joked about it. Instead of drawing closer to me he joked. He didn't advise me, didn't tell me what and how. I learned by myself from experience."

The discourse revealed that David was aware of the possible reasons for his parents' behavior. "I understood that my father, who had experienced a very difficult childhood (the Holocaust), found it hard to understand his child. I understood his remoteness toward me. Maybe because of the times he had undergone he was not an open person. Children who grow up in a free home, without any worries, probably have parents who have more time, are more open, and then the child is more open. ... Maybe I perceived my father as closed because he had no time to talk to me. We didn't even eat together. All the time there was work, and the result was closure. I understood. I didn't think for a moment that he didn't want to talk to me. I understood that he was busy." Thus, although David showed little preoccupation with his parents' behavior toward him, he also expressed understanding to some degree.

When asked to state five words that best represented his relationship with his daughter, he gave precisely the opposite words to those he used to describe his relationship with his parents: "A lot, lot of openness, understanding, awareness, mutual sensitivity ... I'll give you an example. I remember that the first boyfriend Sharon had. I'm sure she told her mother about it too, but soon after she runs to tell me, because I have been open with her since she was very young. First she comes and tells me, in detail. Unbelievable, this is openness."

David described the open and respectful relationship with his daughter: "Economic issues should not bother her. She has to find her way and go forward." At some point Sharon had something of a weight problem. "I didn't interfere, I relied on her to know what to do. ... I only encouraged her to perform better at sports ... Not that I don't intervene at all. My attitude is that you shouldn't intervene too much, but you shouldn't be in a situation that you don't have time, as I experienced from my parents. I don't want to influence my daughter's personality. I want to let her learn about life herself, to know what's best for her, and let her experience life."

Reading these examples raises the question of whether David's lenient attitude was not also a subtle expression of the distance that characterized his upbringing. David also described Sharon as a very aware and considerate person, and he explained the mutual sensitivity as follows: "There are difficult periods in life, like economic problems, and she is aware of it. She knows that I am ill and I need silence. She is aware that if I come back from work furious she won't disturb me, she won't nag me. She is aware of her parents, her father. She is sensitive toward me ... When she shares with me, I set everything aside and listen to her." The sensitive daughter compensates for the father's past deprivations, but he is also sensitive when she wants him to listen.

Equally compelling was yet another instance where David's "proclaimed" attitude of openness and availability concealed an additional layer recalling David's personal experience with his father over issues of emerging sexuality: "In my opinion she feels fine. We help her and support her during her adolescent experiences. My wife's openness and mine helps her move on more smoothly. Sometime I even joke with her. Maybe because I am too open. Once, for example, I saw an ad for bras in the newspaper and asked her, 'Why don't you buy a bra like this one?' She laughed and said, 'What, can't I decide for myself what bra to buy?' You see, we don't make such conversations taboo, but I don't overdo such things either. It was the only joking around we had in the last three years."

Case Summary. A remarkable aspect of David's parenting is his strong wish to correct his difficult experiences with his parents who were distant and not sensitive to or even aware of his needs as a developing adolescent. David tries to enact a *corrective script* in his relationship with his daughter. However, he seems to be so enthusiastic in his mission that he almost overdoes it. Where his parents did not discuss with him sexual issues, and removed relevant books to the attic, David is open with his daughter. He even brought such a book to *his daughter in bed*. It sounded from the interview as if David was trying to *undo his unfavorable past* as described by Shabad (1993). In doing so he acted in a somewhat discordant manner, evoking to some extent his own insensitive upbringing.

Interestingly, his involvement as a parent that seems like the opposite behavior to that of his own parents, but in fact it contained some traces of his adolescent experience. David's father, who was described as a remote person, joked about the girlfriend. David repeats a similar behavior with his daughter in a sexually loaded experience. Bretherton and Munholland (1999) described how previously established schemas are difficult to change as they operate outside the conscious awareness. The incident with the bra gives the impression that David was not fully aware of what he was doing when he teased his daughter. An affect-laden incident that he had experienced with his father was reactivated in a similar incident with his daughter (Tomkins, 1978; p. 211).

We don't know for certain what helped David to partially correct his experiences. It seems that his wife has more positive background and manages well with their daughter, and probably supports him as well. His daughter's good-hearted personality, her tolerance, and willingness to accept his awkward gestures probably help too. Nevertheless, the partial awareness and the ability to reflect on the painful experiences without being flooded by uncontainable anger and disappointment enable David to raise his daughter far better than he himself was raised. However, continuous preoccupation with the past, as evinced to some degree by how David talked about his parents, interferes with the complete resolution of past difficult experiences (Pianta, Marvin, Britner, & Borowitz, 1996). As a result, David is trying too hard and is probably acting to *undo* his own past rather than just providing a *corrective* experience of parenting (especially in his eagerness for boundless openness in the relationship with his daughter).

The Unaware Coercive Mother and her Daughter: Re-enactment of Past Experiences – Like Mother (and Grandmother), Like Daughter

Dana is 52 years old, married, and a mother of two sons and one daughter. The interview focused on her relationship with Rachel, her youngest daughter, who is 16. When recounting her early experiences with her parents, Dana presented a very difficult relationship with her mother. "Mother could relate to us only by criticizing. She was coercive. It was expressed in many aspects of life. My mother loved to tell me how to comb my hair. She liked my hair in a particular way; she remarked about it all the time. She decided what should I wear and how my hair should look. When I was older they found out that I had a boyfriend. I was by then at a boarding school because I couldn't stay with her anymore, so they came to the boarding school to force me to break up with my boyfriend. I was very independent; I didn't want her to dictate every detail of my life. It was unbearable. She always saw the negative side."

Dana repeatedly describes the coercive pattern of her mother. It sounds as if all the mother–daughter interactions were driven by the mother's lack of respect for her daughter. During the interview Dana speaks in a stream of angry sentences and adds an additional diagnosis, saying that her mother had an "emotional handicap." She tells that during her adolescence her mother's derision for her was very painful. "On the one hand she gave me a lot of food – OK, I can understand. But then I gained weight and she ridiculed me for being fat. It was destroying me. She needs everything perfect." Dana went on to say that still today she has deep resentment toward her parents. "This is the reason that I married so early. I simply could not go back home, I couldn't be with my mother." Even when she spoke about the pride her father felt, she resented it. "I didn't like it at all. It was quite weird. They decided that I was beautiful. I was fat as a child and I don't see that I was so beautiful at that age. I was just swollen child with swollen face. Seriously, I think that now in my fifties my appearance is better than in those days. My personality is more shaped and seems to me more interesting than in the past, and whenever my father came across somebody (during childhood) he always said, proudly, 'Do you know my daughter?'"

When asked to explain why her parents treated her that way, she answered: "I won't take the blame, because if I'm guilty I deserved that treatment, so this is a bit too much, isn't it? I wasn't a difficult child. Maybe I was a difficult child in insisting on my view. I took responsibility for myself and my life, and that's what made them angry. I think that the main reason was castration of emotions and my mother's inability to communicate."

When describing her relations with her daughter, Dana tries to portray a positive and close relationship that may have some reasonable difficulties from time to time: "I always loved to see her. It made me feel good that she is at home. It gave me a real good feeling. I boast about her. I was proud of her . . . I boast about her, and this is not a healthy thing." This theme echoes her father's pride in her, which she could not bear as a child.

When describing the trust in the relationship with her daughter she said: "I think she has full confidence in me, that I'll help her in every situation and will be with her in everything. I try hard to keep what she tells me in confidence, and I let her to go out with friends. There are things that bother me. Once I did something not nice – I read something she wrote, and later I realized that I had really abused her trust, and I was sorry I did that. I did something that I shouldn't have done, but sometimes naturally there are things you are afraid of." Thus, although Dana acknowledges the inappropriateness of her behavior (interestingly, when trying to demonstrate the trust between herself and her daughter), she provides justification and tries to normalize it.

While conflictive incidents came up in Dana's descriptions (e.g., forcing her daughter to finish her homework, letting her travel with friends, choosing her clothes, reading her personal notes), she continuously tried to suggest that her relationship with her daughter had improved in recent years. In particular, she repeatedly claimed that she developed significantly in her way of parenting. It is interesting, however, that her accounts reflected fluctuations between inappropriate over-involvement and shedding responsibility.

"Now that she is older she is more independent and it is easier. At the peak of the problems I used to do everything with her. And I learned to let her do things. Once I made a silly mistake. She had a homework assignment. Instead of her doing it, I saw that the material could be found in the encyclopedia. So I bought the whole encyclopedia. My son joshed me because instead of letting her do it and copying just one page I bought the whole encyclopedia. You can't imagine how terrible it was. I had to return the encyclopedia. She didn't appreciate at all the fact that I went and searched for her. I told myself, from this day on she'll do her homework on her own. It doesn't bother me if she gets a lower grade, from now on she does everything by herself."

In another reference to learning, she says: "I had a method and I told her, after you finish your homework, you can go to a friend. There were incidents where she deceived me. She told me she had finished her homework and I opened her exercise book, not trusting her. She had told me not to look at it but I did, and it turned out that she hadn't done her homework. I was not willing to give up. I went and took her at her friend's. I did it by force." To some extent Dana is probably aware of the gap between her claims as to how she parents her daughter and the reality. So when reflecting on the similarities between her experiences with her parents and her own parenting she adds: "Maybe I too wanted her to do certain things but I didn't force her that way. I don't think there is real similarity between the relationships."

Dana speaks about her daughter's burgeoning autonomy: "I used to buy her all her clothes, and she started getting angry with me. But this year I let her buy whatever clothes she wanted. This year I told her something I shouldn't have said. Suddenly she began a diet. It became evident that she was eating 1200 calories, and not 1800 as she told me. I was very angry, I said something I shouldn't have, but I hope it helped. I told her that if something happened to her, something would happen to me too. I used this because I knew she depended on me, and maybe would also be afraid that something would happen to me. Because she knows my situation is not the most marvelous lately. I don't know if it's good or not, but I felt that in this case it was permissible because it was for her own good, and also for my own good. . . . There are other things that quite scare me, and I don't like with the way she dresses. She has a miniskirt which in my opinion is dangerous to wear these days . . . I don't know if she'll listen to me, I'm not sure. She won't go out dressed like that, because today it's very dangerous, but anything else, I don't mind."

Case Summary. Dana described a very difficult, disdainful, and intrusive relationship with her parents, especially with her mother. She distanced herself from her parents and felt continuous anger toward them. She resented her mother's intrusiveness and pressure on her, but unconsciously in her relationship with her daughter she creates compulsive repetition of the past she so hated (Fraiberg et al., 1975). She is highly intrusive, while trying to provide rational justification for her misdeeds. Her ambivalence toward her daughter's autonomy calls to mind Stierlin's (1981; p. 55) delegating mode, in which the daughter's mission is to protect her mother's fragile ego by sparing her conflict and ambivalence.

On the semantic level she explicitly states her wish to raise her children differently from the way she was raised. But actually she is repeating the past, maybe because on the emotional-experiential level she is still the young child wishing for revenge, which she enacts against her daughter, thereby creating another victim. The pseudo-reflection does not involve correction, because actually she imitates her mother's behavior through the mechanism of "identification with the aggressor" (Silverman & Lieberman, 1999). In fact, she insists that there are no similarities between the relationships. She resembles mothers of ambivalent children as described in George and Solomon's (1999) study. Those mothers promoted dependency and appeared insensitive to their children's cues. They were characterized by cognitive disconnection, manifested in their inability to integrate positive and negative, and they were immersed in heightened caregiving, and appeared ineffective. Actually, the improvement in Dana's daughter's behavior occurred after her older son returned to live in his parents' home. For two years he took the role of parental figure, and stepped in trying to educate his younger sister after Dana herself had given up. As Dana noted, he succeeded where she herself failed.

From Submissive Son to Submissive Father: Re-enacting the Victim Role

Jacob, in his early fifties, is a father of two daughters. Jacob was interviewed with regard to Tamar, his second daughter. Jacob was the older of two sons in an immigrant family.

At the beginning of the interview, Jacob said that he has nothing special to say about his adolescence: "Like everybody, I was a good kid, a good student, obedient, I liked sports, I was OK." Elsewhere in the interview, he said: "It's difficult to remember. It was 40, 35 years ago, really nothing special." Yet when he was further encouraged, an interesting story emerged.

"Nothing special. I was with my parents all of the time. Don't remember anything special. I left home when I was 17 to study in a different town, I was quite independent but I didn't like being alone so I went back home. . . . I respected them. I was never disobedient. They were very controlling. I was afraid of my parents, never told them what was going on at school. Afraid to tell the truth, what grades I got. They always preferred to hear the good things but it wasn't always good. I had to take care of my younger brother and was responsible for cleaning the house."

About his relationship with his mother he said: "I was afraid of her." "She should have been warmer with me." He recounted that his mother forced him to study, to take care of his younger brother, to go on vacations with her and his father, to dress the way they wanted; they even took him to the barber's and decided on his haircut. "She shouldn't have forced me to do things I didn't like . . . I don't know – we had a very remote relationship. I didn't kiss her a lot. I don't know. I was also shy. When I started working she took the money. She gave me what I needed. I know they needed the money. If it was the norm – I would have accepted it. It was beyond the norm. With clothes, they bought me what they thought I needed. I wanted to go to a summer camp, just for a week and they said the whole family would go together." Jacob's accounts (following encouragement of the interviewer) further exposed feelings of being told how much to read and what to read, and very critical reactions from his mother once, when he brought his girlfriend home.

The father is described as a very weak person. For example, he had to ask his wife's permission to take Jacob fishing with him. Yet the father was also described as warm, taking Jacob to the beach or to a sauna, or helping him once when he needed money.

When asked to reflect on his parents' behavior toward him he commented: "This is how education has to be. In my time that was the way. I succeeded, I'm not a criminal. They controlled my brother less, and he's 43 now and still hasn't found his way in life. No real profession, no family. I have a family, I have a profession. I was kept tight and I've got somewhere in life." This idealized description sounded different when Jacob talked more specifically about his family. After repeating the positive aspects of his upbringing, he added: "I think it had an additional effect. I'm too remote from my children. Not open with them. Don't tell them what's going on with me, like my parents. There are children who know more about their parents."

Jacob's description of his relationship with Tamar was short and laconic. After each sentence he had to be encouraged to elaborate. When asked to describe his relationship with Tamar, he said: "I don't know. Not a good relationship.... I'd like more warmth, more cooperation, more trust. That's –.... Not good. Like cat and mouse. I wish it was like cat and milk. I don't know what to do first, to take the cat to the milk or the milk to the cat. If I'm the cat then who's the milk? I don't know.... I come home, say hello, and expect that at least somebody will answer me, yes, hello, how are you, – nothing. I didn't open my mouth against my parents. They do open [their mouths], nothing held back, bad language, that's all I get.... I don't know. Everything. I want to see, a TV program, she can see it with me, – no.... Very rarely do I hear a thank you, and I go out of my way."

"I wish they'd appreciate my hard work. I don't know, as if they don't believe me.... And when I say something – Who's asking you? Why do you push your nose in?... I hear all kind of words, dummy, moron. I don't know either to throw her out or if I should leave.... It's like I said, I keep quiet but I'm exploding inside. That's what I do. I'm afraid that one day it'll burst out. I'm afraid. When it does come out, me or my daughter – she'll have to leave. It has already reached the level of hatred, mutual.... These days I don't want to get home before my wife. I don't want to be with my children alone, because I know that something will happen. This is a catastrophe.... Once I tried the other way, to be calm, to be nice. Not to buy them off with money. It doesn't help.... Sometimes it gets to extremes. I may come into the apartment: Look how you're dressed. Don't go into my room. Have you done the shopping?... At times I fall asleep on the couch in front of the TV. At 2 o'clock she'll come with her friends, wake me up – Go to your room. Noise full blast, and I work very hard and I get no consideration."

It was very difficult for Jacob to describe the abusive relationship he has with his adolescent daughter. It sounded as if Tamar acted like the abusive parent, and Jacob, the father, was the frightened child. When asked to consider whether he saw any connection between the relationship he had with his parents and his current relationship with Tamar, Jacob replied: "It's probably the genes. I don't know. Maybe what I didn't do to my parents. I kept it within myself, they don't keep it within themselves. It's a different time. Maybe if I were an adolescent now, I'd behave exactly like them."

Case Summary. During the interview with Jacob, his dismissing state of mind was very apparent. Repeatedly he claimed that he did not remember as "it was 40, 35 years ago" (when he was an adolescent). Jacob described a very controlling, arrogant, and to some extent unpleasant adolescence for which he was still angry with his mother. However, despite this resentment, he identified with the aggressor (Shabad, 1993) and praised this pattern of upbringing. Moreover, he claimed that had his parents not been that controlling, as they were with his brother, he would not have ended up having a profession and a family.

Interestingly, Jacob did not enact an authoritarian pattern of parenting. On the contrary, he was so weak with his daughter that the roles were reversed and he was intimidated by her as he had been intimidated by his mother. The same pattern of relations seems to have been enacted in each generation; except that Jacob, then the child and currently the father, remained the victim (Brazelton & Cramer, 1990) and Jacob ascribed it to the genes. Yet his final statement reveals an additional dynamic: "It is a different time. Maybe if I were an adolescent now, I'd behave exactly like them." Jacob's irresistible wish to undo the past has led him to allow his daughter to play out his wishes and to enact what he could not do as an adolescent (Shabad, 1993; Stierlin, 1981). This demonstrates the mechanism of projective identification, "a fantasy of getting rid of intolerable experience by evacuating it into an object and then asserting control over the disowned parts, which are felt to now reside within and be a part of the other" (Silverman & Lieberman, 1999; p. 177).

Mother Who Succeeded in Creating Favorable Experiences for Her Daughter – Successful Correction of Difficult Past Experiences

Sarah in her late forties, the mother of Danielle, aged 15, described a difficult experience with her own mother. She had an older brother in her parental family, and Danielle is the younger of her two daughters.

"Look. I was afraid of my mother. My mother was a very rigid woman, and my father was a 'high flyer.' He was a very clever man but he was occupied with his own world. I never shared with my mother what is happening; nor did she ever ask what was happening because she didn't care. I'm the youngest child in the family, and she probably was glad that I was growing up and that the children would leave home. My mother was a very rigid woman, and therefore I was afraid of her and afraid of confronting her because she was very highly strung. A woman that you should keep away from, and that's why I chose to stay at a distance. It's better to read, to enter the imaginary world, than to get into to any deep connection with her. . . . I preferred doing what she wanted than getting yelling and anger. Once she hit me as hard as she could to take out all tension she had; from that time on I preferred backing off than getting hit again". . . . Describing another episode of powerful hitting, she described how she hid but her mother found her and took out all her rage beating her relentlessly ... "Every day you never knew what to expect. I didn't know what mood she'd be in. You always had to be on your guard. Even when I started getting my periods I didn't tell her. I didn't tell her anything because of her unpredictability. Everything was hidden."

Sarah recounted that her mother did not let her go out during adolescence. However, she said that she had a very supportive older brother with whom she had a very close and special relationship. Since her mother did not want her to go out, her brother decided to invite her to go along when he went out with his girlfriend. He promised their mother to take good care of her, and they indeed spent the time together. She mentioned that otherwise she would not have been allowed to go out at all.

When asked whether adolescence was a meaningful time for her in shaping who she is today, she answered: "A lot. Because I was treated like that, I swore that my children would receive totally different treatment. Because I had no one who understood me, I tend to understand them, listen to them, feel them, talk with them, go out with them, spend 'quality time' with them. Not to yell, hit ... to be patient. Although at times I get home very tired from work, I don't let myself be impatient, and I keep telling myself to listen, because it's very important that there's somebody when you come home after an eventful day that you can share with, talk about things. So I listen and I join in what has been happening with them. It is immensely important for me."

About her relationship with her daughter, she says: "I think there's a lot of love between us, kissing and hugging and 'I love you,' notes with I love you. It's fun being with her, hugging her, and going out with her." Asked about problematic aspects with her daughter, Sarah says that Danielle is a perfectionist and likes to be perfect, so she is very stressed before exams. Describing how she handles this, Sarah says that she talks with her, gives her massages, hugs and kisses her, and showers love on her. She uses this strategy because she did not receive it in her own childhood, but also because she gets it from her husband and she knows it helps. "This love and warmth helps. Maybe I can't help her in the exam but I can help her get to the exam more relaxed and calm."

Referring to the similarity or dissimilarity of this relationship with her own relationship with her parents, Sarah says: "I let her be an adolescent, I was not allowed to be an adolescent at all. I let her say what she thinks, sometimes crying if she feels bad. I let her behave as she wants, and not be closed up in herself ... it's very different from my adolescence. I really understand the adolescence scene. I constantly prepared myself that when my daughters grew up there might be screaming and anger. It didn't happen. Maybe because I expected this and I prepared the ground well, and there is a lot of understanding and good connections, things didn't turn out that way. I wanted to give my daughters the things I never had, that I missed. I knew what I was missing. It's just the opposite from what I got. I give them a lot of warmth, a lot of support, love and understanding, because I want them to know they have support, they have backing and they have always somebody to turn to with good things as well as with bad things. There will be always someone that will support and love them no matter what, in everything they do."

Case Summary. Sarah, like many other parents, swore not to repeat her mother's behavior when raising her own children. Yet, unlike many parents, she was successful in establishing a warm and respectful relationship with her daughter, expressed in their joyful times together and her ability to comfort her when distressed, as well as respecting her autonomy and accepting her moodiness. This resembles a dynamic described by Way and Leadbeater (1999) of the adaptational pathways of adolescent mothers. In their study, one half of the adolescent mothers who succeed and accomplished high achievements at school spoke of their need to do well in school and be independent because their parents were "not there" for them for a variety of reasons. The absence of maternal emotional support may have become an incentive for increased responsibility, and strengthened the determination to succeed.

What might have helped Sarah to construct and enact a corrective script? From Sarah's recounts of her relationship with her mother, we learn that to protect herself she choose to distance herself from her mother and build her own imaginary world.

By enhancing her separateness from her mother, Sarah might have been able to develop a more accepting and flexible parenting. Yet it was probably not only her determination. Several times in the interview Sarah described her supporting and close relationships with her older brother and her relationship with her husband. Her older sibling was the one she could turn to when she was a child. He was supportive, helpful, and understanding. His brotherliness and responsiveness toward her probably promoted her capacity to internalize a more benevolent internal working model. As she mentioned, from her husband too she learned to act differently. The corrective experiences with her brother and her husband might have allowed her to develop a more balanced model. This is similar to the dynamics of the *earned secure* (Pearson et al., 1994), where later exposure to a more benevolent model of relationship can contribute to the reorganization of representational models. Finally, Sarah acknowledged her wishes during adolescence, but she recognized that the past is irreversible, and she is not immersed in it (Shabad, 1993). It seems that corrective experiences helped her work thorough this painful past and free her to see her daughter as she is, and not as a mirror of herself as an adolescent.

Intergenerational Transmission of Parenting Adolescents:
Overt Behaviors and Covert Motives

Central Themes in Adolescence. As seen in the five cases presented, parenting adolescents is indeed a challenging and demanding task even when the parents themselves experienced favorable adolescence, and even if their offspring evince an easy temperament and personality. Although the dyads we presented are quite different from each other, shared themes emerged when parents talked about their own adolescence or about their adolescent children. First, it seems that the emotional, physical, and sexual maturity of adolescence activated adolescents' and parents' concerns. It was manifested in the need to receive or share information regarding these issues, in concerns relating to eating habits, physical appearance, and style of dress. Going out with friends and dating become central issues on which parents and adolescents need to come to terms. Additionally, the sexual maturity of the adolescents provoked internal conflicts in both parties regarding closeness, physical as well as emotional.

Second, concerns related to the separation-individuation themes emerged also in the narratives. The adolescents' need for developing intrapsychic separation from parents might incite difficulties as well as the need of adolescents to keep a domain of autonomy within the parental home. The issues of what to share and what not to share with the parents, parents' respect of the privacy of one's room or one's possessions, parents' respect of one's autonomy over one's body (appearance, hairstyle, clothes), and the degree of autonomy of one's emotional and psychological world play a central role in our interviews. The ability of parents to let go and to respect their adolescents' autonomy in dating, doing homework, leisure activities, or choosing friends is a core question they struggle with. Parents' capacity for containment and tolerance is highly challenged (especially during middle adolescence), when adolescents wish to draw away from parents and simultaneously to create renewed closeness with them (Josselson, 1980). This becomes even more complicated when unresolved separation-individuation issues of the parents themselves are involved. The increased conflicts, de-idealization, and undermining parents' authority might prove painful and unbearable for some parents, as revealed in their narratives. Thus central themes of the intergenerational transmission of parenting experiences become more salient during adolescence.

Resolution of Difficult Experiences. Chronic and cumulative difficult childhood experiences could leave deep scars on one's life and personality. Parenting one's own child arouses those shadows of the past and increases the possibility of repeating or reconstructing one's difficult experiences. While normative development promotes flexible representational models, difficult childhood experiences might narrow in some ways one's flexibility and one's ability to update representational models. As Silverman and Lieberman (1999) suggested, "when interactions with a parent produce representations of relationships with a bad object, the already established identification leaves the child helplessly implicated. These unthinkable representations are relegated to the unconscious but make themselves felt in the form of repetitions that continue to organize emotional experiences. The external object is thus protected while its badness is perpetuated in the internal world" (pp. 173–4).

In addition to the strong impact of their own experienced upbringing, the parents' efforts to enact a different parenting from what they received were impressive to listen to and observe. In some cases parents were successful in constructing a different and more flexible pattern of parenting. Yet in many instances parents struggled with their past, tried to correct it or undo it, but ended up repeating the themes from their own childhood. In some cases, for example the case of Dana, the mother was not even aware that she was repeating her mother's behavior, but was trapped in her belief that she was a better mother.

Why are some parents able to construct new models or scripts while others are not? In line with other researchers (Main, 2000; Pianta et al., 1996), we suggest that the capacity to reflect on these painful experiences, to "mourn" the lost "ideal" childhood or ideal parent, and to resolve this mourning, might determine whether difficult experiences are transmitted to one's own children. Lack of resolution perpetuates the use of modeling, thus imitating unconsciously adverse parenting, via mechanisms such as identification with the aggressor, projective identification, re-enactment, and undoing. Like Shabad (1993), we expand the definition of mourning to cover a wider range of difficult experiences one may need to resolve. "It is not the actual physical loss of a parent, but an intangible subjective sense of loss concerning the hopes, illusions, and ideas one has in regard to that parent" (Shabad, 1993; p. 66). Referring to loss and trauma, attachment scholars (Bowlby, 1973; Main & Hesse, 1990) have posited that loss of an attachment figure or trauma experiences require a reorientation of thinking about the loss/trauma and a reorganization of previous representations of the relationship to fully acknowledge the changed reality. Failure to complete the mourning process leads to the continued existence of multiple conflicting representational models, and is considered lack of resolution.

Bowlby (1980) identified two main disordered variants of mourning. The first, termed *chronic mourning*, involves (in its more extreme form) unusually intense and prolonged emotional responses to the loss. There is a disability to reorganize one's life, which frequently becomes and remains sadly disjointed. The second variant is termed *prolonged absence of conscious grieving*. In this type the bereaved's life continues to be organized. However, such people may suffer physiological symptoms and interpersonal difficulties, which are derivatives of the mourning, though disconnected, both cognitively and emotionally from the loss that led to them. Although these two variants seem very different, Bowlby argued that "in both, it may be found the loss is believed, consciously or unconsciously, still to be reversible. The urge to search may therefore continue to possess the bereaved, either unceasingly or episodically, anger and/or self-reproach to be readily aroused, sorrow and sadness to be absent. In both variants the course of mourning remains uncompleted. Because the representational models he has of himself and the world around him remain unchanged his life is either planned on a false basis or else falls into unplanned disarray" (Bowlby, 1980; p. 138).

Though Bowlby referred to actual loss of a parent, as indicated above we expand these descriptions to the need of parents to resolve other difficult experiences as well – their "lost" childhood. Under the circumstances of unresolved mourning of difficult experiences, parents may project onto their children their unfulfilled wishes, anger, or parts of themselves that they are not aware of. In the cases we presented above, one case – Dana – can be viewed as exemplifying *chronic mourning*, where the mother is still entangled and preoccupied with her loss of a "good" mother and is still angry with her mother for not being a better mom. Thus, she thus does to her daughter what her mother did to her, while proclaiming that she has changed. Another case – Jacob – exemplifies *prolonged absence of conscious grieving*, in which despite a miserable childhood he thinks it had a favorable effect on him. Interestingly, Jacob, unlike Dana, repeats not the role of the parent but the same role he played as a child – submissive and victimized. Though the two sides of the interactions may be learned, in the new relationships formed with their children the parents may re-enact the past parental role or the past role of the child. In the words of Crittenden (this volume), "Actions that are based more upon past then present conditions tend to either replicate the past or reverse the error, without correcting it." The two ways of unsuccessful resolutions of past difficult experiences may lead to one of these routes. In the case of *chronic mourning* and preoccupation, the parent is driven to enact the role of the parent in the family of origin, and in the case of a dismissive *absence of conscious grieving* he or she is driven to enact the role of the child in the family of origin.

Successful mourning processes, in contrast, involve becoming relatively free from the compulsion to repeat the past, or from the compulsive need to correct it. It is the inability to acknowledge the painful past and to fully understand and accept its irreversibility that sustains rigid representations, thus perpetuating painful experiences. "It is through consciously reclaiming and elaborating on previous unconscious wishes to undo traumatic theme that one is also able to gain access to a vision of one's ideal childhood and, in so doing, open up with renewed hope to the possibilities of less circumscribed life for oneself and one's children" (Shabad, 1993; p. 62). This results in more flexible models that allow improvisation when required (Byng-Hall, 1995). Breaking the cycle of difficult experiences requires genuine resolution of those experiences, not just compelling oneself or others to change forcefully their still painful or disconnected scripts. This was well demonstrated in a recent study (Shulman et al., 2001) showing that the more integrative perception of parental divorce was related to more adaptive romantic relationships of young adults who experienced that divorce.

Overcoming past experiences can also be helped by an alternative attachment figure. For example, the exposure to a healthy and positive spousal attachment figure was found to improve an individual's parenting (Belsky, Youngblade, & Pensky, 1989), probably through the support received and the possible development of a current coherent and *earned secure* state of mind (Pearson et al., 1994). Thus, inappropriate models of self and others may be revised or replaced when individuals have a corrective experience such as a supportive and sensitive relationship, whether with a significant other, a friend, or a psychotherapist (Bowlby, 1988; Lieberman, Weston, & Pawl, 1991; Ricks, 1985; van IJzendoorn, Juffer, & Duyvesteyn, 1995).

Two of our cases reflect to some extent each of these routes of correction. In David's case, partial correction was possible probably due to some reflection on the past, some understanding of the parents' background that led them to be so distant and demanding, and partial containment of the anger and disappointment that these experiences in the family of origin incited. In the case of Sarah, it was probably her capacity to distance herself from the abusive mother, but in particular the corrective experiences with her brother and husband, that contributed to her capacity to rework her difficult experiences and construct flexible parenting models.

In sum, the cases presented here demonstrate the powerful grip of experiences in one's family of origin, revealing that the past continues to play an active role in present life. It is also impressive to observe how parents try to correct and undo their past, in many cases unsuccessfully. "Finding the safe and integrative balance between past and present conditions and between adult and child perspectives is a difficult process and requires extensive and ongoing integration" (Crittenden, this volume). Yet the ability to achieve flexible and integrative reflection of the past seems to enable people to accept the imperfection of their parents, themselves, and their children, to relinquish the need to fulfill all longed-for wishes, and to pave the way to breaking the intergenerational transmission of adverse parenting and healing difficult past experiences.

Clinical and Research Implications

At the clinical level, it might be important to identify at-risk families and intervene to prevent subsequent maladjustment. Parents who had difficult adolescence experiences might be of special interest, and could benefit from interventions that foster examining past experiences and their reflections in their current relationships with their adolescent children. It has been argued that remnants of traumatic experiences keep penetrating the conscious and the unconscious until they are properly remembered, mourned, and worked through (Kellerman, 2001). Pianta and colleagues (1996) indicated that resolution of the trauma is reflected in re-orientation to the present and future, a realistic view of the child, and a balanced view of the impact of trauma on the self. Thus, resolution of difficult experiences and relinquishing unfulfilled wishes might free parents from the unfinished business of their past and help them observe and understand themselves and their children as they really are.

To gain deeper understanding of the process of resolution of past difficult experiences, parents can be asked to fantasize that they have the possibility to relive their adolescence and describe how they portray it. Parents' portrayals might expose their longed-for wishes and the extent to which they come to terms with their experiences in adolescence. It is also possible to adopt the guidelines of Main and Goldwyn (1998) and of Pianta et al. (1996), namely to examine carefully the way parents discuss their past experiences. Inquiring into the resolution of difficult experiences in general, not just attachment or trauma-related themes, may enrich clinical understanding of clients' immobilization and resistance to change. Examining the resolution of difficult experiences may also indicate the potential routes for elaborating those experiences, mainly through corrective close relationships and reflections (Crittenden et al., 2000; Shabad, 2001).

Until recently, clinical and empirical writing focused mainly on adolescents' perspectives, whereas parents were mainly investigated as a way to understand and/or improve their children's adjustment. It is interesting to note that although our study involved a middle-class non-risk sample, it seems that many of the parents undergo an emotion-loaded and relatively vulnerable period during their children's adolescence. Providing parents with updated and accurate information regarding normative as well as problematic developmental processes of parents and adolescents seems essential. Empirical research should be directed toward studying parents of adolescents and the developmental processes they undergo as a research target in itself. The distinct gratification and diverse difficulties of this period during the "parenting career" should be delineated. More systematic study of the emotion-laden themes of this period is warranted. For example, the CCRT procedure (Luborsky & Crits-Christoph, 1998) that asks people for interpersonal memories relating specifically to their own adolescence, as well as to particular situations involving their relationships with their adolescent child, may identify and shed light on these themes. Finally, future studies should examine parents' well-being and competence (Steinberg & Silk, 2002) and the various contributing variables to individual differences in parents' psychosocial functioning during this challenging period.

References

Belsky, J. & Cassidy, J. (1994). Attachment: Theory and evidence. In M. Rutter & D. Hay (Eds.), *Development through Life, A Handbook for Clinicians.* Oxford: Blackwell, pp. 373–402.

Belsky, J., Youngblade, L., & Pensky, E. (1989). Childrearing history, marital quality, and maternal affect: Intergenerational transmission in a low-risk sample. *Development and Psychopathology, 1*, 291–304.

Blos, P. (1962). *On Adolescence: A Psychoanalytic Interpretation.* Oxford: Free Press of Glencoe.

Bowlby, J. (1973). *Attachment and Loss*: Volume 2. *Separation and Anxiety.* New York: Basic Books.

Bowlby, J. (1980). *Attachment and Loss*: Volume 3. *Loss.* New York: Basic Books.

Bowlby, J. (1988). *A Secure Base: Clinical Applications of Attachment Theory.* London: Routledge.

Brazelton, T. B. & Cramer, B. G. (1990). *The Earliest Relationship: Parents, Infants, and the Drama of Early Attachment.* Boston, MA: Addison-Wesley.

Bretherton, I. & Munholland, K. A. (1999). Internal working models in attachment relationships: A construct revisited. In J. Cassidy & P. R. Shaver (Eds.), *Handbook of Attachment: Theory, Research and Clinical Applications.* New York: Guilford, pp. 89–111.

Byng-Hall, J. (1995). *Rewriting Family Scripts: Improvisation and Systems Change.* New York: Guilford Press.

Cassidy, J. (1994). Emotion regulation: Influences of attachment relationships. *Monographs of the Society for Research in Child Development, 59(2–3)*, 228–83.

Collins, W. A. (1995). Relationships and development: Family adaptation to individual change. In S. Shulman (Ed.), *Close Relationships and Socioemotional Development. Human Development.* Westport: Ablex Publishing, pp. 128–54.

Crittenden, P. M., Lang, C., Claussen, A. H., & Partridge, M. F. (2000). Relations among mothers' procedural, semantic, and episodic internal representational models of parenting. In P. M. Crittenden and A. H. Claussen (Eds.), *The Organization of Attachment Relationships: Maturation, Culture, and Context.* New York: Cambridge University Press, pp. 214–33.

Cummings, M. E. & Schermerhorn, A. C. (2003). A developmental perspective on children as agents in the family. In L. Kuczynski (Ed.), *Handbook of Dynamics in Parent-Child Relationships.* Thousands Oaks: Sage, pp. 91–108.

Esman, A. H. (1985). A developmental approach to the psychotherapy of adolescents. *Adolescent Psychiatry, 12,* 119–33.

Fonagy, P., Steele, H., & Steele, M. (1991). Maternal representations of attachment during pregnancy predict the organization of infant-mother attachment at one year of age. *Child Development, 62,* 891–905.

Fraiberg, S., Adelson, E., & Shapiro, V. (1975). Ghosts in the nursery. *Journal of the American Academy and Child Psychiatry, 14,* 387–421.

Freud, A. (1958). Adolescence. *Psychoanalytic Study of the Child, 13,* 255–78.

Gecas, V. & Seff, M. A. (1990). Social class and self-esteem: Psychological centrality, compensation, and the relative effects of work and home. *Social Psychology Quarterly, 53,* 165–73.

George, C., Kaplan, N., & Main, M. (1985). *An Adult Attachment Interview.* Unpublished manuscript, University of California at Berkeley.

George, C. & Solomon, J. (1999). Attachment and caregiving: The caregiving behavioral system. In J. Cassidy & P. R. Shaver (Eds.), *Handbook of Attachment: Theory, Research, and Clinical Applications.* New York: Guilford Press, pp. 649–70.

Gould, R. L. (1972). The phases of adult life: A study in developmental psychology. *American Journal of Psychiatry, 129,* 521–31.

Greenberger, E. & O'Neil, R. (1990). Parents' concerns about their child's development: Implications for fathers' and mothers' well-being and attitudes toward work. *Journal of Marriage and the Family, 52,* 621–35.

Hesse, E. (1999). The adult attachment interview: Historical and current perspectives. In J. Cassidy & P. R. Shaver (Eds.), *Handbook of Attachment: Theory, Research, and Clinical Applications.* New York: Guilford Press, pp. 395–433.

Josselson, R. (1980). Ego development in adolescence. In J. Adelson (Ed.), *Handbook of Adolescent Psychiatry.* New York: Wiley, pp. 188–208.

Kellerman, N. P. F. (2001). Psychopathology in children of Holocaust survivors: A review of the research literature. *Israel Journal of Psychiatry and Related Sciences, 38,* 36–46.

Levinson, D. J. (1978). Eras: The anatomy of the life cycle. *Psychiatric Opinion, 15,* 10–11, 39–48.

Lieberman, A. F., Weston, D. R., & Pawl, J. H. (1991). Preventive intervention and outcome with anxiously attached dyads. *Child Development, 62,* 199–209.

Luborsky, L. & Crits-Christoph, P. (1998). *Understanding Transference: The Core Conflictual Relationship Theme Method.* Washington: American Psychological Association.

Lyons-Ruth, K. & Block, D. (1996). The disturbed caregiving system: Relations among childhood trauma, maternal caregiving, and infant affect and attachment. *Infant Mental Health Journal, 17*, 257–75.

Main, M. (2000). The organized categories of infant, child, and adult attachment: Flexible vs. inflexible attention under attachment-related stress. *Journal of the American Psychoanalytic Association, 48*, 1055–96.

Main, M. & Goldwyn, R. (1998). *Adult Attachment Rating and Classification Systems*. Unpublished manuscript, University of California, Department of Psychology, Berkeley.

Main, M. & Hesse, E. (1990). Parents' unresolved traumatic experiences are related to infant disorganized attachment status: Is frightened and/or frightening parental behavior the linking mechanism? In M. T. Greenberg, D. Cicchetti, & E. M. Cummings (Eds.), *Attachment in the Preschool Years: Theory, Research, and Intervention*. Chicago: University of Chicago Press, pp. 161–82.

Main, M., Kaplan, N., & Cassidy, J. (1985). Security in infancy, childhood, and adulthood: A move to the level of representation. In I. Bretherton & E. Waters (Eds.), *Growing points of attachment theory and research. Monograph of the Society for Research in Child Development, 50* (1–2, serial no. 209), 66–104.

Paikoff, R. L. & Brooks-Gunn, J. (1991). Do parent-child relationships change during puberty? *Psychological Bulletin, 110*, 47–66.

Paikoff, R. L., Brooks-Gunn, J., & Carlton-Ford, S. (1991). Effect of reproductive status changes on family functioning and well-being of mothers and daughters. *Journal of Early Adolescence, 11*, 201–20.

Pearson, J. L., Cohn, D. A., Cowan, P. A., & Cowan, C. P. (1994). Earned- and continuous-security in adult attachment: Relation to depressive symptomatology and parenting style. *Development and Psychopathology, 6*, 359–73.

Pianta, R. C., Marvin, R. S., Britner, P. A., & Borowitz, K. C. (1996). Mothers' resolution of their children's diagnosis: Organized patterns of caregiving representations. *Infant Mental Health Journal, 17*, 239–56.

Ricks, M. H. (1985). The social transmission of parental behavior: Attachment across generations. *Monographs of the Society for Research in Child Development, 50 (1–2)*, 211–27.

Rubin, K. H., Booth, C., Rose-Krasnor, L., & Mills, R. S. L. (1995). Social relationships and social skills: A conceptual and empirical analysis. In S. Shulman (Ed.), *Close Relationships and Socioemotional Development. Human Development*. Westport: Ablex Publishing, pp. 63–94.

Salt, R. E. (1991). Affectionate touch between fathers and preadolescent sons. *Journal of Marriage and the Family, 53*, 545–54.

Scharf, M. & Shulman, S. (1998). *Adolescence Experiences' Interview*. Unpublished manuscript, University of Haifa.

Shabad, P. (1993). Repetition and incomplete mourning: The intergenerational transmission of traumatic themes. *Psychoanalytic Psychology, 10*, 61–75.

Shabad, P. (2001). *Despair and the Return of Hope: Echoes of Mourning in Psychotherapy*. Northvale: Jason Aronson.

Shulman, S., Scharf, M., Lumer, D., & Mowrer, O. (2001). Parental divorce and young adult children's romantic relationships: Resolution of the divorce experience. *American Journal of Orthopsychiatry, 71*, 473–8.

Silverman, R. C. & Lieberman, A. F. (1999). Negative maternal attributions, projective identification, and the intergenerational transmission of violent relational patterns. *Psychoanalytic Dialogues, 9*, 161–86.

Slade, A. & Cohen, L. J. (1996). The process of parenting and the remembrance of things past. *Infant Mental Health Journal, 17*, 217–38.

Snarey, J. R. (1993). *How Fathers Care for the Next Generation: A Four-decade Study*. Cambridge, MA: Harvard University Press.

Steinberg, L. & Silk, J. S. (2002). Parenting adolescents. In M. H. Bornstein (Ed.), *Handbook of Parenting. Vol. 1: Children and Parenting*. Mahwah, NJ: Erlbaum, pp. 103–33.

Steinberg, L. & Steinberg, W. (1994). *Crossing Paths: How Your Child's Adolescence Triggers Your Own*. New York: Simon & Schuster.

Stierlin, H. (1981). *Separating Parents and Adolescents: Individuation in the Family*. New York: Jason Aronson.

Tomkins, S. S. (1978). Script theory: Differential magnification of affects. *Nebraska Symposium on Motivation, 26*, 201–36.

van IJzendoorn, M. H. (1995). Associations between Adult Attachment representations and parent-child attachment, parental responsiveness, and clinical status: A meta-analysis on the predictive validity of the Adult Attachment Interview. *Psychological Bulletin, 117*, 387–403.

van IJzendoorn, M. H., Juffer, F., & Duyvesteyn, M. G. C. (1995). Breaking the intergenerational cycle of insecure attachment: A review of the effects of attachment-based interventions on maternal sensitivity and infant security. *Journal of Child Psychology and Psychiatry, 36*, 225–48.

Way, N. & Leadbeater, B. J. (1999). Pathways toward educational achievement among African American and Puerto Rican adolescent mothers: Reexamining the role of social support from families. *Development and Psychopathology, 11*, 349–64.

12 Interplay of Relational Parent–Child Representations from a Psychoanalytic Perspective

An Analysis of Two Mother–Father–Child Triads

Hadas Wiseman, Ruth Hashmonay, and Judith Harel

Abstract

In this chapter a psychoanalytic perspective is applied to the examination of parents' representations of their relationships with their child, and to the interplay between these representations and the child's relational representations. A review of the psychoanalytic object relations and attachment perspectives on parent–child relational representations is followed by the illustration of the application of the Core Conflictual Relational Theme method (CCRT; Luborsky & Crits-Christoph, 1998) and the Working Model of the Child Interview (WMCI; Zeanah et al., 1986) to two mother–father–child triads. The CCRT identifies the content of relational themes in relationship narratives, while the WMCI assesses the parent's working model of the child and the relationship. Links between the parents' and child's relational themes and representation organization are presented in order to demonstrate the shared and unshared aspects of the inner worlds of parents and children, and the implications for clinical work with young children are discussed.

In this chapter, we apply a psychoanalytic perspective to parents' representations of their relationships with their child, and to the interplay between these representations and the child's relational representations. By applying the Core Conflictual Relational Theme method (CCRT: Luborsky & Crits-Christoph, 1998) and the Working Model of the Child Interview (WMCI: Zeanah, Benoit, & Barton, 1986) to the analysis of two mother–father–child triads, we will illustrate both the relational themes (content) and the cognitive aspects (organization and coherence) of the representations of the working model of the parent–child relationship (Gabarino, 1998). Our aims are fourfold: (1) To review the psychoanalytic perspective on parent–child relational representations; (2) to demonstrate the application of the CCRT method to the study of the content of relational themes, or schemas, in relationship

352

narratives, in combination with the WMCI, which allows the identification of the parent's working model of the child and the relationship; (3) to distinguish between mother- and father- relational representations of their child; and (4) to elucidate conscious and unconscious aspects of parent–child relational representations, conflicts, and defenses, and the shared and unshared aspects of the inner world of parents and children. We begin with a review of the psychoanalytic perspective, followed by the presentation of the two cases (Joy and Noa).

Psychoanalytic Theory on Representation Development

Psychoanalytic theorists share the notion that the relationship established between the infant and its caregivers, in particular the mother, lies at the heart of representation development (Klein, 1932; Fairbairn, 1952; Winnicott, 1958, 1971; Balint, 1968; Guntrip, 1971; Sandler & Sandler, 1978, 1998; Blatt & Lerner, 1983; Kerenberg, 1976). Internal mental representations of self and other that are formed in an internalization process from the infant's experiences with his/her caregivers are assumed to affect personality development and future relationships.

According to object relations theory, infants establish from birth both real and fantasized object relations (Klein, 1932). In fact, "object relations" mean "internalized object relations" which are different from observable, actual interpersonal transactions between self and other. If the infant, who is initially object-seeking, does not reach optimal intimacy with his mother, several less adaptive developments might arise, such as splitting between different systems of self and other (Fairbairn, 1952), and the development of a "false self" (Winnicott, 1965).

Historically, the term *representations* was introduced by Edith Jacobson (1954, 1964) from an ego psychology perspective. She explained that representations are formed on the basis of the experienced internal and external worlds, and that they could be subject to distortions and changes irrespective of the physical reality. She also claimed that the child's perception of the other directly shaped the structure of the experience of the self.

According to the Sandlers' structural approach (Sandler & Sandler, 1978, 1998), representations of self and other in interaction are formed on the basis of the everyday interactions between mother and infant, and also on the basis of fantasies and memories the individual has about himself/herself alone and in interaction with others. They further suggest that infantile and childhood relationship patterns may be actualized or enacted in adult relationships. It is assumed that representations of the self and the other, connected by an affective element, are the building blocks of the mind (Kerenberg, 1984). The level of integration between self-other-affect depends on personality organization (normal, neurotic, borderline), and is related to defenses formed against unconscious threatening representations.

Contemporary psychoanalytic relational theorists emphasize mutuality and intersubjectivity between the individual and his/her external relationships in representation development. The mother, no longer an object of the infant's drives or needs, is acknowledged as a separate object, a subject, with an important inner world of her own. A major developmental achievement for the child, according to the relational perspective, is the child's ability to see his/her mother as a subject, an achievement attained through reciprocal processes between mother and child (Benjamin, 1988). The relationships between mother and infant, or psychoanalyst and analysand, are dialectic in nature, creating the "analytic third," who is neither subject nor object, but a mutual creation of the couple (Ogden, 1994).

Stern (1985, 1995), a psychoanalytic developmentalist, offers a theory of "interfaceable minds," explaining representation development through mutual mental states. Stern's model describes a dynamic interaction between the behaviors and representations of both the infant and the mother. The mother's representations include a combination of representations of herself (e.g., as person, daughter, wife, mother), which are enacted in the interaction with the infant. The infant's representations of his/her interaction with the mother will include memories, prototypes, rules, and models of himself/herself with his mother. These will in turn influence the way the infant will perceive, interpret, remember, act, and feel about the interaction and will form a "schema of a-way-of being-with," which may also be influenced by inner fantasy. Stern (1983) distinguishes between three ways of being with another, which may exist separately or together in one action: self-other-complementing, self-with-other-state-sharing, and self-other-state-transforming. In "complementing," self and other are in a state that is impossible to create without another, and they perform complementing actions in which the interpersonal behavior with the other is the aim (e.g., mother holds baby and baby cuddles to her). In "state-sharing," self and other share the same mental state, and the central focus of the relationship between the self and other is on the similarity of experience (e.g., mother and child are vocalizing together). In "state transforming," the neurophysiologic and mental states of one of the partners are changed by the action of the other (e.g., the crying baby is soothed by mother's voice). According to Stern's view (1983), experiences of "being-with," in normal development, will act constructively to form and integrate the affective and cognitive components of the experiences of being with another. These three "ways-of-being-with" will be illustrated further in our analysis of the two cases.

Focusing on the links between parental representations and the child's representations in normal development, Stern (1995) claims that in a process of enactment, which is partially conscious, the caregiver's representations are transmitted to the child through the caregiver's behavior in their interaction. The child, in turn, must show a certain amount of acceptance towards the parental enactment. Stern describes how the mother's active scheme system gives meaning to the interaction with the infant, and causes her to notice certain events and ignore others. In this way, the mother's scheme system influences the moment of meeting with the infant. Thus, an unconscious circular dialogue occurs between events and scheme.

Attachment Theory and Representation Development

Central to representation formation is Bowlby's attachment theory (1969, 1973, 1980), influenced by psychoanalytic theory, but diverging from it in a number of major points (Fonagy, 2001). Bowlby, like many of the object relations and relational theorists, ascribes importance to the mother's real presence, claiming that emotional stability is a result of security in the attachment relationship with the mother, and emotional difficulties result from insecure early attachment ties to her. Bowlby and later attachment theorists (e.g., Bretherton & Munholland, 1999; Main, Kaplan, & Cassidy, 1985) claim that the infant will form "internal working models" on the basis of the type of early attachment ties between himself/herself and his/her caregivers. These working models, which include models of the self and other, will influence the infant's capability to regulate, interpret, and predict his/her own behaviors, thoughts, and feelings, as well as those of attachment figures, and will create expectations for future relationships. The concept of "internal working models" is similar to the concept of object representations and self-images in systems theory, and seems to share characteristics of the concept of representation in psychoanalytic theories (Bowlby, 1973).

Working models develop as children mature and learn that the goals of the attachment figures and of the child are not always alike, creating a "goal-corrected partnership" (Bowlby, 1969). This contains "an interplay of working models" between the parent's representations and the child's (Bretherton & Munholland, 1999). This active dynamic relationship between parental and child's representations has been considered meaningful for understanding the relationship and interactions between parents and children. Another important characteristic of working models is that they include a subjective element, which represents the individual's history of personal attributions, in addition to a mutual element, which is characteristic of the participants in the attachment relationship and in society in general (Bretherton & Munholland, 1999; see also Mayseless' chapter (this volume) for an overview on attachment and parent representations).

One of the major propositions of attachment theory has been the primary emphasis on real-life events, as opposed to a person's fantasies or subjective perceptions of such events. It is this emphasis on the observation of behavior as an indicator of a person's emotional responses, as opposed to relying mostly on verbal reports, fantasies, wishes, or dreams, that appears to have impeded the assimilation of attachment theory into psychoanalytic practice with children and adults (Lieberman & Zeanah, 1999). However, the focus on internal representation and working models of the self in relation to attachment (Bretherton, 1984; Main, 1991; Zeanah & Benoit, 1995) provided an impetus for the current rapproachment between psychoanalysis and attachment theory (Fonagy, 2001; Lieberman & Zeanah, 1999; Slade, 1999).

A major lacuna in attachment theory (Diamond, Blatt, & Lichtenberg, 2003), addressed by Sandler's model, is the relationship between fantasy and internal working models of attachment. Integrating the psychoanalytic theory of fantasy with attachment theory, he postulates that "the origins of fantasy derive from the wished for and feared states related to early experiences of felt security, or lack of it, in relation to the attachment objects" (Sandler, 1995/2003; p. 12). Wishes involve self-representations, object representations, and interaction between the two. For example, a child's wish to cling consists of both a mental representation of clinging to someone else, as well as a representation of the object responding to the child's clinging in a particular way.

Distinguishing Mothers' from Fathers' Representations

In discussing parental representations and their link to the child's representations, there is strong reason from both the psychoanalytic and the attachment perspectives to distinguish mothers' representations from fathers'. From the psychoanalytic perspective, the importance of the father to mental life is through the Oedipus complex, as a fundamental intrapsychic construct and as significant in the child's development (for review see Etchegoyen, 2002).

Abelin (1975) stressed the father's important role in enabling the toddler to experience "early triangulation," that is, to perceive and internalize the relationship between the two most invested-in love objects, and that the child already grasps his/her frustrated wish at the age of a year and a half. However, although the parents' roles are not identical, the two parents' relationships to the child develop side by side from the baby's earliest weeks (Abelin, 1975).

The father's importance for the child's mind development was described by Britton (1989) as involving the way that the child must accommodate his own perspective to the third person's perspective, such that the oedipal situation opens the child's mind to thinking. Stern (1995) argues that the father's representational world is generally equivalent to that of the mother's, but that the degree of similarity should be evaluated. He postulates that the father's representational world goes through less change with the infant's birth, and that the process of reorganization of representations with the birth of the infant takes longer than the mother's process. The supporting role the father needs to assume towards the mother has its roots in the father's family origin and culture.

Fonagy and Target (1995) emphasize that the child needs to experience the father as someone who observes the child's relationship with the mother and makes an attempt to find his/her image in the mother's mind. The child finds in the father not only a perception of himself/herself as a psychological entity, but also the father's perception of the child's relationship with the mother. Even if there is damage in the relationship between the mother and the infant, the child can still enter an intersubjective relationship with someone who sees the child in interaction, which is significant for the psychological self. In periods when the mother cannot reflect upon the child's relationship experiences because, for example, of primary maternal preoccupation, the father's ability to reflect to the child his/her relationships is essential for the development of the child's ability to perceive the self in object relationships.

Bowlby (1969) identified the father as a potential attachment figure, and research has shown that fathers are capable caregivers and that their children form attachment relationships to them (Belsky, Gilstrap, & Rovine, 1984). Research also shows that the type of attachment to each parent is not dependent on the type of attachment to the other parent (Cox, Owen, Henderson, & Margand, 1992; Schneider-Rosen & Burke, 1999), and that fathers and mothers differ in the form of interaction they form with their infants (Lamb & Oppenheim, 1989). Lately, new voices have been calling for a reconsideration of the father's role in children's internal and external world due to the increased involvement of fathers in their children's lives (Fitzgerald, Mann, & Barratt, 1999; Cabrera et al., 2000; Etchegoyen, 2002).

Research on Links between Parental and Child's Representations

To date, research on "interplay between representations" has centered on the link between parents' and child's attachment representations. By means of the Adult Attachment Interview (AAI), it has been shown that the structural characteristic of these interviews with the parents, in particular their coherence, predict classification of their child's attachment (George, Kaplan, & Main, 1985; van IJzendoorn, 1995). Coherence was assumed to be a reflection of the caregiver's capability for meta-cognitive monitoring, described as the ability to organize a single working model, and was found to be essential for predicting the infant's secure attachment (Main, 1991).

Researchers interested in parents' representations of their children developed interviews following the AAI format that ask parents to describe their perceptions, subjective experiences, and interactions with their children and their relationship with them (e.g., Aber et al., 1989; Bretherton et al., 1989; Zeanah & Barton, 1989). Referring to the mother's perceptions of the infant, George and Solomon (1996) suggest that such perceptions are influenced not only by her attachment relationships and representations, but also by her own experiences from childhood, adolescence, transition to parenthood, and meeting with the infant itself (George & Solomon, 1996). Similarly, Bretherton et al. (1989) suggest the importance of considering the parental perspective. Secure attachment will be transmitted if the mother is capable of seeing attachment matters from her infant's point of view, an ability that goes beyond a mere reflection of the mother's attachment experiences (Bretherton & Munholland, 1999).

George and Solomon (1999) have outlined a behavioral systems model of caregiving, postulating that "caregiving behavior is organized within a behavioral system that is independent from, but linked developmentally and behaviorally to, attachment" (p. 651). They developed a semi-structured caregiving interview to assess the representational schemes of the caregiving system. They found that mothers of secure children were best characterized as flexible in their mental representation related to care providing.

Building an important bridge between psychoanalytic theory and attachment theory, Fonagy et al. (1991), extended Main's (1991) work on "metacognitive monitoring," by defining the concept "reflective function." Reflective Function (RF) refers to the ability to perceive and understand the self's and others' behavior in mental terms, such as wishes, beliefs, goals, values, and affects (Fonagy & Target, 1998). The tendency to incorporate mental state attributions into internal working models of self–other relationships depends on the opportunity that the child had in early life to observe and explore the mind of his primary caregiver (Fonagy, 2001). By understanding the child's mind, and relating to the child as an "intentional" being, the caregiver encourages the child's acquisition of an understanding mind, that is, reflective function, which is closely linked to attachment (Fonagy, 2001). The capacity for RF is relevant to the different relational representations involved in parent–child representations (i.e., attachment representations in relation to one's parents, representations as a parent to one's child, and the child's relational representations of the parent). A secure parent, for example, will have a good RF, will be able to see from the child's point of view, be empathic to the child's emotions, and respond to the child's attachment signs with caring behavior. The parent's acknowledgment of the child's wishes, feelings, and intentions will enable the child to see himself/herself as a thinking and feeling being, and to develop mentalizing ability and reflective function. The development of the reflective function allows the child to make others' behavior meaningful and predictable, and permits him or her to respond adaptively in a range of interpersonal situations (Slade, 1999). This association between parents' RF and the child's internal state has been demonstrated empirically by Slade et al. (2001), who found a high correlation between mother's reflective function and the attachment classification of the caregiver and the child.

Applying the CCRT Method and the WMCI to the Study of Relational Parent–Child Representations

While it is agreed that the interaction between the parent and the child includes a meeting between the child and his parents' representations and the parents' mental functioning (Bowlby, 1988; Stern, 1995; Fonagy & Target, 1998), research has mainly focused on attachment working model of the parents (state of mind with respect to attachment) and their child's attachment behavior (e.g., George, Kaplan & Main, 1985; van IJzendoorn, 1995). However, the links between parents' representations of their child (working model of the child) and child's relational representations of his/her parents have still not been investigated, in normal or at-risk populations.

One method of studying relational representations is through narratives. These enable us to learn about a person's emotional and developmental aspects as well as about the person's close relationships as represented in the narratives the person tells about significant relationships. Although the narratives that are told might not reflect representations exclusively (e.g., they may include the subject's understanding of the assignment or the way the person wants to be perceived), they do, however, reflect the dynamic nature of representations (Wolf, 1993). In this chapter we briefly present two narrative research tools that we applied to the analysis of parent–child relational representations (Hashmonay, 2005).

The first method we employed was the *Core Conflictual Relationship Theme (CCRT) method*, originally developed by Luborsky (1977) to study transference in psychodyanamic therapy hours. The conceptualization of the CCRT was influenced by Freud's structural theories of personality and psychopathology (Luborsky Crits-Christoph, 1998). The CCRT is a method for identifying from an interview (psychotherapeutic or other) the central relationship patterns that characterize a person. According to Luborsky (1977), central relationship patterns consist of three basic components: the wish (W), the responses from other (RO), and the response of self (RS). The Wish component includes a wish, desire, or intention that the person has towards the other (e.g., to be loved and understood, to be assertive and independent); the RO refers to an actual, anticipated, or fantasized response from the other (e.g., strong, anxious, helpful); and the RS refers to the person's own actual, anticipated, or fantasized response of the self in the form of thought, emotion, behavior, or symptom (e.g., feels appreciated and accepted, opposes and hurts others, feels depressed). The three components of the CCRT are extracted from narratives, called Relationship Episodes, or REs, that the person tells about specific interactions that occurred with other people. The CCRT is comprised of the most frequent Wish, RO, and RS across the REs, and the relationships between them, complementary or in conflict, representing the person's central relationship theme. The term "theme" was used traditionally by CCRT researchers to refer to the composite CCRT. In this study we followed Barber et al. (2002) in using the term "interpersonal theme" to describe any single wish or response within a specific relationship.

Initially, the CCRT was identified only from relational narratives told spontaneously in psychotherapy sessions. Later on, Luborsky (1998) developed a specialized interview, called the Relationship Anecdotes Paradigm (RAP), designed to elicit narratives to identify the CCRT components in the same way as the narratives drawn from psychotherapy sessions. This method of interviewing enabled researchers to study narratives outside of the psychotherapy sessions (Barber et al., 1995) and to study narratives in individuals who were not in psychotherapy (Wiseman & Barber, 2004). The relational narratives told by the interviewee allow learning, through the loosening of defenses, about the unconscious aspects of central conflicts as with the telling of dreams.

To study the interpersonal themes of the parent's relationship with their child, the parents were asked to tell two relational narratives about a specific interaction with their child. The instructions for our adaptation of the RAP interview for the parents were as follows: "Please tell me about some incidents or events, each about an interaction between yourself and your child...". The accounts should be about *specific* incidents, not just amalgams of several incidents. For each of the two specific incidents, the parent was asked to tell when it occurred, some of what the child said or did and some of what the parent said or did, and what happened at the end. The RAP instructions indicate that the event in the narrative "... has to be about a specific event that was personally important or a problem to you in some way" (Luborsky, 1998; p. 110). The REs that the parents told were fully transcribed, and the authors of this chapter rated them for the two cases using the CCRT standard categories, and when needed, adding tailor-made ratings (for details on the CCRT method and issues of scoring, see Luborsky & Crits-Christoph, 1998). Each of the three raters rated the material independently, and then the final ratings were arrived at through consensus among the three raters.

The second method we used to assess the parent's representation of the child and the relationship with the child was *The Working Model of the Child Interview (WMCI)* developed by Zeanah et al. (1986). The WMCI was developed within the framework of attachment theory in order to detect the specific working model that parents have of their children. The underlying assumption is that parents can develop specific working models for each of their different children. Hence, the WMCI is designed to reveal more about the specific representation the parent has of the relationship with the child than an assessment of the parent's general aspects of the working model in relation to attachment figures (e.g., by use of the AAI; Bretherton, 1999). This assessment tool was also aimed at aiding psychotherapy processes with troubled infants and their families, through addressing the dynamic system of ongoing interactive behaviors and representations between parents and their child (Zeanah & Benoit, 1995).

The WMCI is a one-hour semi-structured interview which yields a classification of the parent's representation of his/her child and the relationship with the child: Balanced, Disengaged, or Distorted. The interview is conducted separately with each parent, videotaped and transcribed, and judges rate the interview on 15 Likert scales in order to reach the parent's WMCI classification. The questions of the interview refer to the child and the parent's relationship starting from the pregnancy, through early infancy and up until the present as well as in the anticipated future. The aim is not so much to learn about the actual developmental facts or to receive an accurate personality description, but to learn about the parent's *subjective experience* of the child and his/her relationship with the child. Parents are asked to describe, for example, their emotional reactions during pregnancy, the child's development and personality, and the relationship between the parent and the child. Specific examples are asked to support general descriptions in order to evaluate formal characteristics of the representations, such as coherency and flexibility to change. The emotional tone of the representations (e.g., joyful, angry, anxious) as well as two thematic characteristics ("Child Difficulty" and "Fear for the Child's Safety") are evaluated.

A *balanced* representation is one in which the parent's narrative is rich, coherent, flexible and straightforward, portraying a picture of who the child is and a truthful sense of the relationship between parent and child. The parent is involved in the relationship with the child without sensing his/her parental responsibility as a burden, conveying sensitivity and positive feelings towards the child and an appreciation of the significance of their relationship for the child's personality development.

A *disengaged* representation is one in which the parent's narrative conveys emotional distancing from the child, and in certain cases even to a degree feelings of rejection and aversion towards the child. The descriptions of the child and the relationship with the child are general and unelaborated (e.g., "he is a normal kid"); at times containing a cognitive quality to them; and reveal, particularly around emotional distress, lack of sensitivity towards the child.

A *distorted* representation, although conveying more parental involvement in the relationship than in the case of the disengaged representation, is characterized by a certain distortion in the representation. Distorted representations are sometimes characterized by an unsuccessful struggle on the part of the parent to feel close to the child, and they may convey confusion and contradictions. The parent's descriptions reveal, for example, preoccupation with a specific matter (e.g., the child's disruptive behavior), or confusion and anxiety over raising the child and their relationship with the child. The parent may conceive the child inappropriately, such as in role-reversed representations, or exhibit a strong sense of self involvement and an incapability of seeing to the child's needs.

In this study, we propose the application of the CCRT method in order to identify the themes of the parent's representation of the relationship with the child, combined with the application of the WMCI, which enables the identification of the parent's working model of his/her child and the relationship with the child (balanced, disengaged, or distorted). Indeed, a parallel can be drawn between the working model a person has and the central theme a person holds of his/her relationship with a particular person (Luborsky et al., 1995). The major difference between the two is that the central theme adds to the thematic (content) understanding of the representation, whereas the working model emphasizes the cognitive aspects (organization and coherence) of the representations (Bretherton, 1999; Gabarino, 1998; Shaver, Collins, & Clark, 1996). In this regard, Stern (1995) suggested the need to consider four models of the representational world that are used to organize the clinical material about parental representations: The *distortion* model evaluates to what extent the representation (subjective reality) has been distorted from some objective view of reality; the *dominant theme* model evaluates how much representational space is left to view the baby in ways other than the ways dictated by the content of a particular dominant theme; the *narrative coherence* model evaluates the coherence, comprehensibility, consistency, and emotional balance of the representation as narrated; and the *ontogenetic* model evaluates the out-of-developmental-phaseness of representations (e.g., remaining stuck on phase-specific representations or holding a representation that is in advance of the appropriate developmental phase). By combining the application of the CCRT with the WMCI in this study of parental representations of the child, we will demonstrate the advantages of combining the dominant theme model with the narrative coherence model.

To study the child's representations, we used an adaptation of the story stem technique (Bretherton, Oppenheim, Buchsbaum, Emde, & the MacArthur Narrative Group, 1990), referred to as "the MacArthur Story Stem Battery" (MSSB). The story stems elicit the child's responses to dramatic beginnings of stories. The adaptation that we used included story stems developed by Ben-Aaron, Eshel, and Harel (1999) that evolved around seven themes (i.e., performance, frustration, failure, child's request from parents, conflict around limit-setting, fulfilling parents' wishes in the context of re-union, and a frightening situation). The MSSB is used effectively for learning about preschoolers' early emotional meaning making, early relationship experiences, moral development, representations of attachment figures, and of parental and self-representations. It is also useful for learning about the thematic and organizational characteristics of the child's representations, identifying different groups of children (e.g., with attachment disorders), and can assist in learning about the child's capacity to regulate emotions and engage others in this process. In this story-stem technique, by the use of dolls (Buchsbaum & Emde, 1990), the child's presentation of what the dolls do or say appear to contain a variable mixture of depictions of relationships events that may have occurred along with fantasies about these relationships (Luborsky et al., 1998). For a full review of coding procedures and the latest findings related to the MSSB, see Emde, Wolf, and Oppenheim (2003). In our study, the stories told by the children were analyzed by the CCRT method, as were the narratives told by the parents.

We now present two cases drawn from a larger sample of four- to five-year-olds and their mothers and fathers who were recruited through preschools with a normal population (Hashmonay, 2005). Each parent was interviewed individually by a trained interviewer, and underwent our parent-version of the RAP interview followed by the WMCI, and their child participated in the story-stem task. We have chosen to present two cases of well-functioning girls, whose relational representations seemed closely connected to their parents', reflecting an "interplay" with their parents' working models. In presenting the two triads, we first present an analysis of one RE of each parent in relation to the child, followed by an overview of the organization of the parents' working model of the child as revealed by the WMCI. The cases conclude with one narrative told by each child in the story-stems task.

Case 1: Joy and her Parents

Joy is four years and seven months old, and is the first-born; she has a baby sister (nine months old).

The Mother's RE in Relation to Joy

Mother: Can it be a positive interaction? *(ahhm)* I let Joy know that it is not easy to be a parent. So, when she said: "Mommy pick me up," I would often say: "No, I'll get a bent back at the end, or it'll hurt me; you must take care of mommy like mommy takes care of you." Since then, when she sees me carrying things, she says: "Mommy, can I help you so it won't hurt you, so it won't be heavy for you?" We live on the third floor so from the day she could walk she climbed the stairs alone, because I told her: "What will happen to me in another five years when I have more kids?" Since she was very small I have insisted that she climb the stairs alone, even if it took her an hour, and that shows independence and empathy towards the parent.

In response to the interviewer's request that she focus on one specific incident, mother said:

Last week, when we got home from the supermarket, she said: "Can I help you with the groceries? You're carrying baby sister and a bag, and it must be heavy for you." So I told her: "No thank you, Joy, I don't want you to carry too much [giggles]. It's not good for you either." So Joy said: "Maybe you give me this bag, it doesn't look too heavy, it looks fine." So really I usually do try to give her something so she knows it isn't easy to carry, then it's also fun for her: When she eats the cornflakes she'll remember that she carried them from the supermarket. We talk a lot about it being hard for mommy. So she always looks at others and says: "That kid – I saw that he only wanted to be held, and his mother picked him up and his poor mother." That makes her feel kind of good about herself.

Interviewer: How did you feel during this interaction? (Interviewer tries to elicit RS.)

Mother: Each time I really get excited [giggle]. It is something that Joy absorbed from childhood, that I like to be helped, to be spoiled, "Mommy I love you," so she really learned this, and really does it a lot. It kind of made me not feel like her mother. No, kind of a little like my daughter takes care of me too, and, because actually my mother died when Joy was one year old. So, like, I miss this part, a spoiling mother, and I'm kind of always looking for it from others. So this is something that I work on myself not to exaggerate with, because she doesn't have to be the compensating part, but in a way it is kind of fun for me, so I try not to exaggerate, to get it from others, not only from her. I want her to be empathic towards me and I'm aware that it's my need to be spoiled, that she actually gives this to me. These are reinforcements, so that I'll be able to go on.

The CCRT method, when applied to this RE, indicated the following themes:

Wishes:	to be helped and be taken care of, to be understood; that Joy will be empathic towards mother. Secondary wishes are to feel good and that Joy will be independent.
Responses of Other:	Joy is helpful and takes care of mother, and is perceived as understanding mother's needs and as happy, and she loves mother.
Responses of Self:	Mother is happy, feels comfortable and loved by Joy; she is aware of her need that Joy take care of her, but is somewhat ambivalent about it.

The main outcome in this interaction, from mother's point of view, seems positive, as mother's wishes are complemented by her daughter's responses, even though some ambivalence is evident in mother.

The thematic content from the above analysis suggests that the central pattern in mother's represented relationship with Joy is of *role reversal*. We further explore how this pattern developed and how it is organized on the representational level through the analysis of the WMCI interview.

The WMCI with Mother. Mother reported in the WMCI that Joy's conception was planned rationally, because "it was time to have a child." Upon first seeing Joy at birth, mother responded with rejection, refusing to see her, saying she looked scary: "I saw her and couldn't look at her from the stress and shock, I said suddenly – 'take her, take her,' and then when I needed to breast-feed her after six hours, I cried, 'I don't know her, I don't want her' . . . I didn't feel depressed, I felt happy, proud and detached." Mother chose the name Joy (although changing the real name we still kept its meaning) because she wished her newborn baby will be happy, believing the most important thing in life is happiness.

The first weeks at home were very confusing for mother, who did not know how to react to Joy, who cried constantly. Mother persisted in breast-feeding, although she was exhausted and addicted to coffee, and felt that Joy too had become addicted. When Joy was a few months old, her maternal grandmother got very sick and mother was busy attending to her, sometimes not even knowing with whom Joy was staying. Mother described how, during the first year of Joy's life, both mother and Joy did not stop crying. Mother did not reflect on any possible emotional meaning this first year might have had on Joy. There were no remembered difficulties (e.g., not with separations in daycare, which Joy began at six months, and not when mother went abroad every year for a few days, "not thinking about Joy"). The difficulties began, however, around the time of the interview (Joy aged 4.5), when Joy began kindergarten and got a little upset separating in the mornings. These recollections illustrate how hard it was for mother to assume the caregiving role following Joy's birth and during the first year, and to show sensitivity to her baby's needs. These difficulties were perhaps due to unresolved issues about becoming a mother, which were intensified by her mother's illness and death during that same period.

Mother is preoccupied with her own unmet needs and her explicit desire that Joy provide her with caregiving and empathy in place of her own mother. Although involved in thinking about her relationship with Joy, she focuses on Joy as a source of fulfillment for her need to be cared for, and on Joy not burdening mother with her own needs. For example, mother sees it in a positive light that Joy turns to other mothers in kindergarten in the morning, and asks them to play with her when she has trouble separating. Focusing on Joy's point of view is experienced by mother as a burden: "I feel I am not always spontaneous with Joy. I think what to say to her, and sometimes I think I answered wrongly, then three hours later, I say: 'Joy, I am sorry about what I said, I actually should not have said it,' and it's tiring, this whole thing."

Mother's involvement in her own anxieties over dependency, her unresolved loss, and her need that Joy compensate for the loss of her own mother seem to result in a *distorted representation* of Joy and in the quality of *role reversal*. This is further illustrated in mother's idiosyncratic response to the question in the WMCI interview asking her to reflect on what may be a difficult period in Joy's future development:

> "Joy's most difficult period of life will be if I die when she is still young [and childless], unlike me, who had Joy to help me recover from the loss of my mother."

The Father's RE in Relation to Joy

Father tells an RE with Joy when she was one and a half years old. Both parents were attending her daycare party, where Joy performed:

> "She was absolutely amazing, she got up and danced, she was the only one who got up, and turned around doing butterflies, and that made me feel so proud, and it was fun to see her that way, it was amazing. Without talking about it, my wife and I changed our original plan, and decided to take her with us abroad [on a vacation]. It is amazing how such an interaction causes you suddenly not to give up on the need to be with the child, and not leave her, because she is such a great kid, and so amazing, and so nice."

Father's primary *Wish* that can be inferred from this RE is to feel good in relation to Joy's successful performance. His secondary wish is to be close to a successful Joy.

Responses of Other: Joy is successful, cooperative, mature, and a source of self-esteem for father.

Responses of Self: Surprise (discovers Joy), pride, love, and feeling good.

Again, as in mother's RE, the outcome is positive, as Joy fulfills father's wish to feel good and wins approval and closeness (the parents decide to change their original plan to leave her, and instead they take her with them abroad).

Father's WMCI. Father's Working Model of Joy and their relationship, as elicited from the WMCI, is characterized by *disengagement* due to his emotional distance, especially from negative or painful feelings about Joy and about their relationship (e.g., father's reaction to Joy being hurt was: "When your child is hurt, you feel a little pain and sorrow, but nothing terrible, just a little pinch in the heart."). Father minimizes Joy's dependency needs, and there is little evidence that he is willing to comfort Joy when distressed (e.g., father's reaction to Joy's bleeding nose: "She was frustrated, it happens to her occasionally, but she knew it was not her fault. I didn't feel bad for her, she didn't cry, she knows how to go and get a tissue by herself and she tries to stop the bleeding.").

Father appears to show a lack of sensitivity to Joy's point of view. He ascribes Joy's good behavior to good parenting, aimed to prepare Joy for life, whereas difficult behavior (e.g., difficulty and sadness at separating in the mornings) is ascribed to what is perceived by him as children's tendency to manipulative behavior. Father's main descriptions of his relationship with Joy are of fun and playing activities, emphasizing Joy's good and mature behavior, in fulfillment of his expectations.

Both parents' working models share lack of sensitivity to Joy's needs, and are unable to reflect on her emotional experience and to understand Joy's difficulties. Both see her more as an adult than as a child. Their representations can be distinguished in that mother imposes a distortion of role reversal on the representation, whereas father's representation focuses primarily on seeing Joy as mature and well-behaved, while denying negative experiences and dependency needs. Mother acknowledges her own dependency needs, and wonders if Joy is trying to please her, whereas father's representation of Joy and their relationship is more rigid and less open to self-observation or self-criticism.

Joy's Relational Representations. Of Joy's responses to the seven story stems, we chose to present the story that best illustrated her representations of her relation to her parents. This was the story stem that is intended to elicit representations with regard to themes around the *child's performance*, that is, *child makes animals from play-dough with friend, and parents enter the room.* Joy's first response to the question: "What happened next?" was:

> "The dog jumped on mommy and daddy. And then they fell and got up and got hurt on their heads. And then they went to the hospital and the doctor took care of them. And then their grandmother took them to the hospital to visit mommy and daddy, first mommy and then daddy and they brought them delicious cookies. (*What did mommy say to her about the play-dough animals she prepared?*) And then, grandmother was with them all the time, and then when she was healthy, she saw the play-dough zoo and so did daddy. And it is nice. (*What did she tell mommy?*) That she had fun with grandmother. (*What did she tell daddy?*) Also, that she had fun with grandmother, and she [her friend] told them too. (*What did she feel like?*) Happy. First she was sad and now she is happy. (*And what did she think to herself?*) Fun."

This idiosyncratic and incoherent story told by Joy involves a unique situation that Joy created, in which parents are not able to respond to the child. On a subconscious level, the *Wish* in the story might be that parents get hurt, and also perhaps, to hurt (punish) parents. On the manifest level, the wishes are that the parents get taken care of, will be able to respond to her, and not leave her. Meanwhile others (grandmother) will take care of Joy, maybe a memory of the vacations when the parents left her with grandmother and expected her upon their return to say that it was fun.

Joy's *Responses of Others* are that the parents (in this story she does not distinguish between father and mother) are unable to respond to their child's performance, they are hurt, therefore helpless and cannot be relied on (perhaps an enactment of their emotional vulnerability) and are in need of treatment and help. Another significant other, grandmother, plays an important role in Joy's RE: the wishes toward grandmother are that she help the child, nurse the parents, and control the situation. Joy perceives other-grandmother as helpful, available, in a powerful position, and nurturing. Only after receiving treatment are the parents perceived as able to respond to their child. Joy seems to be saying that her parents still need a lot of caregiving for themselves (by other adults) in order to be able to parent her.

The *Responses of Self* are of loneliness (as revealed through a theme Joy created of separation from parents that she interjected into the story), of being "unseen," and of being helped by other-grandmother. A response of sadness is acknowledged, as well as a change of mood to happiness, as a result of a change in parental emotional availability.

Interplay of Joy's and Her Parents' Relational Representations. Joy's relational themes as revealed by the CCRT ratings of her responses to the story stems, are disorganized, incoherent, and emotionally fearful. This situation, in our opinion, reflects the interplay between parents' unbalanced representations of Joy and their shared difficulty in reflecting psychologically on Joy's inner world. Table 12.1 presents a summary of the interplay among the relational themes and representation organization of mother–child, father–child, and child–parents in Joy's case.

The interplay can be organized around Stern's (1983) description of the three different forms of self-other representation of experiences of being with each other, namely "complementing," "sharing," and "transforming." Mother's wish to be helped and taken care of by Joy, and father's representation of Joy as competent and mature, are complemented by Joy's representations of both parents as helpless, in need of treatment and incapable of dealing with negative experiences. Mother's wishes that Joy will be empathic and understanding of her have, perhaps, led Joy not to allow herself to acknowledge her own needs. Therefore, on the manifest level, Joy has a complementary representation of herself as a happy child, who has fun as expected of her, but perhaps at the expense of her inner resources. When analyzing the narratives, in search of the more unconscious hidden self representation, we may infer that Joy also represents herself as lonely,

Table 12.1. *Interplay among Mother–Father–Child Relational Representations*

		Joy's Case			Noa's Case		
		Mother	Father	Child	Mother	Father	Child
CCRT	Wishes	To be helped, taken care of, & understood by Joy; that Joy will be empathic to mother and make her feel good; that Joy will be independent.	To feel good in relation to Joy's successful performance, to be close to a successful Joy.	Parents get taken care of; to hurt parents, parents help Joy; to feel accepted, understood, & to feel good.	To feel stable, confident, & have control over Noa; that Noa will be independent & self-controlled.	Noa will succeed, be self-confident and independent; to support Noa.	Both parents: to be helped, understood, to be protected, to feel secure. Mother: help me, understand me. Father: to hurt him & be accepted by him.
	RO	Joy is helpful, takes care of mother, is understanding, happy & loves mother.	Joy is successful, cooperative, mature, & a source of self-esteem for father.	Both parents: unresponsive, hurt, need treatment, helpless; capable of helping after receiving help.	Co-operative, understands mother, sooths mother; injured and persuaded by mother.	Dependent, not confident; trusts father, proud, happy, cooperative and independent.	Both parents: helpless and capable of helping. Mother: attends to her own needs first; Father: pays attention, helps, gets angry.
	RS	Happy, comfortable, loved by Joy, ambivalent.	Surprise, pride, love, feels good.	Helpless, lonely, unseen, sad and happy.	Wounded, guilty, embarrassed; reassured, accepted, & understood.	Helpful, responsible, successful, takes care of Noa. Proud and happy.	Helpless, alone, guilty, cautious, ambivalent, sad and happy.
WMCI/ Child's Coherence		**Distorted Role Reversed**	**Disengaged Suppressed**	**Narratives incoherent**	**Disengaged Suppressed**	**Balanced Restricted**	**Narratives coherent**

unseen, and anxious. Still, Joy's ability to create a complementing representation of self and other, which is perhaps due to her parents' wishes and high expectations of her, enables Joy to have a certain degree of mental differentiation between herself and parents. As a result, Joy can create a helpful solution for herself, as revealed in a competent and compensating RO of grandmother.

Joy's narratives in relation to father, and the father's narrative in relation to Joy, suggest that her representation of "the way-to-be-with father" is to share positive experiences (even at the price of denial). Father's representation of himself as emotionally remote and denying negative affect (in the WMCI) is reflected in Joy's complementing representation of herself as lonely, unseen, and sad when in need. Both parents fail Joy in her need of "state transforming," as clearly transpires from her other narratives, but also echoed in the parents' narratives (when sad, she may not cry with daddy; when lonely, she is not reassured by mother picking her up). Joy copes with the situation by her representation of her grandmother as caring and helping in state transforming, helping child and parents to feel happy.

The striking interplay between the parents' representations of Joy and her own representations illuminates Joy's emotional development and the family interaction. The parents enable Joy to be mature and to have only positive feelings, by being available to her only when she fulfills their needs. She has too few, if any, state-transforming experiences with her own parents and many experiences of role-reversed complementing. These role-reversed complementing representations that are tailored to her parents' needs, at the expense of having complementing representations tailored to her needs, leave her overwhelmed by her own anxiety and limit her own potential for a richer and truer self. Left to her own devices, Joy develops a competent "false self" (Winnicott, 1965), is able to turn to other adults for help, and employs a variety of defenses (e.g., denial, reaction formation). Nevertheless, her inner world contains negative affects that tend to overwhelm her and make her prone to confusion and incoherence.

Case 2: Noa and Her Parents

Noa is five years and four months old, her mother's first-born child, sister to a one-year-old baby brother. She is her father's second child; he has a daughter from a previous marriage.

Mother's RE in Relation to Noa

> Mother: I feel embarrassed that I do not have a significant interaction to tell about. The truth is that I am not home so much, she is with a nanny, and it's fine that I have little time to spend with her. I'm not good at it,

it's very difficult for me with kids, it's hard for me to go down to the level of things that interest them. Most of the time that she is at home she watches TV, which doesn't involve an interaction between her and me. We go places where the attention is to something else; it's a lot of fun for me to go places with her. Now that you mention it, I do remember an interaction. We went to a children's play and I slipped and fell, and she slipped after me. She was covered with blood. I managed, she managed to calm down. I can count on her in critical moments that she won't let me down. I felt guilty because she fell because of me and I made her cry. She recognizes when I'm stressed and doesn't bother me. When I need her in a certain way, she adjusts herself. She's easily persuaded, and I can get her to do things, even though on a regular day she may cry for hours. When she fell she understood it was not appropriate to cry. I told her it was my fault she fell; I showed her nothing terrible had happened. After that I didn't feel guilty any more, even though I was very embarrassed. I was to blame, and she calmed me down.

In this RE, mother's *Wishes* are to feel stable and confident and have control over Noa, that Noa will be independent and self-controlled, and that mother will not be let down by her.

Responses of Other: Noa is cooperative, understands mother, is injured but still soothes mother, can be counted upon in times of stress, does not need mother's attention.

Responses of Self: Mother is injured, anxious, guilty, and embarrassed, yet feels reassured because she is accepted and understood by Noa.

The outcome of this interaction pleased mother, as she found Noa's behavior soothing. Noa behaved as expected, complying with mother's wish not to cry, so mother was able to deal with her own guilt feelings.

The WMCI with Mother. Noa's mother's responses to the WMCI questions on the birth and first year were that Noa was a wanted baby (mother married father only after ascertaining she could become pregnant), and was loved from first sight by mother. Mother generally describes Noa as a very easy baby and child, who could be counted on not to cause trouble. Mother breastfed Noa enjoyably for three months, but stopped abruptly when she went back to full-time work with no hesitation or difficulty. Since then Noa has been taken care of by a nanny, an older woman from a foreign country, whom Noa loved very much and was attached to (e.g., according to mother, when distressed in kindergarten, Noa called for nanny and asked to visit her on weekends). Mother finds it upsetting when Noa at times cried without apparent reason for hours on end, and believes that the most difficult issue Noa has had to deal with was the arrival of her brother.

Mother does not perceive herself as meaningful to Noa and finds it very difficult to attend to Noa's dependency needs. For example, she does not think that Noa expects anything from the relationship, and thinks that she does not give Noa what a mother is expected to give, feeling that she and her husband "should not have a permit to be parents." It seems mother perceives herself as potentially harmful, and her caregiving is embodied by finding Noa a better caregiver than herself. Although mother does find Noa a substitute caregiver and is aware sometimes of being detached from the relationship with her daughter, mother's representation did not qualify for a balanced representation (e.g., showed substantial lack of sensitivity to some of her daughter's needs). Hence, we evaluated her representation as *Disengaged Suppressed*.

The Father's RE in Relation to Noa

> Father: The first time she slid alone down a water slide, about a month ago, something that before she had been very afraid of, she is not very brave. She was excited that she was able to do it the first time. I was happy for her that she may have gotten some self-confidence, and become a little more independent. At first she slid with me, but I gradually left the slide, each time adding another meter and a half or two, until she slid alone. And she survived it. Each time I gave her a positive reinforcement. I said: "Well done," and "Here, you see, you don't have to be afraid," and "Daddy's taking care of you, you've nothing to be afraid of." She cooperated even though she was scared at the beginning, but she was very happy the moment she did it. She was pleased. At first she said, "Don't leave me," and I said: "I'm not leaving you, and I'm next to you, and you know daddy doesn't want anything bad to happen to you." I wanted her to slide for fun and for her self-confidence, which I think she lacks. I believe that knowing how to swim contributes a lot to personal confidence.

Father's *Wishes* are to support Noa, and for her to succeed, to be self-confident and independent, and have fun. *Responses of Other* are Noa is dependent and afraid, she trusts father, and as Noa masters the sliding, she is perceived by father as proud, happy, cooperative, and independent. *Responses of Self* are that father feels helpful, responsible, successful; he takes care of Noa, is proud and happy, and feels comfortable. The outcome of this RE is positive, as it is free of conflict.

Father's WMCI. Father's representation of Noa and their relationship is *balanced-restricted*. Father values the relationship with Noa (e.g., feels guilty and a sense of loss that he does not have more time to spend with her), keeps her in mind, and is sensitive and respectful of her point of view (e.g., understands it is not easy for Noa with her baby brother; remembers favorably how Noa said, in a moment of anger, it was a pity that mother went to the trouble of having her brother). At the same time, father is somewhat emotionally distant, not having enough confidence in himself and in the importance of the relationship for her (e.g., she should not acquire my bad personality), though he is generally comfortable in the caregiving role, and likes being close to Noa, enjoys pampering her, and contains his negative affects in stressful situations.

Noa's Relational Representations. To illustrate Noa's representations of her relation to her parents, of the seven story stems we chose to present her response to the story stem that is intended to elicit representations with regard to themes around a *frustrating situation* for a child. A *child is sitting next to parents, not succeeding in copying a picture from a book.* Noa told the following ending to this story stem:

> She (the protagonist) said: "Mommy, can you draw this drawing and I will color it?" And mommy said: "Not now, later, after the news is over." And Lucky barked: "Please, please help her." And mommy didn't understand [brings dog closer to mother, dog barks, puts dog on mother's lap]. She sat on her and then mother understood and said: "Oh! Alright then, the news is long anyway. I'll draw the hand this way [mother doll draws], sweetheart, now you can color it. [Mother doll sits back on sofa and says to dog:] "Come Lucky" [dog is seated on mother's lap]. (*What will her father do about the drawing she didn't succeed in copying?*) He'll fix it so now she has two drawings. (*What else can she do?*) She can play, and by mistake, not on purpose, spill paint. And not on purpose, some completely white cow [introducing imaginary cow into the story], soft and silky, by mistake, she thought it was a page, and then by mistake, mistake, she drew on it, and daddy got a little angry, but in the end he took it to the laundry, and when the cow came out of the wash it was shiny and sparkling! (*How does she feel?*) At first she was sad, after that she was happy. (*What did she think to herself?*) That she had a little bit of a sad day and a little bit of a happy day.

In this RE the *Wishes* in respect to mother are that she help and understand Noa; in respect to father, to hurt him and that he will accept and forgive. *The Responses of Other – Mother*: she attends to her own needs and delays the gratification of the child's needs (does not pay attention, ignores her). She does not help and does not understand, but when she does understand (after child insists) she is helpful. *Responses of Other – Father:* he pays attention to her, is helpful (fixes drawing) and angry, solves problems. *Responses of Self:* Noa feels alone, and is not heard (she needs the dog to talk for her). She feels guilty, cautious (spills paint but the spill seems planned and she is cautious rather than impulsive), sad, and ambivalent. The story told is relatively coherent and logical, with two surprising events (dog explains the child to mother; child spills paint) and a positive resolution (father helps to clean the paint that the protagonist spilled).

Interplay of Noa's and Her Parents' Relational Representations. A summary of the interplay among the relational themes and representation organization of mother–child, father–child, and child–parents in Noa's case are presented in Table 12.1. Mother wishes Noa to be independent and self-controlled, and holds a complementary representation of Noa as cooperative with mother and easily persuaded. Mother is aware of her own limitations in caregiving. Complementary to this, Noa represents mother as someone who helps but needs very loud and clear expressions of the need for help; even then her help might be limited. Mother's self-representation, which contains opposite qualities (e.g., guilty–accepted, embarrassed–reassured), is complemented by Noa's representation of mother as not consistently available emotionally and therefore confusing. Mother's representation of Noa in the falling incident indicates state sharing representation in which both are upset but calm down through self-control. In Noa's narrative she turns to mother to help her in "state transforming," but mother fails to help her although she tries, and Noa has to find her own solution. Father is represented by Noa as capable of "state transforming" in situations that are frustrating (with the drawing) and aggressive (the cow), but not always available emotionally (e.g., Noa does not immediately turn to father for help when she does not succeed with drawing). Interestingly, father represents himself as "transforming" Noa's experience from fear to competence in the slide situation. The difference between Noa's and father's representation of him as state-transforming may be related to specific aspects of the situations involved, such as achievement and competence versus fear of an imaginary creature.

Perhaps the fact that neither mother nor father has a distorted representation of Noa enables Noa to represent her relationships autonomously and coherently. In addition, the parents' ability to hold representations that include guilt feelings shows a certain degree of reflectiveness, which is paralleled in Noa's ability to reflect on her own feelings relatively non-defensively and to use her reflective functioning to move freely between fantasy and reality, when she is stressed.

Discussion

Interplay of Parent–Child Relational Representations

In our analysis of parent–child representations of the parents and of their child, we set out to explore the interplay of mother–father–child relational representations in two triads. Each triad was unique and showed different ways in which parents' and child's representations could interface. In both cases the mothers were limited in their ability to reflect on their daughters' feelings. In the first triad this was due to role reversal, and in the second it was due to mother's mistrust of her own ability to be a protective parent. The two girls differed in their relational themes and in their levels of organization, reflecting an interface between parents' and child's relational themes and representations.

In the first case, Joy's responses to the story stems revealed polar relational themes, such as perceiving others (RO) as "helpless" and "capable of helping," and her responses of self (RS) of feeling "sad" and "happy." These contradictory themes might be explained as linked to Joy's mother's impending distorted role-reversal representations, and father's disengaged representations, leaving Joy vulnerable to her mother's impingements, which are further imposed due to Joy's low level of reflective functioning. Mother, herself low in reflective functioning (i.e., unable to see things from Joy's point of view, to be empathic to her emotions, and to respond to her attachment signs with caring behavior), enacted her representations of Joy in their relationship, leading Joy to accept mother's distorted representation of her, which evolved into Joy's schema of a "way-of-being-with" the other (Stern, 1995). Perhaps by complying with her mother's obtrusive wishes, Joy has remained incapable of developing and organizing her own true self, instead developing "a false way-of- being-with" the other as a protection against expressing her "true self" (Winnicott, 1965) and putting the relationship with mother at risk. As Bowlby (1988) suggested: "... *a child's self model is profoundly influenced by how his mother sees and treats him; whatever she fails to recognize in him he is likely to fail to recognize in himself*" (p. 132).

The work of Lyons-Ruth on disorganized attachment in infancy (Lyons-Ruth, Bronfman, & Atwood, 1999) can contribute to understanding Joy's polar relational representations. According to her relational diasthesis model, the more the parent needs to regulate his/her own fearful arousal rather than the child's, the more distorted the child's relational representations become, and the more discontinuous and self-contradictory are the internalized models (Fonagy, 2001). Joy's relational polarities might therefore be linked to her mother's preoccupation with her own attachment needs, unresolved feelings about the loss of her mother, and her difficulty containing them, at the expense of her daughter's attachment needs. Father's representation of Joy, as successful and mature, excluding her negative experiences, does not provide Joy with an alternative representation of herself. Joy cannot trust her father in order to learn about herself and about reality, further limiting her capability to think and reflect non-defensively and realistically, and to develop her true self. It seems that Joy's parents show relatively low reflective functioning, whereby they do not see Joy as an intentional being in some crucial aspects of her. This low reflective functioning sustains the processes of projection and Joy's identification with her parents' projections make it more difficult for her to free herself from these intruding parental representations. These dynamics contribute to Joy's polar relational representations and disorganization and impede the development of her own true self.

In the second case, Noa, unlike Joy, was not threatened by impinging representations, given that Noa's mother showed a dismissing orientation in her working models of Noa, and her father displayed a restricted-balanced representation. The mother distanced herself from Noa, because she did not trust her ability to be a protective parent to her. However, Noa's mother did not leave an emotional vacuum for Noa, providing her instead with a caring nanny. Moreover, Noa's father, holding a more balanced representation of Noa, tried to see Noa's point of view and was more able to be sensitive to her needs and her perspective. This particular representation interface may perhaps explain the development of Noa's ability to deal more freely with her inner true feelings, creating an inner existence not as frail as Joy's, and not as split off from her awareness. It also enabled Noa to be creative and develop advanced mentalizing functions, which further served her as adaptive coping mechanisms.

Addressing the issue of reflective functioning in these two cases, it appears that Joy's mother was unable to reflect on her daughter's mental state, since she was preoccupied with her own depression. Mother actively demanded that Joy be sensitive to mother's mental state, while ignoring Joy's mental state. From the narrative told by Joy, she indeed seemed sensitive to her mother's mental state (e.g., describing mother's need of treatment), but she remained unable to reflect on her own mental state (e.g., could not answer questions about what the protagonist thought). Noa was more able to reflect on her feelings and thoughts, and showed awareness of mental functioning (e.g., could describe the transformation in feelings the protagonist went through), exhibiting an ability to "play with reality" (Fonagy & Target, 1996; Fonagy, Gergely, Jurist, & Target, 2002) in times of need. We postulate that

Noa's father's balanced representation of her was linked to Noa's ability to use her reflective functioning and to move freely between fantasy and reality when she was stressed. In keeping with recent writings on the role of fathers (Target & Fonagy, 2002), Noa's father fosters her independence (slide story) and promotes her symbolic thought. It is also conceivable that Noa's nanny as a "surrogate mother," with whom Noa had a trusting relationship (approved by mother), further contributed to her positive emotional and mental development.

The two dyads show the links between the parents' and the child's representations, and the ways we think they influence the child's development. The possibility of one parent "correcting" the other parent's relational limitations is an important factor in parenting. In the same vein, the cases also show the importance of relations with "significant others," beyond the parental couple, as potential positive influences on the child. This last point seems particularly relevant today as many infants and young children are cared for by alternative caregivers.

Many other aspects may be linked to the differences between the representation developments in the two cases that are beyond the scope of our study, such as differences in constitution and temperament between the two girls (e.g., Noa was an "easy baby," in contrast to Joy, who was difficult to sooth). Similarly, one would need to consider the parents' personality, attachment history, marital quality, and other personal characteristics in the two triads.

Implications for Psychotherapy

The cases presented indicate that parent's representations of their relationship with their child are linked to their child's relational representation. This supports the psychoanalytic position regarding the importance of parental representations, projections, and fantasies that the parent brings to the relationship with the child as a possible source of influence on the child's developing capacity for symbolization. Therefore, consideration of the links between the child's and his parents' representations is essential in therapeutic work with young children, making it possible to separate the parent's perceptions of the child from distortions transferred to the child. Working with parents and their child simultaneously the therapist can help parents see how their feelings affect their child and to analyze less conscious aspects of their representations. For example, in Noa's case, the therapist can help mother understand that Noa needs the dog to express her own feelings, perhaps because Noa is represented by mother as a child who does not need mother's attention, and help mother see why she developed such a representation. The therapist becomes an "intermediary between them," having access to both "complementary and interacting representational systems and emotional worlds" (Slade, 1999).

The two cases presented here were drawn from a non-clinical sample of families who volunteered to take part in our study. Still, one might wonder, should therapy be needed due to future difficulties, which would be the treatment of choice? As in both cases each parent–child dyad showed specific patterns of mutual relations between their representational worlds, we suggest that the mother–child and father–child psychotherapy developed by Ben-Aaron and her co-workers (2001) would be particularly suitable in these cases, as it addresses the mother–child dyad and equally the father–child dyad. In this dynamic approach to brief treatment of relational disturbances in young (three-to-seven-year-old) children, the mother–child dyad and the father–child dyad meet with the same therapist in weekly alternating sessions so that the child attends therapy at least once a week. The therapist also has regular meetings with the parent dyad. This treatment format enables the therapist to directly observe and experience the child's relationship with each parent, instead of extrapolating it from the transference, or learning about it from parental reports (see Fonagy's introduction to Ben-Aaron's et al. [2001] manual).

With the growing emphasize on "implicit relational knowing" as different from the "declarative knowing" of relations (Lyons-Ruth, 1999; Stern et al., 1998), the direct mode, which is at the heart of this mother–child and father–child psychotherapy model, becomes outstandingly important. It is claimed that our earliest and most important ways of being with significant others, are stored in implicit memory and become accessible only through behavior with the specific other. Declarative knowledge develops later and is only a partial aspect of our relations, that part that we can talk about or symbolize in other ways (Lyons-Ruth, 1999; Stern et al., 1998). Thus, by observing the dyads in therapy one can learn about their implicit ways of being with one another. The therapist attends to the dyad at the level of interactive behaviors and simultaneously at the level of meanings and representations of self and other. The therapist creates an atmosphere of trust and safety, and uses her/his containing and reflective functioning *to help the parent help the child.* In this secure framework, the parents and the child are encouraged to use their reflective functioning to improve the behavioral and representational aspects of the relationship. The therapist, who is present in the three dyads, makes links between the different representations and promotes the attainment of more coherent, comprehensive, and balanced self and other representations.

In both of the cases that we presented, the therapist's role would be to provide a secure framework and facilitate the parents' ability to reflect on the relationship as enacted and as represented. The aim is to differentiate between their own and their child's needs and wishes, and to create more adaptive representations and interactive behaviors. In Joy's case, for example, one of the goals would be to release Joy from mother's projections and to help mother become more containing of Joy's fears and needs, by initially containing them by the therapist (Bion, 1967). However, once Joy is freed from complementing her mother's need to be cared for by her own daughter, mother may be obliged to face her own problems and she will be motivated to seek individual therapy. Joy's father will be helped to construct a more comprehensive representation of Joy, thus enabling her to develop herself more fully and coherently.

In Noa's case, the therapist would provide a secure framework that would validate mother's role and enhance her sense of competence as a parent, thereby helping Noa become better known to her mother. In therapy meetings with her father, the therapist could evaluate whether father was aware of Noa's difficulty in expressing negative feelings directly towards him (the cow story) so that he could help her express these feelings, without Noa feeling guilty. Father's ability to transform Noa's negative states would be further enhanced. Through this kind of therapy, both fathers would be able to gain more confidence in their roles and become more involved in their daughters' lives. This is particularly crucial in Joy's case, given her father's disengaged representation of his relationship with Joy, alongside mother's reversed representation. Considering the developmental needs of both girls at the Oedipal phase, father's involvement seems even more important.

The CCRT framework is clearly relevant to psychotherapists working with children and their parents in both a psychoanalytic and attachment oriented therapy. The CCRT can be applied to both parents' and children's narratives told in a psychotherapeutic evaluation or during the course of therapy, in order to reach a comprehensive understanding of the interplay occurring between parents' and child's representational worlds. Relying on the parent-version of the RAP and the story-stem task with the children has the advantage of being more compatible with the "playful" and "storytelling" mode of therapy than the formal common diagnostic tools. Understanding the child's inner and outer relational world is crucial in determining the type of therapy the child can best benefit from. Also, the nature of the transference that will develop in therapy may possibly include the components of the CCRT that have been identified in the relational narratives (Luborsky & Crits-Christoph, 1998). The therapist's awareness, perceptiveness, and ability to listen and identify such relational themes during the course of therapy can facilitate the understanding of intrapersonal and interpersonal processes.

Conclusion: Relational Themes and Relational Organization

To the best of our knowledge, this is the first study that applied the CCRT framework to the study of the relational themes told in narratives by mothers and fathers about their five-year-old child. Research on children's narratives using the CCRT method (Luborsky et al., 1995) showed that children's relational themes remain stable between the ages of three and five. Applying the CCRT to both parents' and their child's narratives, as we have demonstrated in this chapter, appears to be a useful way of analyzing narratives from a relational perspective searching for the self-other representations.

The analysis presented reveals links between relational parent–child themes and representation organization. The first case seems to show that when a distorted theme, such as role reversal, existed in a narrative, it was correctly speculated that the representation organization was distorted role-reversed. In the second case, mother's relational themes, which included wishes to have control over other, and to be stable and confident, with difficulty containing negative feelings of guilt and embarrassment, was shown to have a disengaged organization. The father's relational themes, which included wishes for the child to gain autonomy while at the same time seeing the child's dependency needs and containing free expression of good and bad feelings, went with a balanced representation. This indicates that themes and organization structure are closely related, and that themes can be significant in helping to understand a person's representation structure.

The interplay that we presented was based on the relational narratives that were told by mother, father, and their child and on the parents' WMCIs at one point in time. This does not permit us to make more than speculative statements on how the child's relational representations evolved. Therefore, it may be only speculated that the different forms of the children's "self-with-other" representations are a reflection of different types of early experiences of being-with the other, namely, self-other complementing, mental state sharing, and state transforming (Stern, 1983).

The analysis of relational narratives using the CCRT method can allow us to gain knowledge of specific relational themes that characterize the person. Combining psychoanalytic information (gained from methods such as the CCRT) and representation organizational aspects (gained from attachment methods such as the WMCI or AAI) enables us to gain a rich and deep understanding of both the content as well as the coherence and organization features of parent–child relational representations. Stern (1995), in referring to the usefulness of the four clinical models of the representational world, states: "Most experienced clinicians probably use an eclectic mix of all four models without thinking much about it, depending on the clinical material presented. Nonetheless, specifying the models they use may clarify and facilitate their clinical endeavors" (p. 40). In this study we demonstrated how the combination of the use of the CCRT method and the WMCI can inform the clinician in a structured and systematic way about the relational representations worlds of the mother–father–child in order to plan the suitable clinical interventions. Two recent other studies have reported on the links between relationship themes, as identified by the CCRT method, and attachment states of mind, as measured by the AAI, the first with an adolescent sample (Waldinger et al., 2003), and the second in a clinical case study of an adolescent male patient (Ammaniti & Sergi, 2003). Integrating psychoanalytic and attachment research methods, as we attempted in this study, can be seen as part of the recent inclination (e.g., Fonagy, 2001) towards bridging the gap between these two theories, and finding their points of interfacing.

Acknowledgments

We thank Tal Ashkenazy for her skillful assistance in conducting the interviews presented in this chapter; and special gratitude to the parents, who participated with their child in our project, for agreeing to have parts of their interviews presented in this chapter. All identifying details have been changed.

References

Abelin, E. L. (1975). Some further observations and comments on the earliest role of the father. *The International Journal of Psycho-Analysis, 56*, 293–302.

Aber, J. L., Slade, A., Cohen, L., & Meyer, J. (1989, April). *Parental representations of their toddlers: Their relationship to parental history and sensitivity and toddler security.* Paper presented at the Biennial Meeting of the Society for Research in Child Development, Baltimore, MD.

Ammaniti, M. & Sergi, G. (2003). Clinical dynamics during adolescence: Psychoanalytic and attachment perspectives. *Psychoanalytic Inquiry, 23*, 54–80.

Balint, M. (1968). *The Basic Fault.* London: Tavistock.

Barber, J. P., Foltz, C., & DeRubeis, R. J. (2002). Consistency of interpersonal themes in narratives about relationships. *Psychotherapy Research, 12*(2), 139–58.

Barber, J. P., Luborsky, L., Crits-Christoph, P., & Diguer, L. (1995). A comparison of core conflictual relationship themes before psychotherapy and during early sessions. *Journal of Consulting & Clinical Psychology, 63*, 145–8.

Belsky, J., Gilstrap, B., & Rovine, M. (1984). The Pennsylvania infant and family development project: I. Stability and change in mother-infant and father-infant interaction in a family setting at one, three and nine months. *Child Development, 55,* 692–705.

Ben-Aaron, M., Eshel, Y., & Harel, J. (1999). Relational themes in mother-child and father-child dyads of 4.5–6.5 years old children as seen in free play interactions, teaching interactions and evoked story stems. *Paper Presented at the IPA Research Seminar*, UCL, London.

Ben-Aaron, M., Harel, J., Kaplan, H., & Patt, R. (2001). *Mother-child and Father-child Psychotherapy*. London and Philadelphia: Whurr.

Benjamin, J. (1988). *The Bonds of Love*. New York: Pantheon Books.

Bion, W. R. (1967). *Second Thoughts*. London: Heinemann.

Blatt, S. J. & Lerner, H. (1983). Investigations in the psychoanalytic theory of object relations & object representations. In J. Masling (Ed.), *Empirical Studies of Psychoanalytic Theories*. Hillsdale, NJ: Erlbaum, pp. 189–249.

Bowlby, J. (1969). *Attachment and Loss: Volume 1. Attachment*. London: Hogarth Press and the Institute of Psycho-Analysis.

Bowlby, J. (1973). *Attachment and Loss: Volume 2. Separation: Anxiety and Anger*. London: Hogarth Press and the Institute of Psycho-Analysis.

Bowlby, J. (1980). *Attachment and Loss: Volume 3. Loss: Sadness and Depression*. London: Hogarth Press and the Institute of Psycho-Analysis.

Bowlby, J. (1988). *A Secure Base*. London: Tavistock Routledge.

Bretherton, I. (1984). Representing the social world in symbolic play: Reality and fantasy. In I. Bretherton (Ed.), *Symbolic Play: The Development of Social Understanding*. New York: Academic Press, pp. 1–41.

Bretherton, I. (1999). Updating the "internal model" construct: Some reflections. *Attachment & Human Development, 1*(3), 343–57.

Bretherton, I., Biringen, Z., Ridgeway, D., Maslin C., & Sherman, M. (1989). Attachment: The parental perspective. *Infant Mental Health Journal, 10*, 203–21.

Bretherton, I. & Munholland, K. A. (1999). Internal working models in attachment relationships. A construct revisited. In J. Cassidy & P. R. Shaver (Eds.), *Handbook of Attachment: Theory, Research, and Clinical Application*. New York: Guilford Press, pp. 89–111.

Bretherton, I., Oppenheim, D., Buchsbaum, H., Emde, R., & the MacArthur Narrative Group. (1990). *The MacArthur Story-stem Battery*. Unpublished manual, University of Wisconsin-Madison.

Britton, R. (1989). The missing link: Parental sexuality in the Oedipus complex. In J. Steiner (Ed.), *The Oedipus Complex Today*. London: Karnac Books, pp. 83–102.

Buchsbaum, H. & Emde, R. (1990). Play narratives in 36-month-old children: The portrayal of early moral development and family relationships. In A. J. Solnit, P. Newbauer, S. Abrams, & A. S. Dowling (Eds.), *The Psychoanalytic Study of the Child*. New Haven, CT: Yale University Press, pp. 129–55.

Cabrera, N. J., Tamis-Lemonda, C. S., Bradley, R. H., Hofferth, S., & Lamb, M. E. (2000). Fatherhood in the twenty-first century. *Child Development, 71*(1), 127–36.

Cox, M. J., Owen, M. T., Henderson, V. K., & Margand N. A. (1992). Prediction of infant–father and infant–mother attachment. *Developmental Psychology, 28*, 474–83.

Diamond, D., Blatt, S. J., & Lichtenberg, J. (2003). Prologue – Attachment research and psychoanalysis III: Further reflections on theory and clinical experience. *Psychoanalytic Inquiry, 23*, 1–11.

Emde, R. N., Wolf, D. P., & Oppenheim, D. (2003). *Revealing the Inner Worlds of Young Children: The MacArthur Story Stem Battery and Parent-Child Narratives.* New York: Oxford University Press.

Etchegoyen, A. (2002). Psychoanalytic ideas about fathers. In J. Trowell & A. Etchegoyen (Eds.), *The Importance of Fathers.* New York: Taylor & Francis, pp. 20–41.

Fairbairn, W. R. D. (1952). *Psychoanalytic Studies of the Personality.* London: Routledge.

Fitzgerald, H. E., Mann, T., & Barratt, M. (1999). Fathers and infants. *Infant Mental Health Journal, 20* (3), 213–21.

Fonagy, P. (2001). *Attachment Theory and Psychoanalysis.* New York: Other Press.

Fonagy, P., Gergely, G., Jurist, E. L., & Target, M. (2002). *Affect Regulation, Mentalization, and the Development of the Self.* New York: Other Press.

Fonagy, P., Steele, H., & Moran, G. S., Steel, M., & Higgitt, A. (1991). The capacity for understanding mental states: The reflective self in parent and child and its significance for security of attachment. *Infant Mental Health Journal, 13*, 200–17.

Fonagy, P. & Target, M. (1995). Understanding the violent patient: The use of the body and the role of the father. *The International Journal of Psycho-Analysis, 76*, 487–501.

Fonagy, P. & Target, M. (1996). Playing with reality: I. Theory of mind and the normal development of psychic reality. *International Journal of Psycho-Analysis, 77*, 217–33.

Fonagy, P. & Target, M. (1998). Mentalization and the changing aims of child psychoanalysis. *Psychoanalytic Dialogues, 8*, 87–114.

Gabarino, J. J. (1998). Comparisons of the constructs and psychometric properties of selected measures of adult attachment. *Measurement and Evaluation in Counseling and Development, 31*, 28–44.

George, C., Kaplan, N., & Main, M. (1985). *Adult Attachment Interview.* Unpublished manuscript, University of California at Berkeley.

George, C. & Solomon, J. (1996). Representational models of relationships: Links between caregiving and attachment. *Infant Mental Health Journal, 17*, 198–216.

George, C. & Solomon, J. (1999). Attachment and caregiving: The caregiving behavioral system. In J. Cassidy & P. R. Shaver (Eds.), *Handbook of Attachment: Theory, Research, and Clinical Application.* New York: Guilford Press, pp. 649–69.

Guntrip, H. (1971). *Psychoanalytic Theory, Therapy, and the Self.* New York: Basic Books.

Hashmonay, R. (2005). *Interplay between representations: Links between mothers' and fathers' representations of their child and the child's relational representations and adjustment.* Unpublished doctoral dissertation, University of Haifa, Israel.

Jacobson, E. (1954). The self and the object world: Vicissitudes of their infantile cathexes and their influence on ideational affective development. *Psychoanalytic Study of the Child, 9*, 75–127.

Jacobson, E. (1964). *The Self and the Object World.* New York: International Universities Press.

Kerenberg, O. F. (1976). Object relations theory and clinical psychoanalysis. New York: Aronson.

Kerenberg, O. F. (1984). *Severe Personality Disorders: Psychotherapeutic Strategies.* New Haven, CT: Yale University Press.

Klein, M. (1932). *The Psychoanalysis of Children.* Reprinted as *The Writings of Melanie Klein, Volume 2.* London: Hogarth Press, 1975.

Lamb, M. E. & Oppenheim, D. (1989). Fatherhood and father-child relationships: Five years of research. In S. H. Cath, A. Gurwitt, & L. Gunsberg (Eds.), *Fathers and Their Families.* Hillsdale, NJ: Erlbaum, pp. 11–26.

Lieberman, A. F. & Zeanah, C. H. (1999). Contributions of attachment theory to infant-parent psychotherapy and other interventions with infants and young children. In J. Cassidy & P. R. Shaver (Eds.), *Handbook of Attachment: Theory, Research and Clinical Applications.* New York: Guilford, pp. 555–74.

Luborsky, L. (1977). Measuring a pervasive psychic structure in psychotherapy: The Core Conflictual Relationship Theme. In N. Freedman & S. Grand (Eds.), *Communicative Structures and Psychic Structures.* New York: Plenum Press, pp. 367–95.

Luborsky, L. (1998). The Relationship Anecdotes Paradigm (RAP) interview as a versatile source of narratives. In L. Luborsky & P. Crits-Christoph (Eds.), *Understanding Transference: The Core Conflictual Relationship Theme Method.* Washington, DC: American Psychological Association, pp. 109–20.

Luborsky, L. & Crits-Christoph, P. (1998). *Understanding Transference: The Core Conflictual Relationship Theme Method.* Washington, DC: American Psychological Association.

Luborsky, L., Luborsky, E. B., Diguer, L., Schaffler, P., Schmidt, K., Dengler, D., Faude, J., Morris, M., Buchsbaum, H., & Emde, R. (1995). Extending the Core Conflictual Relationship into childhood. In G. Noam & K. Fisher (Eds.), *Development and Vulnerability in Close Relationships.* Hillsdale, NJ: Erlbaum, pp. 287–398.

Lyons-Ruth, K. (1999). The two person unconscious: Intersubjective dialogue, enactive relational representations and the emergence of new forms of relational organization. *Psychoanalytic Inquiry, 19(4),* 576–617.

Lyons-Ruth, K., Bronfman, E., & Atwood, G. (1999). A relational diathesis model of hostile-helpless states of mind: Expressions in mother-infant interaction. In J. Solomon & C. George (Eds.), *Attachment Disorganization.* New York: Guilford, pp. 33–70.

Main, M. (1991). Metacognitive knowledge, metacognitive monitoring, and singular (coherent) vs. multiple (incoherent) model of attachment. Findings and directions for future research. In C. Parks, J. Stevenson-Hinde, & P. Marris (Eds.), *Attachment Across the Life Cycle.* London: Routledge, pp. 127–60.

Main, M., Kaplan, K., & Cassidy, J. (1985). Security in infancy, childhood and adulthood: A move to the level of representation. In I. Bretherton & E. Waters (Eds.), *Growing Points of Attachment Theory and Research. Monographs of the Society for Research in Child Development, 50* (1 2, serial No. 209), 66–104.

Ogden, T. (1994). *Subjects of Analysis.* Northvale, NJ: Aronson.

Sandler, J. (1995/2003). On attachment to internal objects. *Psychoanalytic Inquiry, 23,* 12–26.

Sandler, J. & Sandler, A. (1978). On the development of object relationships and affects. *The International Journal of Psycho-Analysis, 59,* 285–96.

Sandler, J. & Sandler, A. (1998). *Internal Objects Revisited*. Madison, Connecticut: International University Press.

Schneider-Rosen, K. & Burke, P. B. (1999). Multiple attachment relationships within families: Mothers and fathers with two young children. *Developmental Psychology, 35*, 436–44.

Shaver, P. R., Collins, N., & Clark, C. L. (1996). Attachment styles and internal working models of self and relationship partners. In G. J. Fletcher, J. O. Garth, & J. Fitness (Eds.), *Knowledge Structures in Close Relationships: A Social Psychological Approach*. Mahwah, NJ: Erlbaum, pp. 25–61.

Slade, A. (1999). Representation, symbolization, and affect regulation in the concomitant treatment of a mother and child: Attachment theory and child psychotherapy. *Psychoanalytic Inquiry, 91(5)*, 797–830.

Slade, A., Grienenberger, J., Bernbach, E., Levy, D., & Locker, A. (2001). Maternal reflective functioning and the caregiving relationship: The link between mental states and mother infant affective communication. Paper presented at the *Biennial Meeting of the Society for Research in Child Development*, Minneapolis, MN, April 22.

Stern, D. N. (1983). The early development of schemas of self, other, and "self with other." In J. D. Lichtenberg & S. Kaplan (Eds.), *Reflections on Self Psychology*. Hillsdale, N.J.: Analytic Press, pp. 49–83.

Stern, D. N. (1985). *The Interpersonal World of the Infant*. New York: Basic Books.

Stern, D. N. (1995). *The Motherhood Constellation: A Unified View of Parent-Infant Psychotherapy*. New York: Basic Books.

Stern, D. N., Sander, L., Nachman, J., Harrison, A., Lyons-Ruth, K., Morgan, A., Bruchweiler-Stern, N., & Tronick, E. (1998). Non-interpretative mechanisms in psychoanalytic therapy: The "something more" than interpretation. *International Journal of Psychoanalysis, 79(5)*, 903–21.

Target, M. & Fonagy, P. (2002). Fathers in modern psychoanalysis and in society: The role of the father and child development. In J. Trowell & A. Etchegoyen (Eds.), *The Importance of Fathers*. New York: Taylor & Francis, pp. 45–66.

van IJzendoorn, M. H. (1995). Adult attachment representations, parental responsiveness, and infant attachment: A meta-analysis on the predictive validity of the Adult Attachment Interview. *Psychological Bulletin, 117*, 387–403.

Waldinger, R. J., Seidman, E. L., Gerber, A. J., Liem, J. H., Allen, J. P., & Hauser, S. T. (2003). Attachment and core relationship themes: Wishes for autonomy and closeness in the narratives of securely and insecurely attached adults. *Psychotherapy Research, 13*, 77–98.

Winnicott, D. W. (1958). *Collected Papers*. New York: Basic Books.

Winnicott, D. W. (1965). Ego distortion in terms of true and false self. In *The Maturational Processes and the Facilitating Environment*. New York: International Universities Press, pp. 140–52.

Winnicott, D. W. (1971). *Playing and Reality*. Middlesex, UK: Penguin.

Wiseman, H. & Barber, J. P. (2004). The Core Conflictual Relationship Theme approach to relational narratives: Interpersonal themes in the context of intergenerational communication of trauma. In A. Lieblich, D. P. McAdams, & R. Josselson (Eds.), *Healing Plots: The Narrative Basis of Psychotherapy*. Washington, DC: American Psychological Association, pp. 151–70.

Wolf, D. P. (1993). There and then, intangible and internal: Narratives in early childhood. In B. Spodek (Ed.), *Handbook of Research on the Education of Young Children*. New York: Macmillan, pp. 42–56.

Zeanah, C. H. & Barton, M. L. (1989). Internal representations and parent-infant relationships. *Infant Mental Health Journal, 10*, 135–41.

Zeanah, C. & Benoit, D. (1995). Clinical applications of a parent perception interview. *Child Psychiatric Clinics of North America, 4*, 539–54.

Zeanah, C., Benoit, D., & Barton, M. (1986). *Working Model of the Child Interview*. Unpublished manuscript, Brown University, Providence, RI.

13   Why Do Inadequate Parents
Do What They Do?[1]

Patricia M. Crittenden

Abstract

Understanding why threatened parents behave in ways that seem, from the perspective of less threatened people, to exacerbate the risk to their children requires consideration of the process of generating and selecting among dispositional representational (DR) models. This chapter addresses six forms of DRs from a memory systems perspective (Schacter & Tulving, 1994). These are described in a developmental framework in which neurological maturation interacts with experience to generate developmental pathways. The outcome of the pathway, at any given moment, is an emergent, ever-changing set of DRs that both shape individuals' perception of the world and their relation to it and also guide the transformation of mental representations to enacted behavior. It is argued that preconscious memory systems regulate important aspects of parental behavior because they promote safety and that reflective, integrative, and verbal processes may be infrequent, especially among risk parents, because integrative processing itself can expose parents and their children to danger. The chapter points to the paradox that protection and preparation for reproduction, which are essential and universal components of parenting, appear to be precisely the functions that are distorted in cases of risk, that is, cases of child maltreatment and parental mental illness.

Everyone has seen parents treating their children in unacceptable ways and wondered why they did that. Everyone has been horrified at the "inhumanity" of parents whose abuse and neglect of their children has garnered media

[1]   I would like to thank Clark Baim, Lynn Benjamin, Steve Farnfield, Stuart Hart, Kasia Kozlowska, Andrea Landini, Jennie Noll, and Ute Ziegenhain for their suggestions on earlier drafts of this chapter. I am especially appreciative to Ofra Mayseless for this opportunity, for her imagining that something interesting could come from it, and for her near-endless patience and assistance as I developed the ideas presented here.

attention and wondered how they could do those things. Each of us who is a parent has, on occasion, acted in ways that appalled us – and we wonder why we did that. This chapter considers how parenting behavior is generated in terms of what information is brought to bear on the task, how we employ the information, and which aspects of the task have priority when not all can be managed or when success is at risk. Doing so highlights the importance of protection and preparation for reproduction as essential and universal components of parenting. It also points to the paradox that these appear to be precisely the functions that are distorted in cases of risk, that is, cases of child maltreatment and parental mental illness.

The Problem. If one considers only the effects on children of dangerously inappropriate parental behavior, one may think the parents are malicious. But if one considers the developmental process through which adults have learned to make meaning and organize their behavior, other explanations become possible. In particular, over-zealous attempts at reversal and correction of childhood experience (i.e., over-compensation) and over-application of learned safety measures (i.e., compulsion) are frequently observed among well-meaning, but endangering parents.

Following the developmental process of making meanings that organize behavior requires that one note both (1) the distortions that functioned self-protectively for the parents in the past and also (2) the maturation-induced changes, especially sexual motivations, that were applied to distorted childhood representations. It is proposed here that dangerous parental behavior can be seen as having comprehensible and self-protective roots in adults' early development and that this development is an on-going process, that is, not one that is arrested at some early stage (Bowlby, 1969/1982). Central to this conceptualization is the notion that without adequate reflective integration (a) childhood strategies may be applied inappropriately to adult contexts, (b) errors of attribution and behavioral response may be carried forward without awareness, and (c) new distortions and errors may be added in response to newly maturing capacities. This combination can endanger children.

The advantages of taking such a complex view of inappropriate parental behavior are that (1) professionals can develop understanding of and compassion for parents, (2) professionals can talk to parents in terms that are meaningful to parents, thereby increasing the probability of engaging the parents' cooperation, and (3) parental change may become more likely.

Resolving the Problem. Understanding why parents behave in ways that endanger their children requires consideration of the process of generating and selecting dispositional representations. Dispositional representations (DRs) are the outcome of mental processing of information that dispose us to behave in particular ways. This term is used as a replacement for the older and less precise construct of "internal working models" both because it clarifies the "disposing to action" function of representation and also because it emphasizes the transient, in-process quality of representing (as opposed to the retained and static quality of models). This chapter addresses several ways of representing the relation of self to context from a memory systems perspective (Schacter & Tulving, 1994). These are described in a developmental framework in which neurological maturation interacts with experience to generate developmental pathways (Bowlby, 1969/1982). The outcome, at any given moment, is an emergent, ever-changing set of dispositional representations that (a) shape individuals' perception of the world and their relation to it and (b) guide the transformation of mental representations to enacted behavior. The ways in which multiple DRs interact to generate parental behavior are the focus of this chapter.

From a mental health perspective, understanding the minds of parents whose behavior is maladaptive is crucial to enabling them to change. Change requires that we build a bridge from their reality to ours and then help them to cross it. To do this, we must carefully differentiate behavior from its meanings because the former is objective, that is, we can all agree on what happened, and the latter is unique to each person. That is, for any exchange between parent and child, the parent's intent provides meaning from their perspective, whereas the effect on the child provides meaning from our perspective. It is easy to see that these meanings might be quite different such that, if we try to communicate at the level of attributions, we will often miscommunicate. This is especially likely because professionals' terms often imply moral censure of maltreating parents' behavior (e.g., "abuse," "abandon") and a lack of meaning for mentally ill parents' behavior (e.g., "personality disorder," "bi-polar," "psychotic"). If parents do not share these meanings, our terms will build walls of misunderstanding, rather than bridges to cooperation. The emphasis in this chapter will be on describing parental behavior and discerning its meaning to parents.

Parenting and Protection

Experience with danger is proposed to be central for parents' attribution of meaning because it influences (1) which representations are deemed most predictive of future conditions and (2) the process by which conflicting representations are resolved into behavior. This leads to the unexpected conclusions that (a) preconscious memory systems regulate important aspects of parental behavior because they promote safety and (b) reflective, integrative, and verbal processes may be infrequent, especially among risk parents, because integrative processing itself can expose parents and their children to danger.

The central role of parents is to protect their children until they reach reproductive maturity. When there are problems (i.e., when there is maltreatment, psychopathology, or sexual dysfunction), the function of protection is almost always distorted. Thus, the central issue addressed by this chapter is *how parents' protective behavior is organized with regard to their children.* The answers offered are in the form of theory-based hypotheses, specifically hypotheses derived from my Dynamic-Maturational perspective on self-protective strategies (Crittenden, 1995, 1996, 1997a, 1997b, 2000, 2002).

Safety, Comfort, and Sex

Three aspects of protection are considered: safety, comfort, and sexual behavior. Safety is promoted through close affectional bonds with a protective person. Spouses form mutual attachments to one another and children form attachments with their parents; these relationships function to promote protection.[2] Although the importance of physical safety is obvious, an important issue is how parents behave when self-protection and protection of one's children are, or appear to be, in conflict.

Psychological protection is also necessary and this is tied to comfort. Comfort is crucial because a safe child who feels uncomfortable, that is, unsafe, will both feel anxious and also behave as if threatened. This may endanger the child unnecessarily (for example, the child may use risk-taking to elicit protection) or may interfere with sexual and reproductive behavior (for example, the child might use coy/flirtatious behavior to attract comfort and, instead, elicit sexual attention). In addition, there can be conflict between self-comfort and comforting one's children. In the most worrisome cases, parents who feel threatened *by* their children deceive their children regarding safety or comfort

---

[2] Parental and child attachment have often been differentiated as child "attachment" and parental "bonding" or "caregiving." A more functional approach is offered here. Rather than relying on the construct of behavioral systems, here "attachment" refers to behavior that serves a self-protective function. When the self is extended to include one's progeny (i.e., one's genetic future), behavior that involves protecting the child is considered "attachment."

(for example, a parent who intends to punish the child may invite the child to approach with apparent affection – and then attack).

Sexuality stands out because of its overlap in function and form with protection. Specifically, both attachment and sexuality function to bring individuals together and to maintain closeness with enduring affectional bonds. Furthermore, both use the same behaviors to accomplish this: smiling, calling, extended eye contact, touching, caressing, holding, embracing, kissing, etc. Only genital contact is largely limited to the sexual/reproductive function. Finally, feelings of anxious arousal and sexual arousal are quite similar and can be confused. The extensive overlap in function, behavior, and feeling between attachment and sexuality creates particular circumstances for families in which one or the other system malfunctions. Because one system can elicit or substitute for the other, the essential functions of protection and reproduction appear over-determined to the point of being almost failsafe processes. Thus, in families with attachment problems, sexuality may provide a pathway to achieving closeness and comfort.

The mental processing that leads to behavior, including attachment, caregiving, and sexual behavior, is referred to as "representation." The neurological and psychological aspects of representation are discussed first, and then they are applied to inadequate or dangerous childrearing.

The Process of Mental Representation

Much of our approach to intervention and treatment is based on symptoms and focuses on behavior change. If the basis for behavior lies in the information processing that precedes action, our interventions might better be targeted to the point where the process goes awry, rather than solely on outcome behavior.

Mental Representations. A mental representation is a network of firing neurons. The neural response to externally generated information represents the state of the *context* at that moment. The neural response to internally generated stimulation represents the state of the *self* at that moment. Together, these generate the neurological representation of "*the self in this context now.*" This representation motivates and organizes individuals' behavior; in Damasio's terms, it *disposes* the self to a particular response (Damasio, 1994). Although the process is not yet fully understood, consideration of how past representations affect the array of dispositional representations (DRs) can inform our understanding of how parental behavior is organized.

What Is Retained from Past Experience. The brain does not keep or store memories (or internal models). Instead, the array and strength of synapses between neurons reflect past experience (Schacter, 1996). Both frequent reactivation and intense stimulation strengthen synapses (Schacter, 1996). Strong, numerous, interconnected synaptic networks are more easily triggered than those with fewer and weaker connections. Thus, what is retained over time is not an "internal representation," but rather a neural network, with each sequence having a probability of firing in response to certain stimuli. In any given moment, these probabilities generate chains of activated neurons that represent "the self in this context in this moment," that is, the *when* and *where* of existence. Because danger is an intense experience, it has a disproportionate impact, compared to its frequency, on information processing.

What Kinds of Dispositional Representations Are There?

Six types of representation are described below. They vary in (1) whether they are "cognitive"[3] (temporally based) or "affective" (intensity based), (2) whether they are preconscious and non-verbal or conscious and potentially verbal, and (3) whether they are available in the early years of life or only later. Figure 13.1 displays these six ways of representing the relation of self to context graphically.

Implicit, Pre-Verbal Representation. The temporal order in which sensory information is perceived is crucial. In Piagetian terms, this is sensorimotor representation. In information processing terms, it is *procedural memory* (Tulving, 1979). Behaviorally, it is learning theory (Skinner, 1938). Temporal order is also the basis for implicit causal attributions (Crittenden, 1997a; Schmahmann, 1997). For example, a young child may learn that after he makes noise, his mother hits him. Such a child may learn to inhibit vocalization both without awareness of the reason and also without limitation regarding the context or circumstances. Alternatively, the child may discover that being helpful reduces the probability of being hit – even if one has been noisy. This child may become compulsively helpful, again without being able to put the idea in words. Procedural representation is rapid, preverbal, and preconscious – and it may be inaccurate. It is information about *when* in the sequence of events a particular event might occur.

---

[3] The term "cognitive" is used here in the restricted meaning of "based on temporal order." It is does not, as used here, refer to a wider range of cortical processes.

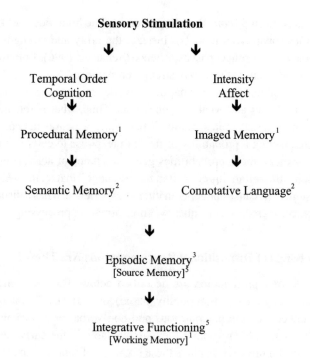

^{1} These three memory systems are functional at birth.
^{2} Semantic memory and connotative language begin to function after about two years of age.
^{3} Episodic memory begins to function after about three years of age.
^{4} Source memory begins to function after about seven years of age.
^{5} Integrative functioning is always present, but is very limited until the school years and not mature until the thirties.

Figure 13.1. Six memory systems as a function of cognitive and affective information. (Copied with permission; copyright of P. Crittenden).

Changes in the intensity of stimulation activate the limbic structures (Le Doux, 1994).[4] This affects somatic arousal, that is, heart rate, breathing rate, etc., in ways that heighten sensory awareness and prepare the body to fight, flee, or freeze (Selye, 1976; Le Doux, 1994). Changes in autonomic state produce sensory stimulation that is itself processed through the limbic system. This can produce an escalating feedback loop of self-arousal, for example, rapid breathing feeds new somatic stimulation back to the brain, thus leading to even more arousal. Associative learning connects sensory aspects of

^{4} Innate, genetically based differences in the perception of change in intensity contribute to temperamental differences in emotional lability.

contexts with experienced outcomes, thereby increasing the set of sensory stimuli that elicit arousal (Pavlov, 1928). For example, a child who was punished in the headmaster's office might later feel uncomfortable in any office.

Arousal changes how individuals feel, literally, and psychologically gives rise to "feelings" (Bowlby, 1980; Damascio, 1999). In Tulving and Schacter's terms, this is "perceptual memory" (Tulving & Schacter, 1994); in the terms used here, it is *imaged memory*.[5] Imaged memory represents sensory aspects of the context and, like procedural representation, it creates a disposition to act that is preverbal and preconscious – and possibly erroneous. Imaged representations are information about *where* an event might occur. Both procedural and imaged representations are probabilistic and reflect past experience with predictability and unpredictability.

Explicit, Verbal Representation. Procedural and imaged representation are functional in humans at birth. With maturation, both can be processed further in ways that make them verbal. Beginning in the third year of life (i.e., two years of age), cortical processing can render procedural information verbally explicit in the form of generalized, context-free information (Tulving, 1987). The classic form of semantic representation is a when/then or if/then statement. On the basis of such statements of contingency, individuals construct notions regarding how one *should* behave. Thus, *semantic memory* generates verbal dispositional representations regarding how things are – or ought to be. Such representations are often used by parents to instruct children and to explain parental behavior. Whereas procedural and imaged information is always self-generated and self-relevant, verbal information can be generated by other people and retained neurologically without corresponding sensori-motor experience. Therefore, semantic DRs can be "borrowed" from others and implemented without self-relevance.

The verbalized form of imaged information is *connotative language* (Crittenden, 2002) which begins to be experienced, in the form of stories, rhymes, and songs, in the preschool years and to be generated by children during the school years. For example, school-aged children's taunting chants have the power to elicit strong emotional reactions in other children. Like semantic information, connotative language can be self-relevant or borrowed; both can generate emotional states in the self or others. That is, the way we tell our stories affects the way we and others feel and, thus, what we are disposed to do.

---

[5] The term "imaged" was selected because it reflects both subjective experience and also usage in the trauma literature.

Cortical Integration. By about three years of age, all four sorts of DRs can be integrated to yield episodic recall of specific events. Episodes contain the temporal order of events and the sensory context in a verbal form. Young children cannot construct episodes without guidance in the form of questions and elaborations by parents (Fivush & Hamond, 1990). In teaching children to construct and tell episodes, parents both influence the representation of the episode (with omissions, additions, and distortions) and also teach children what should be omitted, added, and distorted when constructing an episode. This affects how children attribute meaning to experience.

A subtype of episodic memory is tagging information by the occasion in which one garnered it. The source may be an occasion, what another person said, or the conclusions that one drew oneself. Knowing the source of information is crucial to being able later to evaluate its likely accuracy or veracity, given current circumstances.

Working memory is the fitting of a representation from another memory system to immediate physical circumstances, for example, thumb sucking as a self-comforting behavior is a procedure, but to be implemented, working memory must fit the movements to the positions of the body in real time.

Integrative functioning, on the other hand, carries out integrations of DRs that change the meaning of information. Procedural, imaged, semantic, connotative, and episodic DRs can be compared, contrasted, and integrated cortically to yield a best-fitting representation of the relation of self to context at this moment. Integration, however, is a slow, all-encompassing process that depends upon multiple, concurrent inputs from all over the brain. The advantage of integration is that it permits the best fit of self to current circumstances. The disadvantage is that it consumes the breadth of the brain (thus leaving little capacity for scanning the environment) and progresses slowly (thus leaving the individual unresponsive to external stimuli for a long time). In this time, danger could come close without the individual being aware of it. Thus, the closer in time and space the danger is perceived to be, the less the individual will dare to dally in reflection and the more likely he or she will be to act on a less fully processed and possibly erroneous dispositional representation from procedural or imaged memory. Integrative capacity improves as a function of maturation into the mid-thirties. Thus, self-protective integration will require maturation, sufficient safety to promote reflection, and sufficient exposure to threat to provide relevant information about danger.

Selection of a Dispositional Representation upon which to Act. If all the DRs provide a similar picture of the relation of self to context, behavior proceeds unimpeded. All the excitement occurs when the various dispositions are in conflict. For example, the procedural representation predicts dangerous outcomes (so the individual is disposed to act defensively) whereas in imaged representation the individual feels comfortable (and, therefore, is disposed to attend to other things). But semantically, one has rules that require (or forbid) certain actions, and episodically one recalls a similar situation and how one acted and that it turned out badly (or well). As one considers these possibilities, one tells oneself a story, using minimizing (or arousing) language. Each of these representations generates a disposition to behave. Given sufficient time, the mind can sort through these, evaluating, combining, and contrasting them so as to generate an integrated and comprehensive solution to the problem.

Time is crucial. More complete processing takes longer. Under conditions of perceived danger, time cannot be wasted and processing may need to be aborted in favor of protective action (Damasio, 2003). This is desirable because it reduces the probability of injury or death. It is undesirable because it occurs before full analysis of the ambiguities and uncertainties has been completed. As a consequence, the protective action may be based on erroneous information and may not be necessary. There is, in other words, a trade-off between accuracy and speed.

The outcome is that older and less endangered people will engage in more reflective thought than others. Parents who were exposed to danger in their childhood would be expected to over-estimate the probability of danger and more often to abort integrative processing in favor of self- or progeny-protective action. Thus they would have fewer alternative and less elaborate DRs. When low intelligence is added, the risk of inappropriate behavior rises.

The crucial points to take from this discussion of information processing are that:

(1) Many sorts of DRs are generated by the brain.
(2) The most rapidly protective DRs are preconscious and, therefore, vulnerable to error retained from the past.
(3) The more one has been exposed to danger in the past, especially in the first years of life,
    a. the more facilitated preconscious protective neural networks will be;
    b. the less experience one will have with integrative processing;
    c. the fewer alternative DRs one will have available to apply to current circumstances.

How Do Parents Affect Children's Representations?

From the earlier sections, one might presume that parents who were mistreated in childhood would necessarily repeat that process with their children.

Although there are data supporting this process, the data leave the majority of the variance (78%) unaccounted for (van IJzendoorn, 1995). That is, more often parents' DRs do *not* match their children's. Instead, both corrections and reversals of the parental error are common. To understand this, one must consider the process of intergenerational "transmission" of DRs.

What Is Transmitted. Beginning with communication between two adults, each adult has all six kinds of dispositional representations. One DR regulates behavior in a particular moment and the first person acts. That is, what gets out of the mind is not the representation itself, but rather, behavior. The other person perceives this behavior as sensory stimulation: temporally ordered stimulation and intensity-based stimulation. Perception itself, however, is colored by previous experience, such that one perceives what one expects to perceive; according to Gregory (1998), 80% of perception is memory. The second person's brain processes this already distorted information as networks of activated neurons and generates a set of DRs. On the basis of one or a combination of these, the second person acts – producing behavior that the first person perceives as sensory stimulation, etc.

The DRs (i.e., the networks of firing neurons) never get out of the person's brain. They exist only in the moment of synaptic firing and cannot be directly shared with another person. What "gets out" is behavior, but even behavior is not transmitted directly, but rather is perceived in the form of temporal order and intensity of stimulation. At this point, the recipient's brain begins transforming the incoming information to generate its own dispositional representations of the relation of self to the other person. These representations may – or may not – be similar to the first person's representations, but they are never identical.

Parent–Child Transmission. The situation between parents and children is the same – with one exception. Parents, being adults, have six functioning memory systems. Infants have only three and older children are developing the other forms of representation. Anything the parent does, no matter how complex, will be represented in a simpler form by infants and children. That is, infants' and children's dispositional representations *cannot* be the same as their parents'. Parents cannot give or transmit their *representations* to their children. Instead, parents act creating an environment in which infants and children perceive certain stimulation and then generate their own representations of the relation of self to context. Like parents' representations, children's representations vary in the emphasis on temporal or affective information used to organize behavior and this may reflect – or reverse – the parents' emphasis.

From Representation to Strategy

The terms "pattern of attachment" and "quality of attachment" have been used to refer to the ABC patterns described by Ainsworth (Ainsworth, 1979). They are also considered strategies for eliciting care from attachment figures and internal representational models of how to elicit care. That is, as Ainsworth's work developed, it moved from being strictly descriptive (patterns of attachment) to awareness of the interpersonal function of the patterns (strategies) to awareness of the mental processing that underlay behavior (internal representational models). Although academic discussion of these reflects a historical progression, the three are inseparable and co-occurring aspects of the same phenomenon, a trinity, if you would. This section of the chapter considers both what constitutes a self-protective strategy and what the array of possible self-protective strategies might look like.

An Expanded Model. The Dynamic-Maturational Model of attachment expands the Ainsworth model to include self-protective strategies that require greater neurological and physical maturity than infants have (Crittenden, 1995). Individuals using the Type A subpatterns organize their behavior around cognitive procedural and semantic contingencies and discard as unreliable or misleading imaged and connotative information (i.e., affect). In infancy, this is displayed as inhibition of anger, fear, or desire for comfort and is accomplished by keeping the attachment figure out of perception (by "avoiding" looking at the attachment figure). By the end of the second year of life, maturation gives children the ability to inhibit even when perceiving the attachment figure and Type A children become more subtle; they look but with an object raised between them and the adult. This keeps the adult from feeling rejected while still avoiding intimacy. Also in the preschool years, children learn to substitute inhibited negative affect with false positive displayed affect, for example, smiling when angry or frightened. The distortions of cognition begin in infancy as highly predictable behavioral responses. By three to four years of age, these are taking verbal form as exaggerations of probability (that can be identified by such "absolute" words as "always," "never," "very, very," etc.) As the numeral of the pattern increases (from A1–2 to A7–8), the extent of distortion in cognition and affect increases, as does the compulsiveness with which the strategy is applied to daily problems. That is, an individual classified as A1 (idealizing of attachment figures) or A2 (negating of self) uses a strategy that is mildly biased toward temporal contingencies, but in the face of clear disconfirming information, can change strategy, whereas an individual using an A7 or A8 strategy

P. *Crittenden*

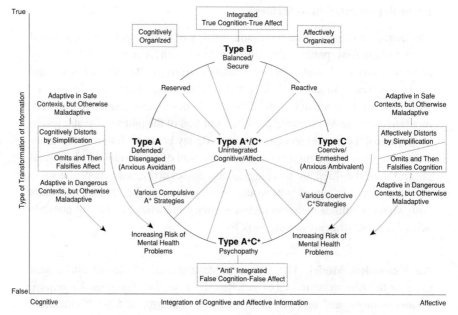

Figure 13.2. The Dynamic-Maturational Model of attachment. (Copied with permission; copyright of P. Crittenden).

(delusional idealization or externally assembled self) relies almost exclusively on temporally organized and distorted information and applies the strategy without variation to both appropriate and inappropriate conditions in spite of clear, strong, and highly self-relevant disconfirming information. The intermediary substrategies are A3 (compulsive caregiving), A4 (compulsive compliance), A5 (compulsively promiscuous), and A6 (compulsively self-reliant). Strategies are considered "compulsive" to the extent that they require the individual to act in a rapid, reflexive, and unchanging manner. Three points are important. First, cognition takes two forms, procedural action and pre-scriptive semantic guides. Second, as the numeral increases from A1–2 to A7–8, the source of semantic prescriptions becomes increasingly outside the self (i.e., parental directives to moral/religious standards to people claiming to represent or be the source of guidance). Third, as the numeral increases, there is an increase in both the extent of distortion of information and also the uniformity with which the strategy is applied to all perceived threats, appropriately and inappropriately. See Figure 13.2.

Individuals using the Type C substrategies are biased toward acting on the basis of their feelings (i.e., affect, as represented by imaged and conno-tative information) and find temporal contingencies to be unpredictable or misleading. Type C is a more complex organization than Type A. In infancy, it is experienced as simple arousal leading to mixed feelings of anger, fear, and desire for comfort. These motivate approach with aggression, escape, and approach with requests for comfort, respectively. Any one of these responses might be the most adaptive response to a given situation, but used together they are incompatible and ineffective. By the end of the second year of life, maturation gives children the ability to regulate these feeling states both internally (such that behavior becomes focused) and also interpersonally (such that displayed affect is used to affect others' response). Thus, a preschool-aged child might usually approach problems with angry aggression, but, when faced with adults' anger, shift to disarmingly coy bids for comfort (while hiding evidence of anger). The Type C strategies include C1 (threatening), C2 (disarming), C3 (aggressive), C4 (feigned helpless), C5 (punitively obsessed with revenge), C6 (seductively obsessed with rescue), C7 (menacing), and C8 (paranoid). Three points are important. First, desire for comfort, anger, sexual desire, fear, and pain constitute a gradient of increasingly arousing affective states that transform arousal into coherent action. The more arousing states become more prominent as the numeral increases from C1–2 to C7–8. Second, as the numeral increases, these states are increasingly generated and maintained by the self. Third, as the numeral increases, there is an increase in both the extent of distortion of information and also the uniformity with which the strategy is applied to all perceived threats, appropriately and inappropriately. See Figure 13.2.

Thus as individuals deviate away from Type B, they become increasingly locked into a strategy without sufficient regard to current circumstances. Using integrative processes, on the other hand, reflects mental balance with regard to the type of information used to generate behavior and this, in turn, creates the greatest probability that (1) distortions in representation will be discovered and corrected and (2) occasion-specific and effective self-protective solutions will be found to life's threats. That is, psychologically balanced individuals have the greatest probability of being safe and feeling secure. Put another way, the Type A and C strategies use past representations to organize behavior (with working memory fitting the old solution to the current context), rather than considering *whether* the solution fits the context. The Type B strategy, on the other hand, is a strategy for using information to generate new solutions to problems.

Trauma, Depression, Disorientation, Disorganization, and Reorganization. In the Dynamic-Maturational Model, danger refers to events and "trauma" to certain kinds of psychological responses to dangerous events.

There are five ways in which a strategy can be modified and modification may occur after exposure to danger.

When individuals are exposed to danger, they garner new information on its antecedents and context, their behavior and feelings, and consequences. If they discriminate accurately that which is unique to the past and that which is relevant to the future (dismissing from current representation the irrelevant information and carrying forward the relevant information), they are considered resolved with regard to that dangerous experience. Sometimes resolution changes individuals' understanding of the relation between themselves and their context such that both their internal processing of information and also their strategic organization of behavior are modified in ways that increase the fit of person to context. That is, exposure to danger can be the impetus to correction of omitted, distorted, erroneous and falsified information, such that individuals *reorganize* (R) in a more adaptive manner. On the other hand, if individuals make errors in this discrimination, either dismissing that which is relevant or carrying forward that which is not relevant (or both), they are considered *unresolved* (U). Dismissing lack of resolution causes signals of danger to be omitted from representation. Preoccupying lack of resolution causes people to respond as if there were danger when there is not. Both errors make prediction less accurate, the former by under-estimating the probability of danger and the latter by over-estimating its probability. *Depression* (Dp) occurs when the individual has concluded that no action will effect any change; arousal drops, sometimes in life-threatening ways. *Disorientation* (DO) occurs when sources of information are confused such that the individual's behavior is sometimes in their own best interest and sometimes not – without their being able to identify this. Instead, without knowing it, they may act on DRs from earlier ages or from other people, especially attachment figures. When adults are not oriented toward specific interests (their own or others), behavior becomes incoherent. *Disorganized intrusion of negative affect* (DX [desire for comfort, anger, sexual desire, fear, or pain]) occurs when inhibited negative affect intrudes explosively and without coercive interpersonal organization; this increases arousal rapidly and intensely. Such intrusions are only possible in a compulsive Type A strategy, can function to reverse depression, and are sometimes associated with psychotic breaks.

How Does Perception of Danger Affect Behavior?

The attachment literature treats parental representations as being different from attachment representations (George & Solomon, 1999). The perspective offered here is more general. Representations are simply networks of firing neurons that represent the relation of self to context at a particular moment in time and dispose the self to some response. DRs elicited when safety or reproduction are threatened are more intense and temporal relations are learned in fewer trials than DRs not related to attachment. That is, stimuli signaling danger to the self, progeny, or opportunity for sexual reproduction receive preferential attention.

Threatened individuals often take extreme risks to protect themselves and their children or to gain access to reproductive partners. That is, many of the things that one does to protect oneself – or one's children – are themselves dangerous. What except extreme danger would make a person jump from an upper floor window – as some people did from the World Trade Center on September 11? Why would parents send their children away to be raised by strangers – as did some Jewish parents in Nazi Germany? Why would anyone permit their body to be cut open – as is done in surgery? Why would someone beat their wife – as many husbands do? What would cause a person to hit their own child – as far too many parents do? The answer to all of these questions is the same: fear of greater danger if this very dangerous action is not taken.

Applying this notion to the first three examples is straightforward. The second example, however, is important in showing that parents treat children as an extension of self such that their survival can be more important than protecting the self. That is, children are parents' genetic future and, thus, are protected as a part of self (Dawkins, 1976). The final two examples, spousal and child abuse, are more perplexing because they seem counter-intuitive and morally reprehensible. Nevertheless, the most common reason for spousal abuse is fear of sexual unfaithfulness (Dobash et al., 1992; Wilson & Daly, 1992). That is, the attacking man is protecting his reproductive opportunity. The most frequent reason for striking children is to teach them not to do something that the parent believes is dangerous (Holden & Zambarano, 1992). Framed this way, these relatively frequent forms of danger can be included in the same motivational model as more extreme and unusual forms of risk-taking.

Thus one principle can account for a great deal of dangerous human behavior, including most forms of inadequate childrearing:

> The more dangerous the threat is deemed to be, the more risk will be incurred to prevent or overcome the threat.

Furthermore, the greater the perceived danger, the more rapid and incomplete the processing of information and, therefore, the more vulnerable the representation is to error. Finally, the specific error is likely to be one that treats current conditions as being similar to past conditions.

404 *P. Crittenden*

Representation and Inadequate Childrearing

In the sections below, these ideas are applied to different forms of inadequate childrearing to illustrate how the universal aspects of DRs can inform our understanding. The ideas are organized by *psychological functions* and not by parental behavior, outcome to the child, or psychiatric diagnosis. Nevertheless, associations with maltreatment and psychopathology are offered to help the reader to visualize six different clusters (see Figure 13.3).

The discussion is organized around how parents integrate *self*-representations with representations of their *child* to organize parental behavior. The interplay among DRs determines what and whose needs are given priority, what meanings are attributed to them, and what action is taken. The clusters are divided into cognitively (Type A) and affectively (Type C) based representations, with a gradient of increasingly severe transformations of information (from true to erroneous and false) and increasing intrusion of the effects of

Distortions of normal child-protective behavior

(1) Type A: Parents who exaggerate the probability of danger to their children by relying on past contingencies, thus over-protecting (and sometimes physically abusing) their children;

(2) Type C: Parents who overlook the probability of danger by failing to predict outcomes and responding on the basis of feelings, thus under-protecting (and sometimes neglecting) their children;

Distortions that emphasize self-protective behavior

(3) Type A: Parents who transform (forbidden) desire for comfort into (acceptable) sexual desire and respond to children's need with sexual behavior (thus sometimes sexually abusing their children);

(4) Type C: Parents who exaggerate the probability of danger to themselves, protecting themselves at the expense of their children (and psychologically maltreating their children);

Distortions that substitute delusional information for accurate information

(5) Type A: Parents who misconstrue powerful forces as threatening both themselves and their children, thus responding with irrational protective measures (and both psychologically and physically maltreating their children);

(6) Type C and Dp A+ DX [negative affect]:   Parents who misconstrue the child as a source of threat, thus intentionally attacking, abandoning, or even killing the child.

> **Figure 13.3.** A clustering of parental representation organized around a patterned gradient of covarying psychological processes. (Copied with permission; copyright of P. Crittenden).

trauma (from limited to pervasive). It is not expected that Type B parents would behave in these ways (except in rare cases when actual threatening conditions prevent the time needed for integration).

A Set of Hypotheses. The basic hypothesis is that, as past threats become more prominent and children less accurately a part of parents' DRs, parenting becomes less adequate. At the extreme, a delusional representation of the child may motivate life-threatening parental behavior. Although the gradient is structured around psychological functions, there is a rough concordance with symptom-based diagnoses such that parents fitting clusters 1 and 2 rarely carry a diagnosis or, if they do, it is a mild Axis I, stress-based diagnosis, whereas parents in cluster 3 and 4 often have personality disorders (Axis II, enduring and maladaptive personality characteristics) and many parents fitting clusters 5 and 6 have had delusional or psychotic episodes.

It is noteworthy that these hypotheses are often consistent with what mal-treating and mentally ill parents say about themselves and inconsistent with what the professional literature says about them. They reflect an attempt to reconcile parents' words with the evidence of their harmful actions in ways that might a) change professionals' understanding of the parents, b) permit parents to recognize themselves in the descriptions (thus reducing denial), and c) change the sorts of interventions that are offered. Throughout, the goal is to explain existing evidence with a set of new and potentially informative hypotheses. See Figure 13.3.

There are four bases for the hypothetical clusters offered: (1) empirical studies, especially of physical and sexual abuse and neglect, (2) observa-tions of parent–child interactions, Strange Situations, and Adult Attachment Interviews (AAI) of disturbed children and adults, (3) clinical experience with troubled families, especially in child protection, and (4) theory regard-ing self-protective attachment strategies (Crittenden, 1997, 2000, 2002). The clusters are intended to connect what is known empirically with the richness of clinical practice and the meaning-generating function of theory.

Distortions of Normal Child-Protective Behavior

(1) Type A: Parents Who Exaggerate the Probability of Danger to Their Children by Relying on Past Contingencies, Thus Over-Protecting (and Sometimes Physically Abusing) Their Children. Parents often punish children's dangerous behavior in order to teach them safe behavior (Critten-den, 2005). This is true regardless of whether they scold, spank, or hit children hard enough to hurt them. Strangely, this explanation is accepted when there is no injury and yet rarely believed when the child is hurt. Nevertheless, outcomes do not define motivations and the same psychological process can account for both ordinary physical punishment and injurious punishment (but see subsequent sections for parents who attack or kill their children without apparent cause).

Ordinarily, our evaluation of whether a parent's action was appropriate or not depends upon both the outcome to the child and also our evaluation of the danger. For example, if a parent broke a child's arm jerking him off train tracks in front of an oncoming locomotive, most people would consider it a justifiable act that saved the child's life. The same event might be considered abusive if the child had been peddling a tricycle toward an empty street. This example highlights that it is not simply severity of injury that defines child abuse, but rather a comparison between the parent's dispositional representation of the situation *prior* to action and an authority's *after* action is taken (Crittenden & Claussen, 1993).

Parental Behavior and DRs. Parents who abuse their children are not usually mentally ill (Kolko, 1996). Instead, it is proposed that they make errors in estimating danger and its implications for their own behavior. These errors are drawn from their experience of having been exposed to danger in their own childhoods (Aber & Zigler, 1981). Abusive parents are likely to overestimate the probability of danger and respond protectively too frequently and strongly (Crittenden, 1998). For such parents, mildly threatening situations may elicit recall of dangerous consequences (i.e., procedural DRs that initiate compulsive behavior) or sensory images (i.e., imaged DRs that elicit intense arousal) or both.

What happens next depends upon the extent to which parents integrate representations from the past with those of the present. When parents both mistakenly accept their childhood DR without question and also place themselves in the adult role (as they should), they may be disposed to act in an authoritarian manner, possibly repeating the sorts of behavior used by their parents. Alternatively, parents may have reflected sufficiently upon their experience to have decided to raise their children differently. In these cases, parents may take the child's perspective and behave too permissively, thus reversing the pattern. Finding a safe balance between past and present conditions and between adult and child perspectives is difficult and requires extensive and ongoing integration (Crittenden, Lang, Claussen, & Partridge, 2000).

Most abusive parents have clear and meaningful representations of children as needing protection to the point being vigilantly focused on identifying (dangerous) misconduct or disrespectfulness. The problems in organizing a response are (a) simple procedural distortion of over-estimation of danger based on past experience, (b) intense fear of negative consequences that impels a quick response, and (c) a limited array of response alternatives. This may trigger a protective, albeit authoritarian (cf. Baumrind, 1971), response that can lead to injury (Crittenden, 2005). It is important to understand that the punishment was intended by the parent to be protective and is deemed abusive by others. That is, given time and safety, these parents reach appropriate conclusions, but under the pressure of perceived threat, they act dangerously on preconscious DRs. This suggests the intrusion of unresolved trauma.

Errors of over-estimating of danger are relevant to immigrant populations, especially when parents have moved from relatively dangerous to relatively safe countries. Such parents use childrearing strategies that were accepted and even essential to safety in the country in which they were learned, but which seem unnecessarily strict or dangerous by the standards of the new country. Without explicit consideration of the two contexts, misapplication of parenting strategies is likely to occur.

Outcomes to Children. Children of authoritarian parents both know that what they do is important to their parents and also try to avoid parental attention. Children's feelings of being competent depend upon parental satisfaction with their behavior or upon their finding alternate attachment figures who support their development. Some (over)achieve and become very successful. Others, however, remain locked in anger, fear, and failure, carrying this into their childrearing. Most do not become abusive parents themselves (Aber & Zigler, 1981; Kolko, 1996) although an important minority of these becomes overly permissive.

(2) Type C: Parents Who Overlook the Probability of Danger by Failing to Predict Outcomes and Responding on the Basis of Their Feelings, Thus Under-Protecting (and Sometimes Neglecting) Their Children. Some parents raise children in crisis-ridden, multi-problem environments. The central problem generating crises is the parents' failure to predict and prevent problems. Instead, parents respond only when the intensity of the signal is very high, that is, when it elicits affective arousal. This often forces the parent to choose, under pressure, what to attend to (for example, the crying baby, the overflowing toilet, the eviction notice, the gossipy neighbor, or the fighting preschoolers). The parents' behavior appears unpredictable unless one notices that intense sensory input and impending danger capture parental attention preferentially. So in the example, the baby and preschoolers vie for the mother's attention while her interest is in gossip, and the eviction notice gets no response – until the family's belongings are on the curb.

Parental Behavior and DRs. The problem is that there are competing triggers to parental action. In this cluster, the most compelling DRs are those tied to parents' own feelings and motivations. Parents run from crisis to crisis, solving problems and soothing children in a just-too-late pattern that maximizes everyone's arousal. In addition, the children's intense focus on the parent satisfies the parent's own need to feel important and loved.

Nevertheless, these parents care for their children and try to protect and comfort them. That is, when children are prominent in the parents' DR, they are cared for almost adequately, but achieving and holding that state is difficult. Instead, competing sensory signals interfere with parents' attention and temporal information is not used to predict children's needs. Consequently, the parents respond only after the children have imposed themselves, in intensely imaged ways, on the parents. When the parents do respond, they do so with a sense of urgency that precludes access to semantic ways of framing the situation or reflective thought that could integrate competing DRs. Because the behavior was organized preconsciously, semantic explanations offered later often fit poorly and raise doubt in professionals.

Outcomes to Children. Under such circumstances, children learn to be vigilant regarding parents' attention, to heighten their signaling, and to compete with siblings. They exaggerate and alternate displays of negative affect. If caregivers habituate to intense signals, children may take even more extreme protection-eliciting action, that is, provocative or risk-taking behavior. This becomes part of a dynamic process between parent and child. This "coercive strategy" (Crittenden, 1992) can lead to disorders of attention, arousal, and conduct, and these, in turn, can prevent academic learning and satisfactory peer relationships.

The next two clusters have in common that the parent places too great an emphasis on their own need for comfort and protection, unknowingly using that information to organize their caregiving behavior. Correspondingly, children are treated as being more mature and competent than they are. In addition, these two clusters form a transition from parents largely without psychiatric disorder to those with serious psychiatric disorder.

Distortions that Emphasize Self-Protective Behavior

(3) Type A: Parents Who Transform (Forbidden) Desire For Comfort into (Acceptable) Sexual Desire, and Respond to Children's Needs with Sexual Behavior, Thus Sometimes Sexually Abusing Their Children. Two decades of research seeking profiles of incestuous abusers have largely failed (Murphy & Smith, 1996; Veneziano & Venziano, 2002). Similarly, treatment seems ineffective (Shine, McClosky, & Newton, 2002). Possibly the problem lies in two assumptions: (1) that sexual abuse is about sex or power and (2) that abusers are predators who intentionally entrap children. If these assumptions are in error, research and treatment based on them are unlikely to be successful.

A different perspective is offered here. First, desire for comfort transformed into sexual desire is hypothesized to be the motivating affect in sexually abusing parents. Semantically, these parents are hypothesized to intend to reverse the isolating and threatening experiences that typified their own childhoods. That is, affectionate behavior, including sexualized affection, may be abusers' expression of desire for comfort and closeness as well as their offer of comfort to their children. Second, the developmental pathway to incest may be a series of experiences that accrue over childhood and adolescence and that culminate in a form of attachment tied to dismissing the self, focusing on others' needs, and expressing affection in sexualized ways. Third, to ensure that their children will not experience the isolation and humiliation that they experienced, abusers may try take their children's perspective. That is, sexual abusers may be unusually attuned to their children's signals of anxiety or desire for comfort. The resulting closeness is likely to be satisfying for both parent and child. In the literature, this is called "grooming" the child; here a different set of motivations is imputed to the same behavior.

Adequate developmental studies of sexual abusers do not yet exist. AAIs of sexual abusers, however, suggest a developmental pathway to their current functioning (Crittenden, 2000; Haapasalo, Puupponen, & Crittenden, 1999). These include (1) lack of family intimacy and comfort, (2) bullying attacks from fathers or step-fathers (i.e., physical abuse), (3) witnessing violence to their mothers (i.e., abuse to their protective attachment figure), (4) mocking and shame for seeking comfort (i.e., psychological abuse), (5) abandonment, lack of supervision, and separation (i.e., neglect), (6) feeling singled out or marked for mistreatment, (7) internalizing problems, (8) exclusion from symmetrical peer attachments (best friends and peer groups), (9) inclusion as victims in peer bullying, and (10) precocious sexual activity (Bumpy & Hansen, 1997; Duane, Carr, Cherry, et al., 2003; Garlick, Marshall, & Thornton, 1996; Hunter, Figueredo, Malamuth, & Becker, 2003; O'Halloran, Carr, O'Reilly, et al., 2003; Levant & Bass, 1991; Smallbone & Dadds, 1998, 2000; Salter, McMillan, Richards, et al., 2003; Starzyk & Marshall, 2003). The great majority of abusers were not themselves sexually abused although most were abused psychologically or physically or both (Murphy & Smith, 1996). Based on their AAIs, many sexually abusive men idealize their intimidated mothers and exonerate their fathers. That is, they identify with victims in ways that suggest a desire to protect and care for vulnerable, picked on, and uncomforted people. It is proposed that the compulsive patterns of attachment (Types A3–8) that involve inhibition of their own desires and negative feelings in favor of meeting others' expectations and soothing their feelings can account for these data; this is consistent with abusers having internalizing problems, an external locus of control, and low expressed anger (Beck-Sander, 1995; Fisher, Beech, & Brown, 1998; Marsa, O'Reilly, Carr, et al., 2004). This brief review suggests a series of developmental risks whose cumulative effect increases the probability of becoming a sexual abuser. Paradoxically, these risks are not directly tied to sexuality; rather they consist of lack of comfort until adolescence when sexual desire may initiate the first satisfying experience of closeness and comfort.

Parental Behavior and DRs. Most sexual abuse by parents is touching, not sexual intercourse; moreover, very little involves violence (Herman, 1992; Russell, 1986; Trickett et al., 2001). Furthermore, families in which there is sexual abuse rarely complain and usually support the abuser, preferring to remain together. When accused of sexually abusing their children, most abusers deny doing so (Barbaree, 1991; Maletzky, 1991). As with physical abuse, this may indicate a difference in semantic meanings. Did they touch the child? Yes. Did they "abuse" the child? No – because they intended to comfort the child. The point is that our labels tied to outcomes may not fit abusers' intent. The relation between intent and action, however, may be quite complex.

Sexually abusive parents' motivation may reflect a series of transformations. Semantically, they may organize around ensuring that their children do not experience the isolation, lack of comfort, shame, or domination that they experienced. Because this is a semantic *reversal* strategy, it is not under-girded by procedures and images drawn from the parents' own experience. Procedurally, they may try to reverse experienced dominance hierarchies by creating a symmetrical parent–child relationship. This creates risk that children will be treated like adults. Abusers' experience with closeness and intimacy may be tied to adolescent sexual relationships, such that sexualized affection becomes the source of their procedural and imaged DRs of affection. In addition, like other parents using compulsive strategies, incestuous parents adapt their behavior to the child, but they may misconstrue the meaning of children's coy, attention-seeking behavior as being flirtatious.

Regardless of whether the adult's response is based on empathic caregiving or sexual desire, affectionate behavior consists of behaviors that are common to both the attachment and sexual behavior systems, for example, caressing, hugging, kissing, reassuring. This suggests a means by which disparate affects can be substituted for one another. Because there are semantic dictates against sexual acts with children, sexually abusive adults probably rationalize comforting/sexual action as being justified by worthy motives: "She wanted it"; "I was only comforting him"; "We were only being close and affectionate." Abusers may also displace the source of their dispositions. Parental behavior should be based primarily on child needs; in incest, parents' need for comfort and intimacy may be denied and displaced onto children. Finally, abusive adults already experience shame for their normal feelings and hide their comfort-desiring behavior. Adding actually shameful acts that also must be hidden changes their psychological state very little. That is, the alarm bells of conscience and the practice of hiding "shameful" behavior are already so pervasive that adding new eliciting conditions changes little or nothing for the adult. The warning system fails because it has been activated excessively and, thus, it does not discriminate risk from non-risk. This complex array of reversals, substitutions, distortions, and displacements may combine in the sexually abusive parent to promote the fusion of affectionate and sexual behavior with children.

Because stepparents are less inclined than biological parents to define the child as an extension of self, they may be more likely to act on their own desires. In addition, because stepchildren can threaten or dilute stepparents' reproductive success, higher rates of mistreatment are found among non-biological parents (Wilson & Daly, 1996). That is, desire for comfort may motivate many biological sexual abusers, but be a less prominent motivation among stepparents.

The crucial hypotheses offered regarding incestuous caregiving are that (1) its roots are in normal comfort seeking that is punished and inhibited in childhood, first satisfied in romantic relationships, and, in that form, applied to children, (2) incestuous parents have themselves been seriously and repeatedly victimized psychologically, physically, and sometimes sexually, and (3) abusers act on the confluence of personal motivations and child signals that elicit affection.

Punishment is unlikely to correct the mental processes leading to such distorted DRs, and even treatment must be managed carefully and compassionately. It is sadly ironic that treatment of sexual offenders often emphasizes their taking our perspective by empathizing with their victims, changing their behavior, and taking responsibility for their moral transgressions. This may both misconstrue their intentions and also reify their already distorted self-denying, victim-glorifying strategy. If so, our treatments may function to increase the probability of future offending and, thus, to make sexual abuse appear untreatable.

Child Outcomes. Children who are sexually abused experience intense and confusing affectional bonds to their parents. Expressing desire for comfort and fear as coy behavior may constitute a contribution by children to their abuse, albeit one over which they have neither control nor responsibility. However, when the abuse is part of an enduring relationship, child and parent adapt to one another. Thus, over time, the sexually abused child becomes a complicitous victim (Herman, 1992; Russell, 1986), contributing signals that initiate intimacy, reinforcing the parent's attention, and participating in keeping the intimacy private. An obvious risk is over-attribution of self-responsibility by the child. In addition, there are physiological, emotional, and intellectual effects that extend into late adolescence and adulthood (Trickett et al., 2001, Noll et al., 2003a; 2003b). A particular concern is that changes in the child's behavior may attract other, more endangering abusers and romantic partners. The child's complicity and the presence of strong affectional bonds makes treatment of incest more difficult than treatment of random and isolated stranger attacks.

(4) Type C: Parents Who Exaggerate the Probability of Danger to Themselves and Protect Themselves at the Expense of Their Children (Thus Psychologically Neglecting Their Children). Some parents are unable to function as protectors of their children. Instead, they act on representations that portray *themselves* as needing comfort or protection, thus focusing too extensively on their own feelings and needs while concurrently understanding too little about those of their children. Their errors are (a) failing to resolve past loss or trauma, and sometimes (b) structuring adult relationships in ways that create current risk. In many cases, this means that a genuinely loving and caring parent has unpredictable moments of psychological absence and/or actively keeps the child from having the information needed for the child to understand the parent's behavior. In spite of being psychologically unavailable in crucial ways or at crucial moments, these parents rarely pose a physical threat to their children. Some parents in this cluster have diagnosed psychiatric disorders, including depression, substance abuse, anxiety disorders, and PTSD, whereas others self-medicate or gravitate to support groups for parents of problem children. Such parental need results in a more pernicious and less obvious form of inadequate care than simple abuse or neglect.

Four patterns suggest the nature of parents' psychological functioning and some of its effects upon children. They are ordered from clarity of interpersonal contingencies to complex and largely obscured causal relations.

(1) Non-caregiving parent–child relationships (e.g., parental withdrawal, role-reversal, and spousefication);
(2) Triangulation of the child into the marital relationship;
(3) Disorientation among incompatible representations that then motivate contradictory behavior;
(4) Unpredictable and extreme changes in mood and caregiving.

Parental Behavior and DRs. Role-reversing parents are motivated more by their own need to feel safe and protected than by a desire to comfort and protect their children. In moments of conflicting need, they generally protect themselves, even at the expense of their children. Very withdrawn (depressed, traumatized, or sorrowing) parents are an example. In some cases, the parents psychologically abandon the children, having little or no relationship with them. In others, one or more children are able to establish a relationship with the parent by caring for the parent as if the parent were the child (cf., compulsive caregiving, Bowlby, 1973; Crittenden, 1992).[6] In more extreme cases, parents who lack adult partners or have very distant or rejecting partners may treat the child as a spouse. ("Parental" children function as parents for their siblings. Depending upon the children's ages, the responsibilities given to the parental child, and the adult support offered, this varies from a desirable form of family management and preparation for parenthood to a burden that leaves all the children unprotected.)

Triangulating parents try to protect the children from the marriage or, in more severe cases, engage children in protection of the marriage. In the former case, the child is prevented from knowing the conditions that motivate parental behavior. In the latter condition, triangulated relationships use children in ways that children cannot understand while also preventing them from seeing the actual causes of parental behavior. There may be a gender effect in triangulated relationships with mothers triangulating daughters into the marital relationship and daughters responding with passive-aggressive strategies, eating disorders, and drug use. Fathers and sons may more often use directly aggressive strategies such as extreme risk-taking and anti-social behavior.

---

[6] As with all of the high numeral patterns in the Dynamic-Maturational Model, it is not the designated behavior itself that is the problem, but rather it is compulsive or obsessive application to all aspects of the parent–child relationship. In the case of compulsive caregiving, that means both that the child gives care when it is needed and within range of what the child can manage developmentally as well as when it is not and also that the child is uncomfortable (i.e., anxious) being the cared for person.

Disoriented parents are anxious, but without evident focus for their agitation. Their affective states are unstable and not tied closely to current conditions, being generated by a shifting array of incompatible DRs from different periods in their life, different people, and, particularly, dismissed childhood traumas. Each DR by itself is reasonable, but combined, they leave parents out of sync with daily life, puzzled about contingencies and unable to discern the effects of their behavior on others. Even more important, they leave the parent without a "self," without a perspective regarding who they are and what they desire from which they can connect with other people. In this confusion of arousal-without-perspective, children's physical needs are met with kindliness while the children themselves are not treated as social and psychological beings.

The fourth group of parents displays unpredictable and dangerous changes in contingencies and arousal, for example, parents with bi-polar disorder or those who abuse substances. The changes can be between negative and positive affect, one negative affect and another, low and high arousal, submissiveness and vindictiveness, or awareness of the child and lack of awareness. Such changes place excessive demands upon children to adapt to the parent's state. In some cases, the parents feel so threatened themselves that there is simply no place in the family priorities for one or more of the children.

In all four subgroups, the triggers to parental action are hypothesized to be primarily within and about the parent. Unlike incestuous abusers, however, these parents take too little account of the information from or about the child who, therefore, is largely missing, as a unique person, from the parent's DRs. In addition, parents distort their self-representation such that the self appears vulnerable, childlike, and blameless while over-estimating the child's competence or power. Often this is expressed semantically as statements regarding children's maturity (in the case of role-reversing children) or resistance to caregiving and guidance (in the case of oppositional or withdrawn children). In a sad irony of misunderstanding, parents' effort to protect the child from the parent's threatening experience denies the child essential information about causal relations, thus greatly harming the child's development. In addition, as the child's efforts to be cared for become more distorted, both parents and professionals become convinced that the child is either highly competent and resilient or irreparably damaged.

Child Outcomes. Children in these situations face the problem that their state neither triggers parental protection, nor does the parent adapt to their characteristics or developmental needs. Moreover, their self-protective strategy both distorts their own development and maintains the distorted family process.

Although many children respond to parental withdrawal with compulsive caregiving, others rebel or themselves withdraw. There is particular risk for the siblings of successful role-reversing children in that, once the protective function is fulfilled by one child, other children may have fewer possibilities for organizing a successful strategy. Thus some children within a family may organize compulsively, others coercively, and others may settle into non-strategic depression (Jean-Gilles & Crittenden, 1990).

In triangulated families, cross-generational relationships may be established in which the child colludes with one parent to demean or expel the other. In some cases, the child concurrently attempts to seduce the opposite gender parent, often with sexualized behavior. This weakens the marriage further and leaves adolescent children angry, confused, and unable to extricate themselves from their childhood family. The outcomes are various forms of the coercive strategy: in childhood, psychosomatic distress and passive risk-taking; in adolescence, severe disorders such as eating and conduct disorders; in the transition to adulthood, full-fledged personality disorders, that is, stuck forms of passive resistance.

Children of disoriented parents cannot soothe the parent, nor will the parent fight with them, nor are they used by the parent. Indeed, they cannot elicit contingent responses from the parents at all. Even explosive coercive displays do not engage the parent. Trying to coerce a disoriented parent is like trying to wrestle with fog. That is, nothing the child does connects (or relates) them to the parent. Instead, the children are treated with benign irrelevance, rather like the way one absently pats a pet. Lack of contingency and shared affect drives humans crazy. These children retreat to internal worlds of self-generated contingencies and private affective states – that increase their isolation. Such children use a failed form of the preschool Type C strategy and often have autistic characteristics. Without contingent and affectively attuned responses (even anger is contingent and attuned and, therefore, strategically useful to children), children lack the basic inputs needed for development.

Children from mood-dysfunctional families sometimes become "co-dependent" or "enablers" as they try to accommodate their parents' changing needs for protection and comfort. For example, when the parent is aroused and angry, the child may behave with compliance or submission, but when the parent is frightened or anxious, the child may take charge and manage the household, siblings (as a "parental" child), and even the parent (i.e., role reversing). A/C combinations are frequent, combining an array of useful substrategies.

When children are unable to find any strategy that elicits attention from their parents, they are at risk for psychological withdrawal, escape into a world of fantasy, and depression. Children in these families are at risk for somatization, problems with self-identity, and depression; in extreme cases, there may be risk of suicidal thought, threats, and action. Although children in this cluster cannot easily discern them, real conditions still motivate parental behavior. This is less true of the clusters described below.

The sections below describe parental behavior that is associated more nearly with parents' psychiatric disorder than maltreatment. In information processing terms, this means more transformations that are more likely to include erroneous and false information. The literature in this area is less developed, both empirically and conceptually. Instead, the studies that exist can be characterized as "variable research" in which parent diagnoses are correlated with child variables without clear understanding of the causal relations among them. In the sections below, functionally similar conditions are clustered and described in terms of representational processes and the probable effect of these on children. The following sections, therefore, constitute the beginnings of an agenda for further research.

Distortions that Substitute Delusional Information for Accurate Information

(5) Type A: Parents Who Misconstrue Powerful Forces as Threatening Both Themselves and Their Children, Thus Responding with Irrational Protective Measures. Parents who fear danger in irrational ways combine many of the distortions described above and add to them one crucial transformation. Because they rely on erroneous information generated in early childhood during exposure to danger, these parents are confused about the current presence and source of danger. Because the threat was – and is – not real, it cannot be disarmed; consequently, the parents' efforts to protect themselves and their children cannot – and do not – relieve their perception of threat. Such parents take repeated extreme and irrational protective measures (e.g., repetitive actions, excessive cleansing, bizarre forms of punishment) on behalf of themselves and their children.

Such behavior appears to be the developmental outcome of a childhood history of severe neglect, often combined with gratuitous and uncontrollable abuse. Many of these adults had no committed caregiver early in life to provide structure or offer comfort when they could not yet manage this themselves. Superstitious behavior may have created the perception of control. In adulthood, the parent's fears are at least semi-delusional (in that they are self-generated and violate boundaries of time and space), and their attempts at self- and child-protection are often desperate and dangerous (Salmon, Abel, Cordingley, Friedman, & Appleby, 2003). Many of these parents have psychiatric diagnoses such as severe personality disorder, bi-polar disorder, schizophrenia, and major depression. Dysregulated arousal is common to these.

There is a wide array of organizations of delusionally threatened parents. A few are described here, but the list is not exhaustive. They include parents who:

(1) Shame children for normal feelings and behavior through semantic belief systems (including religious beliefs) that denigrate feelings and/or find humans to be inherently sinful (for example, diapering older children, putting derogatory signs on children);

(2) Engage in compulsive rituals (intended to protect the self or child) while neglecting basic life needs of the child;

(3) Apply semantic rules that forbid essential protective action (for example, using faith-based rituals instead of medical care);

(4) Apply semantic rules that require punishment in ways that threaten children's survival (such as confinement, extreme fasting, etc.).

Parental Behavior and DRs. Many adults who have delusions faced frequent, severe, and unpredictable childhood threats, leading the child to associate many ordinary conditions with threat. For example, being alone or going out alone are normal and safe conditions, spilling or soiling are ordinary, not knowing what will happen next occurs frequently without dangerous consequences, etc. For adults who have been abandoned, had numerous placements in care, been punished for drawing attention to themselves, or left uncertain that basic life needs would be met, these ordinary conditions may instigate extreme self-protective behavior. That is, there was once actual threat, but the adult has not discriminated between threatening and non-threatening aspects of the past situation; all are responded to as if they were threatening. Moreover, because the threat is experienced preconsciously, the rationale for behavior cannot easily be discovered by, nor communicated adequately to, others, thus making it difficult to correct.

Compared to parents in cluster 3 who distort and substitute affectionate feelings, parents in cluster 5 focus almost exclusively on the bad aspects of themselves and their children. In addition, they show punctilious reliance on external authority that can lead to dangerously inappropriate application of rules. Often they rocket between extremely low arousal (e.g., depression, excessive tiredness, and suicidality) and excessively high and non-strategic arousal (e.g., inappropriate sexuality, self-injury, and manic states). Their behavior includes preoccupation with illusory self-protective schema in agitated states and isolating withdrawal in depressed states such that children's basic care may be overlooked. In addition, these parents have a tendency to see their progeny as an extension of self and, therefore, marred or vulnerable as is the self. As a consequence, they may humiliate, abuse, or ritualistically cleanse their children (Kelley, 1996).

In adulthood, parents in this cluster have severe problems with intimate relationships including both isolation from normal social support and inordinate reliance on strangers and organizations. This exposes them to risks of intimacy with potentially dangerous people (for example, promiscuous sex) and excessive reliance on delusional people (e.g., religious cults). They are particularly vulnerable to authorities that prophesy dire outcomes and require painful sorts of propitiation because these are consonant with their childhood experience.

The death of Victoria Climbié (Laming, Crown report, 2003) illustrates many of the issues. At age eight, Victoria was taken from Africa to England by her great-aunt to be educated. However, she was frequently absent from school because of incontinence and illness. Indeed, she was admitted to hospital and brought to social services' attention several times. Nevertheless, everyone found her engaging, "a ray of sunshine" (p. 41), and having "the most beautiful smile that lit up a room" (p. 11). Her demeanor and verbal denials of abuse were such that the physical evidence of her injured and wasting body were disregarded. As the great-aunt's boyfriend said in court, "You could beat her and she wouldn't cry... she could take the beatings and pain like anything" (p. 11). The great-aunt had asked for help (claiming the boyfriend sexually abused Victoria) from the childminder, protective services, and the church. Only the church responded, saying that Victoria was a "wicked girl" (p. 28) and "possessed by an evil spirit" (p. 42); the pastor offered prayers "for deliverance from witchcraft, bad luck and everything bad or evil" (p. 46). Victoria died of organ failure consequent to at least 128 injuries and severe neglect, including sleeping each night enclosed in a black plastic bag containing her urine and feces. Her great-aunt and the boyfriend were convicted of murder.

What were they thinking of?! How could the great-aunt both seek to educate Victoria, ask for help, warn of sexual abuse, and seek spiritual guidance and also participate in criminal abuse and neglect? How could Victoria be so appealing and also an incontinent evil spirit who needed isolation and punishment? The photos of Victoria are haunting. They show her dressed well, with matching hair ribbons, and having a huge smile, very bright but unfocused eyes, and arms stuck stiffly to the sides of her body. In the words of the Crown report "some important tell-tale sign has been missed" (p. 11).

The signs are in the report, but their meaning was misinterpreted. The discrepancy between events and Victoria's affect openly amazed many people, but was not considered a warning sign. Even the Inquiry Report itself does not suggest that this little girl who "twirled" in the hospital corridors (p. 11) might be suffering at that moment and hiding her true feelings under the guise of false positive affect. But how could a little girl, taken from her family, be happy, even joyful – especially when in hospital? Why would strangers see happiness whereas her great-aunt saw a wicked, devil-possessed incontinent monster? Is it possible that Victoria used the extreme compulsive behavior typical of maltreated and orphaned children? That is, was she compulsively compliant with her caregivers (inhibiting even expression of pain) and promiscuously friendly with strangers? Both displays are based on fear as a motivating internal state, fear of abuse in the first case and fear of abandonment in the latter. It may be that only Victoria's body could tell the truth.

When we try to understand the great-aunt, we are faced with the contrast between good intentions and heinous child abuse. Splits between semantic beliefs and behavior can be understood if the aunt, too, felt overwhelmingly frightened and had been traumatized. Her extreme religiosity suggests an intense need to do the right thing – as defined by external authority. The boyfriend fits the step-parent role in incest. But nothing is known about these substitute parents.

A similar case in Canada throws light on the parents' experience. For 13 years, an aunt who adopted her two orphaned nephews caged and tethered them, diapering and beating them to prevent their soiling and punishing disruptively "unmanageable" behavior. At school, the boys were withdrawn, obedient, and academically accomplished; after school, even into their teens, they returned home to the cage and diapers. Understanding the adoptive mother's behavior requires understanding her developmental history. As a child, she had been severely abused such that she sustained permanent physical injuries. The abuse continued in her marriage to a man whose anger elicited such fear that she engaged in protective rituals (both truly protective and irrationally protective, but in both cases compulsive). In adulthood, she was diagnosed with (1) PTSD (i.e., a psychological disorder of dismissing from awareness some aspects of past threat while retaining excessively other aspects) and (2) chronic physical pain from past injuries (Wente, 2004). The role of current pain in keeping past threat perceptually present is important as is her daily experience of fear of her husband. The adoptive mother's DR is likely to be one of unresolved trauma within a compulsive A strategy. Equally confirming of the rationale offered here is the response of the boys. Once rescued and given psychological treatment, the two adolescent boys were able in court to forgive their adoptive mother (Wente, 2004).

The trigger for such parental behavior does not include an accurate representation of the child. Instead, the representation is highly distorted and infused with personal, idiosyncratic meaning. It should be noted that the characteristics are given threatening meanings by the parent; that is, the child is not abnormal. In sum, these parents act with intention, believing they are doing the right thing. Their responses range from irrationally reasoned by the parent, to reliance on external authority, to privately accessible instructions that cannot be challenged by others (for example, delusional voices). Long periods between instances of danger reinforce the compulsive rituals whereas intermittent danger confirms the need for the "protective" measures. Thus, errors are rarely corrected and risk escalates.

Outcomes to Children. The outcomes to children of these very serious forms of inadequate parenting consist of more symptoms and more serious symptoms than more ordinary abuse, neglect, or sexual abuse as well as misleading symptoms (Burke, 2003; Waterman et al., 1993; Young et al., 1991). When children cannot see or make meaning of parents' endangering behavior, they feel confused and threatened. Children need adequate (for their age and intelligence) explanations for what parents do. That is, they need DRs in each relevant memory system that can enable them to predict, in self-relevant ways, what their parent is likely to do and how that may affect them. Furthermore, when parents define children as flawed, children find it almost impossible to develop a responsible, empathic, and integrated self-representation. It should be noted, however, that when parents' behavior becomes blatantly irrational (especially when other adults clarify that the parent is mentally ill), children are able to define the parent as crazy or mentally ill and to protect themselves psychologically. This, however, is not a full resolution of the problem because it does not address (a) children's lack of safety and comfort, (b) the role-reversing quality of asking children to empathize with and forgive inappropriate parental behavior when no one has first understood their perspective, and (c) the void in the construction of self left by parents who cannot organize caregiving behavior around children's signals.

It should be made clear that parents in all the clusters described above love their children and express it in ways that children recognize. Were this not the case, it would be much easier for children to protect themselves from their parents' endangering behavior. The complexity of parents' dispositional representations is, in other words, a problem for their children. It is less apparent that the parents in the final cluster love their children in a meaningful way.

(6) Type C and Dp A± DX [Negative Affect]: Parents Who Miscon-strue the Child as the Source of Threat, Thus Attacking, Abandoning, or Even Killing the Child. This section is the most speculative of the sections in this chapter. Little research exists and sound research designs are almost impossible to implement. Nevertheless, it is proposed that parents who endanger the lives of their children in systematic or apparently inten-tional ways differ greatly from parents whose motivation is to protect the child, protect the self, or even correct/purify the child (Gelles, 1991). These parents are confused about the source of the danger and consider the child to be a threat. Therefore, they take extreme measures to protect themselves, including repeated sadistic abuse, infanticide, and murder, sometimes in the form of sui-cide/murder. These parents sometimes have severe psychiatric diagnoses, for example, bi-polar disorder, borderline personality disorder, psychotic depres-sion, schizophrenia, and/or psychopathy (Howard & Hannam, 2003). Many, however, are undiagnosed and do not easily fit within current diagnostic sys-tems. Nevertheless, they have in common that they actively endanger their children because they perceive the child as a threat or because they see no solutions to problems. Several sorts of behavior are included:

(1) Terrorizing and deceptive aggression to, or fearful withdrawal from, children resulting from over-estimation of threat to themselves and confusion of their child with the source of threat;
(2) Forbidden acts, such as sexual abuse, followed by overwhelming feelings of shame associated with the child victim, who, therefore, must be destroyed;
(3) Murder of children who are perceived by the parent as threatening the parents' survival (e.g., some infanticide, killing of unwanted children, killing of children who jeopardize parents' safety);
(4) Murder (usually combined with suicide) intended to save the child from the unending misery that the parent perceives in life.

Parental Behavior and DRs

These parents humiliate, attack abusively, and sometimes murder their chil-dren. Sometimes this is preceded by abuse or neglect; in other cases, murderous acts seem to appear with no forewarning. Because psychological maltreatment deceives children about causal relations, associates children's comfort-seeking with humiliation and shame, or misconstrues children as powerfully malevolent, it robs children of the ability to make sense of experience and of their contribution to outcomes. As with the examples in cluster 5, little systematic research exists although individual cases are uncovered occasionally and capture public attention.

Crucial to understanding the parents' perception of extreme threat associated with the child is their sense of having no protector for themselves and of being abandoned by people who could support them. This perception is usually both accurate and also exaggerated. For example, in cases of infanticide, the mother almost always experienced the pain and fear of childbirth completely alone. Frequently this occurred because the pregnancy was hidden or denied because the father or the mother's parents would reject the mother were they to know she was pregnant. The distortion is the mother's avoidance of everyone, even medical personnel (Crittenden & Craig, 1990). The DRs of mothers who kill their children reflect their desperation and belief that there is no possibility of help (Milgrom & Beatrice, 2003).

Two cases of child homicide illustrate the two subtypes (Type C and Dp A+ DX[negative affect]) in this cluster. In 1994 Susan Smith fastened her two preschool-aged boys into the car, then pushed it down a slope into a lake where the boys drown. She then claimed they were kidnapped and, for a week, together with her estranged husband, gave tearful interviews to the media while the police searched for the supposed kidnapper. When the sunken car was discovered, Ms. Smith was accused (and later convicted) of murder. Ms. Smith was depressed and had recently received a letter from her boyfriend breaking off their relationship in part because he did not want to raise another man's children (Meyer & Oberman, 2001). It is noteworthy that her mother's infidelity had triggered her father's sexualized revenge suicide and her brother had died similarly. Susan herself was known for precocious sexual activity and was chosen as the "Friendliest Female" in high school. The issues of seduction, revenge, deception, and sexuality stand out starkly against a background of failed protection. In a desperate and deceptive bid to be protected by a man, Ms. Smith may have sacrificed her children to win back her husband or retain her lover.

The oscillation between depression and intense arousal in a compulsive A strategy is exemplified by Andrea Yates. Mrs. Yates methodically drowned her five young sons in the family bathtub, then called the police and confessed, making no effort to defend or protect herself. She later explained that she believed she was possessed by the devil. Mrs. Yates had been treated for recurrent post-partum depression that included a previous suicide attempt and psychotic breaks. Because her husband's religious beliefs required it, she continued to have babies against her will at approximately 18-month intervals. Her husband's beliefs also required home schooling of the children such that she was never free of them. In spite of her chronic depression and expanding family, family photos show all members, including Andrea, with huge, toothy smiles, wide enough to crack one's cheeks. After the deaths, Andrea had several psychotic episodes and threatened suicide. The elements of false positive affect, obligation to obey, severe depression, and religiosity coalesced to enable a parent to believe that her children must be killed. On the surface, she explained it as protection of the children from herself. Functionally, however, the deaths served to free her from both her existing children and the possibility of having to bear future children. Protection of self and progeny were in such conflict that Andrea's short-term self-protective action defeated the ultimate function of protecting one's genetic future.

These cases differ from those in cluster 5 in that they are not predicated upon a semantic parenting strategy that is systematically implemented over a long period of time. To the contrary, the dangerous behavior of cluster 6 parents is unique to one or a few specific occasions in which some aspect of short-term, immediate protection overwhelms long-term, ultimate goals. Moreover, these parents know they are doing the wrong thing. Depending upon their underlying strategic organization, they try to deceive others about it (Type C) or willingly submit to punishment (Type A). The risk for such behavior is continuously present in the sense that parents act on some immediate and unpredictable threat, albeit self-perceived, which triggers their dangerous behavior. Knowing the nature of that threat could help to protect both parents and their children. Possibly, for Andrea, the danger increased as her youngest child approached six months of age – the time when she should soon become pregnant with the next child.

Outcomes to Children. Under such conditions, children find it difficult to organize adaptive self-protective strategies. Because the child's behavior is not the trigger that initiates parental threat, children cannot prevent or prepare for the parents' endangering behavior. That is, parents who mislead their children regarding danger and comfort or who falsely identify their children as a source of danger terrorize their children in ways that children cannot predict, control, or regulate. This can lead to depression and other serious forms of psychopathology. Physically, injury and even death are possible outcomes.

Conclusions and Clinical Implications

The function of theory is to span the gap between what we know and what we want to know. Clinically relevant theory is more systematic, comprehensive, and internally coherent than the case-specific clinical hypotheses while also being more differentiated and complex than a summation of empirical findings. It accounts for both structural similarities across clinical cases and also variation away from central tendency in empirical data.

This chapter set out to explain inappropriate parental behavior. In the process, it described how the mind generates dispositional representations and offered a conceptual structure for parental behavior, including (1) the use of causal contingency and affect to generate meaning and organize behavior, (2) the motivations underlying various forms of inadequate parenting, (3) parents' use of sexual behavior with children and children's use of sexual signals to attract too distant parents, and (4) the implications to children of parental inadequacy.

Many relevant topics have been omitted. Surely there are genetic relations between parent and child, child effects on parents, and reciprocal effects between parents and children. In an effort to maintain focus on the process of representation and its application to parental behavior in cases of inadequate caregiving, these topics have not been pursued.

Why Do Parents Engage in Harmful Forms of Caregiving?

The hypothesis that forms the basis for this chapter is that all parents seek to protect themselves, their children, and their reproductive opportunity. This is crucial because danger is a universal human experience; no life is free of it and successful reproduction requires surviving it (Bonanno, 2004). Survival does not, however, require comfort. If one must choose between anxious discomfort with a higher probability of survival and complacent comfort and the possibility of not recognizing or being unprepared for danger, the former seems more adaptive. Surely, our species seems genetically biased *toward* the anxiety disorders (Benjamin, Mller, Hamer, & Murphy, 1996), with the "comfort disorders" having no name – and no surviving representatives. Moreover, there is no response to danger (mental or behavioral) that is adaptive in all circumstances. Therefore, the ability to transform and even distort information to generate behavior suited to ever-changing and unpredictable conditions is essential to our species and to each individual – even if it causes psychological suffering in many cases and physical risk in a few cases.

Representing the Childrearing Context

Parents, like everyone else, generate representations from an integration of the self-in-the-present with aspects of the self-in-the-past. Representations, however, are always active neural processes, in the sense of being generated in the present (as opposed to being recalled from some mythical storage facility in the brain). That is, representing is a *verb*, an active *process* connecting self to context (and not a noun, a thing that can be kept over time). Multiple representations, each disposing the individual to some action, are produced concurrently by the human brain. The advantage of parallel processing is that a wide range of possible constructions of the situation can be brought forward rapidly. The limitation is that the elaboration of each parallel stream is only partial; therefore, each DR could be in error. When there is sufficient time, the array of DRs can be compared, contrasted, and integrated cortically to generate a best-fitting DR to guide the individual's behavior in the current circumstances. However, when danger is very near, "fast and frugal" processing (Gigerenzer, Todd, and the ABC Research Group, 1999) is safest; the drawback is increased error. Parents who have been exposed to danger often use rapid processing, thereby both carrying forward uncorrected error and engaging unnecessarily in risky self- and child-protective strategies. When the threat has been very great or very frequent or both, parents may have had little experience with reflection and, therefore, be unprepared, even under safe conditions, to reflect and reorganize their psychological processing and strategic behavior.

A Conceptual Model of Inadequate Childrearing

It is unfortunate that the child maltreatment literature is almost exclusively concerned about effects on children and often content to think of parents as "perpetrators" or "offenders." The criminal justice approach is even more skewed away from a psychological and systemic perspective. The literature on mentally ill adults, on the other hand, sees the same individuals not as parents, but rather as victims of disease conditions – thus, largely overlooking the risk experienced by patients' children.

Strangely, parental mental illness is rarely included as a form of maltreatment of children. Indeed, it is often considered an explanation or extenuating circumstance. More startling, the professionals who treat adults rarely express more than passing interest in the welfare of their patients' children. Nor do child psychotherapists routinely consider seriously enough the probability of disorder in the parents (Chronis et al., 2003; Schultz & Shaw, 2003). Nevertheless, children of parents with behavioral or psychiatric disorder must cope with an environment in which parents' dispositional state is (a) crucial to their physical and psychological safety, (b) highly variable, and (c) often misleading or inscrutable. This can wreak havoc with children's development.

One reason for these discrepancies lies in misunderstandings regarding appearance and reality. Most cases of child abuse and neglect (cluster 1) look like what they are. That is, the situation is dangerous, but visible, and the parents distort information, but only in moderate ways. This is easier to identify, easier to treat, and less damaging to children than the situations in clusters 2 and 3. Parents in clusters 2 and 3 split appearance and reality. When the children act out intensively, the parents look normal, but deviate in subtle or actively deceptive ways. We tend not to focus on the parents' contribution. The children's behavior should be our clue to look more closely. When children look happy and adjusted under severely negative conditions, that too should alert professionals that something is severely amiss. We tend not to recognize the severity of risk that these discrepant situations signal, often until it is too late to protect the children. Looking behind appearances is very difficult, but is necessary if we are to protect both children and their parents.

One of the goals of the theory offered in this chapter is to connect developmental processes across generations around the issue of protection in a manner that permits us think productively about parental motivation – without having to dehumanize troubled parents or to construct a different psychology, an abnormal psychology, for them. The outcome could be better coordination between child protection, child and adult psychiatry, and criminal justice in which issues of morality and punishment do not block understanding of the needs, experiences, and strategic attempts at resolution of both children and their parents.

Treatment

If we accept that inadequate parents, like all parents, organize around protection of self and progeny and that past exposure to danger affects current information processing, then what are the implications for intervention and treatment? This is not a chapter on treatment, but several implications follow directly from what has been offered here.

A. Formulating functional hypotheses (i.e., diagnostic formulations that focus on interpersonal processes rather than on symptoms) to guide treatment planning requires that one keep in mind that:
   1. Appearance is not reality. Obvious danger is often less worrisome and intractable than hidden danger. Watch out for happy children – who should not be happy. Watch out for innocuous parents with desperate children. Both discrepancies are misleading. Identifying that Victoria's smiles are false can not only save her life, but also permit her great-aunt

to be helpful to Victoria – as I believe she wanted to be. Recognizing that acting out and autistic-like children do this because they do not get meaningful responses – neither positive or negative – can help us to help both parent and child. But, of course, we must not accuse or blame the parent. That is threatening and they (like you and I) will fight.

2. Danger tends to be associated with Type A, compulsive A's. Uncertainty, threats and deception tend to be associated with Type C. But parent and child can and often do use opposite strategies – as do siblings. To be helpful, we must consider the entire family constellation.

3. The systemic and self-protective approach offered here makes clear that no one is to blame; everyone is trying to understand how to protect themselves and their children. If blame can be avoided, parents will not be distracted by having to defend themselves.

4. Child therapists should more carefully evaluate the psychological functioning of their patients' parents before drawing conclusions about or making treatment plans for the children. Adult therapists should consider very carefully the welfare of their patients' children.

B. Pre-conditions necessary to implement any treatment plan:

1. People who feel endangered cannot be expected to think reflectively, nor to trust anyone who further endangers them. So if there is real external danger (in the family, neighborhood, etc), it must be removed or the parent and child must be protected from it. We ourselves should avoid threatening parents because threat hijacks information processing and prevents integration. Knowing what threatens the parent can help us to avoid creating a source of threat. For sure, anything that shames, bullies and humiliates, or isolates parents from their children risks exacerbating their feeling of threat and promoting precisely the self-protective strategies that have already failed. This includes establishing too close a relationship with their child (one that excludes or shames them) and threatening to remove the children or send the parents to court/prison. Such acts threaten all parents. If we do these things, we must expect parents to define us as dangerous and to defend themselves from us.

2. To establish a connection to a threatened person, we must use nonjudgmental language. Behaviorally descriptive language works best. Our attributions of negative intent (abuse, fondle, etc.) put a wall of misunderstanding (that elicits anger or fear) between ourselves and parents. If, on the other hand, if we presume a protective function, we can often connect and then the parents will help us to discover how they arrived at their actual behavior. In that case, we might be able to be helpful to both parent and child.

Functional diagnosis and preparation for treatment should co-occur because a cooperative stance from professionals facilitates the diagnostic process and a functional diagnosis can alert professionals to less obvious forms of threat within the family.

C. Managing dispositional representations, that is, treatment strategies:

1. The Dynamic-Maturational Model focuses on competency. Parents arrive at treatment with competency using one or more strategies. These strategies not only help them in their lives (where they were developed), but also protect them from the threats of psychotherapy. Treated as strengths, they can be looked at openly and thought about. Treated as the source of the problem and a deficit, parents might prefer not to acknowledge them and, instead, use them to close the therapist out or engage the therapist collusively. Both patient and therapist can be misled into thinking either that the patient is resistant and refusing of therapy or that the problems are outside the patient.

2. Every strategy is the right solution to some problem. Our job is not to get rid of "bad" strategies, but to increase each person's repertoire of strategies and the specificity with they are applied to life's problems.

3. Treatments should be directed toward specific memory systems – with awareness of which systems parents and children are using and the ways in which they are distorted. For example, Type C individuals might benefit from behavioral techniques that create clear temporal and causal contingencies whereas Type A individuals might benefit from imaging techniques, especially somatic techniques, that raise awareness of inhibited feelings. We have the techniques already; we need only select them with greater precision.

4. If the Dynamic-Maturation Model is more or less accurate about the psychological organization of Types A, B, and C, then A and C are psychological opposites. In that case, they might need opposite forms of treatment. Moreover, the treatment that helped a Type A person, might augment the distortion of a Type C person. For example, behavioral strategies might harm a Type A individual and imaging strategies might augment the already exaggerated arousal of Type C individuals. It might matter very much that we understood the psychological and strategic organization of parents and chose our interventions with that in mind.

In conclusion, this is a speculative chapter that challenges current understanding and practice regarding parents whose behavior endangers their children. Nevertheless, the ideas that are offered are consistent with existing data – even though there are not data to affirm that this interpretation is correct. The question becomes: Is it true? Truth itself is elusive. True about the past, about the process that generated the inappropriate parental behavior? Truly predictive of future danger? True from the parents' perspective? The children's? Professionals'? True ethically or pragmatically? If pragmatically, for what purpose? To punish or to protect and reduce suffering? As was noted at the beginning of this chapter, the brain has not evolved to capture the past accurately; it is evolved to transform information from the past to predict the future.

The theory offered here is intended to offer professionals new ways to represent the experience of very endangered parents and children. It is hoped that this will enable us to protect both parents and children better. That is, the proper test of these ideas is whether or not their application increases the safety and comfort of children and their parents in the future.

References

Aber, L. & Zigler, E. (1981). Developmental considerations in the definition of child maltreatment. *New Directions for Child Development: Developmental Perspectives on Maltreatment, 11*, 1–30.

Ainsworth, M. D. S. (1979). Infant-mother attachment. *American Psychologist, 34*, 932–7.

Barbaree, H. E. (1991). Denial and minimizations among sex offenders: Assessment and treatment outcome. *Forum on Corrections Research, 3*, 30–3.

Baumrind, D. (1971). Current patterns of parental authority. *Developmental Psychology Monographs, 4*, 72.

Beck-Sander, A. (1995). Childhood abuse in adult offenders: The role of control in perpetuating cycles of abuse. *Journal of Forensic Psychiatry, 6*, 486–98.

Benjamin, J., Mller, C., Hamer, D., & Murphy, D. (1996). Association of anxiety-related traits with a polymorphism in the serotonin transporter gene regulatory region. *Science, 274*, 1527–30.

Bonanno, G. A. (2004). Loss, trauma, and human resilience: Have we underestimated the human capacity to thrive after extremely aversive events? *America Psychologist, 59*, 20–8.

Bowlby, J. (1969/1982). *Attachment and Loss: Volume I. Attachment.* New York: Basic Books.

Bowlby, J. (1973). *Attachment and Loss: Volume II. Separation.* New York: Basic Books.

Bowlby, J. (1980). *Attachment and Loss: Volume III. Loss.* New York: Basic Books.

Bumpy, K. & Hansen, J. D. (1997). Intimacy deficits, fear of intimacy, and loneliness among sex offenders. *Criminal Justice and Behavior, 24*, 315–31.

Burke, L. (2003). The impact of maternal depression on familial relationships. *International Review of Psychiatry, 15*, 243–55.

Chronis, A. M., Lahey, B. B., Pelman, W. E., Kipp, H. L., Baumann, B. L., & Lee, S. (2003). Psychopathology and substance abuse in parents of young children with attention-deficit/hyperactivity disorder. *Journal of the American Academy of Child and Adolescent Psychiatry, 42*, 1424–32.

Crittenden, P. M. (1992). Quality of attachment in the preschool years. *Development and Psychopathology, 4*, 209–41.

Crittenden, P. M. (1995). Attachment and psychopathology. In S. Goldberg, R. Muir, & J. Kerr (Eds.), *John Bowlby's Attachment Theory: Historical, Clinical, and Social Significance.* New York: The Analytic Press, pp. 367–406.

Crittenden, P. M. (1996). Research on maltreating families: Implications for intervention. In J. Briere, L. Berliner, J. Bulkey, C. Jenny, & T. Reid (Eds.), *APSAC Handbook on Child Maltreatment.* Thousand Oaks, CA: Sage, pp. 158–74.

Crittenden, P. M. (1997a). Patterns of attachment and sexuality: Risk of dysfunction versus opportunity for creative integration. In L. Atkinson & K. J. Zuckerman (Eds.) *Attachment and Psychopathology.* New York: Guilford Press, pp. 47–93.

Crittenden, P. M. (1997b). Toward an integrative theory of trauma: A dynamic-maturational approach. In D. Cicchetti & S. Toth (Eds.), *The Rochester Symposium on Developmental Psychopathology, Vol. 10. Risk, Trauma, and Mental Processes.* Rochester, NY: University of Rochester Press, pp. 34–84.

Crittenden, P. M. (1998). Dangerous behavior and dangerous contexts: A thirty-five year perspective on research on the developmental effects of child physical abuse. In P. Trickett (Ed.). *Violence to Children.* Washington, D.C.: American Psychological Association, pp. 11–38.

Crittenden, P. M. (2000). A dynamic-maturational exploration of the meaning of security and adaptation: Empirical, cultural, and theoretical considerations. In P. M. Crittenden & A. H. Claussen (Eds.), *The Organization of Attachment Relationships: Maturation, Culture, and Context.* New York: Cambridge University Press, pp. 358–84.

Crittenden, P. M. (2002). Attachment theory, information processing, and psychiatric disorder. *World Journal of Psychiatry, 1*, 72–5.

Crittenden, P. M. (2005). The origins of physical punishment: An ethological/attachment perspective on the use of punishment by human parents. In M. Donnelly & M. A. Strauss (Eds.), *Corporal Punishment of Children in Theoretical Perspective.* New Haven: Yale University Press, pp. 73–90.

Crittenden, P. M. & Claussen, A. H. (1993). Severity of maltreatment: Assessment and policy implications. In C. J. Hobbes & J. M. Wynne (Eds.), *Bailliere's Clinical Paediatrics: International Practice and Research.* London: Bailliere Tindall, pp. 87–100.

Crittenden, P. M. & Craig, S. (1990). Developmental trends in child homicide. *Journal of Interpersonal Violence, 5*, 202–16.

Crittenden, P. M., Lang, C., Claussen, A. H., & Partridge, M. F. (2000). Relations among mothers' procedural, semantic, and episodic internal representational models of parenting. In P. M. Crittenden & A. H. Claussen (Eds.), *The Organization of Attachment Relationships: Maturation, Culture, and Context.* New York: Cambridge University Press, pp. 214–33.

Damasio, A. R. (1994). *Descartes' Error: Emotion, Reason, and the Human Brain.* New York: Avon Books.

Damascio, A. R. (1999). *The Feeling of What Happens; Body and Emotion in the Making of Consciousness.* Fort Worth, TX; Harcourt College Publishers.

Damasio, A. (2003). *Looking for Spinoza: Joy, Sorrow, and the Feeling Brain.* New York: Harcourt Inc.

Dawkins, R. (1976). *The Selfish Gene.* New York: Oxford Press.

Dobash, R. P., Dobash, R. E., Wilson, M., & Daly, M. (1992). The myth of sexual symmetry in marital violence. *Social Problems, 39,* 71–91.

Duane, Y., Carr, A., Cherry, J., MacGrath, K., & O'Shea, D. (2003). Profiles of the parents of adolescent CSA perpetrators attending a voluntary outpatient treatment program in Ireland. *Child Abuse Review, 12,* 5–24.

Fisher, D., Beech, A., & Brown, K. (1998). Locus of control and its relationship to treatment change and abuse history in child sexual abuse. *Legal and Criminological Psychology, 42,* 141–8.

Fivush, R. & Hamond, N. R. (1990). Autobiographical memory across the preschool years: Toward reconceptualizing childhood amnesia. In R. Fivush & J. A. Hudson (Eds.), *Knowing and Remembering in Young Children.* New York: Cambridge University Press, pp. 223–48.

Garlick, Y., Marshall, W. L., & Thornton, D. (1996). Intimacy deficits and attribution of blame among sexual offenders. *Legal and Criminological Psychology, 1,* 251–8.

George, C. & Solomon, J. (1999). Attachment and caregiving: The caregiving behavioral system. In J. Cassidy & P. R. Shaver (Eds.), *Handbook of Attachment: Theory, Research, and Clinical Applications.* New York: Guildford Press, pp. 649–70.

Gelles, R. J. (1991). Physical violence, child abuse, and child homicide: A continuum of violence, or distinct behaviors? *Human Nature, 2,* 1991, 59–72.

Gigerenzer, G., Todd, P. M., & the ABC Research Group (1999). *Simple Hurestics That Make Us Smart.* New York: Oxford University Press.

Gregory, R. (1998). Snapshots from a decade of the brain: Brainy mind. *British Medical Journal, 317,* 1693–5.

Haapasalo, J., Puupponen, M., & Crittenden, P. M. (1999). Victim to victimizer: The psychology of isomorphism in a case of a recidivist pedophile. *Journal of Child Sexual Abuse, 7,* 97–115.

Herman, J. L. (1992). *Trauma and Recovery.* New York: Basic Books.

Holden, G. W. & Zambarano, R. J. (1992). Passing the rod: Similarities between parents and their children in orientations toward physical punishment. In I. E. Sigel, A. V. McGillicuddy-DeLisi, & J. J. Goognow (Eds.), *Parental Belief Systems: The Psychological Consequences for Children.* Hillsdale, NJ: Erlbaum, pp. 143–72.

Howard, L. M. & Hannam, S. (2003). Sudden infant death syndrome and psychiatric disorders. *British Journal of Psychiatry, 182,* 379–80.

Hunter, J. A., Figueredo, A. J., Malamuth, N. M., & Becker, J. V. (2003). Juvenile sex offenders: Toward the development of a typology. *Sexual Abuse: Journal of Research and Treatment, 15,* 27–48.

Jean-Gilles, M. & Crittenden, P. M. (1990). Maltreating families: A look at siblings. *Family Relations, 39,* 323–9.

Kelley, S. J. (1996). Ritualistic abuse of children. In J. Briere, L. Berliner, J. Bulkey, C. Jenny, & T. Reid (Eds.), *APSAC Handbook on Child Maltreatment.* Thousand Oaks, CA: Sage, pp. 90–9.

Kolko, D. J. (1996). Child physical abuse. In J. Briere, L. Berliner, J. Bulkey, C. Jenny, & T. Reid (Eds.), *APSAC Handbook on Child Maltreatment.* Thousand Oaks, CA: Sage, pp. 21–50.

Laming, Lord. (2003). The Victoria Climbié inquiry: Presented to Parliament by the Secretary of State for Health and the Secretary of State for the Home Department by Command of Her Majesty. London: Crown Copyright.

Le Doux, J. E. (1994). Emotion, memory, and the brain: Neural routes underlying the formation of memories about primitive emotional experiences, such as fear, have been traced. *Scientific American,* June, 50–7.

Levant, M. & Bass, B. (1991). Parental identification of rapists and pedophiles. *Psychological Reports, 69,* 463–6.

Maletzky, B. M. (1991). *Treating the Sexual Offender.* Newbury Park, CA: Sage.

Marsa, F., O'Reilly, G., Carr, A., Murphy, P., O'Sullivan, M., Cotter, A., & Hevey, D. (2004). Attachment styles and psychological profiles of child sex offenders in Ireland. *Journal of Interpersonal Violence, 19,* 228–51.

Meyer, C. & Oberman, M. (2001). *Mothers Who Kill Their Children: Understanding the Acts of Moms from Susan Smith to the "Prom Mom."* New York: New York University Press.

Milgrom, J. & Beatrice, G. (2003). Coping with the stress of motherhood: Cognitive and defense style of women with post-natal depression. *Stress & Health, 19,* 281–7.

Murphy, W. D. & Smith, T. A. (1996). Sex offenders against children: Empirical and clinical issues. In J. Briere, L. Berliner, J. Bulkey, C. Jenny, & T. Reid (Eds.), *APSAC Handbook on Child Maltreatment.* Thousand Oaks, CA: Sage, pp. 175–92.

Noll, J. G., Horowitz, L. A., Bonanno, G., Trickett, P. K., & Putnam, F. W. (2003b). Revictimization and self-harm in adolescent and young adult females who experienced childhood sexual abuse. *Journal of Interpersonal Violence, 18(12),* 1452–71.

Noll, J. G., Trickett, P. K., & Putnam, F. W. (2003a). A prospective investigation of the impact of childhood sexual abuse on the development of sexuality. *Journal of Consulting and Clinical Psychology, 71(3),* 575–86.

O'Halloran, M., Carr, A., O'Reilly, G., Sherrin, D., Cherry, J., Turner, R., et al. (2002). Psychological profiles of sexually abusive adolescents in Ireland. *Child Abuse and Neglect, 26,* 349–70.

Pavlov, I. P. (1928). *Lectures on Conditioned Reflexes: The Higher Nervous Activity of Animals.* (Vol. 1, H. Ganett, Trans.) London: Lawrence & Wishart.

Russell, D. E. H. (1986). *The Secret Trauma: Incest in the Lives of Girls and Women.* New York: Basic Books.

Salmon, M., Abel, K., Cordingley, L., Friedman, T., & Appleby, L. (2003). Clinical and parenting skills outcomes following joint mother-baby psychiatric admission. *Australian & New Zealand Journal of Psychiatry, 37,* 556–62.

Salter, D., McMillan, D., Richards, M., Talbot, T., Hodges, J. Bentovim, A., Hastings, R., Stevenson, J., & Skuse, D. (2003). Development of sexually abusive behavior in sexually victimized males: A longitudinal study. *Lancet, 361,* 471–6.

Schacter, D. L. (1996). *Searching for Memory: The Brain, the Mind, and the Past.* New York: Basic Books.

Schacter, D. L. & Tulving, E. (1994). What are the memory systems of 1994? In D. L. Schacter & E. Tulving (Eds.), *Memory Systems 1994.* Cambridge, MA: Bradford, pp. 1–38.

Schmahmann, J. D. (Ed.) (1997). *The Cerebellum and Cognition*. New York: Academic Press.

Schultz, D. & Shaw, D. S. (2003). Boys' maladaptive social information processing, family emotional climate, and pathways to early conduct problems. *Social Development, 12*, 440–60.

Selye, H. (1976). *The Stress of Life*. New York: McGraw-Hill.

Shine, J., McClosky, H., & Newton, M. (2002). Self-esteem and sex offending. *Journal of Sexual Aggression, 8*, 51–61.

Skinner, B. F. (1938). *The Behavior of Organisms*. New York: Appelton-Century-Crofts.

Smallbone, S. & Dadds, M. (1998). Childhood attachment and adult attacment in incarcerated adult male sex offenders. *Journal of Interpersonal Violence, 13*, 555–73.

Smallbone, S. & Dadds, M. (2000). Attachment and coercive sexual behavior. *Sexual Abuse: A Journal of Research and Treatment, 12*, 3–15.

Starzyk, K. B. & Marshall, W. L. (2003). Childhood family and personological risk factors for sexual offending. *Aggression & Violent Behavior, 8*, 93–105.

Trickett, P. K., Noll, J. G., Reiffman, A., & Putnam, F. W. (2001). Variants of intrafamilial sexual abuse experience: Implications for long term development. *Journal of Development and Psychopathology, 13(4)*, 1001–19.

Tulving, E. (1979). Memory research: What kind of progress? In L. G. Nilsson (Ed.), *Perspectives on Memory Research: Essays in Honor of Uppsala University's 500th Anniversary*. Hillsdale, NJ: Erlbaum, pp. 19–34.

Tulving, E. (1987). Multiple memory systems and consciousness. *Human Neurobiology, 6*, 67–80.

van IJzendoorn, M. (1995). Adult attachment representations, parental responsiveness, and infant attachment: A meta-analysis on the predictive validity of the Adult Attachment Interview. *Psychological Bulletin, 117*, 387–403.

Veneziano, C. & Veneziano, L. (2002). Adolescent sex offenders: A review of the literature. *Trauma Violence and Abuse, 3*, 246–60.

Waterman, J., Kelley, R. J., McCord, J., & Oliveri, M. K. (Eds.). (1993). *Behind Playground Walls: Sexual Abuse in Day Care*. New York: Guilford.

Wente, M. (2004). The Blackstock secret: Anger greets sentence for couple who caged two boys. *The Globe and Mail*, Toronto, July 6, 2004.

Wilson, M. & Daly, M. (1992). The man who mistook his wife for a chattel. In J. H. Barkow, L. Cosmides, & J. Tooby, (Eds.), *The Adapted Mind: Evolutionary Psychology and the Generation of Culture*. London: Oxford University Press, pp. 289–322.

Wilson, M. & Daly, M. (1996). Violence against step-children. *Current Directions in Psychological Science, 5*, 77–81.

Young, W. C., Sachs, R. G., Braun, B. G., & Watkins, R. T. (1991). Patients reporting ritual abuse in childhood: A clinical syndrome: Report of 37 cases. *Child Abuse & Neglect, 15*, 181–9.

Index

AAI. *See* Adult Attachment Interview
abandonment, 253, 421
ABC patterns of attachment, 399–401
Abelin, E. L., 356
Aber, J. L., 10, 42, 47, 48, 54, 66, 69, 158, 212
abuse, 6, 277, 278, 339, 340, 388. *See also*
    child abuse; child homicide; sexual
    abuse; Smith, Susan; Yates, Andrea
    Canadian case of, 419–420
    Climbié's, 418–419
    parental, 88, 277, 340, 388, 406, 408–410
    spousal, 403
abusive parenting, 88, 340, 388
acceptance scales, 247
Ackerman, J., 309
adaptive parenting, 91
adolescence
    assessments in, 26
    attachment/caregiving system's
      differentiation in, 269
    case studies of, 329–343
    characteristics of, 231–232
    developmental tasks of late, 219, 226–229
    George on, 112
    intergenerational transmission of parenting
      during, 319
    mastery and, 320
    parent's experiences in, 319
    PRI-A and, 209
    themes in, 343
Adolescence Experiences Interview, 329
adolescent(s). *See also* Israeli/Jewish
    adolescent research project
    anger of, 415
    autonomy of, 211
    change of, 211

compliance of, 340
coping of, 219
dominance goals of, 89
father's ambivalence towards, 323
flexibility in parenting, 331
flooded/out of control, 283
incestuous fixations among, 320
increasing autonomy of, 211
independence demands of, 320
individuation/differentiation by, 219, 320
interactional modes with, 323
interviews with, 179, 319
intrapsychic separation of, 343
limits given to, 330
mothers of, 208
outcomes, 254
parenting representations of, 213
parents and, 88, 209, 211–213, 319, 320,
    324, 338
parent's representations of, 213
peer relationships of, 211, 321
as proxies, 323
research projects involving, 209
role-reversal of, 339, 340
self-definition of, 212, 219
self-image of, 211
separation-individuation of, 343
sexual/physical maturity of, 320, 343
siblings cared for by, 338
social realm of, 211
undervaluing parents by, 320
Adult Attachment Interview (AAI), 5, 6–8
    adapted PDI's similarity to, 51
    adult's assessed via, 7
    attachment studied with, 44, 180, 245
    autonomous secure parents and, 181

Adult Attachment Interview (AAI) (*cont.*)
  classifications used in, 44, 281
  coding of, 7, 24, 280
  construct of, 44
  details of, 6
  development of, 7
  E3 (living in the war zone) classification,
    284
  father's classifications on, 182
  individuals with dismissing, 181
  Israeli/Jewish adolescent research use of,
    221, 222
  IWMs and, 7
  Lack of Resolution in Mourning, 268
  Main's work on, 268
  mother's classifications, 116, 280
  mother's differentiating statements on, 280
  mother's representation of mothers and,
    152
  PAI's differences with, 45
  PAI's similarity to, 45
  PDI's similarity with, 47
  questions on, 6
  relationships assessed in, 42
  representations assessed by, 25, 45, 94
  scales, 7
  sexual abusers and, 409–410
  Strange Situation and, 7
  unresolved classifications of, 181, 265,
    290
adulthood, emerging, 219
adults. *See also* parent(s)
  AAI's assessing of, 7
  attachment, 94, 244, 267
  autonomous, 44
  autonomous-secure, 7, 180, 181
  avoidant, 244
  corrective parenting script of, 203
  dismissing, 7, 44, 94, 181
  DRs of, 398
  love relationships of, 68
  parents idealized by, 180
  preoccupied, 7, 44, 45–54, 94
  unresolved, 7, 44, 45
affect dysregulation, 276, 278
affection, 18, 19, 179, 192–194, 201
  sexualized, 409
affective attunement, 117–118
affective experience
  children's, 11
  parent's, 11
affective load, 6

affective mirroring, 121
affective organization, 113–119
affective tone scales, 125
  IFEEL categories and, 131
  WMCIs, 132
affects, negative, 116
African American(s)
  children, 54
  self-efficacy and, 83
aggression, 10, 287
agreeableness scales, 54
Ainsworth, Mary, 119, 185, 267, 268, 399. *See
    also* ABC patterns of attachment
alcoholism, 277
Allen, J. P., 231
AMBIANCE coding scheme, 12
Ammaniti, M., 21
amnesia, childhood, 200
anger
  adolescent's, 415
  blocked goals and, 117
  children's, 11
  coding, 64
  dysregulating, 286
  empowerment and, 65
  mother's, 49, 64
  parent's, 12, 49, 277
ANOVAs, 225
Antonioli, M. E., 21
anxiety
  disorder, 424
  high, 91
  maternal, 14–15
appearance, reality v., 426
arousal
  depression v., 422
  dysregulated, 417
  feelings and, 395
  self-, 394
  somatic, 394
Asian children, 54
assessments. *See also* Attachment Concerns
    and Close Relationships Questionnaire;
    Attachment Doll-Play Assessment;
    Attachment Story Completion Task;
    Child Behavior Checklist; Child Rearing
    Practice Report; Children's Apperception
    Test; Differentiation of Self Scale;
    Emotion-Focused Coping test;
    MacArthur Story Stem Battery; Mental
    Health Inventory; Mother Father Peers
    questionnaire; Parent-Child Early

Relational Assessment; Reynell
Developmental Language Scale;
Separation-Individuation Test of
Adolescence-SITA; story stem technique;
Three Boxes Procedure; Ways of Coping
test
adolescence, 26, 222
aspects of, 26–27
autonomy promotion, 25
doll play, 270, 271
emerging adulthood, 223
foster parent investment, 296
grandfather's, 242
monitoring of, 25
mother-child interaction, 56
parenting representations, 8–23, 26, 47,
210–211
relationship, 42
associative learning, 394
Atkinson, L., 93, 94, 117–118
at-risk families, 347
attachment(s), 5. *See also* attachment security;
Dynamic-Maturational Model; Parent
Attachment Interview; secure attachments
AAI and, 44, 180, 245
ABC patterns of, 399–401
adolescence and, 269
adult, 94, 244, 267, 290
affective processes in, 109
ambivalent, 15, 16
Bowlby's description of, 44
caregiving and, 244, 269
childrearing and, 253–254
children's, 12, 31, 209, 269
classifications of, 273, 275
compulsive patterns of, 410
concerns, 240, 244–246, 247–248, 250–252,
253–254
disorganized, 266–269, 376
disorganized-controlling, 267, 290
disruption of, 300
fathers and, 240, 244–246, 250–252, 253,
333
form of, 44
infants and, 13, 19, 45, 109, 120, 267, 268,
376
insecure-avoidance, 67
IWMs of, 44–46
maternal representations of, 17, 61, 210, 245
mental models of, 28
minimization/mobilization links with, 7,
94–97

mothers and, 210, 245
neurobiology of, 299
parental side of, 8, 9
patterns, 42, 265, 266, 399
relationships, 31, 113
RF and, 358
scales relevant to, 24
secure, 12, 13, 19, 109, 120, 209, 331
sexuality and, 392
son's representations of, 210
state of mind associated with, 7, 27
strategies, 4, 20
systems, 269–270
theory, 4
attachment approach
social cognitive approach differences with,
98
social cognitive approach similarities with,
97–98
attachment behavioral system, 27, 28. *See also*
behavioral processes; behavioral systems;
behaviors
caregiving behavioral system's connection
to, 244
safety regulating system as, 29
Attachment Concerns and Close Relationships
Questionnaire, 247–248
Attachment Doll-Play Assessment, 270
Attachment Q-Sort Security, 9, 46
Attachment Story Completion Task, 9, 46,
149, 156, 157, 161–162
attachment theory, 3, 41, 87, 150, 153
family behavior patterns and, 327
intergenerational transmission and, 325
lacuna in, 356
psychoanalytic conceptualizations and, 319
psychoanalytic theory and, 319, 358
real-life events and, 356
representation development and, 355–356
attribution(s)
accurate, 84
automatic, 90
benign, 131
emotional arousal and, 85
incorrect, 84
malevolent, 116
mother's, 125–126, 130
parent's, 84, 85, 86
styles of, 85
theory, 83–87
authoritarianism, 85, 88, 340
automatic cognition, 79, 89–97

autonomous-secure adults, 7, 180, 181
autonomy
  adolescent's increasing, 211
  adult, 44
  daughter's, 336
  foster mother's, 309
  mother's, 11, 14, 18, 20, 48, 220, 226
  promotion of, 25, 247
  son's, 220
  state of mind of, 325, 328

Bakersman-Kranenburg, M., 99, 269
Baltimore Study (Ainsworth), 185
Bandura, A., 82
Baron, M., 46, 210
Barton, M. L., 46
Bates, B., 309
Baumgartner, E., 21
behavioral processes, 116
behavioral systems, 5. *See also* attachment
    behavioral system; caregiving behavioral
    system
  coordination of, 5
  function of, 29
  IWMs of, 5–6, 42
behaviors
  causes of, 84
  child-protective, 405–406
  distortions emphasizing self-protective,
    408–416
  DRs and parental, 406–407, 408, 409–410,
    411, 413–414, 417–420, 421
  embedded interactive, 49
  family patterns of, 327
  foster children's maladaptive, 306
  gender-typed, 255
  maternal, 59, 61
  meanings that organize, 389
  mentally ill parent's, 390, 405
  mental models guiding, 63
  parent's emotion consistent, 116
  parent's irrational, 420
Belsky, J., 48, 49, 177, 178
Ben-Aaron, M., 168, 363, 379
Benoit, D., 15, 46, 117–118, 125, 141, 158,
    210, 213
Berger, B., 42, 47, 69
Biasatti, L. L., 246
Biederman, J., 93
biological dyads, 298, 300, 303
bipolar disorder, 413–414

Biringen, Z., 45, 112, 165
birth order, 62
Block, D., 326
Block, J. H., 241, 242, 252
body, fear's influence on, 117
Bogat, G. A., 17
Bonferroni adjustment, 229
Booth, C., 327
Bowlby, J., 5–6, 28, 31, 43–44, 201, 269, 345,
    355, 357
Bowlby's Theory, 5–6, 41, 65, 150
boys, 48
  comfort seeking behavior of, 62
  mothers of, 62
  mothers of girls v. mothers of, 59
Bradley, R., 298, 303
Braungart-Reiker, J. M., 122
Brazelton, T. B., 322, 323, 324
Bresgi, I., 42, 47, 69
Bretherton, I., 8, 28, 45, 46, 65, 158, 185, 213,
    244, 251, 255, 269, 334
Britton, R., 357
Brody, L., 93
Buck, M. J., 80, 241, 243
Bugental, D. B., 86, 89, 92, 99
Bugental's Parent Attribution test, 95
Button, S., 14, 51, 65, 164
Byng-Hall, J., 203, 327

Canada
  abuse case of, 419–420
  father study of, 180
Candelori, C., 21
caregiver(s). *See also* metapelet
  adolescent self as, 112
  alternative, 296
  biologically unrelated, 296
  children as, 30
  difficulty perceived by, 142
  father's capability as, 357
  infant signaling of, 111
  infant's relationship with primary, 109
  investment of, 17, 20, 27, 297, 298–299
  maternal v. non-maternal, 300, 302
  metacognitive monitoring capability of, 358
  multiple, 301
  "rejecting," 50
  representations, 21, 143–144, 297–298
caregiver investment, 17, 27, 297, 298–299
  child effects on, 303–305
  evolutionary perspective on, 298–299

influence of, 298
moderators of, 303
caregiving, 3, 5
adolescence and, 269
aspects of, 62
attachment reciprocal to, 244, 269
behavior systems model of, 109, 358
biology and, 298, 299
complexity of, 46
development of, 269
dysregulated, 287
incestuous, 411
intergenerational transmission of, 265
IWMs of, 3, 28, 29, 31–32
kibbutz and, 301
maternal positive, 56
mental models of, 164
negative emotions aroused in, 117–118
positive, 56
prenatal representations of, 17
sensitivity, 141
strategies for, 14
system, 269
caregiving behavioral system, 27, 28, 29,
    269–270
attachment behavior system's connection to,
    244
emotion's activation of, 110
parenting within, 31
unique role of, 112
Caregiving Interview (CI), 270, 280
caregiving representations, 27–28, 30, 31, 94
assessments, 96
conceptualization of, 266
mother's state of mind and, 224–226
past mediating effect of present in, 290
prenatal, 17
WMCI and, 96–97
care-receivers, 28, 30
Carter, A. S., 122
case studies. *See also* Israeli/Jewish adolescent
    research project; Israeli married men
    study; Israeli mother/children
    longitudinal study; Michigan Family
    Study; middle-class mother of
    kindergarten children study; Minnesota
    Longitudinal Attachment Study; National
    Institute of Child Health and Human
    Development Study of Early Child Care
adolescence, 329–343
Canadian father, 180

relational parent-child representations,
    364–375
Cassidy, J., 41, 46, 117–118, 119, 130, 267
categorical systems, 50
CAT. *See* Children's Apperception Test
causal inference, 84
causality. *See* social causality
CBCL/2–3. *See* Child Behavior Checklist
CCRT. *See* Core Conflictual Relational
    Theme
Center for Epidemiological Studies
    Depression Scale (CES-D), 54
cerebral palsy, 52
CES-D. *See* Center for Epidemiological
    Studies Depression Scale
Chamberlain, P., 300, 302
change. *See* generational change
child abuse, 153, 403, 406, 426. *See also*
    sexual abuse; Smith, Susan; Yates,
    Andrea
foster children and, 303
Child Behavior Checklist (CBCL/2–3), 248
childcare, 54
child-centered goals, 81
child homicide, 422–423
childhood
relationships with parents in, 247
replicative script from, 203
child maltreatment, 65, 177, 309. *See also*
    abuse; child homicide; sexual abuse;
    Smith, Susan; Yates, Andrea
parental mental illness and, 425
Child-Parent Attachment Project (CPAP), 42,
    50–53
childrearing, 79
attachment concerns and, 253–254
attitudes towards, 241–243
fathers and, 182, 239, 242, 244–246,
    249–250, 252
inadequate, 404–423, 425–426
Child Rearing Practice Report (CRPR), 241,
    246–247, 257–258
children. *See also* foster children;
    mother-child; mother-father-child triads;
    preschool children
affective experience of, 11
African American, 54
aggression of, 287
ambivalent, 337
anger of, 11
Asian, 54

children (*cont.*)
  assessing parenting representations with, 210–211
  attachments and, 12, 31, 209, 269
  attacking/abandoning/killing, 421
  caregiving by, 30
  as care-receivers, 30
  cerebral palsy and, 52
  characteristics of, 55, 58–59
  childcare's effects on, 54
  compliance of, 340
  D-controlling, 270, 276–278, 279
  delusional representations of, 405
  developing mind of, 357
  disabilities of, 19
  disorganized-controlling, 265, 266, 270, 271, 275, 277
  doll play of, 270, 271
  DRs of, 398
  DRs of mother's killing, 422
  enmeshment construct and, 55
  epilepsy and, 52
  father perceived as self by, 357
  father's activities with, 177
  father's control of, 254
  first v. later born, 58, 62
  gender of, 62
  helplessness/abdication of, 283
  higher IQs of, 58
  high-risk, 296
  inhibited, 14
  insecure-avoidance attachment of, 67
  insecure/secure, 279
  intentional being of, 358
  intervention evaluations of, 89
  IWM of, 117, 325
  kindergarten age, 265, 270
  knowledge of, 87–89
  labeling of, 323
  language competence of, 55
  lovable self-representation by, 154
  maturing of, 68
  mother figure representation by, 161–162
  mother's descriptions of, 266
  mother's hatred for, 33
  multiple, 51
  narratives of, 153, 165–166, 168
  Pacific Islander, 54
  parental comfort for, 42
  parental values internalized by, 99
  parenting views of, 168
  parent's attributions about, 84
  parent's fear of, 339
  parent socialization of, 81
  parent's psychological neglect of, 412–413
  parent's representations of, 113–119, 166
  perspective of, 87
  point of view of, 51
  preschool, 10, 153, 252
  pre-symbolic/symbolic representations of, 15, 279, 378
  protection and, 405–406, 407, 408
  psychological withdrawal by, 416
  representations of, 94, 151, 153–154, 245, 363, 368–369, 374–375, 397–398
  responsiveness of, 87
  reunion-based attachment of, 270
  role-reversal of, 271, 282, 283, 415
  secure, 358
  self-representation development of, 155, 403
  sexualized behavior of, 415
  sexually abused children, 412
  socialization of, 80
  state of mind of,
  Strange Situation and, 153, 180, 245
  studies of developing, 52
  teacher's and, 31
  temperament of, 14–15, 303
  terrible-twos of, 11, 49
  therapy and, 378, 427
  transmitting problems to, 239
  underprotecting, 407
  values instilled into, 81
  variables of, 88
Children's Apperception Test (CAT), 153
child therapists, 427
chronic mourning, 345
CI. *See* Caregiving Interview
Climbié, Victoria, 418–419
Cocci, V., 21
co-dependence, 415
coding scales, 24, 48
  narrative style (process scales), 216–219
  parent's representations of adolescent, 213
  parent's representations of parent-child relationship, 214
  parent's representations of self, 213
coding scheme(s), 8–23, 33. *See also* Life Events coding
  AAI, 7, 24, 280
  AMBIANCE, 12

anger, 64
approaches, 210
CI's system of, 280
CPAP-PDI, 51
development of, 47
diversity of, 26–27
emotion's, 27
focus of, 27
global methods of, 50
interview, 7, 24, 46, 55, 209
interview transcripts and, 7
limits of, 27
mother's experiences, 266
PAI's, 11
PDI's, 13, 14, 45, 64
PRI-A, 212
validity of, 25
WMCI, 141
Zeanah's WMCI, 141
coercion, 334
cognition(s), 27. *See also* social cognition
automatic, 79, 89–97
constructs of, 79
controlled, 79, 89–97
distortions of, 399
forms of, 400
negative event, 91
parenting, 33, 81–89, 91–94, 98
parent's emotions influence, 130
cognitive processes, 116
Cohn, D. F., 326
Cohn, J. F., 122
Coleman, P. K., 158, 213
Collins, N. I., 247
comfort
boys seeking, 62
disorder, 424
importance of, 391–392
parent's providing, 42
sexual abuse and, 409
communication, 192–194
compensatory hypothesis, 178
competence
maternal, 25, 163, 218
measures of, 213
parental, 24
rating scale, 12
compliance, 340
conceptualizations, psychodynamically
oriented, 322–325
Concordia Longitudinal Risk Project, 239

connotative language, 395
content focused scales, 26
Coolbear, J., 16
coping, 19, 93
adolescent's, 219
foster children's, 306
ineffective parental, 291
son's, 208, 220, 226–229
strategies, 93
Corbin, J., 185
Core Conflictual Relational Theme (CCRT)
method, 348, 352, 359
application of, 352, 359–364, 380
components of, 360
details of, 352, 359, 360
narratives and, 381
psychotherapy's use of, 380
RE and, 365
response from other (RO) component of,
360, 365, 367, 369, 372, 373, 374,
375
response of self (RS) component of, 360,
365, 367, 369, 372, 373, 375
themes identified using, 360, 362, 369
Wish component of, 360, 365, 367, 368,
372, 373, 374
corrective parenting, 203, 334
corrective scripts, 333, 342
cortical integration, 396
Corwyn, R., 303
Cowan, C. P., 326
Cowan, P. A., 326
Cox, S. M., 16
CPAP-PDI, 51
coding system of, 51
composite, 55, 59
constructs of, 57
content scores of, 51
descriptive analyses of, 57–58
enmeshment construct of, 52
future research possibilities, 66
intercorrelation calculations, 57
predictions using, 57
scales, 53
worry construct of, 52
CPAP. *See* Child-Parent Attachment Project
Craik, K., 43
Cramer, B., 22, 324
Cramer, B. G, 322
Cramer, B. G., 323
Critis-Christoph, P., 361

Crittenden, P. M., 33, 345
Crnic, Kl., 49
Crowell, J. A., 95
CRPR. *See* Child Rearing Practice Report

Daly, K., 180
Damasio, A. R., 392
danger
    actions from extreme, 403
    corrections in face of, 402
    Dynamic-Maturational Model and, 401
    exaggerating probability of, 405
    fear of greater, 403
    overestimating of, 407
    overlooking probability of, 407
    perception of, 402–403
Darling-Fischer, C. S., 183
daughters
    autonomy of, 336
    fathers and, 320, 331–334
    mothers and, 320, 334–337, 340–343
    narrative of, 371, 377
    trust for, 335
Davidov, M., 89
Davidson, R. J., 91
D-controlling children, 270, 276–278,
    279
Dean, K., 46
death, loss through, 276
delusions, 400, 405, 417
dependence-independence, 11
dependency, 337
depression, 64
    arousal v., 422
    depressive realism as, 302
    parent's, 177
    postpartum, 422
derision, 335
developmental psychology, 3
development, theories of, 150
DeWolff, M., 120
Differentiation of Self Scale, 224
difficult experiences, 324
    breaking cycle of, 346
    resolution of, 344–347
Dimmock, J., 51
discipline, 41, 194–197
    maternal representations of, 61
    men and, 194, 195, 196
    mothers and, 194
disengaged representations, 16, 125, 128, 130,
    144, 362

dismissing
    adults, 7, 44, 94, 181
    mothers, 18, 95, 96, 118–119, 120–122,
        226, 232
    parents, 181
    state of mind, 325, 339
disorganized controlling children, 266, 270,
    271, 275, 277
disorganized-disoriented (D) group, 268
dispositional representational (DR) models,
    388
    adult's, 398
    brain's generation of, 397
    generating/selecting, 390
    incompatible, 414
    intergenerational transmissions of, 398
    interplay among, 404
    mothers who kill children, 422
    parental behavior and, 406–407, 408,
        409–410, 411, 413–414, 417–420, 421
    parents v. childrens, 398
    selection of, 396–397
    semantic, 395
    synaptic firing and, 398
    types of, 393, 396
    universal aspects of, 404
distortions, 125
    cognitive, 399
    defined, 125
    delusional v. accurate information,
        416–421
    normal child-protective behavior, 405–406
    protection, 391
    representational, 16, 47, 125, 130, 132, 144,
        362
    self-protective behavior and, 408–416
distress, infant's, 116, 132, 269
divorce, scale for, 13
Dix, T. H., 81, 85, 86, 116, 118
doll play, 270, 271. *See also* Attachment
    Doll-Play Assessment
    assessments, 271
    flooded, 271
domains, parenting, 50
Donovan, W. L., 85, 86
Dozier, M., 20, 309
DR models. *See* dispositional representational
    models
Duncan tests, 225
dyads, 300
    biological, 298, 300, 303
    father-child, 48, 379

mother-child, 12, 53, 56, 155, 265, 379
mother-daughter, 48
mother-infant, 46, 121, 123, 151
mother-son, 18, 48
parent-child, 42
Dynamic-Maturational Model, 391, 399
accuracy of, 428
competency focus of, 428
danger in, 401
eliciting of, 403
trauma in, 401
dysregulation, 279, 280, 287
affect, 276, 278
arousal, 417
disruptions in care and, 300
mother-infant, 300

early childhood, narrated self of, 154
earned secure individuals, 201
Edwards, J., 80
Egeland, B., 201
Eichberg, C., 268
Elias, P. K., 85
Emde, R. N., 154, 242, 243, 363
emotion(s)
activation of, 110, 116, 127–130
arousal of, 85
behavioral processes and, 116
caregiving and negative, 117–118
coding, 27
cognitive processes and, 116, 130
consistency of, 116
dysregulated, 279
engagement of, 130–136
Frijda's definition of, 117
infant's development of, 109, 111
investment of, 10, 298
IWM self-management of, 117–118
maternal activation of, 109
mother's negative, 149, 164
parent's unavailability of, 120
positive, 117
representations and, 27
emotional dance, 120, 121
emotional investment, 298
interview reflecting high level, 305–306
interview reflecting low level, 307, 309
emotional processes, 118–119, 120–122
Emotion-Focused Coping test, 223
emotion regulation, 17, 79, 91–94, 96, 99
foster children problems with, 309
infant's, 109, 111, 117–118, 122

IWM's role in, 113
strategies, 109, 117–118, 136
empowerment, 65
enablers, 415
engagement processes, 116–118, 130
enmeshment, 52, 55
thought process, 14
epilepsy, 52
episodic memory, 396
episodic memory systems, 6
Epstein, S., 247
Eshel, Y., 363
Etchegoyen, A., 356
experiences. *See* difficult experiences
extraversion scales, 54

family/families
at-risk, 347
behavior patterns of, 327
dysfunctional, 415
scripts, 327
triangulation, 415
violence, 276, 277, 278
family of origin, 182, 185, 188
father's, 357
grip of experience in, 319
parent difficulties in, 327
substance abuse in, 276
Family Story Collaborative Project (FSCP),
141
fantasy, psychoanalytic theory of, 356
Faraone, S. V., 93
fatherhood, 178
fathers. *See also* Israeli married men study;
men
AAI classifications of, 182
abandonment fears of, 253
ambivalence of, 323
attachment concerns of, 240, 244–246,
250–252, 253
as attachment figures, 333
authoritarian, 242
authoritative, 242
caregiving capability of, 357
categories of, 242
childrearing by, 182, 239, 242, 244–246,
249–250, 252
children's activities with, 177
child's perception of self in, 357
controlling attitude of, 254
daughters and, 320, 331–334
dissatisfaction of, 182

fathers (*cont.*)
  engaged, 203
  family of origin, 357
  fathering and, 178
  father's perceptions of, 249–250, 251, 252
  father's relationship with own, 242–243, 256
  flooded/out of control, 282
  gender identity issues of, 240
  good, 179
  grandfathers and, 185
  Great Britain study of, 204
  increased responsibility by, 240
  intergenerational studies of, 202
  interviews with, 183
  men's comparison with, 193, 194, 195
  men's compensations for, 190
  men's self-rating as, 178
  mothers as perceived by, 249–250
  mother's inputs to, 256
  motivations of, 327
  narratives of, 371
  new, 182, 203
  nurturing, 255
  optimal, 203
  parenting attitudes of, 251–252
  parent's relationship with, 240–244,
    249–250, 251–252, 253
  permissive, 242
  practices of, 243
  pre-children's birth AAI of, 182
  pride of, 335
  rejecting, 189
  representations of, 33, 177
  REs of, 367, 373
  role of, 240–241
  role-reversal of, 339, 340
  self-reports by, 239, 254
  stimulating, 242
  strict, 252
  study of Canadian, 180
  submissive sons to submissive, 337–340
  therapy sought by, 202
  toddler's supported by, 202
  as victim, 337–340
  WMCIs of, 367–368, 373–374
father-son relationships, 179
Fave-Viziello, G. F., 21
fear
  adolescent's, 338
  body's reaction to, 117
  of mother, 340

feedback loops, 5
feelings
  arousal and, 395
  sadistic, 287
Feldman, S. S., 95
fetus, 300
filial relationships, 32
first-born male toddlers, 11
Fisek, G. O, 22, 23
Fisher, P, 300
Floyd, K., 179
Fogel, A., 29
Folkman, S., 223
Fonagy, P., 12, 155, 158, 164, 213, 357
foster care, caregiver representations and,
  297–298
foster children, 296. *See also* This is My Baby
  Interview
  age of placement of, 304
  case study of, 304
  challenges of, 297
  coping by, 306
  emotion regulation problems of, 309
  foster parents pushed away by, 306
  late placed, 306, 307, 309
  maladaptive behavior of, 306
  negative self-view of, 310
  neuroendocrine functioning of, 300
  newborn, 304
  placing of, 300
  prior abuse of, 303
  relational difficulty of, 306
  younger, 304
foster mothers
  autonomous, 309
  biological preparedness of, 299
  biological v., 20, 297, 299
  disadvantages of, 299
  internalizing"mother" role by, 304
  investment of, 20, 298
  pregnancy and, 297
  separation from, 304
foster parents, 20
  barriers facing, 296
  biological v., 297
  commitment of, 302
  complications faced by, 302
  factors inhibiting, 303
  foster children push away, 306
  intervention, 311
  investment of, 296, 298, 302–303

motivations for becoming, 302
sacrifices of, 301
younger foster children and, 304
Fraiberg, Selma, 152, 321
Frederickson, B., 117
Fremmer-Bombik, E., 182
Freud, Anna, 320
Frijda, N. H., 117
FSCP. *See* Family Story Collaborative
  Project
Furman, W., 62

Gelfand, D. M., 82
gender, 62
  behavior typed by, 255
  father's issues concerning, 240
  maternal representations based on, 63
  mental models and, 63
  parental attitudes based on, 63
generational change, 203–204
George, C., 12–14, 28, 44, 49, 95, 96, 112,
  158, 165, 213, 231, 337, 358
Gergely, G., 136
"ghosts in the nursery" (Fraiberg), 152
girls, mother of boys v. mothers of, 59
global rating scales, 50
goal corrected partnership, 355
goals
  adolescent's dominance, 89
  anger and blocked, 117
  child-centered, 81, 82
  childrearing, 88
  parent-centered, 81, 82
  parenting, 81–82
  partnership and, 355
  relationship-centered, 82
  safety-centered, 82
  short v. long-term, 81
Golby, B., 251
Goldberg, S., 117–118, 119, 136
Gondoli, D. M., 89
grandchildren, 188
grandfathers, 185, 242
Granot, D., 154
Great Britain study, 204
grieving, absence of conscious, 345, 346
Grossman, K., 182, 202
Grossman, K. E., 182
Grusec, J. E., 32, 82, 88, 89, 243
guilt, 323
Gunnar, M., 300

Haft, W. L., 117–118
Haglili, E., 245
Handbook of Attachment (Cassidy & Shaver),
  4
Hans, S. L., 16
Happaney, K., 86, 90
Harel, J., 363
Hastings, P., 82, 88
hatred, 33
Hazan, C., 247
Helenius, H., 22
helplessness, 279
  children's, 283
  maternal, 272
  representation of, 265
  scales, 49
  trauma and, 271
Hesse, E., 268, 277
heuristic thinking, 91, 97
Hirshberg, L., 46, 210
Hirshfeld, D. R., 93
Hishber, L. M., 46
Holden, G. W., 80, 241, 243
Holmbeck, G. N., 213
homicide. *See* child homicide
Honig, A. S., 242, 254, 255
Hopkins, J., 16
Huebner, D., 158
Huth-Bocks, A. C., 17

idealization, 180, 322, 338, 400
identification, 328, 337
IFEEL task. *See* Infant Facial Expressions of
  Emotions from Looking at Pictures task
Ilicali, E. T., 22, 23
illusory control, 85–86
  high, 86
  low, 86
  moderate, 86
  mother's, 85–86, 97
incest, 320, 408, 409, 411
independence-dependence, 11
individuals
  anxious, 91, 93–94, 97
  dismissive, 95
  preoccupied, 95
  repressive/sensitizing, 91
individuation
  adolescent, 219, 320, 343
  indicators of, 224
  son's levels of, 19, 219

infancy
  disorganized attachment in, 376
  eliciting descriptions of, 210
  maternal sensitivity during, 156, 157
Infant Facial Expressions of Emotions from
    Looking at Pictures (IFEEL) task, 123,
    125–126
  affective tone scales and, 131
  details of, 125
  infant's scored using, 126
  mother's emotion attributions and, 130
  psychometric properties of, 126
Infant Mental Health Journal (George &
    Solomon), 4
infants, 7
  acceptance of, 142
  affective displays of, 121, 126, 131
  ambiguous facial expressions of, 123
  ambivalent, 45–54
  assessing parenting representations with,
    210–211
  attachment, 45, 267, 268
  attachment security, 13, 19, 109, 120
  autonomous-secure parents and, 180
  avoidant, 44, 65
  caregiver's and, 109, 111, 143–144
  dismissing parents of, 181
  disorganized, 45, 268
  distress of, 116, 132, 269
  early placed, 304
  emotional dance of parents and, 120, 121
  emotional development of, 109, 110–111
  emotion regulation of, 17, 109, 111,
    117–118
  facial expressions of, 90
  first year of life of, 110, 111
  hand gestures of, 90
  IFEEL and, 126
  interoceptive state of, 110
  IWMs of, 355
  maternal representations of, 123–125
  minimizing/maximizing signals of, 326
  mother dysregulation with, 300
  mother's internal feelings communicated to,
    132
  mother's perceptions of, 358
  negative affects in interactions with, 116
  parent representations of,
  physical characteristics of, 304
  primary caregiver's relationship with, 109
  psychological preoccupation with, 142

  relational cocoon of, 110–111
  "schema of-a-way-of-being-with" of, 354
  secure attachments of, 358
  self-regulation by, 109, 111, 117–118, 121
  self's differentiation by, 109
  sensitive parents and, 120
  signaling caregiver by, 111
  6-month-old, 122
  Still Face procedure and, 122, 126
  Strange Situation observations of, 12, 13,
    17, 65, 181
  well-being of, 9
  working models of, 130, 132–136
information-processing, 79, 86, 87, 93, 244
insecure-avoidance attachment, 67
Insel, T. R., 299
integration, 396
interactions
  longitudinal study of, 150
  maternal affect during, 165
  modes of, 323
  mother-infant, 151
interfaceable mind theory, 22, 151, 354
intergenerational modeling, 178
intergenerational similarity, 43
  intergenerational differences v, 177, 179,
    185
intergenerational transmissions, 177, 201–203,
    265, 398
  of attachment security, 327
  attachment theory and, 325
  case examples of, 328–337
  of difficult experiences, 324
  DRs and, 398
  of parenting, 319, 321–322, 343–347
internalization, 30
internal working models (IWM), 5, 111–113
  AAI and, 7
  associations between, 31
  of attachment, 44–46
  of attachment relationships, 113
  of behavioral systems, 5–6
  behavior's relationship to, 42
  in Bowlby's Theory, 5–6
  caregiving and, 3, 28, 29, 31–32
  change resistance of, 43
  children's, 117, 325
  defined, 111
  dysregulated, 279, 280
  elucidation/clarification of, 6
  emotion regulation and, 113

emotion self-management and, 117–118
flexibility of, 6
infant's, 355
mental representations as, 41
organization of, 32
parent's, 8, 31, 112, 116
systems theory and, 355
interventions
children's evaluations of, 89
foster parent, 311
psychotherapeutic, 23
interviews, 3. *See also* Adolescence
Experiences Interview; Adult Attachment
Interview; Attachment Concerns and
Close Relationships Questionnaire;
Mother Father Peers questionnaire;
Parent Attachment Interview; Parenting
Representations Interview-Adolescence;
This is My Baby Interview; Working
Model of the Child Interview
adapted PDI's semi-structured, 51
adolescent's, 179, 319
coding of, 7, 24, 46, 55, 209
irrelevant answers on, 181
maternal representations during, 21
men's, 179, 183
parent, 10, 170–171, 209
R, 22
representations and, 32
segregated, 184
structured/semi-structured, 4, 23
taping of, 6, 55
Invernizzi, R., 21
investment
caregiver, 17, 20, 27, 297, 298–299
emotional, 10, 298
foster parent's, 20, 296, 298, 302–303
Israeli/Jewish adolescent research project, 209,
210–213, 219, 220, 222
AAI used in, 221, 222
adolescent's report, 222
basic training assessment, 222–223
Differentiation of Self Scale, 224
emerging adulthood assessments, 223
Emotion-Focused Coping test, 223
hypothesis of, 220–221
indicators of individuation, 224
Intimacy Status Interview,
late adolescent assessment, 222
measures, 222–224
Mental Health Inventory (MHI), 222

peer's report, 223
Problem-Focused Coping test, 223
procedure, 221–222
results, 224–230
PRI-A used in, 221
sample, 220–221
secondary appraisal scale, 223
Separation-Individuation Test of
Adolescence-*SITA*, 224
Ways of Coping test, 223
Israeli married men study, 178
analysis procedure of, 185
father's profile, 183
findings of, 185, 200
men's memory issues in, 186–189
PAI used in, 184–185
procedure, 184
quotes from fathers in, 186, 187–188, 189
sample, 183
segregated interviews in, 184
societal influences in, 203
Israeli mother/children longitudinal study,
156–169
Attachment Story Completion Task, 156,
157, 161–162
children's parenting representations in, 166
domains addressed in, 158
mother-infant interaction at 12 months, 157
parenting interview in, 170–171
parenting representations at 6 years,
157–159
PCERA used in, 157, 159
PDI used in, 157–158
research design, 156, 157
WIPPSI, 156, 157
IWM. *See* Internal Working Models

Jacobson, Edith, 150, 353
Jaffee, S. R., 178
joy-pleasure/coherence dimension, 11, 48
Juffer, F., 99
Jung, K., 242, 254, 255

Kaplan, M., 42, 47, 69
Kaplan, N., 41, 44
Kanaker, K. H., 158, 213
kibbutz, caregiving on, 301
Kimberly, K., 154
kindergarten age children, 265, 270. *See also*
middle-class mother of kindergarten
children study

Kindler, H., 182
Kivenson-Baron, I., 158, 222
Kogan, N., 122
Kranenburg, M., 48

labeling, 323
Lack of Resolution of Mourning (LRM), 268
Lack of Resolution of Trauma (LRT), 268
Lambermom, M., 48
Lambert, J. D., 185, 251
language
  competence, 55
  connotative, 395
  parent's use of, 64
Lazarus, R. S., 223
Leadbeater, B. J., 342
learning, associative, 394
Leavitt, L. A., 85
letting go, 212, 232, 343
Levendosky, A. A., 17
Levy, D., 79
Lewis, C., 204
Lieberman, A. F., 344
Life Events coding, 272, 275, 277, 278
  categories, 276
  results of, 277
Lifton, N., 158
Likert scales, 15, 361
Likert-type scales, 46
Lipsett, L., 46
longitudinal study. *See also* Concordia
    Longitudinal Risk Project; Israeli/Jewish
    adolescent research project; Israeli
    married men study; Israeli
    mother/children longitudinal study;
    Minnesota Longitudinal Attachment
    Study; sleep/infancy longitudinal study
  interaction/representation, 150
  NICHD's, 53
  parenthood, 239
loss
  lack of resolution of, 266–269, 272
  mothers unresolved for, 290
  of parent, 345
loss, lack of resolution of, 266–269
love, 7, 68, 192–194
low power schemas, 86–87
LRM. *See* Lack of Resolution of Mourning
LRT. *See* Lack of Resolution of Trauma
Luborsky, L., 166, 359, 360, 361
Lundell, L., 89
Lyons-Ruth, K., 268, 277, 290, 326, 376

MacArthur Story Stem Battery (MSSB), 363
MacKay, S., 117–118, 119, 136
MacKinnon, C., 85
Magai, C., 132
Main, M., 41, 44, 154, 181, 267, 268, 271,
    272, 275, 277, 325
maltreatment. *See* child maltreatment
MANOVAs, 216, 219, 225, 226
Marvin, R. S., 14, 19, 42, 50, 51, 52, 158,
    213
Maslin, C., 45
maternal representations, 17, 21, 151–153
  of attachment, 17, 61, 210, 245
  child characteristics and, 58–59
  differentiation/organization of, 42
  dimensions of, 41
  of discipline, 61
  gender based, 63
  infant's, 123–125
  maternal characteristics and, 59
  post therapy, 22–23
  subjective aspects of, 152
  of teaching, 61
maturation. *See also* Dynamic-Maturational
    Model
  neurological, 388, 390
  procedural/imaged representation and, 395
maximization, 326
Mayseless, O., 18, 154, 158, 245
McDonough, S., 17
McShane, K., 89
measures of attachment. *See* Adult Attachment
    Interview; Attachment Concerns and
    Close Relationships Questionnaire;
    Attachment Story Completion Task;
    Strange Situation
measures of parenting representations. *See*
    Caregiving Interview; Parent Attachment
    Interview; Parent Development
    Interview; Parenting Representations
    Interview-Adolescence; Working Model
    of the Child Interview
Meins, E., 164
Melson, G. F., 29
memory, 200–201. *See also* amnesia,
    childhood
  absence of childhood, 201
  averages, 43
  brain and, 393
  episodic, 396
  events and, 91
  imaged, 395

men's issues with, 186–189, 200–201
  perceptual, 395
  preconscious, 391
  procedural, 393
  retranscription of, 269, 291
  semantic, 6, 395
  systems, 6, 388
  working, 396
men. *See also* fathers; father-son relationships;
    Israeli married men study
  childhood experiences of, 189
  comparison with father's by, 193, 194, 195
  comparison with mother's by, 192–193
  compensating for father's by, 190
  discipline and, 194, 195, 196
  interviews with, 179, 183
  joint activities and, 197–200
  memory issues of, 186–189, 200–201
  modeling statements by, 189–190
  mother's as models for, 177, 202, 204
  parental model missing for, 202
  parenting beliefs of, 182
  parent's descriptions by, 191
  self-rating by,
  sexually abusive, 409–410, 411
  shared time and, 197–200
  societal influences on, 203
Mental Health Inventory (MHI), 222
mental illness, 413–414, 425
mental models, 28, 43
  activation of, 43
  behavior guided by, 63
  of caregiving relationships, 164
  child's gender and, 63
  pleasure-coherence dimension of, 66
  relationships and, 43
mental representations
  IWMs as, 41
  limitation's measuring, 50
  parent's, 41
  process of, 392–393
  transformation of, 388
metacognitive monitoring, 154, 326, 358
metapelet (non-maternal caregiver), biological
    mother v., 31, 301
MFP questionnaire. *See* Mother Father Peers
    (MFP) questionnaire
Michigan Family Study, 122–123, 141
  mothers recruited for, 123
  protocol of, 123
  Still Face procedure used for, 123
middle-childhood, 267

middle-class mother of kindergarten children
    study, 266
  adult attachment classifications distribution,
    275
  case history I, 282–284
  case history II, 284
  case history III, 287–289
  Life Events coding categories, 275, 276,
    277
  measures, 273
  procedures, 273
  results, 273
  sample, 272
mid-life challenges, 320
military service, sons and, 208
Miller, A., 17
Milligan, K., 117–118
Mills, R. S. L., 327
mind-mindedness, 164
mind reading, 155
minimization, 79, 91
  infants and, 326
  mobilization linked with, 94–97
  mothers, 97
  parental, 92, 326
Minnesota Longitudinal Attachment Study,
    201
mirroring. *See* affective mirroring
Mistry, J., 29
mobilization, 79, 91
  minimization linked with, 94–97
  parental, 92, 93
modeling
  hypothesis, 178
  men's statements on, 189–190
modeling compensatory hypothesis, 178
monitoring
  assessing, 25
  metacognitive, 154, 326, 334, 358
moral standards, 10
Moran, G., 155
Morman, M. T., 179
Morog, M., 51
mother-child
  dyads, 12, 53, 56, 155, 265, 379
  interactions, 51, 56, 59–61, 63
  representational links between, 154–156
  role-reversal in, 267
mother-father-child triads, 352, 376
  RF and, 377
Mother Father Peers (MFP) questionnaire,
    247. *See also* peer relationships

mother-infant
  dyads, 46, 121, 123, 151
  interactions, 267
  psychotherapy, 22
mothers. *See also* foster mothers; maternal
    representations
  AAI and, 116, 152, 280
  adequate, 216
  adolescent's, 208
  affective tone of, 162
  affects of, 53, 118, 165
  anger level of, 49, 64
  anxiety of, 14–15
  attachment of, 17
  attachment representations of, 61, 210, 245
  attachment strategies and, 20
  attributions of, 125–126, 130
  autonomous, 11, 14, 18, 20, 48, 220, 226
  balanced, 15, 47, 96, 124, 128, 130, 131,
    136, 216, 233
  behavior of, 59, 61
  biological, 20, 297, 299, 300, 301
  boys/girls and, 59
  caregiving representations of, 31, 224–226
  characteristics of, 54, 59
  children attachment classification with,
    265
  children killed by, 422
  child's representation of, 161–162
  coercive patterns of, 334
  cognitions of, 27
  competence of, 25, 163, 218
  compliance spoken of by, 52, 58
  constricting, 271
  daughters and, 320, 340–343
  day-care givers v., 31
  D-controlling children and, 270, 276–278,
    279
  dependency promoted by, 337
  derision from, 335
  disciplinary practices of, 194
  disengaged, 47, 97, 128, 132
  dismissing, 18, 95, 96, 118–119, 120–122,
    226, 232
  of disorganized-controlling children, 265,
    266, 270, 271, 275, 277
  distorted classification of, 16, 47, 125, 130,
    132
  education of, 61
  father's perceptions of, 249–250
  father's relationship with own, 242–243, 256
  fear of, 340
  first born children and, 62
  flooded, 216, 233
  hatred by, 33
  helplessness of, 272
  hostility of, 133
  IFEEL and, 130
  illusory control, 85–86, 97
  infant dysregulation with, 300
  infants perceived by, 358
  insecure/secure children and, 279
  internal feeling's communication by, 132
  lack of resolution of, 268, 289
  later born children and, 62
  low power, 86–87
  men's comparison with, 192–193
  as men's models, 177, 202, 204
  metacognitive capacities of, 155
  Michigan Family Study recruitment of, 123
  mind reading capacity of, 155
  minimization by, 97
  mother's representation of, 152
  negative emotionality of, 149, 164
  neutralizing by, 63
  non-autonomous, 20, 220
  parenting representations of, 18, 112,
    210–213
  parenting variables of, 162–163
  parenting views of, 168
  past relationships of, 152
  PDI taken by, 149
  perspective-taking skills of, 89
  positive caregiving by, 56
  preoccupied, 18, 95, 96, 226, 231–232
  problems transmitted by, 239
  protective/regulating role of, 162
  psychological adjustment of, 54
  questionnaires filled out by, 22
  rage patterns of, 265, 276, 277, 278, 280
  real presence of, 355
  reflective capacity of, 162
  representations of, 22, 52
  REs of, 364–365, 371–372
  restricted, 216
  ridicule from, 335
  role-reversal of, 267, 282, 289, 365
  sadistic feelings of, 287
  self-description by, 96, 266
  self-representation by, 210
  sensitivity of, 156, 157, 162–163, 164
  sons influenced by, 208, 329–331

state of mind of, 224–226, 266, 267, 268
Still Face procedure and, 126, 132–136
Strange Situation observations of, 12
as subject, 354
surrogate, 378
toddlerhood representations of, 49
unavailability of, 121
unaware coercive, 334–337
unresolved, 265, 290
WMCIs of, 123, 365–367, 372–373
worry narrative of, 52
mother-son dyads, 18, 48
mourning, 265
chronic, 345
processes of, 346
variants of, 345
MSSB. *See* MacArthur Story Stem Battery
multiple regression analyses, 55, 59
Munholland, K. A., 28, 244, 334
murder, 421
Muzik, M., 17

narrative(s). *See also* Relationship Anecdotes
Paradigm; Relationship Episodes
analysis, 143, 153, 165–166, 168
CCRTs and, 381
children's, 153, 165–166, 168
daughter's, 371, 377
father's, 371
mother's worry, 52
parent's, 360
relational, 360
representational representations and, 359
research tools of narratives, 359
style (process scales), 216–219
National Institute of Child Health and Human
Development (NICHD) Study of Early
Child Care, 53
hypotheses of, 53
longitudinal design of, 53
measures of, 54–56
multiple regression analyses of, 55
outliers in, 55
participants in, 53
PDI of, 53, 54
procedures, 54
reliability of, 55
University of Virginia site of, 53
NEO Personality Inventory, 54
scales used in, 54
neural networks, 393

neurobiology, 299
neuroticism scales, 54
neutralizing, 51, 63, 67
Newson, E., 204
Newson, J., 204
NICHD. *See* National Institute of Child Health
and Human Development
Nicholson, E., 16
nurturance, 29

object-relations theories, 152
O'Connor, T. G., 50, 51
Oedipus complex, 356
"On Attachment" (Bowlby), 43–44
openness, 331, 333
Oppenheim, D., 363
outcomes, observation of, 25
overprotection, 79, 405

Pacific Island children, 54
Padron, E., 201
PAI. *See* Parent Attachment Interview
Pajulo, M., 22
Palkowitz, R., 179
Papousek, H., 90
parent(s). *See also* adults; foster parents;
stepparents
abusive, 88, 277, 340, 388, 406, 408–410
achievement/compliance orientation of, 41
adolescents and, 88, 209, 211–213, 319,
320, 324, 338
adult idealization of, 180
affective processes of, 11, 111
anger of, 12, 49, 277
attachment of, 8, 9
attacking/abandoning/killing children by,
421
attitudes of, 62, 242, 251
attributions of, 84, 85, 86
autonomous secure, 180
balanced representations, 124
biological, 300
bipolar disorder and, 413–414
childrearing goals of, 88
children causing fear in, 339
children internalizing values of, 99
children's representation's influenced by,
397–398
comfort provided by, 42
competence of, 24
delusionally threatened, 417

parent(s) (*cont.*)
depression of, 177
developmental needs of, 319
disengaged representations, 125
dismissing, 44, 181
distorted representations, 125
DRs of, 42, 406–407, 408, 409–410, 411, 413–414, 417–420, 421
emotional dance of infants and, 120, 121
emotion-consistent behavior or, 116
family of origin difficulties of, 327
father's relationship with, 240–244, 249–250, 251–252, 253
foster parents v. biological, 297
gender difference and, 63
grandchildren and, 188
guilt induced by, 323
infant representation by, 110
inner/mental world of, 3–5, 27, 32
insecure, 326
insensitive, 120
interactional modes of, 323
interviews of, 10, 209
intrusiveness of, 337
irrational behavior of, 420
IWMs of, 8, 31, 112, 116
language used by, 64
letting go by, 212, 232, 343
life-span issues of, 321
limits set by, 330
loss of, 345
love from, 7
love of, 7
low scoring, 45
men's descriptions of, 191
mentally entangled, 93
mentally ill, 390, 405, 425
mental representations of, 41
mid-life challenges of, 320
mind of, 3–5
minimization by, 92, 326
mobilization by, 92, 93
modeling by, 328
motivational system of, 208
multiple children of, 51
narrative of, 143, 360
negative affect avoided by, 51
nontraditional, 62
openness to change by, 142
over-involvement by, 336
past's influence on, 319, 324, 344
perceptions of, 21, 141

positive emotions of, 117
protector role of, 13, 82, 390–392, 412–413
psychological neglect by, 412–413
regulatory process impact on, 143
repressive, 92
resentment of, 335
role-reversal by, 413
schemas of, 84
secure, 359
self-descriptions from, 47, 51, 320
self-report's by, 255
sensitive, 88, 119, 120
separation-individuation of, 343
socializing children by, 81
substance abuse by, 414
threatened, 388
toddler questions asked of, 47
traditional v. nontraditional, 62
triangulating, 413–414
use of language by, 64
Parent Attachment Interview (PAI), 8–10
AAI's differences with, 45
AAI's similarity to, 45
adult's representations assessed with, 45
analysis of, 11
coding scheme for, 11
development of, 45
emphasis of, 24
focus of, 8
Israeli married men study's use of, 184–185
issues focused on in, 9
parent-child relations in, 200
predictions using, 50
relationships assessed in, 42
Parent-Child Early Relational Assessment (PCERA), 157, 159
parent-child relationships, 150–151
idealization of, 322
intergenerational, 186
Parent Development Interview (PDI), 10–12, 47, 69, 96. *See also* CPAP-PDI
AAI's similarity with, 47
coding of, 13, 64
coding scheme, 14, 45
describing constructs of, 70–74
edited version of, 49
emphasis of, 24
George/Solomon modifications of, 12–14
Israeli mother/children longitudinal study and, 157–158
mothers taking, 149
NICHD Study of Early Childcare's, 53, 54

parenting representations assessed by, 10, 47
Pianta's modifications of, 14–15
questions on, 47, 69
rating scales of, 49, 70–74
Parent Development Interview (PDI), adapted
    version, 50
AAI's similarity to, 51
parent's self-view measured by, 51
semi-structured interview of, 51
parenting
adaptive, 91
adolescent specific aspects of, 211–213
affective organization of, 113–119
anger dimension of, 49
attitudes, 241
authoritarian, 340
caregiving behavioral system and, 31
challenges of, 114–116
children's views on, 168
classifications of, 50
cognition, 33, 81–89, 91–94, 98
competency, 149
corrective, 203, 334
discontinuities in patterns of, 182
domains of, 50
emotion-laden process of, 110
emulating negative, 181
flexibility in, 326, 331, 342
goals, 81–82
good, 100
hassles of, 49
helplessness in, 142
high illusory control and, 86
inadequate, 405
insensitive, 120
intergenerational differences in, 191
intergenerational transmissions of, 319,
    321–322, 343–347
IWM's of, 112
maladaptive, 97
men's egalitarian beliefs about, 182
mother's view on, 168
motivational system, 4
negative affects of, 116
positive, 48, 178
prenatal development and, 300
process of, 88
protection and, 13, 82, 390–392, 412–413,
    424
psychoanalyst's arguments about, 79
relationships, 46
resentment of, 142

self-efficacy, 80, 81, 82, 83
sensitive, 88
state of mind, 11
strategies of, 13
styles, 88
successful, 322
types of, 242
variables, 162–163
vignettes on, 114–116, 117–118, 119
Parenting Representations
    Interview-Adolescence (PRI-A), 18–19,
    209, 212
administration of, 208
adolescence components of, 209
coding of, 212, 218
Israeli/Jewish adolescent research project
    use of, 221
scales, 18
parenting representations, 53, 159–160
AAI categories associated with, 25
of adolescent, 213
assessments of, 8–23, 26, 47, 210–211
attachment theory and, 4
central facets of, 232
of children, 113–119, 166
coping as, 19
distortion model of, 363
domains of, 220
dominant theme model of, 363
flooded, 18
foster children and, 297
intergenerational, 177
Israeli children's, 166
maternal v. non-maternal caregiver's, 300,
    302
measuring, 65
models of, 363
mother-infant interaction and, 159–160
mother's, 18, 112, 210–213
narrative coherence model of, 363
negative markers of, 220
ontogenic model, 363
of parent-child relationship, 214
PDI's assessment of, 10, 47
pre-birth of child, 21–22
psychoanalytic perspective of, 352
psychoanalytic theory and, 352, 378
of self, 213
sons coping and, 226–229
son's psychosocial functioning and,
    229–230
theoretical level of, 27

Parke, R. D., 254
Parker, K. C. H., 16
past experiences
  overcoming, 346
  parent's attempt to undo, 319, 324, 333,
    344
  preoccupation with, 334
  present's influence on, 319
  reenactment of, 334–337
  retention of, 393
  unresolved, 328
PCERA. *See* Parent-Child Early Relational
    Assessment
PDI. *See* Parent Development Interview
Pearson, J. L., 326
peer relationships, 211, 321. *See also* Mother
    Father Peers (MFP) questionnaire
Pempa, 82
perceptual memory, 395
perspective-taking, 51, 87–89, 93
Phelps, J., 48
Pianta, R. C., 14–15, 19, 42, 50, 51, 52, 55,
    158, 213, 347
Piha, J., 22
Pinto, A., 93
pleasure-coherence dimension, 66
postpartum depression, 422
Poulton, L., 117
power schemas, 86–87, 89
preconscious memory, 391
pregnancy, 21
  biological adaptations of, 299
  eliciting descriptions of, 210
  foster/biological mothers and, 297
  WMCI's concentration on, 23
prenatal perceptions, 21
preoccupation
  adult, 7, 44, 45–54, 94
  individual, 95
  mother's, 18, 95, 96, 226, 231–232
preschool children, 10, 153, 183, 252
  disorganized classification of, 267
  maltreated/neglected, 309
present, past's influence on, 319
PRI-A. *See* Parenting Representations
    Interview-Adolescence
pride, 335
primiparous women, 21
Principle Component factor analysis,
    247
Problem-Focused Coping test, 223

problem solving, 19
process scales, 216–219
projection, 167, 322
promiscuity, 418
protection, 168, 397
  aspects of, 391
  of children, 405–406, 407, 408
  children's narratives regarding, 168
  distortions of, 391
  mother's regulation and, 162
  parenting and, 13, 82, 390–392, 412–413,
    424
  psychological, 391
  reproduction, 388
  risk-taking elicits, 391
  self-, 391
psychiatric disorder, 421
psychoanalysis, 3
  conceptualizations of, 319
  parenting behavior and, 79
  relational perspective in, 152
psychoanalytic theory, 152, 153, 354, 355
  attachment theory and, 319, 358
  fantasy and, 356
  parenting representations and, 352, 378
  representation development and,
    353–355
psychodynamic theory, 167
Psychological Inquiry (Bell & Richard), 4
psychological protection scale, 13
psychology. *See* developmental psychology
psychosocial functioning, 19, 219, 229–230,
    231
psychotherapy, 67
  CCRT's relevance to, 380
  interventions of, 23
  mother-child/father-child, 379
  mother-infant, 22
puberty, onset of, 211

Q-sort, 246. *See* Attachment Q-Sort Security
    246

rage patterns, 265, 276, 286
  elements of, 290
  mother's reporting, 277, 278, 280
  suppressing, 286
Rapee, R. M., 14
RAP. *See* Relationship Anecdotes Paradigm
Read, S. J., 247
reality, appearance v., 426

reflective function (RF), 12, 155, 326, 358
  attachment and, 358
  mother-father-daughter triads and, 377
  secure parents and, 359
Regan, C., 46, 210
regulation
  emotion, 79, 91–94, 96, 99
  infant's emotion, 17, 109, 111, 117–118
  mother's protection and, 162
  self-, 90
Reid, J., 300
Reinhold, D. A., 85
"rejecting" caregivers, 50
rejection, 6, 49, 50, 80, 96
relational representations, 127
  children's, 368–369, 374–375
  method of studying, 359
  polar, 376
relationship(s). *See also* parent-child
    relationships
  AAI/PAI assessment of, 42
  abusive, 339
  adult love, 68
  as affective bonds, 137
  assessments of, 42
  attachments, 31, 113
  children-teacher, 31
  client-therapist, 31
  close, 153–154
  cross-generational, 415
  declarative knowing of, 379
  father-son, 179
  filial, 32
  foster children and, 306
  goals centered on, 82
  implicit relational knowing, 379
  intergenerational comparison of, 192
  IWMs related to behavior in, 42
  mental models of, 43
  mother's past, 152
  non-egalitarian, 32
  organizing/reflecting emotional experience
    of, 111–113
  parenting, 46
  peer, 211, 321
  representations of, 127
  schemas, 9
  self-other, 358
  templates/working models of, 110
Relationship Anecdotes Paradigm (RAP), 360,
    364, 380

Relationship Episodes (RE), 360
  CCRT method applied to, 365
  father's, 367, 373
  mother's, 364–365, 371–372
representational models, 42. *See also*
    dispositional representational models
representation development
  attachment theory and, 355–356
  psychoanalytic theory and, 353–355
representations, 10. *See also* dispositional
    representational models; maternal
    representations; mental representations;
    relational representations
  AAI's assessments of, 25, 45, 94
  assessing aspects in, 19–21
  balanced, 15, 47, 96, 124, 128, 130, 131, 362
  broadening focus on, 46
  caregiver, 21, 143–144
  caregiving, 17, 27–28, 30, 31
  children's, 94, 151, 153–154, 245, 363
  defined, 392, 402
  delusional, 405
  disengaged, 16, 125, 128, 130, 144, 362
  distorted, 16, 47, 125, 130, 132, 144, 362
  emotions place in, 27
  father's, 33, 177
  foster children and parent's, 297
  foster parent's, 20
  helplessness, 265
  imaged, 395
  inadequate childrearing, 404–423
  internal world of, 150
  interplay between, 357, 369, 371, 375,
    376–378
  interviews and, 32
  Jacobson's introduction of, 150, 353
  longitudinal study of, 150
  mother's, 22, 52
  post therapy maternal, 22–23
  prenatal caregiving, 17
  preverbal/verbal, 393–395
  procedural, 6, 395, 396
  psychoanalytic perspectives of, 152
  relationship, 127
  representational, 359
  Stern's narrative model of, 151
  threat, 265
  Type A (cognitively based), 404
  Type B, 405
  Type C (affectively based), 404
repression scales, 247

repressors, 91, 92–93
coping of, 93
dismissive individuals as, 95
dismissive mothers as, 95
encoding of, 92
parents as, 92
self-esteem of, 92
social limitations of, 92
thinking limitations of, 92
reproduction, 388
RE. *See* Relationship Episodes
resentment, 335
resignation/anxiety scales, 126
response from other. *See* Core Conflictual
Relational Theme method
response of self. *See* Core Conflictual
Relational Theme method
Reynell Developmental Language Scale, 55
RF. *See* reflective function
Rickel, A. V., 246
Ridgeway, D., 45, 46
ridicule, 335
R interview, 22
risk
children and, 296
intergenerational transmission of, 239
protection and, 391
threats and, 403
Robert-Tisot, C., 22
Robinson, J., 154, 242
Rochester, M., 117–118, 136
Roisman, G., 201, 202
role-reversal
children's, 271, 282, 283, 415
father-adolescent, 339, 340
mother's, 267, 282, 289, 365
parent's, 413
Rose-Krasnor, L., 327
Rosenblum, J., 93
Rosenblum, K., 17
Rubin, K. H., 327
Ruddick, S., 29
Rudy, D., 32, 243

sadistic feelings, 287
safety-centered goals, 82
safety regulating system, 29. *See also*
attachment behavioral system
Safier, R., 14
Sameroff, A. J., 17, 85
Sandler, A., 353
Sandler, J., 353

Sandler, L., 356
Savonlahi, E., 22
Sayre, J. M., 52, 53, 65
scales
AAI, 7
acceptance, 247
affective tone, 125
agreeableness, 54
attachment, 24
autonomy promotion, 247
coding, 24, 48
competence rating, 12
content focused, 26
controlling, 246
CPAP-PDI, 53
Differentiation of Self, 224
divorce, 13
expressive/nurturance, 246
extraversion, 54
global rating, 50
helplessness, 49
independence encouragement, 247
Likert, 15, 361
Likert-type, 46
neuroticism, 54
PDI's rating, 49, 70–74
PRI-A, 18
process, 216–219
psychological protection, 13
rejection, 49, 96
repression, 247
resignation/anxiety, 126
secondary appraisal, 223
secure base, 12, 49, 96
uncertainty, 49
WMCI, 17, 46
Scharf, M., 18, 158, 222
schemas
low power, 86–87
maladaptive self-, 97
parent's, 84
power, 86–87, 89
previously established, 334
"schema of-a-way-of-being-with," 354
self-protective, 418
threat-based, 97, 99
Scheungerl, C., 269
Scheurer-Englisch, H., 182
Schmitz, S., 154
Schnarch, Ruth, 222
scholars, 3
Schwartz, G. E., 91

SCORS-Q, 9
scripts, 327
  childhood replicative, 203
  constructing new, 344
  corrective, 203, 333, 342
  painful/disconnected, 346
  replicating flexible, 329–331
secondary appraisal scale, 223
secure base scales, 12, 49, 96
security regulation, 29
Seifer, R., 85
self
  children as, 155, 403
  complementing, 354
  individuation/differentiation of, 219
  mental representations of, 353
  models of, 325, 346
  narrated, 154
  representations of, 154, 213
  state sharing, 354
  state transforming, 354
self-arousal, 394
self-differentiation, 109
self-efficacy, 82–83
  African Americans', 83
  constructs, 84
  mediating influence of, 83
  parenting and, 80, 81, 82, 83
  preoccupation and, 82
  variables of, 82
self esteem, 24, 92, 252, 253
self-other relationships, 358
self-protection, 391, 396, 399, 408–416, 418
self-regulation, 90
  affective, 126
  infant's, 109, 111, 117–118, 121
self-reports, 239, 254, 255
self-understanding, 213
semantic memory systems, 6, 395
sensitivity, 118–119, 120–122, 162–163
  caregiving, 141
  emotion-salient components of, 120
  mother's, 156, 157, 162–163, 164
  parental, 88, 119, 120
sensitization. *See* repression-sensitization
Separating Parents and Adolescents (Stierlin), 323
separation, 6
  adolescent's intrapsychic, 343
  distress, 11
Separation-Individuation Test of Adolescence-SITA, 224

sex
  affection and, 409
  promiscuous, 418
  protection and, 391
  safety, comfort and, 391–392
  unfaithfulness with, 403
sexual abuse, 408–410
  AAIs of, 409–410
  of children, 412
  Climbié's, 418–419
  comfort and, 409
  men and, 409–410, 411
  stepparents and, 411
  types of, 410
  violence and, 410
sexuality
  attachment and, 392
  children's, 415
sexual maturity, 320, 343
sexual offenders, 409–410
  motivations of, 410
  shame of, 411
  treatment of, 411
Shabad, P., 324, 333
Shamir-Essakow, G., 14
Sharabany, R., 245
Shaver, P. R., 247
Shears, J., 242
Sherman, M., 45
siblings, caring for, 338
Sigman, H., 93
Silverberg, S. B., 89
Silverman, M., 158
Silverman, R. C., 344
similarity. *See* intergenerational similarity
Slade, A., 10, 42, 47, 49, 112, 158, 213
  affective attunement and, 117–118
  mother's parenting representations and, 112
  PDI interview and, 69
sleep/infancy longitudinal study, 246
  Attachment Concerns and
    Close-Relationships Questionnaire used in, 247–248
  Child Behavior Checklist used in, 248
  Child Rearing Practice Report used in, 246–247
  discussion, 246–248
  limitations, 254–255
  measures, 246–248
  method, 246
  Mother Father Peers questionnaire used in, 247

sleep/infancy longitudinal study (*cont.*)
  parental beliefs/attitudes, 246–247
  results, 248–251
Smith, Susan, 422
Snarey, J. R., 178, 179, 201, 326
social causality, 9
social cognitive approach,
  attachment approach differences with, 98
  attachment approach similarities with,
    97–98
socialization, 80, 81
  adolescent, 211
  desirable outcomes of, 81
  dichotomous approaches to, 81
societal change, 182, 191
Solomon, J., 12–14, 28, 49, 95, 96, 158, 165,
    181, 213, 231, 267, 337, 358
somatic arousal, 394
son(s). *See also* adolescent(s)
  attachment representations of, 210
  autonomous, 220
  coping by, 208, 220, 226–229
  individuation levels of, 19, 219
  mandatory military service of, 208
  mother's influence on, 208, 329–331
  non-autonomous, 220
  Nurtured Mother Nurturing her, 329–331
  psychosocial functioning of, 19, 229–230,
    231
sons
  autonomy of, 220
  military service and, 208
  submissive fathers to submissive, 337–340
Sourander, A., 22
spousal abuse, 403
Srouge, L. A., 201
standards
  moral, 10
state of mind
  attachment and, 7
  autonomous, 325, 328
  children's,
  dismissing, 325, 339
  manifestations of, 325
  mother's, 224–226, 266, 267, 268
  parenting, 11
  secure, 325
  women's, 266–267
Statistical Abstract of Israel, 221
Steele, H., 155, 158
Steele, n., 158

Steinberg, L., 213
stepparents, 411
Stern, D. N., 22, 150, 151, 154, 300, 354, 362,
    369
Stierlin, H., 323, 324, 337
Still Face procedure, 121–122
  infant response to, 122
  maternal emotional display during, 132–136
  maternal hostility and, 133
  maternal/infant affective behavior during,
    126
  Michigan Family Study and, 123
  scoring, 126
  segments of, 126
  WMCI and, 133
story completions. *See* attachment story
  completions
story stem technique, 363, 364, 368, 374, 380.
  See also MacArthur Story Stem Battery
  (MSSB)
Strange Situation, 9, 121, 122
  AAI's, 7
  Ainsworth's, 267
  AMBIANCE coding scheme during, 12
  children's representations studied in, 153,
    180, 245
  classifications, 16, 45
  infant's attachment security in, 13, 19
  infants observed in, 12, 13, 17, 65, 181
  mothers/infants observed in, 12
  predicting children's behavior in, 180, 245
  preschool version of, 14
Strauss, A., 185, 200
stress, 303, 327
Structural Equations Modeling, 17
substance abuse, 276, 277, 414
surrogate mothers, 378
symbolization, 15, 279, 378
synapses
  DR's and, 398
  strengthening of, 393
systems, categorical, 50
systems theory, 355

Target, M., 155, 158, 164, 357
Taylor, S. E., 91
teachers, 31, 245
teaching, 41, 51, 56, 61, 66
temperament, 14–15
terrible-twos, 11, 49
Teti, D. M., 82

Theran, S. A., 17
therapists
    child, 378, 427
    intermediary role of, 380
    secure framework provided by, 380
therapy
    father's seeking, 202
    maternal representations post, 22–23
    young children and, 378
thinking
    anxious, worrisome, 93
    heuristic, 91, 97
    repressor's limited, 92
This is My Baby Interview (TIMB), 20,
        305–306, 307, 309, 313
    acceptance/commitment examined in,
        309
    coding system, 313–315
    development of, 312
    preliminary findings of, 309
    scoring of, 20
threat
    preconscious experience of, 417
    representation of, 265
    risk and, 403
Three Boxes Procedure, 56
Tiedje, L. B., 183
TIMB. *See* This is My Baby Interview
toddlers, 10
    early triangulation of, 356
    father's sensitive support of, 202
    first-born male, 11
    maltreated, 65
    mother's representation by, 49
    parents questioned about, 47
transitions, 219, 226–229
transmission. *See* intergenerational
        transmissions
trauma, 7, 19, 265
    Dynamic-Maturational Model and, 401
    helplessness and, 271
    lack of resolution of, 266–269, 272
Trehub, S. E., 117–118
triads, 352, 376
triangulation, 356, 413–414, 415
turf erosion, 80
Type A (cognitively based) representations,
        404
Type B representations, 405
Type C (affectively based) representations,
        404

uncertainty scales, 49, 96
Ungerer, J. A., 14
University of Virginia, 53
unresolved
    AAI classifications, 181, 265, 290
    adults, 7, 44, 45
    loss, 290
    mothers, 265, 290
    past experiences, 328

values, 81, 99
van Busschbach, A., 48
van IJzendoorn, M. H., 48, 99, 120, 269, 327
Verbal Comprehension Scale of Reynell
        Developmental Language Scale, 55
victim, 337–340
vignettes, parenting, 114–116, 117–118, 119
violence, 276, 277, 278, 410
von Eye, A., 17
von Klitzing, K., 154
vulnerability, intergenerational transmission
        of, 239

Walsh, R. O., 85
warmth/affection, 18, 19, 214
Waters, E., 46
Watson, J. S., 136
Way, N., 342
Ways of Coping test, 223
Weinberger, D. A., 91, 92
Weiner, B., 84
well-being, infant's, 9
Westen, D., 158, 213
Whaley, S. E., 93
WIPPSI, 156, 157
withdrawal, children's psychological, 416
WMCI. *See* Working Model of the Child
        Interview
Wolf, D. P., 363
Wolfe, J., 89
women
    depressive disorders in, 64
    harsh treatment reported by, 278
    primiparous, 21
    state of mind of, 266–267
working memory, 396
Working Model of the Child Interview
        (WMCI), 15–18, 352, 361
    affective tone scales and, 132
    application of, 352, 359–364
    Balanced classification of, 47

Working Model of the Child Interview (*cont.*)
  caregiving representations with, 96–97
  classifications, 144
  coding, 141
  details of, 124, 352, 361
  development history of, 46
  emphasis of, 24
  father's, 367–368, 373–374
  global categories in, 46
  maternal representations assessed using, 17
  modified version of, 139–141
  mother's, 123, 365–367, 372–373
  pregnancy concentration of, 23
  sample questions, 140–141
  scales of, 17, 46
  Still Face procedure and, 133
  typology classifications of, 128, 144
  validity, 139–140
  yields from, 124
working models
  characteristics of, 355
  interplay of, 355
worry, 52
  CPAP-PDI and, 52
  findings regarding, 52
  mother's narrative of, 52

Yates, Andrea, 422–423
Yediot Acharonot (Israeli newspaper), 255

Zambarano, R. J., 85
Zeanah, C. H., 15, 21, 46, 96, 158, 210, 213
  distortion defined by, 125
  infant's distress and, 116
  WMCI's coding scheme and, 141
Zimmerman, P., 113, 182
Zwart-Woudstra, A., 48

Recent books in the series (*continued from page iii*)

Development Course and Marital Dysfunction
Edited by Thomas Bradbury

Mothers at Work
By Lois Hoffman and Lise Youngblade

The Development of Romantic Relationships in Adolescence
Edited by Wyndol Furman, B. Bradford Brown, and
Candice Feiring

Emotion, Development, and Self-Organization
Edited by Marc D. Lewis and Isabela Granic

Developmental Psychology and Social Change
Edited by David S. Pillemer and Sheldon H. White